W9-AAF-458

Mythology of the Americas

The Hamlyn Publishing Group
London, New York, Sydney, Toronto
Hamlyn House, The Centre,
Feltham, Middlesex
First Published 1970

ISBN 0 600 30017 X

Originally published as
North American Indian Mythology © Cottie Burland 1965
Mexican and Central American Mythology © Irene Nicholson 1967
South American Mythology © Harold Osborne 1968

Printed in Italy by O.G.A.M. Verona

Mythology of the Americas

Cottie Burland

Irene Nicholson

Harold Osborne

Hamlyn

London New York Sydney Toronto

Contents

North American Indian Mythology

Mexican and Central American Mythology

South American Mythology

The flyer.

Colour Plates

North American Indian Mythology

Mexican and Central American Mythology

South American Mythology

North American Indian Mythology

Cottie Burland

Author's Note

A wooden construction and mask from Vancouver Is. It represents a sea monster with a separate headpiece of a duck on top of a human head. It was used in the spring dance ceremonials when its ferocious appearance was intended to drive the salmon towards the shore.

North American Indian cultures cover a special range of human activities. In comparison with the cultures of the Old World they encompass societies which range from late Palaeolithic, comparable with the Magdalenian of France, right up to an advanced Neolithic, which can compare well with the earliest town building cultures of the Middle East such as the pre-Flood cities of Mesopotamia. In North America, therefore, we are dealing with myths arising from a recently living group of cultures which reflect a way of life lost to European and Asian tradition in the mists of prehistory.

The signposts I have followed have been the archetypal gods; the vaguely defined Power Above, the Earth Mother, and that curious universal figure the Trickster. Between mankind and these greater powers there are a host of other spirits: some are the animal souls, others, in the agricultural cultures, are the spirits of the plants, particularly the divine Corn Maidens. Sun, Moon, and the Twins who are Morning Star and Evening Star are there to remind us that our religions are largely conditioned by observation of the character and rhythms of these lights in the sky. As we deal with advancing civilisation we find the simple legends of the world-under-the-earth become the wonderful and elaborate creation myths. By using this method of selection by subject and by the gods concerned we have been able to find a pattern within the confusion of many hundreds of stories.

Of the many records available, I have made a point of choosing the older sources as far as possible because they are likely to reflect the mind of the Indian most clearly. The major sources for many of the Eskimo legends are the publications of the Canadian Department of Mines; for Northwest Coast myths the publications of the Canadian National Museum, particularly works by Dr. Marius Barbeau; for most of the myths from the United States the publications of the Bureau of American Ethnology, Smithsonian Institution.

A Chilkat blanket with a repeated killer whale design. This type of design is known as the 'hocker' motif and its distinctive feature is the figure with limbs outstretched in frog fashion.

Introduction

The North American continents is an immense, roughly triangular land mass. It extends from the permanent ice-cap of the Arctic to the sub-tropical regions of California and Florida. In the west there are great mountain chains running from north to south, spreading out into two main regions with a dry valley between them in the neighbourhood of Utah. Over to the east coast there are other, much older, mountain ranges, the Appalachians and, in the north, a low rocky plateau of archaean rock known as the Algonkian shield. Between these two major mountainous areas there are wide stretches of alluvial plains, the valley of the Mississippi and Missouri and the prairie region. To the north the plains were scoured out during the last glacial period and the glacial moraines have produced a region where the low sandy hills have dammed up the waterways to form the Great Lakes system and Hudson Bay. Within this whole vast area there are few natural barriers which would hinder the passage of man.

The general evidence suggests that men first entered America at the stage of the late palaeolithic hunters, a stage rather similar to that of the Aurignacian and Magdalenian periods of Western Europe. The period of earliest migration is completely uncertain. There is some evidence that hunters capable of making fire and cooking animal bones lived in central North America as early as 50,000 years ago, but there is very little evidence of large-scale occupation taking place before the ending of the last glaciation about twelve thousand years ago. The route of immigration was from Siberia across the Bering Strait. At the period of the last glaciation this whole area was above sea level. There was a land bridge some 200 miles wide, extremely cold, but still traversable by the ice-hunting tribes. Once over into the American continent these primitive hunters would have found the mountain chains under ice caps, but along the whole of the eastern fringe of the Rockies, towards the Great Plains, there was an ice-free corridor, dry,

A fired-clay effigy head from a 5,000-year-old camp site near Council Grove, Kansas.

bitterly cold and windy, but passable for skin-clad hunters, which led down into regions of more equable climate.

For millions of years the animal population of the Americas had thrived, and there can be no question that the country was ideal for hunters. Of these very ancient times we have no clear echoes in American Indian legends. There are one or two tales, collected among the Nascopie of Labrador, which tell of creatures able to push over trees. It is not certain whether these were folk tales of the mammoth, or whether they were ultimately derived from stories told by European visitors (the Norsemen, for instance, for four hundred years from the year 1,002 visited the coasts of Newfoundland and Labrador to collect timber for use in the Greenland settlements). It may well be that Indians in contact with these Norse visitors were regaled with stories of strange lands far away, where creatures like the elephant were found.

In the Great Plains region there is a story about a water serpent who swallowed up the rivers, and this may have a historical background in the sudden period of drought which caused population movement in this region and in the south-western area of the United States in about the twelfth and thirteenth centuries.

All ancient immigration into the Americas was by the race which we know as Amerindian. The physical remains, from nearly every archaelogical site in the Americas, show mixed human types, with the ratio of long to broad heads that is to be found within any given group. The later arrivals were somewhat different. They were the large, strong-featured Indians of the central plans region, and the smaller and highly specialised peoples who developed the Eskimo cultures. It is quite clear that the ancestors of the American Indians were already a mixed race, of mongoloid affinities, from the time of their first entry into the American continent.

The hunters of North America paid great attention to their tools, often making them decorative as well as efficient. This halibut hook comes from the Haida Indians of the Northwest Coast. The figure shows a bound witch seated above a wolf's head.

There is no evidence of a planned invasion at any period. The likelihood is that people found their way into the country in family groups, during hunting expeditions. Finding the land full of game, with extra resources of wild berries, edible tubers and other plants, they settled down, making their way from place to place, and leaving no trace for the archaeologist, beyond an occasional camp fire and a few stone implements scattered throughout the land over which they roamed. On linguistic grounds we may suppose that at some time more than a thousand years ago there was a movement of tribes along the foothills of the Rockies and then eastwards across the Great Plains into the Atlantic seaboard areas. It was probably part of a great spiralling migration of tribes which was still in progress when the European settlements along the east coast first began to be developed.

There were some hundreds of distinct linguistic groups in the North American population and few of them had anything in the way of a migration legend. They generally assumed that man was created first in the regions that they themselves inhabited. At the time of the discovery of North America by Europeans the Indians had no written records, so it is useless to hope for much depth in the time scale of their legends. Many of the eastern tribes had mnemonic systems, such as the famous Wampum belts of the Iroquoian tribes. Among the

Ojibway there were bark paintings which recorded pictorially a sequence of events in the mythical stories of tribal heroes. But in general stories were passed down by elders of considerable repute to the youngsters. Not everyone could be a custodian of the native histories; the job fell only to those with either specially trained memories or with a special aptitude for telling the stories.

There is a wide variation in stories from the different regions because of the great cultural diversity of the North American continent. In the north there is the Eskimo, an ice-hunting people, whose culture was upper palaeolithic in type and who lived in very small tribal groups, usually consisting of less than a hundred individuals. In the northern forest area, north of the Great Lakes, the forest tribes, mostly of Cree origin, were living as a forest-hunting people with their life dependent on the migration of caribou, and the tracking of deer, beaver, and smaller animals.

In the eastern woodlands, that is to say the north-eastern United States, the tribes were beginning to settle in farming villages, at the time of the Discovery; and the federation of the Iroquois nations about a century before the arrival of the Europeans was made possible by their settled economy. They lived in villages of bark-covered longhouses, which they called wigwams. Between one village and another there was easy transport by means of birch-bark canoes, which not only carried parties of young men on the warpath, but also served as the vehicles of inter-tribal trade. These tribes already possessed a basic farming culture that was more important than the hunting side of their economy. They had learnt about maize agriculture from tribes to the south of them and had themselves established apple orchards and cared for many other vegetables including pumpkins and beans. This, then, was a typical neolithic culture in which independent tribes were quite capable of confederating to form a state unique in America north of Mexico.

Farther to the south, in the warmer areas, such tribes as the Cherokee were living in confederations of villages which might contain two thousand individuals. Each village was under the authority of a chief, or sometimes of a chieftainess, and most of them formed into loose confederations for better trading relationships between each other and the tribes around. They were an advanced agricultural people, and their whole ceremonial life was linked to the passage of the seasons and the development of the crops.

The whole of the central plains region south of the Great Lakes was inhabited, before the introduction of the horse in about 1750, by tribes practising a mixed economy. They lived among the small patches of woodland in the river valleys, building earth houses to withstand the winter snows and living in skin tipis in the hunting seasons, to enable them to become more mobile. Their hunting of the migrating herds of buffaloes brought ample food supplies. As well as using their stone-tipped spears and arrows, they resorted to stratagem, creating pitfalls by planting rows of upright posts that would serve to divert part of the migrating herd over a cliff, so that the fallen animals could be more easily slaughtered at the base. This was a very different life from that of the wild horsemen who depended almost

A North American Indian with the large, strong-featured face typical of the plains tribes.

An Eskimo man, drawn in the sixteenth century by John White. The heavy furs and skin boots worn by the northern tribes enabled them to survive in the icy conditions they encountered as they entered North America from Asia.

entirely on buffalo meat in the century before the final destruction of independent Indian life in the late nineteenth century. The legends of these Indians of the plains reflect the world of the hunter, especially in the idea of the Great Mother beneath the earth; they also display an interest in agricultural matters such as the water supply. At least half of the foodstuff of the village in earlier times was produced by women working on their garden plots to grow vegetable food.

On the Rocky Mountain borders of the Pacific, and on the island chains of Vancouver Island and the Queen Charlotte Islands, there lived highly specialised groups of seafaring tribes. They had no agriculture whatever, although some leaves, berries and tree roots formed part of their diet. Their tools were beautifully made, late neolithic, implements: axes, adzes, flaked blades for spears, and so on. They made magnificent canoes from the great cedars of the mountains, and lived in large family houses made of timber, carved and painted richly with the family crests of the owners. The abundance of fish, seal and sea-lion enabled them to achieve quite a high cultural stage and to live in considerable comfort without resorting to agriculture. Since wars between villages and clans were common occupations, the stories have a tendency towards the heroic adventure tale. The medicine men were interested in stories about the origins of animals, the coming of civilisation and the life after death.

To the south, in the main Rocky Mountain-Pacific Coast areas of the United States, the country was inhabited by very poor hunting tribes who practised a little agriculture to supplement the vegetable resources available in the form of acorn flour and wild roots and berries. The wildness of the country and the general aridity tended to make conditions so hard that tribes remained small and poverty-stricken. This was some protection, since their richer eastern neighbours of the plains felt no advantage, and indeed no honour, in raiding such poor and primitive people.

Feather prayer sticks from a Zuñi pueblo. They were carried in the prayer ceremonies to symbolise the link between the spirits and man which was marked by the sacrifice of an eagle every year. British Museum.

In the south-western areas, Utah and Colorado, Indian culture reached its highest point in North America. For many centuries there had been agricultural life centring around large mud-built villages along the river valleys in the desert. Some of these Indians, notably the Hohokam people, practised irrigation, digging trenches running from higher to lower levels of the river system so as to fertilise their fields. But when the climate deteriorated in the twelfth century, many of the village settlements became untenable and agriculture was concentrated on the fertile parts of the river valleys, while the villages were moved into the waste-land beyond.

However, the droughts had stricken the Plains tribes as well, and they developed the habit of raiding the more settled Indian communities. This was partly guarded against by the removal of the villages into caves and into fortified pueblos, or town settlements, on the tops of isolated mesas. The tribes of Pueblo Indians were of more than one linguistic group but they had a basic common culture that was conditioned by the circumstances of their life. They had the most clear-cut mythology of all the North American peoples, and the most carefully organised system, in which religion and social life were carefully planned on the basis that a man growing up in the community would move from one office to another, holding power alternately in civil and religious fields. Thus the chief, who was really the law-giver and adviser to the community as a whole, reached his political position only after having been thoroughly initiated into the religious and traditional knowledge of his people.

The approach to the mythology of North America is through different levels of culture. It is not a journey through time. The contemporary state of tribes in the sixteenth century varied from the very simple life of stone-age hunters, with no agriculture at all, to the organised town settlements of the Pueblo Indians and the Cherokee. In fact, in the lower Mississippi area tribes such as the Natchez built settlements on mounds and were the only people in the North American continent to be divided into castes of aristocrats, priests and commoners in a highly organised social system with very advanced social contacts between the towns. Their craftsmanship was also of a high order. Nearly all of this, however, was destroyed in the first century of the European invasions of the continent and little was left to tell us about the way of life of these advanced tribes.

Bird cults are found all round the Pacific coast from Asia to America, and birds were a common feature of design. This woven hat comes from the south-west region of North America where basketwork reached an exceptionally high standard, and depicts an owl.

The Pueblo Indians had the most fully developed mythology of all the North American peoples. They believed in spirits called kachinas, who had specific functions to perform in the agricultural festivals. This Indian painting shows Tawa, the sun kachina. Bureau of American Ethnology, Smithsonian Institution.

The Eskimo

A fish with a woman's head which represents the fish's spirit nature. The Eskimo believed that all animals had souls that could be charmed to bring them to the traps of the hunter. Soapstone carving from Cape Dorset.

Eskimo folk-tales hold the position of myths as there is almost no formalised group of beliefs about a pantheon of gods. The material is limited by the nature of Eskimo experience. No Eskimo would recount legends of the great forest, or of a life in which people dug the ground in order to make plants grow. His natural environment was very grim, although it had a fantastic beauty of its own.

Life for the Eskimo was always precarious. A season of successful hunting meant that there would be comfort and the euphoria of success for everybody. It would bring about periods of jollity and happiness, and of eating and drinking to excess. But it was also a time of preparing stocks of dried meat in readiness for the times when success was not so widespread. Food would be hidden in caches and, although it may be that it was never dug up again by the same family, it would last for a very long period and remain edible.

The summer hunting of walrus and whale on the open sea inlets provided exciting material for adventure tales. The winter periods of waiting for fish and seals at blow-holes in the ice gave occasion to many strange stories of ghosts and fantastic creatures who appeared from the darkness. The world of the Eskimo was always filled with mystery. Birds flew to unknown lands uttering cries which were taken as a presage for good or evil. The aurora borealis danced in the sky, and the people saw in it images of their own families and friends who had passed out of this world and were now dancing happily around fires in the heavens. They would call out greetings, and ask them to send good luck to their descendants upon earth. The sea itself, the great source of life to the Eskimo, was the home of powerful spirits, notably a very, very ancient fertility mother.

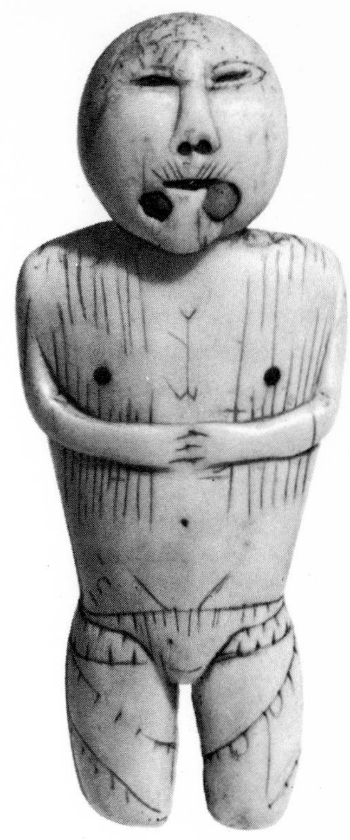

The Shaman

The religious ideas of the Eskimo were never formalised. The only kind of religious gathering was the impromptu attendance at seances organised, or rather inspired, through the angakok or shaman. If the angakok felt that he was being overcome by the spirits of nature, or the souls of the dead, he would retire to his tent and start beating a rhythm on his drum while he sat swaying regularly, lifting his head, holding the tambourine-like drum high above his head and beating on it. People would come together, to sit quietly and watch him falling into a trance. As his words came struggling out, they would strive to hear them. Sometimes they were under the impression that other beings, often in animal shape, were there in the hut. This was possibly the kind of materialisation well known to spiritualist circles. It was principally a subjective phenomenon caused by the concentration which the audience directed towards their shaman. The prophecies usually referred to minor domestic matters, but sometimes they assumed group importance when they pronounced words from the spirits telling of the coming of shoals of fish, or of movements of seal or caribou. There is no careful record which compares prophecies with actually observed phenomena, but there is every reason to think

The religious life of the Eskimo centred around the seances at which the shaman communicated with the spirit world. This small ivory doll was used as a charm in the ceremonies. The two circular inserts on the face are trade beads and represent the labrets, or lip-plugs, customarily worn by the northern tribes. Bank Is. 1800–1880.

A wooden dance mask of Negafok, the cold-weather spirit, wearing a sad look because spring is coming and he must leave the people. The mask is too delicate to be worn and is simply held before the face. Kuskokwim River, Alaska.

that the skilled angakok was acutely aware of the state of the weather, and the activities of the local animals, which would give him clues. He would probably not be able to express these delicate impressions in ordinary, everyday talk, but when in a trance this inner knowledge of the situation was projected and appeared in the strange sing-song recital.

The spirit world

The Eskimo was dependent on the natural world; therefore he felt there was some relationship between his own inner personality and that of everything around him. Bears were not merely soulless animals, but creatures with a spirit of their own, which could be charmed to bring them to the traps and pits of the hunter only when this was necessary. Fish were not just animals which swam in the sea but animated creatures provided by the Old Woman who lived under the sea. Spirits of all kinds daily watched over the people and guarded their welfare.

There are a number of Eskimo stories which deal with the stars and with the sun and moon. The sun and moon were usually regarded as sister and brother, engaged in a race in which the moon, first close to his sister the sun, gradually slips behind her until she overtakes him at the end of his course. This is a perfectly natural observable phenomenon and has given rise to the same story in almost the whole range of humanity. Movements of the planets were observed to be irregular, so they were not very important to the seasonal calendar. However astronomy was most important for a hunting people like the Eskimo, as a guide to the time of year. The position of the stars at the time of the migration of the caribou, or the appearance of the fish shoals, was very important for the hunter, and the whole community needed to know what the position of the stars was just before the freeze up of the long winter nights, and just before the breaking of the ice in the spring.

The times when the ice froze, or broke up, were periods when the whole way of life of the people would change with the aspect of the natural world. There were times when they migrated from camp sites on the land to positions on the sea ice, or when the ice-hunting area had to be abandoned to return to the old land camps. Near the camps on the land there were usually carefully buried caches of food, mostly consisting of dried fish and dried seal meat and sometimes containers filled with whale blubber. This stored food was in a curious condition, often dry and mouldy, smelling like old cheese, but nevertheless nourishing. And of course, at the period when the camp was being established again in the spring, it was necessary for the people to have immediate resources of food available until they could begin regular hunting again. The presence of such caches of food, sometimes forgotten or lost over many years, led to stories of spirits who revealed special supplies of food to wandering heroes.

The Eskimo had no hierarchy of gods. They relied on the generalised power of spirits to guide them. It was only natural that they felt that the spirits of the grandparents would look after the children left upon earth. The nearest thing to a true deity was the Old Woman who lived under the sea. In various parts of the Eskimo lands she was known under different names. Sedna was the one in use in the central area.

Sedna

The basic legend makes this personage a typical example of the great Earth Mother concept common to all mythologies. A central Eskimo story tells how once there were two giants. Nobody knows how they came into being or who they were. They just existed, living, as Eskimos do, by hunting. They had a child, a girl, who grew up rapidly and showed a terrifying inclination to seize on flesh and eat it whenever she could find it. She was abnormally hungry, even for a giant's child. One night she started to eat the limbs of her parents as they slept. They awoke in horror, seized the frightening child and took her in a umiak (one of the large, skin-covered boats used for transport and whale hunting) far out into the deeper parts of the sea. There they started cutting off her fingers. As the fingers fell into the water they turned into whales, seals, and shoals of fish. The giant parents became even more frightened by this so they threw the child into the sea and paddled themselves home as fast as possible. The story recounts that they lived to be very, very old and finally fell asleep and were frozen to death in the way common to many Eskimo people. The demon girl, living under the waters, became Sedna the great mother of all the sea creatures. It was she who caused storms on the sea, and she who governed the migration of her myriads of children — the whales and walruses, the seals, and fish of all kinds. The Eskimo did not conceive of change of any sort but believed that she was always there and could always be approached by the shaman in his trance.

Two figures carved from walrus ivory. The man, clutching his stomach in a characteristic gesture, is probably a shaman. In his visions he often sought knowledge from under the sea about the movements of fish and seals. James H. Hooper Collection.

On occasions when shortage of food threatened, the Angakok would go into a trance, and his sould would soar over the sea until he came to a great whirlpool. There he would be drawn down and find himself in a beautiful tent under the sea, furnished with the skins of all manner of sea animals. There, seated on the bench, was the great, dark lady herself. She would listen to the requests of her people, sung as a hymn by the soul of the shaman. He would dance and contort himself in front of her to engage her attention and amuse her, so that she would feel favourably inclined towards his people. Eventually she would give him a message, either threatening that the people would die unless they moved to another place, or promising that food would come abundantly from her inexhaustible stores. The soul of the shaman would then be returned to his body. He would become conscious after the trance and sing a magical song recounting what Sedna had told him, and the people would act in accordance with her wishes.

Ancestral spirits

The Eskimo had no conception of a supreme spirit, although some tribes thought that there was one ancestral spirit who came to each family to direct its welfare. But in many regions it was felt that there was an overlord of all the ancestral spirits, very much in the way that

European peasants believed in a king of the fairies. This overlord could be approached by shamans and begged to give information, but more reliance was placed on the information given in dreams by the family's ancestors, and on the conjectures of hunters who believed that they had been blessed by the spirits so that they could sometimes understand the speech of birds and animals. The prophecies of the hunters, of course, were again a way of manifesting the information that they had accumulated by observing the natural world around them.

Many of the myths of the Eskimo give us a valuable picture of life as it was lived by the people. The stories take one into the ice-hunters' igloos or to the caribou hunters' skin tents. We find all their curious customs reflected. Somewhat surprisingly we find that in spite of the harsh and cruel environment the Eskimo were an extremely sensitive people. It was sometimes necessary for them to abandon a child, or even to deliberately allow their old parents to freeze to death. It was an absolute necessity from time to time, when living as a member of a small band searching for enough food to eat, that when things were really bad the weaker members should be sacrificed for the welfare of the whole. Nevertheless every story, in which events of this kind happen, refers to the sorrow of the people, the pain they felt at this sacrifice, and this has led to stories of a romantic cast in which the old people remain under the ground, and find means of attracting their descendants and giving them useful information, or in which the abandoned child, particularly the abandoned girl, finds a new life of her own, and comes to a wonderful land where she marries a fairy prince and comes home rich in furs and ivory to her aged parents.

These primitive myths really show a picture of a human community fighting its environment, making use of everything possible to sustain life and usually winning through the struggle. From both archaeology and the stories of Arctic travellers we know that the struggle for existence was not always successful and that whole tribes simply disappeared from history after an unsuccessful hunting season.

Right, above: An Alaskan spoon showing a man shot through the middle and a spirit with evil intentions above. The Eskimo attributed bad fortune as well as good to the influence of spirits. British Museum.

Right, below: The woman in the sun, a stone-cut by Kenojuak, an Eskimo from Cape Dorset.

A modern Eskimo lithograph of a caribou spirit.

The people in the sky

The following account of the stars was given by Eskimo from Smith Sound in north-west Greenland. These people lived so far north that they were able to see the Great Bear to the south of the zenith.

To them, as to all the Eskimo, the sun is a beautiful girl who carries her torch through the sky as she is chased by her brother the moon, whose name is Aningan. The moon man has a house in which he rests with his demon cousin Irdlirvirisissong, who is a kind of female clown who sometimes comes out into the sky and dances to make people laugh. But if anyone such as a visiting angakok is nearby, they had best look sideways, for if they laugh she will dry them up and devour their intestines.

The moon is a great hunter, always in front of his igloo. His sledge stands piled high with seal skins. He has a sledge team of spotted dogs which sometimes leave the sky and shoot down to earth like shooting stars. The mother of the sun is the planet Jupiter, and she is dangerous to magicians. They have to be wary lest she should eat their livers.

Some of the main constellations of stars also have myths attached to them, connected with their forms. There was once a bear who was chased by a fine pack of dogs. They all ran so hard that they left the earth and came up into the sky where they form the Pleiades, which the Eskimo believe to be Nanook the Bear and the hunting dogs. Over the heads of the Smith Sound Eskimo a giant caribou looks down — he is the constellation Ursa Major. Opposite him, across the sky, are the stones which support a cooking lamp — this is Cassiopeia. Between the two, on the edge of the sky, are three steps cut in a snow bank linking heaven and earth — these are the constellation Orion, sometimes on a dark night the ancestors dance and light fires — this is the joyful bridge of the aurora — perhaps in some way related to the Gullabrig, the bridge to the sky described in Norse folk-lore.

Stories from the Labrador Eskimo

Among all the Eskimo a great spiritual power is attached to the angakok, or shaman. Usually the candidate for these powers is inspired to wander in a deserted area when he reaches the age of puberty. After a few days he becomes dissociated through hunger and anxiety and then the tornaq, or spirit, appears to him, usually in some near-human form. There is a dialogue between them. The frightened aspirant is promised strength and visions. He returns to his family and for a time lives a normal life, but spells of inspiration come, and eventually he seeks to be accepted as an assistant to an experienced magician. Later in life the angakok gives public seances for his tribe. He starts by chanting and beating his drum until he falls into a trance. In this state there is always a display of shouting, and struggles which look like a fit. He will scream in strange languages and suffer sickness and nausea. Every now and then his words make sense to his audience, for some of them know the ancient dialects commonly used by magicians. Finally, exhausted and shaken, the magician returns to consciousness and tells of his journey to the land of the spirits, how he has met the chief of the tornaq, or journeyed to the moon.

Thus, through the ecstatic trance and prophetic powers of their angakok, the people are always in contact with the spirit world of their mythology. There can be little doubt that the angakok usually experiences the visions he describes. He is a natural shaman first before he has learned the little arts of deception which belong to the professional calling. The visions are of the nature of highly dramatised archetypal dreams, and because the angakok is so steeped in tribal traditions the setting for the vision is already prepared for him. It is a translation of local Eskimo life on to a larger scale or in a different place: the igloo of the moon man is thought of as a fine igloo up in the sky along the road of the moon. The dead live in an underworld that is not very happy, rather like this world only darker, and too often they are hungry because their descendants on earth fail to give them little offerings from the good hunting on earth. It was all very matter of fact and it was felt to be quite practical that the ancestors should inspire the hunter and receive a share of the catch. Life was like that, and for the Eskimo seemed likely to go on in the same way for ever.

The Fishermen of the Northwest Coast

Principal tribes: Haida Kwakiutl Tlingit Tsimshian

The Indians who lived along the coast of America, from southern Alaska through British Columbia and south as far as Oregon, were a highly specialised group of people. They were of typical North American Indian stock physically, with the characteristic straight black hair, somewhat Mongolian eyes, and reddish-brown skin colour which varied considerably within any one tribe.

This particular group of people made use of a highly specialised natural environment. The coast is rocky, with many deep, fiord-like indentations, and scattered off-shore islands. The structure was determined geologically by the incursion of the sea into valleys of the Rocky Mountains as they slowly sank lower in the ocean. Many of the valleys were steep-sided and highly glaciated. The whole country was heavily wooded, the chief timber trees being cedar and Douglas fir.

The Indians themselves were conditioned, probably over many thousands of years, to a life of fishing and hunting. The ocean was prolific. There were immense numbers of fish, herds of seal and great numbers of sea birds. In the woods of the mainland animal food was available. In some regions there were plentiful caribou and deer; in all areas there were bears and many smaller edible mammals. Vegetable products consisted mainly of wild seeds and berries and there were a number of edible roots which could be pounded up and made into something resembling a hard, unleavened bread. Edible fungi and mosses were also sought out. Agriculture was not practised.

The Northwest Coast Indians were, in theory at least, a pre-agricultural stone-age population when the first Japanese fishermen and European sailors visited their coasts. However, the degree of comfort, and almost of civilisation, in their lives was quite remarkable, when compared with that of the other Indian tribes. Their fishing was conducted from magnificent water-craft. Dug-out canoes, sometimes forty or fifty feet in length, capable of holding crews of thirty and forty

The interior of a house in Nootka Sound, Vancouver Is. At the back are two posts, carved with the totem emblems of the family. Fish hangs from racks near the floor to dry in the smoke from the fire. A woman on the left wears the basket-work hat typical of this region. From a drawing by John Webber, 1778.

men, were the common means of transport. Villages were normally built near the mouths of the rapid mountain rivers. Such a site was a convenient place for beaching the canoes, and a sheltered background was important because it helped to deter raids by other tribes.

The Northwest Coast Indians had a tremendous sense of the importance of winning military victories over their neighbours. Prestige raids, both for killing rival tribesmen and for kidnapping slaves, were commonplace events. The raids were naturally more intense in regions where there were tribal or linguistic differences. The main tribal groups were the Kwakiutl of the north and the Tlingit and Haida of the south and Queen Charlotte Islands.

Village life

On the islands, the Haida Indians were supreme and enjoyed isolation from their warlike neighbours. They developed a remarkable proficiency in carving wood and stone. There was little knowledge of metal before the time of the white men, although nodules of natural copper were beaten out to make ceremonial objects, such as the copper shields, which had a high value. Some of these are to be found in museums today, although almost all have been made from copper sheeting taken from the bottom of wrecked or abandoned ships.

The villages consisted of clustered houses, each of which was inhabited by a different family group in the tribe. A house might hold some forty or fifty people, although most were considerably smaller

The beaver, one of the totem animals of the North-west Coast. This Tsimshian Indian head-dress ornament is made of intricately carved wood inlaid with abalone shell. British Columbia.

than this. They were built of heavy, squared timber-framing with elaborately carved corner posts and usually a strong post with decorative carving in the central doorway. In later times, when the Indians obtained fine steel tools in trade with the white man, they developed larger and larger doorposts, which after about 1830 became the great totem-poles for which this region is famous.

The totem

The population was quite large. Inhabitants of a village would vary in numbers from one or two hundred up to as many as a thousand individuals. The organisation of fishing expeditions, hunting and war parties demanded that there should be a system of government that was to some extent permanent. This took a form similar, in some ways, to the feudal system in Europe. The important families of the tribe were divided into totemic groups. These were not unlike the clans of Scotland in their social organisation. They dedicated themselves to the honour of a family totem, almost like a clan ancestor. Thus there were Bear people, Killer Whale people, Cannibal Spirit people, Salmon people, Beaver people and so on. This did not mean that they believed themselves to be descended from those particular animals, or even to have had a common ancestry, in the way understood by Australian aborigines. They usually named themselves after an ancestor who, in one of the heroic legends of the people, had a special relationship with the totem ancestors; the totem had much the nature of a family crest. The people of the bear totem would have bear symbols on their clothing, and their houses would be built with finely carved totem-poles exhibiting representations of the bear.

The carving of the totem on the pole had an important bearing on social custom. If a stranger from another village came visiting in times of peace, the first thing he did was to look at the totem-poles to see which house belonged to members of his own totemic group. He could then go there expecting to find protection, food and shelter. He was accepted as a kinsman, to be supported against other families in the village and against any raiding by other tribal groups while he stayed there. This was a very important point, because it allowed the spread of tradition from one group to another. It also preserved ancient customs by making sure that in every region within visiting distance of others the old stories were repeated, and the old beliefs about the spirits, the origins of fire and other myths, were basically the same despite linguistic differences between the main tribal groups.

Stone and wood sculpture

The basic structure of life depended largely upon the use of tools capable of cutting down big trees and shaping them into the magnificent houses and canoes which were the means of tribal life. The normal stone-age hunter, with his chipped arrow heads and flaked stone knives, such as were used by the Eskimo, could never deal with forest country. The Northwest Coast Indians, however, developed efficient axes and adzes made out of hard polished stone. Sometimes

Right: An Eskimo woman in furs with her baby on her back. A sixteenth-century watercolour by John White. British Museum.

their tools had very handsome sculptural decoration on them. The blades were lashed by hide thongs to wooden handles and were quite as efficient as the white man's steel, although much slower.

There is a wide range of stone sculpture known from this area although it is all on a small scale. It was produced by beating and chipping at the stone with other pieces of rock, and then polishing and grinding the shapes so obtained with sand and wood until a smoothly contoured surface was achieved.

Weaving, as such, was not known among these tribes, but they produced textile fibres by beating out cedar-bark, and sometimes by spinning dogs' wool combed from their hunting dogs. These fibres were hung on a framework and then twined by the fingers. There was no true warp and weft weaving, only this system of finger twining. The technique was used to make cloaks that were worn tied over the chest. They were big enough to wrap from shoulder to knees. They also made little wrap-around aprons which reached from the hip to just above the knee, and fringed skirts which were worn by the women. Both sexes wore quite beautifully made hats, sometimes of elaborate design, made in basketry.

The shoals of salmon

Good tribal organisation and a simple but very efficient technology enabled the Indians to exploit their surroundings very successfully. They were particularly fortunate in the immense shoals of salmon which every year ascended and descended the rivers and were trapped by the million. Not only was the fish eaten fresh, it was also dried, and great quantities of salmon oil were extracted during the drying process, to be stored in wooden bowls. Some of these bowls, even after nearly two hundred years of storage in museums, still ooze salmon oil every summer when they warm up after the winter cold.

It is natural that the folk tales of the Northwest Coast Indians should be concerned with hunting adventures, both on sea and land, the relationship between family and totemic groups, and, of course, the various war cults. War itself was a very common activity at seasons when hunting was not necessary. After the salmon fishing was over and preserving was done, there was a period when people could think of adventure, and this often took the form of raids on settlements which were not so close that their help was needed during the fishing season. These raids produced stories of heroic bravery and sometimes strange cruelties. Any stratagem was considered fit for use against an enemy, so some of the tales tell of the curious tricks by which groups of people were trapped and killed or enslaved.

Slavery was a misfortune and the slave, although normally treated kindly, as a rather low-grade human being, was the chattel of his or

The tools of the Northwest Coast Indians were often decorative as well as efficient. This ancient knife has a blade beaten out from raw copper, the blade is lashed with hide thongs to an ivory handle in the form of a hero being swallowed by a whale. James H. Hooper collection.

her owner. When the great chiefs held a potlatch festival, in which they gave presents to all the members of a visiting group, they sometimes demonstrated their contempt for property by clubbing slaves to death.

The Potlatch Festival

The potlatch festival was a means of giving away wealth to gain social prestige, and also of exchanging useful goods. The group which received the gifts was bound in honour to hold a potlatch festival themselves later, in which they gave back goods exceeding in value those that they had received. Thus there was a constant transfer of wealth in the form of carved wooden chests, blankets, personal ornaments, tools and in fact all the manufactured goods of the people. It was socially important to make things for use as gifts in these ceremonies as well as for personal everyday use. But there was very little real trade in the normal sense of the word; occasionally blankets or beautiful small carvings were exchanged for food or other objects of value. Normally each village community subsisted on the food gathering and craftwork of its own members without needing to trade with any outside peoples at all.

Ceremonial life

The ceremonial life was richest in the dark months of winter, when the long nights were enlivened by dramatic performances by societies who enacted totemic legends, and by the retelling of myths by the elders, who thereby preserved the tribal lore. Children, although at first frightened by the strange animal masks and paint of the actors in these dramatic recitals, gradually came to learn the stories, and to visualise them within the limits of the tribal art style.

There is not sufficient archaeological evidence to show how long the Northwest Coast artistic styles of representing the legendary creatures of the stories had existed. But this style must have persisted for many centuries, possibly for thousands of years, before the white man came. Many of the objects of daily life were history books in themselves: chiefs had wooden war helmets that had been worn in famous battles of the past, and there were ancient war canoes and sometimes ruined house sites which were associated with stories. Historical and religious legends were closely linked.

Principal gods

The mythology was based on the world of nature, conceived as the abode of spirit powers as well as of men. Animals could be heroes as

Kwakiutl potlatch figure. The potlatch festivals provided an opportunity for the Northwest Coast tribes to display their wealth and grandeur by giving away property. This figure, holding a beaten-copper shield, was a representation of its owner's affluence.

Carved wooden figure from Vancouver Island showing the shaman in his trance and his vision of a wolf-spirit above. British Museum.

well as humans, but with the difference that in the heroic tales the totems act like humans but can still change into animal form at will. There was probably some general consensus of opinion that there might be some power, the Chief of the Sky People, who was more powerful than the ordinary spirits, and some idea of inescapable fate, but nothing is clearly formulated. There was the customary Old Woman who lived under the sea, who seems to form a myth in most parts of the world, and is, in fact, a psychological phenomenon. From this general view of the way of life of the Indians we can turn to a study of their stories.

The mythology of the Indians of the Northwest Coast is slightly more advanced than that of the Eskimo, but we find no clear traces of deities, apart from a Sky Being, Sun, Moon and the trickster-creator known as the Raven.

Many of the characters in the stories are totem creatures not entirely animal and not entirely human. They are in many ways archetypal forms, but are projected in a special way so that they are not immediately recognisable as mythological deities. The concept of a single godhead is foreign to any primitive culture, and we must expect the stories to display much of the nature of what we would consider folk-lore. The individual spirits were seen in visions by the shamans but they were never formally worshipped. There were neither regular ceremonies, nor temples, in the whole of the region; civilisation had not yet taken the vital step of organising the myths into a truly religious tradition.

The Lord of the sky

The Lord of the Sky is referred to in some of the tales as an old chief. Once the sky was much nearer to the earth than it is now, and this old chief was sometimes annoyed by the constant shouting of children, the beating of drums, and the hullabaloo of war parties. Unable to rest, he would cause the mountains to move or induce earthquakes, with the intention of destroying the offending tribe or giving it a fright.

These characteristics are not unreasonable if one is postulating a sky god. However, it is possible that these legends are derived ultimately from the talk of European visitors. There is something unnatural in this idea of the elderly chief living in his house above the skies. Much more natural myths are those of Raven and the Old Woman who had the Sun in her house, or of the wondrous land under the sea where the killer whales and sea birds had their ceremonial homes. These are more authentic Indian beliefs.

Opposite page, right: When the myths were recounted to the tribe, masked actors impersonated the main characters. This wooden mask, with deep-set orbits and fur eyebrows, was known as a 'Whistling Grandmother' and symbolised the malevolent spirits who breathe out illness and cause children to die. British Museum.

Semi-divine spirits

The spirits of the dead were thought of as going into an underworld where they could occasionally be reached by their descendants. It was clear to the Indian story tellers at the winter ceremonies that one might go to the land of the dead and find one's relatives. But one could never expect to return if food was accepted in this other land. This is a strikingly international conception of the dangers of visiting the other world and recalls the Greek myth of Persephone who ate part of a pomegranate while she was in the underworld and had to spend part of her life there ever after.

Some of the legends are very beautiful, and we find that the wondrous, semi-divine creatures — the great Thunderbird, the sea-dragons, the men who work marvels — are part human, part animal, and part spirit. The mythological world of the Northwest Coast was the world of the hunter where anything might happen and where spiritual forces were always active. These things are not formalised, except in so far as a traditional folk-tale about a strange event was passed on from generation to generation. In early times the story-teller was under the strict censorhip of the audience, most of whom had heard the tale every year since they were children. They protested at any variation, but alterations were made in more recent years. The myths were often recited during the winter months, when actors wearing masks and robes would endeavour to impersonate the characters described.

The powers of nature were personified to some degree and as such they took revenge when creatures of the natural world were deliberately injured. It was one thing to catch salmon for food; the salmon spirits and river spirits were not worried by this, it was the reason why salmon existed. If people caught more than they needed, however, and then threw the fish, away, or carelessly tortured the salmon when they were caught, then retribution from the spirit world could be expected. This often occurred in the form of a volcanic eruption.

A wooden mask with three hooded water birds. It was worn in tribal dances by the person enacting the role of the Lord of the Sky. Vancouver Is. 1890–1900.

The Wolf Clan and the salmon

A story from the Nass River illustrates this. It tells how, in a canyon near the head of the river, there existed a wonderful place where the tribespeople could always find food, salmon and wild berries. The villagers who lived nearby were wealthy enough to trade with others and much respected. As time went on, the younger people forgot the old traditions; sometimes they killed small animals and left the carcasses for the crows and eagles to eat. Their elders warned them that the Chief in the Sky would be angered by such foolish behaviour, but nobody heeded them. In one case, when the salmon season was at its height and the fish were swimming up river in their myriads, some of the young men of the Wolf Clan thought it amusing to catch salmon, make slits in the fish's backs, put in pieces of burning pitch pine, and put them back in the water so that they swam about like living torches in the river. It was spectacular and exciting, and they did not think about the cruelty to the salmon, or the waste of a good food fish. The elders as usual protested and as usual the young people took no notice. At the end of the salmon running season the tribe made ready for the winter ceremonies. But as they prepared they heard a strange noise in the distance, something like the beating of a medicine-drum, and grew worried. As there was nothing very threatening about it, the young people began to say, 'Aha, the ghosts wake up, they are going to have a feast too.' The old people guessed that the young men's thoughtlessness in ill-treating the salmon had brought trouble on the tribe. After a while the noises died down, but within a week or two the beating of drums became louder and louder. Even the young warriors became very careful about what they did, because they were frightened. The old people noted the young men's fear, and said it would be their fault if the tribe perished. Eventually a noise like thunder was heard, the mountains broke open, and fire gushed forth until it seemed that all the rivers were afire. The people tried to escape, but as the fire came down the river, the forest caught fire and only a few of them got away The cause of the conflagration was said by the shamans to be entirely due to the anger of the spirit world at the torture of the salmon. Thus the powers of nature insisted on a proper regard for all their creatures.

Ceremonial rattle of puffin beaks. Round ones like this were believed to be used by witches to call up storms. Kodia, South Alaska. 1868. British Museum.

Bear Mother

Another group of stories from the Northwest Coast which has become famous concerns the Bear Mother. The stories can be paralleled with much European folk-lore. The theme is that of the young woman who wanders away from her own country and goes into an animal's den, under the impression that she is entering a human household. She loses her sense of time and after what she considers to be a short period is rescued by her relatives. But she has in fact been away long enough to become the mother of animal cubs. The European stories are concerned with the world of the fairies, where Thomas the Rhymer, or some other hero, goes to the underground house of the Fairy Queen and is lost there, without knowledge of time, for a long period.

In the Haida story of Bear Mother, there is an interesting picture of everyday life linked with the mythical world of the Bear Spirits.

The princess Rhpisunt, daughter of the chief of the Wolf Clan, was gathering berries on the mountains with two other young women. As Rhpisunt was walking up into the hills she stepped on a bear's excrement and her foot was smeared. This made her very angry; she said, 'This bear was a dirty beast and heedless of where I, a lady, stepped, as if it were somebody important.' She kept grumbling about this all day; whenever she saw one of her friends she would shout out angry remarks about the bears. As the day went on she wandered from the others, farther into the forest. At last she had filled her basket, and turned to go back to their canoe. She had not gone very far when the strap of her basket snapped. All the berries spilled on the ground. She scraped them up and started on her way again. When she called out to her companions there was no answer. Again she felt the straps slipping, so she sat down for a while and tightened them.

Soon she met two young men. One of them spoke to her. 'Beautiful lady, we were sent to bring help. Let us take your pack and lead you.' She didn't recognise them, but she thought they were very handsome, especially the young man who was the leader. Rhpisunt had no care that the trail did not lead down to the canoe but away into the mountain. It was a very good trail, and she went along laughing and chattering all the time. Soon they came to a village with a very large house in the centre. The leader took the princess to the house saying, 'Stay here till I see my father.' He went in and she heard a loud voice

Overleaf, left: A carved wooden half-figure wearing a mask. Large Eskimo figures such as this are rare. Point Barrow, Alaska.

Overleaf, right: A mask with feather attachments, representing a woman. Eskimo masks were usually delicate and imaginative and ranged from the horrific, designed to scare away evil spirits, to the amusing or gentle. Anvik, Alaska.

A ceremonial blanket of a Haida chief, from Prince of Wales Island, showing a bear outline made from shells. This picture emphasises its horrific aspect, but the Indians generally felt a sympathetic, if respectful, relationship to the bears.

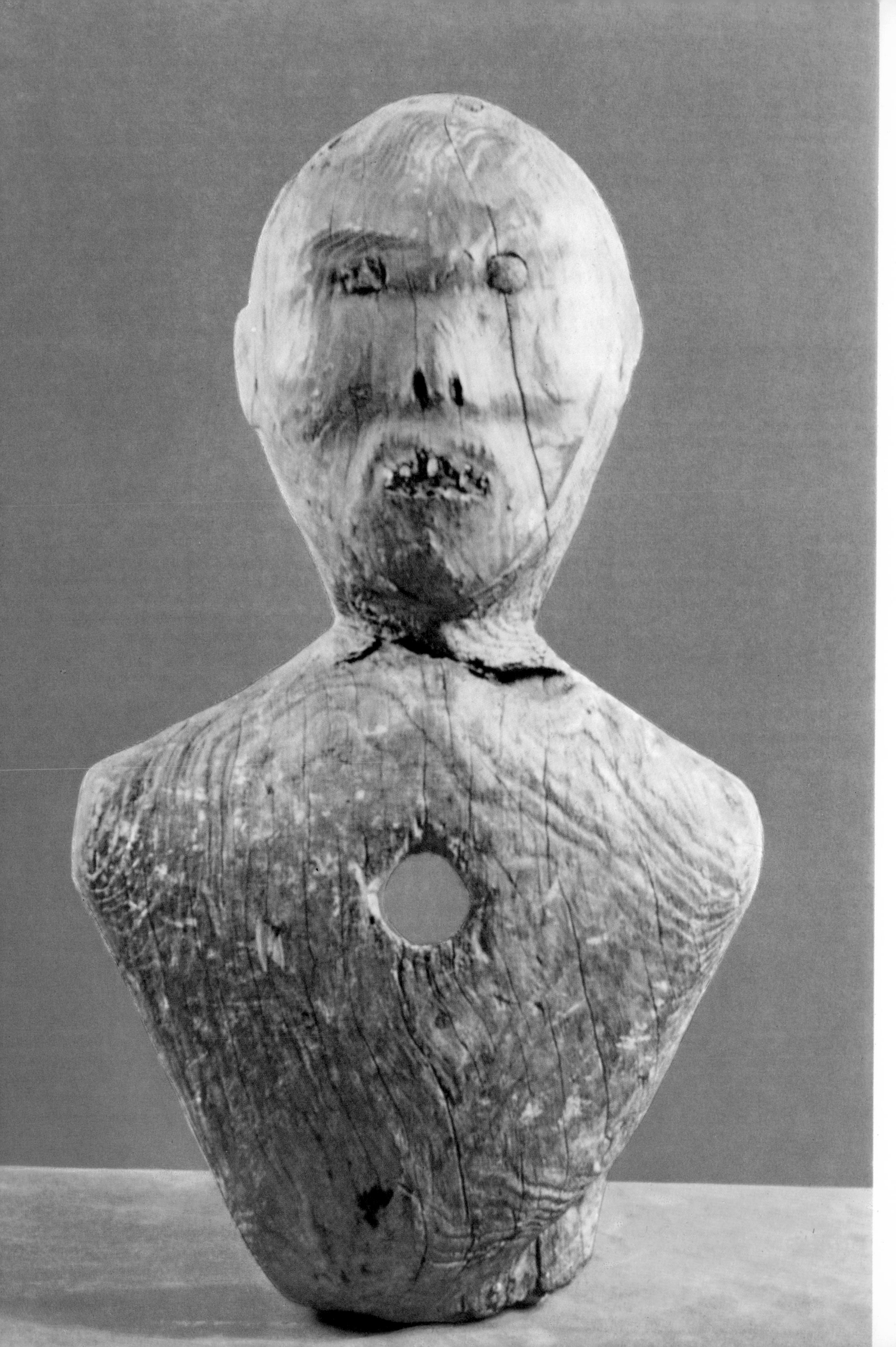

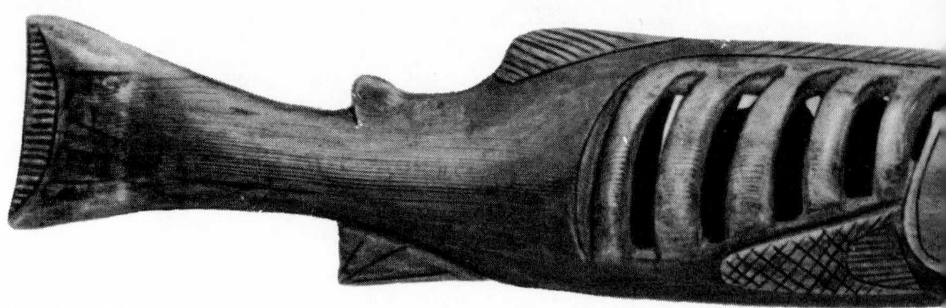

Tlingit soapberry spoon with a rattle handle representing a salmon. The importance of the salmon to the fishermen of the Northwest Coast is reflected in their account of the misfortunes which befell the Wolf Clan when its tribesmen abused the fish.

Opposite page: The princess Rhpisunt who was carried off by the Bear People. Her flat head is a deformation caused by pressure of a light cradle board during infancy. In parts of the Northwest Coast region and the Northern Forest a flat head was held to be a mark of beauty. British Museum.

coming from inside. Did you find what you went seeking?' 'Yes, she stands outside.' 'Bring her in, that I may see my new daughter-in-law.' Then the young man came out, calling, 'Follow me, my father would see you.' She followed him and saw a huge man sitting at the back of the house. Beside him sat a woman with her eyes closed. Inside bearskin coats were hanging everywhere. Old slaves went around as if near death, sleepy and quiet. The great chief called out, 'Bring the girl here, she must, sit near me, and beside you. Spread mats that she who visits me may sit down.' The slaves laid down mats at the feet of their master, and here Rhpisunt and the beautiful young man sat down. While the chief was speaking to his servants the princess felt somebody pinch her. Looking down at her side, she saw a little old woman who said to her, 'Have you any wool or fat? I am Mouse Woman. If you have any wool or fat, I can help you.' The princess took off her woollen earings and some decorations from her hair and gave them to Mouse Woman. After the little old woman received these ornaments, she disappeared. She soon came back and said, 'The Bear People have taken you. They were offended that you insulted the bears when you stepped on their mess today, and that is why Bear Chief was angry. Now do you have any fat? If you have any to give me I'll protect you. The chief's anger is still great.' The princess had some mountain goat fat which she used to rub on her face to keep her skin smooth. She gave this to the little woman who went away again. She returned. 'When you go outside to relieve yourself, dig a hole to hide your excrement. As soon as you've finished cover it up. Then take a piece of your copper bracelet and put it on top, and do this every time. The Prince of the Bears will make you his wife. Be careful. You will always be watched. All these old slaves have been lured away by the Bear People because like you they made fun of the bears. Some of them mutilated the bears that they killed, and many have perished for breaking the taboo of the Bear People.'

The chief sent messengers to call friends to a party to welcome the new princess. Before long Rhpisunt went outside to relieve herself and dug a hole as usual behind the bushes. When she had covered it all up, she laid on the earth a piece of copper that she broke off one of her bracelets. Then she sat down and watched. The bears, who had been spying on her, rushed to the place where she had sat and

A painted drum and drumstick from the Tsimshian Indians. Drums were made by treating skins with glue and then stretching the reinforced skin over a frame. They were used in religious ceremonies to call up the spirits.

found a piece of copper. They were surprised. 'Look, she's right when she says that our excrement's unpleasant. She leaves real copper behind her.'

They took the copper to the chief. Soon the guests began to arrive. When most of them were there, the chief spoke, and his wife at last woke up and noticed that among the company were many real human beings. She was a terrible creature herself. Her breasts were human heads which were alive and moving about, and bright rays of light shone from her eyes in the underworld house. Bear Chief spoke to his guests and said, 'This is my daughter-in-law. Whenever you see her in danger, you will protect her. Her children will be the grandchildren of the Bear People.' Then great bowls of mountain goat fat were brought in. These had been made by magic from the cosmetic fat that Rhpisunt had given to the little Mouse Woman.

From now on she was married to the bear. She found that the Bear People never used dry wood for their fires; only water-soaked wood from the bottom of rivers would burn in this underworld. Whenever any of the Bear People went out, they always took with them their bear coats. Once outside they put them on and behaved as animals. Sometimes bears would go out and never return, and then someone would announce that 'Our brother's lip plug has fallen out.' Lip-plugs, or labrets, were valued highly on the Northwest Coast and these words meant that they had lost their most precious possession, their life. When the time came to move to the winter village, where the houses were warmer, Rhpisunt knew that she was pregnant. She discovered that the new village was hidden among the trees, almost in sight of her own old earthly home. They moved to the houses, and she found that her husband had made a new home in a cave high in a cliff.

At home in the village of Niskae, people had missed Rhpisunt long ago. The chief had sent search parties out. They had followed her trail and found the spot where she had dropped her fruit basket. Then they came to a place where, alongside her footprints, the were great bear's footprints on either side of her. They felt certain she had been killed by the bears. They hunted all over the country, hoping to find her body, because bears never eat human beings; but the old medicine man stated that she was not dead, that she would return, and that she was now not far away. All the hunters went into the hills; they

killed many bears but found no sign of the princess. The Bear People were very unhappy that so many of their number had been killed, and the Bear Prince told his wife that they would go to a safe refuge, not far away from her father's village, where she could have her babies in peace. They climbed up into the mountain by a very narrow and dangerous path, but they were safely away from any hunters. Before long the princess gave birth to twin cubs, who grew very fast and were very lively and beautiful.

Among the people from Niskae were the three brothers of Rhpisunt, who all went out seeking her. Her youngest brother and his dog Maesk decided that they would not give up the search as quickly as the other hunters. They roamed far and wide and found nothing. Then they thought of the places where it seemed impossible to go. They arrived at the foot of the cliff, underneath the cave where Bear Mother Rhpisunt and her husband were living. The dog began to howl and her younger brother realised that this meant that she was somewhere very near and that he would have to climb the steep cliff. He slipped back quietly to the village and at every spare momenthe practised climbing steep, rocky slopes. The Bear Prince watched from the cave. Every time the hunters came near, he took his family safe into the depths of the cave and said magic words so that the hunters soon became tired and went away. But one day he was very quiet and unhappy. He told his wife that the dog Maesk and his young brother-in-law would find him and would kill him. Bear Mother was sad, but realised that she must watch for her brother.

One day she saw him on the trail underneath the mouth of the cave and dropped a ball of snow down the side of the mountain. It fell near his feet. When he picked it up, he could see her handprint on it. He held it to his dog's nose and the dog recognised his mistress's scent and began to howl. The younger brother looked up and saw something move across the mouth of the cavern. The hunter and his dog came steadily up the cliff, moving from one tiny hold to another. The Bear Prince knew that his end was near. He said, 'Let me go to my den, I shall be quite helpless; do not let them mutilate my carcass. When they have skinned me, tell them to burn my bones, and then I may go on to help our children. As soon as I am dead they will turn into humans and become skilful hunters.'

He then preparad to meet his fate. The young hunter came up and did as the bear had prophesied, smoked him out and then speared him. Bear Prince then sang the magical song that he wished the princess and her brother to learn. They promised him they would give the bearskin to his father-in-law, so that he should always have good fortune and the children should be happy in a rich household. All was done as he commanded. The two little bear cubs trotted along with their mother and uncle and came to the village of their grandfather. As they entered the door of the chief's house, they took off their bearskin coats and become two handsome little boys. Later on, when the magic song and the bear coat had made the chief very wealthy, and the little boys had grown up to be great hunters, their grandfather made a high pole for them to climb up. From the top of the pole they would look out and see smoke coming from the village of the Bear

Left: A carved wooden headdress known as 'The Mystery of the Sea'. These headdresses were worn by men enacting scenes from the myths, and the rich decoration and ermine skins reflect the ostentatious nature of the Northwest Coast Indians.

Tlingit totem poles in South Alaska featuring the Beaver and the Eagle.

People and their other grandfather's home. Eventually their mother Rhpisunt became an old woman, and after she had died, they left the village, leaving their dog behind. They put on their bear coats when they reached the forest and joined the Bear People. Ever after the tribe had good fortune when they reminded the Bear People that they were relatives and should help them with their hunting. All these events are believed to have happened at a village on the Nass River, and the story is owned by the people of the Wolf totem house.

Raven the trickster

For some reason that is not quite clear many different peoples in the world have thought that the act of creation was some kind of trickery, and that the spirit who brought the world out of the waters had demonic qualities and a talent for deceit. This is faintly echoed in the story of Genesis, though here the serpent, rather than the Creator, is the deceiver. But among primitive people the treachery of the Creator is always startlingly clear. From the tribes of the Northwest Coast of America the stories of the Trickster concern Raven. This remarkable personality brought man many of his most wonderful gifts, but he could never refrain from making fools of people.

Raven and the moon

One day Raven learnt that an old fisherman, living alone with his daughter on an island far to the north, had a box containing a bright light called the moon. He felt that he must get hold of this wonderful thing, so he changed himself into a leaf growing on a bush near to the old fisherman's home. When the fisherman's daughter came to pick berries from the wild fruit patch, she pulled at the twig on which the leaf stood and it fell down and entered into her body. In time a child was born, a dark-complexioned boy with a long, hooked nose, almost like a bird's bill. As soon as the child could crawl, he began to cry for the moon. He would knock at the box and keep calling, 'Moon, moon, shining moon.'

At first nobody paid any attention, but as the child became more vocal and knocked harder at the box, the old fisherman said to his daughter, 'Well, perhaps we should give the boy the ball of light to play with.' The girl opened the box and took out another, and then another, box from inside it. All the boxes were beautifully painted and carved, and inside the tenth there was a net of nettle thread. She loosened this and opened the lid of the innermost box. Suddenly light filled the lodge, and they saw the moon inside the box, bright, round like a ball, shining white. The mother threw it towards her baby son and he caught and held it so firmly they thought he was content. But after a few days he began to fuss and cry again. His grandfather felt sorry for him and asked the mother to explain what the child was trying to say. So his mother listened very carefully and explained that he wanted to look out and see the stars in the dark sky, but that the roof board over the smoke hole prevented him from doing so.

So the old man said, 'Open the smoke hole.' No sooner had she

Haida slate carving showing the pain suffered by Rhpisunt when she nursed one of her unnatural children. The projecting lower lip is caused by the insertion of a labret, or lip-plug.

Opposite page: A man wearing a bearskin, illustrating the concept of interchangeability of bear and human described in the story of the Bear People. Wood. Nootka Sound. British Museum.

opened the hole than the child changed himself back into the Raven. With the moon in his bill he flew off. After a moment he landed on a mountain top and then threw the moon into the sky where it remains, still circling in the heavens, where Raven threw it.

Many of the stories about Raven describe his everyday adventures. Raven once met the wife of a fisherman. He had stuck a red robin feather in his head and this attracted her attention. She asked how she could get a red feather like that for her own hair. Raven said he could easily get lots of them for her, so he and her husband went out to hunt for robins on an island. Raven rushed ahead of the fisherman and gathered pieces of rotten wood which he threw away among the trees, charming it so that it changed into robins. Then Raven showed the fisherman where he could get the beautiful red birds, sending him deeper and deeper into the bush.

Raven then slipped away, hurried to the canoe, paddled back to the shore, and turned himself into a man just like the fisherman. The fisherman's wife was quite sure that it was her husband who had returned home, so she was not surprised when he went straight to the special fishing pool where the finest fish were preserved and took some of them out to prepare himself a meal. As he finished eating, the fisherman returned saying that he had been fooled. He threw down the bagful of red feathers, which immediately changed back into a heap of rotten wood. He then chased Raven round the house, clubbing him into insensibility.

Then he threw away the body into the water. The drifting carcass was swallowed by a large halibut, but Raven resumed his own shape inside the halibut and so tormented it that it swam ashore, where a number of Indian fishermen seized it and began to cut it up and eat the delicious fat. To their astonishment Raven burst out of the

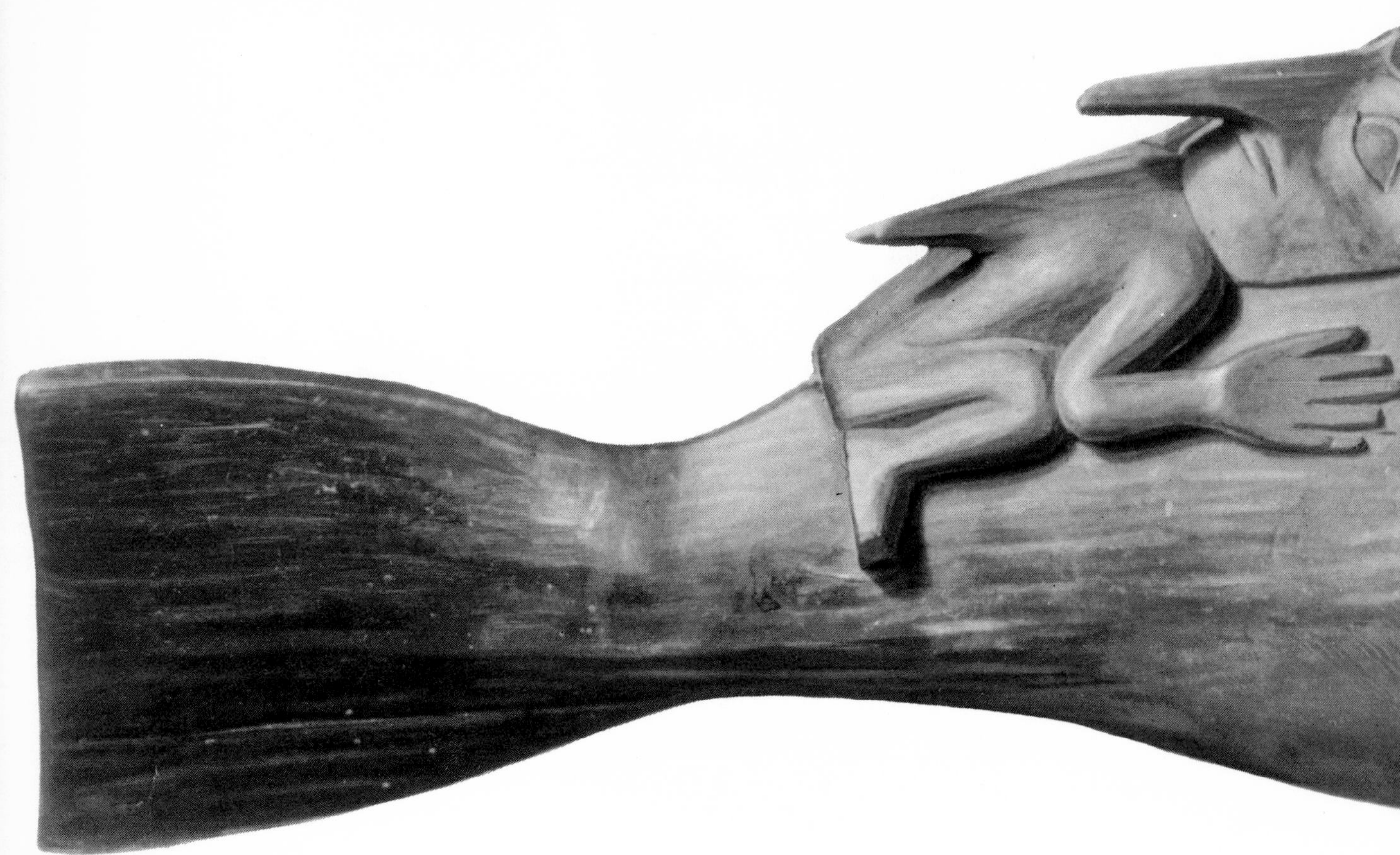

The great enemy of the fishermen of the Northwest Coast was the killer-whale. This carved wooden Haida headdress shows a sea monster carrying men away on his back.

fish and flew away. He screamed and cawed as ravens do, but the fishermen mistook it for profane language and were shocked. Raven flew on and then alighted and changed himself into an old man and walked back to the shore. He could hear the fishermen talking about the foul bird that had slipped through their hands. He suddenly came among them and burst out laughing. 'I have now changed myself to an old man. I'm bent on destroying you unless you leave at once.' The whole tribe fled, leaving everything in the village to Raven.

The Lady Hanging Hair

Some of the legends told by the Indians of northwest America are surprisingly similar to those of ancient Europe. Here is one reminiscent of the story of Scylla and Charybdis. It tells of a dangerous whirlpool, Keagyihl Depguesk, which means 'Where it is turned upside down'. The people who lived in this particular region sorrowed when many of their bravest young men were sucked down into the waters.

Just across the river there lived a very gentle spirit whose name was Hanging Hair. She dwelt among the trees. When the wind blew the trees so that their branches swayed and hung down over the water, people thought that they could see this beautiful spirit. She protected those who lived nearby. It was she who called a great feast to arrange that Kaegyihl Depguesk should be disappointed of his prey. She invited all the monster powers of nature from the rivers and along

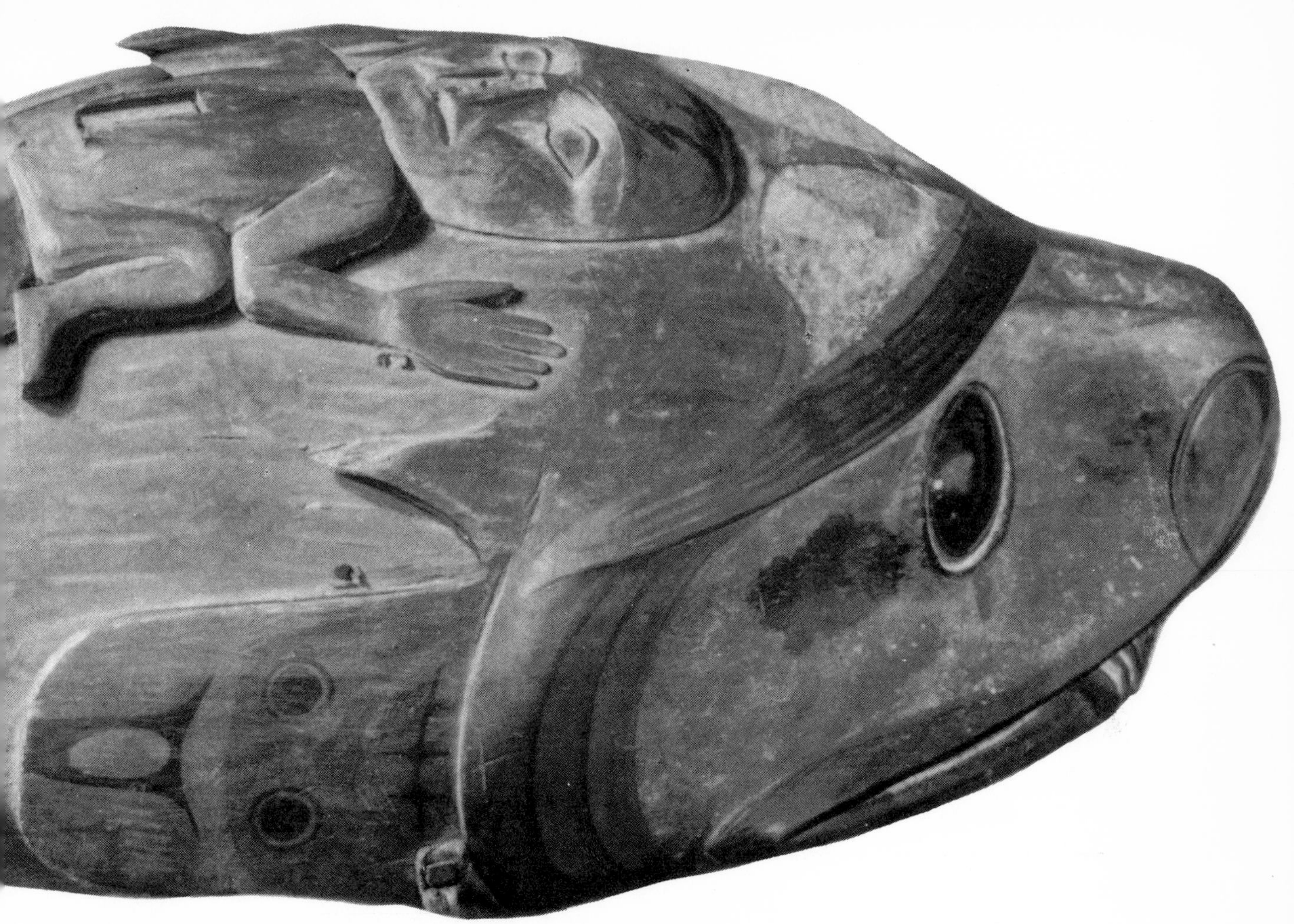

the coast. Some of the guests came roaring along in a storm wind, others calm and gentle in the smooth water. Each one demonstrated his own particular skills, some falling as cliffs, some freezing as pieces of ice, some burning like forest fires, but all entering peacefully into the Festival House, which was under water.

Hanging Hair gave each one, even Kaegyihl Depguesk, his own place on the bench around the wall. Then from her store the hostess brought out the very precious and tasty kidney fat of mountain goats, placing some in front of each of the guests. By magic each piece became a large ball of the most perfect fat, and they ate of it until they were full. At the end of the feast, when everybody was in a good mood, the lady Hanging Hair said that it was time they should have more consideration for human beings, that people who made offerings to the spirit of the whirlpool must not be cheated and destroyed, and that the powers of Kaegyihl Depguesk must be greatly reduced. Solemnly the monsters spoke in turn and finally agreed to shake the earth so that a high bluff, which deflected the water in the river, would be moved to another place, thus reducing the force of the water flowing through the whirlpool. When all the monsters were agreed, the earth shook, the wind blew and the forest fire burnt trees, but nobody in any of the villages was injured. When the storms had subsided, the high bluff had been broken down. The river was now quiet and broad, and the terrible whirlpool was no more than a gentle eddy that actually helped the fishermen on their way.

Opposite page: Two rattles from the Northwest Coast. The top one is made out of beaten copper and was used to call up spirits. The lower one represents a bear and was used to call up bears for the hunt.

The Thunderbird

There are many stories of supernatural creatures. Some tell of the Thunderbird, an eagle with an extra head on its abdomen, which was powerful enough to carry off whales in its talons. Sometimes men actually saw the Thunderbird. One story tells of two hunters who travelled up a river until they arrived at a lake high in the mountains. They made their camp and wrapped themselves for warmth in ferns and leaves. In the middle of the night they heard a tremendous noise coming from the lake. They looked into the water and there they saw an enormous bird. As it arose, a flash of lightning came from its beak and two children stood beside it. The monster bird spread its wings and the sound of them was a roaring of thunder, and lightning flashed again from its beak as it rose. Then it slowly sank back into the lake and when only the beak was visible it released another tremendous flash and roar. The local people, as well as the hunters, witnessed the scene, and feared for the men who were so close to the terrible bird. Their joy was great when they met the hunters unharmed.

The child who grows to full stature in the space of a few minutes, or days, is a recurrent figure in North American mythology. On the Northwest Coast he is represented by Stoneribs, and the event is depicted in this carving from Nootka Sound. 1778. British Museum.

The fantastic worm

Other stories tell of dragon-like creatures. In some ways they resemble the Norse stories of huge and dreadful worms. One story from southern Alaska tells how a chief's daughter had a woodworm for a pet. She fed it with her own milk and as it grew bigger she took food for it from the storeboxes of her parents. When it was two fathoms long she made up a cradle song for it, 'You have a face already and can sit up.' As it grew, she sang, 'You have a mouth already. Sit right up.' Those who overheard these strange songs began to wonder what it was she sang to. The girl's mother peeped into the hut where, according to custom, the girl was secluded because of her first menstruation and saw the enormous worm. The people in the village were frightened, especially as some of them had noticed that the boxes in which they stored oil supplies for winter food had been emptied by some creature that tunnelled in underneath the ground. They blamed the worm.

The chief tried to persuade his daughter to come out of the seclusion hut and, knowing that she could not disobey, she changed her song into a mourning song for the worm and returned to he father's house. As soon as she had gone the villagers attacked the worm and cut it in pieces. The starvation that threatened them through the loss of their oil supplies was soon averted by good fortune and fishing. The girl explained that the tribe's success was due to the spirit of the worm and that it must now be regarded as a symbol of one of the totem clans of the Tlingit people.

The killer whales

In ancient times the greatest powers of the sea were the spirits of the killer whales. There is a heroic legend of a great hunter who met the killer whales in their enchanted home underneath the sea and still escaped. The name of the hunter was Gunarhnesemgyet. Once he killed a white sea otter and skinned it. As he did so a little of the blood ran from the skin into the fur. He gave the skin to his wife to clean, and while she was busy washing it on the sea shore she happened to put both feet upon it and it drifted away. A large black whale came up and caught the skin on his back. The woman held on to his dorsal fin and cried out for help from the villagers, but the whale travelled at tremendous speed and dived under the sea with her. Gunarhnesemgyet grabbed his hunting weapons, ran to his canoe and with a friend pursued the whale as fast as he could. He followed until he came to the place where the whale had dived. Here he took a long leather line, tied it to his boat and held on to it as he dived to the bottom of the ocean, where he found himself in another kind of world. He met a number of Cormorant People there, all blind. He approached them and cut their eyelids open so that they could see. In return they told him the way that he must travel. They warned him not to return by the same route but to follow a roundabout way to avoid capture.

Gunarhnesemgyet followed the trail that had been shown to him. He had gone some distance when he heard the sound of wood being chopped and saw a woodman who had broken the stone wedge that he used to split trees. He was weeping because his master, the Lord of the Killer Whales, would be angry with him. When Gunarhnesemgyet heard his story he put the wedge into his mouth, then took it out, blew upon it, made it whole and gave it back to the woodman. In return the woodman told him that he was cutting wood for Gunarhnesemgyet's wife who was building a fire inside the house of the killer whales. He also warned him that the whales would use magic to put a fin on her back so that she would become one of them. At Gunarhnesemgyet's request the woodman slipped several pails of water from the spring into the house. Gunarhnesemgyet hid near the door and pushed in a long stick and spilt the pails of water on to the hot stones in the fireplace. Steam gushed from the fire and the house was filled with white mist. In the confusion Gunarhnesemgyet rushed to his wife crying, 'Come, escape!' They made for the door. Gunarhnesemgyet put some magical medicine into his mouth and blew it towards the chief of the killer whales. The whale gradually began to swell, until he became so huge that he blocked the door. In an attempt to shrink him, his wives rushed over and urinated on him, but the shrinking was slow and it was some time before the whales could pass through the door. When the whales caught up with the pair they had reached the line attached to the canoe and shaken it. Gunarhnesemgyet's companion felt the tug on the line and hauled up Gunarhnesemgyet and his wife. Meanwhile the Cormorant People had set traps into which they put a special herb which the killer whales swallowed and which put them to sleep. Eventually Gunarhnesemgyet and his wife they reached the safety of home, and the killer whales returned to their own world.

Mythical heroes

The story of the strong man with magic powers is another heroic myth found in every mythology. In European myths he is usually

A Haida grave-post carved with the deceased's totem. It shows, from top to bottom, a bear's head, a human head, a fish (possibly a killer whale) and at the base a stylised raven's head. Natural History Museum, Vienna.

helped by gods or goddesses, but in the Northwest Coast stories the hero has a supernatural power within himself. Some of the stories concern Stoneribs, who was the son of Volcano Woman. It is said that as soon as he began to walk, he was able to make his own bow and arrow and shoot birds. Soon after his first adventures he heard voices crying in the winds. People farther to the south needed his help.

He left his mother and walked down to the seaside where he sat and watched the sea from underneath a cedar tree. An eagle flew across the water, seized a halibut and threw it on the beach. The boy picked up the flat fish and noticed that on its body there was a strip of copper, which he interpreted as a mark given to it specially by his mother, the Volcano Woman, for she had charge of all the copper in the world. He shot his arrow through the fish and tried to skin it, starting at the head and working towards the tail, but he was unable to do this. A voice from the cedar tree told him that he was working the wrong way. So he skinned the fish starting at the tail. Then he stretched out the skin to dry to make himself some clothing.

With the aid of the magical garment he could turn himself into a supernatural being, able to swim in the sea like a halibut. In this disguise he swam rapidly southwards towards the voices crying for help. He came in to the shore, changed back into human form and crept through the bushes. He saw a canoe full of fishermen chased by finback whales which wrecked the canoe and killed the fishermen. He could still hear voices crying faintly for help and when he came to their village he saw a woman crying and with her a baby screaming with hunger. There was no food. When he peeped into the house he saw only a few starving people lying about, unable to speak. He removed the child and took its place magically in the cradle. He gave unexpected power to the woman so that she could feed her new baby and he grew up magically to the full size of a man.

He went out to help the people collect some mussels for food. Before setting off in the canoe he took his bow and arrows, shot a blunt arrow at the side of the canoe and called out the name of the great sea monster Qagwaai twelve times. Then, with the other tribesmen, he jumped into the canoe. Soon they saw the great sea monster, in the form of a killer whale, swimming after them with its mouth wide open. The boy took his arrow and shot at its head; it dived down, only to reappear and chase them again. Once more it opened its mouth ready to swallow them all, but the boy jumped into the gaping mouth and disappeared inside the monster. As Qagwaai dived deep into the ocean, the boy wished for his magic power and then shot his arrow right through the monster, killing it from within. By killing Qagwaai Stoneribs punished the whales for killing so many tribesmen.

When the monster was cast up on the beach, the boy emerged, skinned it, and dried the skin in the sun. He put the skin over himself and was able to swim out to sea with the same power and speed as the dead monster.

He moved farther south to other islands, where he saw a great wooden house. Somebody within called out, 'Come, stay with me tonight.' He entered the house where he found a great monster. The monster gave him a box to lay his head on while he slept. As soon as

A grotesque mask in the form of a human face with a raven's mouth. It is surrounded by a ring of heads and may represent Raven rogether with his other personalities.

his head touched it the box burst open. At this the monster realised that his visitor was something strange, and dried to trap him. It cried out 'Stone door, close yourself! Smoke, hole, shut yourself!' And at once the house closed itself up. Stoneribs was trapped; he was still in the form of Qagwaai the whale, and wondered how he could save himself within the space of a house that was only just big enough to hold him. He noticed that there was a narrow slit at the bottom of the stone door and remembered that he still had the halibut skin tied to his belt. He quickly put this on and the large and bulky whale was changed to a small flat halibut. Then he put his thin tail under the crack in the stone door and pushed. The stone shattered, salt water rushed into the house and he swam away.

Later he arrived safely at another inlet where he once more changed skins and became the magical whale. A gigantic crab spread out its legs to capture him. He was caught by one of its pinchers, which nearly squeezed him to death, even though he was in whale form. Again he put on the halibut skin and, again suddenly reduced in size,

An ivory-headed shaman's rattle in the shape of a loon. The head on the bird's back represents its spirit. The loon features in Northwest Coast mythology as a messenger from men to the world of spirits. Late eighteenth century. Vancouver Island. British Museum.

At the potlatch festivals slaves were sometimes clubbed to death as a demonstration of their owner's contempt for property. Kwakiutl slave-killer. Pre-1900. British Columbia.

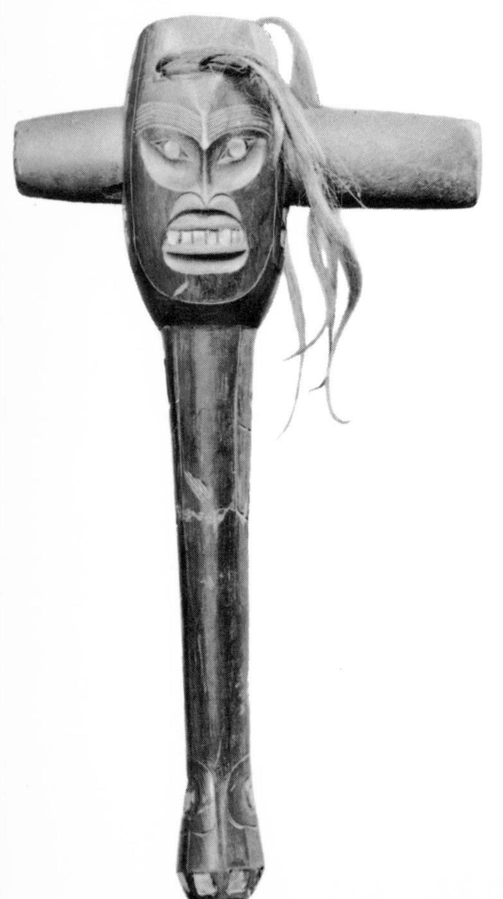

slipped between the legs of the crab and escaped leaving the large whale skin in the trap. Disguised as a halibut he swam on and eventually managed to come up in a safe bay where he took his halibut skin off and hung it up to dry while he sat down warming himself in the sun. Suddenly he heard a noise and was just in time to see an eagle steal his halibut skin and fly away with it. He called other birds to attack the eagle, but he heard a voice from the woods telling him that he must not touch the eagle, that the skin had only been lent and now it had been taken away as magically as it had come. So he decided to travel no more and returned in his normal human form to his mother. Proud of her courageous son she gave him a new name; instead of Stoneribs he was ever after called Crystalribs.

The lazy boy

There are many other tales told of mystical heroes with spiritual power that gave them the ability to overcome natural obstacles. One young boy was a lazy and over-sleepy child, and everybody called him names and laughed at him. When the men were away hunting or fishing he would go to the sea and wash himself with magical herbs so that he became stronger and stronger in secret. But whenever other people were near he would pretend to be as lazy and foolish as usual. Whenever trouble came to the tribe they always left him to the very last before asking him for help. However, he had such strength that people became aware he was a supernatural being.

As time passed, the world seemed to threaten the tribespeople and they did not know what to do. The forest trees and the mountains slowly moved in, crushing the settlements, driving people away, killing them. The chiefs and magicians all tried their magic powers, but without success. Finally the people decided that the only thing to do was to abandon their homes and crowd themselves into the canoes and get away to sea. Just as they were stepping into the last canoe the young hero awoke from his sleep in the corner and said, 'Why is everybody so excited? Why are they going away?' The chief replied, 'If you could keep awake you'd know that the forest is pushing us into the sea. Whole villages have vanished while you slept.'

The young man then rose up and went to the back of the house. There he began to pull up trees, roots and all, to build a barricade. He pushed it forwards, sweeping the entire forest back into the hills. He kept on pulling up trees by the roots, and so made it forever impossible for the forest to move again. He returned to the village and said to the people, 'It is well that you have only little things like this to worry you.' And without another word he curled up on a warm bed near the fire and slept again as though he had never been disturbed. Soon after this, the spirits who control the shape of the earth started flattening the hills. Once again the people prepared to run away, but first told the young man. He was quite unconcerned and went to sleep again, but when the people's fears grew he took action. First he chewed some of his magical herbs and bathed, then he called the loon to his aid. He said, 'Go to my grandfather and tell him what is happening. I must help the people. I must push the mountains and hills back and divide them, so that the rivers can flow through them.' At once the bird flew off with the messages. When, later on, the young man heard the loon calling him he knew that his grandfather had sent him the magical powers he needed. He threw back the hills and the mountains, and broke them apart, so that rivers ran between them and it was no longer possible for them to cascade down bringing destruction. Then the young man returned to his uncle's house, lay down and fell asleep.

The people acclaimed and feared him as the greatest of all magicians and medicine men. But one night a large canoe landed and a man disembarked with his servants, saying, 'This is the place where our master sleeps. We are seeking him', and they walked straight to the chief's house where the young man lay. They said, 'Master, great chief, your grandfather is ill and sent us. You have done everything that can be done. Your mission is finished. Your canoe is waiting.' He answered and said, 'I am ready.' Then he turned to the chief and said, 'I must go to my grandfather who has grown weak. I must relieve him of his work of holding up the earth on a long pole. Now I shall hold it in his place. But remember, never ridicule somebody you do not know. Now you can rest assured that no more harm will befall the world.' And he joined his strange visitors.

Now whenever the young man spreads his arm or moves his feet he causes earthquakes and when the medicine men wish to send a message to him the loon is his messenger.

The myths of the Northwest Coast Indians are influenced by the dominating features of their lives. Thus the salmon and bears which are important food animals to the tribes play a part in their myths and have spirits that have to be placated. Other creatures, dangerous to man, such as the eagle and the whale, are feared for their supernatural powers as well as their physical powers. Parallel to the stories of the supernatural monsters are stories of the mythical hero with supernatural powers of his own, who can oppose them on equal terms. In their emphasis on force and cunning, all these myths reflect the aggressive life of tribes of this region who depended on hunting for their livelihood.

The Hunters of the Northern Forests

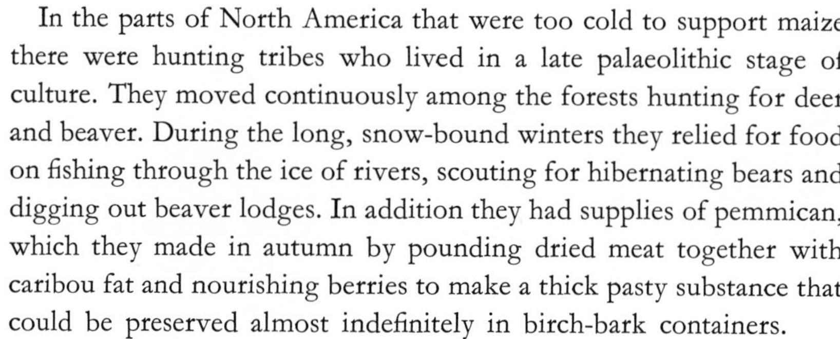

In the parts of North America that were too cold to support maize there were hunting tribes who lived in a late palaeolithic stage of culture. They moved continuously among the forests hunting for deer and beaver. During the long, snow-bound winters they relied for food on fishing through the ice of rivers, scouting for hibernating bears and digging out beaver lodges. In addition they had supplies of pemmican, which they made in autumn by pounding dried meat together with caribou fat and nourishing berries to make a thick pasty substance that could be preserved almost indefinitely in birch-bark containers.

Principal tribes: Algonkian Chippewa Cree Nascopie

In the summer the forests teemed with life. Rivers could be navigated in birch-bark canoes that were used more for fishing than as a means of transport, although tribal territory sometimes extended over some hundreds of miles. In this land then, there were small communities of several families travelling over their hunting territories and occasionally meeting together for ceremonial occasions. Their clothing was made entirely from skins, and even in early times covered them completely as a protection against the cold of winter and the attacks of the mosquitos in the summer. No half-naked tribe could survive in these conditions.

The Cree

These Indians of the Northern forests were mostly members of the great Cree nation, divided into widely separated bands, but all speaking a common language. In earlier times their culture was based on the possession of good, flaked-stone tools. They used arrow heads, scrapers and knives, but as they had no need to cut down trees they never invented heavy stone axes. The forest itself was a home in which both the hunter and the hunted lived with some degree of comfort. The number of animals, though quite large, was not sufficient to support a settled population. The hunters added to their diet all kinds of wild berries, and some of the grasses produced edible grain which was beaten up to make paste or boiled for gruel.

A box in which the feather headdress of a Chippewa Indian was stored in between ceremonies. The lid bears a pictograph record of one of the ceremonial chants and could only be read by an initiate. Wisconsin. 1850–75.

Ancestor spirits

The mythology of the Cree people was based on the spirits of the hunt. They believed in an earth spirit who was another of the animals; and in an ill-defined sky being who displayed a general interest in the human race. But the root of their religion lay in their close relationship with their ancestors. It was felt that the 'old people' were always near, ready to assist the tribe with advice or warning. Occasionally, people who were endowed with shamanistic faculties would fall into a trance and visit the camps of the ancestors underneath the earth. But as in most legends of this kind, it was emphasised that the visitor should accept no hospitality at the hands of his hosts. Once the food of the dead had been eaten by a living man his spirit was captured by its new environment and his body, lying in trance in the upper earth, simply died.

The movements of the forest people were dependent upon the seasons and they had many legends about the winds and about the positions of the sun and stars. As is usual in such a mythology the animals could speak and tell stories, for the whole of nature was an integrated community of animals and men. The world of the primitive hunter was extremely limited, not only in its human contact but also in the development of myths and stories. The relationship between the family and the spirit world was as simple as its relationship with the other families who made up the small tribal group.

The development of more complex beliefs came from contact with more advanced people, or from the adoption of an agricultural routine. This step forward was a vital one in all human societies. Its importance is observed, for example, in the biblical story of Cain and Abel, where the favoured brother was the one who made offerings of the fruits of agriculture rather than those of hunting. Once men learnt to dig the earth in order to grow grain, they took on a completely new relationship with the world of nature, and from this new relationship a new body of myths evolved.

A finely embroidered knife-sheath. The forest tribes paid great attention to their knives and arrows as they were dependant upon hunting for most of their food supply.

Fertility spirits

The new mythology centred around the fertility spirits, who were often a group of goddesses who in many ways mirrored the development of a woman's life. Not surprisingly they were often linked with the monthly phases of the moon. The idea of a protective old father also begins to appear, although in North America this was never a very clearly defined concept. The Great Spirit was a vague generality, a being who did not have contact directly with the shaman but who was known to preside over the activities of the forces of nature. These forces were imminent everywhere; as thunder and hail they had the power to destroy the crops and so reduce man to starvation; as warm winds and rains in the right season they brought blessings. For the primitive agriculturist a whole new world developed in which closer observation of nature became important.

Myths of stars and seasons

Because crops maturing at different seasons demand a much more complex knowledge of the calendar than is found among simple hunting peoples astronomical myths also become more numerous and detailed. The development of agriculture is therefore accompanied by a tendency to divide the sky into regions in which the sun and the planets would appear at different seasons of the year. This in its turn leads to a mythology based on the inter-relations of the planets and their special influences as they move from one part of the heavens to another. There is also a much more complex mythology about rainbows, clouds and thunderstorms.

For example, among the Algonkian tribes there was the cycle of legends which Longfellow described in his Song of Hiawatha. Only the name Hiawatha was wrongly used as it was actually the name of an Iroquois chief who was one of the founders of the Five Nations. But this cycle of stories represents the generalised mythology of an Algonkian group who had rudimentary agriculture but still lived largely by hunting. Their social structure was reflected very clearly in the myths, and there was also a very strong emphasis on the rhythms of the seasons. But the break with the simple hunting mythology of tribes like the Cree was by no means complete. Ancient traditions lingered on among the agriculturists, and remained a strong influence among those tribes who still subsisted largely by hunting.

Village festivals

The new agricultural life was accompanied by greater sophistication in the stories, since they were no longer mere anecdotes recited among members of the family, but began to form part of the oral literature of large communities when settled villages became possible. In the North American forest climate villages usually had two sites, one for winter living, the other for summer living. On moving from one site to another the whole community would have a few days of festival in which stories were told and myths enacted before an audience often of more than a thousand people. On the great occasions when tribal meetings brought people from several villages, it was not impossible for as many as seven or eight thousand people to come together. The stories began to assume definite epic form, in which recognisable heroic archetypes went through a series of adventures. The mythological epics of the farming tribes are completely distinct from the more primitive stories, which have one or two episodes of an emotional character but no continuous theme.

The figure of the deceiver, who is also a culture-bringer and a creator, is a common one in North American mythology. The figure varies considerably in psychological significance, sometimes suggesting merely the spirit of uncertainty, in other forms a strong demonic power. This first story comes from the Eastern Cree Indians.

Wisagatcak and the creation of the world

The Trickster Wisagatcak built a dam of stakes across a creek in order to trap the Giant Beaver when it swam out of its lodge. He waited all day, until in the evening he saw the creature swimming towards him. He was ready to spear it, when Muskrat suddenly bit him from behind and made his spear stroke miss. So he gave up hunting that night. Next morning he decided to break down the dam, so he levered the stakes of the dam out of place. The water flowed out, and kept on flowing. But the level of the creek did not fall. The Giant Beavers had worked magic against Wisagatcak because he had broken the dam. All the land was covered. As the waters rose Wisagatcak pulled up some trees to make a raft and collected many different kinds of animals which were swimming about in the waters. For two weeks the Beavers made the waters rise until no land was left. At the end of the two weeks Muskrat left the raft and dived down but could not find any earth, and stayed below the surface so long that he died. Then Raven left the raft; he flew for a whole day yet saw no land, only water in all the four directions. Then Wisagatcak made his own magic and called Wolf to help. Wolf ran round and round the raft with a ball of moss in his mouth. As he ran, the moss grew and earth formed on it. Then he put it down and they danced around it singing powerful spells. The earth grew. It spread over the raft and went on growing until it made the whole world. The Cree storytellers enforce this myth by pointing out how sometimes the water that is now beneath the earth pours out as a spring from under the rocks.

A witchcraft doll from a Chippewa medicine-bundle. This small wooden figure was used by the headman in Bad Medicine rites to bewitch people. Manitoba. 1850–1900.

Left: Cree drum with a thunderbird design. The destructive forces of thunder, hail and wind were given increased prominence in the myths of the forest people as they took up agriculture and accordingly came to depend on fine weather.

The brothers who created the world

The Algonkian creator force was the hero Gluskap, who had a destructive wolf-brother Malsum. When their creator died, Malsum made rocks, thickets and poisonous animals, while Gluskap took the body of this mother earth to form the pleasant plains, the food plants, animals, and the human race. Malsum tried to find out what magic could kill his rival, and in jest asked him what could kill him, adding that only fern root could cause his own death. Gluskap replied that an owl feather was the only thing that could slay him. So one evening

Malsum took the feather of an owl's wing and used it in place of an arrow head to shoot his brother. Gluskap fell dead but immediately after, by his great magic, he recovered. Suspecting his brother's treachery he went into the forest and sat by a stream declaring that only a flowering reed would kill him. A toad hearing this hopped away and, asking for the power to fly as a reward, told Malsum the secret. But Malsum refused to give the toad the power of flight, and said it would look silly with wings. To be revenged the creature hurried back to Gluskap and told him of his danger. Gluskap thereupon plucked a large-rooted fern stem. With it he struck down Malsum and killed him, driving his evil magic below the earth. Unlike his brother, Malsum was unable to revive; he became a cruel and vindictive wolf.

Left in peace Gluskap completed the creation of the world from the body of his mother. He drove away many evil creatures and conquered the stone giants. But he was often of a whimsical turn of mind. In one case, when four men came to him begging that he would help them, he asked them what they wished. One wanted to become gentle instead of quarrelsome, another wished for enough riches to get himself a home and not be a despised beggar, a third, who was laughed at by the tribe, wanted to become an ordinary man, as stately and respected as his fellows. The fourth wanted to be taller and more beautiful than other men so that he could rule over everyone. So Gluskap gave each a box of medicine. The first three found it gave them their wishes; and so did the fourth, since he grew, tall and stately, into the first and greatest of all pine-trees.

Gluskap had one fault: pride. He had done such wonderful things and conquered so much evil that he would not believe that anyone could defeat him. But one day a poor woman told him that she knew one person who could withstand all his powers. He refused to believe her, but she persuaded him to come into her bark lodge. Making himself as small as an ordinary man, he entered. There, sitting on the floor newly dusted with white ashes, was a baby boy. The great Gluskap sang and the child smiled. He told it to walk, still the child only smiled. He changed himself into strange shapes and the child laughed happily, but it would neither walk nor talk with him. He grew angry and shouted, whereupon the child burst into tears, but still neither walked nor talked. The great wonder-worker was defeated.

Eventually Gluskap left the land in a birch-bark canoe, travelling towards the sunrise, for his work was completed, but it was believed he might return one day.

The myths of the forest Indians show the development of a more sophisticated mythology as the tribes turn from a life of hunting to an agricultural routine. The transition can be seen in the story of Wisagatcak, where a typical hunting myth about a man being punished by the spirits for his ill-treatment of animals develops into the story of creation. The primitive hunting tribes did not have creation myths. The growth of large settled communities made possible regular trival festivals which gave rise to the epic legend in which a hero, such as Gluskap, goes through a series of adventures. This transition from hunting to agricultural preoccupations, which is evident in the myths of the Northern Forests, is almost complete in the Eastern Woodlands.

Many of the North American tribes kept medicine-bundles in which were stored objects and fetishes associated with the mythical history of the tribe. This Algonkian medicine-pouch is made out of an animal's skin and hung with fur charms.

Left: A box drum from the Haida Indians of the northwest coast. The design represents a bear, an animal very familiar to the tribes of the region. Drums of this kind were usually to be found hanging from the ceiling.

The Farmers of the Eastern Woodlands

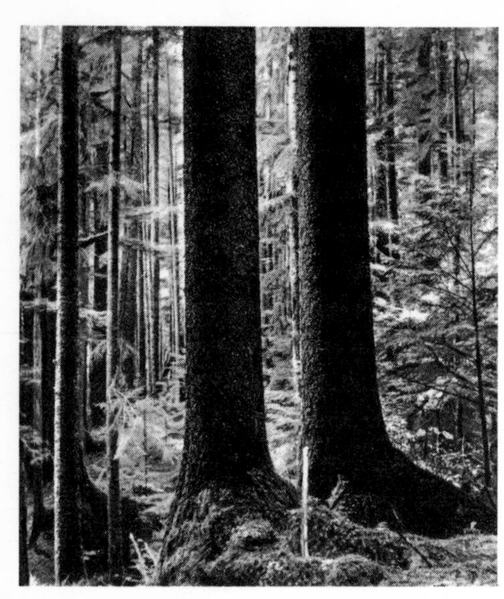

The Indian peoples south of the St Lawrence River down to Delaware Bay, and inland to the region of the Great Lakes, were grouped in many tribes, speaking three main languages. Most of them were members of the Iroquois people, known as the Five Nations. Like their southern neighbours the Lenape or Delaware, and their northern neighbours the Algonkian tribes, they inhabited temperature woodland country where the heavy snows of winter were followed by warm moist summers, in other words the climate of New York today. All had a good knowledge of agriculture when they were discovered by the white man. There was a good deal of hunting for deer and moose, as well as for the fur-bearing animals, beaver, squirrel and fox. The rivers and lakes provided good fishing.

The importance of agriculture

Agricultural life was based mainly on the cultivation of maize, which had spread, over a very long period of time, from the Mexican plateau through the American southwest, proceeding mostly by trade and barter along the rivers until it reached the region of the eastern woodlands. Agricultural techniques were fairly simple. Digging sticks were used to break the ground, and the earth was piled up into small hillocks in which maize seeds were planted. Fields were carefully weeded and tended by the women and children. After a few years a field would be abandoned and another piece of land cleared while the original area lay fallow. It was rapidly covered by scrubby undergrowth and remained fallow sometimes for fifteen or twenty years.

The fields surrounded villages of wigwams; which were not mobile tents but long-houses made of bark. A framework of bent saplings was built in the form of a row of arches, sometimes fifteen or twenty feet high and twenty feet wide at the base. This arched structure was covered by sheets of birch and elm-bark to make a weatherproof covering. Screens divided the wigwam into family apartments, each with its own fireplace and smokehole in the roof.

A big village, and they were not uncommon in what was in the circumstances an advanced community, might consist of three or four long-houses each over a hundred feet long.

Transport was primitive, since the horse was not introduced until after the occupation of North America by Europeans. People travelled on foot with packs on their backs, but by far the most popular form of travel was by birch-bark canoe. These light canoes, which could easily be carried by a couple of people, were ideally suited to the mountainous forest country. It was often necessary to leave one river system and carry the boat across to another group of rivers in order to travel from one important village to another. It was possible for most of the crew to step out and carry the load in bundles on their backs while two of their number carried the canoe itself to the next river and prepared it for reloading at a landing stage.

Principal tribes: Delaware Huron Iroquois Lenape Wyandot

Hiawatha and the Five Nations

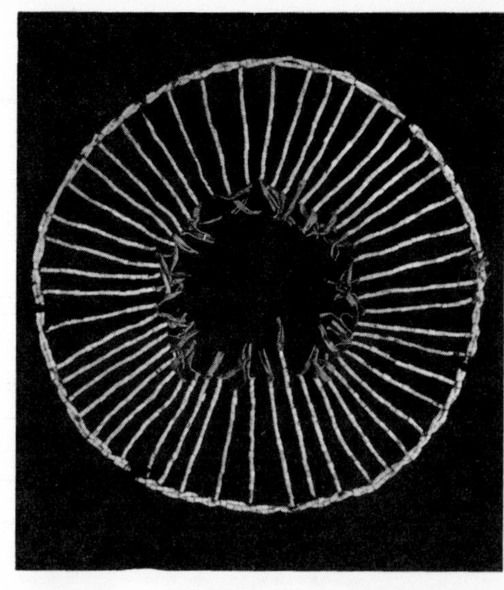

A wampum circle with fifty pendant strings, one for each sachem, or chief, of the confederation of the Five Nations. It was entrusted to the Mohawk nation at the foundation of this federation which united the Seneca, the Cayuga, the Onondaga, the Oneida and the Mohawk into the group known henceforth as the Iroquois.

The Iroquois were an important people because they built up a tribal federation which united five separate Indian nations, all speaking the same basic language, who had previously been constantly at war. This union was brought about only a century or so before the arrival of Europeans by a chief of the Mohawk tribe. He was invited to the Council of Hereditary Chiefs because of his intellectual distinction, and was appointed one of the Lone Pine chieftains who were chosen from among distinguished tribal members regardless of their family. His name was Haio hwa tha, pronounced Hiawatha by the white men. We was able to convince the Council that if Indian life was to continue, the bitter and murderous wars between the five Iroquois tribes must be replaced by federation and regular mettings for united ceremonies. They must prepare plans for spreading the confederation further and further from tribe to tribe until, one day, they would unite all the Indian nations of North America. However, this was not to be; they became involved in the wars between the French and the English and their own tribal organisation was badly undermined, although ceremonial meetings, their system of chieftainship, and above all their great respect for the powers of nature, all continue to the present day.

It is plain that the Iroquois plan was a piece of advanced political thinking. In practice it developed as an organisation for allowing crops to be grown in peace and for organising tribal wars far from their own territory so that no harm would come to the Iroquois people. On one occasion they even raided the Black Hills of Dakota. From this region, a thousand miles from their homeland, they carried prisoners tied on their backs. They were brought back to the great festival so that they could be tortured to death in the ceremonial of fire, by which they were burnt in various parts of their body, for a day or more. It was considered a matter of great importance for a prisoner to be able to show no fear of pain, and to continue singing his death song, praising his own bravery and reviling his captors until he finally became unconscious. This barbarous practice, like the hunting of scalps, was fairly widespread in ancient America, although there is some reason to think that it grew worse when the European powers recruited Indians as allies in their own struggles to achieve dominion. The ancient clubs, spears and arrows were then reinforced by the tomahawk which was not an Indian invention at all.

Records of tribal history were kept through mnemonic objects, usually strings of wampum beads. A wampum belt would be carried over the arm of the Keeper of the Wampum at the great festivals and the stories connected with it recited to the people. This one has a medicine bag attached in the form of a tortoise – the animal which was believed to support the world. British Museum.

Iroquois beliefs

The religious life of these tribes was much more organised than that of the hunting tribes. It centred very largely around shamanistic practices where the usual accompaniment of dance, song and trance was to be observed. But there was also a highly organised theology. The concept of supreme power among the Iroquois was expressed in the idea that all existence was a struggle between a duality of light and darkness, of good and misfortune. The concept of evil, as we know it, is not characteristic of primitive religion in any part of the world.

Right: A large wooden carving of the Thunderbird. This mythical creature was believed to have an extra head on its abdomen. Its wingbeats sounded like thunder-claps, and lightning flashed from its beak. Haida Indian. Northwest Coast. British Museum.

A classic wooden mask with a fringe of human hair. Hair taken from an enemy's scalp was believed to possess supernatural power and, after purification, was often used in this way to give protection to the owner.

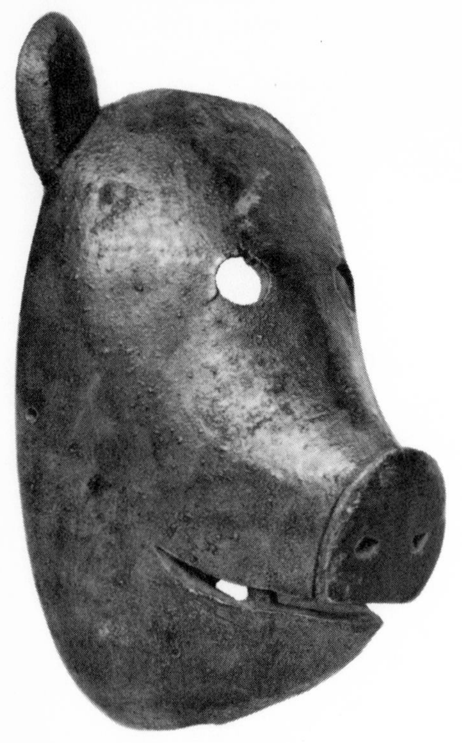

Iroquois masks were designed to emphasise their symbolic importance, not their beauty. This mask reflects the importance of the pig as a food-animal to the Iroquois, just as the corn-husk masks reflect the importance of agriculture.

Although primarily an agricultural people, the Eastern Woodlands tribes still depended on hunting for their meat and felt a special relationship to the animals they hunted. This mask is made from the head of a deer and was worn at ceremonies designed to bring better hunting to the tribe.

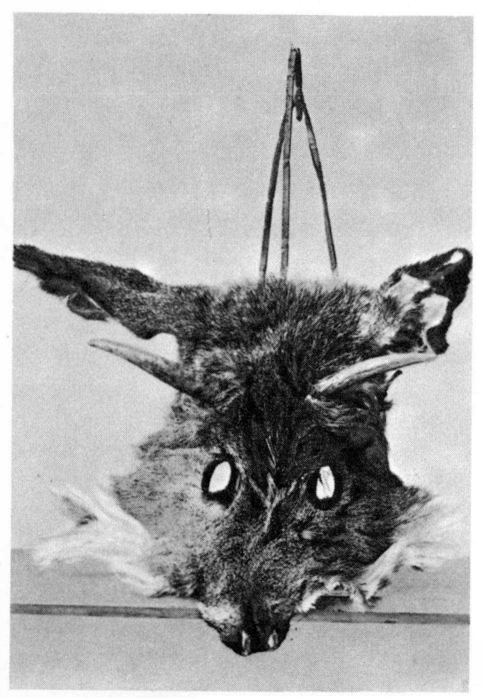

What was called bad was what was unlucky in material affairs. Great respect was paid to the sun and to the moon and stars; in particular, the Morning Star was very important. The passage of the seasons and the growth of crops made the people aware of the importance of the calendar. As among all American Indians the four directions, north, south, east and west, were important to their beliefs. In many of the legends spirits behave in different ways according to which of the four regions their activities take place in. The universe was believed to be directed by spiritual powers of a mysterious nature to whom men must constantly pray for assistance and guidance. Offerings must be made to them, though human sacrifice was rare except for the prestige killing of prisoners. The first of the harvest, and certain portions of hunted animals were acceptable gifts to the spirits. In the ceremonial observances at the great annual festivals of religious societies in the main settlements of the confederation, and in the 'False Face' ceremonies in which masked dancers impersonated the spirits of nature, offerings of corn and food were made.

The Iroquois believed there was a land of the dead somewhere far away. Warrior spirits in particular were thought to inhabit the sky, and some stories associate them with the appearance of the aurora in the northern heavens. There was an underworld Mother of Animals and, of course, a great number of ancestral spirits. Not only did the ancestors watch over men in their daily activities, they could also be visited in dreams, when they would be found living in beautiful villages underneath the earth, in a condition which seems to have been rather better than that of life on the surface. There was neither war nor sickness and they never lacked skins and food.

These groups of Indians have altered so much in their centuries of close contact with Europeans that it is difficult to discover much about their earlier life. The first objective accounts of them come a century after the first white settlements. It appears that they lived in the bark wigwams described earlier. Their basic tools were made of stone. They did much wood carving, of which very little has survived, but what there is is pleasant in its simplification of natural form. They wore less clothing than in historic times. Leggings, breech clout and cape was the costume of the men. Women wore knee-length skirts to which was added a large skin cloak in bad weather. It is difficult, in view of the almost complete lack of archaeological material, to know much about the daily life. More of it is preserved in folk-lore than in any other way. But probably the social organisation has been preserved carefully because tradition in tribal life was always important.

Wampum belts

Records of tribal history and remarkable adventures were kept through a system of mnemonic objects. These were usually strings or belts of wampum, made of great numbers of beads of white and purple shell. Wampum was a valuable article of exchange, and a fathom, that is a string of wampum as long as a man's arm-span, was a unit of value recognised over the tribal territories of the north-eastern region.

Keepers of the Wampum were important tribal dignitaries; they kept the store of historic strings and belts in special wooden boxes. At the great annual tribal gatherings the belts were brought out and the stories associated with them were recited to the people, so that everybody should be acquainted with the tribal history and tradition. Young men who showed promise were taken to be servants and assistants to the Keepers of the Wampum so that they in turn should learn the tradition more thoroughly. In time they would be able to take over the great responsibility of preserving the unity of the tribe through its historic past.

Most of the Iroquois myths that we now know were first recorded by missionaries and traders in the late seventeenth and the eighteenth century, but we have no real check on their earlier forms. However the custom of holding faithfully to tradition can probably be assumed to have existed among the Iroquois long before the European arrival.

A seventeenth century wooden club from the east coast region. Under the federation tribal war was conducted by the Iroquois far from their own territory, so that their own lands were not endangered.

The supreme spirit

Religion among the Indian tribes of the eastern woodlands is reported to include the concept of an All-Father of the type of Odin or Zeus, but it is more probable that this concept had derived from contact with European Christians, which began with the visit of Vinlanders from Greenland about the year 1002. The concept, found among the Northwest Coast Indians, of a sky house, where an angry old chief lived, was no doubt an explanation of meteorological phenomena. The Indians of the great forests had a wider concept of nature, and their thinkers postulated a supreme spirit, all-embracing, but without form and having little contact with men. The concept was more like an abstract notion such as Time, thought of as the bearer of fore-ordained events. For most people this Great Manitou, or spirit, was an ever present emotive force that took second place to the world of nature spirits who were concerned with daily events.

The whole world seemed imbued with life to the primitive agriculturist. The Iroquois and their kindred tribes knew of the spirit forces which drove rivers, danced with the rain clouds, swept through the trees, and changed the face of the land in spring and autumn. The food crops were blessed by protective feminine spirits, five sisters who were sometimes glimpsed as they rustled among the corn or shook the stems of squash and pumpkins.

Agricultural festivals

As elsewhere agricultural life demanded a different rhythm from hunting. The hunters' two seasons of animal migration were replaced among the Iroquois by six regular festivals based on the stages of growth. The first festival of the year involved a cleansing ritual in which public confessions of the past year's misdeeds were made while holding white wampum. In ancient times the people tickled their throats with wooden swallow-sticks until they vomited, thus cleansing themselves before the world of spirits and humans as a preparation for the ceremonies held to celebrate the first rising of sap in the maple trees. (Maple sugar was an important food item.)

The other festivals were those for planting corn, collecting the first strawberries, the appearance of the ears of green corn in the maize fields, the festival to celebrate the harvest and finally the great White Dog festival of the new year, in which the Power Above was thanked, and a white dog sent to the skies as a messenger. At every stage of the ritual year there was a reminder of the relationship between the spirit world and the real people. The festivals were always a great social occasion, with a great deal of jollification. But the rituals were very serious, and even the wild behaviour of the masked beggars of the False Face Society had an important ritual meaning.

In this outward expression of the myths there are parallels with the agricultural rituals of Europe which are very striking, and which include carnivals, masked begging by children and mummers plays. Man has a tendency to develop a sympathetic magical relationship with nature, and to mime and mask the desired events. Since agricultural pursuits are so closely linked with fertility and the wonders of sex, the festivals were often occasions of free and happy licence, without the usual social inhibitions. This part of the celebrations has persisted through time, even after the close link between human behaviour and favourable harvests has been abandoned as an article of faith.

Because of the long contact between the Iroquois and European missionaries and traders, it is probably best to study the myths of these woodland Indians through the stories of the less acculturised people such as the Hurons, who never amalgamated in the Iroquois manner. The following is a creation legend reported in earlier times from the Iroquois as well as more recently from Huron and Wyandot story-tellers.

The creation of the world

The first people lived beyond the sky because there was no earth beneath. The chief's daughter fell ill and no cure could be found. A wise old man was consulted and he told them to dig up a tree and lay the girl beside the hole. Many people began to dig but as they did so the tree suddenly fell right throught the hole they had made dragging the girl with it.

Below was an endless sheet of water where two swans floated. There was a sound, the first thunder clap, and as the swans looked up, they saw the sky break and a strange tree fall down into the water. Then they saw the girl fall after it. They swam to her and supported her because she was too beautiful to allow to drown. Then they swam to the Great Turtle, master of all the animals, who at once called a council.

When all the animals had arrived the Great Turtle told them that the appearance of a woman from the sky foreshadowed future good fortune. Since the tree had earth on its roots, he commanded them to find where it had sunk, and then to bring up some of the earth, so that it could be put on his back to make an island for the woman to live upon.

The swans led the animals to the place where the tree had fallen. First Otter, then Muskrat and then Beaver dived. As each one came

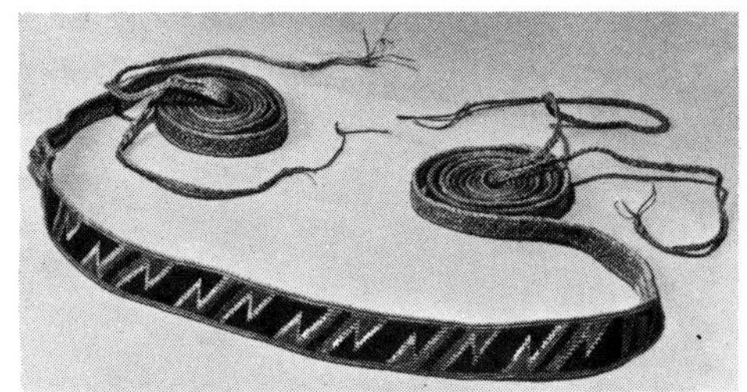

A burden strap used by the Iroquois to carry prisoners back from battle to be ceremonially tortured to death. The wide strap went across the forehead to take the weight of the burden, the rest was used to tie up the prisoner. The moose-hair embroidery had symbolical significance, but its meaning has been lost. British Museum.

Left: A man's shirt made of mountain goat hair trimmed with a fur design representing a brown bear, one of the totem animals inhabiting the Northwest Coast.

up from the great depths he rolled over exhausted and died. Many other animals tried but the same fate overcame them. At last the old lady Toad volunteered. She had been below a long time, until all the animals thought she had been lost, when at last she surfaced and before dying managed to spit a mouthful of earth on the back of the Great Turtle. It was magical earth and had the power of growth. As soon as it was as big as an island the woman was set down upon it. The two white swans circled it, and it continued to grow, until at last it became the world island as it is today, supported in the great waters on the back of the Turtle. But it was dark. Again the Great Turtle called the animals. They pondered for a long time. They decided they should put a great light in the sky. But no one could take it there, until the Great Turtle called Little Turtle and she confessed that she might be able to climb the dangerous path to the heavens. Everyone invoked their own magical powers to assist her. A great black cloud was formed; it was full of clashing rocks, and from their movement lightning flashed out. Little Turtle climbed into this cloud and was carried around the sky, collecting the lightning as she went. First she made a big bright ball of it and threw it into the sky. Then she thought it was well to have some more light so she collected still more lightning but only enough for a smaller ball. The first ball became the sun, and the second the moon. Then the Great Turtle commanded the burrowing animals to make holes in the corners of the sky so that the sun and moon could go down through one and climb up again through the other as they circled. So there was day and night.

Astronomical myths

The sun and moon were credited with human words and deeds. They quarrelled. They were like man and wife. Once the moon passed through the hole at the edge of the sky before her husband. He was enraged and beat her so violently that she disappeared for a time. Again Little Turtle set off, this time into the dark world below. There she found the moon woman who had lost most of her light because she had pined away. She was so thin that instead of a ball she was only a tiny crescent. Little Turtle mended the moon and set her on her course again. She gradually became her own round self; but as the sun passed in the opposite direction he looked away and refused to recognise her. Again she began to pine away. And so it has continued ever since, with the moon hoping and sorrowing each time she passes round her cycle with the sun.

It was after this that the thunder cloud came down and the rain made a rainbow. The deer saw this wonderful bridge and raced up its shining pathway to find a pasture in the sky. Later Little Turtle found that the other animals envied the deer, and allowed many of them to climb the rainbow. They can now be seen as the stars.

This composite legend continues with the birth of the two opposing gods on earth. The idea of a Spirit of Blessing and a cruel Trickster is very common in American Indian mythology. It is almost certainly derived from ancient tradition and the beings are, in fact, archetypal figures derived from certain aspects of the unconscious mind. The

Wyandot version described here divides the whole world into pleasant and easy, and unpleasant and difficult. This division is only part of the concept however. Further study reveals that the two opposing principles are creative usefulness and harsh destructiveness. And to find that the destructive force was reckoned the less powerful by these simple farming tribes people comes as a slight surprise.

Above and opposite page: Details from 'An accurate delineation of New France', made in 1657 by Père François Joseph Bressani and now in the Bibliothèque Nationale, Paris. These early maps often included illustrations which give a valuable glimpse of everyday Indian life as it probably appeared to the early explorers.

The destructive and creative twins

When the Woman Fallen from the Sky was settled on the world island, she realised that she was pregnant with twins one of whom, Taweskare, said he would kick his way through his mother's side. Tsentsa, the other twin, told him he was evil, and that they should be born in the usual way. The Woman had found her mother, who also descended from the sky to help her. But when the time came the evil twin burst forth from his mother's armpit and so killed her. The little boys, however, were strong and healthy and were brought up by their grandmother. Tsentsa's habit was to work for a while and then rest. While he was resting Taweskare would work even harder undoing the good that his brother had wrought. When the fertile plains and undulating valleys were made on the world island Taweskare heaved parts of them up to make barren mountains, and cleft others to make terrible chasms and swamps. The good power made a world of fruit trees and pleasant bushes; the evil one made the fruit small and gritty and put thorns on the bushes. One made fishes smooth, the other covered them with horny scales. For long ages the struggle continued, and later legend shows the evil twin retreating west to create the terrible Rocky Mountains.

Heng, the Thunder spirit. Thunder in the atmosphere meant the approach of spring and so Heng was regarded as a kindly spirit and given offerings at the celebration of the seasonal festivals. Watercolour by Ernest Smith.

The atmospheric powers

The twins Tsentsa and Taweskare had shaped the earth. The powers of nature who succeeded them were very close to man. One of the great seasonal powers was the Thunder. Thunder marked the atmospheric changes which heralded the coming of spring, and basically the farming tribes thought of Thunder as showering blessings. But sometimes Thunder swept in bringing destruction and danger, so they assumed a family of thunder children less responsible than the parent. Herein were the seeds of the highly developed mythology of the rain and lightning spirits of Middle American civilisations. In some ways it recalls the cults of Thor Red-Beard and Jupiter Tonans in Europe. But the woodland Indians took a simpler attitude than the Europeans. They lived close to nature, had no temples, and included Thunder among the Manitous or spirits who were given offerings of prayer and dance at the seasonal festivals.

Thunder was one of seven brothers. He was named Heng, a big, vigorous youngster and a great favourite with the others in spite of the unfortunate clumsiness which caused him to break everything he touched. But in the end Heng's clumsy behaviour so exhausted his brothers that they had to part from him. They took him to an island

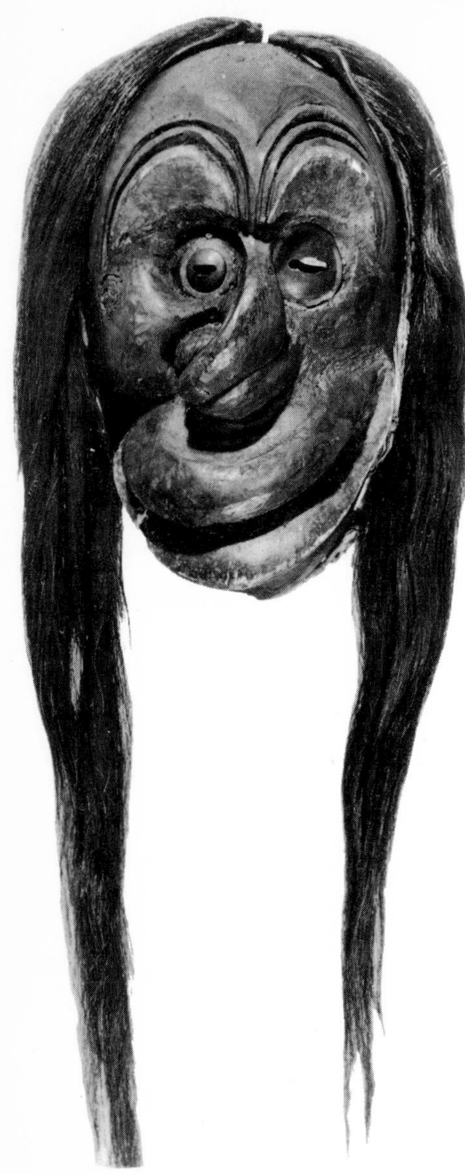

A wooden False Face mask. These grotesque masks were worn in Iroquois ceremonies in the ritual intended to counteract the influence of the malignant False Face spirits. Although usually horrific in appearance, so as to drive away the evil spirits, some of the masks have a rather more humorous aspect.

in a mountain lake. Then they slipped away taking his canoe with them. At first Heng was very angry and stormed terribly, but in time he found his island so pleasant that he made it his home.

Earth and sky spirits

Thunder is a sky power and therefore different from the powers of the earth and underworld. The following myth describes the antagonism at work between the forces above and below, and the feminine force of the earth surface. Part of it derives from simple meteorological observation. The Indians had noticed that lightning was like a serpent, striking both downwards and upwards, and that plants after rain strove upwards from earth to sky to bear their fruit. But apart from the poetic interpretation of fact there are again very deep psychological matters involved. This kind of myth occurs in dramatic dreams, especially as people begin to face the imminent problem of new sex life flowering within them.

In the village among the corn plantations there lived the most beautiful of all young women. She had been so lost in admiration of her own personality that she found no man fit to marry her. But it happened one day that a most handsome young man arrived beside her. As they looked at each other she fell in love, presently promising to marry him. So he called her to follow him, and she cast aside her past habits and walked after him as a good wife should.

They walked a long way, though it seemed almost no distance. At length they reached his long bark wigwam where she was welcomed by his mother and three sisters. Each day the young man would go out to bring in deer meat while the women worked the fields and prepared skins for clothing. One day however he returned very tired. His magic was exhausted. He laid his head in his wife's lap and asked her to clean his hair. As she smoothed the long tresses she felt a terrible change. He had returned to his proper shape and became a gigantic serpent. Her mother-in-law then confessed that they were the Serpent People and told her to run away as fast as she could.

The poor girl, sufficiently punished for her earlier pride, was allowed to escape under the protection of Thunder. Once again her long journey seemed short. She could hear a terrible rustling behind her as the serpent followed, but she crossed the mountains and came to a lake near her home. There stood three handsome men. The tallest cast a shining spear at the serpent and pierced it. At once a roaring black cloud enveloped them all, for the great spearman was Thunder himself.

After this the young men escorted the girl to their father's home on the island, where she married the third son. Eventually they had a baby boy who also had thunder power and when he was four years old his toy arrows would knock down trees.

As the boy was so strong and healthy his mother begged to be allowed to visit her own mother on the earth below. Thunder warned her that if she took the child to show her mother she must never let him shoot at people, even in play. For if he made lightning on earth he must return to the sky at once.

At first all went well. The Thunder Boy played peacefully with his companions, but after a while they began to jeer at him because he never went hunting with bow and arrows. Unable to resist their taunts he seized his bow. He shot an arrow towards the boys. Happily the shot went wide and only set some trees on fire. But his grandfather Thunder swept down in his roaring black cloud and carried the boy away to live high in the sky where he is unable to strike men.

As with all hunting peoples the woodland Indians felt the relationship between man and animals to be close. Even their agricultural activities had not exempted them from hunting as the primary source of food. So there were many animals with whom a special relationship had to be established. Some creatures had ceremonial importance, for instance the eagles which flew highest of all birds and hunted animal prey too. Eagle feathers were a brave ornament to be worn by a chief.

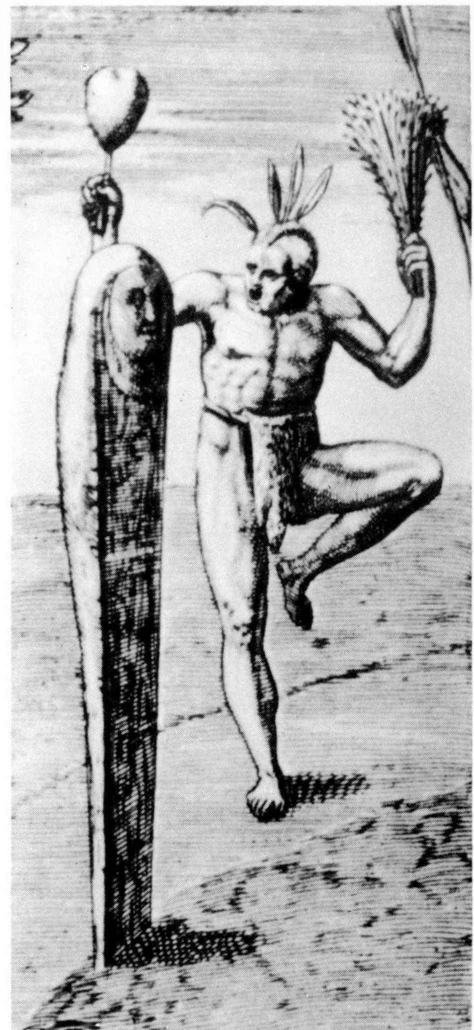

An Indian dancing, from a drawing by John White. He carries a sheaf of corn and a rattle. The artist reported that the dance took place in the evening, to avoid the worst heat felt during the day.

The hunter and the eagle

There is a tale of a hunter who was exceptionally successful in hunting deer. He had a magical power of calling them to eat in the pastures near him where they offered an easy target to his arrows. He was not content with this however. He would call to the eagles, saying that here was fresh meat to take to their eyries. The eagles would descend to eat the meat and then he would shoot them and take their feathers. Everyone warned him that this was dangerous and would bring retribution; but he ignored their warnings.

One day when he called the eagles the gigantic Mother of all Eagles swooped down on him. He fled to hide himself in a hollow log. But Eagle Mother seized the log and carried him to her eyrie. Luckily, he still had his leather carrying-thongs and a little dried meat with him. As the eagle left her nest to seek more food he fed a little of the meat to each eaglet in turn, and then tied up their beaks with his carrying-thong. For two days the Eagle Mother tried unsuccessfully to release her fledglings. Finally she came to an agreement with the hunter. If he would promise to shoot only deer and never to kill an eagle without the permission of the Spirit World, she would return him to earth safely, provided that he first unbound the beaks of her young. The hunter agreed to do so.

Later on his descendants kept his promise for him. Whenever a deer was killed the shaman called the eagles to come and eat in safety.

The myths of the woodland Indians reflect the new and more intimate relationship between men and the world of nature which men experienced when they began to practice agriculture. The struggle to grow crops in face of difficulties of land, climate and disease is reflected in myths, such as the story of Tsentsa and Taweskare, which describe a struggle between light and dark, good and misfortune. The more complicated social organisation which developed in the large, settled, agricultural communities is reflected in the increased complexity of the subject matter of the myths, such as the elaborate creation myth about the Woman Fallen from the Sky, and the relationship they believed to exist between men and the powers of nature is illustrated by the story of the proud young girl rescued from the serpent by Thunder.

The Buffalo Hunters of the Plains

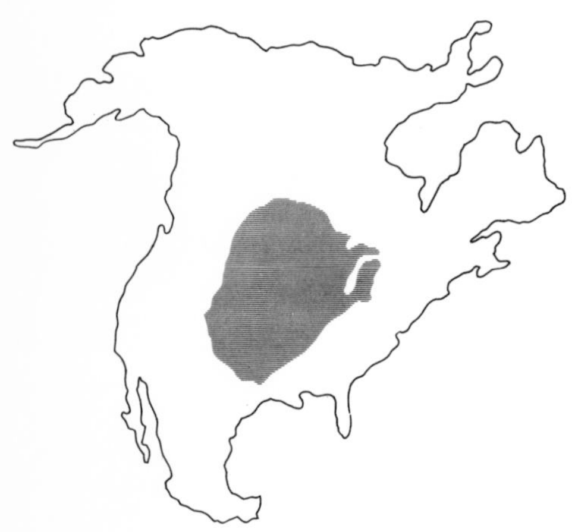

Principal tribes: Arikara Comanche Dakota Mandan Pawnee Sioux

In prehistoric times the Great Plains of North America were an almost unbroken expanse of grass. The lowland stretched for a thousand miles with only occasional hilly ridges. It was intersected by deep-cut river valleys that were often bordered by bluffs. Along these valleys Indian families settled and grouped themselves into large tribes.

When they were first discovered by Europeans they were practising agriculture as much as hunting. They cultivated maize, several varieties of beans and squash and, like the Iroquois, they had fruit plantations. For part of the year they hunted the buffalo and at other times they hunted deer.

The buffalo spirits

The buffalo moved north and south according to season in immense migrations, tens of millions of animals in the herd. They would sweep through everything in their path, and the Indians naturally hoped that they would not trample over their villages. As the buffalo were the main source of their meat supplies, many of the legends naturally related to Buffalo Spirits and the Earth Mother who gave shelter to the archetypal spirits of buffalo in her under-the world home. In times of famine the Indians would pray to her to send out more souls to inhabit the bodies of buffaloes and so bring food to the hungry people.

The horse spread among these Indians only in historic times. Until 1800 all their horses were descended from mounts of the Spanish conquistadores in Mexico, who had brought them from Spain. Many of the horses escaped and wandered free northwards over the fine grasslands. They were captured, broken in and tamed by the Indians, who passed the knowledge of the strange animal and how it could be ridden from tribe to tribe.

Tribal life

The early hunters of the plains must have lived a life very much like that of the palaeolithic hunters of Europe some twelve thousand years ago. They wore very simple skin clothing; leggings and some kind of loose jacket for men, and skirts or loose shifts for women. In cold weather they wore buffalo-skin cloaks.

Hunting was the work of men. They would drive small groups from the buffalo herds over bluffs, or trap stragglers in pitfalls. Often they erected stockaded corrals into which they would drive buffaloes from the rear of the herd.

As well as their regular supplies of vegetable food, they kept stores of dried buffalo meat and pemmican, which was kept in birch-bark boxes and used on long journeys. The search for deer and antelope, beaver, fox, and marten went on all the year round. These animals contributed skin, food and bright, shining teeth to be used as necklaces or as the points of chisels and flaking tools.

The Indian tribes of the plains spoke many dialects although even in ancient times the Dakota seem to have been quite important among the many nations. To the south of the Dakota, another famous tribe, the Pawnee, were active and prominent, preserving some legends which seem to have been brought from somewhere in Central America, perhaps from Mexico in pre-Aztec times. A rather specialised group, retaining many ancient customs, was the Mandan who preserved an interesting and complete mythology.

The pattern of life for these prairie tribes varied with the alternation of summer and winter. In the summer they lived in the tipi, or skin tent on the wide prairie grasslands; in winter they returned to large earth houses near the rivers and the garden plantations. The earth houses were quite large constructions with tree trunks erected as pillars to support a small, square frame, left open as a smoke vent. Encircling the pillars was a low, circular palisade of stakes and brushwood, sunk a few feet below the ground, which formed the walls of a sunken room perhaps twenty or thirty feet across. From these low walls, poles were arranged sloping up to the square central framework. They were covered first with brushwood and then with sods of earth. Seen from outside, the whole house looked like a low conical mound with an entrance at one side and a smoke hole in the top.

The beds were cane structures slung on leather thongs, almost like hammocks, but they were short and square because the Indians slept curled up rather than stretched out straight. In the middle of the house was a fire. The household vessels were usually made of skin, but sometimes pottery was used. The house was a place where the men could chip and flake flints to make arrowheads and spearblades which were sometimes so beautifully made that they can be compared with the best Solutrean work of Europe. The women also worked at sewing and embroidery indoors.

The men of the Plains tribes had various societies, pledged to perform particular duties and to fulfill ceremonial functions. The members of the Dog Society had a special duty to protect the tribe and the costume worn in the Dog Dance, as shown in this painting by Carl Bodmer, emphasised their warlike character. 1832.

The great festivals

During the summer the Plains tribes tended to break up, family

At the Sun Dance ceremony distinguished warriors offered their suffering to the sky spirits. The men taking part ran skewers through their breasts and attached them to a central pole, leaning back so that nearly all their weight was hanging. Then they fixed their eyes on the sun and followed its path across the sky all day, slowly circling the pole. If the warrior succeeded in staying on his feet till sunset he became a medicine-man and won good fortune for his tribe and this happy prospect is reflected in this painting, the work of a Dakota Indian.

groups separating on the prairie in order to enjoy easier hunting. A small group could cut off a section of a migrating herd of buffalo more easily than a whole tribe of people working together. In the great tribal gatherings at spring and autumn festivals, when there were ceremonial dances and initiation ceremonies the families all came together again. Offerings were made to the spirits of sky and earth, and to tribal ancestors. The men belonged to various sacred societies, such as 'Those who are not afraid to die', or the 'Dog Society', or the 'Buffaloes'. These groups had certain magical functions to perform and special costumes to parade at the great festivals. They painted themselves elaborately, and sometimes wore animal disguises.

In times of rest and peace there were mass games, particularly of shinny. This was not unlike hockey, but played with teams of hundreds a side, with a good deal of excitement and usually injuries as well, since under such conditions fights broke out all over the field.

In social life the men had a strong sense of the dignity of warriors. Under the rules of inter-tribal law everything had to be conducted with great punctiliousness. Women, too, delighted in their social life, and worked hard to make beautiful clothes for their husbands. Family ties were strong and there was deep affection between members of a family, who would help each other under all circumstances.

Spirits of the sky

The religious beliefs of the Plains Indians centred on an ill-defined, but all watchful Sky Father. He was an omnipresent power, protecting the people, guarding the world, watching and directing the animals. Between him and the earth there was the realm of eagles, of thunder, of lightning, of the rainbow, of the moving planets and the sun and the moon. These spirits had the power to come down to earth and assume human form if they so wished. Their life in the sky they lived Indian fashion, travelling with their tipis over the prairies or retiring into earth huts during winter, although this winter was not always at the same time as earth's winter. They often intervened in human affairs, inspiring warriors, directing storms, causing rivers to dry up, or altering the path of the migrating buffaloes. They could be propitiated by offerings of human pain. This was the principal reason for the sufferings distinguished warriors inflicted upon themselves in some of the great Sun-Dance ceremonies.

There was a spirit world in which one's ancestors lived in greater and more beautiful villages than those of earth. There were little creatures living within the earth resembling fairies and hobgoblins. In fact, as is usual among primitive peoples, the whole world was imbued with life.

Nesaru and the creation of the world

The Arikara, a typical people of the prairies, believed man came from a previous world under the earth. The first part of their creation myth recalls that of the woodland Indians about the Woman Fallen from the Sky. The great sky spirit Nesaru (known as Wakonda in the Dakota myths) had charge over the whole of creation. Below his sky world there was a limitless lake where two ducks swam eternally at peace. Suddenly they saw Wolf-Man and Lucky-Man. These two both asked the ducks to dive and bring up mud to make the earth. Wolf-Man made a great prairie for the animals to live in. But Lucky-Man made undulating ground with hills and valleys where in the future the Indians could hunt and shelter. Between the two regions the great river began to run as it still does.

Then Wolf-Man and Lucky-Man went under the earth to find the Two Spiders. These were male and female beings, dirty and ugly. The two visitors were very surprised to find that these creatures had no knowledge of how to reproduce their species. The visitors set to work to scrub the Two Spiders. They explained to them the wonderful power of fertilisation. Thus enlightened, the Two Spiders began to give birth to all kinds of animals and to a race of giants.

Nesaru was displeased with these giants, who lived under the earth and would not give obedience to him as the Power Above. So he created maize, and sent down its seeds for the animals to take under the earth. The seeds turned into a smaller race of people, like ourselves. Nesaru then sent a flood which destroyed all the giants without harming the new people who were still under the earth. They developed in their dark underworld, began to wonder if there was a better place, and cried for help. Thereupon Nesaru decided that they should come out into the open world. He sent down a woman from his cornfields, the Corn Mother. She walked far and long, but found no one. Then in the east she heard Thunder, who thrust her down into the underworld.

The people and animals clustered around her in the dark underworld. She called upon the gods and the spirits. The animals were inspired to help her. Badger began the work of digging towards the light but could not bear it as he came near the surface. Then Mole dug further, but the first rays of light blinded him, so he remained in

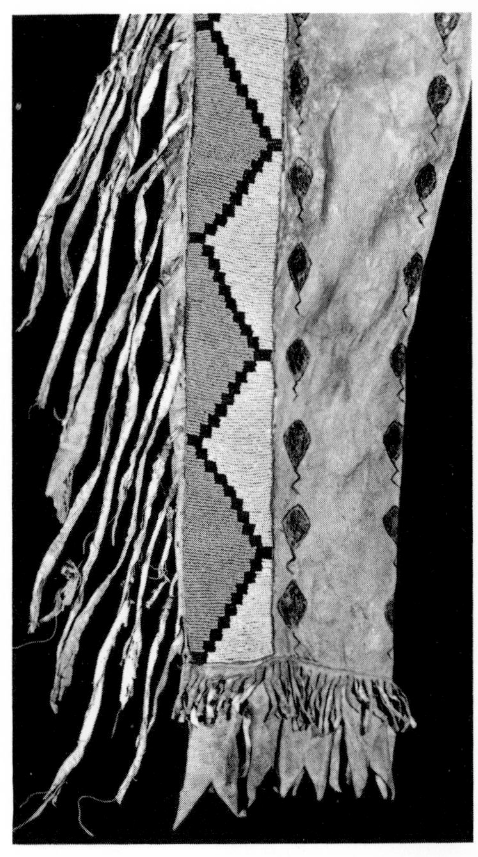

The buffalo hunters lived a very simple life, following the great herds across the plains. Their clothing derived from the animals they hunted and consisted of skin leggings, or skirts, and cloaks. These beaded and painted leggings with the fringed sides follow the traditional pattern of dress. James H. Hooper collection.

Tobacco promoted contentment and was smoked at tribal councils in the central and southern regions of North America. It was sometimes offered to the spirits when their favour was sought. A pipe of the Sioux Indians.

his underground burrows. Lastly, Mouse made the breakthrough but the light was so strong that it cut off the long snout which he once had and he became a short-nosed mouse. Then Corn Mother began to thrust her way into the light. Earth was still tight and close around her. Then Thunder roared again in the east and shook the earth loose so that Corn Mother and the whole creation of humans and animals could come up to the surface.

The people followed the trail westwards from the place of emergence. Many adventures followed. Kingfisher pointed the way, Owl led them through the dark forest, and Loon led them across the lake.

They were given maize to plant, and taught how to play games like shinny. Corn Mother returned to the sky. Left to themselves, the people began to quarrel and fight about the games. Many were killed. But one day they saw beside the lake a wonderful man dressed as a chief. His hair was beautiful and hung down to his waist. He carried a staff hung with captured scalps. It was Nesaru, and he told them how to live at peace together and work under the leadership of a chief. He showed them how to conduct wars, and gave them the rules of honour which included the taking of scalps. These scalps were to be marks of bravery and show which of the warriors was best suited to become a war chief. Then Corn Mother stood beside him to teach them how to grow maize. She told them of the stars, of the planets, sun and moon and the gods in the sky. Lastly she told them that they must take the sacred symbols which would be given to them, and wrap them up to become the sacred medicine-bundles to help them through all dangers.

The people made offerings to the Gods of the Eight Directions of the Sky. Then there was a roaring sound. It was the Wind of the Southeast who had been forgotten. He was like a tornado, and everyone he touched fell dead from disease. But a dog was sent from the sun with medicine to cure them. It told the people about the diseases of man and how to cure them, and explained the reason for the turbulent anger of the Wind of the Southeast. Then the people made the offerings necessary to appease him. They learned to cure diseases. Because of this, whenever the Arikara held a ceremony, they sacrificed a dog so that its spirit would go to take messages to the gods.

Nesaru and Corn Mother left the people, warning them that offerings of tobacco smoke must be offered regularly to the Gods of the Eight Directions. Nesaru left his medicine-bundle among them and Corn Mother gave them a great cedar-tree to represent her.

The medicine-bundle

Among all the Indian tribes, but particularly those of the Great Plains, the concept of the medicine-bundle was central to the practice of religion. There were few sacred buildings of any kind. Those there were included open constructions such as the Sun-Dance Lodge, where people offered their ceremonies to the spirits above and where men would make offerings of their physical suffering because the Indians associated physical and spiritual expression as complementary to the whole. Some of the sacred places were those where great happenings had occurred.

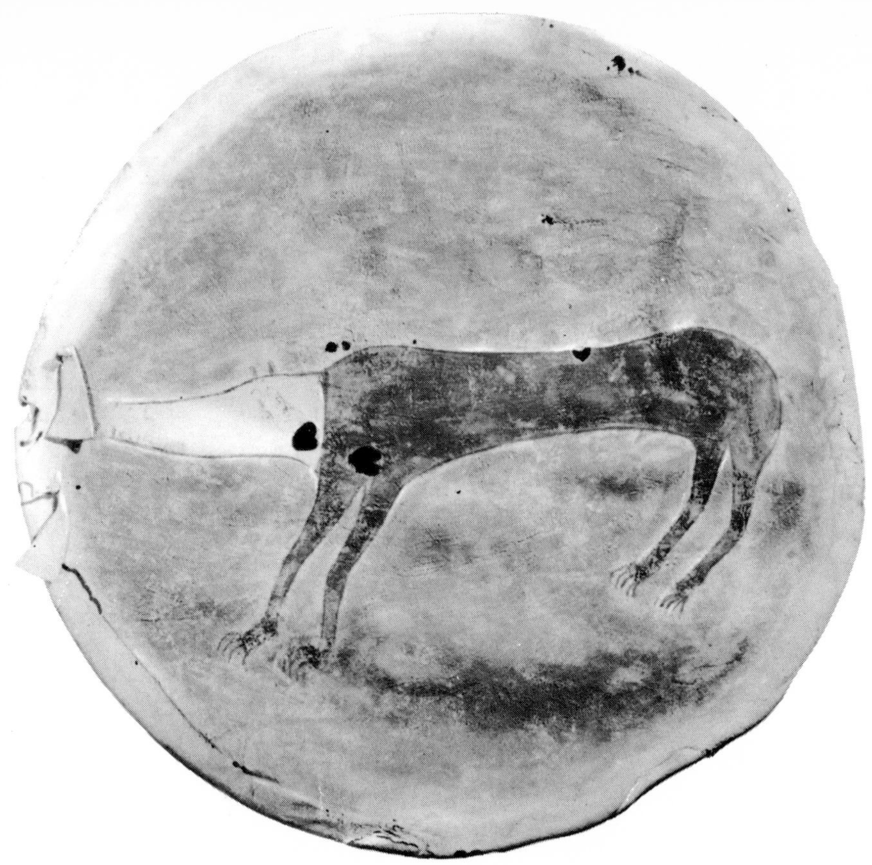

A shield and cover from the Crow Indians. The design on the shield was painted after the warrior had seen it in a vision, and it was the design, rather than the shield itself, that was supposed to afford him protection. Montana. Nineteenth century.

One of the most famous was the 'Sacred Canoe' of the Mandans, which was made of ancient willow boards believed to come from a palisade in which the first ancestors had been rescued from the primeval flood. Instead of sacred places the Indians venerated the medicine-bundles, which were in effect portable shrines. The Indians believed that they contained relics of the first ancestors, or sacred objects given by the gods to protect man and bring good fortune. In this they were almost indentical with the sacred bundles preserved among the highly civilised Aztecs of Mexico, and similar to the sacred bundles, called *tjurungas*, kept by the Australian aborigines and the sacred objects, such as the Palladia, which were preserved in the holy places of classical Europe.

The medicine-bundle, however, was regarded as a form of property. It could change hands, though often only within a family to whose ancestor it had first been entrusted. High values in skins and food had to be exchanged in return for a bundle in a way similar to the medieval practice of bartering the relics of saints between one cathedra and another. The medicine-bundle rights included the songs, dances, and ritual costumes connected with it. The sacred object was the focus of an entire myth, almost a materialisation of an archetype. Its properties are illustrated in the following myth from the Arikara people.

The knot in the tree

There was a time when the autumn buffalo hunt had failed. All the people went unfed. The children cried with hunger. The women begged the chief to call on the keepers of the 'Knot in the Tree'

Right: A False Face mask, known as a 'Speaker Mask'. It was worn at the ceremonies held to drive away False Face spirits from the tribes. Seneca.

medicine-bundle to call for help. So the chief took sacred tobacco, offered its smoke to the gods and asked the priests to open the sacred bundle to make the buffalo come. The priests who guarded the bundle first made the chief clean his tipi and purify the ground inside.

When all was ready the sacred bundle was brought into the tipi. A pole with offerings and gifts for the gods was set up in front of it, and the people were warned that they must sit in complete silence. The priests sang many chants and struck the pole three times, and then four times, invoking the buffalo spirits. They reminded the buffalo that they had promised to come when the poeple, who were in want, performed the ceremony before the buffalo medicine-bundle.

After three days they heard the thunder of the advancing herds. Then the priests sent out some chosen young men to capture a young bull and bring it entire to the chief's lodge. The young men did this, bringing a complete carcass, unmarked save for a single lance thrust. It was laid on the floor of the big tipi while the priests recited the myth of the buffaloes who became people. Thus would the buffalo medicine-bundle be strengthened in its power to protect the people and bring the animals to feed the tribe.

The Indians generally divided the world up into four or eight directions, each of which was inhabited by a spirit who had to be placated. Sometimes the different directions were represented pictorially by different colours, sometimes, as in this embroidered papoose-carrier, by twin mountain peaks. James H. Hooper collection.

There was once a village of the Buffalo, who in those days resembled strong human beings wearing horns. In the Buffalo village they kept the sacred bundle called 'Knot in the Tree'. After singing magic chants for four days the Buffalo priests went to an ancient cottonwood-tree and struck a knot in its trunk three times and four times. Then they heard a sound like people crying and talking under the ground. Soon a great many people came up out of the tree. Cut-Nose was the first man out. The Buffalo people hunted them like animals. Cut-Nose ran fast but many others were clubbed and cut up for a great feast of human flesh. Cut-Nose circled and sped back to the tree avoiding the clubs thrown at him. He leapt inside and warned other people against coming out. The flesh of the human victims was then cut up and the Buffaloes danced as the meat was put on drying frames.

One human escaped. He was a young man who was a very fine runner. He was chased by a white Buffalo-woman but he outdistanced her. He hid among the grape vines and tangled bushes of a ravine.

This young man found small animals to eat as well as berries. He moved from one sheltered place to another. One day he saw a beautiful horned woman dressed in white leather. Her hair hung below her waist. The young man followed her. He saw her go into a fine painted tipi. He followed. She bade him welcome and invited him to sleep with her. So they lay in each others' arms, covered by her robe of white skin. As he looked hungry she gave him some meat. Then he slept. When he awoke there was no tipi at all.

Buffalo-Girl told how the Buffalo people wanted to be turned into true animals, but that the man who could work the magic was not to be found. She had selected him to be the hero. But he must brave the danger of the angry flesh-eating Buffalo-men if he was to win. He must get to the chief's tipi through four rows of guards. She covered him in a buffalo skin and led him as far as the guardian warriors. Some thought they could smell human meat, but others told them that was because they had all became spotted with human blood during the

A buffalo skin painted with scenes of mythological importance. It shows ceremonial dances, and warriors being protected by the mystical designs painted on their shields. It also has a recurring sun motif. It reflects the increased complexity that was introduced into the myths of the Plains Indians with the spread of agriculture and agricultural festivals.

hunt. At last the young man came to the chief's tipi. Buffalo-Girl led him to where he could rest in a pile of animal skins.

He overheard the chief reciting the hunting chants and learned the way to use the ash staff to strike the magic tree when calling the food people. He dared not sleep for fear of betraying himself. In the morning when the chief went out to lead another great hunt, Buffalo-Girl came in and to give him courage, showed him the high racks on which meat was drying. He climbed up and saw human ribs, hands, breasts, and some heads. His anger gave him strength.

Buffalo-Girl next took him to a copse near the sacred tree. There she told him to cut ash staves and trim them into bows. He must take straight twigs and canes to make arrows. He must use strips of skin to make bow strings. For a long time he worked and made as many as he could, ready for the fight. Then Buffalo-Girl went with him to the tree. She called through it to Cut-Nose and told him that when the time came he must take the bow and arrow offered to him and shoot a Buffalo-man. Everyone with him was to do the same.

Next day they took the ash bows to the sacred cottonwood-tree and hid them underneath a buffalo-skin in readiness for battle. The chief came with his warriors. He chanted while he struck the tree three times and then four times. There was a sound of voices, and Cut-Nose emerged. He took his bow and ran quickly beyond the Buffalo-men. Then the other people came up and each took a bow. As they did so they shot at the Buffalo-men, who were so frightened that they fled. Each took with him a piece of the stored human flesh, which he tucked under his armpit. None gave fight, but as each one was hit he turned into a real buffalo and grazed on the prairie grass instead of eating humans.

Buffalo-Girl married the young man, and their children founded the Arikara nation. Now, whenever the 'Knot in the Tree' medicine-bundle is opened, the ceremonies and dances are those which Buffalo-Girl taught the first Arikara. And whenever the Arikara hunt buffalo for food, they leave uneaten the lump under the buffalo's foreleg because it is human meat from their ancestors.

The Okipa ceremony

Among the Mandan the great annual ceremony was known as the Okipa. Dances lasted many days, great men offered their pain for the good of the world, and the sacred legends of the beginnings of things were recounted by the elders among the priests. The story of creation was owned by 'The Lone Man' medicine-bundle.

Above and below: Details from the buffalo skin showing warriors dancing, and a horseman with his painted, protective shield.

Lone Man

Lone Man was walking on the great waters. He did not know how he had come into being. He turned back and followed his tracks and found a blood-striped flower. The red flower spoke, saying that she had given birth to him so that he might go about in the world. He knew there must be something below the waters from which his mother had her life. He saw two ducks and commanded them to bring earth up from below the waters. They brought up four pieces which Lone Man scattered. The pieces formed four directions, and bore grass and fruit trees.

Lone Man went to many places, and everywhere new things came into being. After many adventures he came across Coyote, who called himself First Man. They quarrelled about their names and about who was the elder. Lone Man speared First Man, who died. Lone Man waited a time and saw that First Man had become a skeleton and the spear was broken. He was pleased that he had proved he was the elder. But as he moved his spear, the bones clicked together again and First Man Coyote stood alive once more before him. So they decided to hunt together. They made different kinds of country, and filled them all with animals. Then they discovered that the Indians were living on the land.

Lone Man wanted to be one with the Indians so he looked around to find a woman who would take him inside her body so that he could be born. He saw a girl chewing maize, but thought she might break him up before he got inside. Then he saw another very beautiful

woman, who was fishing with her mother. He became a dead buffalo floating in the stream, with some kidney fat showing through a wound in his back. The girl snatched the tasty fat and swallowed it. She suddenly felt strange and called her mother. She became big with child and gave birth to a fine boy with magical black marks on his forehead.

The child grew with unprecedented speed. Soon he was a young man. He desired beautiful clothes. Spotted Eagle Hoita lived nearby. He had a fine white buckskin coat. The young Lone Man called Wind and it blew the coat far away. The Rain and Sun made the coat more beautiful than ever. It was found by some travelling Indians, who said it was far finer than the coat worn by Hoita. They brought it with them to the village and gave it to Lone Man. This offended Hoita, who went off in a huff and took all the animals with him to the Dog Den and kept them there. Lone Man sometimes saw animals pass by to the north. He was disturbed about the migration. He met Mouse-Woman who warned him that his property was being turned into animals which all became white and went northwards. On her advice he turned himself into a white hare. He came to the Dog Den, and managed to hide safely.

Hoita led the animals in a magic dance and sang a chant that would make a famine in Lone Man's village. The power of the dance came from the beating of the drum made from a great roll of hide. Once Lone Man had learned this he slipped away in search of a more powerful medicine-drum. He called all the creatures but none could help except the Giant Turtles who supported the earth in the waters. As they could not move without destroying the earth Lone Man made a copy of their form, stretching leather over it to make a drum and decorating the neck with feathers. He made the frame of oak, because it was oak-wood which held the earth on the back of the Giant Turtles.

When Lone Man played on his new medicine-drum Hoita was perplexed. He sent the animals to find out what it was, but one by one Lone Man trapped them and gave them to his people. Hoita then realised he was defeated and released the remaining animals from Dog Den, telling them to scatter, so that wherever the Mandan people travelled they should find the food which they asked for.

Lone Man was persecuted by a being known as Maninga; but by trickery and cunning he defeated him. Maninga retreated, but four years later returned tor a last test of strength. He came as a great flood. At this time there were five Mandan villages full of people, and as the flood came higher the villages were abandoned one by one. Lone Man led his people up to the last village. There he planted a sacred cedar-tree to represent himself and the people. Then he built a small stockade of willow planks. It was called the Great Canoe, though it never floated. As the flood grew, it lapped the sides of the Great Canoe. Maninga drew clear in order to destroy the Mandans. But Lone Man knew that he was fond of shell ornaments and threw the most precious shells over the stockade wall. Maninga let the flood recede so that he could pick them up. Then the magic of the turtle-drum was made and Maninga was swept away with the receding waters. The cedar-tree stood for many centuries, and some of the

Left: Two Indian ceremonial dances. *Top:* The Chippewa Snowshoe Dance was performed to thank the Great Spirit for sending the first snow of the winter, for thick snow made it easier for the hunters to chase the game on their snowshoes. *Below:* The Buffalo Dance was performed far to the south, in the Great Plains region. All the tribesmen were expected to keep a buffalo head in their tents to wear when the dance had to be performed to bring about the return of their herds. The dance continued until the buffalo came, fresh dancers taking over from those who fell out exhausted.

The medicine man, in addition to prophesying about the future and curing the sick, was expected to produce favourable conditions for hunting and farming. Sometimes he performed the ritual which would bring back the buffalo herds, at other times, as this painting shows, he might attempt to bring rain. Mandan medicine man by George Catlin. Nineteenth century.

stockade that the Indians believed to be the remains of the Great Canoe, can still be seen at the old Mandan village on the left bank of the Upper Missouri in North Dakota.

After many victories over the hostile powers of nature Lone Man departed to the south west, leaving the Mandans with the cedar-tree memorial, and the great medicine-bundles used in the Okipa Ceremony.

The Nuptadi robe

The story of the medicine-bundle known as 'Nuptadi (Young Grandmother) Robe' sheds some light on early Indian custom, for the robe itself is a very old and small garment like an apron, not worn by any tribe in historic times, and the tale begins with clear evidence that it dates from the days before the horse.

The early Indians harnessed dogs to drag a travois of trailing wooden poles to carry their possessions when they moved camp. One day as a boy was sitting on a travois First Man Coyote, who made the earth, ran by. The dog, seeing a coyote, chased it, dragging travois and boy with him. Lost and far from his village, the boy found a bow and some arrows and thanked the spirit who had left them. Then he saw a buffalo bull, shot at it, and felled it although he did not pierce its hide. He sought a sharp stone and cut open the back of the bull to extract the rich kidney fat. Then, as he needed something hard to make tools, he took a leg bone from the bull and struck it against a stone until it broke. A splinter flew off and where it fell he found a baby girl.

The boy had proved himself. Coyote reappeared in human form. He told the boy to bring some sage. Then he set it on fire. He passed the baby girl through the smoke four times. Each time she grew older. When the last smoking was over the girl was big enough to cook and make fine buffalo robes, and the boy had become a young man. Coyote was satisfied that they could now support each other, and left them.

A red stone pipe bowl of the east Dakotas. Smoking was very often a ceremonial activity and pipes were decorated with religious scenes. The carving on this pipe shows a shaman receiving instruction from a bear spirit.

In Pawnee mythology the bodies of two dead star rulers were placed on burial frames in the sky. This reflects the Indian custom of placing the bodies of their dead on frames near the village. The body was painted and oiled, dressed in its best robes and supplied with arms and provisions. A buffalo skin from a freshly-killed animal was tightly bound round the body. Other robes were soaked in water to soften them, then bandaged round the body and tied fast so as to exclude the action of air. Later, when the flesh had quite dried away, the bones were buried in crevices. Funeral scaffold of a Sioux chief by Carl Bodmer, 1834.

They both worked well and built themselves a sound tipi to live in. One day the girl asked her foster-brother if he should not find himself a wife, for there were some girls approaching and by the time they had built themselves their winter earth-house the girls would come.

Sure enough, two beautiful girls arrived, and the boy asked them if they would stay as his wives. They agreed, although they warned him that his foster-sister had complained of his violent temper.

Soon after their arrival the wives warned the young man that his foster-sister needed an extra human scalp to ornament a new robe that she was making. Curious, he looked at the bundle containing the robe when she was out, burning sweet grass and praying that he would not be overcome by magic as he did so. He saw that it was a shell robe, with a man's scalp under each of the clam shells sewn on it. An empty space on the shoulder clearly awaited another scalp. Then he recalled that she cooked and ate her meat secretly. Now he guessed that she was a supernatural creature who ate human flesh. When his foster-sister came back, she passed the bundle containing her new robe and then touched her foster-brother's garments. As she did so they gave off a flash of blue fire. He also had supernatural powers. He ran to the white skin tipi of his wives, and in the ensuing combat managed to shoot his foster-sister who told him that her time on earth had come to and end. Now he must take her magic shell robe and perserve it, so that her powers might benefit the Mandans. As she died he took the robe and made the magical Nuptadi Robe bundle with it.

The Pawnee

Well to the south of the Great Plains lived the Pawnee. They moved

gradually northwards, planting and hunting until, when the white men met them, they were hunting around the Platte River. They spoke one of the Caddoan languages spoken by their remote ancestors. They were a confederation of smaller tribes who shared a common culture. The name Pawnee, derived from a word meaning 'a horn', was adopted because their young men used to gather up their hair and coil it back over their foreheads as a queue bound with hide and stiffened with grease. The Pawnee were famed for their courage and intelligence. They put up a brave resistance to the white invaders but eventually abandoned the old customs and adopted new ways.

The ancient Pawnee tribes were especially interested in the gods of the sky. There were among them astronomers who watched the movements of the planets and decided the most propitious times for making offerings. They particularly venerated the North Star as a beneficent creator god, and went in fear of the magical South Star, who was a force of opposition belonging to the underworld. Morning Star, who led the sun up into the sky, was their protector. Evening Star, who drove the sun down to the darkness, was a dangerous enemy spirit who sent his daughter to hinder the creative powers of the Morning Star, although eventually, when she had been pierced by magic arrows and lay dying, she gave great blessings.

The morning star myth

One of the more important bundles was the 'Morning Star' bundle. The story connected with this bundle consisted of two halves, one telling the myth of Morning Star and the Evening Star Girls. Its ritual climax occurred in four-yearly cycles. The young warriors had to creep up to an enemy camp and capture a young woman. She was kept a while and treated kindly so that she could carry good messages to the gods. Then, on the appointed day, she was stripped naked and painted half red and half black to symbolise the Morning and Evening Stars. Then she was tied to a scaffold and the young warriors killed her with a shower of arrows. Her blood was believed to revive a blessing given to the people long ago and to ensure better fortune over the following four years.

The moon basket

The other part of the sacred bundle enshrined a more pleasant stellar myth connected with the Moon Basket.

When the world was created, the gods decided to make the First People. Two mud figures were made, one of a girl and one of a boy. The boy was given a bow and arrows so that he might hunt for food. Then, while the earth was still in darkness the gods made all the animals pass in front of the boy. He was to shoot one, and whichever he shot would determine the conditions they would create for him. The boy hesitated, fearing to shoot an 'unfavourable' animal, and waited until the last creature came by. His arrow sped true, for he had magical strength and a black and white buffalo cow fell in its tracks.

Left: A buckskin Ghost Dance shirt with a design of Thunderbirds and stars. The design was revealed to the owner in a vision. Arapaho. Oklahoma.

The condition determined by his choice was the alternation of light and darkness, of day and night.

The young man and woman hunted in the forest, and built themselves grass huts as they needed shelter. One evening they heard a distant drumming that went on and on and seemed to come from the near distance. It lasted all night. They made up their minds to discover the cause and on the next evening followed the sound and soon distinguished voices singing sacred chants. In a forest glade they came upon a small plantation of maize and a well constructed lodge where a festival was in progress. As they approached, a woman asked them into the lodge. They entered and in the dim light they saw the central altar where four old men, painted with red earth mixed with grease, chanted and beat the medicine-drums for the dance to begin. The dancers were a great crowd of girls. This was the house of Moon Lady and her daughters the stars.

The round dance began. The First People were told to watch so that they would understand the dance of the stars.

The old men who led the chant were Wind, Cloud, Lightning, and Thunder, the four powers of the sky. During the dance the Evening Star Woman stood in front of the altar, slightly to the west. In the sacred basket she held the Moon. In front of her to the east, there danced four other women, who were the daughters of Big Black Meteor Star (possibly Algol or Capella) who stands to the north-east in the sky of the Pawnees. Big Black Meteor Star was the star of magic, who would later be the instructress of the medicine men. Her daughters danced to the west, each carrying a basket in which there were two white skins of swan's necks and two white fawn skins. They laid their baskets with the symbols at the feet of Evening Star Woman and the dance ended.

The basket was a magic one. When the Indians made copies for the dance on earth, they were not allowed to use a knife but had to break the withies by hand, and when it was woven they lined it with mud and water. This symbolised creation. The swan's neck skins and the fawn skins represented the two pairs of gods who stood in the west, the region of Evening Star Woman.

The First People were given the basket they had learned to make, together with twelve sticks and many plumstones. This would remind them that Tirawa Atius the Power Above, made the moon (who was mother of the stars) and the twelve great stars (probably the Pleiades). The sticks and the plumstones were to be thrown down in a gambling game so that people should play and understand the mysteries of the movement of the stars through the apparent falling of chance.

This was the story of the medicine-bundle that contained the Moon Basket. In places where neither houses nor lights obsure the night sky one can learn a little of the reverence with which the Pawnee, like all ancient peoples, regarded the stars. The heavens showed the continuation of regular movement in the dance of life; the sudden changes of fate were shown in shooting stars. They believed that one day they would see in the sky the signs which would mean the end of the world. The Pawnee thought that the Pole Stars, North and South, would move together when the end came.

The end of the world

In earlier times the Pawnee believed that the world would end in a different way. The elders sang about Tirawa Atius the Power Above. They chanted to the beat of the drums, they rattled their gourds as they sang before the medicine-bundle. There was a time when Tirawa Atius had placed giant people on the earth. But the giants grew proud and had to be destroyed. Storms came from the north-west, the waters rose and rain poured down. The race of giants was destroyed; the last of them were supposed to have died on a hill in Kansas. (The bones discovered there, on which the Indians based their myth, have been shown by modern science to be dinosaur bones).

Human beings were made. In the north-west Tirawa Atius set a great buffalo bull to hold that corner of the sky. Each year the bull lost a single hair. When all the hairs had fallen out the world would come to an end for the present human race.

Tirawa Atius had placed the gods in the sky: the groups of four deities for each quarter of the heavens, the moving stars, the Sun and Moon.

Painted shield-cover from Kiowa, Oklahoma. It is coloured red and black and shows a bear charging out from between two thunderclouds towards a row of flying bullets.

An Apache beadwork collar, part of the regalia worn in the religious ceremonies.

He would consult with them all if he had to threaten humans with destruction. Morning Star was appointed to rule over the lesser gods, and together with Evening Star had power of giving life to the people on earth. Sun and Moon also gave life but they were not great powers like Morning Star.

The Pawnee believed that when the end was coming they would be warned by the moon changing to a dark colour and then to black. On the day that the cataclysm was to take place the sun would become dim quite quickly and then suddenly all would be dark, darker than in an eclipse, and that darkness without light would be the end for the human race. Sometimes the South Star was given permission to move through the heavens to look on the North Star so that it could rest assured that North Star was in the right position. Then it would move back and the stars resume their dance.

And in the heavens there were warnings of death too. At the first great council of the gods two of the star rulers died, one old and one young. Their bodies were wrapped and placed on frames, just as the Indians wrapped their dead and placed them on high racks so that their bones should be nearer the stars. There were two burial frames in the sky which always moved around the North Star (Ursa Major and Ursa Minor).

The North Star was aware of fate and warned the people that when the South Star moved through the heavens it came a little further north each time. One day it would swing high enough to capture the People on the Frames. On that night the ruler of the earth and its people would change and the South Star would then assume complete dominion.

As the end came nearer there would be meteor showers, and the sun would change colours like a rainbow before the final darkness. The final commands for the destruction would come from the west and be obeyed in the east. The skies would move. The North Star would command and the South Star carry out the work. The stars would come to earth and the Indians would become stars too and live in the place ruled by the South Star, which is their true home.

The important role played by the sun, moon and stars in Pawnee mythology grows out of their experience of the movement of the stars across the vast sky of the prairies. In the regular patterns of the stars in the night sky the Indians saw a symbol of the pattern of life and expressed this in veneration of the Sky Father. The Mandan myths are exceptional among the myths of the Buffalo hunters in that they deal with more complicated subjects, such as the story of Lone Man and the universal theme of creation, and tell them in a more vivid and elaborate style.

The spread of agriculture throughout the tribes of the plains is reflected in the myths about Corn Mother and the coming of maize, but the major pre-occupation of the Plains Indians, the hunting of the great buffalo herds, is illustrated in what is probably the most typical of their myths, the Arikara story of the Buffalo people.

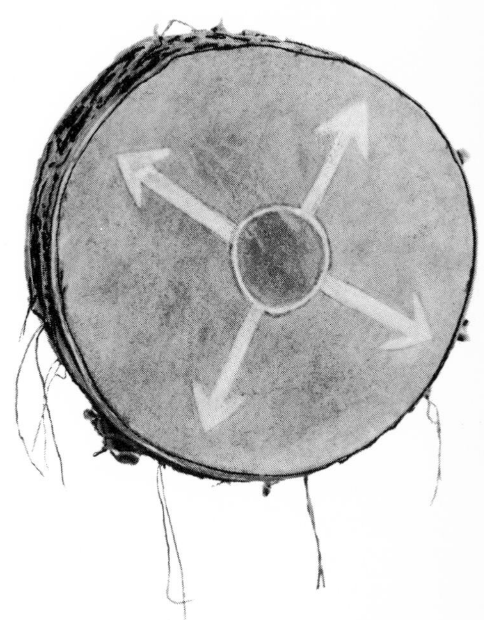

A buffalo-hide drum with a painted design illustrating the four quarters into which the world was divided. The Pawnee had an elaborate mythology about the sky in which the heavens were divided into four quarters and the Morning Star and Evening Star were great powers.

The Hunters of the Great Desert

Principal tribes: Apache Navajo Papago

In the south-west the tribes were mostly small groups of people living on what they could gather under the semi-desert conditions. On the Pacific coast, around the region which is now Los Angeles, tribes were few and poor, living on shell fish and a few small wild animals. Inland they collected acorns from the local species of oak, beat them into flour strained through water to remove the tannic acid, and baked the paste on hot stones to make a fine, almost tasteless, wafer bread. These people have typical hunting mythologies and ancestor tales but they are of the simple type already represented in our collection of Eskimo stories.

The Navajo

On the edge of the great desert regions and on the borders of the prairie lived the Navajo people. They were basically hunters, although they had retained a little agriculture similar to that practised by the Pueblo Indians who lived on the hilltops of this region, subsisting by semi-desert farming. In pre-Columbian times the Navajo hunters lived rather impoverished lives because of the gradual reduction in available game with the slow but progressive dessication of the whole region that had been going on for a thousand years.

The homes of the Navajo tribesmen were called hogans. They were conical huts built from timber, with a small square entrance and an open top through which smoke from the fire escaped. Sometimes they had an outside covering of earth to lend warmth during the winter. New ones could easily be built, and no one was ever strictly tied down to a single dwelling place. When the tribes travelled in search of game they built temporary shelters out of bushes and grass.

At the time of the discovery of North America by the white man clothing was simply a kilt, and the usual leather moccasins common to all the American Indian tribes. The simple life of hunting and gathering edible seeds was associated with a very rich mythology which reveals that in earlier times, when the country was more fertile, the Navajo had long been agriculturists. Their tiny catch-crop plantations of maize in the sixteenth century must once have been carefully organised fields, as is shown by the great importance of the corn spirits in Navajo ritual life.

The Shaman

The Indians of the south-west had a very loosely organised system of tribal government because poor living conditions compelled them to split into small groups. Great medicine men, shamans, as we would call them today, were known to all the tribes. These men often exhibited neurotic symptoms, but they were considered to be in close contact with the spirit world of ancestors and gods, and with the spirits of maize, the rainbow, the sun, thunder and all the powers of nature. A powerful Navajo shaman could be expected to advise on future events, to guide people in the proper ritual for curing illness, or for protecting crops. He was regarded as a holy man.

His initiation, like that of the shamans, of the northern Indians, the Eskimo, and the Plains tribes, was by selection from the spirit world. The boy of eleven or twelve would follow the usual custom of going out into the wild alone for perhaps three or four days to seek a spirit protector. He would travel far without seeking food, praying for help and protection from the spirit world. At the end of this period he would be favoured by a vision. Sometimes spirits would appear in animal form, sometimes in human, bigger and more powerful than men, like the Rainbow Maiden or the Thunder Spirit, or the Spirit of Hail. Any of these beings could appear; all could impress the sensitive youngster. In some cases they would promise to guide and direct the young man through life: it was possible for a young girl to have a similar experience.

Once he had had his vision of his spirit-protector, the young shaman would return to his village and recount his dreams and visions to his relatives. If his relatives found the visions significant, he would be introduced to the religious societies where he would learn the chants describing the gods and the spirit world, and the proper rituals for healing and for seeking inspiration.

Many Navajo medicine men had a tendency to think of themselves as magically changed into women, and would often do woment's work such as cooking and even wear women's clothing. They were beings set apart and regarded as rather strange, but also as people blessed by the spirits. As such they were not under any obligation to account for their actions to the other members of the tribe.

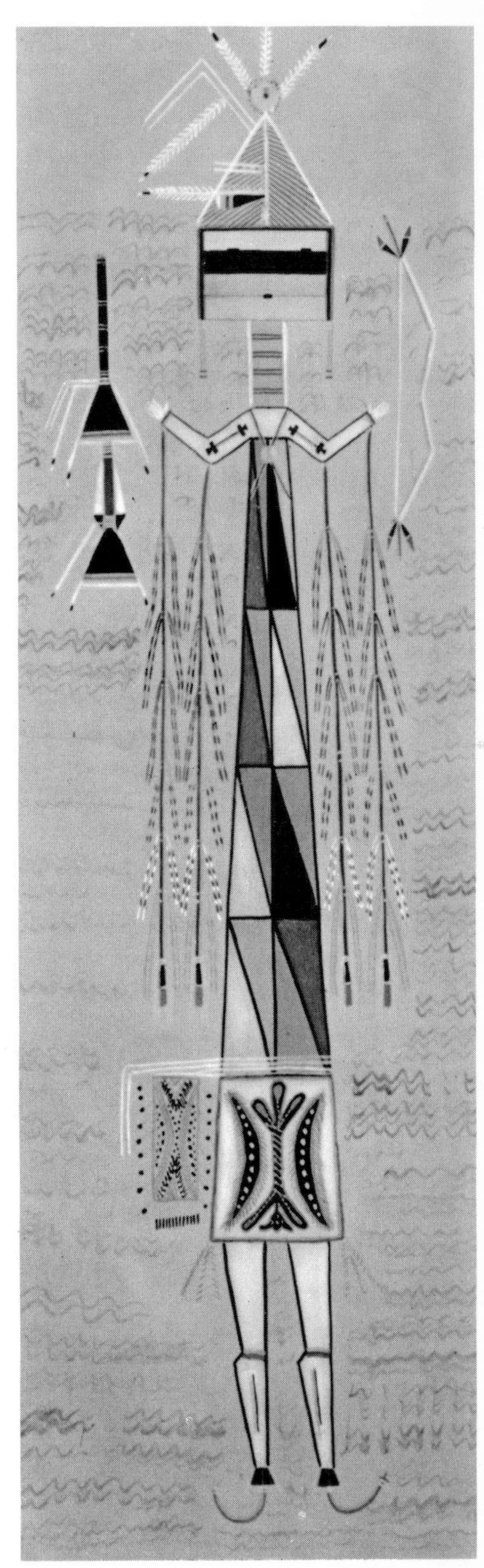

The sand-painting was a distinctive feature of the religious life of the Indians of the Southwest. It was made to the accompaniment of one of the ceremonial chants and wiped away when the chant ended.

Navajo sand-paintings

Navajo beliefs were illustrated by their system of sand-paintings, carefully made for special ceremonies and for the curing of the sick. These beautiful works of traditional art are now preserved in many of the museums of the world, but originally they were made and shown only to the accompaniment of the sacred chants that revealed the mystical happenings that occurred when the painting rituals and their power of blessing were first given to man.

The relationship of the Navajo to the spirit world was one in which sacrifices were offered to the spirits in the certainty that blessings would be sent to man in return. There would be food, there would be animals, there would be hope, and life and understanding would continue among men. Luckily these legends were kept intact among the Navajo. At the beginning of this century one of their greatest medicine men recited them into phonograph cylinder records for Miss Mary Wheelwright, who founded the Museum of Navajo Ceremonial Art at Santa Fé. Here many of the sand-paintings, as well as sound recordings and published accounts of the Indian mythology, can be studied and by such means an almost complete record of Navajo religion has been preserved for our own time.

Montezuma

We know a little of the more primitive background of the Navajo from the mythologies of the scattered desert peoples such as the Papago, whose creation legend makes the typical First Man figure into a dual-natured demiurge who was once called First Man but who later became Montezuma. The name reflects the Aztec influences that were carried northwards by the Spanish invaders.

The story tells how he created a human race, how he helped them and occasionally brought trouble to them, how four attempts were made to kill him, and how four times he came to life again to bring still greater scourges. He even created a huge eagle which destroyed many of the first people. The quarrel between the people and the god became irreconcilable. The time came for a new human race to be released from their home underneath the earth. They attacked and destroyed the previous people. Then, after Montezuma had taught them how to hunt and grow maize, he went away to an underground house farther south.

In this legend the basic myths of many American Indians are present in a very simple form. Whether the behaviour of the Montezuma of Papago mythology reflects the behaviour of Mexican mercenary warriors advancing with the Spanish conquerors in the sixteenth century cannot of course be proved, but it may well be so. Raids on the desert Indians by people from the south are suggested by the presence of an Aztec type of leather shield in the personal treasure of a great Apache Chief Cochise, now preserved in Exeter.

The Navajo conception of mythology is not very different from the Greek conception of a cycle of plays presenting the myths. To the Greeks the plays were a poetic expression of the relationship between gods and men. The Navajo expressed this relationship in remembered chants and in the planning and making of symbolic designs. The sand-painting, made during the ceremony and then

A leather shield from the personal treasure of the Apache chief, Cochise. This type of leather shield, with its double serpent design is Aztec in style and suggests that the Central American tribes sometimes raided the desert tribes of the Southwest; the influence of the Aztecs also seems to be reflected in the Papago legend of Montezuma.

wiped away, was an expression of the understanding between the spirits and the shaman, who depicted them in colours made from sand and flower pollen. A curing ceremony might last from four to nine days, and the ceremonies were all linked with the appropriate myth.

The Navajo developed a series of lengthy and complex myths which preserved their general form through long periods of entirely oral transmission. Some variation was permitted, since each shaman had inherited variations from his teachers, and indeed each shaman might be inspired to improvise in order to clarify his story.

The emergence myth

The most important of the Navajo myths was the emergence myth, the story of creation. The version which follows dates from 1882 when the Navajo were not greatly influenced by European thought.

The present world is the Fifth World. In the First World there were three beings in the darkness: First Man, First Woman and Coyote (the trickster-creator). The First World was too small for them. They travelled to the Second World, where there were two men who became Sun and Moon and where there was a dim and misty light. In the east was blackness, in the south blueness, in the west yellowness and in the north whiteness. Sometimes the blackness would intensify and overshadow all the world, leaving night, soon the colours would glow again, bringing day; each of the four colours concealed a personage who lived within it. When the three beings arrived in the Second World, Sun tried to make love to First Woman and there was discord. Coyote, who knew everything, called the dwellers of north, south, east and west to arbitrate. They decided that the Second World was too small and they should all climb to the Third World where there would be room for Sun to separate from First Woman for ever.

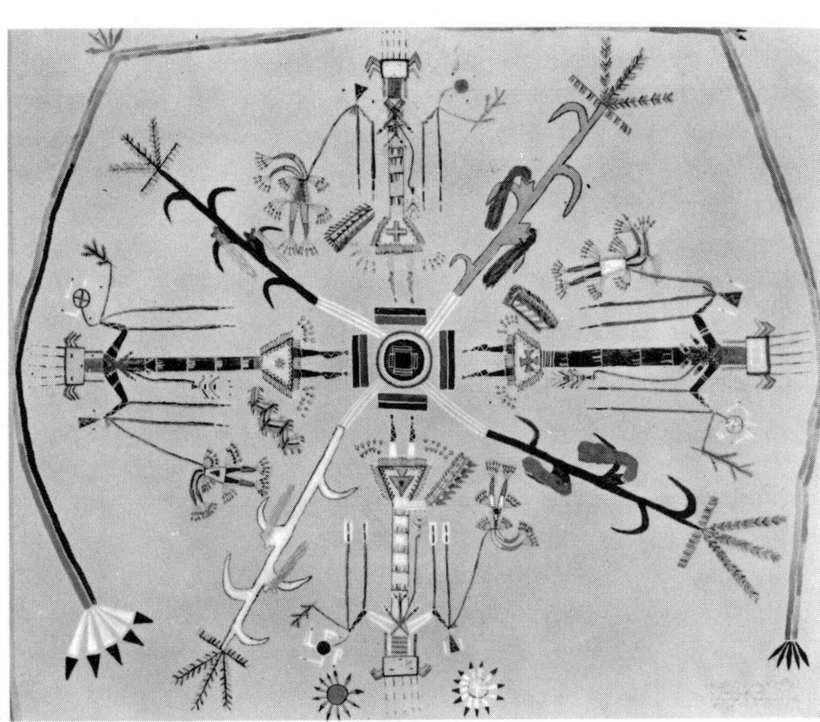

A replica of the Moisture in the Mountain chant which is part of the Mountain Chant group. In the centre is a lake from which four stalks of maize are growing, between them stand some of the characters from the myth. The sand-painting is part of a healing ceremony during which the supernatural powers who figure in the myths are summoned to the assistance of the petitioner. J. F. Huckel collection.

They ascended to the Third World, a wide and beautiful land like the earth. At the corners there were four mountains. At the foot of the mountains there were lakes. And on the slopes of the mountains there were people. The newcomers were met at the Place of Ascent by the mountain people. They were welcomed and warned that all would be well for them in this wider world so long as Tieholtsodi, the water-monster, was left in peace.

Now Coyote ignored the mountain people's counsel. He was inquisitive and went to look at the great waters. He went to the eastern waters and found two of the children of Tieholtsodi who were so attractive that he took them off to his home wrapped in a blanket. The monster searched the four corners of the world for his children. Unable to find them he guessed that they must be with the new people. The only way he could recover them was by using his power over water. Thereupon the four oceans filled and the water began to rise. All the people held council and determined to escape the flood by removing the mountains of the four directions to pile them one on top of the other in the middle of the land. Still the flood rose. The people planted a giant reed on the top of the piled-up mountain.

When the reed was fully grown it reached the sky and pierced into the Fourth World. The ancestors and the animals they had found in the Third World all climbed inside the reed. Last to come was Turkey who was to sound the alarm when his feet were wet by the flood. When he did so they began to climb up inside the giant reed. On the fourth night they emerged from the top of the reed into the Fourth World. Even now turkeys have light-coloured tail feathers to show where their ancestor had his tail feathers washed by the flood.

The Fourth World was larger again than the Third. It was dim, lit only by three great mists of light, and obscured from time to time

by misty darkness. The mountains and seas were like those of the Third World but in the central plain flowed a great river. On the north bank lived human beings, and on the south other people, who were in animal form. Time passed swiftly in that world. The year resembled a day. But trouble was to follow.

A vicious quarrel developed in which each sex claimed to be the source of sustenance and life. The women argued that they made fire, prepared cotton, planted the fields and made pottery. They also bore the children. The man countered that they hunted and worked hard clearing the fields and building the houses, and—most important—that they knew the ways of the gods and performed the dances and ceremonies needed to make the crops grow. In the end men and women decided to separate. The men made a boat and crossed the river in the central plain, leaving the women to cultivate their little fields without the propitious dances and ceremonial.

So it continued for four years. The women dug no new ground, and their crops grew less and less. The men dug fresh soil and each year they produced better crops; they also had planty of reserve food from hunting. But the men were aggrieved that they should have to work so hard tending the fields, while the women were not happy about sowing new ones. They agreed that they were indispensable to each other, and joined forces again.

Having learned this salutary lesson in social discipline, man might have been expected to develop in peace. But Coyote was still among them, still holding the children of the water-monster Tieholtsodi. The world, so recently made more secure by the new understanding between men and women, was threatened by another danger. The ground became soft, the waters burst in, and again the flood menaced the people. Again the mountains of the four directions were piled together in the central plain. Again a great reed was planted and again grew to the earthen sky above the Fourth World.

Badger was the one who went first, digging away the earth above them. But when he found that he was emerging into a muddy lake, there was consternation. No one had any idea what to do, and the flood was rising. Locust alone felt that he might be able to slip through and find a way. So up he went. He flew to the surface, and there he saw four beautiful swans, who were like the lights of the underworlds, black in the east, blue in the south, yellow in the west and white in the north. The swans questioned Locust and he told them his sad story. But they imposed a magical test before admitting anyone. They demanded that everyone who came up into their world should take an arrow, thrust it into his mouth, pass it right through his body and draw it out of his anus. Then the process had to be reversed and the arrow returned from the mouth. The swans were able to do this without difficulty, but Locust realised that people could not do it. So he agreed, on condition that the swans in turn would do as he did. He took an arrow, thrust it apparently through the middle of his chest, drew it out at the other side, and then returned it the same way. The swans did not know that Locust was different from other creatures because he had only a narrow spine in the middle of his body, joining the head to the rest, beneath which the arrow could pass safely. They

A typical basket from the Southwest region, with a geometrical design.

Opposite page: A woven hat featuring a sea-monster. The need for man to behave well towards animals is emphasised in many North American myths, from the Northwest Coast story of the Wolf Clan and the salmon to the Southwest story of Coyote and the children of the sea-monster Tieholtsodi.

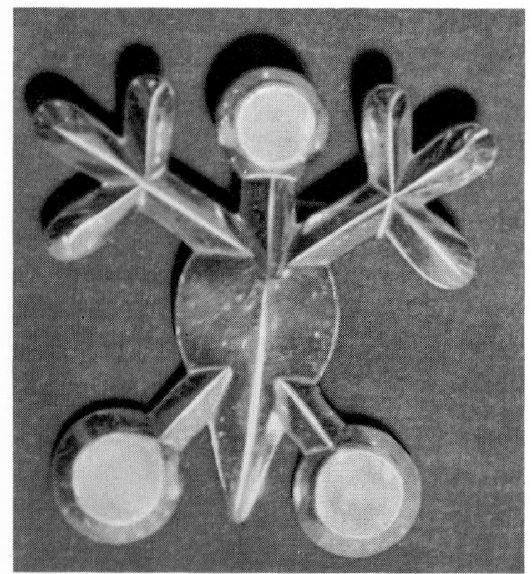

agreed that in view of the phenomenal powers on both sides there need be no further ordeals.

The way was opened and up surged people and animals, hard pressed by the pursuing flood. Each carried a bundle of his most precious possessions. They climbed into the marshy lake, but still the water below surged after them. Suddenly they saw the horns of Tieholtsodi appear in the midst of the land. Overcome with a sense of some hidden guilt, they all came together and showed what was in their packs. Unable to do otherwise, Coyote was forced to reveal the stolen monster-children. His fellows promptly cast them back to their parent. The three monsters swam away, and the waters receded to the underworld.

At the Place of Emergence the people found themselves standing on an island in the middle of a swamp. They prayed to the god of darkness in the east, and he cut open the surrounding cliffs with his curved knife. The remaining waters drained away but the swamp was dangerously soft and the the people still could not move. Anxiously they prayed to the Four Winds. A gale arose and for four days they waited. Then the earth dried out and hardened, and they reached the shores of the swamp in safety. As the earth was not yet properly formed, they took piles of mud to make the four mountains at its corners. The mountains hardened and grew as the earth expanded. When the boundaries were marked, they took Sun and Moon and threw them up into the sky. At first Sun was too near the earth. On four successive days the earth was expanded and the Sun flew higher. On the fifth day Sun stood still at its zenith. Everything was in danger of being burned.

The need for death

The people discovered that Sun must be placated by human death, otherwise he could not move. A great chief's wife offered herself. As her life's breath ebbed away, her body grew cold and then vanished. Whereupon the Sun moved once more. This was the first intimation that every day someone, somewhere in the land, would die. The people were afraid of this prospect until a wise man went to the Place of Emergence and, looking down, saw the dead woman sitting happily by the river of the Fourth World combing her hair. She told him that all the people of the Fifth World must return to live in the Fourth after death. The wise man fell sick soon after this and one night the Moon stood still. The wise man died and Moon continued on its nightly way. Coyote, interpreter of these signs, told the people that, just as every day one of the Navajo must die, so every night someone else, not necessarily a Navajo, must die.

From this interpretation came the belief that death would quickly come to those who gazed on the faces of the dead. Such sights were avoided by covering the faces quickly and by burial. And no Navajo ever ventured to look for the Place of Emergence.

The dispersal of the tribes

When death had been established as essential to the progression of day and night, and as the price of existence in this Fifth World, the tribes of Indians were divided, each resuming its own way of life. Those who had been mountain dwellers in the Fourth World were the mountain tribes of the Fifth; those who had lived in the plains were the plains dwellers. The Navajo remained at the centre, where there was a mountain surrounded by four peaks. In the centre of the land was a small crater lake. They never visited it but adored it from afar as the Place of Emergence. When they first emerged they were no longer able to understand each other. Their language had developed into many separate tongues. For this reason it was decided that people who spoke different languages should live in different places.

First Man, First Woman and Coyote were still with the people. But they were not satisfied with the sky. The Sun and Moon alone did not provide sufficient beauty. So they searched for glittering stones and found some mica dust. First Man placed the Star Which Does Not Move at the pole of the heavens. Then he placed the seven stars (Ursa Major) to grow around it. Then he placed the four bright stars at the four quarters of the sky, and designed the groups of stars around them. Next Coyote picked up three shining red pieces of stone and threw them up to become three red dwarf stars. Then in a hurry Coyote scattered the remaining mica dust so it did not fall into exact patterns but scattered the sky with irregular patterns of brilliance.

The three then turned their attention to time, and made the Moon change her shape to mark the seasons. They set out the twelve new moons in front of them and Coyote named them in sequence, and so the year was longer than before when there had been only one Moon.

In the first year of the new time, the world was set in order. For the first time snow fell. It was soft and not cold, and was a very good food, It could be made into wafer bread and eaten. But Coyote felt thirsty, so he put the snow into a pot and melted it over a fire. Ever since then snow has turned into water when it is warmed. First Woman was angry that they had been deprived of the good food. But Coyote told her that she did not understand the purpose of snow. Henceforth snow would melt in the spring and flow down the mountain sides to bring new grass for the animals to eat. It would nourish the fields in which the maize plants and beans would grow fruitfully, and would bring them better food without the labour of hunting and farming. And so it was. Coyote brought seeds of all food plants from the Fourth World and distributed them to the people.

The plagues sent to men

Then there was peace and wealth for all. It should have brought happiness, but the humans were presumptuous and claimed that all happiness was of their own making. They were careless and stupid. First Man and First Woman were unhappy about them, and determined to punish them by creating monsters who would destroy them. There was the giant Yeitso and his children who pursued human prey. Delgeth, the flesh-eating antelope, was made, and the giant who kicked travellers off mountain trails. The People who Killed by

A fringed Apache shirt with a mythological design painted on it.

Opposite page: Modern Navajo silverwork featuring supernatural figures.

Detail of the Apache shirt showing a horned figure, the symbol of the medicine man throughout the southern regions, wearing an amulet around its neck.

Lightning in their Eyes were made: they lived in a house of jewels so beautiful that travellers were tempted to enter and were slain. All these evils were loosed on the people and many men perished.

Now the time came when First Woman felt that man had suffered too much. She was sad in her heart as a mother is sad for a sick child. She went out, and near her mountain of the north-west she found a little girl lying on the ground. She took the child with her to the House of the North-west. In four days the child grew up. Estanatlehi was her name. She was the means of freedom for the people. As she went walking in the woodlands she saw a handsome man. She told First Man and First Woman but they could see no tracks. But on four successive days she saw him, and lay with him in happiness. Then First Man saw him and knew that he was Sun.

Estanatlehi told her parents that a screen was to be built near the house, so that she could meet Sun in private. For four days Sun visited her there. Then he departed. Four days later the Twin Brothers were born. In four more days they became men, and in another four they decided that they must leave home to seek their father. On the fifth day they went away and met a man in the mountains who told them that Sun dwelt in a land beyond the mountain Tsotsil. So they journeyed on eastwards.

They came to the House of the Sun. It was guarded by the Bear and the Serpent, but they were allowed to pass. Inside the hogan sat the wife of the Sun with her two children. She warned the strangers to leave before the Sun returned. But her two children welcomed the visitors as 'brothers' immediately and, wrapping them in skins, hid them on a shelf. The Sun came home. He heard that two men had come to visit his wife and was angry. He stormed into his hogan demanding to see the visitors. His wife told her children to tell him about them, and when he heard, he pulled down the bundle and the two young men fell out.

The mountains at the corner of the earth were as hard as iron. Sun cast the two young men down on each of the four peaks in turn, but although they were pierced through by the rocks they immediately became whole again. They had been tested in the four directions and now Sun recognised them as his new, deathless sons. Next they must be tested with gifts. He opened the eastern doorway and they beheld limitless herds of horses. They did not desire them. He opened the southern doorway and they beheld mountains of fine clothes. But they desired nothing. He opened the western doorway and they saw jewels of shell and turquoise and coloured stone. They wished for none of them. He opened the northern doorway, and there were all the animals desired by hunters. But they asked for none. Having tested them, he asked them what they desired. They told him that their kinsmen were being devoured by monsters and they wished for magic weapons. They chose a coat studded with iron ore, a great knife, a black and red wind charm and a bundle of thunderbolts.

Then Sun told them they must first destroy Yeitso the terrible giant in the east. He warned them that Yeitso was another of his sons, but that he must now be destroyed. Sun would help by depriving Yeitso of his magic armour when the right moment came. Then the

Above and far right: Two spirits from the Shooting Chant, holding sacred objects. The figures in the sand-paintings represent the spirits who are being invited to take part in the ceremony.

Twin Brothers were taken to the sacred sweat bath and purified. Next day father Sun took them under his arms and flew over the world. High in his path he allowed them to look down. They were over the mountain Tsotsil. The elder brother could not recognise the land below, but the younger of the Twins recognised Tsotsil, the Lake of Salt, and then their home on earth. Then the Sun wrapped them in a thunderstorm and sent them down to the peak of Tsotsil where Yeitso dwelt.

On Tsotsil there was a spring. Every time the giant drank at it he dried it up. There the Twins lay in wait for him. But Tsotsil saw the young men reflected in the water when he came and challenged them and they answered. He cast his thunderbolt at them, but they avoided it and went to another quarter of the peak. Four thunderbolts were cast in the four directions and each time the Twins avoided them. Yeitso had no more thunder power. Then a great black storm overtook them and the great thunder from Sun struck the giant and stripped off his armoured robe. The Twins rushed upon him and attacked him with the big knife. They hacked off his head and threw it into the valley, where it became a rocky hill. Then the blood of the giant began to flow towards it, so with the big knife they cut a ravine so that the blood could not bring the head back to life. The stream of blood halted and turned into a flow of black rock. Then the Twins seized the burnt and shattered armour of the giant and put it into the basket in which he used to carry his victims, and returned to their mother's hogan.

Next day they said they must kill the giant flesh-eating antelope, Delgeth. Estanatlehi their mother, told them it was impossible, for Delgeth lived in the centre of a wide plain where he could see all who approached him. So they decided that they should divide their forces. Elder Twin Brother (Nagenatzani) went to fight the flesh-eater, while Younger Twin Brother (Thobadestchin) stayed to help his mother.

Nagenatzani reached the edge of the plain. He moved among the rocks looking for a way and found none. Then the ground-rat came along and suggested burrowing underground to the centre of the plain. He did this and emerged under the heart of Delgeth. Then he made four burrows radiating from it. Nagenatzani wriggled through the burrow and shot an arrow through the heart of the flesh-eater. In his death throes the antelope ripped up the ground of the burrow where his enemy lay hidden, but Nagenatzani moved to the next burrow. Four times this happened, but in the last burrow Nagenatzani saw the terrible horn rip the ground towards him, stop short and then turn over. He left his hiding place and saw the gigantic carcass. But only when he saw a squirrel scamper over the body was he sure that the monster was dead. The squirrel painted his face red and brown with the blood, and Nagenatzani slit open the carcass and took a length of intestine filled with blood as proof of his victory.

The next struggle was against the great birds who fed their young with human beings. The male devoured men, and came with thunderstorms and lightning flashes. The female destroyed women and came with the female rains, sudden showers that brought no lightning. This pair lived on a high mesa with precipitous sides. They would seize their human victims and drop them from the sky on to a ledge where they were smashed and then devoured by the fledglings in the nest. Nagenatzani offered himself as bait. He carried his thunderbolts and the huge intestine bag filled with blood. The cloud and the thunder came, and the giant bird seized him and hauled him high into the sky before releasing him. The intestine bag hung below him. Swiftly he fell but the bag cushioned his fall. It burst and the blood splashed all around.

Nagenatzani found himself in the nest. Four times the young birds attacked him, and four times he hissed at them and they withdrew. Then he asked them when the parent birds would come back, and learned that they returned with the female rains and the male rains. Suddenly the bodies of two women fell on the ledge and were shattered. A moment later a man's body was broken in the same way. The clouds gathered, there was rain and then thunder over the mesa. The parent birds were returning. The male bird settled on a crag above the eyrie. Nagenatzani cast his thunderbolt at it, and it fell on the rocks below the nest. Then the mother bird swooped nearer the nest; with another thunderbolt he destroyed her too. Then Nagenatzani picked up the fledglings one by one. The first he threw to the skies and named it Atsa, the eagle. It became full grown at once. He named the others too; they became the various birds of prey.

Now Nagenatzani was alone. He could not fly. He was on a ledge with no way up and no way down. Then far below him he saw Bat-Woman moving. He called for help. Three times she disappeared from view but the fourth time she told him to stand back because he must not see how she came up. He went back to the rock wall and in a few moments Bat-Woman was beside him with her basket on her back. She warned him that he must be prepared to get into her basket and trust her, though he could hardly see the thongs which held the basket to her back. He must also keep his eyes shut because he must

Below, right: Father Sky and Mother Earth from the Hail Chant. Throughout the southern region of North America the myths speak of these two as the creators of the world and of the race of men. Father Sky is characterised by the stars painted down his front and Mother Earth is represented by the maize symbol.

Below, and opposite page: Modern Navajo silverwork – silver was traditionally a favourite Navajo medium for decoration.

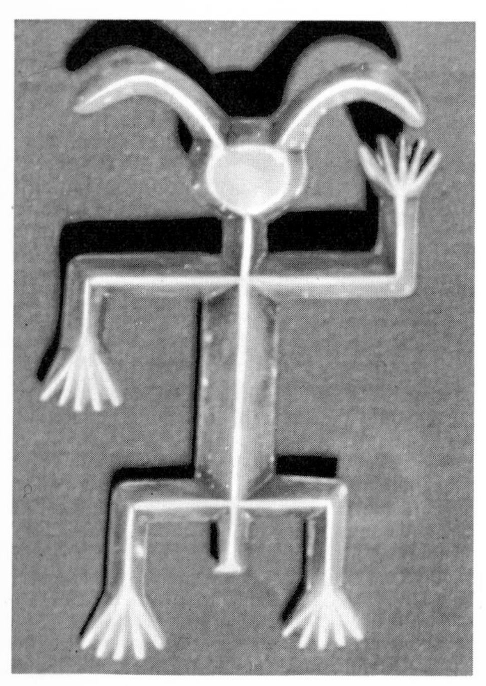

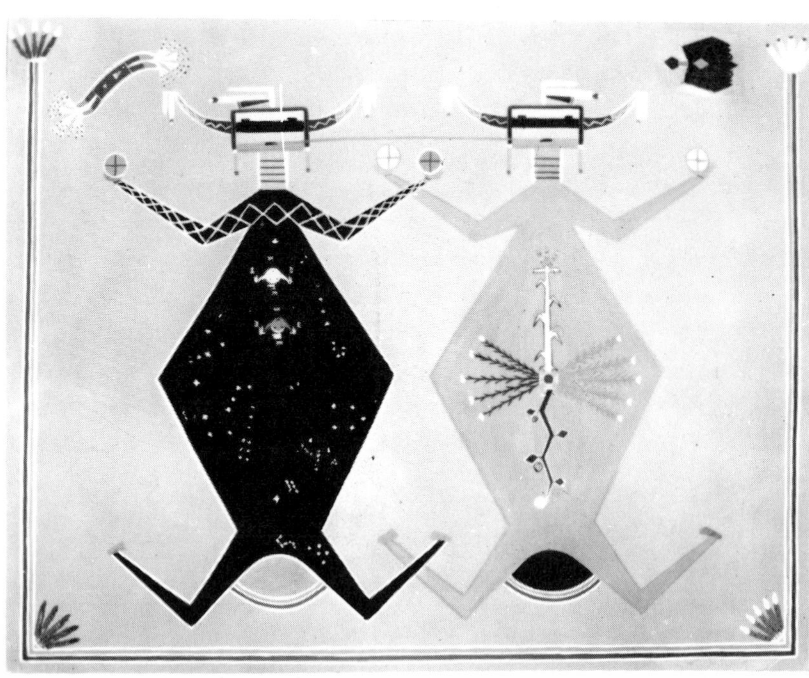

not discover how she flew. He climbed into the basket and covered his eyes. They swooped from the cliff and gently flew down. For a moment he opened his eyes and they began to fall, but Bat-Woman threw her blanket over him and the gentle descent was resumed. They reached the earth.

Then Nagenatzani, from the bodies of the monster birds he had shot down, took the wings for himself and the feathers for Bat-Woman. She valued them greatly, but he warned her that she must not walk over the field of yellow flowers in front of them. But on her way back she forgot and started to cross the flower field. Suddenly she heard a twittering and calling in her basket. The feathers had turned into song birds. Bat-Woman was so delighted that she released the birds to make people happy everywhere.

Again the Twins danced with Estanatlehi to record the great victory. But there were yet other trials to be undertaken by Nagenatzani while his brother Thobadestchin helped to cultivate the earth at home.

The Ogre who kicked people off mountain paths was the next to be conquered. He himself never fell because his coarse hair grew into crevices of the rock to hold him. Nagenatzani walked along the path. He extended his wand and the kicker struck out. The young man dodged behind his legs. The kicker was angered. Four times this was done. The kicker danced with rage, then with the big knife Nagenatzani slashed through his hair. As the Ogre crashed, a wailing sound was heard. The hero ran down to find that the kicker had fallen on his wife and family who were now busy cutting up his body and eating it. More birds were made; the Ogre's wife and children were swung into the sky and changed into the carrion eaters.

The last task of Nagenatzani was to go to where the people with the Lightning in their Eyes tempted people into their beautiful palace and then killed them. He took his knife and some salt from the Lake of Salt. Like other visitors he was allowed into the palace. But he was the child of the Sun and had thunderbolt protection. He was not stricken. Four times the tempters tried, throwing lightning against him, and each time their eyes stuck out further from their heads. Then he threw the salt on the fire, where it exploded in coruscating yellow flames which burned the eyes of the tempters and made them powerless. He took his big knife and killed and then scalped them. He took the scalps home, and there was a great scalp-dance to celebrate the final victory over the monsters.

Now the only people who were still fulfilling the curse that First Woman and First Man had laid on their people were the descendants of Yeitso the giant. So the Twin Brothers went together to a sacred spot that Sun had told them about. There they put down the black and red wind charm. They danced around it singing magical songs. The winds began to whirl, gathering power until they could uproot and toss great trees about. Then they were directed to the mountains where the enemy lived. The destruction was complete. There were no more giants left.

The work of the Twins Nagenatzani and Thobadestchin was accomplished and all dangers to the human race were ended, though

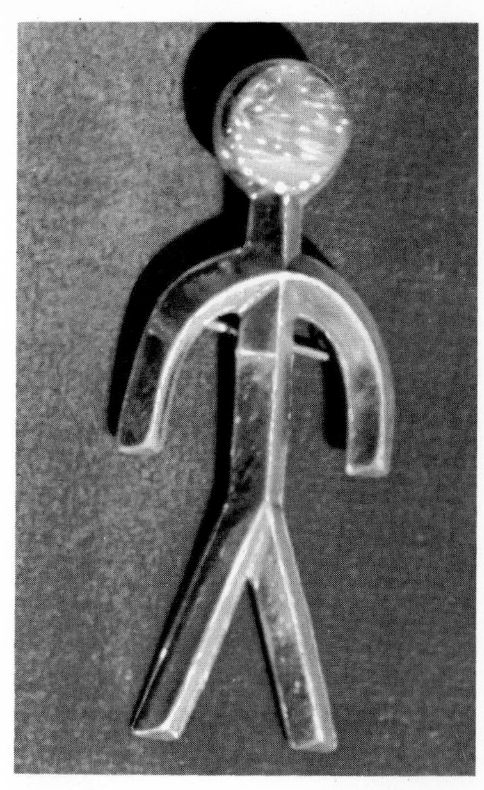

Overleaf, left: Two Mandan Indian dances, painted in the nineteenth century by Karl Bodmer. *Top:* A war-dance. The warriors carry staves but no other weapons and are known as 'They who are about to die'. Each hoped to win honour by being the first to touch an enemy with his staff. *Below:* The Buffalo Dance, commemorating the time when the buffalo hunted men, and the change that took place at the sacred tree from which man emerged from the earth.

Overleaf, right: Products of the Plains Indian culture. *Left:* A quillwork tobacco pouch with a Thunderbird design. Smoking featured in their ceremonies because it promoted peace and well-being. (James H. Hooper collection.) *Top:* An Apache storage basket with a hunting design divided into the four magical directions. *Centre:* Buffalo skin drum showing a Thunderbird, a tipi, and a symbol representing the shaman in meditation. (British Museum.) *Below:* Drum showing the sun surrounded by scenes which may represent the groups of stars. (British Museum.)

few were left alive after the plagues which First Man and First Woman had released. The Twins took the magical arms back to their father the Sun. But they found Sun was not happy. He was so proud of them that he wished to visit their mother again. He therefore ordered them to return to earth and build two fine lodges. In the west was to be the Palace of Estanatlehi, where each day Sun could see her beauty as he came to the end of his journey. At the opposite end of the sky, in the east, were to be the homes of First Man and First Woman, the parents of Estanatlehi. He said he could pass by now without desiring First Woman as he once had, since it was shameful for a man to look in his wife's mother. Thus it was done, and because of this Navajo men would never look at the faces of their mother-in-laws for fear trouble should follow.

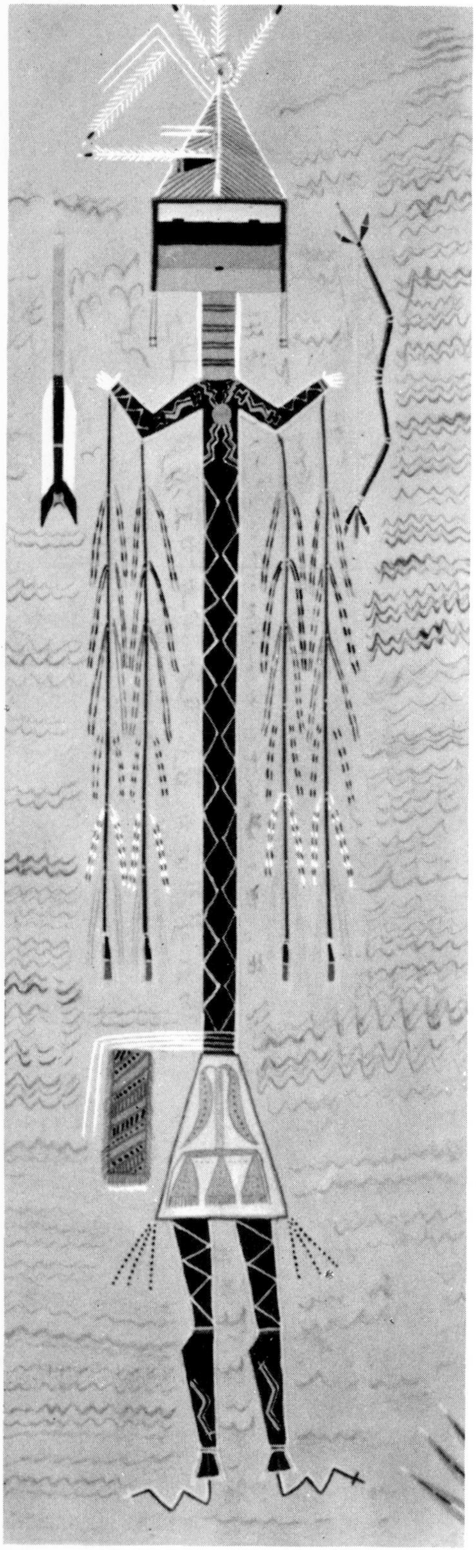

The repopulation of the world

Now when all this was done Sun consulted with Nagenatzani and Thobadestchin. They told him that earth was without people; so few were left that they could never repopulate it. Sun told them to explain to their mother that more people were needed and she would know the way to make them. So they returned to Estanatlehi to give her the message.

Their mother took two baskets. One she filled with flour ground from white maize, the other she filled with flour ground from yellow maize. Then she shook her breasts. From the right breast dust fell into the white flour. From the left breast fell dust into the yellow. Then she moulded the flour with water into a firm paste. From the white mixture she modelled a man. From the yellow mixture a woman. She warmed them and then placed them under a warm blanket. She watched over them as they lay together all night.

When morning came they were living people. Estanatlehi gave them a special power so that in four days they had children who grew up immediately. The new people, and their children, continued to have children every four days until the country was repopulated again, but stopped before they became as numerous as the ancient peoples had been when they sinned and brought punishment upon themselves. The new people were placed to live in four houses at the corners of the world. They were the first four clans of the Navajo. Then Estanatlehi began her journey to the House of the West, having decided to create more people. As she went she made four more clans from different coloured maize, taking the skin from the centre of her breasts to mix with the flour. This was believed to be the reason why women had special beauty in their nipples.

The eight people Estanatlehi made on her journey to the House of the West were ancestors of the four new clans that completed the numbers of the Navajo nation. With them the mother sent Bear, Puma and Wild-cat to hunt for them and to protect them.

The world was now completed and people were created to live in it subject to the orders of the gods. Nagenatzani and Thobadestchin went to dwell in a mountain cave near the junction of two rivers, where they are sometimes seen reflected in the waters. Estanatlehi

One of the holy people from the Shooting Chant. The ceremonial chants of the Navajo were recited as part of a healing rite.

went to her home in the west and became the Goddess of the Sunset-land. She sent everything that was good for the Navajo: the snow, the spring, the summer, the growing plants and maize to cover the hills and valleys. She was much loved by the people. But on the eastern borders of the sky lived her parents First Man and First Woman. They were envious of the new human race and wanted to send plagues such as those which destroyed most of the last human race. From them came sickness, wars and the white men.

Another of the Navajo myths recounts the adventures of the sisters who discovered a world of beauty and is called the Beauty Chant. It was used by shamans for curing, and is interesting from a medical point of view because at one point the patient was given a deliberate shock, through the appearance of the shaman acting the return of the Snake-Man near the end of the chant, to help to effect the cure. The greater spirits do not appear in this legend, and its recounting of the activities of animal spirits recalls the legends of simpler people. The world shown here is one where natural powers function in a way similar to the ways of nature spirits in European classical mythology. The basic difference is that in the European stories the gods have anthropomorphic forms whereas the American Indians use theriomorphic creatures who simply act like humans.

An animal fetish used in rituals designed to make the animals return when game was scarce. It is stuck with precious shells and recalls the myths about the people who lived under the ocean who were supposed to possess special powers. These powers were acquired by Bear and Snake after the raid on the House of Shells, described in the Beauty Chant. British Museum.

The beauty chant

Bear, Snake, Frog and Turtle set out to raid a village of people who lived under the great ocean. Frog and Turtle went alone into one of the hogans, intending to capture a couple of girls alive. The people of the village rushed out and the two adventurers had to kill the girls and take their scalps. The elder girl's hair was decorated with white shell, the younger one's with turquoise. The warriors hid the scalps in their robes and dashed out of the hogan. When the villagers attacked them, Frog made himself small enough to hide inside Turtle's shell, which was so strong that even blows with heavy stone axes failed to break it. Then the villagers decided to throw them into an oven where the fire would destroy them. Turtle was terrified, but Frog was a water creature and squirted water so well that he put the fire right out. When the oven was opened up the two creatures emerged unhurt. Then the villagers foolishly threw them into a stream, and both swam to the other shore, where they displayed the scalps with the jewels of the House of Shells.

Now Bear and Snake, who had been look-out men, were told by the wind to go along the coast to meet Frog and Turtle coming up out of the sea.

As they neared home they met eight people from their own village who asked which of them had the scalps. But they refused to say. Two of the villagers, who had daughters at home, said they would give the girls to whoever could shoot farthest. They wished to establish who was strongest so that he might then take the jewelled scalps by force. The eight and the four all shot. All were young except Bear and Snake, who said they were too old to shoot; but all the same they were the winners of the competition. The other ten were so angry that they hurried away leaving Bear and Snake to follow after them. But they did not get far before they were caught up by the elder pair. Three more competitions were held. Each time Bear and Snake were the winners. But no one would let the girls go to them. So the whole party went back to the home village to hold a scalp-dance. This time Bear and Snake did not hurry after the others but camped a little way outside the village and made themselves a shelter of sage-bush.

The people in the village began the scalp-dance, the drum and singing began. All the young people began to dance. The girls were all there, including the two who had been promised as prizes. As they danced the two girls became aware of a strange and wonderful scent. There was no way to find out where it came from except to follow it.

The scent led the girls to the sage-bush shelter, where they were delighted to find two handsome young men. Bear-Man was clothed in black and Snake-Man was coloured like a rainbow. They were bedecked with rich and beautiful jewellery. The elder girl asked Bear for some of the tobacco with the wonderful scent. But he said the young men at the dance would be angry. Snake, however, said they should come inside and then the young women would be allowed to smoke the pipes. The girls, struck by their beauty and kindness, had fallen in love. Bear gave his white shell pipe to the elder girl, and Snake gave his turquoise pipe to the younger. One breath of the smoke each, and they lost consciousness. Next morning they were given incense to revive them. They woke to find the sun was up and Bear and Snake had become old men. The girls were terrified but only the younger girl, Glispa, tried to escape. She found that she was tied to Snake's ankle by a blue racer snake. Whenever she moved he woke up. Whenever she was quiet he slept. She managed to loosen the snake at last and reached the door, only to find an army of snakes all hissing at her. The more frightened she became the more they hissed. Forcing herself to appear calm she walked between them and escaped. After a while she heard human voices, the voices of her relatives from the village. They were very angry and she knew that if she was found they would kill her. She looked back and saw that Snake was chasing her. Quickly she made her way to a river and waded downstream so that she could not be trailed by her scent. When she came to the mountains near the Place of Emergence, she circled round them. She grew thirsty and suddenly there was a lake in front of her. Snake-People came to her gently and asked whence she had come. She told her story. When she had finished, they lifted up the lake, and told her that it was only because she had told the truth that she was allowed to enter their world.

She came to fields of maize and ate. She met Snake-People who offered her bowls of water, and she drank. She found that they lived in adobe houses like the Pueblo people. They invited her into a house in which they assured her she would be safe from the old man. She stayed and was fed with a magical porridge made of pollen, and she found that however much she ate, the bowl never emptied. While she was living here the Snake-Man reappeared at a feast, once more in the form of a young and handsome man, dressed in his all-coloured clothes. Glispa was happy to see that he was young again. She knew that she

Right: Images set up on poles representing spirit beings. These poles were often set up outside individual houses as a form of protection against malignant spirits.

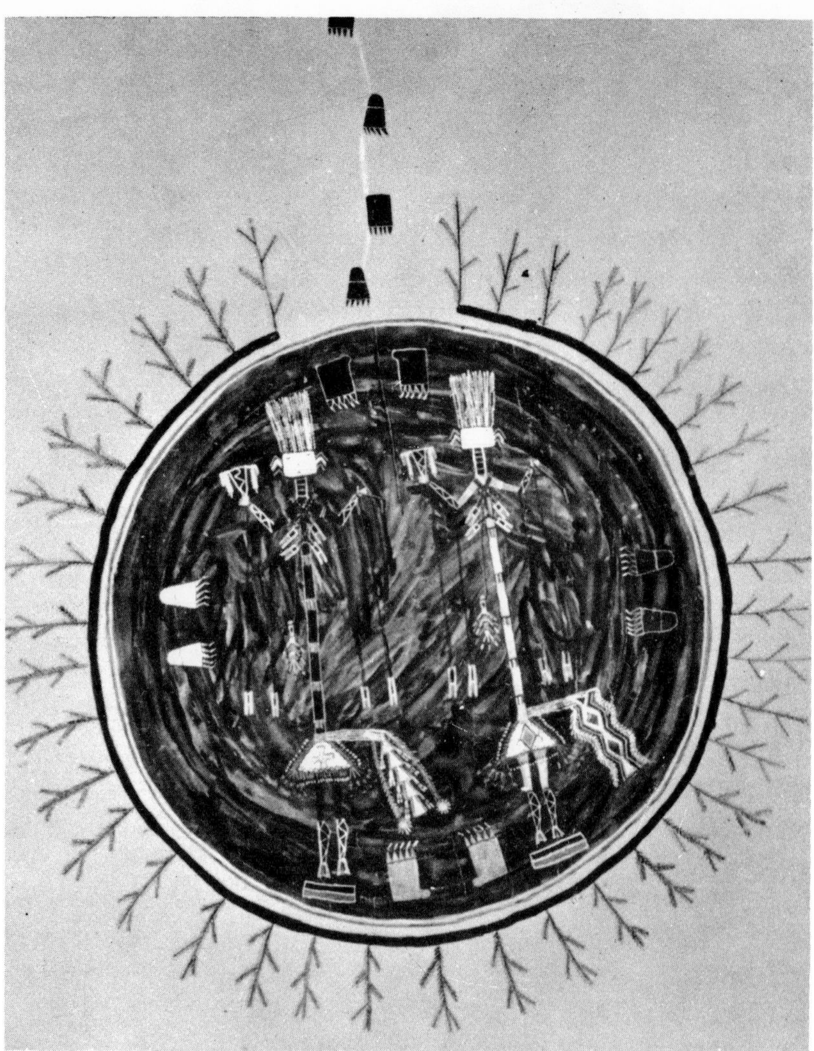

A detail from the Mountain Chant showing the maiden who became a bear – another version of the Northwest Coast story of Bear Mother.

The Southwest Indians excelled in basket work and often decorated them with both human and animal figures.

was happier than ever before, so she laughed with him and ate beside him. He explained that he was a great and powerful shaman who knew the whole of the Hozoni Chant and the accompanying sand-painting rituals. It was a healing chant and she learnt it very quickly. For two years she lived with the Snake-People and was happy. Then she became home-sick. Snake said that the time was come when she should visit her people and teach the Hozoni Chant to her brother so that he could bring healing to his people.

So Glispa returned to her people. Any fears she had were unfounded. Time had passed and their anger was forgotten, they welcomed her as one returned from the dead. She tried to teach her brother how to perform the healing ceremonies, but he could not remember the sequence of movements or the colours when making the sand-paintings.

After a time Glispa took some fine maize kernels, and as she sang the chants and directed his hands she laid a single kernel at each important point. Four kernels marked each song. Then they were left all night in the rows as she had laid them. Next morning maize was gathered and boiled into a gruel. Then she had a captive slave bring the food in a basket specially woven for the ceremony. After her brother had eaten the gruel his memory no longer failed him. He learned all the ceremonies, the chants, the sand-paintings and the feather prayer-offerings. Glispa sang ceremonies over her brother with herbs, trees and sand and he became a great shaman and acquired power to initiate others whom he knew to be fitted for the office.

The celebration of the Beauty Chant, by the Navajo, lasted four days and four nights while the people took ritual steam baths to symbolise their cleansing from the ignorant past. As the nocturnal ceremonies were nearing their conclusion the return of Snake-Man was described. At this point the shaman, disguised as Snake-Man, would suddenly appear. This was intended to shock the patient, and thus cure him, probably with the suggestion that this might be the serpent calling him to the underworld just as in the myth Snake-Man had called Glispa to return to the world beneath the lake.

The Beauty Chant, like many others, had the specific purpose of bringing health and well-being to those for whom it was performed. The Emergence Myth was of still greater power. Its recital could hea l the sick, initiate the aspirant to religious experience, and unite the people with the world of nature. In effect, the ancient chants of the Navajo people were a form of psycho-therapy which helped the sickly to heal their divided spirit or to reclaim their missing soul (for sickness was thought of as a matter of the spirit more than of the body).

This linking of the myths with healing ceremonies were probably the major factors in preserving them. Both onlookers and participants felt that they themselves were involved in the myths, and that their integration with the world of nature and with the spirits was thereby renewed. In its own way the ritual must have conveyed an emotional balance similar to that attained through regular participation in the ceremonies of the more complex civilisations of the Old World.

Overleaf, left: A sand-painting design reproduced on a textile. The elements included in the design varied not only according to the Chant which it illustrated but also had to take account of the particular ailment of the patient for whose benefit the Chant was being performed.

Overleaf, right: Two sand-paintings from the Hail Chant.
Top: The Storm People stand four-square on the rainbow bars facing the cardinal points. In the centre are the sun (top) and moon (bottom) and on either side the male and female winds. The male Storm People, holding lightning and hailstones, stand on the right of their partners who are dressed in white clouds and carry light rays. *Bottom:* The Thunder People, surrounding a central stalk of black maize topped by a yellow-breasted blackbird. All their masks are made of yellow evening light with white stripes of dawn at the forehead.

A basket-work tray from the Pima Indians of Arizona. The figure at the top is called Siuhu and figures in several Piman legends. He is surrounded by a maze because he was believed to live far in the mountains where the trails became so confused no-one could follow him. The tray is woven so tightly it could be used to hold water.

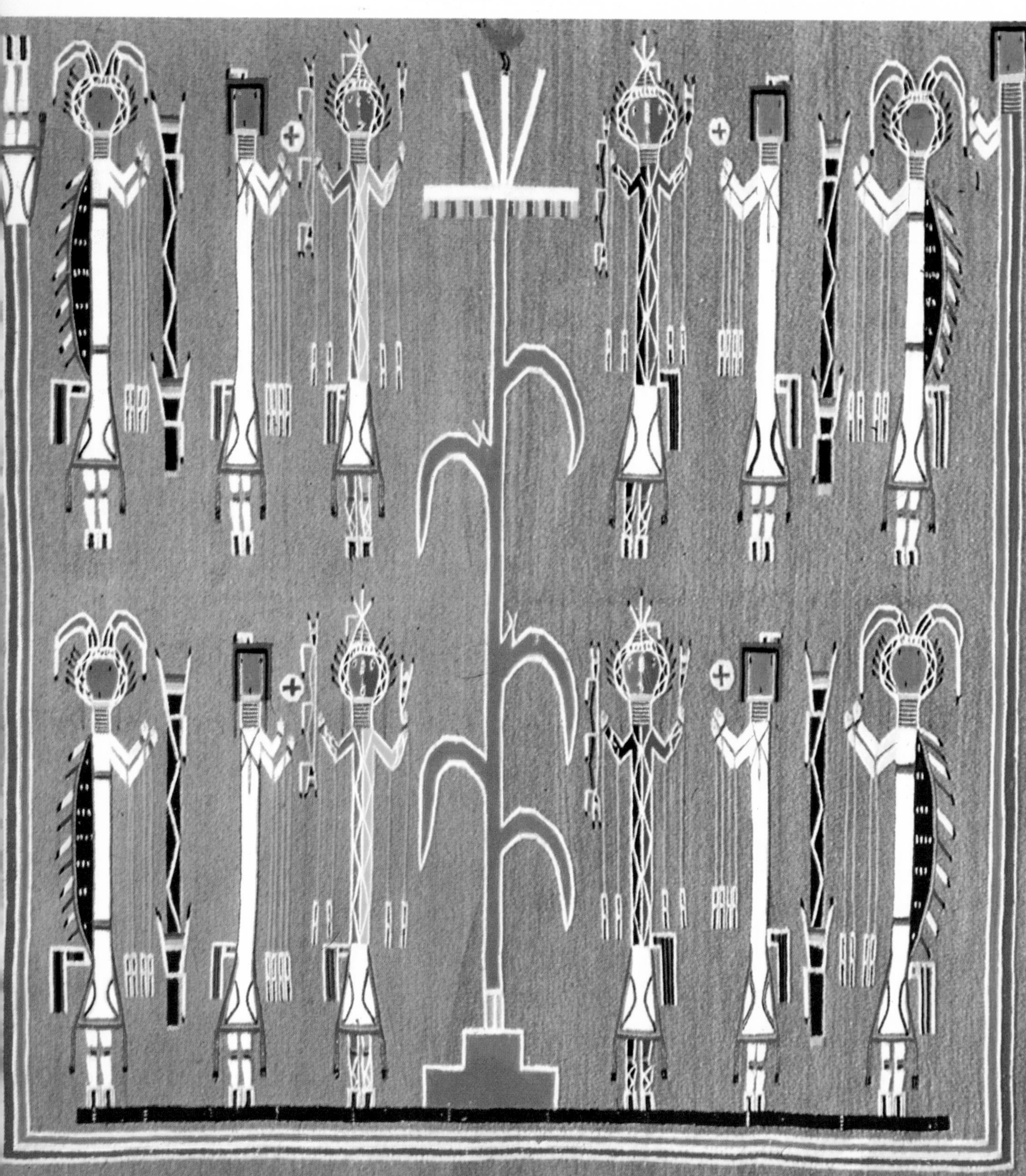

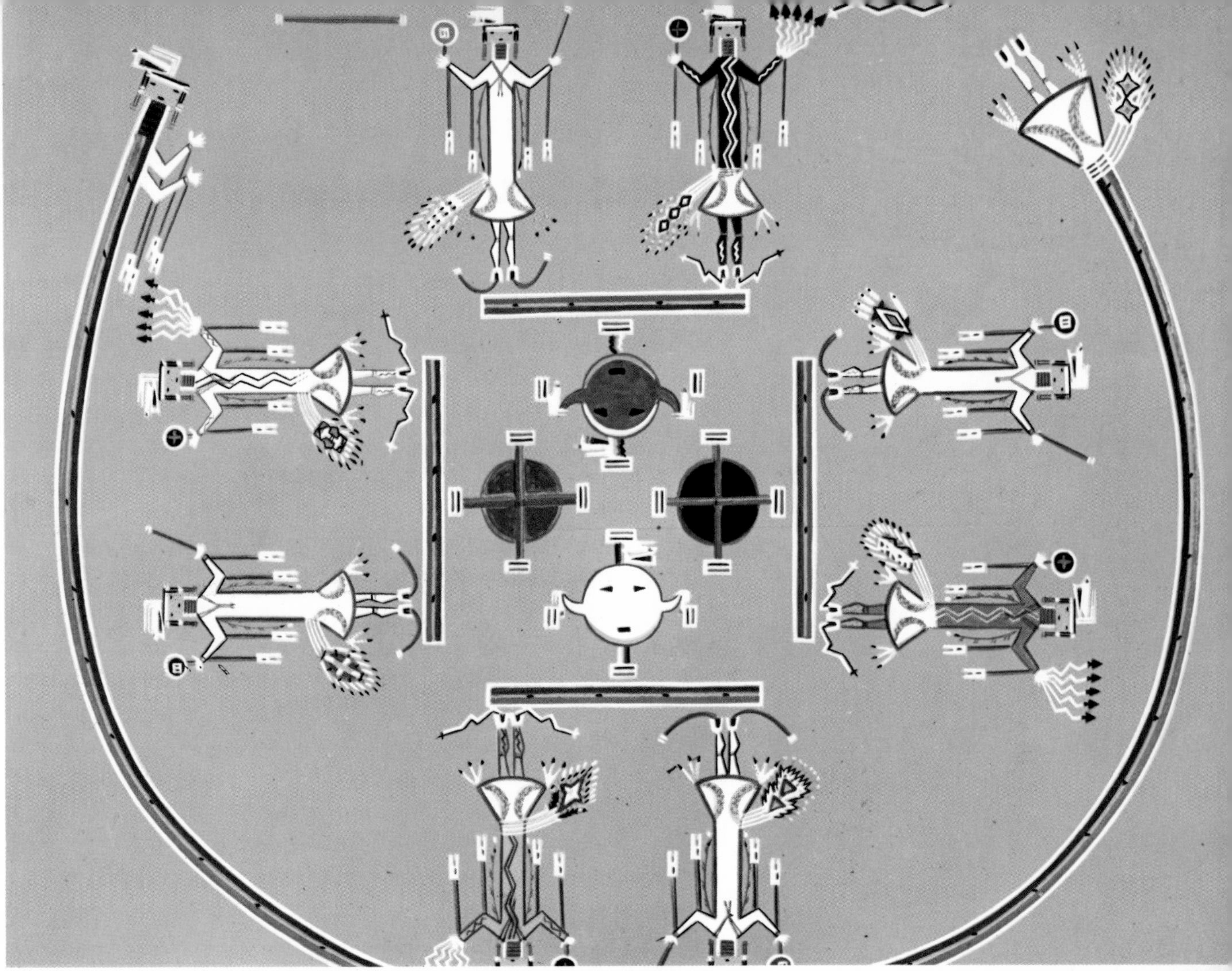

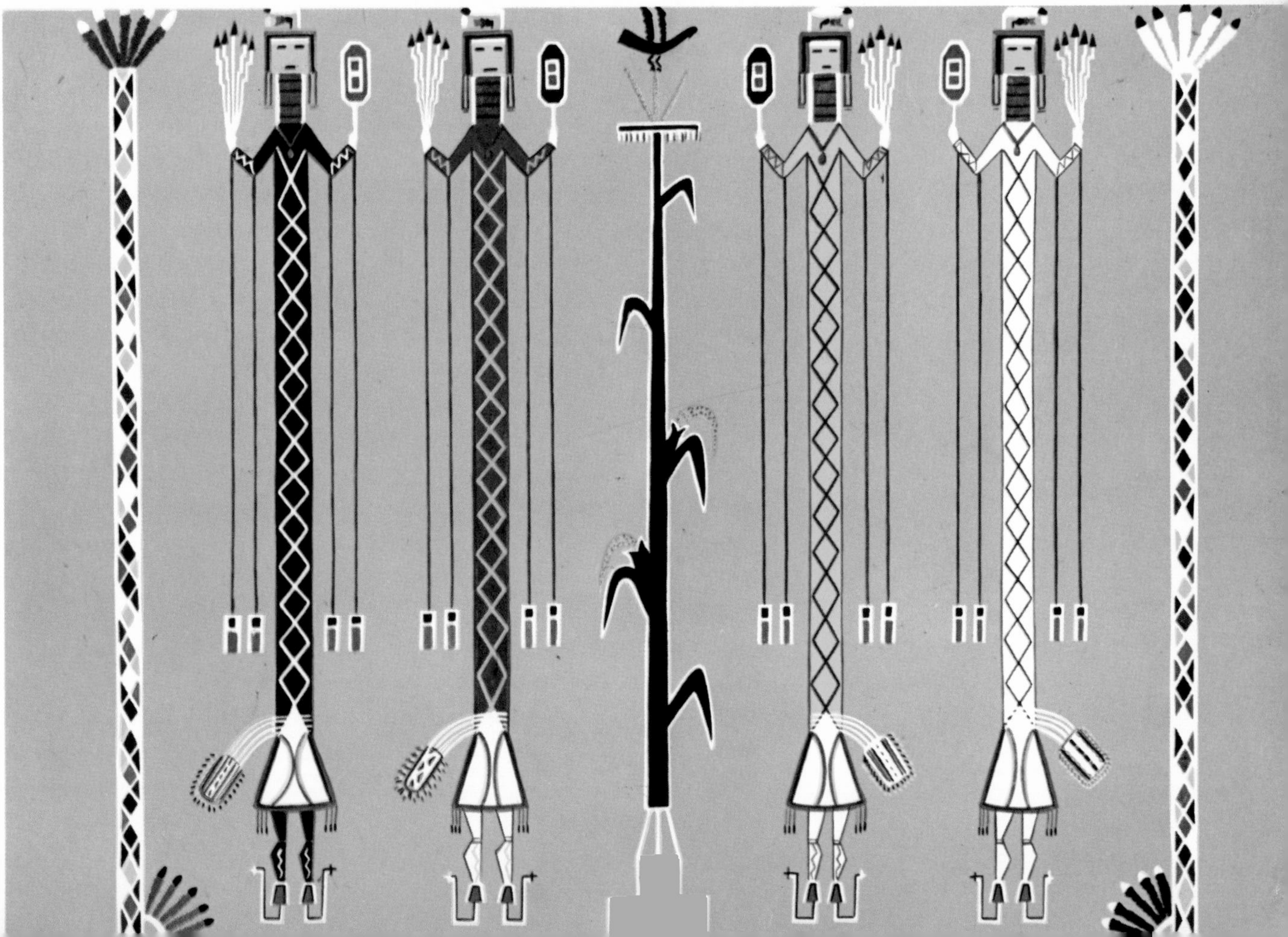

The Mound Builders in the Southeast

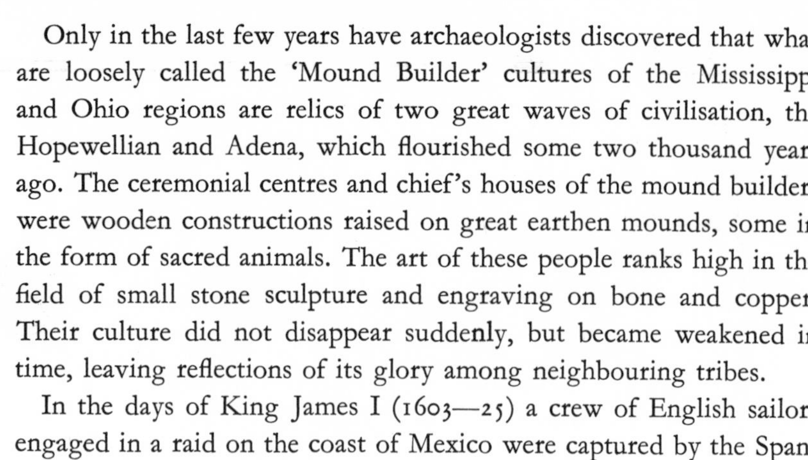

Only in the last few years have archaeologists discovered that what are loosely called the 'Mound Builder' cultures of the Mississippi and Ohio regions are relics of two great waves of civilisation, the Hopewellian and Adena, which flourished some two thousand years ago. The ceremonial centres and chief's houses of the mound builders were wooden constructions raised on great earthen mounds, some in the form of sacred animals. The art of these people ranks high in the field of small stone sculpture and engraving on bone and copper. Their culture did not disappear suddenly, but became weakened in time, leaving reflections of its glory among neighbouring tribes.

In the days of King James I (1603—25) a crew of English sailors engaged in a raid on the coast of Mexico were captured by the Spaniards and jailed in Mexico City. Most of them died under torture or were executed, but five men escaped from prison and proceeded to walk across North America. They were picked up by an English ship on the New England Coast. Unfortunately, they were taken to be questioned by the English authorities about their adventures, in case they could give military information useful in the wars with Spain, and to ensure their uninhibited replies they were stretched on the rack. Apparently they had some idea of what was expected and told a satisfyingly detailed story of their journey through the Natchez, Creek and Choctaw country in which they had seen fine palaces of timber and stone built on huge earthen mounds and decorated with pearls and diamonds, people wearing fine clothes and jewels, and plates made of gold everywhere. In the first edition of his great work on the voyages of English navigators Hakluyt quoted their short account in the Star Chamber records, but in the second edition he omitted it as altogether incredible. However, it seems to have been an exaggeration of real facts; the jewels were nothing more than lovely smoky river pearls like those which a Cherokee princess offered to the Spanish explorer De Soto, and the plates of gold described were partly true, although there was, no doubt, much more copper. As to the marvellous accounts of empires, the truth is represented by the loose confederation of the Creek towns and the small *imperium* of the Natchez whose eight towns included those of two subject tribes. One could wish that somewhere among the records of Elizabethan and Jacobean travels there had been some less ingenious account than that told by men who had suffered greatly under the Inquisition, travelled far across mountains and forest only to be racked for information at home.

Similarly, the magnitude of the disaster of De Soto's expedition resulted in only a partial account being given of his journey among the Creek towns, but at least this is strictly factual and reveals the existence of a material culture not unlike that of the western European tribes in the time of Julius Caesar, allied to a similarly advanced social structure.

Principal tribes: Cherokee Choctaw Creek Hitchiti Natchez

The Natchez

Of all the tribes, the Natchez probably remained most nearly at the level of the ancient civilisation of the Hopewellian Mound Cultures. There are surprising parallels between the Natchez and some central American cultures, excluding the later phase of Aztec civilisation. It appears that there were early connections between the mound builders and the people whose cultures were later to flower richly in Mexico, but that this contact had ceased centuries before the Aztec era. Perhaps the change of climate which cut the contacts between Mexico and the south-western Indians was responsible for the break. Certainly between the Panuco River and the Mississippi there was a stretch of desert and swampland, which by the time of the time of the European invasions would hinder communication.

The Natchez became involved in struggles against the French, and the final tragedy came when the French granted land, which included the site of the chief and sacred town of the Natchez, to French settlers for use as plantations. They saw only a poor wooden village built on ramps of earth, which was all that remained after nearly a century of intermittent wars with the white men. After the final desperate battles the remaining seven hundred Natchez were sent to settle among neighbouring tribes. They preserved some of their old traditions in a weakened and distorted form. As their numbers decreased, and knowledge of their old language faded, the ancient traditions became confused. When anthropologists recovered accounts of the myths from the last few speakers of the old tongue, they gathered mixed and distorted legends. The same process is reflected in Britain, in the way that the sacred Celtic chant to the Lady of the Underworld has became the English nursery rhyme 'Sing a Song of Sixpence'.

An incised conch shell from the Spiro Mound, Oklahoma. It portrays an eagle man and probably represents a ceremonial dancer. A.D. 1200–1600.

The Creeks

A similar, but much less complete, process affected the development of Creek myths. The loose confederation of neolithic villages broke up on contact with white settlers, but the main tribal ceremonies

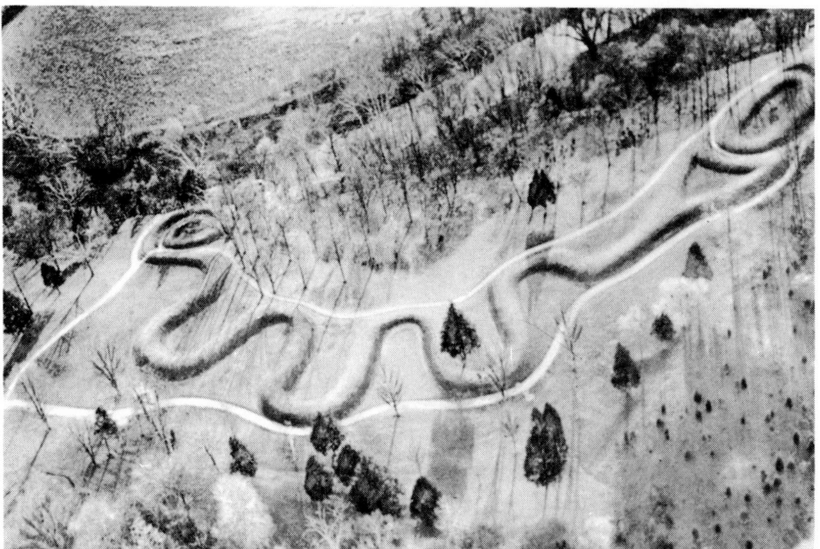

The many mounds in the form of birds, bears and other animals, found in the Mississippi and Ohio regions are relics of a civilisation which flourished in North America about two thousand years ago. The Great Serpent Mount (1,350 feet long) is the largest, situated in Ross County, Ohio.

A sandstone pipe-bowl from a mound in Boone County, Kentucky. It shows old mother frog who played a part in the creation of the world in many southern myths. British Museum.

were preserved by the Creeks and the language kept alive. Much was saved by the efforts of the Creeks themselves. An important aspect of their handling of new experiences was the process of gradual assimilation. They absorbed many folk-tales from the European settlers into their mythology, and many from the negro slaves from West Africa. The Creeks in turn had a considerable influence on negro folk-tales, especially in the imposition of their own concept of the Trickster Spirit, personified as the Rabbit, on to the cycle of Ashanti stories about Anansi, the Trickster. In Jamaica Anansi suffers a spelling change and is often called Nancy, but in the south-eastern United States he took over the name of his Creek Indian archetype and has since charmed the world as Brer Rabbit.

The coming of fire

The following account of Rabbit comes from a Hitchiti Indian myth. He is the Trickster of the legend describing the coming of fire and is very like Raven in the stories of the Indians of the Northwest Coast. Although the stories are different, the relationships are the same. The degeneration of myth has made it into a confused tale about 'people' instead of about the Sky People and the First People on the earth below, but the detail of the myth makes the identification clear.

A dance was to take place on the village square where the Sky People were going to celebrate Puskitá, the Green Corn Festival of purification. They would make fire afresh. The dancing square was the only place where one was allowed to make fire. But Rabbit thought there should be fire in other places. He thought for a long time. Then he had his friends rub his head with pine until his hair stood on end. Everyone thought his new creasted headdress looked so fine that they made him leader of the dance.

A fragment of a garment brought back to England by some early explorer and known as Powhatan's Mantle, though there is no evidence to prove that it ever did belong to the south-eastern chief of that name. The shell decoration is typical of North American art.

The dancers followed him, circling the four directions of the sacred fire logs. As they passed the east, Rabbit bent low, as if to throw the offerings of tobacco to the fire. People said that when Rabbit danced he always acted extravagantly, and did not notice how low he bent. On the fourth round he set his headdress on fire, and ran away so fast that they failed to catch him. Then the people worked magic and made a great rain which lasted four days. They thought the stolen fire would be put out by then and allowed the sun to shine again. Rabbit, however, had run into a hollow tree and made a fire there in shelter, emerging when the sun shone. So again the people made rain. Every time Rabbit came out he lit new fires, but the rain put most of them out. The First People saw these fires and were quick to light firebrands at them. After this they had fires in their homes, and whenever the rains put them out the people who had fire shared it with the others. In the end the rains stopped, everybody was allowed to have fire, and Rabbit was remembered for bringing fire to the Hitchiti.

The origin of tobacco

The culture of the Indians of the south-east contained variant attitudes to many of the myths, mainly because climatic and economic influences were different from those in other regions. The origin of tobacco is an example. In the plains, where it was not native, it was a marvellous star plant. But in the south-east tobacco was linked with sex to account for its power of giving peace.

A young man and a girl travelled together, fell in love and left the path for the happiness of intercourse. They were so pleased that they agreed to marry. Later, on a hunting journey, the man returned to the place where they had first united and there found a pretty flower with scented leaves. He took it back to the people and told of the discovery. They said, 'When it is dried, we will smoke it, and name it "Where We Came Together".' The elders of the tribes claimed that because the man and woman were so completely at peace and happy when tobacco was made it has been smoked ever since at councils for promoting peace and friendship between the tribes.

The origin of maize

This is another story in which some elements of the world above the earth have been applied to people of the present world. It has, however, preserved most of its simplicity. It attributes the origin of maize to the creative female magic of an old woman who must have been some kind of earth-mother goddess.

An old woman lived alone. She trod her own paths from the house until they were smooth. One day, on one of the paths, she saw a clot of blood. She covered it with a jar. Later she removed the jar and found a baby boy underneath. When he grew up he called her Grandmother. When he was seven she made him his first bow and arrows. He went out with them and came back full of questions.

'What is it, Grandmother, that has a bushy tail and runs up trees?' 'It is a squirrel. Shoot it and bring it home to eat'. He did so. Then he went out again. 'What is it that flies from tree to tree?' 'It is a bird and good to eat. Shoot it and bring it home'. And another day, 'I saw a big animal with big feet and its body leaning forward. It had no tail and its ears were round. What can it be?' 'That is a bear and good to eat. Shoot it and bring it home.' By asking these questions, day after day, he learned the names of all the animals and which of them were valuable as food.

Now he went hunting everywhere, but his Grandmother told him he must never pass a distant blue mountain on the horizon. He hunted many things but never discovered from which creature his Grandmother made the *sofky* maize gruel and the blue dumplings of maize and beans. He knew nothing of plants. He decided one day to peep in through the door when she was preparing food. He saw her remove her dress and straddle a corn sieve. As she scratched one of her thighs, a stream of maize poured down. As she scratched the other thigh, a stream of beans descended. When he came in and would not eat, the Grandmother guessed that he had discovered her secret. She told him that now he had solved the mystery he must leave her and go beyond the blue mountain. To protect him, she made a magical headdress of intertwined rattlesnakes and blue jay-birds which rattled and sang when he put it on.

A stone mask from Tennessee. Masks such as this, which were too heavy to be worn, and which have no eye apertures, were probably used to cover the faces of the dead. Some of the southern tribes believed that if one looked on the faces of the dead one's own death would be hastened.

Drawing made by John White in 1590 of the Natchez custom of keeping the bodies of the dead on frames in sacred buildings. This custom is reflected in the story of the flood when those who had died were told they would continue to live on in spirit. British Museum.

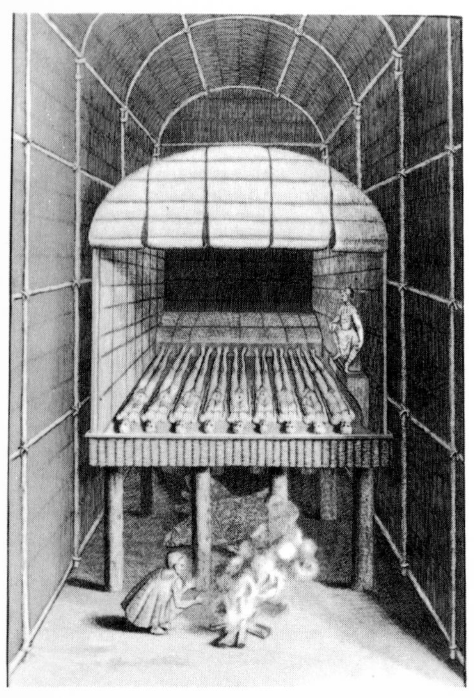

Now Grandmother told him that all was ready for his journey. He must marry the first girl that he met, and then return. As he left he was to shut the door, with Grandmother inside, and set fire to the house so that nothing would remain but ashes. He did so and the fire consumed everything just as Grandmother had decreed.

The orphan boy went out over the mountains. He came to a village where men were playing a ball game. They stopped to watch him with his marvellous headdress of rattlesnakes and jays. Rabbit was there, and he said he would walk along the path with him. They came to a lake where there were many turtles. Rabbit said, 'Come! When I say "jump" we will dive in and each catch some turtles.' Orphan Boy agreed. Rabbit called out 'Jump'. Orphan Boy set his marvellous headdress beside the lake and jumped in. Rabbit snatched the hat and ran away as fast as he could.

Orphan Boy caught his turtles. The men were sorry for him when he told of his loss and brought him to the village. There he entered the first house and was welcomed by a beautiful young woman. He made a hole near her house and put the turtles in it. He returned and she accepted him as her husband. Next he saw her mother and told her, 'There are turtles in the ground. Go and bring some, and cook for us all.' She followed his directions and found many fine turtles. In this way Orphan Boy proved that he was a good provider.

Soon Rabbit was brought in, having been seized for stealing the magical headdress. It had neither rattled nor sung since Rabbit stole it, but, as soon as Orphan boy touched it, the rattlesnakes buzzed their rattles and the blue jays sang. Rabbit asked to be thrown among the dogs. The tribespeople thought that this would certainly make an end of him, but as soon as he was thrown amongst them, the dogs went to sleep and Rabbit ran off unharmed, ready for further mischief.

One day Orphan Boy took his wife to the river. He told her that if he could swim across four times they would be able to catch enough fish for all the people of the village. She believed him and called all the people. He swam across four times and hundreds of fine big fish came up for them. Rabbit was envious and said he would do the same and swam across four times. The fish appeared, but all so dead that their eyes had turned white and their bodies rotten. The people chased Rabbit out of the village and warned him never to come back.

Having provided for the villagers, Orphan Boy and his wife went on the journey over the mountains, back to the place where Grandmother had been burnt. There they found the ground covered by a fine crop of maize plants and beans. Each maize plant was wearing a skirt of earth around its base, and that is why the Indians subsequently made little skirts of earth for their maize seed to sprout through. They believed that maize was really old Grandmother.

The flood

The myths of the Creek Indians have changed less than those of the once mighty Natchez. Some of the original content of the Natchez myths still survives, but gives the impression that many of the legends have been mixed. In the flood story that follows, there are three social groups of people among the survivors. They probably represent the Suns, the Nobles, and the Commoners of ancient Natchez society, but the myth provides no clue as to the origin of the social differentiation although this was probably explained in the original.

The story tells of the Dog who warned his master to make a raft because all things would be overwhelmed by a flood. As the water rose the Dog and the Man saw the mountains burst open and strange monsters emerge. But the waters drowned everything except Man and his Dog, lifting them above the clouds where they saw a wonderful world of land and trees. But Dog told Man that he must return to the place he had come from and that this would be impossible unless he threw Dog into the flood. Much against his will, Man threw Dog into the waters and they began to subside. Dog warned Man not to land until the ground had had seven days in which to dry. When this had happened Man saw people coming to him because he still had fire on the raft. Some were naked, some wore rags and some wore beautiful clothes. The three groups divided the fire between them. Then a noise was heard in the east and an Old Man appeared to say that although their bodies had been dead for various periods they would continue to live in spirit.

The myth reflects the Natchez custom of drying the bodies of the dead and keeping them on frames in sacred buildings. There are similarities between this myth and a longer story about the seventh son of a cannibal giant who had already destroyed six sons. The seventh escaped and jumped up a tree in the night. When morning came he was terrified to discover that the tree was really a horn of the great water serpent who was now swimming up the river. Canoes loaded with deformed people drifted by. They all laughed at him because he was riding on the serpent. But at last a canoe full of girls drew alongside him. They were sorry for him, and told him to spit towards them. He did so and they came nearer until he was able to board the boat.

The canoe continued on its course along the great river for so long a period that he married one of the girls, who bore his child while they travelled on. They came at last to where the seventh son's mother lived. At first she hid from him, doubting his identity because she lived in darkness and all kinds of animals, especially the rats, came to her pretending to be her son. But when she saw her grandchild she danced for joy and led all three to the place of a great chief.

The chief had many wives but he always blinded them. When he saw his visitors arrive he prepared to welcome them. The old mother had taken command. She would not approach the chief unless he made his wives all lie down to make a pathway for them. So he ordered the wives to lie side by side. Then the old mother became young again and led her son and grandson over the women. The chief married the mother, but the son did not want her eyes removed and the chief had him thrown out. When the son returned her eyes had been removed. The son set them back in their sockets but the chief had him removed a second time and on his return he found her dancing blind before the chief who was beating a magic drum. The young man restored his mother's eyes again, desperately seized the magic drum and

A medicine rattle from Carolina, over 200 years old. The severe, geometric decoration is typical of the more advanced art of the southern region. British Museum.

rushed his family to the canoe. The chief and his blind wives were unable to stop them and the family escaped, with the son beating the magic drum, towards the west.

This story is possibly an account of a voyage through the stars and a visit to the underworld. The principal characters are probably Moon (the mother) Sun (the chief) and Morning Star (the son).

The image of the head with antlers is one of the oldest, and most widespread, of man's symbols. This example comes from the Spiro Mound, Oklahoma. It is carved in one piece and was probably worn at the Deer Ceremony to promote good hunting. A.D. 1200–1600.

The rolling heads

The North American Indians as a whole had an obsessive ghost story about heads with no bodies, the Rolling Heads. The story is to be found in almost every tribe, though there are local variations. The Natchez version of this takes place in the warm swampy terrain of their homeland. It has a definite mythological character, although confused by the lapse of time. The hero and heroine seem to have control over the powers of nature, and it is probably another myth about the Moon and the Morning and Evening Stars. The characters have many adventures which finally end in the trapping of the destructive power.

Two brothers lived together. One day a woman came and said she wanted to live with them. They decided that she should be the wife of Younger Brother. Later the brothers went out fishing. A big fish came up. The only way they could think to catch it was for the Elder Brother to tie a hickory-bark rope round the Younger Brother, throw him into the water, and drag him ashore with the fish in his arms. They tried this, but the fish was too big and swallowed Younger Brother, snapping off the rope. Elder Brother ran along the bank asking the animals to help him. With the exception of Kingfisher they were all terrified of the fish and ran away. Kingfisher perched on the fish and hammered with his long bill on its side until it died and drifted to the bank. There Elder Brother cut it open; but only the head of Younger Brother remained, the rest of him had been reduced to powder. The head spoke, instructing Elder Brother to wash it well and place it on a log. The head said that he would visit the house in the morning and would sing as it came, and his wife was to be warned he could no longer act as her husband.

That night Elder Brother took the woman as his wife. Next morning the head flew through the air and sat on the roof singing. On hearing that Elder Brother had taken his wife, it plotted to kill him. It asked them to come out to pluck fruit from the trees. It then flew to a tree and began to eat the fruit, throwing the skins at the woman to provoke Elder Brother to climb after him, but Crow warned them to escape while they were able.

Elder Brother and the woman fled. But the head saw them and came rolling along the ground, screaming at them. They ran for the house of the Mud-wasp, where the head, in close pursuit, demanded that the woman should be handed over. The Mud-wasp denied that she was there, but the head could not be deceived, he had already seen the imprint of the woman's buttocks where she had slipped in the mud.

Mud-wasp then told the woman to lie down. He took her genitals

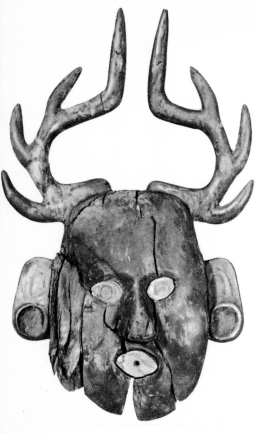

Below and opposite: Tobacco pipes of the Hopewell Culture from mounds in Ohio. The animals are all involved in the creation myth that tells how they came out of the bamboo cane of the woman married to the Rolling Head. First century A.D. Squier and Davis collection. British Museum.

and, with a few magical cuts, changed her into a man. To confuse the head he took the two men outside asking them to show their skill by shooting a row of four pots. The new man's arrows pierced all four. But Elder Brother pierced only one. The head was convinced by this that the better shot was a man also. He invited the new man to hunt deer with him. When he saw the manner in which the other hunted his suspicions returned and he renewed the chase. They came to a swampy creek. The head suggested that they should jump in and swim across. The new man leapt in with the head. Underwater he sang a charm which told the Rolling Head that this was his home and he should stay there. Then he turned back into a woman and escaped, leaving the head imprisoned beneath the waters of the creek.

As she continued her journey she found she was pregnant. She gave birth to several babies, which she put in the joints of a big bamboo that she carried with her. She came to the house of a chief, who married her because she was so attractive, although he already had many wives. She became his favourite. This made the others ashamed and angry. They challenged her to a contest to see who could make the most parched maize. She went to her old friend the Mud-wasp for advice and he told her to open the top joint of her cane. Kingfisher flew out. While the other wives were working hard, Kingfisher went to all the villages and collected parched maize for her and so she won the contest.

Next, to test her attractiveness, the other wives proposed a contest to discover which of them had the most beautiful pubic hair. Again she was advised to open a joint of the cane. This time Humming Bird flew out, and wove the iridescent down of humming-bird breasts into her hair. Once again she triumphed. She was then challenged to play a ball game. The rival wives decided that while the game was in progress they would attack and kill her with their shinny sticks. Friendly Mud-wasp said she must now open the whole cane and let out all her children. She did so, and living creatures came streaming out. Among them were storm and thunder, who swirled the dust in the air and confused the women, and lightning, who struck them down.

In triumph and with all her children around her, the woman went on her way, and as she travelled she sent her offspring out in different directions to people the earth as she followed her path along a westward journey.

This myth from the warm swampland of the Natchez country contains some of the elements found in the myths of the Creek tribes: the journey, the danger threatening a particular woman (the moon), the hostility of a chief (the sun) or his wives and the woman's rescue by her children (the stars). Its confused nature is typical of the myths that have survived in which the original distinctions have been blurred by the passage of time. The stories themselves speak only of 'people' although it is possible to indicate the Sky People, First People and spirits of the natural world who must have featured in the original myths and it is unlikely that we shall ever know their exact form. In contrast to this confusion, the myths of the Indians of the desert country of the south-west, described in the next chapter, are the best preserved of any in the whole continent.

The Dwellers on the Mesas

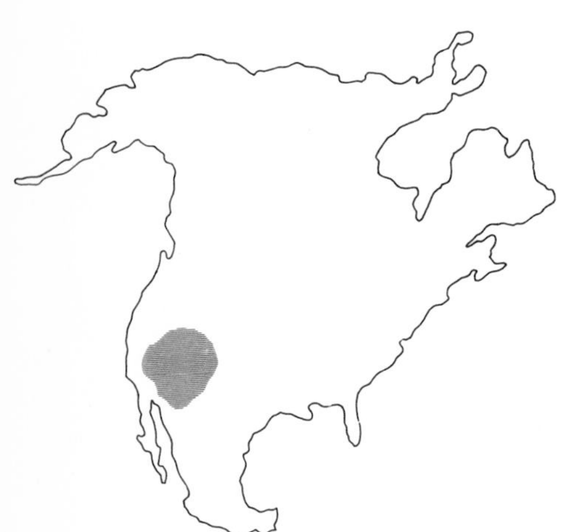

Principal tribes: Hohokan Hopi Zuni

In the south-west region the most highly organised Indian communities lived in large villages called *pueblos* by the first Spanish discoverers. The villages were built on the mesas, the high rocky tableland, typical of this region. Some of the villages were built of stone, others of adobe. There was a common culture among the Pueblo Indians, but they were divided by language into four distinct groups. They were fairly widely scattered through the arid, near-desert country of what is now Colorado, Utah, New Mexico and Arizona.

The distinctive civilisation of the Pueblo Indians had been forced on them by the necessities of their situation. In past centuries the fertile lands where they had grown their food were devastated by increasing drought. Raids by the prairie tribes increased and the settled communities were forced to find easily defensible spots from which they could emerge to cultivate the remaining fields whenever possible. After a period of cliff-dwelling the towns were moved to commanding sites on the flat-topped mesas. Each was near a water hole, and the people went out daily to cultivate their plantations. Often the cultivated plots were some miles distant from the towns, so in periods of danger the warriors went out to protect the women at their work.

The Pueblo tribes were of mixed origin. Some had been settled cultivators in pre-drought times, others were remnants of simpler people from the west who found it safer to live with their neighbours

Right: Eototo, a kachina from the Hopi pueblo of Walpi. Eototo played an important part in the celebrations that marked the departure of the kachinas, for they were believed to be absent from the people for half of the year.

rather than to fight them. The mixture is evident in their myths as well as in some local differences within a particular linguistic group.

Life in the Pueblo

Considerable social organisation was needed for the pueblo way of life. Single-room dwellings were clustered together like cells in a three or four tiered beehive. The various matriarchal groups within the tribe usually lived in adjacent quarters and there was a group of men to keep the peace between dissident groups when quarrels arose. There were many religious societies, some organised on a clan basis, some dedicated to the service of particular spiritual powers. These societies had underground meeting rooms known as kivas, which were entered through a hole in the foor. Here the tribespeople held their religious ceremonies, mostly for men only, and arranged their outdoor activities, especially those which included processions of masked dancers inspired by the kachinas as the spirits and powers of nature were called.

Tribal organisation was necessary for social reasons. Each of the religious societies had a leader, and the various clan groups had chiefs. Government was conducted through meetings of the council of elders rather than by dictatorship by any one group. Women occupied a respected place in society and descent was normally through the female line.

Under desert conditions growing, gathering and storing food was always a communal concern. Each family looked after its own livelihood, but they banded together for protection. Each family group was required to maintain reserves of grain, so that if the crops failed in any one year there would be approximately half rations available from stored reserves kept in huge baskets and pottery vessels.

This way of life was reflected in the agglomeration of family apartments which made the town one large complex of solid building. There were occasional courtyards opening on to a plaza by means of alleyways, and beneath the courtyards lay the underground kivas. The

The spirits worshipped by the Pueblo Indians were known as kachinas. This is Momo, the bee kachina. He carries a miniature bow and arrows and in the dance he imitates the hum of a bee and goes from one spectator to another shooting blunt arrows at them. If any of the children cry with fright, he squirts a little water on the supposed wound.

general plan is similar to a structure such as the Minoan palace of Knossos. Pueblo towns often had dependent villages and were, in effect, independent communities who traded a little between themselves and sometimes united to repel raids by the wilder tribes from the plains. But, in the main, the Pueblo Indians were peaceful and sought to occasion no hatred from neighbouring people.

All the North American Indians used body painting at important ceremonies and those of the south had the most elaborate designs of all. In addition they wore feather headdresses, turquoise and shell jewellery and circular amulets round their necks.

Pueblo crafts

Pueblo craftsmanship was not highly developed. The people carved wood a little, worked with turquoise and shell to produce beautiful jewellery, and made pottery by pinching coils of clay together to make pots and then firing them in heaps of brushwood and buffalo dung; neither potter's wheel nor kiln was used by the Pueblo Indians. Weaving was developed, with cotton, rabbit fur and yucca fibre as the staple yarns. Clothing in the old days was very simple. The rough ground led to the development of pads worn under the toes and later to hide moccasins. Youngsters normally went naked, but when a girl married it was the duty of her husband to weave her a blanket as her first article of clothing. Men wore kilts for great occasions, otherwise a small simple breechclout. The elaborate leggings and shirts of the men, and the pretty boots, gowns and shawls of the women of more recent times, evolved through contact with the outside world.

The pictorial arts were highly formalised in the regional styles already described among the Navajo. Traditional figures painted in mineral colours decorated ceremonial boards, the walls of kivas, and the masks and headdresses worn by the dancers who impersonated the kachina spirits in the ceremonies.

Among the Pueblo Indians we find a civilisation which in its early stages developed in comparative isolation. After the initial Spanish

The Pueblo Indians were fond of ornaments made from turquoise and shell. This shell was worn as an amulet in the winter solstice ceremony. Zuñi pueblo. British Museum.

invasion their struggles were on a small scale and conditions were ameliorated by the Spanish missions. Yet these struggles were nonetheless bitter, involving much cruelty on both sides and helped to perpetuate the isolation of the Pueblo Indians through a reputation for recklessness and cruelty which they hardly deserved. In modern times the contact with the United States, although sometimes unsuccessful, has led to increasing understanding and helpfulness on both sides, and during the last half-century the arts of the Pueblo Indians have made a considerable impression on artistic taste in America. The religious dances and processions of the kachinas have became more and more a tourist show, but there have also been intellectual contacts between Indian elders and anthropologists which have resulted in the preservation in literary form of much of the ancient tradition.

The myths that follow show the specially Pueblo Indian character of the mythology for the archetypal deities dress and behave as Pueblo Indians. Projected unconsciously from the hearts of the people themselves, they appear to them as visionary beings who have the power of giving blessings and receiving love. What follows is the beginning of the story of creation as told in the town of Zuñi round about 1880.

The creation of the world

Before creation began there was only the 'one who contains everything', Awonawilona; otherwise there was blackness and nothingness. Awonawilona created life within himself; the mists of increasing and the streams of growing flowed from him. He assumed a form and was the maker of light, the sun. When the sun appeared the mists gathered together and fell as water, becoming the sea in which the world floats. From within himself Awonawilona formed seed and impregnated the waters. Then, in the warmth of the sun, green scum formed over the great waters and became solid and strong. It was divided and became Earth Mother of the Four Directions and Sky Father who covers everything.

Earth and Sky lay in union and the fourfold womb of Earth conceived all creatures. Then she separated from Sky. She would not give birth yet; all must be prepared. So Earth and Sky assumed the forms of man and woman and discussed the creation of the earth. Earth Mother held a bowl of water and described how the mountains should be made to divide land from land, and stand around the rim of the world. She spat into the water and stirred it with her fingers making foam arise. She drew milk from her breasts to give it life. So she indicated the coming of life, and showed how children should be nourished. She breathed upon the foam, and mists and rainbows arose as clouds floating above the sea. Then Sky breathed and rain fell from the clouds. This showed how man would find warmth and life near Earth Mother and cold from Sky Father, whose breath would bring fertilising rain to Earth again. The Indians believed that because of this warmth ever remains with women and coldness strengthens men. The Sky opened his hand. Within every crease there lay innumerable grains of shining maize. In his thumb and forefinger he took some of the shining grains and placed them in the sky as

Right: Three south-eastern Indians as they appeared in the sixteenth century. Water-colours by John White. *Left:* A priest, *top:* a woman of Florida and *below:* a warrior wearing ceremonial paint. British Museum.

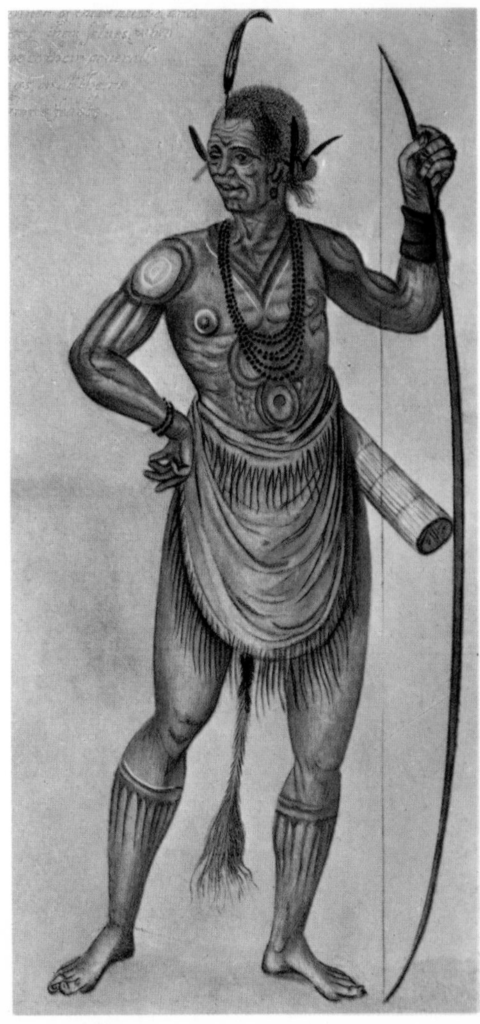

A Hopi Indian dance wand with a painted kachina figure, decorated with feathers and maize-stalks. Pueblo dances were the dramatised expression of a prayer to the spirits and were formal, elaborate and disciplined.

brilliant stars to be a guide to humans when the bright sun was hidden. They marked the six regions of the sky in which stars would move: north, south, east, west, upwards and downwards. Then he blessed the breasts of Earth Mother, saying that the golden grains would spring from her to be food for their children.

Then Earth Mother and Sky Father parted and assumed their cosmic forms again. Within the innermost of the four wombs, the Place of Generation, life began to quicken. The beginnings of creatures were formed, dark, horrible and writhing in the darkness. They had neither knowledge nor cleanliness and crawled over one another crying for escape to a better world. As time passed they became wiser and more like the form they were finally to have. Among them was One Alone, the sacred master Poshaiyangkyo, who was able to escape. He found a path from the inner womb and followed it, where no-one else could go, outwards and upwards until he came to the light. There in the swamp of creation, wallowing in the waters, he came seeking the sun and praying for the beings still imprisoned.

Sun Father cast his beams down upon the foam around the earth. He impregnated this Foam Mother and she give birth to twins, the Preceder and the Follower, of the right hand and the left. Sun Father imparted to them some of his wisdom. He also gave them gifts: their mother the Foam Cloud, the rainbow, the thunderbolts and the fog-shield that makes clouds.

The blessed Twins were given dominion as if they were creators ruling all creatures. They used the rainbow to raise Sky Father above the earth so that warmth could come to the surface. Then they flew towards the road of Poshaiyangkyo, and the Place of Generation. They cleft the earth with the thunderbolts and, being small, they descended on threads of spider-web. They came to the deep inner womb where they went among the developing creatures to instruct them and lead them from womb to womb until they could be born on the earth.

When all the creatures were ready the Preceder and the Follower found grass, vines and trees and bound them together to make a living ladder. Where their hands pressed they formed the places where new buds and branches would grow. The Twins led the way up the ladder to the second womb and all the creatures tried to follow. Many fell back however and were later thrown up by Earth in the form of monsters. The second womb was called the Place beneath the Navel. It was broad and high but dark as the earth under storm clouds. The people and the animals increased in number and soon had to struggle to climb the living ladder to a third, and wider world. The Twins sent up the animals and men divided into six groups; yellow, brown-grey, red, white, black and all-colours-mixed. As before, many fell on the way and were later rejected as monsters, cripples and idiots. But in spite of all trials the climb was successful and the fittest creatures survived. At length they entered the world of the Vagina of Earth. The light in this world of sex-birth was like a valley in starlight. Here they discovered the nature of sex and united to bring new life to birth. They developed in many ways. Again they increased in number, and soon, led again by the Preceder and the Follower, animals and men climbed the living ladder of growth into the Womb of Birth, where the light was like the dawn coming in the sky. The Twins began to instruct men, telling them that first of all they should seek the Sun, who would teach them the way of life of the upper world. Each of the tribes understood according to its ability. Their numbers increased until the Twins once again led them onward, this time into the outer world, the World of All-Spreading Light and Seeing.

When men first reached this outer world it was dark. They were strange creatures, black and scaly, with short tails, owls' eyes, huge ears and webbed feet. They were adapted only for the underworld and were hardly able to stand upright. They saw the great star Sirius and thought it must be Sun because its beams hurt their eyes. Then they saw the Morning Star still more brilliant, and they mistook that for Sun. But then the sky grew brighter still. The first sunrise was terrible with the howling and terror of the newly-emerged human race. Gradually they grew accustomed to seeing in daylight. When they saw how strange they looked, they made themselves wraps, and sandals to pad their feet against the stony ground.

The new light meant that people discovered many new things. In order to learn all about their wonderful new world, they sought among themselves for people who had been wise even before they came out of their great Earth Mother, the priests. The first of them was Yanauluha. He brought a vessel of water from the great ocean, seeds of plants, and a staff which had power to give life.

The medicine staff of Yanauluha was very beautiful, painted with many colours, and decorated with feathers, shells, and precious minerals. The shells rattled and called the people to see the wonderful staff as it was raised. The priests and people gathered round. Yanauluha lifted the staff, balancing it on one hand while he tapped it sharply with the other.

Suddenly four eggs appeared, two white and two blue. The people were told that these were in fact the seeds of those living things which would make the summer time more fruitful. They rushed forward to take them. Those who were anxious and eager to get fine things for themselves seized the blue eggs. Those who were not in such haste were content with the white ones. Then the eggs hatched out. The blue eggs produced little coloured birds with rough skins which looked as if they might later be very beautiful. The people fed them well and that made them very greedy by nature. Then feathers grew, shiny black feathers. The newly hatched ravens flew away, laughing raucously at the people who had expected to find beauty in them. Then the plain white eggs hatched and from them flew brilliantly coloured macaws, who were sent off to their home far to the south amid the general rejoicing of the people at seeing such beauty.

After this event the nations were divided into two social groups. The Winter People were thoe who had chosen Ravens and they were strong and active and many in number. The Summer People were gentler and slower; their numbers were less but they were the wise and prudent members of the race. From these two the kindred groups were selected at a great council of the people. A few of the totem groups were given the functions of hereditary priests with powers to control the weather and other natural forces.

A bird carved in black basalt inlaid with turquoises, from a Zuñi pueblo. The Pueblo Indians included birds and animals in their creation myth about the journey made to the Place of Emergence.

Overleaf, left: A stone pipe in the shape of a crouching figure, from Moundville, Alabama. *Overleaf, right, above:* A death's head effigy jar from a mound in Mississippi County, Arkansas. The incised decoration, which represents the traditional body-painting, shows Aztec influence. *Below:* An incised shell gorget from the Spiro Mound, Oklahoma. It was worn suspended on a string around the throat, as a good luck charm, and also reveals Central American influences.

Below and opposite: Two war god statuettes of the Zuñi Indians. The Zuñi have two war gods of whom images are made for use in regularly recurring ceremonies. They can only be carved from the wood of pines that have been struck by lightning.

The journeys of man

The emergence of man was completed and the social order established. Men next had to learn how to live in the world under the sun. But the world was new and tormented, with vast swamps inhabited by monsters, desolate plains of broken rock, and earthquakes. It was necessary for men to seek more secure dwelling places. On the journey they were led by the beloved Twins who told them to rest awhile at a camp called the Place of Uprising which faced the sunrise. At this camp they were instructed to travel towards the east, where Father Sun arose, until they came to the Navel of the Earth. Only there would they find peace and stability.

The people resumed their journey. As yet the world was hardly formed: people were still physically imperfect and fearful in spirit, surrounded by monsters, giants and volcanoes. The Twins held a council and called on Father Sun. In a great hymn they begged for wisdom. The Sun decided that the earth must be broken and turned like a field being dug for planting, and so he and the Twins let fall thunderbolts and lightning. The people cowered in what shelter they could find while the earth was stricken and churned around them. Finally came peace; the monsters had all been destroyed by the thunder and lightning and many perils had disappeared for ever. Sometimes in the rocks one can see the bones of the monsters and great areas of broken and scorched rocks which the Zuñi believed resulted from this primeval catastrophe. Then the people rested, protected by the fog-shield of the Twins, before continuing their journey to find the centre, the Navel of the Earth.

Eventually they came to the place where tree-trunks stood in the waters. It was a rich and peaceful land. They thought they had at last reached the Navel of the Earth and built themselves homes. They discovered people who had preceded them, and who were angry and warlike. From them they learned to fight and kill and they became warriors. The day came when the earth shook once more. The leaders sounded the white shell trumpets and the best of the people followed them. Those who were reluctant to leave their homes and property were abandoned and overwhelmed by the destructive force.

The next stage of their journey brought the people to the Place of Mist on the Waters. The mist was the smoke from the fires of a large town. The town-dwellers were peaceful. They told their visitors that they were the elder brothers of men, the People of the Seed. There was much discussion and a council was held at which it was established that it was better to hold to the way of peace than to make war.

After the council they all went to the plains and camped under the cedar and hemlock trees, building a great bower within which sacred symbols were made and prayers chanted. The ceremonies lasted a long time and included dances in which the boys and girls blessed the plants with caresses. Wherever they touched them, the plants burst into coloured flowers with beautiful tendrils. Then the Gods of the Four Seasons appeared from the east, and the food plants prospered. Man was now capable of living freely in the wide world. The events of creation had run their course.

A witchcraft fetish jar from a Zuñi pueblo. It was used in a ceremony held for the punishment and purification of witches and when not in use the fetishes, carved from elk and deer antlers, were kept inside the bowl and 'fed' with sacred corn meal through a circular hole.

The myth continues with an account of the gradual development of civilisation. Man discovered death; some degenerated and fell back into the lake which led to the lower world. Priests were made and ritual societies developed. The gods and kachinas walked with men and in time men lost their tails and became fully human. Those who dwelt at the centre accepted all the movements of the earth and the warnings of the sacred shell trumpets and marched as the gods directed until finally they came to the lands around Zuñi. The myth is long and elaborate and describes many gods and spirits. It is all preserved in the chants and ceremonies which were performed until modern times.

The people and the environment

One of the problems presented by the mythology of the Pueblo Indians is the richness and complexity of the material. The relationships between man and natural forces, the animal and the vegetable kingdoms, form the subject of a vast collection of myths which was combined and recombined in long ceremonies in which the myth was re-enacted by costumed actors.

The result was the integration of the people of the pueblo with their natural environment. There was no important event that was not related to man and the gods. Eagles were kept for a year by every family in the pueblo and then killed and sent to the gods to report on the world of men. Man depended on the blessing of the gods; the gods depended on the prayers and magical ceremonies of the people. The social system was naturally disrupted by the impact of the new and wider world of the white man; but there is evidence that the new ways have been assimilated without loss of all the ancient belief. A new relationship between man and his environment is evolving and it may be that the influence of American Indian philosophies and attitudes to life will become more important in the future.

Left: Three kachina dolls representing lightning, corn and snow and hail. Kachinas are an innumerable group of beings embodying the differentiated powers of life and almost every living thing has a kachina. They are impersonated by dancers in the great festivals and represented also by dolls which are taken home after the ceremony. British Museum.

Above: Karwan and Mana, two kachina figures, who take part in the Powamû ceremony when the beans which have been artificially sprouted in the kivas are brought out into the plaza and there distributed.

Right: Water jar of the Pueblo Indians. The design was intended as a good luck charm, to guide the hunters' arrows to the buffalo's heart. Late nineteenth century. British Museum.

The Past and the Future

The Indian cultures of the North American continent cover a unique range of human activities. They show how the evolution of ideas is intimately linked to the ascending scale of cultural efficiency. At the simplest level of the wild hunters the relationship of man to the spirit world is one of the search for help in obtaining the necessities of daily life. The ancestral spirits as well as the supernatural powers of earth and sky are implored to bring the animals to the hunter. The most powerful spirits seem little different from human beings. But with the advanced groups of agriculturists, it is evident that the more powerful spirits are looked on as gods with well-defined functions, and inferior to an almost unknowable First Cause or Great Spirit. The myths describe everyday matters as well as cosmic events and link the whole of creation with man through the emergence myths.

Man has to offer prayer and suffering to the gods who are brought into a relationship with the community through rituals which include enactment and recitation of the myths.

Probably the individual's views about the myths in any given tribe also followed an evolutionary sequence. The more backward and the younger individuals would experience the myth in a distinctly more primitive way than the wiser, older chiefs who had a greater knowledge of man and nature in relationship to each other. The shamans were always a special group. Their visions were conditioned by the degree of development of the tribal myths. But in the dissociated condition of the shamanistic trance the type of revelation was fairly consistent. The shaman was a prophet rather than a priest. True priesthood hardly existed in the North American Indian cultures. The owners of medicine-bundles had the right to conduct ceremonies, and among the Pueblo Indians the elders who led the activities of the various religious societies had special responsabilities for organisation. But nowhere was there a specialised caste of priests. From the Pueblo Indian stage of development with its leaders of religious societies it is only a small step to a permanent priesthood mediating between man and the spirit world, but it was not fully achieved.

Considered separately the spirits and gods of American Indian myths can be classified as archetypal forms arising from the unconscious. The shaman, who dissociates more easily than most people, naturally receives more visions. In the typical shamanistic vision the shaman visits the gods and is able to talk with them. But there is no mention of the shaman being absorbed into the divine personality because his religious understanding is conditioned to the idea of gods who are separate entities from himself. The Indians were able to project their essential beliefs into the form of exterior deities but did not realise that the archetypal projections were really part of the individual psyche. Possibly some specially advanced individuals realised that a further stage of religious development might occur when man would be absorbed into the deity, thus making man and his beliefs one whole again, but the myths offer no evidence that this realisation occurred. If the myths truly reflect the condition of the human psyche under primitive conditions of life they constitute a little more evidence for the hope that humanity is evolving towards higher spiritual possibilities as the cultural background develops.

The time scale of human development is almost infinitely variable but within any given community the development of the mind, the social structure and the economic system are the factors which together give a picture of the whole culture. This book describes the myths that give an important insight into the psychology of a people. It also describes the level of material culture in each group under discussion. Only in this way can we begin to understand the nature of the differences which underlie the ideas common to all men.

When these myths were recorded most of the American Indian tribes were already dispersed. Only among the Eskimo, the Pueblo and the Navajo peoples did the mythology represent a living religious cult. A few centuries of change had largely altered the religious observances of the other tribes into either social observances or folk-

Opposite page: A spirit, a modern Eskimo interpretation of a traditional mythological theme.

A group of Pueblo Indian priests taking part in a Rain Dance. At the beginning of the century ethnologists began taking a serious interest in the North American Indians and made photographic and sound records of their religion.

lore. In particular the traditions of the Indians of the south-eastern States had become the heritage of only a few old people.

At the present day the process has continued much further and many Indians have found that the traditions have only been preserved through the work of the white ethnologists at the turn of the century, who made records of what survived. This does not mean that the myths have totally lost their power; but they are assuming more and more the nature of folk-tales. Here and there one may find a true shaman with gifts of prophecy and healing, who has preserved some traditions, but such people are few. Some of the tales told to Indian children preserve a little of the past, and many of the folk-customs intended to bring good luck and avert bad, have remained.

Only the more important tribes among the Indians have retained same of the ancient tribal organisation and still reverence the ancestral traditions. The Iroquois people, particularly, remember the ancient ceremonial and place it successfully in a modern setting. The Pueblos still sing some of the ancient chants and the religious dances are publicly performed, though probably largely for the benefit of the tourists. On the whole the modern Indian thinks of the ancient traditions as echoes of a past which is no longer important. But the impact of the new culture has not totally destroyed the past.

Now that the heritage of Indian blood has come to be highly regarded in many American families the philosophy behind the myths has been sought after and preserved. A notable piece of preservation has been the collection of Navajo sand-paintings which are changed at the appropriate seasons in the Museum of Navajo Ceremonial Art at Santa Fé. This allows visitors to appreciate that the ancient sand-paintings illustrated the relationship between man and nature, and the passage of the stars in the heavens. In such ways the myths are becoming part of the cultural heritage of America, and ultimately of all men throughout the world.

Left: A Smoki ceremonial. In each pueblo village were one or more kivas – underground rooms, often entered through a hole in the roof. They provided a meeting place for the many religious societies and some ceremonies were held there.

A small wooden figure of an evil spirit, from Greenland. The harsh conditions of Eskimo life gave rise to myths about malignant spirits who had to be placated with offerings.

The Indian myths have affected modern art to some extent, but more through their technique than their philosophy. Similarly with the very active tradition of the Pueblo potters and weavers. The beauty of the craftsmanship is universally accepted but the meaning of the designs very rarely matters even to the craftsmen themselves.

The Eskimo have a new way of life, and new possibilities of graphic expression. One notices that the modern soapstone carvings and the new lithographs have great elegance and good rhythmic form and spatial relationships, but few of them reflect the folk-tales which survive from the old myths of man and the spirit world. When they do they are made for an alien viewer and, like so much magic, become aesthetic expressions without any genuine contact with myth.

Perhaps the best way to appreciate the ancient myths of the world is to regard them as an expression of the deepest beliefs of the people who made them. They have faded with time simply because the ways of human life have changed. Yet every nation has its heritage of tradition and that tradition has influenced the quality of intellectual life in its present day representatives. One hopes that the many fascinating pictures of the American Indian past which have been preserved in their myths will prove to be both acceptable and enlightening to the modern world.

Right: During the twentieth century the North American Indians have revealed an increased pride in their traditions and history, illustrated in their art. The buffalo hunt springs from a more romanticised view of the past. This was painted by a Navajo artist, Quincy Tahoma.

'The enchanted owl', a sophisticated stone-cut, the work of a modern Eskimo artist, Kenojnak, Cape Dorset.

Mexican and Central American Mythology

Irene Nicholson

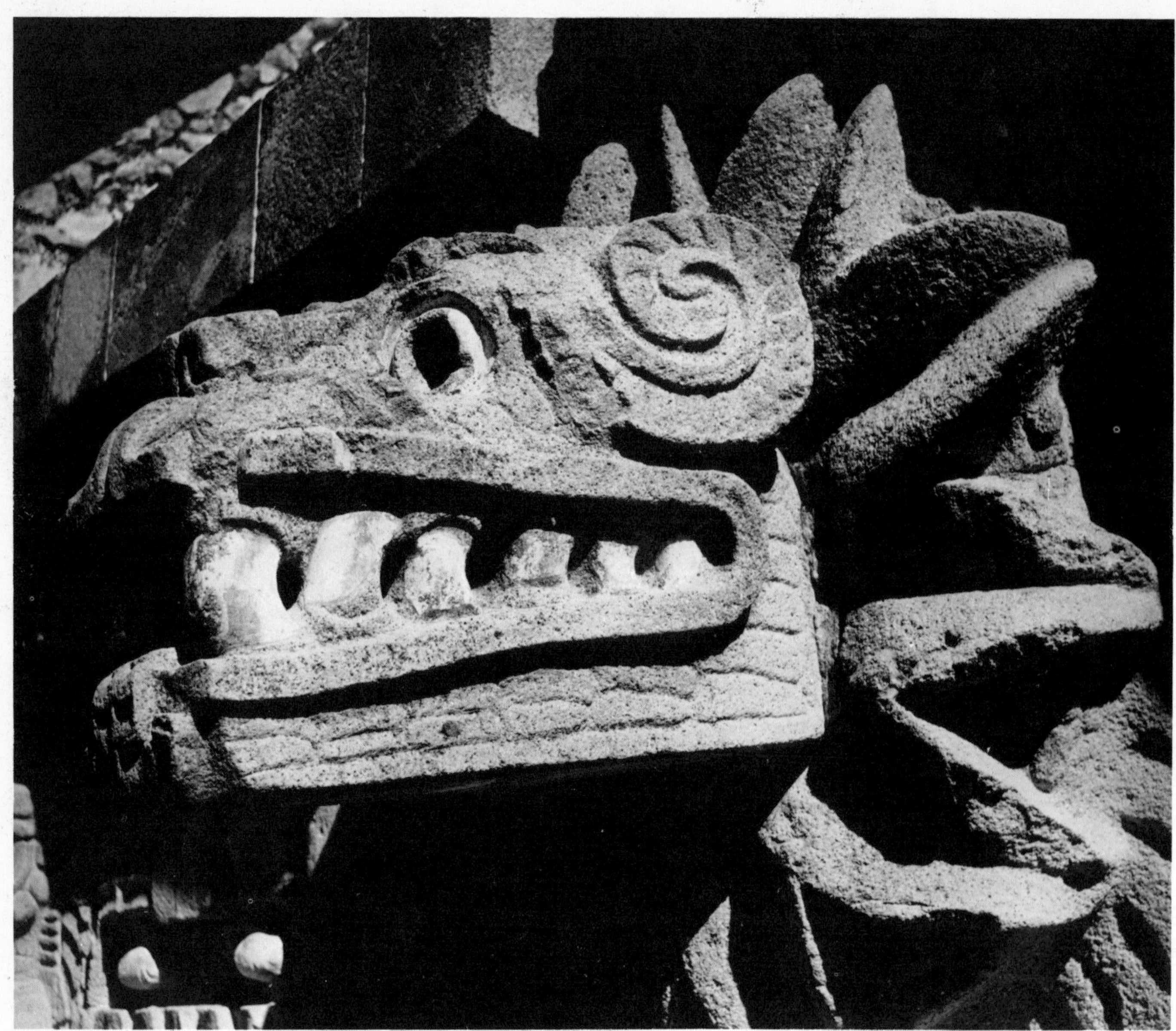

Quetzalcoatl, the plumed serpent, was represented in every artistic medium. This image appears repeatedly on his pyramid at Teotihuacán, where the great size produces an aggressive effect that belies the gentle and compassionate nature of this god. Eighth century A.D.

Introduction

The myths of Mexico and Central America create a world compact of jewels and flowers and birds, bright as a kaleidoscope and as everchanging. No single event can be trapped by logic because the myths belong to another world, both more instinctive and more emotional. Each god can be his twin or his corollary. Each story can be interpreted in several different ways according to the context and the reader's understanding. The symbols are few and concentrated, manipulated with such economy that each is made to serve a wide range of philosophical and religious ideas; and this device helps to stress the underlying unity of all knowledge, the relativity of subjective truth against the permanence of the objective, itself far from immobile but alive and vibrating about its still centre.

The images used as symbols are limited and may even seem monotonous until we begin to search for their deeper meanings. Shells, jewels, flowers, birds, maize, hearts, arrows, thorns of cacti: these keep recurring; but they are skilfully handled to produce all the concepts needed for a lofty philosophy and a complete cosmology, both of which are entirely at variance with the mistaken idea that the basic religion of middle America was founded on human sacrifice and the tearing out of hearts.

The human acts of blood rituals and licensed homicide came later, and were a distortion of what must once have been an extraordinarily complete vision of the place of man and of organic life in the universe.

If the gods had possessed names as easy to pronounce as Venus and Hermes, and if the stories had been handed down to us in more coherent form instead of piecemeal, usually gathered by friars who – in spite of their laudable efforts to preserve the ancient ideas – could scarcely have been expected to understand them or be sympathetic toward them, they might by now be as familiar to every school child as those of the Greeks and Romans. But we stumble over Cinteotl (Cin-te-otl); Huitzilopochtli (Huitz-i-lopoch-tli) is a tongue-twister; and it is bothersome to have to unravel the exact relationship between Quetzalcoatl (Quetzal-co-atl) and Ehecatl (E-he-catl) – both of them gods of wind among other things, and up to a certain point interchangeable. The picture becomes even more difficult when gods and men acquire a single identity, as when Quetzalcoatl the plumed serpent becomes identified with Topiltzin, a real-life figure born in the latter part of the tenth century who was the last king of the Toltecs.

None of the problems presented by the myths of Mexico and Central America is really insuperable provided we refuse to be caught up in needless detail and can see the broad principles upon which the stories were built. Created would be a misleading word to use, because these myths seem to rise out of that deep well of knowledge lying unfathomed in the human mind – hidden by that logical brain so overworked in many of the activities of modern life. Fundamentally the stories have a simplicity of intention that gives them the directness of a deliberately wrought and profound work of art. We shall, therefore, try to keep the picture as clear as possible and shall make no attempt to sort out, list and enumerate all the hundreds of names of gods that can be reduced in the last analysis to one – and on a less unified level to a few of the basic aspects of this all-powerful creator of the universe – Ometeotl.

It is important to let the religious, philosophical, and cosmological concepts speak for themselves. When they have done so, we shall see just how it happened – inevitably and tragically – that a religion of love and of consciousness became debased into a cult of the master race.

We need here to beware of a rather odd argument that has sometimes been advanced to explain the human sacrifices in the midst of a religion whose inner aim was the same as that of all great systems of thought: consciousness, love, and union with the creator of the universe. The argument goes something like this: Aztec sacrifices were not a religious perversion, but represented the heights of worship in the western hemisphere. Europeans ought to be able to understand this, because the western world does not consider the crucifixion of Christ as perversion. We have no right from our vantage point in the twentieth century to assume that human sacrifice is necessarily degenerate and immoral.

But this argument refuses to admit the existence – beneath our subjectively formed social rules of behaviour – of an objective voice within us which, if we listened to it attentively, would tell us the difference between real and changing right and wrong. To admit that other, subjective and very unreliable voices can easily be mistaken for it is not to say that a basic distinction between right and wrong does not exist. It is a little difficult to see how the practice of slaughtering enemies wholesale and with particularly cruel and painful techniques, in order to satisfy deities in heaven, could ever be condoned by a responsible elite or priesthood anywhere in the world.

A Zapotec funerary urn. The head represents a jaguar, the form given to the god Tepeyollotl who was 'Heart of the Mountain' and propitiated as being the cause of earthquakes. The Zapotecs were unlike most of the Mexican peoples, being more peaceful and speaking a different tongue, but like the others their religion was dominated by the figure of the plumed serpent. Fourteenth-century clay.

The Zapotec culture was eclipsed by the Mixtec, one product of which was the intricately decorated walls of the great palace at Mitla. The motifs have a meaning which also appears in the *Codex Zouche-Nuttall*, but their application in architectural terms has not so far been determined. Eighth to eleventh centuries A.D.

A toy, or possibly a votive offering, from Nopiloa. The wheel was not used by the Aztecs at the time of the Conquest; kings and nobles were carried in litters and war was fought on foot, probably because of the difficult nature of the ground in much of the realm. But this figure shows that the wheel was known. Totonac, sixth to ninth centuries A.D.

A ceremonial axehead in marble, with a deer seated within the headdress. Fom the Veracruz region.

Intentionally or otherwise, this argument has also the effect of reversing the whole idea of the crucifixion and of the Aztec sacrifices. It reverses, as it were, the arrow of events. Aztec sacrifices were a central ritual of the religion itself, though not in its original form. It became debased, and those who were sacrificed were not the misunderstood, maligned, and martyred; but the hapless enemy tribes who, according to the view of the master race, could quite well be sacrificed to feed the sun god. It would be difficult to find in history another religion that made the massacre of enemies not merely a common practice but a central ritual. Christian ritual is *not* based on the killing of an enemy but on the perpetuation of Christ's martyrdom, killed as he was by the *enemies* of his religion. The Aztec sacrifices simply cannot, in other words, be explained away by a kind of sleight-of-hand that turns the enemies of a religion into its most faithful adherents.

Another very general illusion is that the Aztec and Maya myths are those of a primitive people who wanted better crops, rain in due season, and sunshine to whiten the silken beards of maize. This kind of naive philosophy was very likely the outermost clothing of the mythology, just as it was the outer clothing of the Eleusinian and Egyptian mysteries and of hundreds of mythologies all over the world. It may well account for some of the simpler rituals elaborated to fit the mood of the more superstitious sections of the community; but behind it lay a much deeper and more profound view. It took into account not only man's material needs, but his desire to probe the eternal puzzle of his life and its meaning.

Agricultural propitiation ceremonies could never of themselves have developed into the rich symbolism of the plumed serpent or the extraordinary idea of the humble, suffering god who was brave enough to save the world from destruction when the sun stood still. The philosophy of sacrifice and of death and rebirth, is on another level entirely. Only from this point of view can any good sense be made of the myths of creation and regeneration that belong to two of the highest ancient cultures in the New World.

Proof of an intentional and psychologically shrewd stratification of ideas can be found in the three different languages used by the Nahua-speaking peoples who inhabited the high central tableland of what today is Mexico. These were the language of the common people, designed to deal with things at an ordinary every-day level; the language of the nobility, more poetic and cultured but with little depth of wisdom; and the language of the magicians or initiates – in more ordinary terms, the priests. This contained in code form every idea an aspiring man might need to achieve true enlightenment.

By analogy with these languages, then, there was a religion of simple agriculture for the profane, one of hierarchies and moral responsibility for the aristocracy, and an esoteric religion of mystery for the initiates. Similarly, every representation of a god or an abstract idea had its corresponding material image, or idol, for the superstitious; a hieroglyph and an associated colour for the noble interested in heraldry, and a mathematical-astronomical-scientific inner symbolism for the priests.

There is nothing unusual in this practice of stratification; it is a feature of many of the great religions of the world and we find it in many forms within Christianity, especially within the Roman Catholic Church where the multiplicity of saints and martyrs, the examples of humanity striving for union with the divine, is attractive to the majority; while the higher meanings of Christ's teaching can be reached by those who make a stronger effort to understand.

The main mythology of the high Mexican tableland was not created by the Aztecs (the heron-people) but by their Nahua-speaking predecessors, including the Toltecs and others farther back. The pre-Hispanic Mexican population was composed of a variety of stock. There were Nahuas on the high central plateau, Olmecs and Totonacs along the Gulf coast, Mixtecs, Zapotecs and Huastecs farther south, Otomies, Tarascans,

The ball court at Copán, showing the stone rings. Ball courts in different forms existed everywhere in old Mexico among all races and cultures. It has never been determined of exactly what the game consisted but the evidence shows that it was much more a rite than a sport. Toltec, tenth to thirteenth centuries A.D.

and Zacatecans in what is today central Mexico, Cora and Huichol Indians to the west, and various nomadic tribes to the north.

Where these various peoples originally came from is uncertain. 'Why were we not simply *here*?' asks the doyen of Mexico's archaeologists, Alfonso Caso. But there have been all manner of theories, including the idea that they came from Asia across the Bering Straits and migrated southward – the opposite theory being that which the Kon-Tiki expedition tried to prove: that migration would have been feasible westward from South America to Polynesia. There is no reason in fact why migrations should not have taken place in both directions at various times in history.

A seventeenth-century Mexican, Sigüenza y Góngora, believed that Quetzalcoatl – the Mexican plumed serpent – was the apostle Thomas and that all the Indians of the New World were descendants of Poseidon, who in his turn was a great-grandson of Noah.

The Indians may have had more than one origin, for they were of many varying physical types and psychological temperaments, and we can see the enormous diversity of the American peoples in their twentieth-century descendants. There are sharp-profiled, hook-nosed Indians typical of the Redskins of nursery tales; others Chinese in feature, with broad, flat cheekbones and the oriental fold of the eyelid. There are regions where the people are stunted, others where they are tall and muscular. Some are fierce and resistant to advances from outsiders or to any suggestion that their old way of life might change; others are more open, gayer, readier to incorporate themselves into modern life. A Mexican novelist, Gregorio López y Fuentes, puts into the mouth of one of his characters in *El Indio* an analysis of some of these differences: 'What is there in common between the Otomí of the central plain, who wards off cold by drinking pulque and sleeping in the ashes, who lives in hovels roofed with maguey chaff and who eats vermin, and the clean Totonac with his brilliant past? What affinity do you find between the taciturn Tepehua and the rough, warlike Huichol?'

A stone model of a pyramid, discovered in the foundations of Moctezuma's palace of Tenochtitlán. At the top the sun is flanked by Huitzilopochtli and Tezcatlipoca, gods of day and night; while on the right side of the stone an eagle alights bearing human hearts. Below this are the gods whose self-sacrifice set the sun in motion. This being a late, Aztec work, all the gods, and the eagle, bear speech-scrolls signifying war. The stone codifies the Aztec belief in war as a way of securing captives, who were then sacrificed and their hearts offered to the sun in repayment for the divine sacrifice. Aztec, *c.* 1500 A.D.

This is not quite an accurate description, for the Huichol Indians are decorative and artistic rather than warlike; but it reflects the variety of type that exists today and has always existed in this area popularly thought of as the land of the Aztecs.

The Aztecs, consolidating their power in the area only in the fourteenth century of our era, conquered the peoples occupying what is now a broad area of central Mexico, and became the self-styled successors of the Toltecs (master craftsmen), who had been on the high plateau for several centuries previously. The Toltecs were in their turn relative newcomers, and before their day the other Nahua-speaking people – builders of Teotihuacán and earlier sites – had established the general shape of the mythology.

Farther to the south, and intermingling, was the widespread and older Maya culture centred on what are now Yucatán and Chiapas in Mexico, and the isthmus of Central America. Its early formative period goes back to about 500 B.C.; and its classic period, with its arresting art, ranges from the fourth to the tenth century.

To deal with these cultures separately would entail unnecessary repetition; so they will be discussed together and we shall move from one to another as seems fit, bringing in such modern residues of custom and tradition as may be pertinent, and discussing the beliefs of outlying ancient peoples in so far as they throw light on the two distinct basic cultures: Nahua and Maya.

From very far back there must have been interchange between these two. The great Nahua god Quetzalcoatl includes in his name the shy

quetzal bird native to the Maya lands. Both cultures have an idea of a holy place which in time became a specific geographical site – the Tollán or Tula of the Nahuas – but which was probably at first the description used for a spiritual condition. The very name Nahua, the name of the linguistic group of people inhabiting the central Mexican plateau, means 'one who speaks with authority', and we shall see how the idea of a chosen people able to speak for the gods was characteristic of Maya and Nahua religion, incomprehensible in many aspects unless we regard it as representing revelation from a high source. Until the end of the nineteenth century at least, and probably down to our own day, the Mayas have believed in diviners called *H'men*, meaning, according to D. G. Brinton, the nineteenth-century investigator, 'those who understand and can do'. Their authority is believed to come from the gods, who give them insight into creation, and power to make cosmic forces work for and not against the well-being of mankind.

At the time of the discovery of America, legends soon circulated of lands where men were giants with supernatural powers, or alternatively pygmies with capacities unknown to ordinary mortals. The legendary races were never discovered, for the simple reason that the powers ascribed to them are the inner ones hinted at in the myths and would not have been visible to those incapable of seeing more than the physical body.

The difficulties standing in the way of a correct understanding of the ancient myths of America are very great, partly because so much was destroyed by the Spaniards, partly because there are signs that the religion had fallen into extreme decay before the Spaniards had even arrived, but mainly because many of the source manuscripts are chronicles written down by Spanish friars who, however laudable their wish to keep a record of dying customs, could not have been expected to be over-sympathetic with what they regarded, not without reason by the time the Spaniards came, as diabolical superstition. Other useful sources are the 'magic books' or indigenous pictograph records, and these are valuable but probably suffer from the degeneration that had overcome the priesthood. The same objection can be made to the few chronicles written by princes of the ancient royal houses after the conquest, on the encouragement of the Spaniards who patronised them.

The compilations made by the friars were written down in indigenous languages, the sounds recorded phonetically as if they had been Spanish. Bernardino de Sahagún, the chief source, was remarkably modern in his

The painted books of Mexico are an important source of information about the lives and beliefs of pre-Hispanic peoples – but few survived the Spaniards, who believed them to be evil. The *Codex Zouche-Nuttall* is a genealogy interspersed with religious myth. The two leaves shown here read from bottom right, where the Lord Nine Ollin is sacrificed at the dedication of a *temazcalli*, a sweating-house for healing disease. (The Lord was dedicated to the sun god as a boy and the sacrifice, on his fifty-second birthday, is voluntary). Above, the body is dressed as an Ocelot Chief and cremated: the torches are carried by two other chiefs, and more bring offerings. In the next leaf, left, Nine Ollin's brother Eight Deer, Lord of Tilantongo, presides at the place of the plumed serpent seated on an ocelot-skin cushion. Below him, his brother's ashes are adorned with feather headdress and turquoise mask and more offerings are brought by two priests. The final cremation is seen on the far left. A quail is sacrificed as a symbol of the sunrise. The symbols above show where it occurred – at Ocelot-Town on Pregnant Mountain of the War Arrow; the day – 6 Ocelot; and year – 10 House, which was probably 1070 A.D. Mixtec, early sixteenth century. British Museum.

Right: a spear thrower. This elaborately carved device gave added leverage to the arm, and it was with weapons like this that the armies of Moctezuma fought Cortés. The carvings represent the noble orders of Eagle and Jaguar. Aztec, sixteenth century.

Ceremonial axeheads were a feature of Mexican ritual and represent some of the finest pre-Hispanic art. This is a very early example, Olmec style.

methods of questioning the Indians, but if there were any priests left who knew the inner meaning of the ancient lore, they would have been unlikely to submit to cross-questioning by foreigners, nor would they have made the true knowledge known to outsiders.

The Indian princes who chose to write their memoirs were in general those who submitted most readily to Spanish education and became Europeanised. The picture books, or magic books, together with wall paintings that belong to the same category, are elaborate codifications to which the keys have sometimes been lost. They consist of symbolic paintings done by the Indians, sometimes at the request of the Spaniards. Their base is either maguey parchment, leather, or cotton; and they are folded in such a way that they can be opened like a screen. They run to about sixteen feet in length, and are around seven inches broad. Some are evidently historical records, others fiction; but the most interesting are mythological and astronomical. The most famous, the *Codex Borgia,* is a description of the Aztec calendar, the gods and their attributes. Another important codex, the Fejervary-Mayer, relates the gods to the calendar.

The most important of the Maya codices are the Dresden, the Paris, and the Tro-Cortesianus. They are written in glyphs that have only recently been deciphered, and they give us some indication of the Maya gods. There are also glyph steles, and the famous wall friezes at Bonampak in the forests of Chiapas. The latter are paralleled in the Nahua culture by the interesting Nahua-Toltec friezes that have been discovered only in recent years in palaces or priestly homes near the pyramids of Teotihuacán.

From these assorted sources we have to do what we can to reconstruct the mythology. By force of circumstances much that can be said remains highly speculative and controversial; but as new investigations are made it becomes clear that surviving sources show us two broad levels of ancient American thought: the superstitious, pantheistic religion of the populace, and the inner religion corresponding in many ways to the Greek and Egyptian mysteries. Both were confounded and their threads intermingled, and both suffered the degeneration that brought with it human sacrifice and other cruelties. But behind the first there seems to have existed a sound native folklore such as peasants in all parts of the world use for their medicinal and agricultural practices; and behind the second a conception of man's true place and purpose in the universe. If the philosophical ideas are fragmentary, we must remember that so too is our evidence. By piecing together the scrambled and coded myths, the fine wall paintings, the codices, and what we know of the etymology of words that enclose philosophical ideas of no little subtlety, we may try to make some plausible guesses about the pre-Hispanic mind.

Lest the reader be put off by the forbidding names, it should be noted that it is quite easy to split these up into component roots or syllables and then to pronounce them phonetically as if the words were Spanish, remembering that the tendency is for the accent to fall on the penultimate, not on the last syllable.

Accents have been omitted from pre-Hispanic names except where these have become assimilated into the post-conquest Spanish-American scene or where they give an indication of the correct pronunciation.

Historical note

To supplement these introductory remarks, the general reader may find it useful to have the myths placed, however sketchily, against their historical background.

Fossils of the so-called Tepexpan man, discovered in 1949 on the edge of an old lake bed on the high Mexican plateau, and some corn cobs that develop from a small, wild variety to the cultivated 'food fit for the gods', suggest that there were human beings in the Americas 6,000 or more years before Christ. The evidence suggests that these early inhabitants were mammoth-hunters, probably nomad, and that they lacked any true culture. However, by 1500 B.C. they had acquired some artistic techniques, and these were practised at Chiapa de Corzo in the Grijalva basin of south-east Mexico – the earliest site that can properly be considered a human settlement.

A later settlement which was found at Tlatilco in the Valley of Mexico, has been dated at about 800 B.C. and has some characteristics that would appear to link it with sites thousands of miles to the south, in Peru. Tlatilco seems to have been connected with the mysterious Olmec culture of the Mexican Gulf, which some research workers think was the original source of Nahua inspiration. Others believe that the culture spread north from the Maya lands.

The Olmec centre at La Venta in the present state of Veracruz was destroyed deliberately and for no known reason between 400 and 300 B.C., leaving Tres Zapotes, to the northwest, to continue whatever cultural tradition the former had contained. These sites belong to a formative period stretching for several centuries on either side of the birth of Christ, by which time there was already the beginning of a culture at Monte Albán outside Oaxaca. Teotihuacán, on the Mexican plateau, is later and appears to have flourished on either side of 300 A.D. From Monte Albán the Zapotec culture spread to nearby Mitla, and from Teotihuacán to Tula, which is almost due north of Mexico City and which is sometimes supposed to have been the capital of the Toltec empire. Other research workers dispute this, and put the centre of the great Toltec culture in Teotihuacán, the site of the great pyramids and many wall paintings which have come to light in what appear to have been palaces or priests' dwellings. There is no doubt that Toltec culture represents the peak of a long development in art and architecture; but the origins of the myths and the religious and philosophical thought probably go back to earlier Nahua-speaking peoples who were their ancestors.

Broadly one may say that two hundred years before Christ a Nahua-speaking culture had been established in the highland valleys of Mexico, and a Maya culture in Yucatán; and that shortly before the birth of Christ the Nahuas and the Mayas both had glyph writing. A century before Christ's birth there were Maya, Zapotec, and Nahua ceremonial centres, which developed into the strong styles seen in Palenque in the Chiapas forest (seventh century), the great temple of Quetzalcoatl in Teotihuacán (eighth century), and the buildings at Copán in Honduras which can be dated about the same time.

The cult of the plumed serpent, with its Buddha-like compassion, was by this time so fully developed that a little later, in the tenth century, the name of the god Quetzalcoatl was adopted by Topiltzin, king of Tula, the last king of the Toltecs whose empire extended down into Yucatán. By this time the Maya cities had passed their greatest period; and about the eleventh century began a decline, precipitated by invasions from the north. But they were still spreading northward in the thirteenth century, trading along the Gulf from Panama to Tampico, about the time when the Aztecs were completing their long migration southward and beginning to settle in the Valley of Anáhuac in the centre of Mexico.

It was not until 1325 that the Aztecs finally occupied islands on the lake of the Mexican plateau and founded their capital, Tenochtitlán, which

was finally destroyed by Hernán Cortés in 1519. The conqueror's task was made easier by two facts. First, the surrounding peoples were on his side: they hated their Aztec overlords, with their cruel and bloodthirsty excesses, and sided with the Europeans against them. There was also a pall of dread hanging over the Aztecs; the last Emperor Moctezuma was superstitious and believed that Cortés was the god Quetzalcoatl returned – as it was predicted, in that very year – to reclaim his former lands and people. The Aztecs, proud conquerors for a period of two or three centuries, who had taken over the native language, religion, and art and tried to act as if it were their own, were no longer in a state to defend themselves. It is true that Cortés was soon seen to be anything but a returning god, even by Moctezuma, and his son-in-law Cuauhtémoc fought bravely on when the main Aztec armies had capitulated. But for the Aztecs the end of their world had come.

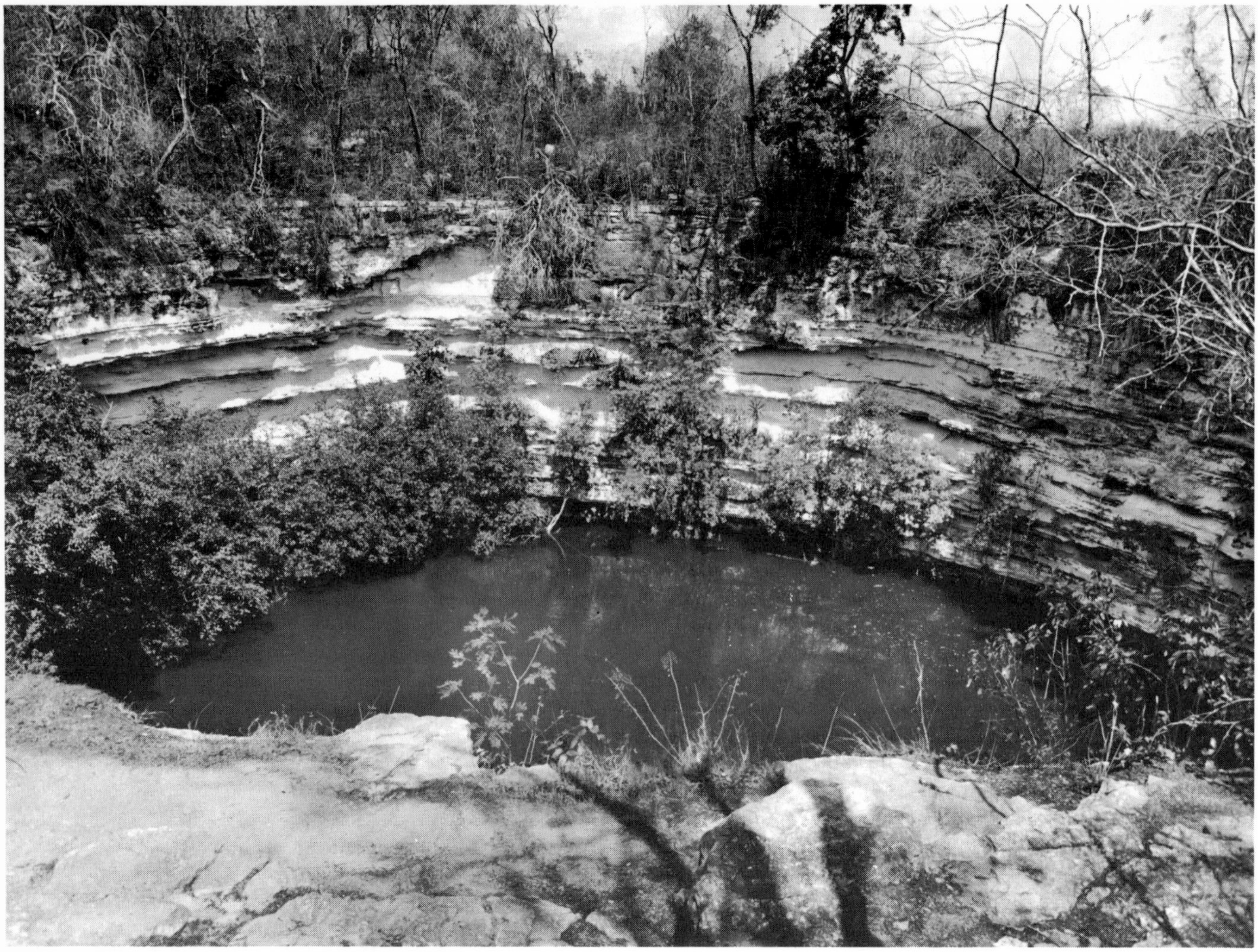

The Yucatecan Mayas held out against the Spaniards until much later. Montejo the younger, the conqueror of Yucatán, was not able to build his capital, Mérida, until 1542, and resistance from the Mayas continued at least until 1546. Even as late as 1622 the Mayas were holding out in the Itzá centre of Petén in Guatemala, and the last Itzá chief was not put to death until 1697. The Itzás themselves may have come from the Mexican Gulf area but were Maya-speaking. They had, however, a close connection with the Toltecs, with whose help they had been able, during the tenth century, to impose their dominion over a large part of Yucatán. The famous sacrificial well at Chichén, their centre, was probably not a place

of human slaughter but of symbolic sacrifice to the gods. Recent exploration of the well has revealed hundreds of tiny rubber dolls which were probably propitiating images thrown down during certain ceremonies.

There were, then, a number of successive Nahua-speaking cultures extending from the early Nahuas, through the Olmecs and the Toltecs, to the Aztecs; and a number of interrelated Maya cultures that at one time or another mingled with the Nahuas. Sandwiched between, and probably a result of mingling, were the Zapotecs of the Mexican isthmus, and the Huastecs who extended along the Mexican Gulf northward from the Yucatán region which is supposed to have been the original home of the Maya Itzá.

One unexplained mystery befuddles modern scholars: how is it that the New World before the arrival of the Spaniards contained ethnic types of such a wide diversity that there have been clay and stone portraits discovered representing practically every known human race? Alexander von Wuthenau, a German art historian who has lived for many years in Mexico and has studied the ancient cultures, has collected an astonishing variety of portraits.

Where did so many different peoples come from? What exchanges were there, before Columbus, between Mexico and Central America on one side of the Atlantic, and Africa and Europe on the other? Between the New World and the Far East? The legends we shall study have traces of oriental influence, and possibly even of Judaism and Mediterranean cultures. One thing is certain: they are older than the sacrifices, and wiser.

Above and bottom left: Mexico and Central America were peopled by races of very diverse aspect, as the illustrations on the succeeding pages will show. Faces modelled during the Totonac culture of the Veracruz region are very European, while there is a distinctly negroid cast to the colossal Olmec heads at La Venta. In striking contrast are two others shown here: on the left is a pre-classic Maya face from Palenque, and above a Zapotec head from Monte Albán.

Top left: the deep limestone pools, called *cenotes*, were the only steady source of water in Yucatán, a region without rivers. The sacred well at Chichén Itzá is surrounded by vertical cliffs sixty-five feet high and offerings were thrown into the water. Originally these were simple votive offerings of clay and rubber; later ceremonies were elaborate, with offerings of gold and jewels. Recent underwater exploration has revealed no sign that human sacrifices, as described by the Spanish friars, took place in this well.

Tonatiuh, the sun god. His heaven was originally the highest, a place for those who had achieved fulfilment on earth, but the Aztecs made it the abode of warriors. Aztec relief, *c.* 1500.

Time and Eternity

'Where there was neither heaven nor earth sounded the first word of God. And He unloosed Himself from His stone, and declared His divinity And all the vastness of eternity shuddered. And His word was a measure of grace, and He broke and pierced the backbone of the mountains. Who was born there? Who? Father, Thou knowest: He who was tender in Heaven came into Being.'

These words from the Maya collection of sacred books, the *Chilam Balam of Chumayel*, set the tone for the myths of creation both of the Maya and Nahua peoples. Unequivocally they affirm a monotheistic doctrine and the timeless quality of the great deity who created the universe. The unknown Maya writer of this *Book of Spirits*, or *Book of the Tiger Priests*, speaks not of *when* there was neither heaven nor earth, but of *where*. He is speaking of a *place* beyond time – not merely of a period when time was not. In Maya terminology this is the 'first time' outside material creation; so that the god-above-all had to descend into the 'second time' before he could declare his divinity. To whom otherwise would he declare it except to himself, the total uncreated essence of all things? The Mayas envisaged an end when creation would return to its beginnings.

'All moons, all years, all days, all winds, reach their completion and pass away. So does all blood reach its place of quiet, as it reaches its power and its throne. Measured was the time in which they could praise the splendour of the Trinity. Measured was the time in which they could know the Sun's benevolence. Measured was the time in which the grid of the stars would look down upon them; and through it, keeping watch over their safety, the gods trapped within the stars would contemplate them.'

This quotation, taken in its context, may be thought to refer to the coming of the Spaniards and the passing of Maya civilisation specifically; but the words reach far beyond any particular time and place and, taken in conjunction with the earlier quotation, reveal the great cyclical concept embodied in the Maya calendar. The Mayas counted not only in days, months, and years, but also in larger periods of time known as *katun* (twenty years), *baktun* (400 years), *pictun* (8,000 years), *calabtun* (158,000 years), and *kincultun* (about 3 million years). The root word *tun* means a stone.

Thus, within the moving procession of the eternal heavens extending to three million years the Mayas felt a stillness, an immobility, something like the immobility of a spoked wheel, which when it is whirled at great speed appears solid and at rest. Everything must turn in its cycle, 'reach completion', and find its quiet place, its 'power' and its 'throne' – in other words its fulfilment and its beginning.

The reference to the Trinity in this quotation may be an interpolation, for the *Chilam Balam* was written down after the Spanish conquest and contains some obvious insertions from Christianity. Nevertheless the fact that the Mayas could so quickly accept a Christian doctrine suggests that it was not incompatible with their own religion. As we shall see later, there were a number of parallels between Maya and Christian thought, including the symbolism of the cross and the idea of death and resurrection.

It is interesting to note in this quotation the reference to the gods 'trapped within the stars'. The supreme god was free, but the forces governing the universe and represented by lesser gods were subject to the laws of time and the revolutions of the heavenly bodies. Freedom was thus relative and depended on the exact position of any particular god in the heavenly hierarchy. Some gods might be aloof from the long, cyclic procession of all created bodies; others would be inside it, fulfilling their duties in smaller cycles perhaps of single galaxies or suns.

An important Maya and Nahua symbol, suggesting a perpetual moving outward to the four points of the created world and inward to a still hub, is the quincunx. This figure is really a cross with its central intersection and the points of its four arms emphasised. Various versions of it occur on pottery, on wall paintings, on the insignia of gods, and carved into temple walls. It had many different interpretations. The Mayas, for instance, had always four *balam* (jaguars or high priests) who stood at the four points of the compass and are still believed to stand invisibly on guard. Together with time, space is thus given a special and miraculous significance. Like the 'first time' outside material creation, there must have been a 'first space'. Indeed the two concepts cannot be separated. Space-time does not of necessity exist. On the highest possible level it merges into the absolute being of the all-powerful god. At any moment since the beginning of creation it might – to the consternation of all living things – have fallen apart. The *balam*, the guardians, hold it together.

Each of the cardinal points of the compass had for the ancients its own

A stone arrow, probably a votive offering to the god of war Huitzilopochtli. Arrows were important symbols to the Aztecs, and in one ceremony they were cast to the four quarters. Fourteenth to sixteenth centuries A.D.

colour: red for the east where the sun rises, white for the north where all is cold, black for the west where the sun sets in darkness, and yellow for the golden warmth of the south. At each point stood a sacred ceiba (silk-cotton) tree, fertilising and feeding life in the four directions. Each tree had its colour, and in each tree nested a bird. It seems, too, that there must have been a central tree, green in colour to represent the fountain of all life.

The position of the colours is not always constant, and the Nahuas often associated yellow with the east, white with the north, black with the west, and red with the south. One gets the impression of a revolving sequence, possibly (though this is speculation) associated with changes in the relative positions of astral bodies.

There is a Nahua poem describing a ritual turning to the four quarters. In this symbolic chant the east is called 'the place where the light emerges' and the eagle, tiger, serpent, rabbit and deer who live there are yellow in colour. South is called 'the place where death comes' and the colour of its creatures is red. West is 'the region of the holy seed ground' and its colour is white. North is 'the land of thorns' and its colour is blue. As the initiate hurls his arrows first in one direction and then in another, he attains to the gods. Finally he places his arrows in the hands of the Old God, the god of Time, who rules over all the cardinal points.

The assertion that the west and not the east is the seed ground suggests a perpetual recreation of life out of death, or at least disappearance in the phenomenal world, and rebirth when light dawns in the east on the following day. As the sun dies or disappears, the seed for its revival is planted.

One of the most important Maya scholars, Sylvanus Morley, notes that the peasants of Guatemala still use symbolic colours in their weaves, black representing war weapons because it is the colour of obsidian; yellow, maize or food; red, for obvious reasons, blood; and blue, sacrifice. Green is a symbol of royalty because the green quetzal feathers were the insignia of kings.

In one ceremony persisting to this day, old colour meanings are transferred to Christianity. Red is east or St Dominic the teacher; north white or St Gabriel of the last judgement; black west or St James the younger; and yellow south or Mary Magdalene – here representing fertility. There seems no reason why these particular figures should have been selected but they have apparently come to stand in the modern Maya mind for the *balam* of old.

In pre-Hispanic times Maya youths painted themselves black until the time came for them to marry, when they changed to red. But black was always used to represent fasting. Prisoners were striped black and white, and priests were painted blue. Throughout ancient Mexico and Central America the colour red was associated with death or mourning. Bones were sometimes painted red, and tombs were frequently stained with a brick-coloured dye.

Steps to heaven and hell

The whole world was supposed to rest on the back of a crocodile – or perhaps four crocodiles corresponding to the four compass points; and these in turn floated on a lake.

From a flat cross-section of the world represented by the cardinal points and diverse colours, there rose a ladder of thirteen rungs leading to heaven; and another leading downward by nine steps to hell. The steps on the ladders are not always consistently named in the various documents, but broadly speaking the topmost rung of the heavenly ladder was occu-

Left: the rain god in his heaven, a light-hearted place of flowers, songs and butterflies. Tlaloc presides, attended by priests, and water flows from his hands while water creatures play at his feet. The happy souls are seen in the lower half. Reconstructed wall painting from Tepantitla. Teotihuacán culture, first to sixth centuries A.D.

Far left: jade plaque found near Puerto Barrientos, Guatemala. It is from this, the oldest dated Maya object, that archaeologists date Maya history. The obverse (above) shows the planet Venus, who was the god Kukulcan. The reverse (below) shows a number of glyphs which give a date according to the Maya calendar, totalling 94,537 days from the beginning of the Maya era. This corresponds to roughly 320 A.D.

pied by the dual god-goddess who is Ometeotl, 'god of the near and close', 'he who is at the centre' or 'within the ring', he to whom we owe the existence of life, self-inventing, self-creating, lord of all Heaven and Earth and even of the Land of the Dead.

The duality of this god was a duality in quality. It stood for the negative and positive, male and female principles in the universe, light and shadow, yes and no. It was not a duality arising from polytheism. The concept was monotheistic and represented the equilibrium rather than the diversity within creation.

The next four steps below the land of Ometeotl are mysterious. Nobody knows more about them than the mere fact that they existed, though the one immediately below Ometeotl was sometimes said to be the abode of innocent children. It is as if these received some special blessing or shelter from the god above all.

Then came a land of tempests and of multiple gods. It would seem that here for the first time strife entered the universe, dividing Ometeotl into his many facets.

Immediately below were two rungs of the ladder belonging to night and day, or to dust and air. Then came a land of shooting stars or fiery snakes; then of birds and of the planet Venus; and, rather curiously below Venus, a place occupied by the Sun and the four hundred warriors created by Tezcatlipoca. Farther below these was the Milky Way, pictured as a female skeleton. The lowest of the rungs in heaven was the land of moon and clouds.

Below: a decorated clay cup from Villahermosa in the state of Tabasco.

Entwined serpents, on a Classic Maya bowl, representing Time. *British Museum.*

Twelve rungs may have been paired, with the thirteenth forming the apex. The nine rungs below the earth would then also have been paired in four steps with a lower pole forming the infernal regions. This pairing no doubt represented the dual nature of matter, growing in its negative and positive aspects ever more rarified and luminous until it found unity in heaven, and ever denser and colder until it descended to the heaviest, lowest point of creation in hell. (The discrepancies between the true cosmic placing of the Sun, planets and Milky Way may be due to a distorted record. We can hardly suppose that people with so accurate a calendar were ignorant of the general positions of the heavenly bodies.)

The nine steps down to hell seem to us more cohesive. First the soul arrived at a river guarded by a yellow dog. Then it had to pass between two mountain peaks, in order to reach one of pure obsidian. Lower still it met bitter winds, then banners, then arrows, then a wild beast. Near the end of its journey it passed through a narrow place, and finally the soul found itself at rest and at peace.

But hell and the lower steps should not be thought of entirely as places to which the wicked went as a punishment (reference to hell as a place for the wicked may be an imposition from orthodox Christianity). Hell was regarded as a necessary point of transition in the circular journey of all created things. These must, by an inevitable cosmic process, plunge into matter and rise again to reach the light. The process takes place in time, and time is important as being the vehicle of man's pilgrimage through material creation and back to his maker. As the sun disappears in the west, the seeds of its rebirth are planted.

The thirteen steps to heaven and the nine to the lower regions should not be confused with three different heavens to which the Nahua dead were supposed to go. The first and lowest of these was Tlalocan, Land of Water and Mist: a kind of paradise where happiness was of a very earthly variety but purer and less changeable. Here men played leapfrog and chased butterflies and sang songs. One fresco from Teotihuacán depicts this scene in a charmingly light-hearted manner. It is a sensual world for the gourmet with discernment. Happiness is conceived of in a simple-minded and materialistic way. The great authority on the ancient Mexicans, Fray Bernardino de Sahagún, says that in this land there was a perpetual abundance of maize, pumpkins, green peppers, tomatoes, beans, and flowers. Tlaloques, benign little mannikins employed by Tlaloc the rain god, are ministers of this paradise of plenty, which is a place of rebirth. It is supposed that after four years of sojourn here, souls return once more to mortal life. Unless we can reach higher, the perpetual round goes on. Most people on earth are probably destined to perpetuate this cycle of birth on earth, death into Tlalocan, and rebirth on earth. Their desires and their pleasures never rise above the simple pursuits depicted in the fresco.

But there was also Tlillan-Tlapallan, the land of the black and the red (black and red in conjunction signify wisdom). This was the paradise of the initiates who had found a practical application for the teaching of the god-king Quetzalcoatl. It was the land of the fleshless, the place where people went who had learned to live outside their physical bodies or, it would be better to say, unattached to them; a place celebrated in many ancient poems and greatly to be desired.

Farther beyond was Tonatiuhican, land of Tonatiuh, House of the Sun, often misrepresented as a military-political abode of warriors; but this is only because the Nahua 'holy war' has been wrongly interpreted as an earthly war against earthly enemies. The third paradise was probably

Right: the Toltec culture flourished at Tula, where these colossal figures once supported the entrance of the temple of Tlahuixcalpantecuhtli, Lord of the House of Dawn – Quetzalcoatl as the morning star. This god was also the culture hero of the Toltecs, who dominated southern Mexico before the coming of the Aztecs and whose influence on the Maya culture is plainly discernible. Eighth to twelfth centuries A.D.

The Lord of the Region of Death, Totonac style; sixth to ninth centuries A.D. Mictlantecuhtli (bottom) ruled over a nether world where there was neither pain nor pleasure, just a dreary eternal existence. The figure of his consort Mictlancihuatl is Aztec, a stone carving from a later period.

reserved for those who had achieved full illumination in the quest for deserved and eternal happiness.

So we have a series of three paradises, each more perfect than the one below and to be attained only by ever more intense spiritualisation and sacrifice of the gross physical world. Men whose desires were for good food and gaiety would go to the Land of Water and Mist, and then return to earth. Those who had acquired some kind of immortality apart from the perishable body would aspire to the Land of the Fleshless. And those who achieved still higher perfection might become worthy of living in the House of the Sun.

One's fate might of course be bad, causing one to go after death to the inferno called Mictlán – a dark place ruled over by the god Mictlantecuhtli and his consort Mictlancihuatl. This place was at the centre of the earth, and much less desirable than the cloudlands of the warrior souls. Nevertheless souls there did not suffer. They merely endured a rather colourless existence – perhaps the worst fate of all.

The great Earth Monster

Before the various paradises existed, the primordial substance seem to have been water. In a Nahua creation myth the great female Earth Monster, with innumerable mouths, swam in the formless waters devouring all she saw. When the gods Quetzalcoatl and Tezcatlipoca (whom we shall study later in more detail) saw how things were they determined that the Earth must acquire form. They changed themselves into two serpents. The first seized the Earth Monster by the right hand and the left foot. The other seized the left hand and the right foot. Together they grappled until the Monster broke in two. Her lower part rose to form the heavens, and her upper half descended to become the Earth. 'As above, so below. As in Heaven, so on Earth'. The entwined serpents are Time itself; and even today there are surviving beliefs suggesting that time was never thought of apart from space. The Nahuas could envisage only a space-time continuum – and the breaking up of the Earth Monster to form heaven and earth is a description of the origins of the linked space-time continuum in the material world.

The Earth Monster is the goddess, says the myth, who sometimes weeps at night, longing to eat human hearts, and she refuses to remain silent so long as she is not fed, and she will not bear fruit unless she is sprinkled with human blood. Life must be sacrificed to the great creature who nurtures life: a simple truth later distorted by the Aztecs who made it a pretext for sacrificing the hearts of their enemies. All living matter returns to earth. Ashes to ashes, dust to dust. But Earth sustains us too, and this the Nahua gods acknowledged after they had dismembered her, by allowing her to produce things necessary to man's well-being. Her hair became long grass and trees and flowers; her skin the lawns and the flowers with which they are studded like jewels. Her eyes became little caverns, wells, and fountains; her mouths, great caves for man's shelter; and her nose, hills and valleys.

Chiapas Indians, descendants of pre-Hispanic peoples, still use the same kind of graphic illustration, as when they say that the rainbow is a wall created to stop the passage of rain, or that the rivers are made with a great plough driving furrows through the land.

Stories of transubstantiation

One wide-ranging creation myth, which explains a series of phenomena from the birth of stars to the appearance of humans on earth, begins

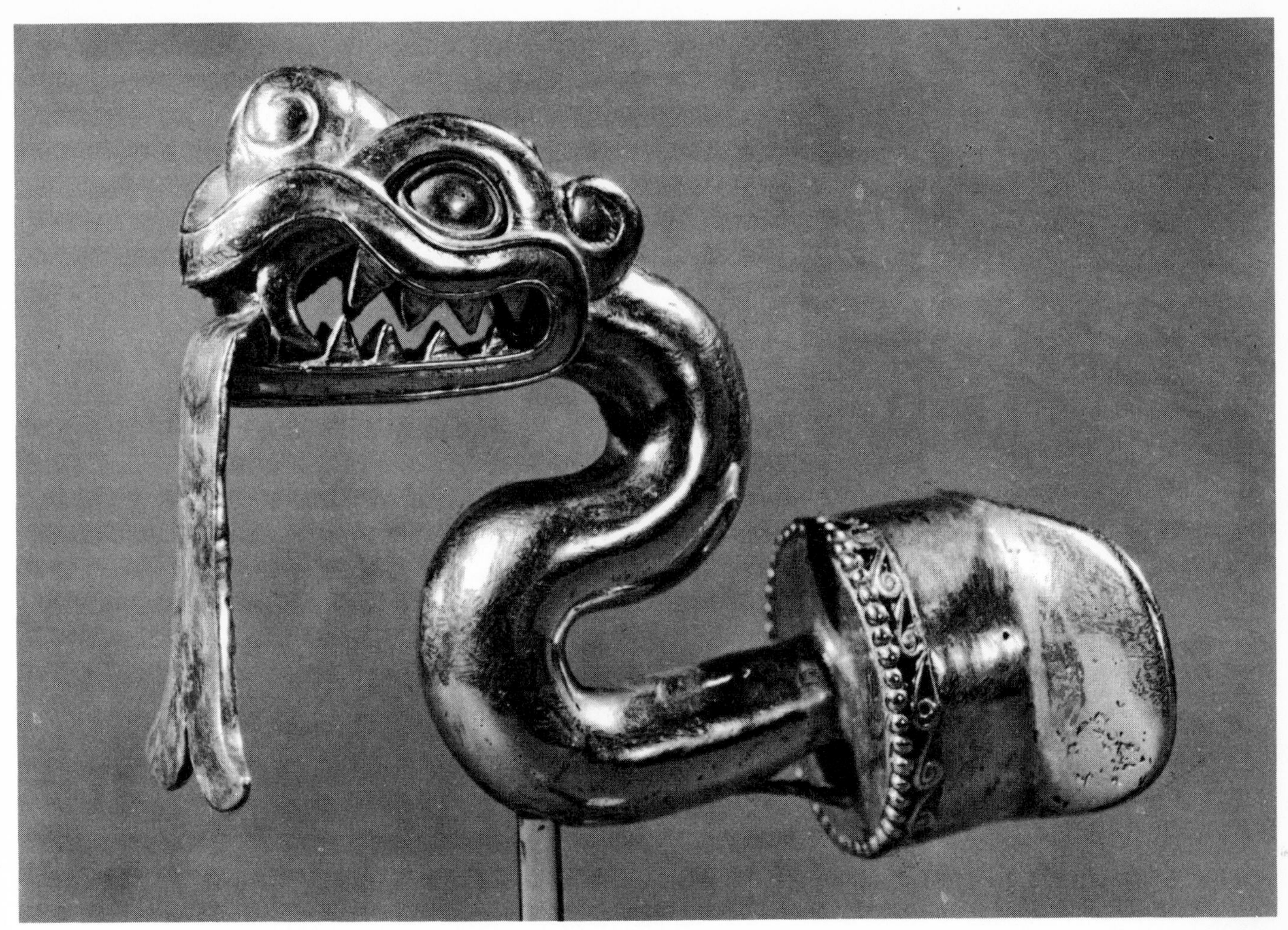

A gold lip-plug in the form of a serpent with a bifid tongue. The serpent symbolised many things to the peoples of pre-Hispanic Mexico, but particularly strength (through Xincoatl) and wisdom (through Quetzalcoatl). It was also a symbol of both earth and time. In the form of serpents Tezcatlipoca and Quetzalcoatl subdued the Earth Monster, who broke into two parts to become Earth and Heaven. Mixtec culture, eighth to eleventh centuries A.D.

with the existence in some heaven of the dual pair Ometeotl, sometimes called Ometecuhtli or Citlaltonac and his consort Omecihuatl or Citlalinicue.

One day the goddess gave birth to a knife of hard stone which she threw to earth, and 1,600 heroes were born. They were alone (many having died in one of the not infrequent calamities that wiped all living things from the face of the earth). These heroes sent an ambassador to their mother asking her to create men who would serve them. Their mother sent a hawk with the message that if their thoughts could be made nobler they would be worthy to live with her eternally in heaven. Not being of a highly spiritual or ambitious turn of mind, the heroes decided that they would prefer to live on earth. So they went to the god of the underworld and asked him to provide them with either a bone or the ashes of past men. These they would sprinkle with their own blood, and from them would issue a man and a woman who would multiply and repopulate the earth. Quetzalcoatl's twin Xolotl went to the underworld and brought back the bone. But the god of the underworld pursued him in anger. Xolotl fell with his bone, which broke into unequal parts. However, he managed to reach the brothers, who sprinkled it with their own blood. Four days later a male child was born, and three days after that a female. Xolotl raised the human pair on the milk of the thistle, and thus humankind was reborn to life on earth.

We see in this story how impossible it is for mankind to exist without some principle entering the human flesh from above. In this case the principle is represented by the blood of the 1,600 heroes, the life-substance of the stars in the Milky Way.

In another story the gods descended into a cave in which a prince was lying with the goddess called Precious Flower. From their union was born a god-child called the Well-Beloved, who immediately died and was buried. Out of the ground, from his body, there sprang many of the plants that were to supply man's basic needs. From his hair grew cotton; from his ears, seed-bearing plants; from his nostrils, a herb which is good for cooling fevers; from his fingers, the sweet potato; from his finger-nails, maize; and so on until he had produced about a thousand varieties of fruits and grain.

On one level the god-child is a material symbol of fertility; on another he represents death and rebirth, just as the Egyptian and Greek mysteries did. In the Nahua myth, however, the equivalent of Persephone came not from the underworld but from above. Even if the stuff of plants and herbs sprang from the buried body of the god-child, life could never have been sustained without an activating principle of a higher order. So it occurred to the wind god that it is well enough for man to rejoice in the fruits of the earth, but he must have love too. It occurred to him, then, to go in search of the maiden Mayahuel, whom he found in the company of many others, all asleep, in the charge of an ancient guardian called Tzitzimitl.

The wind god Ehecatl, a manifestation of Quetzalcoatl. He brought love to mankind when he bestirred the maiden Mayahuel. Their love was made manifest by a beautiful tree which grew up where they alighted on earth. Aztec sculpture, fourteenth to sixteenth centuries A.D.

The wind god bestirred Mayahuel, who awakened and agreed to go with him to earth. Thus the dormant force of love was roused and made active by the wind god. As the pair touched ground, they shot up into a beautiful tree with two great branches. One was known as the Precious Willow and belonged to the wind god. The other – the flowering branch – was the maiden's.

In the meantime old Tzitzimitl had awakened. Discovering that Mayahuel was no longer with her she became very angry. Tzitzimitl evidently represents the forces in nature that have a vested interest in inertia, passivity, and sleep. It did not suit her that love should be awakened and breathed into life by the wind. With an army of young gods who were her henchmen she descended to earth, and there discovered the tree which she immediately caused to split in two. In the flowering branch the old woman recognised the characteristics of Mayahuel. She shared out bits of it among the gods, who devoured them ravenously. The other branch, belonging to the wind god, remained untouched.

When the invaders had returned to their abode in heaven, the wind god changed himself back into his rightful shape, gathered together the bones of the maiden, and buried them in the fields. From them sprang a plant which produced white wine for men.

The story of Mayahuel is the story of the transubstantiation of matter; and the emphasis is on a fusion of heavenly and earthly ingredients. Neither can do without the other. Inertia, or earth, will remain with its possibilities unfulfilled if love – coming from above – does not infuse it with life. But neither can the higher powers work except through the stuff of the dead tree. Matter is the prop and stay of spirit.

The same theme recurs in a story which tells how one day the Sun shot an arrow which split open a rock. From within it were born a man and a woman. They were incomplete, possessing only head and thorax but lacking their lower limbs. They hopped over the ground like sparrows; and only when they had united in a kiss of love were they able to give birth to a complete man, father of mankind. It is interesting here that mankind exists in spirit (in his upper parts), but it is only when he is awakened by love that he becomes incarnate in an earthly form.

Between heaven and earth there must be a bridge; and this is formed

Detail of the rim of the stone of Tizoc, who became ruler of the Aztecs in 1481. A sacrificial stone, there was a depression in the centre which received human hearts. It was two and a half feet thick and eight feet in diameter, and carved with scenes commemorating the monarch's deeds. Victorious Aztec warriors can be seen leading their captives by the hair.

Right: the old fire god Huehueteotl. One of the oldest deities of ancient America, his ceremonies were particularly important at the conclusion of each fifty-two year cycle of time, when old fires were quenched and new ones lighted to keep time moving. Pottery figure from Cerro de las Mesas, Veracruz.

Below: a Zapotec representation of the bat god, the adversary of the valiant twins in the *Popol Vuh* story.

by the gods. After one creation, for example, the Goddess of the Jade Petticoat caused it to rain so hard that all human beings were changed into fishes. Then the gods decided that the heavens must be held up by four giant figures called Falling Eagle; Serpent of Obsidian Knives; Resurrection; and Thorny Flowers. Quetzalcoatl and Tezcatlipoca also helped to prop up the heavens, the former becoming a Precious Tree, and the latter a Tree of Mirrors.

It is difficult to be sure what the four pillars supporting heaven represent; but it would appear that the Falling Eagle symbolises the descent of a heavenly and activating principle into earth; and that the Serpent of Obsidian Knives is a principle of sacrifice needed for the process of incarnation, whose perpetual cycle cannot be escaped except through Resurrection and the growth of flowers. But even flowers have thorns, for nothing in creation can avoid the dual quality of matter with its beauty and its suffering. In the same way the wind god, an aspect of Quetzalcoatl, represents spirit freed from matter, while the god of the smoking mirror, Tezcatlipoca, is the phenomenal world.

How music was made

Tezcatlipoca besought Quetzalcoatl that he should make the journey to the House of the Sun, from which all life comes. He gave Quetzalcoatl specific instructions: that when he reached the seashore he must enlist the help of Tezcatlipoca's three servants who were called Cane and Conch, Water Woman, and Water Monster. Quetzalcoatl was to order these

Left: Chalchihuitlicue, goddess of the Jade Petticoat. In one creation she provided the bridge to heaven, without which mankind cannot exist, by using her power as the consort of the rain god. She caused a downpour that covered the earth, and turned men into fishes that they might use the water as a passage. Pottery figure from Tajín, fourth to ninth centuries A.D.

Below: a clay figure from the early Olmec culture. The kneeling figure is wearing a beast's skin, and is probably an early example of one of the cults which later became the knightly orders.

three to entwine together to form a bridge over which he could pass to reach the Sun. On arriving at the Sun he was to ask for musicians, and was to bring them back to earth to delight the souls of men.

Quetzalcoatl did as he was told, and when the Sun saw him approaching he warned his musicians not to utter a word. Any who opened his mouth would have to return to earth with the wind god. The musicians, clad in white, red, yellow, and green, resisted the temptation to unloose their tongues; but at last one of them relented, gave voice, and descended with Quetzalcoatl to earth where he was able to give mankind the pleasure of music.

In a sixteenth-century Nahua manuscript there is a poem describing this incident:

Tezcatlipoca – god of heaven
and of the four quarters of the heavens –
came to earth and was sad.
He cried from the uttermost depths of the four quarters:
  'Come, O wind!
  Come, O wind!
  Come, O wind!
  Come, O wind!'
The querulous wind, scattered over earth's sad bosom,
rose higher than all things made;
and, whipping the waters of the oceans

Quetzalcoatl (spirit) dances before Tezcatlipoca (matter); a page from the *Codex Borbonicus*. The legends of ancient Mexico demonstrate that the worlds of matter and spirit are coexistent and each has something which the other needs.

and the manes of the trees,
arrived at the feet of the god of heaven.
There he rested his black wings
and laid aside his endless sorrow.
Then spoke Tezcatlipoca:
'Wind, the earth is sick from silence.
Though we possess light and colour and fruit,
yet we have no music.
We must bestow music upon all creation.
To the awakening dawn,
to the dreaming man,
to the waiting mother,
to the passing water and the flying bird,
life should be all music!
Go then through the boundless sadness
between the blue smoke and the spaces
to the high House of the Sun.
There the father Sun is surrounded
by makers of music
who blow their flutes sweetly
and, with their burning choir,
scatter light abroad.
Go, bring back to earth a cluster – the most flowering –
of those musicians and singers.'
Wind traversed the earth that was plunged in silence
and trod with his strength of breath pursued,
till he reached the heavenly roof of the World
where all melodies lived in a nest of light.
The Sun's musicians were clad in four colours.
White were those of the cradle songs;
red those of the epics of love and of war;

Right: two great gods at Teotihuacán. The pyramid usually called after the plumed serpent was in fact shared by the rain god Tlaloc, and symbolic representations of the two alternate on the façade of the pyramid. At one time the serpent masks were coloured, with eyes made of obsidian. The temple which surmounted the pyramid no longer exists.

A gold disk representing the Sun. It was to the House of the Sun that Quetzalcoatl journeyed – at the behest of Tezcatlipoca – in search of music to gladden the heart of man. Mixtec culture.

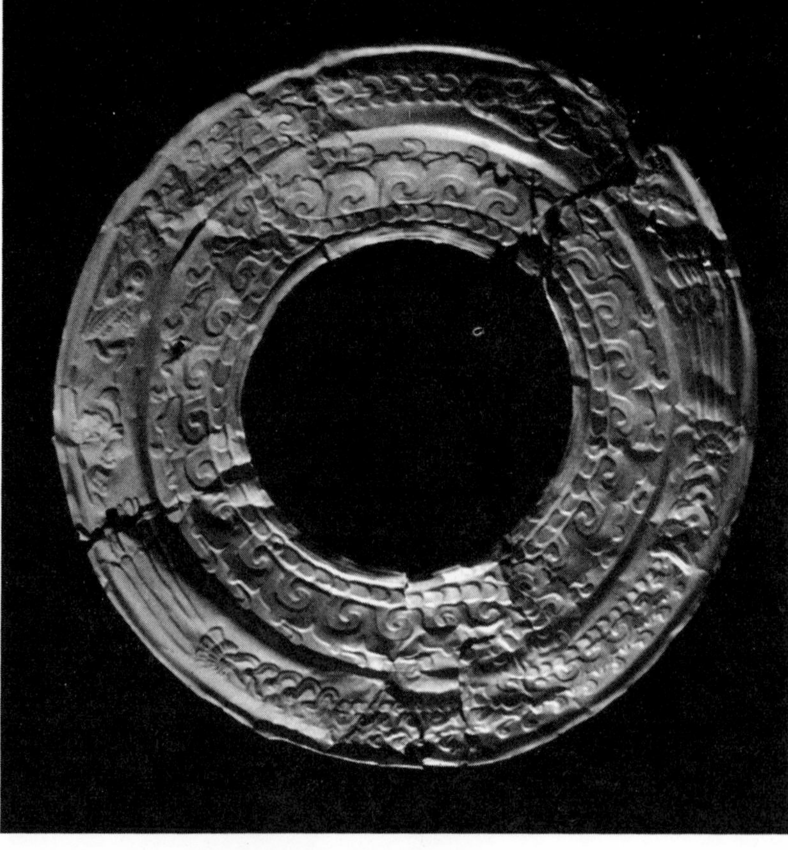

A cast gold pendant from Veraguas, Panama. The upper end shows a jaguar, the lower a crocodile.

sky blue the troubadours of wandering cloud;
yellow the flute players enjoying gold
milled by the Sun from the peaks of the World.
There were no musicians the colour of darkness.
All shone translucent and happy, their gaze turned forward.
When the Sun saw the wind approaching he told his musicians:
'Here comes the bothersome
wind of earth:
Stay your music!
Cease your singing!
Answer him not!
Whoever does so
will have to follow him
back down there into silence.'
From the stairways of light
of the House of the Sun,
Wind with his dark voice shouted:
'Come, O musicians!'
None replied.
The clawing wind raised his voice and cried:
'Musicians, singers!
The supreme Lord of the World is calling you...!'
Now the musicians were silent colours;
they were a circling dance held fast
in the blinding flame of the Sun.
Then the god – he of the heaven's four quarters –
waxed wroth.
From the remotest places,

Monte Albán, general view. One of the most spectacular cities of pre-Hispanic Mexico and one of the oldest.

whipped by his lightning lash,
flocks of cloud whose blackened wombs
were stabbed and torn by lightning
assembled to besiege the House of the Sun.
His bottomless throat let loose the thunder's roar.
Everything seemed to fall flat in a circle
beneath the World's mad roof, in whose breast
the Sun like a red beast drowned.
Spurred on by fear,
the musicians and singers then ran for shelter
to the wind's lap.
Bearing them gently
lest he should harm their tender melodies,
the wind with that tumult of happiness in his arms
set out on his downward journey, generous and contented.
Below, Earth raised its wide dark eyes to heaven
and its great face shone, and it smiled.
As the arms of the trees were uplifted,
there greeted the wind's wanderers
the awakened voice of its people,
the wings of the quetzal birds,
the face of the flowers
and the cheeks of the fruit.
When all that flutter of happiness landed on earth,
and the Sun's musicians spread to the four quarters,
then Wind ceased his complaining and sang,
caressing the valleys, the forests and seas.
Thus was music born on the bosom of earth.

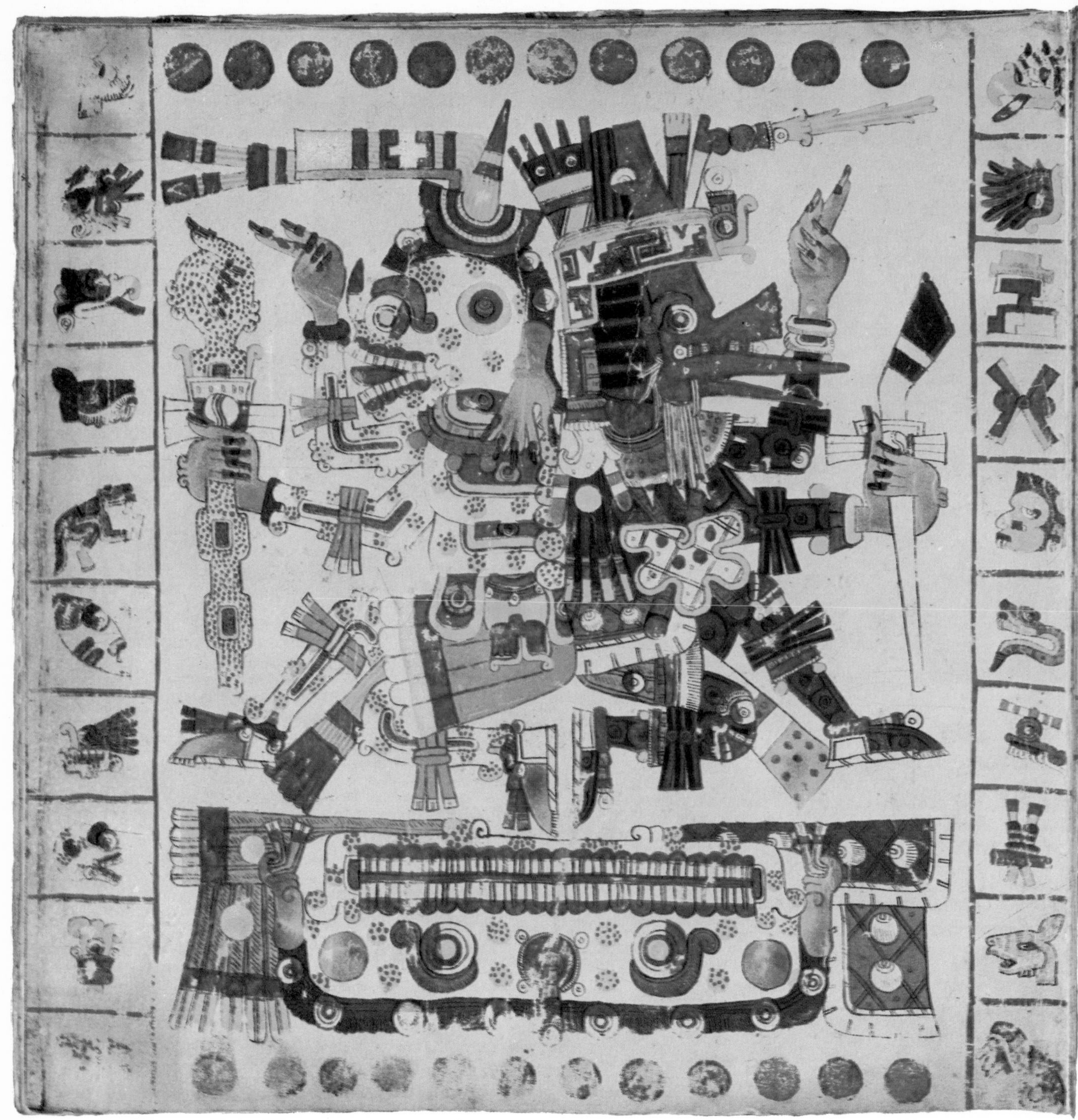

The plumed serpent seen as a performer of miracles. In his manifestation as the wind god Ehecatl, he breathes life into a skeleton figure representing the god of death Mictlantecuhtli. *Codex Borgia.*

The strangely shaped structure at Calixtlahuaca was dedicated to the wind god Ehecatl and recognises his ability to pass where he will.

Thus did all things learn to sing:
the awakening dawn,
the dreaming man,
the waiting mother,
the passing water and the flying bird.
Life was all music from that time on.

Once again, throughout this myth, we notice that matter, the noumenal world, and spirit, the phenomenal, must always be closely intertwined. It even appears that in some cases the phenomenal world rules over the noumenal and Tezcatlipoca has the right to give orders to Quetzalcoatl. There is really no vertical hierarchy here, but only a godly kind of peaceful coexistence, or rather a mutual self-help society in which the noumenal and the phenomenal exchange strength and music, to form the miracle of spirit incarnate.

'Indian time'

The belief that the noumenal and phenomenal worlds were continually interacting one upon the other was probably in part responsible for the attitude toward time natural to all pre-Hispanic peoples and to their descendants today. Workers among modern American Indian communities have noted that the pure indigenous peoples – as distinct from the so-called *ladinos* who have adopted western customs – live in a space-time quite different from ours. It is not just that they are more leisurely, less rushed, and of course totally unaware of clocks. It is rather that – in spite of Einstein, modern nuclear physics, and those events that might by now have been expected to upset our purely sense-based view of time – we continue to think of yesterday, today, and tomorrow as proceeding in a single line and always in one direction. It could be said that our time is horizontal. Indian time, on the other hand, is a completely different conception. It is vertical and static. It moves to no particular appointment in the future. Future and past are extraordinarily confused in the Indian mind, and even the concept of velocity is difficult to grasp, as it was to a Oaxacan Indian who once told me that it would take an hour for me to reach a certain village; and, he added after some thought, 'Two hours if you walk quickly enough.' It is easier for the Indian to describe time in relation to growth or change that is visible, as when peasants measure the distance from village to village in terms of 'a hat and a half' or 'two hats', according to the time it takes to plait the straw as they walk.

To the American Indian the past is not gone forever but is still present somewhere, as it is in the result – the hat – of the handiwork undertaken while walking. The Indians were, however, acutely aware that time, like all else in the universe, is mortal. Fires must be lighted every fifty-two years to keep it going. But the mainspring of this fifty-two year clock (in the old days it had to be wound up by prayers and bonfires) was a cyclical one.

At the end of the fifty-two-year period the fires were put out everywhere in the land. The wooden and stone statues of gods were cast into the water, together with pestles and hearth stones. Homes were swept clean and all rubbish thrown away. At midnight, when time had run out, the Aztecs would kindle a new fire on the breast of a captive, chosen for his noble birth. The captive's heart fed the fire, and if there was not a sufficient blaze it was supposed that the sun would be extinguished and the demons of darkness would descend to devour man, or men might be changed into beasts. Women at this time were held in fear, locked in the granaries and made to wear masks of maguey leaves. Children were also masked, and were kept awake with cuffs and kicks in case they should slumber off and be turned into mice. Everyone waited expectantly for dawn and rejoiced when it finally came, pricking their ears and sprinkling blood on the fire. From the main fire a flame was taken by relays of runners to every temple in the land. Men and women rejoiced at the promise of new life. They put on new garments, redecorated their houses, made new vessels for the rituals, renovated the temples; sacrifices were offered of incense and quail, and amaranth seed cakes were eaten with honey; but nobody was allowed to drink between daybreak and noon. As noon approached, captives were ceremonially bathed and then sacrificed, grains of maize cooked on their fires being distributed to all the people to eat.

A priest of the fire god wearing an elaborate headdress. Pottery figure from Las Remojadas, Veracruz.

The symbol of the cross was known to ancient Americans, who seem to have regarded the horizontal arm as signifying the transitory and the perishable, the vertical one as the eternal and the stable. The vertical arm represented time in the various heavens and underworlds, whereas the horizontal direction was associated with the passage of the sun across the sky.

All the great architectural monuments of Mexico and Central America – Teotihuacán, Tajín, Monte Albán, Mitla, Palenque, Bonampak, Chichén Itzá, Uxmal, Tulúm, Petén, Copán – are expressions of an eternally recurring space-time. The Aztec habit of building one pyramid on top of another every fifty-two years is a manifestation of this, but so also is the massive horizontal planning of the great courtyards and palaces, and the solid base of the pyramids, rising often fairly sharply to their peaks, but firmly set on the ground as if the architects were determined at all costs that they should endure for ever.

The attitude to time is also shown in doctrines concerning free will and predestination. We have seen how immortality could be of different grades, so that a man might pass to a paradise – the Land of Water and Mist – that closely simulated conditions on earth. If he were able to transcend the body, he might continue to the Land of the Fleshless; and thence to full immortality in the House of the Sun. There was a gradual progression from relative darkness to purest light, from earthbound satisfaction to spiritual joy.

The serpent columns at Chichén Itzá. In the long shadows the Chac Mool figure watches eternally at the approach to the Temple of the Warriors in the city founded, legend says, by Kukulcan, the Maya Quetzalcoatl.

Man-Beast Relationships

Other beliefs, some of which have been perpetuated to our day, were of a more superstitious nature though they may have arisen from a true appreciation of the close interconnection of man with the rest of organic life. Before studying various man-beast relationships, we should notice how carefully the pre-Hispanic Indians observed the characteristics of living creatures and how talented they were at giving them symbolic meaning. The ancients sculpted, modelled, and painted animals often naturalistically but more frequently in stylized versions to emphasize the qualities or appearances peculiar to each.

Foremost in the precolumbian bestiary was the snake or serpent, definitely associated with Time in the Maya mythology, more obliquely so in the Nahua. Contrasted with the serpent was the quetzal bird, that shy forest dweller capable of releasing man from Time's bondage; and the vulture who was sometimes pictured in mortal combat with the serpent.

The eagle was placed in opposition to the two cat-like animals, the jaguar and the ocelot. In Maya symbolism the jaguar's day was *Ix*, day of obsidian, the day on which heaven and earth embraced. In a Nahua

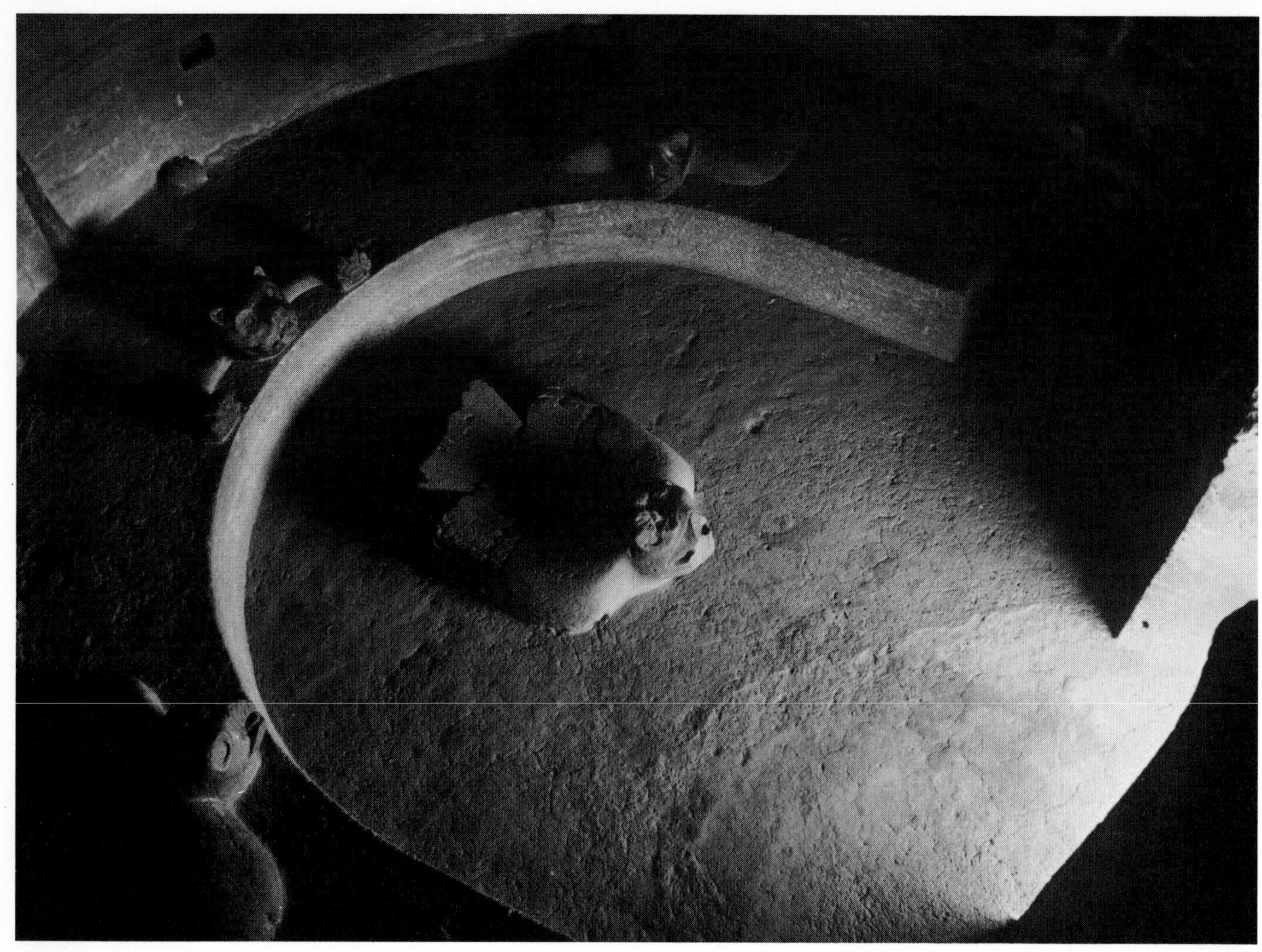

The interior of the sanctuary of the knightly orders at Malinalco. The alternating figures of eagle and ocelot were in fact seats for the chief dignitaries of the orders. The whole is carved from solid rock. Fourteenth to sixteenth centuries A.D.

story describing the rising and setting of the sun, the eagle stood for the day sun and the ocelot for the star on its night journey through the underworld. Two Nahua orders of knighthood were named after the eagle and the ocelot (the American tiger), and one particularly fine Mexican carving shows a knight-eagle with strangely European features looking out from the visor-headdress representing the bird.

The screech owl and the dog were associated by the Mayas with death and burial. Both Nahuas and Mayas had their equivalents of Cerberus, the Nahua dog being Xolotl and the Maya Pek, dog of lightning. Dogs were the first animals on the continent to be domesticated, and they were held sacred, sometimes being bred for particular characteristics such as hairlessness, which is a feature of the dog called today the Xoloitzcuintli. (This Xoloitzcuintli is not to be confused with that other native domestic Mexican dog, the well-known Chihuahua, popular today in the United States. The Xoloitzcuintli is a larger dog and is believed to be the first animal domesticated in the Americas. The race had almost died out a few years ago, but an English dog-lover, Norman Pelham Wright, was able to find a few pure specimens, and there are now about seventy registered with the Mexican kennel club.)

Snail and tortoise, being the slowest creatures, represented the winter and summer solstice. Another type of snail, the sea mollusc, was one of the most important symbols of death and resurrection because its whorled shape fittingly described the cyclic quality of life, growth, and decay. Butterflies, born out of the caterpillar in the chrysalis, were also

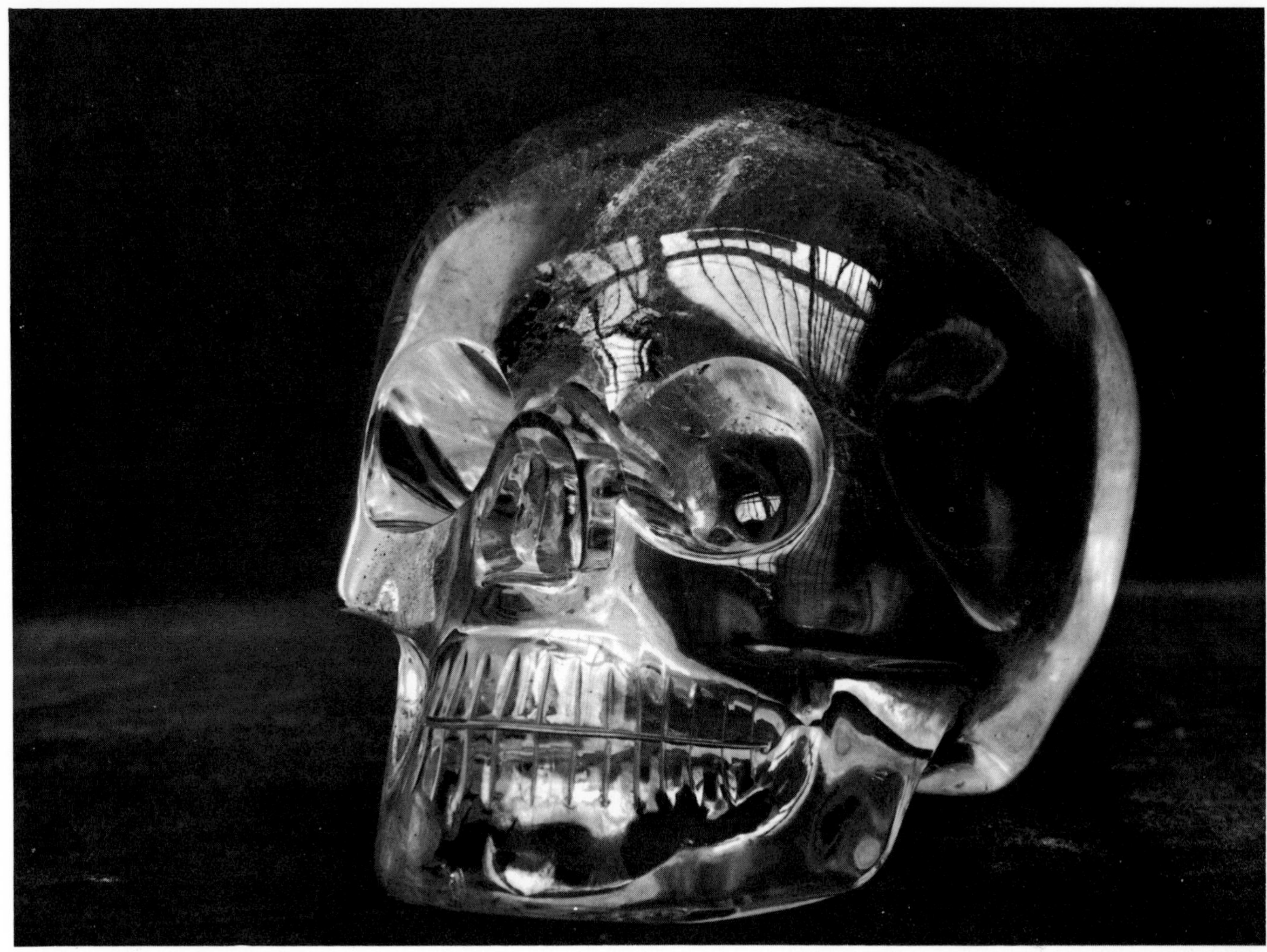

An awareness of death permeated the life of the Mexicans, and provided the motive for some of their finest art. This skull, carved from rock crystal, is Aztec and dates from the fifteenth century A.D.

a symbol of rebirth and regeneration, of happiness and joy.

The Mayas told of a bloodthirsty bat called Camazotz, with large teeth and claws and with a nose the shape of a flint knife, who could easily sever a man's head from his body as he once did to the Maya heavenly twins when they were contending against the powers of evil.

There were mysterious Maya ceremonies connected with bees, which seem to have symbolised chosen people of great industry and potential. In Maya symbolism the fish is also common, being sometimes held in the mouth of a heron; so too the frog, the crocodile, the turtle, and other water creatures. These understandably held much less fascination for the Nahuas, who lived far from the coastlands and were more familiar with the turkey (symbol of Tezcatlipoca), the rabbit who was flung in the face of the moon, and other highland fauna.

Immortality and the soul

The sense of the wholeness and interpenetration of all living things was so strong in the ancient American peoples that they believed a man's fate to be determined by his birthday, and also by his name, which even today is linked with his animal totem. *Naguales* were guardian spirits that took the form of an animal or a bird and presided over a man's fate. A man would receive his particular *nagual* by going into the forest and sleeping among the birds and beasts. There he would either dream of one or, when he wakened, would find himself confronted by his guardian spirit with whom he would be obliged to make a life-long contract. It was supposed that some people had the power of transforming themselves into their *nagual*, in the same way that Gucumatz – one of the heroes of the *Popol Vuh*, could transform himself into a serpent, an eagle, a tiger, and lower forms of life. *Naguals* could become invisible and travel swiftly from place to place.

In modern primitive belief the *nagual* is the first creature to cross the newborn baby's path. Ashes are sprinkled outside the place where the child is born so that the footprints of the animal can be captured and the correct name determined. The animal becomes a kind of second soul to the child, whose physical appearance and psychic features become similar to the *nagual*'s. Some powerful men, for instance, have thunderbolts as *naguals*; others, who seem humble but are really fierce, have a tiger. If a person prays to his *nagual* it will do what he wishes, but he must know how to pray. A man and his *nagual* are not interchangeable, but when a man dies his *nagual* dies, and vice versa.

The identification of the *nagual* with the person can be extended to include almost anything that appears to represent him, and especially his photograph. In many parts even today the peasants fear cameras and turn away from them with the rapidity of a person pursued by death. Something goes out of them, they feel, is diminished, and enters the photographic image. Still worse, if the photograph should fall into the hands of an ill-wisher, damage done to the photograph can be transferred to the subject of it.

The Mexicans believed that soldiers killed in war, or women who died in childbirth such as the one represented in this Totonac clay figure from Veracruz, went to the House of the Sun, where they remained in perfect content.

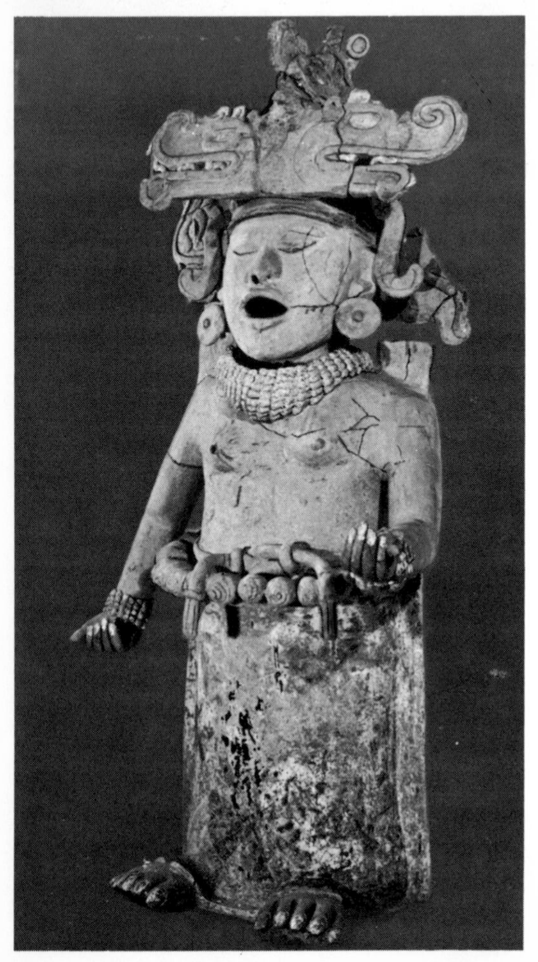

The linking of birth and death to the *nagual* is predestination in its most rigid form. It is also alarmingly accidental, for who can tell whether a coyote or a hare, or even – as in one story – a bicycle (animate in Indian thought) might not be the first to cross a baby's path? Nevertheless fate can be changed by courage in the battle of life as well as on the battlefield itself, by fasting and prayers, and above all by creating a heart and a mind worthy of the gods.

The Chontal Indians of Oaxaca say that a man's soul resides in his heart or breath and has a human shape. When people dream of the dead, they are seeing their souls. During a dream the soul leaves the body and goes to meet other souls. Apart from the soul, and less tied to the physical body, man possesses sense or judgment which resides in the head but which can come and go at will. One may, for example, think mentally of a place and inhabit it for a time in imagination.

The Otomí Indians of the central Mexican plain believe that the soul dies with the body, but the Mexicans and the other people of Anáhuac thought it was immortal. Soldiers killed in war or women who died in childbirth went to the House of the Sun, where they lived happily ever after. Every day the soldiers celebrated the Sun's birth by following it to its zenith, where they were met by the women who led the Sun to its decline in the west. After four years of such duty the souls of the warriors and the women could inhabit the Land of Clouds. They would be transformed into birds of fine plumage and sweet song, and they would be able to fly happily and freely among the flowers and suck their honey. After death the souls of the aristocracy inhabited birds or higher animals; but plebeian souls entered into beetles, leeches, and other insects. One tribe, the Mextecs, believed that a cave in their area, high in the mountains, was a gate to Paradise. In it they buried their dead so that souls could the more easily make their way to the happy land.

There was thus a variety of possible fates for the human soul; one's behaviour in life would determine one's future after death and also the way in which one might or might not return to mortal life.

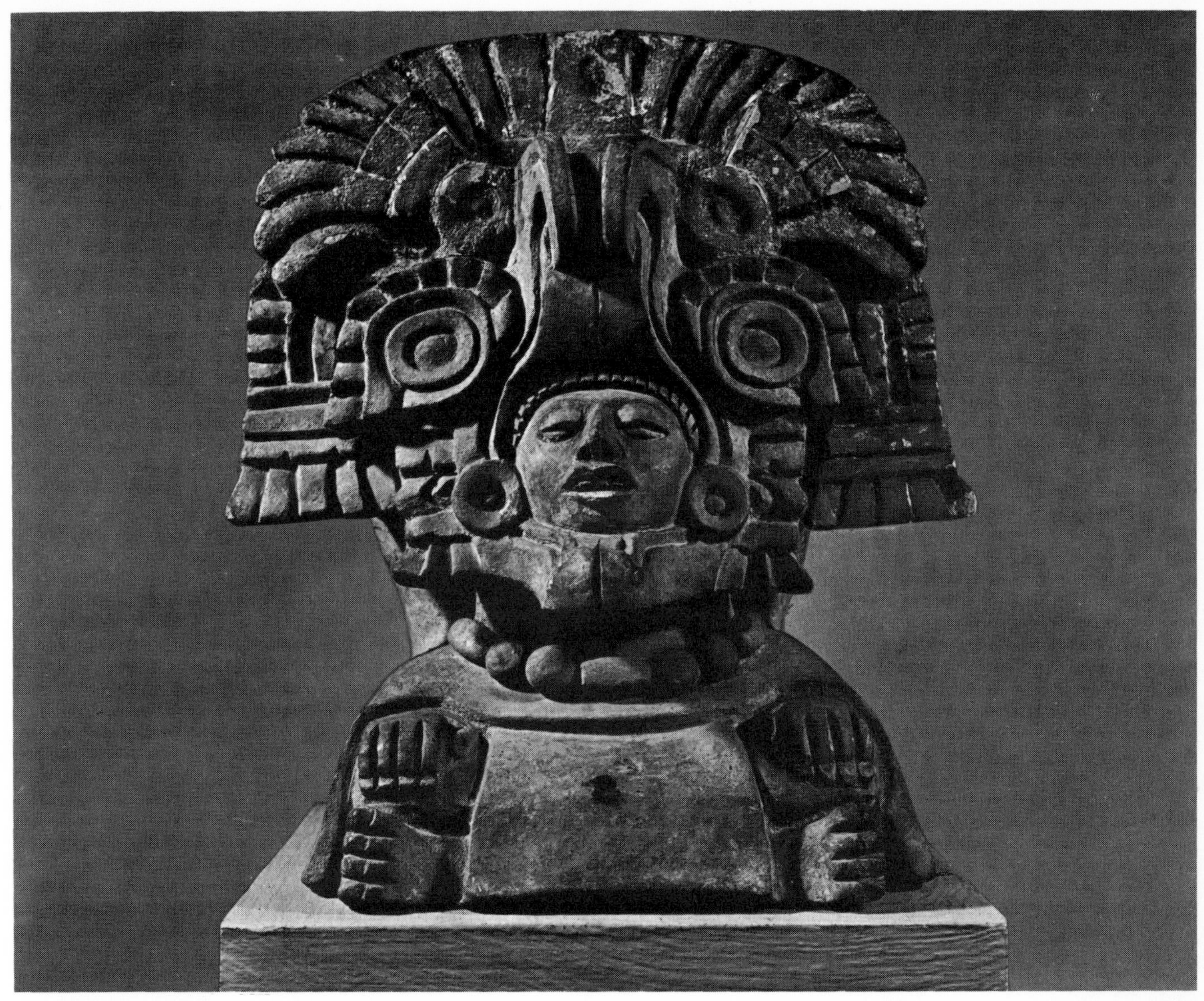

A Zapotec funerary urn, modelled in clay, from Oaxaca. The figure is the butterfly god, the symbol of rebirth.

The Calendar

It is well known that the Mayas and Aztecs had a highly developed calendar system. In their astronomical calculations, myth and science meet. To understand fully the meaning and position of the various gods in the cosmic plan, we must diverge slightly from the main mythological theme in order to study the calendar.

The Mayas, and probably the Nahua-speaking peoples also, regarded days as animate beings, in fact as gods. Time was thus personified and in no way abstract. Every division of time – the day, the month, the year and so on – was a definite object or entity, and it had to be carried by divine messengers which were represented by numbers. If Plato's god was a mathematician, so too was the Maya-Nahua god-above-all. Numbers were his army, protecting his eternal and infinite domain. An important Maya scholar, J. Eric S. Thompson, explains the Maya view by an analogy with our calendar. If we were to take the date 31 December 1965 as an illustration, then there would be six messengers or bearers. The god of number 31 would carry December on his back. The god of number 1 would be carrying the millennium, the god of number 9 the centuries, the god of number 6 the decades, and the god of number 5 the years. At the end of the year there would be a pause, and the procession would reshape itself and start again with the first messenger (1), carrying January, and with the god of number 6 replacing number 5 for the year. In hieroglyphs the messengers were represented carrying their burdens, the weight taken by a strap across the forehead as one can still today see miners raising their loads of ore up the shaft ladders, or peasants carrying wood, charcoal and other wares, trotting with them for incredibly long journeys without tiring. In the hieroglyphs there are also night gods who take over when each day is done.

By the peculiar nature of the calendar, only four gods could start off the load of the new year. Two – Kan, the maize god, and Muluc, rain, would bring good fortune; and two others (Ix and Cauac) were harbingers of disaster.

The cyclical view that the Mayas held of time meant that they saw history in terms of repetition; but the repetition was extended over very long periods for there are inscriptions extant recording a regression of four hundred million years into the past, and others which look at least four thousand years into the future.

Both Mayas and Aztecs based their calendars on cycles of eighteen-day periods arranged in multiples of twenty. Thus 20 × 18 made 360 days. To these were added five days 'outside the calendar' to form a year, in Maya terminology a *Haab*. In both Nahua and Maya lands people were careful not to fall asleep during the daylight hours of these extra-calendar days, nor to quarrel, nor to trip as they walked. They believed that what they did then they would do forever. People tended to confine themselves to their houses, and were careful not to perform any chores or unpleasant activities, lest they should be committed to these forever.

Xochipilli, the young god of flowers and beauty, love and happiness. One of the thirteen who presided over the hours of the day. Aztec carving from Tlalmanalco.

The 365-day year was corrected in such a way that the Mayas fixed the true passage of the earth about the Sun at 365.2420 days, which is only two ten-thousandths of a day short of modern calculations (365.2422). Our Gregorian calendar fixes the year at 365.2425 days, or three ten-thousandths of a day too long.

A *tun* was a 360-day period. A *katun* was 20 × 260 days, or 7,200 days, roughly 20 years and exactly 12.5 cycles of Venus. A *baktun* was 20 *katunes*, or 144,000 days, about 400 years. A *pictun* was 20 *bactunes*, or 2,880,000 days, about 8,000 years. A *calabtun* was 20 *pictunes*, or 57,600,000 days, about 158,000 years. A *kinchiltun* was 20 *calabtunes*, or 1,520,000,000 days, about 3 million years. Twenty *kinchiltunes* formed one *alautun*, or 23,040,000,000 days, over 60 million years.

It so happened that a *katun* could end only on a day called *Ahau*, and every 260 *tuns* the same *Ahau*, numbered in a series, would turn up. Within the greater stretches, history would begin to repeat itself at least to the extent of coming once again under the same cosmic influences. For example, *katun* 8 *Ahau* was believed always to bring disturbances, wars, and political upheavals. In fact an usurping family called Itzá that had ruled over a part of the Maya lands for centuries was not defeated until 1697 A. D., just before the start of a *katun* that spelled tragedy; though whether this coincidence was due to destiny or to an acute suggestibility in the mind of the ruling Itzá, it would be hard to say. The name Itzá means in Mexican a yoke, and the burden of this usurping rule was supposed to have lain upon the Mayas from about the tenth to the sixteenth centuries though there is evidence that some Itzá kings were wise men. One of their greatest prophets predicted that the white man would come. Another high chief, Ta-Itzá, was destined to cause suffering to his beloved princess, Sac-Nicté, who had been betrothed to another prince, Ulmil Itzahal. Ta-Itzá stole Sac-Nicté and presented her to his people in Petén, but the

Details from the Aztec calendar. The planet Venus, Quetzalcoatl, is manifest here as the Morning Star. The two upper sections show (*left*) that on these days Venus is a danger to Princes and (*right*) the days when Venus destroys warriors. The lower section shows the days when (*left*) crops are in danger; when all things to do with mountains are threatened (*centre*) and the days when Venus is inimical to women and the creatures of the great waters (*right*). The figure in the top right-hand corner is Camaxtli, a god of fate, with the twenty day signs attached to parts of his body. *Codex Borgia.*

unhappy princess drowned herself in a lake.

Beautiful ceremonies performed by the Itzá are described in one of the *Chilam Balam:*

'Now the wizards vie with one another in taking the shapes of the blue heron and of the humming bird. Then flowers descend from the source of all and from the folds of the Great Hand – nine flowers. When the hearts of the flowers appear, the priests place four branches of flowers on the burning altar of the Sun.'

Probably, then, the dynasty of the Itzá was not consistenly bad but merely described the whole cyclical round of cosmic fate. It is difficult to believe that the Yucatán temple site Chichén Itzá, called after these kings, was the product of anything but a high culture.

Within the larger cycle of good and bad fate, and within the cycle of the earth about the Sun, a smaller kind of 'year' was made up of a succession of 260 days, divided into twenty groups of thirteen. This is called in Maya terminology the Tzolkin or 'count of days', and in Aztec the *Tonalpohualli.* In both systems the days always had an accompanying number, so that in the Maya calendar, for instance, the days would run 1 *Ik*, 2 *Akbal*, 3 *Kan* and so forth. But in order to describe a given date exactly one would have to add to this designation its position in the 365-day year. Thus in the old calendars there were various 'sliding scales' or intermeshed counts allowing very exact descriptions of earthly time in relation to the heavenly bodies.

Both Mayas and Aztecs also subdivided time into periods of fifty-two days. For example the *Tonalpohualli* of the Aztecs was divided into five parts, corresponding to the four compass points and the centre, and having an exact parallel in the 52-year cycle at the end of which the sun had to be revived or creation would end. We should note here that the number 5 was specifically associated with Quetzalcoatl and his quincunx symbol,

and also with Venus, one aspect of Quetzalcoatl. The synodic revolution of Venus (Quetzalcoatl) is 584 days, and these revolutions were grouped by the Nahuas in fives, so that 5 × 584 equalled 2,920 days, or exactly eight years. At the moment when the solar year and the Venus cycle coincided, feasts and rites were dedicated to Xiuhtecuhtli-Huehueteotl, god of the year, god of the centre, standing at the very hub of the cardinal points, just as the *tlecuil*, or brazier, is the hearth at the centre of all indigenous temples and homes. Therefore the god was often associated with that other form of quincunx, the cross, with emphasis on the connections between each point and the centre. The great incense burners with which the priests paid ritual homage to the gods were often shaped as a cross.

We have, then, multiples of 13 × 20 and of 18 × 20 days, of 52 days and of 52 years, and of synodic revolutions of Venus and the planet's conjunction with the calendar year on earth. There was also a division of 73 days which, multiplied by the 260-day cycle, created the 52 years, bring the meshed cycles even closer. And there were lesser 9-day cycles known as Companions of the Night, although some – including the German nineteenth-century investigator, Eduard Seler – think that this was not a cycle of days but of hours, one deity presiding over each hour of darkness.

The nine companions were the fire god Xiuhtecuhtli; Itztli, god of the sacrificial knife; Piltzintecuhtli, a sun god; Cinteotl, the god of maize; Mictlantecuhtli, god of death; Chalchihuitlicue, the water goddess; an earth goddess and goddess of love, Tlazolteutl; Tepeyollotl, the heart of the mountain; and Tlaloc, the rain god.

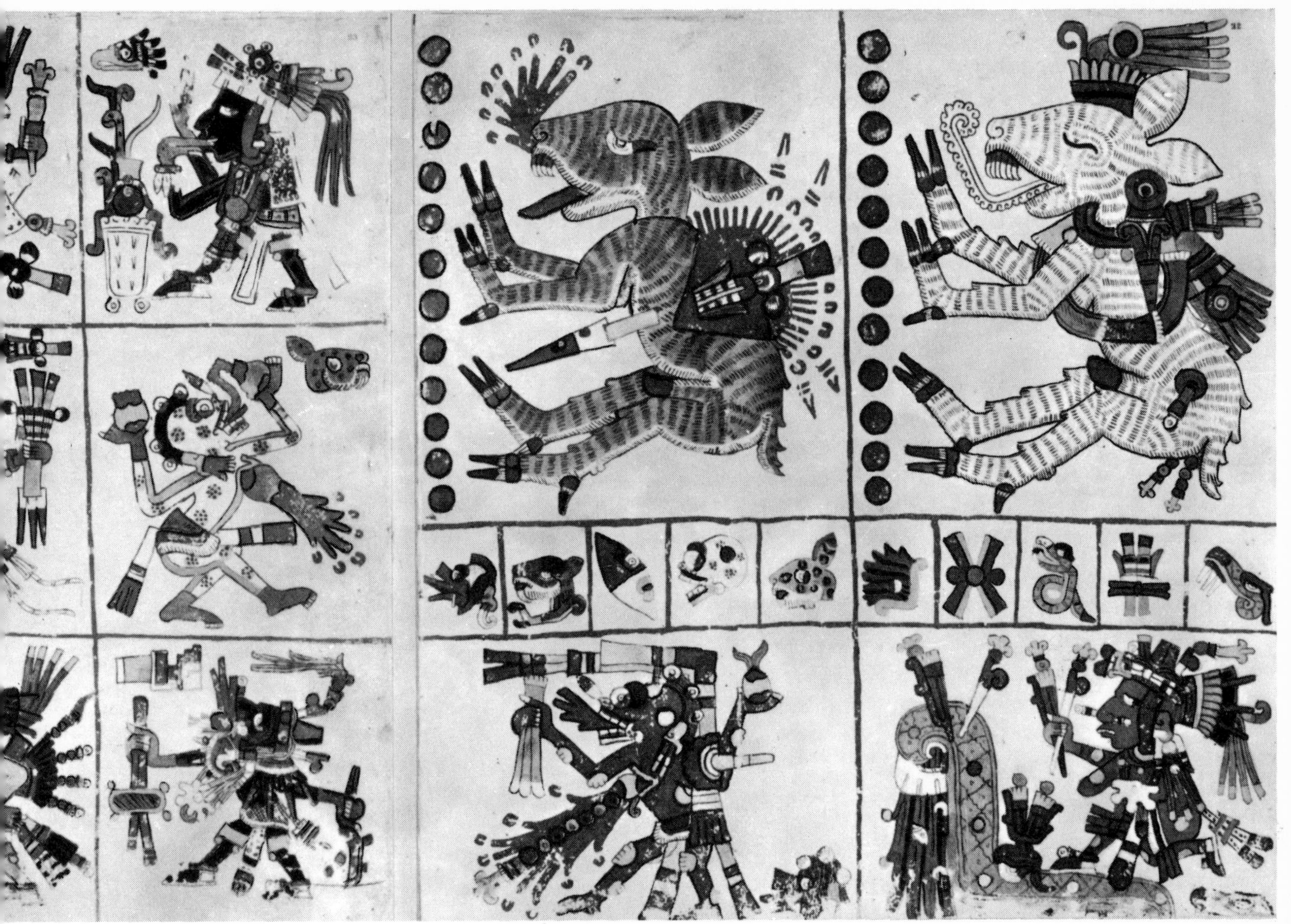

In the same way the thirteen so-called Companions of the Day (some of them duplicated from the night) presided over the hours of daylight; Xiuhtecuhtli; Tlaltecuhtli, an earth god; Chalchihuitlicue; Tonatiuh, the sun god; Tlacolteutl; Mictlantecuhtli; Xochipilli-Cinteotl; Tlaloc; Quetzalcoatl; Tezcatlipoca; Chalmecatecuhtli, god of sacrifice; Tlahuixcalpantecuhtli, god of dawn; and Citlalinicue, goddess of the Milky Way.

The total number of companions adds up to twenty-two hours, so that each ancient Mexican hour must have been longer than that marked by our clocks. Eduard Seler gives us the order of gods for the hours of day and night, with alternative lists from the Mexican investigators given in brackets, in the diagram on page 48.

These Companions of Day and Night are not to be confused with the patron deities of the days, which we shall come to later.

At the end of the 52-day cycles an extra, intercalary period, sometimes of twelve and sometimes of thirteen days, brought the calendar into line with the position of the sun among the stars. The multiple of 13 × 20 days made 260 days; and the cycle of 20-day signs was repeated thirteen times in such a way that only in every 260 days did any given day sign occupy the same place in the 13-day 'week'. The full description of a day could never be merely *cipactli*, *coatl*, or *calli*; a number from one to thirteen had to precede it. A day would therefore be known as One-water-serpent, Two-snake, and so on. No wonder that the priests had their time almost fully occupied with the various calendar-astronomical calculations, and no wonder that numbers such as 7, 9, 13, 20, and 52 were held sacred by the pre-Hispanic peoples.

The twenty Aztec day signs in three leaves from the *Codex Borgia*. The god of each day appears in a separate square, with the accompanying sign in the corner. The first two appear on the bottom of the right-hand leaf. The sequence reads from right to left, continuing on the centre leaf and the leaf on the left, where it follows on the line above, reading from left to the square on the far right of the centre leaf. This continues in the square above and concludes, reading right to left, in the top left square of the left-hand leaf. The first square shows *cipactli*, crocodile, and the last shows *xochitl*, flower.

A clay head of Xipe Totec, an aspect of the shabby and despised god Nanautzin who sacrificed himself in the fire to enable the sun to continue lighting the world. He is also the flayed god and is said to make the seeds germinate in the earth. The skin covering the face is his distinctive representation. Toltec, ninth to thirteenth centuries A.D.

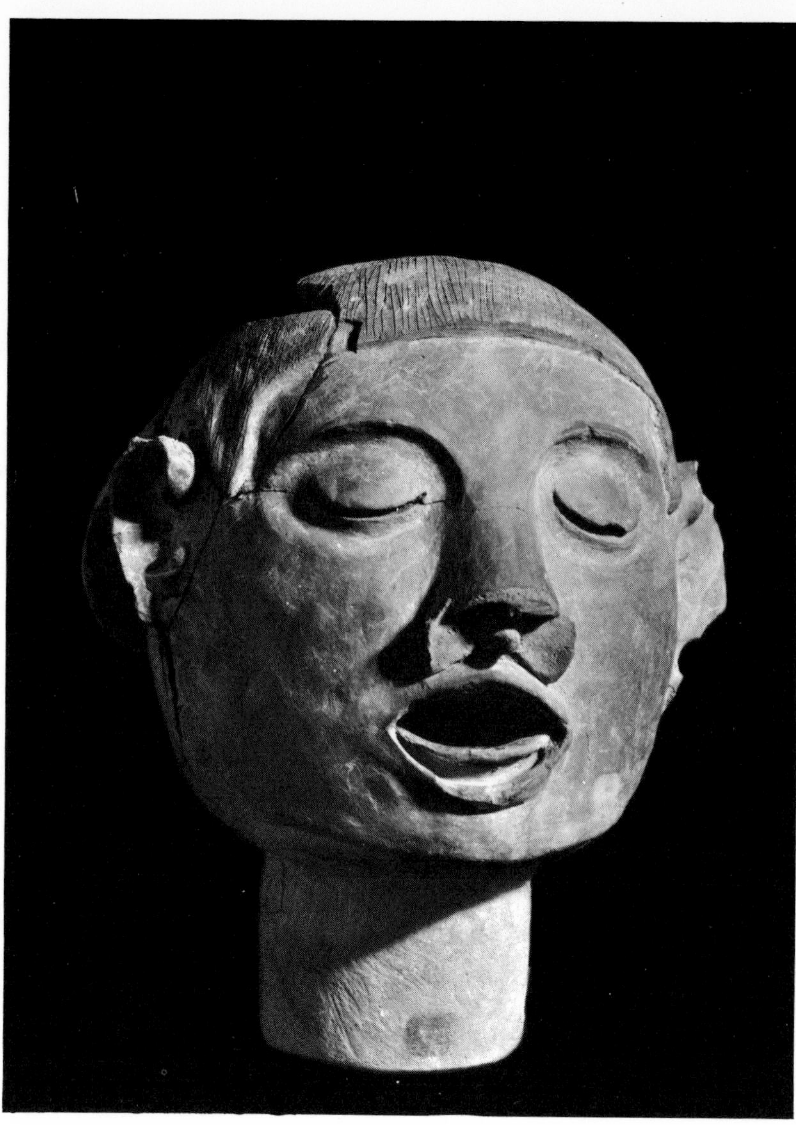

The order of gods for the hours of day and night, according to Eduard Seler.

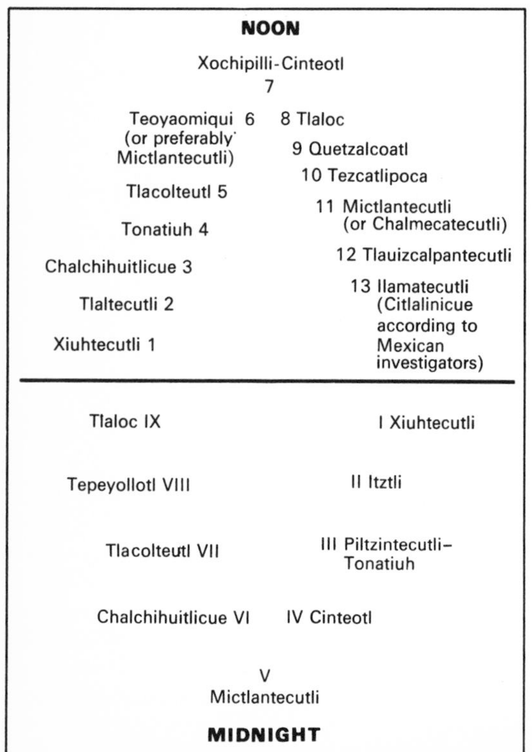

From a modern astronomical standpoint the sliding scale was a surprisingly efficient one. For instance, the agricultural-solar calendar of 365 days, multiplied by two 52-year periods, gives 37,960 days; 146 times the 260-day period also gives 37,960 days; and the synodic revolutions of Venus are 584 × 65, or 37,960 days. So that every 104 years these three sliding scales coincided. Again, five periods of 260 days make 1,300 days, or 44 revolutions of the moon about the earth. Mercury's cycle is 116 days, or about 9 × 13. The 584-day Venus cycle is 2.25 × 260. One cycle of Mars is 780 days, or exactly 3 × 260. Jupiter's cycle is 399 days, roughly 22 × 18. Saturn's cycle is 378 days, or 360 plus 18. By the sliding scale, the cycles of the planets could be calculated with a degree of accuracy that was remarkable.

The footsteps of the god

Before we study the Maya procession of days, which once again is a symbol of birth, death, and resurrection, we should note the detailed account of creation as given in the *Book of the Month* of the *Chilam Balam:*

'When in days gone by the world had not yet awakened, the Month was born and began to walk alone. Then said his maternal grandmother, then said his aunt, and his paternal grandmother, and his sister-in-law: "Why was it said that we should see men on the road?" Thus they wondered as they walked, for there were no men in those days. And then they reached the East, and they said, "Somebody has passed this way. Here are his footprints."

'"Measure it with your foot," said the World Mother, or so they tell.

'Then he measured the footprints of God, the Word. That is why it was called "counting off the world by footprints"... When the Month had been born, he created what is known as a day, and he created heaven and earth in the form of a ladder: water, earth, rocks, trees. He created all things on earth and in the sea. In *One Chuen* he brought forth from himself divinity and created heaven and earth. In *Two Eb* he created the first ladder so that God could descend into the midst of the sky and the sea. Neither land nor stones nor trees existed then. In *Three Ben* he made all things, the whole diversity of creation; things in heaven and in the sea and on the earth. In *Four Ix* heaven and earth embraced each other. In *Five Men* things moved into action. In *Six Cib* the first candle was made, and thus it was that light was created where there had been neither sun nor moon. In *Seven C'haban* the earth was born where there had been none in days gone by. In *Eight Edznab* he rooted hands and feet upon earth. In *Nine Cauac* for the first time there was an attempt to create hell. In *Ten Ahau* bad men went to hell because God the Word had not yet appeared. In *Eleven Imix* stones and trees were made. In *Twelve Ik* wind was created. And that is the reason why he is called *Ik* (Spirit), because in him there is no death. In *Thirteen Akbal* he took water and moistened clay and shaped the body of a man.

'In *One Kan* his spirit was afflicted because of the evil he had created. In *Two Chicchan* evil made its appearance and could be seen by men. In *Three Cimi* death was invented. It came about that God our Father invented the first death.'

At this point in the *Chilam Balam* manuscript there is a blank space corresponding to *Four Man-ik*, the day in which the Spirit passes over.

'In *Five Lamat* he invented the great reservoir of the great sea lake. In *Six Muluc* all the valleys were filled with earth before the world had awakened. And it came to pass that a false voice of God our Father entered into them all, when there was neither voice in heaven nor stones nor trees, in days gone by. And then, one after another, the days were put to the test, and they said: "Thirteen... plus seven form a cluster (of twenty)..." Thus was the month created when earth awakened, and when heaven and earth and the trees and stones were made. All was created by God our Father and by his Word. His divinity appeared where there was neither heaven nor earth, and by its power he became a cloud, and created the Universe. And his great power and majesty shook the heavens.'

These twenty days, the footprints of the god, turn out to be nothing less than the symbolic representation of man's spiritual pilgrimage. They are twenty steps up and down the ladder, beginning with *Imix*, from *Im*, the womb. The first day starts the child off on his journey through life. On the second, *Ik*, spirit or breath is bestowed upon him when he is still within the womb. On the third, *Akbal*, he is born of water (the ancient pre-Hispanic peoples had baptismal ceremonies). On the fourth, *Kan*, he begins to know evil; and on the fifth, *Chicchan*, he gathers together all the experience of his life. On the sixth, *Cimi*, he dies. On the seventh *Man-Ik*, from *Manzal-Ik* (pass through the spirit) he overcomes death.

Now he must plunge into the lower regions; he must struggle to overcome the material state. This is the eighth day, *Lamat*, the sign of Venus. On the ninth day, *Muluc*, he reaps the reward of his effort; and on the tenth, *Oc*, he enters fully into the uttermost depths of matter in order, on the eleventh day, *Chuen*, to burn without flame. In other words, he suffers

Onyx marble bowl, late classic Maya style. On the side shown *top* a priest is presenting a votive jar bearing the *kan* cross. *Bottom*, another aspect of the bowl, the decoration of which records an offering, probably to the North Star god, on a particular day, Imix. The symbols represent the Earth. The inscription on the rim refers to both the god and the day, and to a 'distance number' reading to and from the day 4 Ahau when all twenty-year periods – *Katuns* – ended.

Overleaf, left: the Temple of the Inscriptions at Palenque, one of the great Maya cities. The temple was built about the sixth century A.D. and a crypt was used as a mausoleum for nobles and priests. Right: the temple at Malinalco. The building was begun about 1475 and remained unfinished when the Aztec nation fell to the Spaniards under Cortés. The temple contains a circular shrine of the knightly orders of eagle and jaguar.

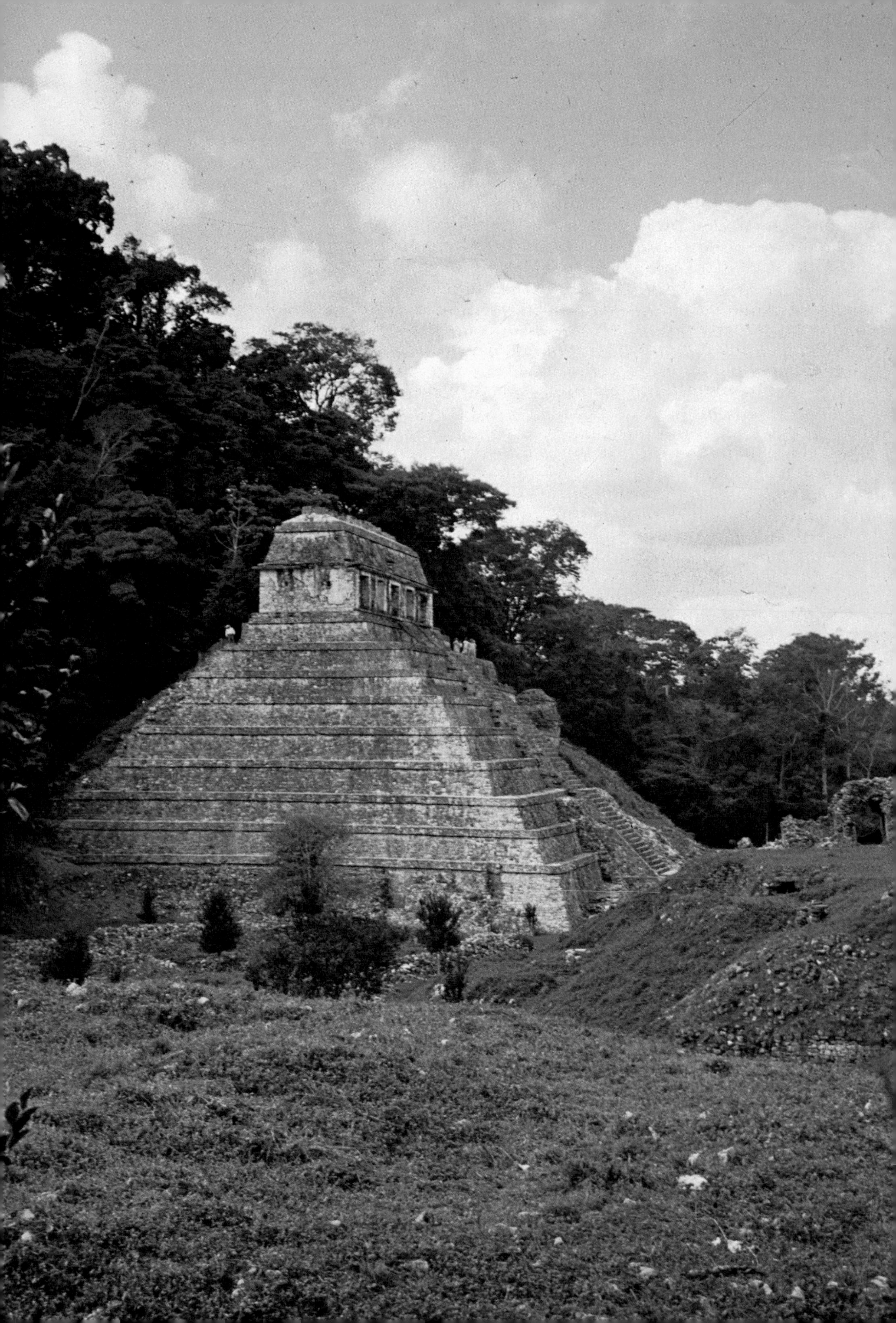

the greatest possible agony. On the twelfth day, *Eb*, he begins to climb the ladder, a long process which continues through the thirteenth day, *Ben*, (which represents growing maize) until on the fourteenth *Ix* (the jaguar god), he is washed entirely clean. This allows him on the fifteenth day, *Men*, to become perfect, but still he does not possess the full light of consciousness, which comes to him on the sixteenth day, *Cib*. On the seventeenth day, *C'haban*, he shakes off the last traces of ash clinging to him from the material world. 'Ash' is the word specifically used and it suggests that he has been purged by fire. On the eighteenth day, *Edznab*, he is made perfect. By the nineteenth day, *Cauac*, his divine nature is manifest. On the twentieth and last day, *Ahau* (god), he becomes one with the divinity.

There could scarcely be a clearer picture of physical birth, followed by death to the world of forms, and a rebirth on the plane of pure spirit. A distinction between the two processes of universal creation on the one hand and the cycle of man's birth and death on the other is clearly made. In the *Chilam Balam* description of the whole of creation, the series of days begins with *Chuen* (burning without flame), whereas the human cycle begins with the womb. The idea of creation beginning with a burning without flame exists in the Nahua myth of creation, where the universe comes into being through the voluntary suffering of the humblest of the gods. The creation of the days, according to the *Chilam Balam* ends with *Muluc* (and by inference with *Oc*, which for some reason is not mentioned in the *Chilam Balam* version). This is the point where the pilgrim enters fully into matter.

The Aztec-Nahua day-names give a more confused picture, but if we begin from the first day of the series, and not from the eleventh as in the Maya journey through twenty steps, we get interesting parallels on some rungs of the ladder. The Aztec days, their compass points, and their patron deities, are as follows:

1. Cipactli. Water-serpent	E	Tonacatecuhtli. Male creator
2. Ehecatl. Wind god	N	Quetzalcoatl. As wind god
3. Calli. Temple	W	Tepeyollotl. Heart of the mountain
4. Quetzpallin. Lizard	S	Huehuecoyotl. God of dance
5. Coatl. Snake	E	Chalchihuitlicue. Water goddess
6. Miquiztli. Death	N	Tecciztecatl. The moon god, he who is to be found in the innermost twist of the conch shell
7. Mazatl. Deer	W	Tlaloc
8. Tochtli. Rabbit	S	Mayahuel. Goddess of drink
9. Atl. Water	E	Xiuhtecuhtli. Fire god
10. Itzcuintli. Dog	N	Mictlantecuhtli. God of death
11. Ozmatli. Monkey	W	Xochipilli. God of flowers
12. Malinalli. Grass or thorns used in penitential acts	S	Patecatl. Husband of Mayahuel
13. Acatl. Reed used for arrow shafts	E	Tezcatlipoca
1. Ocelotl. The Mexican tiger	N	Tlacolteutl. Earth goddess
2. Quauhtli. Eagle	W	Xipe. The flayed god
3. Cozcaquauhtli. Vulture	S	Itzpapalotl. Obsidian butterfly
4. Ollin. Movement	E	Xolotl. Twin to Quetzalcoatl
5. Tecpatl. Stone knife	N	Tezcatlipoca
6. Quiahuitl. Rain	W	Chantico. Fire goddess
7. Xochitl. Flower	S	Xochiquetzal. Flower goddess

Huehueteotl or Xiutecuhtli, the fire god, one of the Companions of the Night. His worship was the occasion for a cruel sacrifice, when human victims were caste alive on burning coals before their hearts were removed. This head is part of a jadeite statue found at Teotihuacán.

The male creator stands with the water serpent at the head of the list. Then wind is breathed into the still formless mass, and a temple is created with wisdom (Tepeyollotl, the heart of the mountain) at its core. After two more days we reach death and the god folded in the shell, ready in the womb to be reborn of water. It is interesting that twice (at the signs Atl and Quiauitl) the day sign and the ruling deity make a firewater pair, representing 'burning water', one of the paradoxes which according to Nahua philosophy had to be solved by enlightenment. Similarly the deity representing 'blossoming war' (the obsidian butterfly, the war within the heart that leads to truth) stands opposite the predatory vulture.

As to the compass points, the years beginning with eastern signs were supposed to be fertile; those beginning with the north, variable; those with the west, good for man but bad for vegetation; and those with the south, hot and waterless. The Companions of Day and Night, and also the patrons of each of the twenty days, spread a special influence, either good, bad, or indifferent, and the science of Mexican and Maya astrology was based on the interpretation of the various combinations of signs. If a child was born on a good sign he was baptised at once; if on a bad, the evil influence might be mitigated by holding his baptism later to coincide with a good omen. The twenty day-signs may have been related each to a given heavenly body, but the chronicles shed little light on this aspect of the calendar. In the Maya series, the order of creation of the days emphasises the essential suffering inherent in matter, and the fact that the spirit must of necessity live within the material world; while the calendar order of the days stresses the corollary, that a man is only fully born and fully alive when he has overcome matter and reached pure spirit. Thus an equilibrium is established between man's inner and outer worlds. Matter must not be denied, but if man lives only in matter, his purpose on earth is not fulfilled. Evidently the Mayas did not make the mistake of submerging themselves in inner light while forgetting the outer world, though it is very possible that the degeneration of both Maya and Nahua religions, which had occurred before the Spaniards arrived in the New World, was brought about because the earlier equilibrium maintained between the two aspects of creation – matter and spirit – was lost.

A priest's head carved in relief in slatestone. The disk formed the back of a mirror which had a reflecting surface of iron pyrites. Totonac style, from the Veracruz region.

Below: a jaguar from one of the carved friezes at Teotihuacán. In ancient Mexico the jaguar was the creature of the era of the Fourth Sun – the era which preceded ours.

Right: an Aztec funerary mask with jade inclusion in the mosaics. The peoples of ancient Mexico were masters of the art of mask carving and decorating, using them to represent their gods, as votive offerings, as cult objects or, as in this case, to accompany the burial of persons of high rank.

The Legend of the Five Suns

It may well be that the era of the Fifth Sun, in which we are now supposed to be living, is in decline. Creatures on earth suffer continual testing by the gods, and if any species fails it perishes with the Sun to which it belongs. Both Maya and Nahua myths affirm this, and there are various versions of the legend of the birth and death of Suns.

In a manuscript called the *Annals of Cuauhtitlán*, one Nahua version relates that the first of five eras – four of which have long since died – was symbolised by an ocelot. This was the reign of instinctive power dwelling in animal form and in the dark. None of its human inhabitants were saved from extinction – the ocelots devoured them all. Then came the Sun of Air, the era of pure spirit that might at some future date become incarnate. But for the moment the necessary redeeming principle was absent, and the men of this age were turned into monkeys. After this came the Sun of the Rain of Fire, but its creatures were destined also to perish, except for the birds who were able to fly to safety. Last of the four Suns was the Sun of Water, during which the fishes of the sea were created. But this Sun perished by flood.

The Four Suns of animal energy earth, air, fire, and water evidently represent the four elements. Each by itself was doomed to die. Only when the Fifth Sun was born – *Naollin* (Four Movements) – was it possible for the separate elements in creation to come together and form the living sun of today. We cannot, however, take it for granted that this Sun is immortal. It can become immortal only if mankind climbs the ladder of redemption which we have seen represented in the names of the twenty days of the Maya calendar. The Nahuas too had a symbolism for this regenerative process that is the chief aim of creation: if the aim is not fulfilled, the world must be destroyed.

A folk dance performed today by groups of Mexican Indians, and which is evidently a vestige of preconquest ritual, represents the Four Suns dancing and dying each in turn. They come to life again only through the power of the Fifth Sun, who gyrates at great speed in the centre. Again we see the four elements inert and helpless when separate, life-giving when joined in movement.

In some versions of the Nahua legend the order of creation is changed. First comes the Sun of Water, then of Air, then of Fire, and then of Earth. One story tells how, when the first Sun was destroyed, a human couple sheltered in a cave and were thus saved from the flood. A man and a woman were also able to escape from the second cataclysm, and they took with them the Promethean gift of fire which was in its turn to destroy the Third Sun. When the Fourth Sun came to an end, man rescued certain nourishing plants and flowers and was able to begin life anew in the era of the Fifth and present Sun.

During one of these ages, the supreme god sent for the human pair, Tata and Nena, and told them to make a hole in a great tree and to hide in it. When the flood came they would be saved, they were told, but only if they were not greedy and did not eat more than a single maize cob each. The man and woman remained safely in their hole until the waters receded. When at last they emerged, they saw a fish, and they made a fire on which to roast it. The gods saw the smoke rise into the air and were very angry. As a punishment Tata and Nena were amputated of a portion of their heads and transformed into dogs. Because they had disobeyed the gods, they forfeited that part of the brain which distinguishes man from animals.

Quetzalcoatl, the morning star or the planet Venus, being swallowed by the serpent, earth, as day breaks and the sun returns. From the *Codex Vaticanus*.

The sanctuary of the Temple of the Jaguars at Chichén Itzá, on the wall of the ball court. The adventures of the twins of the *Popol Vuh* are reflected in much of Mayan art and architecture: they escaped death in a House of Jaguars and defeated their enemies on a ball court.

The Twins of the Popol Vuh

The gods of ancient America were perpetually trying to evolve a living thing that would have the capacity of knowing and worshipping its maker. They found this no easy task, and the Maya *Popol Vuh* is in essence the story of their efforts. The deer and the birds and all four-footed animals could only hiss and scream, says the sacred book, but could shape no word of praise. Above all, they could not pronounce their maker's name. Firmly they had to be told: 'We shall fashion other creatures to obey us. Accept your lot. Your flesh shall be torn apart. Thus shall it be...'

And a little later the chorus of gods cries out in a fit almost of pessimism: 'What shall we do to be invoked and remembered on earth? We have made attempts already with our first creatures, our first creations, but we could not persuade them to praise or adore us. We must try to make obedient creatures who will feed and sustain us.'

So they made a man of clay, but he was too soft and had no mind. He could not stand upright, and he dissolved too easily in water. Then they made men of wood, and these could talk and multiply but had neither souls nor minds. They forgot their Creator and walked on all fours. A flood was sent to destroy them, and even the implements they invented rose against them – the earthen pots, the plates and skillets and the grinding stones – and accused them of hard-heartedness. These inanimate things had been left to blacken on the fire as if they could feel no pain. The dogs who were the wooden men's domestic animals also accused them, and in the commotion that followed the men were turned into monkeys, simulating man but without intelligence.

Next there arose an extraordinary impostor called Vucub-Caquix, who professed to be the sun, the light and the moon: 'My eyes are silver, bright and shining like precious stones, like emeralds. My teeth shine like perfect stones, like the face of heaven. My nose shines from afar like the moon. My throne is of silver, and the face of the earth is alight when I stand before my throne.'

It was obvious to the gods that before true men could be made, this impostor had to be overthrown, and a large part of the *Popol Vuh* is concerned with the war waged against him by the heavenly twins Hunapú god of the hunt, and Ixbalanqué, whose name means 'little jaguar'.

The twins noticed that Vucub-Caquix liked the fruit of a certain tree, so they lay in ambush, and when he came for his daily meal they fired arrows and wounded him. In the ensuing struggle the evil giant was able to unhinge one of Hunapú's arms and to make off with it. In the task of retrieving the arm the twins enlisted the help of an old man and an old woman. These two went in search of Vucub-Caquix and found him suffering from toothache as a result of one of his wounds. Claiming that they could cure his pain, and knowing that his strength lay in his teeth, the old people extracted them and replaced them with grains of maize. They also offered to cure his eyes, which they gouged out so that by now his vaunted beauty had all been taken from him and he was shown up as a hollow-cheeked old creature. The old couple did not fail, while attending the giant, to retrieve Hunapú's arm, which was easily fixed back into position.

A mask of the bat god. In the *Popol Vuh* he is Camozotz, who destroyed the twins' father by tearing off his head. Jadeite, from Monte Albán. The eyes and teeth are made of shell.

This was not by any means the end of the twins' struggle against evil, however, for Vucub-Caquix had two sons who took up the battle on their father's behalf. The elder was Zipacná, 'creator of mountains'. Four hundred warriors were fetching a log to prop up the roof of their house when Zipacná offered to help. He proved strong enough to carry the wood all by himself. The four hundred, who were on the side of the heavenly twins, then lured Zipacná into a deep pit where they hoped to bury him. The giant, seeing the trap, burrowed out an exit from which he was able to escape, leaving the four hundred rejoicing in their supposed victory. Gloating, they waited for the ants to come and devour their victim's corpse; and sure enough they were soon able to observe armies of them carrying bits of hair and finger-nail which Zipacná had cut off to lull the enemy into a sense of false security. Overcome with delight at the apparent success of their plot, the four hundred began a drunken orgy which put them at the mercy of Zipacná, who was still very much alive and only waiting for an opportunity to pull the house down about the heads of the four hundred. Not one of them escaped this disaster, but long after their death they were transformed into stars.

During the day Zipacná used to hunt along the river for fish and crabs, and during the night he carried mountains on his back. Hunapú and Ixbalanqué, wishing to avenge the four hundred, made a model, a delicious-looking and large crab. They put this in a cave at the foot of a high mountain, and then lured Zipacná inside. He was about to eat the apparently succulent crab when the mountain fell on top of him and crushed him.

However the second son of Vucub-Caquix, a demolisher of mountains,

A painted clay figure from Colima showing a dog carrying an ear of maize.

still remained at large. The heavenly twins went in search of him and engaged him in friendly conversation as he was levelling out a mountain. When he asked their names they said they had none but were merely hunters with gun and trap. They offered to lead this second son, Cabraca, to a splendid mountain. On their march he was surprised to find that they did not need ammunition in their blowpipes but could bring down birds with no more than a puff of air. The boys roasted the birds golden brown and Cabraca could not resist this tempting meal. He did not know that the twins had basted the birds with poisonous earth; and so the second son of Vucub-Caquix met his end.

It so happened that the father of the twins, one Hun-Hunapú, had been lured to the underworld to play ball. There he had been defeated and killed, his head hung on a calabash tree as a warning to any who dared interfere with the underworld people called Xibalba. But the calabash tree, which had been barren, immediately bore fruit and was venerated as being miraculous. A maiden heard the story and went in wonder to gaze upon it. Hun-Hunapú's skull spoke to her from its branches, asking her what she wished. 'All the other fruits are only skulls,' he told her, 'and will do you no good.' But the maiden insisted and stretched her hand out toward the skull, which spat into her palm and said: 'In my saliva and spittle I have given you my descendants. Now my head is uncovered. It is only a fleshless skull. Even so are the heads of great princes. It is only the flesh that makes them seem handsome, but when they die men fear their bones. So also is the nature of our progeny, which are like saliva and spittle... They do not lose their substance when they go, but they bequeath it to others. The image of the lord, of the sage, of the orator does not vanish but he leaves it to the sons and daughters whom he procreates. Even so have I done unto you. Return to earth and believe my words for it shall be so.'

The maiden, made pregnant by the spittle, gave birth to Hunapú and

The sacred city of Chichén Itzá dates from the sixth century A.D., and was the largest of the Toltec-Maya centres. The pyramid, seen here from the platform of the Temple of the Warriors, was dedicated to the plumed serpent.

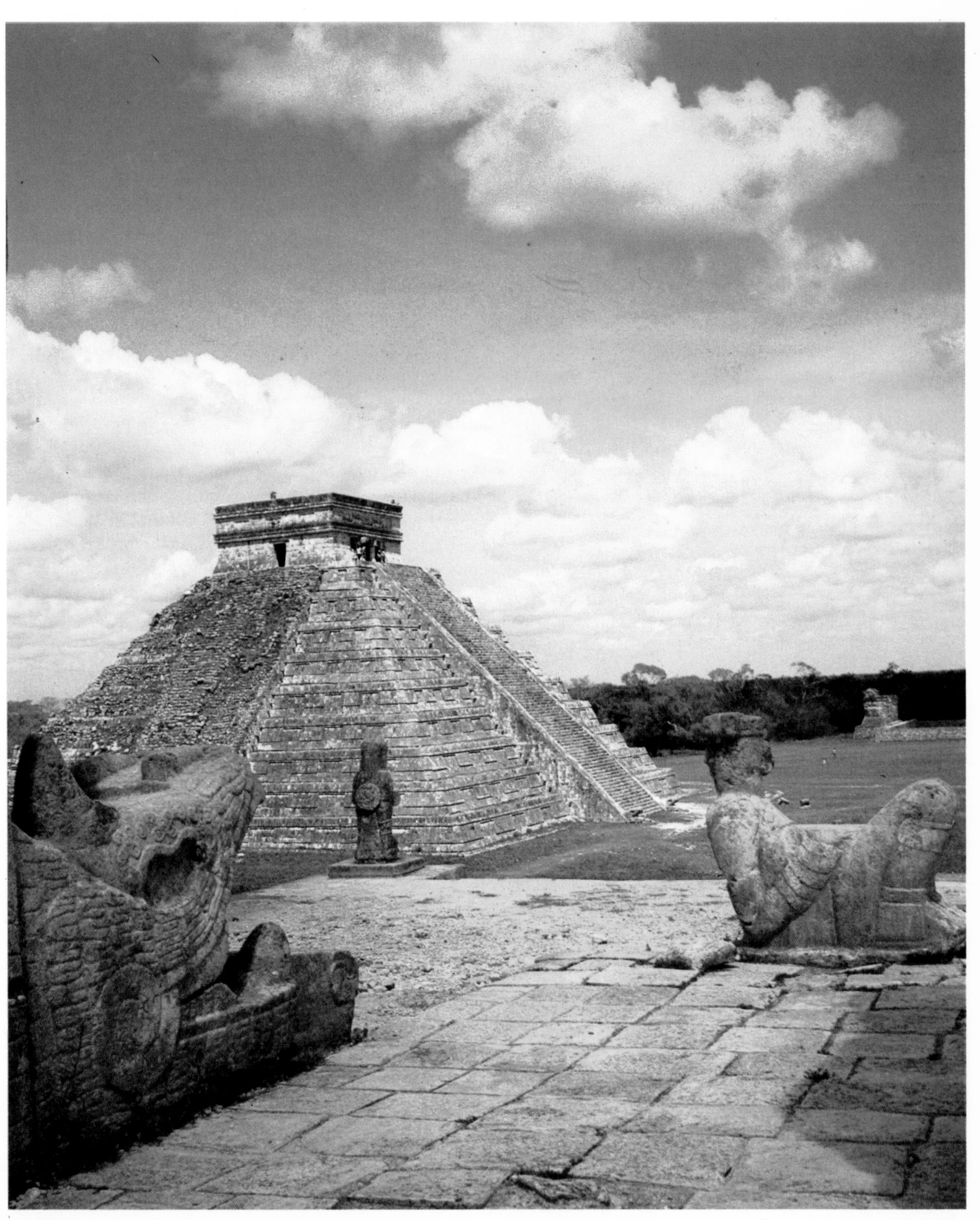

A palmate stone from Veracruz representing a sacrificed man – the incision can be seen which allowed for the removal of the heart. The *palmas* were part of the remarkably heavy accoutrements of the ball game players. Classic Veracruz style.

Ixbalanqué. But these two were at once persecuted by their envious half-brothers who had been models of good behaviour until then but who now idled and played the flute and sang while the twins had to provide them with food. To teach them a lesson, Hunapú and Ixbalanqué changed the jealous brothers into monkeys, and even their doting grandmother could not help laughing at their appearance.

Hunapú and Ixbalanqué believed it was their mission to go down to the underworld to avenge their father's death. In the nether regions they were subjected to a series of trials. At first they were made to enter a place called the House of Gloom and were given pine torches and cigars to provide them with comfort. They resisted the temptation of lighting either, and the next day were able to defeat the Xibalba in a ball game. Nevertheless the Xibalba had still the upper hand. The twins were shut up in a second prison, the House of Knives. Not only did they pass the night unharmed, but next day they were able to enlist the help of the knives and also of ants in order to cut a bouquet of flowers to present to their captors.

Next the twins passed the night in the House of Cold, but they found old logs and made a fire and did not die. Another trial was in the House of Jaguars, but the boys threw bones to the beasts and themselves escaped harm. They passed unscathed through the House of Fire, but nearly met total defeat in the House of Bats where Hunapú's head was struck off. The Xibalba took it to the ball court and hung it up as a trophy.

There now occurred an incident which seems to be connected with the idea of finding a suitable food for man. Ixbalanqué called all the animals together and asked them to choose the food of their liking. Some selected putrid stuff, others grass, others stone, others earth. But the turtle, as he waddled along behind the rest, climbed onto Hunapú's shoulders and took the shape of his head. It was no easy matter to model in Hunapú's features, but at length this was done.

Once more in possession of his full faculties, Hunapú joined his brother in planning the defeat of the Xibalba on the ball court. They caused the ball to bounce far over the court where a rabbit had been stationed in order to chase it and to encourage the underworld people to run after him. This he effectively did, allowing time for Ixbalanqué to steal back Hunapú's real head. When the Xibalba team returned, they found their opponents much stronger and the game ended in a tie.

By now the Xibalba were desperate to end the contest, and decided upon the drastic measure of burning the twins. They prepared a bonfire and then suggested that they should all fly four times over the flames. However, there was no need for such a ruse because Hunapú and Ixbalanqué, knowing by then their prowess had won them immortality, were fully prepared for death and threw themselves willingly onto the flames. Five days later they rose from the dead and appeared in the guise of fishermen, ragged and unkempt but gay enough to put on a dancing show for an assembled company and to work miracles. They burned houses and caused them to reappear undamaged, and cut themselves to bits but returned to life. The lords of the Xibalba were amazed and asked for a repeat performance. The twins feigned reluctance, professing to be ashamed of their ragtaggle appearance, but at length they were persuaded. Having sacrificed themselves and returned to life, they did the same for the Xibalba rulers except that the process of reversal was omitted. When the underworld plebeians saw that their rulers were dead, they admitted defeat and begged for mercy: 'Thus were the lords of the underworld overcome. Only by a miracle and only by transforming themselves could they have achieved their purpose.' They made themselves known to the underworld survivors, for the first time giving their names, and they pronounced sentence on their enemies: 'Because your great power and your race no longer exist, and because you deserve no mercy, you shall be brought low and shall no longer be allowed to play ball. You shall occupy yourselves fashioning earthen pots and tubs and grinding-stones for maize. Only the sons of the undergrowth and the desert shall be allowed to speak to you. The sons of nobles and the civilised vassals shall have no truck with you and shall shun you. Sinners, the wicked and sad, the unfortunate and the vicious, these shall welcome you...'

As to the twins, their grandmother was so delighted with their achievements that she worshipped them and gave them the title 'Those at the Centre'; green grasses grew in the house where they lived. Having avenged their father's death they became centred in themselves, and they were later translated to heaven where one became the Sun and the other the Moon. Their redeeming power was such that the four hundred killed by Zipacná also rose to heaven and became the stars – companions to the twins in the sky.

After this arduous preliminary work, after the descent of the twins to the underworld, their trials and triumph and translation, it became possible once more to return to the task of creating man 'to nourish and sustain' the gods. Four animals gathered together the special food, maize. These were the cat or jaguar, the coyote, the parrot, and the crow: 'Thus they discovered food, and this it was that entered into the flesh of man incarnate, of man made man. This was his blood. Of this was man's blood made. So maize was discovered because of the labour of man's forebears.'

The 'maize stone' from Veracruz. The god of water and the god of fertility preside over the planting of maize to ensure plenty for mankind. Nahua-Toltec culture, thirteenth to fifteenth centuries A.D.

A head modelled in clay, from the Veracruz region. A fine example of Totonac art.

Right: a worshipper, probably a priest, kneels to make an offering. A parrot seems to form part of his costume but it may also have been an offering. This vivid example of Maya low relief carving is from Jonuta in the state of Tabasco.

The first four created men had no parents but were born miraculously out of the effort of the gods. They were intelligent, far-sighted, and could contemplate all heaven and earth without having to move from a single spot. And they gave thanks to their creators.

But their very excellence was their undoing for the gods feared they might become puffed up with arrogance and self-confidence, and they decided to limit their powers. The great god who was the Heart of Heaven blew mist into men's eyes and clouded their sight so that it was like a looking-glass dimmed by breath. Their last state reflects the situation of man to this day: with intelligence of a kind unpossessed by animals, but seeing creation as through a glass darkly.

The final chapters of the *Popol Vuh* seem to be a straight history of the tribes that issued from the first four men and their wives. The author of the tale was an anonymous Guatemalan Indian who lived after the Spanish conquest and was influenced by Christianity. In a preamble he tells us that his version is only a reconstruction of a narrative written down long before but 'concealed from the searcher and the thinker'.

'Splendid were the descriptions and the tales of how all heaven and all earth were created and divided into four parts; how the whole was split and the sky divided. And the measuring rod was brought and was stretched out over the sky and the earth, to the four angles and corners as was told by the Creator and Maker, the Mother and Father of Life, of all created things, He who gives breath and thought, She who engenders children, He who protects people's happiness and that of the human race, the wise man, he who meditates on the goodness of all that exists in heaven and on earth and in the lakes and sea.'

Splendid as the best passages of the *Popol Vuh* may be, one feels that

something has been omitted from the twins' adventures, which flag and appear juvenile at times. It is easy enough to bring miracles out of a hat when all the laws of creation can be suspended at the stroke of a pen, and one does not feel that Hunapú and Ixbalanqué earned their triumph by self-sacrifice or that they acquired their powers by any hard road, as the plumed serpent Quetzalcoatl did. The original story may well have expressed a greater sense of compassion and of genuine effort at spiritual transformation, however, for the basic and familiar clues are all there: the need for worship; the absolute necessity of finding the right food for man; the inevitable process of a descent to the underworld before regeneration can take place; the overcoming of self-destroying pride and vanity and unmerciful power.

A tale told today in the state of Veracruz is very similar in certain aspects to the *Popol Vuh* story and shows not only that Maya influence spread northward along the coast but also that the legend of the origin of maize was and still is at the core of American Indian thought.

The Veracruz maize legend

In the Veracruz version of the story, maize is represented by a clever little fellow called Homshuk. An old couple had discovered him, hatched out of an egg. Even at the moment of his birth his hair was golden, and as soft as the silk down which clings to the ears of maize. After seven days of life his adventures began.

He was jeered at by lesser breeds like minnows and thrushes and other small creatures who declared him ridiculous, not understanding that he was inherently noble and specially endowed. He killed those who made fun of him but his foster-parents became uneasy; they feared the strange child, and decided to murder him while he slept. But they completely misunderstood the child's nature – it was only his mortal shape which lay asleep, his real self was outside, on the roof. The plot recoiled on the head of his foster-father, who was killed instead, and the boy was then persecuted by his foster-mother.

He warned her; 'Let me be. I am very strong and I can destroy you. I am destined to give food to all mankind.'

She paid no heed, and one day tried to destroy him by surrounding him in a curtain of flame. But he managed to escape, and after some wandering made his way to the seashore. There he sat down and began to play on a drum.

The drumming was heard from far away by a great lord, Huracán, who sent a messenger to find out who was making all the noise. To the messenger Homshuk replied;

'I am he who sprouts at the knees. I am he who flowers.'

Huracán thought that the boy was trying to avoid giving his name; he must be an evil spirit, a *nagual*, who wished to remain unknown and thus beyond harm. In the face of what seemed persistent animosity, Homshuk invoked the help of a tortoise who carried him across the sea to the very bastion of Huracán himself.

Here, for offenders against the great lord, there were three kinds of prison. In one there were serpents, in another rapacious tigers, and in another arrows in constant flight. After a night spent in the serpent prison Homshuk was found next morning sitting quietly on the hungry viper's back. The same thing happened with the tigers. The arrows, too, fell harmlessly to the ground and with extreme docility – considering their magical nature – allowed themselves to be made into a bundle for his use in protecting himself, so that he might fulfil the task of providing food for mankind. So the redeemer Homshuk vanquished in turn man's serpentine instincts, his dark tiger nature, and his penetrating, arrow-like, human wickedness. Huracán however was still unable to understand the true nature of his adversary, and invited him to a stone-throwing competition. This Homshuk won with the aid of a woodpecker who, when the lad's stone had been cast, made the characteristic pecking sound which seemed to suggest that the stone was rebounding far away across the ocean. Huracán's stone on the other hand made no sound at all, and Homshuk was conceded the victory.

Then Huracán decreed that Homshuk be swung in a hammock over the ocean, but when Homshuk had reached half way over the water he returned, saying that he could see already how easy the journey was going to be, and that Huracán and his people should go first. After a disastrous voyage Huracán capitulated and offered to keep the lad well watered – it seems as if by now he had taken plant form – so that the maize might grow for man's sustenance.

The details may be different, but the general similarity to the *Popol Vuh* story is clear enough, and we now see that the contest between Huracán, the Heart of Heaven, and the twins (in the *Popol Vuh*) or Homshuk (in the Veracruz story) was a contest not so much between good and evil as between the unharnessed forces of nature (Huracán) and the control exercised by what the Nahua poets would have called a 'man made man', a man who had found the true food, maize, which in so many parts of the world has been a symbol of death and rebirth. The key to an interpretation of the story lies in the fact that Homshuk is hatched out of an egg into a higher life. There is also his pretence at sleep when he was really outside on the roof, surveying the whole scene and in command of it, so that he could kill the incomprehending man, his foster-father, and escape from the old woman. And again there are Homshuk's words to the serpents and the tigers and the arrows: 'I am a strong man, and I must live in order to give food to mankind.' But even more striking is the description he gives of himself, 'I am he who flowers.'

The Veracruz legend forms a link between the *Popol Vuh* and the legends of the Mexican plumed serpent which we shall study later. The struggle between Huracán and the twins, or Huracán and Homshuk, is the same struggle we shall find between the redeeming plumed serpent Quetzalcoatl and the contradictory, wayward Tezcatlipoca. The egg theme and the hatching of a creature with totally new possibilities is echoed in some frescoes found in a priest's dwelling at Teotihuacán near the site of the monumental pyramids.

The Homshuk story is also connected with a theme found in fairy tales the world over, of a very small or very lowly creature whose magical capacities are so great as to give power over giants and other strong adversaries. This theme is common in surviving pre-Hispanic folk lore, as for example in the story of a man who, however many trees he felled during the day, always found them standing on the following morning. A tiny supernatural creature was defeating all his efforts to clear away the timber. There is also the story of a man who mourned his dead wife because he now had nobody to cook for him. To his astonishment, when he returned home one evening he found the floor clean and freshly swept, freshly-prepared maize pancakes and all kinds of food were ready for him. One day, returning home early, the man noticed the skin of his faithful dog lying on the floor and, much to his astonishment, a beautiful woman bending over the cooking pot. Unknown to him, his lowly dog had been his housekeeper.

Left: this Olmec carving from the Veracruz region has a strong resemblance to many Egyptian low reliefs. The bearded figure shown here is probably a priest; the yoke around the waist and the elaborate headdress suggesting a connection with a ball game ritual.

Below: a ball-game marker, carved from stone. From Teotihuacán.

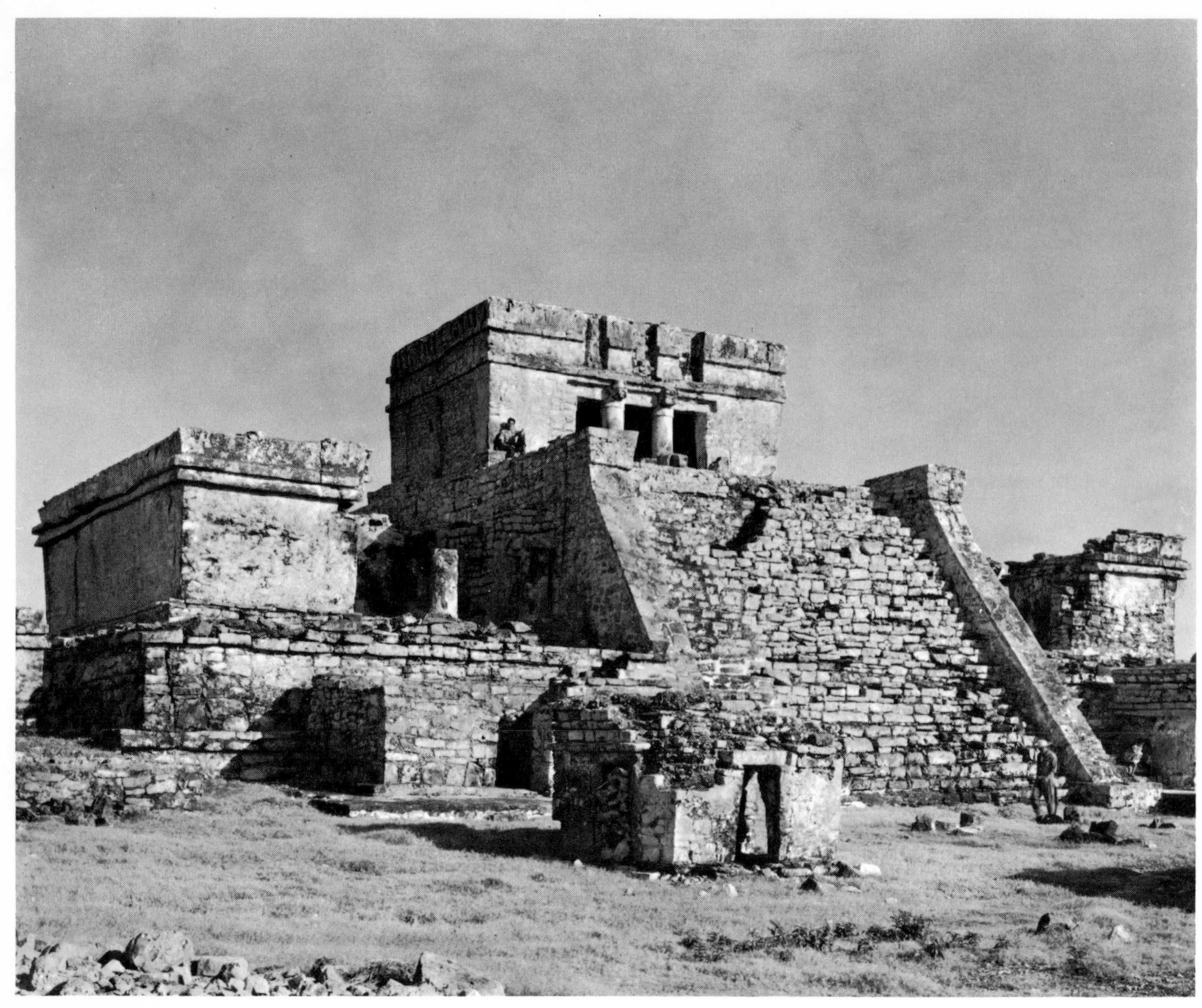

The temple of Tulum, a city founded by the Mayas in the sixth century A.D. near the seashore of Quintana Roo. The holiness of the temple persists – even today it is used by the Indians for religious rites, and they burn the same incense known to the Mayas.

Men of Gold

Returning now to the theme that man, if he is to be truly man, must praise his maker, we find a particularly delightful peasant version of it put by the Mexican novelist Rosario Castellanos into the mouth of her own childhood's nannie. It is probably as near as possible a verbatim account from this illiterate but nevertheless wise and cultured old woman. The story deserves to be quoted in full for its beauty and humanity and because it is evidence that the old myths live still in the minds of the peasants of south-east Mexico and Guatemala – the one-time Maya lands:

'...They were only four in number, the lords in heaven. Each one sat on his chair and rested. For the earth had already been made, just as we see it now, its lap heaped high with bounty. The ocean had already been made, before which everyone who sees it trembles. The wind had already been made to be the guardian over all things. But man was not yet made. Then one of the four lords, the one dressed in yellow, said:

'"We'll make man, so that he may know us and his heart may be consumed with gratitude like a grain of incense."

'The other three agreed with a nod, and went to look for moulds in which to work.

'"What shall we make men of?" they asked.

'And the one who was dressed in yellow took a lump of mud and with his fingers drew in the face and the arms and the legs. The other three watched him and gave their consent. But when the little clay man was finished and was put to the test of water, he crumbled away.

'"Let's make a man of wood," said the one dressed in red. The others agreed. So he who was dressed in red lopped off a branch and with the blade of a knife he marked the features in. When the wooden man was made he was put to the test of water and his limbs floated; they didn't fall to pieces, and his features were not rubbed out. The four lords were satisfied. But when the mannikin was put to the test of fire he began to crackle and lose his shape.

'The four lords spent a whole night in parley until one of them, the one who was dressed in black, said, "My advice is that we make a man of gold."

'And he untied the gold he kept knotted in his handkerchief, and between the four of them they modelled him. One pulled out his nose, another stuck in his teeth, another drew the snail-shell of his ears. When the golden man was finished they tested him in water and in fire and the golden man came out even more beautiful and resplendent than before. Then the four lords looked at one another satisfied. And they set the gold man on the ground, and they waited, hoping he would recognize them and give them praise. But the gold man did not move, he did not even blink: he was quite silent. And his heart was like the stone of the sapodilla, very hard and dry. Then three of the four lords asked the one who had not yet given his opinion:

'"What shall we make man of?"

'And this last one, who was dressed neither in yellow nor in red nor in black, for he wore a garment that had no colour at all, said: "Let's make man out of flesh." And with his machete he cut off the fingers of his left hand. And the fingers jumped into the air and fell into the midst of things, and never suffered the tests of water and fire. The four lords could scarcely make out what the men of flesh looked like, because distance had shrunk them to the size of ants. The effort they made to see the men of flesh inflamed the four lords' eyes, and with so much rubbing of them they grew drowsy. The one with the yellow robe yawned, and his yawn opened the mouths of the other three. And they fell asleep, for they were tired and old. In the meantime on earth the men of flesh scurried to and fro like ants. They had already learned which fruit is good to eat, with what big leaves they could protect themselves from the rain, and which animals don't bite.

'One day they were astonished to see standing in front of them the man of gold. His glitter struck them between the eyes, and when they touched him their hands turned cold as if they had touched a snake. They stood there waiting for the man of gold to speak. The time came to eat, and the men of flesh gave the man of gold a morsel. The time came to go away, and the men of flesh carried the man of gold with them. And day by day the hardness of the heart of the man of gold was softened, until the word of gratitude the four lords had placed within him rose to his lips.

'The lords woke up to hear their names pronounced among the psalms of praise. And they looked to see what had happened on earth while they were sleeping. And they approved what they saw. And from that moment they called the man of gold rich and the men of flesh poor. And they ordered things in such a way that the rich man should care for the poor and shelter them, since it was the rich man who benefited by the poor men's acts. And the lords so ordered it that the poor should

The goddess Mayahuel seated on a shell shared by a serpent and a tortoise. Behind her is a maguey plant in flower. As a farmer's wife she discovered that the juice of the plant, when fermented, made a beverage inducing content – pulque. For this benefit to both gods and men she was made a goddess. *Codex Laud.* Bodleian Library.

The ancient Mexicans were well-versed in the properties of plants which contained vision-inducing drugs, and regarded them as a boon from the gods. This leaf from the *Codex Magliabecchi*, which dates from the years immediately after the conquest, shows an Indian (bottom right) eating a magic mushroom. Xipe Totec, god of the growing seed, can be seen in the upper left-hand corner and the maize goddess Chicomecoatl in the upper right. The god of death Mictlantecuhtli watches, bottom right.

Below: a ceremonial axe-head, Totonac style, carved in the features of an ocelot. From the Veracruz region.

answer for the rich before the face of Truth. That is why our law says that no rich man can enter heaven if a poor man does not lead him by the hand.'

Communicating with the gods

The stress laid in the myths on the need for communication between men and gods demonstrates the enormous importance that was attached to revelation. Communication of this kind could be achieved if the neophyte purified his heart and mind, so that the gods could speak through men in poetry and song, and so that men might communicate their longing to the gods. Whereas the purification of heart and mind required fasting and presumably mental and emotional disciplines (there are many recorded instructions to the students in the colleges suggesting that discipline was rigorous), the process of getting into touch with the deities could be intensified and quickened by the use of drugs distilled from native plants.

The juice of the maguey cactus, today distilled as tequila or fermented to make the poor man's drink, pulque, was widely used by the ancients. So also were tobacco, copal resin for its incense, and a wide range of hallucinogenic plants whose properties are only now being studied by modern pharmacologists and psychologists. There is, for instance, a seed called *ololiuqui* from which the ancients brewed a vision-inducing infusion. A plant called *toluah* of the datura family, is mentioned in the *Codex Badianus* written in 1552 by Martín de la Cruz, an Indian doctor; and there were various mushrooms including *teonanacatl*. The small tuberous cactus, *peyotl*, and the larger species of agave from which mescalin is extracted, have served Aldous Huxley and others for their experiments on states of heightened perception.

It has been found that *ololiuqui* and probably a number of other such drugs are chemically allied to lysergic acid, the most popular modern vision-inducing drug; so it would seem that modern chemists are beginning to catch up with the instinctive lore of pre-Hispanic Indians.

To the ancient Mexicans, plants yielding hallucinogens were sacred and god-given. The *Codex Magliabecchi*, which dates from just after the

Xiutecuhtli as pictured in the *Codex Fejervary-Mayer*. It is believed that the ancient Mexicans, in their sacrifices to the fire god, made use of their knowledge of drugs to dull the sufferings of the victims.

conquest, shows an Indian eating a magic mushroom while the god of the land of the dead keeps guard over him as if showing him the spirits of those who have passed out of earthly life. Sahagún describes how, after having eaten and drunk vision-inducing drugs, the Indians gathered together to dance and sing for sheer joy. He lists dozens of divine plants used by the Indians to such an extent that in 1616 the Inquisition warned against the 'heretic perversity' of those who indulged in them, proclaiming that they received revelations through their use.

All intoxicating drinks, including the hallucinogens, were under the patronage of the goddess Mayahuel who was originally only a simple farmer's wife. One day she saw a mouse in a field and tried to kill it, but it escaped, making circles round her fearlessly and laughing at her. She noticed that it had been nibbling at the stem of a maguey plant, and that some cloudy sap had emerged. Mayahuel collected the sap in a gourd and took it home to share with her husband. As they drank together they became very loving and life seemed very good. So the couple introduced the pleasant beverage to the gods, who as a reward made Mayahuel goddess of pulque, her husband becoming Xochipilli, Lord of Flowers and also incidentally of gambling. A picture in the *Codex Laud* shows Mayahuel naked, seated on a shell shared by a serpent and a tortoise. Behind her is a cactus in flower.

Peyote and hallucinogenic mushrooms, whose properties were known to the ancients, continue to be used both for healing and for divination. The Huichol Indians of west Mexico regard the peyote as a divine plant, and at certain times of the year they make long pilgrimages in search of it. Woollen rhomboid designs represent the eye of the god, and magical drawings of animals and flowers, laid out in wool glued onto a board, are used in the peyote ceremonies. One, in my possession, has a stylised fish at the centre, circled by two snakes that are in turn surrounded by some kind of leafy plant – the whole suggesting that the creator felt himself penetrating down into the primitive fish-serpentine-vegetative part of man's nature to receive an unusually unified view of his own place in it.

Among the Indians so-called 'magic mushrooms' are said to be eaten

only by special sages, who may nevertheless also prescribe them as a cure for certain illnesses; but a cult of them has arisen among some educated circles in the Mexican capital, and workers on their chemistry are watching with some uneasiness the possible results of bringing these ancient and obviously useful but powerful substances into the hands of sophisticated, often atheistic or at least agnostic pleasure-seekers.

The secret lore of the priest caste, which understood how to manipulate these drugs, was handed down from father to son, especially among a sect called the *Xochimalca*, or flower-weavers – that is, bringers of the godly state when the mind flowers into happiness. The use and abuse of hallucinogens may provide a clue to the perplexing riddle of the degeneration of the ancient cultures; for it is evident that the religion of Quetzalcoatl, the original one of redemption and mercy, had become almost transformed by the time the Spanish armies arrived in the New World. The soldiers were not unnaturally horrified by the mass human sacrifices and the superstitious adoration of a proliferation of gods and goddesses, some of whom appeared to be more properly demons. A genuine priesthood aware of its responsibilities and knowing that the ultimate purpose of inducing special states must be union with the godhead, would have been careful how they used their pharmacological knowledge. A degenerate priesthood could very quickly have discovered that the drugs gave them power, and would not have discriminated between evil and good.

For example, there was a herb called *petum* with analgesic properties if used as an ointment on the skin. Used in combination with an hallucinogen, and by a man unable to distinguish between power and cruelty on the one hand, and power allied to virtue on the other, *petum* could become a sinister instrument. A Spanish chronicler called Acosta described how: '...by means of this ointment they became witches, and saw and spoke to the devil. The priests, when smeared with this ointment, lost all fear, and became imbued with cruelty. So they boldly killed men in their sacrifices, going all alone at night to the mountains, and into dark caves, not fearing any wild beasts because they were sure that lions, tigers, snakes and other savage animals that breed in the mountains and forests would flee from them because of this *petum* of their god... This *petum* also served to cure the sick, and for children; and so they called it the divine remedy... so the people went to the priests and holy men, who encouraged the blind and ignorant in this error, persuading them what they pleased and making them pursue their inventions and diabolical ceremonies...'

This is a far cry from Quetzalcoatl, who could not bear to hurt any living thing. But if priests had lost all sense of responsibility, the degeneration is easily explained. As the idea of feeding the sun symbolically with 'hearts made god' became taken literally, so the use of special drugs would fortify the cruelty instead of acting as an adjunct to purification of the emotional life. The Nahuas knew the dangers that might arise when instruments of high knowledge fell into wrong hands, and a story about a poor rag-picker illustrates this. The rag-picker, who worked near the great temple of Huitzilopochtli, found a painted book that told him of a magic casket lying beneath the ninety-third step of the pyramid. It was impossible for him to move the stone alone, so he went in search of a priest, who agreed to help extract the casket provided the spoils could be suitably shared. At night they went together to the pyramid, brought out the casket which was bound by a silver chain, and opened it to find a magic rattle, a mirror that showed the future, a wand of power, a drumstick, and an almanac and book of spells. The priest knew how to make use of these objects, but the outcast rag-picker did not.

So the priest offered to buy the whole box for three hundred pieces of gold. As he was counting out the money, the rag-picker struck him on the head with the wand from the casket, killed him, and took him down to the river where he disposed of the body. Then the rag-picker set about trying to learn the mysteries, but without success. He was filled with fear because strange spirits seemed to play around him night and day. Disgusted with the casket and its contents, he tried to hurl it into the lake, but the priest rose out of the waters, snatched the casket, and then pursued the rag-picker back to the pyramid and killed him. The priest remained in possession of the casket, and one hopes that he used it thenceforth for more constructive things.

In our day a Spaniard, Francisco Guerra, now a research worker at the Wellcome Institute in London, has made a study of the drugs. He was lucky enough to have had the help of an indigenous Mexican botanist, J. Trinidad Pérez Nol, who helped him to gain the confidence of isolated groups of Indians. In a lecture given in London Dr. Guerra said:

'The consumption of up to ten or twelve *teonanácatl* mushrooms, after a period of slight muscular unco-ordination or inebriation, gives rise to a feeling of well-being and enjoyment, explosions of laughter, and the well-publicised coloured visions in three dimensions, followed by a deep sleep. Mazatec Indians still use it for divinations, but... doses of over fifty mushrooms are said to produce intense intoxication and permanent madness. Also when *peyotl* is ingested a feeling of well-being and visual hallucinations of a coloured nature are produced; some of them may be based in the remote past, others apparently cannot be related to any experience. Mental concentration is difficult, and external stimulations are transferred into mental hallucinations... Chemical variations in the molecular structure of mescalin suggests that the spectrum of action of these Mexican drugs can be enlarged and their action on the higher functions of the brain modified extensively.

'The rediscovery of this buried lore among the codices and ancient chronicles of Mexico and its pursuit both in remote Indian villages and in the laboratory has been an exciting adventure. However, the entering of this pharmacological legacy of the New World into the indiscriminating hands of Western civilization, unable to cope with its own drug problems of alcoholism and narcotics, must be regarded with apprehension.'

From Dr. Guerra's evidence it is clear that in ancient times any slackening or laxity among the users of hallucinogens could have brought about degenerate effects. But this was not always so, for the feast of mushrooms, which followed a 'feast of chieftains' and a 'feast of flags', was the supreme feast of revelation.

Sacrifice and humility

In any case, revelation was for the few who could understand the highest level of ancient religion. As we study the almost embarrassing plethora of myths of creation, it becomes clear that there are different levels among them. Some are closely related to physical fertility rites; others – somewhat confused and probably having reached us in degenerate form – present a harsh and not very attractive picture of a universe that is self-devouring and sternly self-perpetuating. Still others penetrate to the very essence of the creative process to emphasise its chief and most poignantly beautiful characteristics: its timelessness, its link with praise and adoration, and the need for sacrifice and humility if anything of value is to be attained.

Of all the myths stressing the sacrificial nature of creation, the most beautiful and complete is that of the creation of the Fifth Sun.

Left: an Olmec ceremonial stone knife from Villahermosa. A knife of hard stone was thrown to earth by the goddess Omecihuatl, and 1,600 heroes were born.

Below: a *macehual*, a young standard bearer of ancient Mexico. These youths were selected at an early age for religious rites, and could aspire to the highest honours in the state. Aztec stone carving.

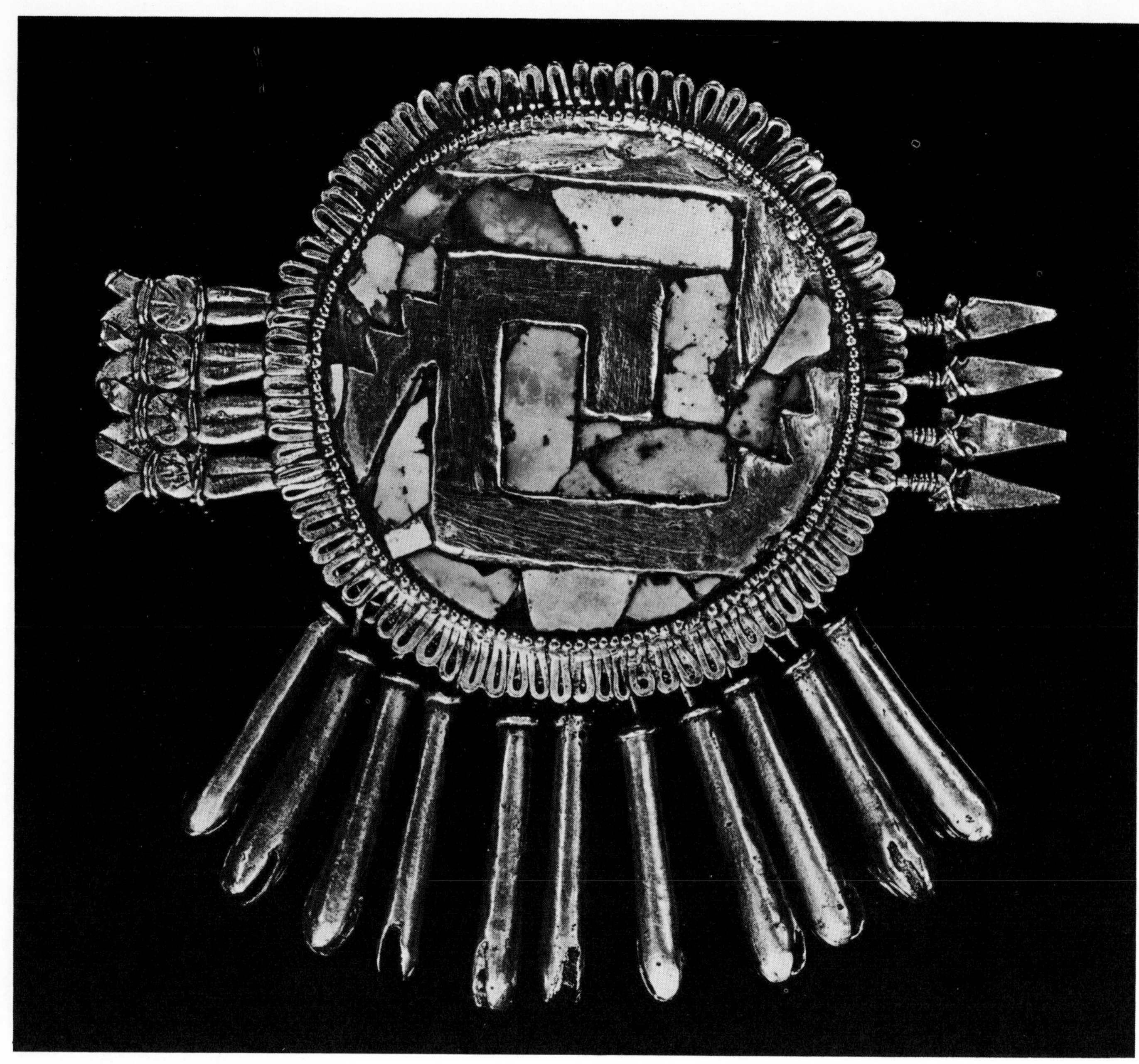

A pectoral in turquoise and gold from the Mixtec tombs at Monte Albán. The round shield and horizontal arrows constitute the sign of war. The war god of the Aztecs was Huitzilopochtli, but in the religious sense he was also involved in the eternal, sacred war between light and darkness and the rising and setting sun.

The Fifth Sun

Before there was day in the world – we are once again in that concept of timeless space – the gods met together and discussed who should have the task of lighting the new era. The gods' committee meeting was not unlike a human one; there was among them a braggart ready to come forward with an easy offer whose implications had evidently not been very carefully weighed.

A god called Tecciztecatl (whom we may remember as the deity of the death's head day, Miquiztli, and who later became acknowledged as the moon god) thought that perhaps he might earn some praise if he under took what at first glance seemed a simple assignment – to give light to the world. But the other gods, being sceptical, or deciding that one alone could not bring to completion so vast a task, asked for a second volunteer. Nervously they looked from one to another, and each in turn made his excuses.

Only one god, to whom nobody was paying the least attention because he was afflicted with scabs, remained silent. Here, it suddenly dawned upon the rest of the company, was useful expendable material.

'Be thou he that shall light the world, scabby one,' they said, not very respectfully, to the god called Nanautzin; and he replied, 'In mercy I accept your order. So be it.'

Then the two – Tecciztecatl and Nanautzin – spent four days in penance. Thus prepared, they then lighted a fire on a hearth built out of rock. Offerings must be made at this solemn time, and Tecciztecatl's – as befitted a proud god – were rich feathers instead of dead branches; nuggets of gold instead of hay; thorns wrought of precious stones instead of those from the maguey cactus; thorns of red coral to replace those obligatory ones tipped with blood; and the finest quality of copal.

But Nanautzin, instead of branches, offered nine green reeds tied in bundles of three. He offered hay and maguey thorns anointed with his own blood; and in place of copal he gave scabs from his sores.

To Nanautzin and Tecciztecatl the other gods built a tower as big as a mountain; and within it the assembled company did penance for another four nights. After the bonfire had burned for four days, and after the receptacles in which the offerings had been made were destroyed, the gods lined up in double file on either side of the fire and facing it. They spoke to Tecciztecatl saying:

'Tecciztecatl, jump into the fire!'

Tecciztecatl made ready, but the fire was large and hot, and he grew afraid, and dared not throw himself in, but turned away. Again he made ready, but shied off. Four times he tried, and four times flinched, and failed to summon sufficient courage. As it had been decreed that nobody was allowed to make more than four attempts, Nanautzin was then called in his place:

'Oh thou, Nanautzin, try thou.'

Nanautzin gathered all his courage together, closed his eyes, and rushed forward blindly, casting himself into the fire. He crackled and burned like one roasting. Ashamed, Tecciztecatl followed the scabby god's example and threw himself onto the flames.

The lowliest of the gods had shown the way; and the Sun, which later was to be made the reason for a demand that men's physical hearts be torn out, owed its very life to a greater, voluntary sacrifice.

The unblemished youth

It should be evident that the voluntary sacrifice of life for the sake of redeeming the world is a very different matter from mass murder and the tearing out of the hearts of unwilling victims. The earliest human sacrifices in ancient America were probably voluntary. At one of the most important feasts in the calendar, for instance, that of the god Tezcatlipoca, a single youth was killed apparently with his own consent. This boy was taken to be the earthly image of Tezcatlipoca, and for a year before his death he was made the centre of extraordinary reverence, cherished and treated with the greatest respect. He was taught to play the flute, to fetch and carry the reeds and flowers required for offerings. He was taught to hold himself well, to be courteous and gentle of speech. Those who met him kissed the earth and paid him reverential bows. He was free to walk about by day and by night, but he was always accompanied by eight servants dressed like palace lackeys. His vestments were those of a god.

Twenty days before he was to be sacrificed the keepers changed his clothes for those in which he would end his life. They married him to four virgins who had also received a careful upbringing and who were

Praying hands carved from stone. A pillar ornament from the Gulf Coast region.

given the names of four goddesses. Five days before the appointed feast, honour was paid to the youth as to a god, there being much feasting and dance. Finally the youth was placed in a canoe covered with a canopy. With him went his wives, and they sailed away to a place where there was a low hill. Here the wives were abandoned, and now only the eight servants accompanied the youth to a small and poorly equipped temple. Climbing its steps, on the first of them he broke one of the flutes he had played during his year of prosperity and cherishing; on the second he broke another, on the third another, and so on until he reached the highest part of the temple where the priests were assembled waiting to kill him. They stood in pairs. Binding his hands and his head, they laid him face upward on the block. A knife of stone was plunged into his breast. It gouged out his heart which was offered immediately to the Sun.

The ceremony was a myth acted out in real life. The myth was about man, who must learn to glorify god through sensual things, through fine clothes and music and dance, before he is worthy of breaking the senses one by one and losing his life in order to gain it.

The deified heart

The sacrifice of the youth was linked with a profound philosophical idea that only the true, the deified heart is worthy to become nourishment for the great star that maintains life on earth. The Nahua peoples believed that we are born with a physical heart and face, but that we have to create a deified heart and a true face. The ordinary word for heart was *yollotl,*

A Chac Mool figure from Chichén Itzá. The influence of the Toltec culture was strongly felt in certain periods of Maya history, and similar figures have been discovered in the great Toltec centre of Tula. They represent attendants of the rain god Tlaloc (or the Mayan Chaac) and these figures, adorned with shallow dishes to catch the rain, were carved to resemble the lumpy shape of floating clouds.

a word derived from *ollín*, movement. Thus the ordinary human heart is the moving, pumping organ that keeps us alive; but the heart that can be made by special efforts in life is called *Yoltéotl*, or deified. The phrase used to describe the face that we must make if we are to be truly men is *ixtli in yollotl*, which signifies a process whereby heart and face must combine. The heart must shine through the face before our features become reliable reflections of ourselves.

Thus heart-making and face-making, the growth of spiritual strength, were two aspects of a single process which was the aim of life and which consisted in creating some firm and enduring centre from which it would be possible to operate as human beings. Without this enduring centre, as the Nahua poet tells us:

> ...you give your heart to each thing in turn.
> Carrying, you do not carry it.
> You destroy your heart on earth.
> Are you not always pursuing things idly?

If we are unable to create this second heart and face, we are merely vagrants on the face of the earth. The idea of vagrancy is expressed in the word *ahuicpa*, which means literally 'to carry something untowardly' or without direction. There is another word, *itlatiuh*, which means to pursue things aimlessly. *Ahuicpa tic huica* means 'carrying, you do not carry it' – and this directionless carrying was believed by the Nahuas to be typical of man's ordinary state on earth. By accident we do not achieve direction, any more than we can be sure of travelling from London to Edinburgh by going to a station booking office and asking for the first ticket that comes to hand, or by thoughtlessly boarding the first bus that comes along because it happens to be moving.

But of course this idea of feeding the sun with a symbolic heart, created within a man's psyche, was very soon distorted. Offerings to the gods made in flowers picked from the meadows and the cornfields became offerings of enemy hearts torn out. As the friar Bernardino de Sahagún tells us:

'They used to make the prisoner climb on to the stone, which was round like a millstone. And when the captive was on the stone one of the priests... took a rope, which went through the eyelet of the millstone, and bound him by the waist. Then he gave him a wooden sword, which instead of knives had bird feathers stuck to the edge; and gave him four pine staves with which to defend himself and overthrow his adversary.'

In this way the prisoners were made to fight and kill one another, or alternatively the hearts were torn out by their captors. Either way it was the end of them, and the sun was left metaphorically licking its chops. The whole gory process is a long way from the Nahua ideal of creating the heart *Yoltéotl*, or of the Maya idea described by a modern student Domingo Martínez Paredez: 'One god who gave life and consciousness, and another who fashioned him, that is, who not only gave consciousness to man but at the same time formed and gave him human shape: only he had the virtue of being able to raise man above the other animals. So in Maya anthropogeny there exists the concept not only that consciousness is given to man, but also that it must be formed, and it is the gods' task to do this.'

This is the central idea and purpose of the Quetzalcoatl or plumed serpent myth, for Nanautzin is one manifestation of Quetzalcoatl. He is the plumed serpent in his lowliest state, but his self-sacrifice saves the universe from extinction and opens up latent possibilities not only for the heavenly bodies but also for man.

Tezcatlipoca, god of the smoking mirror, was patron of the knightly order of tigers (ocelots, the Mexican tiger). In this form he is pictured here, carved on one of the elaborate yokes which represented part of the accoutrements of the ball players. An unblemished youth was sacrificed, with his own consent, each year to this god. From Tajin, seventh to eleventh centuries A.D.

Overleaf, left: pottery figure of a seated Maya worshipper, probably during the month *Yaxkin*, which celebrated the firing of the fields to make ready for the new sowing. On that occasion all clothing and appliances were coloured blue and traces can be seen on the figure. The lips have been cut, probably in the offering of blood to the maize god Yum Caax. Late classic Maya, from Campeche.
Right: a barefoot Maya priest, modelled in clay. An example of the standard of pottery achieved in the culture centre of the island of Jaina off Campeche, which flourished about the sixth century A.D.

The side wall of the pyramid at Xochicalco, representing Quetzalcoatl as the plumed serpent.

The Quetzalcoatl myth

The myth of the plumed serpent is dazzling in its beauty. It is the complete fairy tale. All things change perpetually into something else, everything is elusive, intangible, yet permanent and true. The great bird-serpent, priest-king Quetzalcoatl, is the most powerful figure in all the mythology of Mexico and Central America.

From Teotihuacán on the high plateau to Chichén Itzá in Yucatán and farther south, he is a dominant motif on ancient monuments. Sometimes, with his open jaws, bifid tongue, and articulated spinal column, he is misinterpreted and misused. In modern Mexico he frequently appears on friezes, mosaics and paintings that are as sentimental, as far removed from the originals, as Victorian Gothic from Chartres. What the Eiffel Tower is to Paris, what the lions in Trafalgar Square are to London or the Statue of Liberty to the U.S.A., even so is Quetzalcoatl to post-revolution Mexico seeking to re-establish its old traditions.

In the incarnate form which he is supposed to have assumed at a certain moment in history, Quetzalcoatl was a great lawgiver and civiliser, inventor of the calendar or Book of Fate. He was a compassionate king who, like the Buddha, could scarcely bear to hurt any living creature. Demons tried constantly to persuade him to homicide and human sacrifice but – as the anonymous author of the *Codex Chimalpopoca* tells us 'he would never agree, because he loved his vassals the Toltecs, and his sacrifice was always of snails, birds, and butterflies'.

No one knows just who he was or whence he came. He therefore becomes fair game for every romancer, from D. H. Lawrence with his back-to-instinct philosophy, to others who equate him with Christ or turn him into a green and emerald Irishman. There are theories that he arrived in Mexico from Celtic lands or even from lost Atlantis.

Almost certainly there was more than one historical Quetzalcoatl. In ancient times the name was given to any priest who was supposed to have reached enlightenment. Laurette Séjourné, a French archaeologist living and working in Mexico, believes that Quetzalcoatl was a king living about the time of Christ. If it was he who discovered that maize was a good staple diet for human beings, then he must surely have existed much earlier. Carbon-14 datings show that maize was cultivated in the middle Americas about eight or nine thousand years ago. But the dates are tentative, some people having put them at eighty thousand years ago, which seems unlikely.

It is beyond dispute that a flesh-and-blood king did exist who was a great civiliser and lawgiver, an innovator in arts and crafts, and a man who stood high above his fellows in understanding and rectitude. So moral was he that he could never have condoned the human sacrifices that became, as we have seen, one of the central rituals in the religion of the Mexican high plateau. Such degeneration could scarcely have taken place quickly, even if aided and abetted by indiscriminate use of drugs. Therefore it can be assumed that the man Quetzalcoatl lived many centuries before the Aztecs, who arrived in Mexico at a late period, during the fourteenth century of our era.

A series of priests called Quetzalcoatl, however, adopted the name of the founder of their religion, and these were supposed to be 'perfect in all customs, exercises, and doctrines'. They lived chastely and virtuously, humbly and pacifically, comporting themselves with prudence and tact. They were supposed to be responsible, austere, loving and merciful and compassionate, friendly to all, devout and godfearing. This at any rate was the ideal pattern of the priest of the Mexican religion. That the truth often fell far short can be deduced from the bloodthirsty practices carried out in their name; but the first Quetzalcoatl, the man who created the myth, must have been of a different calibre.

Historically the facts are few. If we turn to the myth we shall see that it embodies a series of truths on different cosmic levels and which are in themselves ample proof of the existence at some time in the land of a great religious innovator. The Quetzalcoatl story exists: somebody must therefore have created it. If our aim is to study and understand it, it is really irrelevant whether the man who made it was the king of Tollan, as he is sometimes called, or whether he belonged to the civilisation of the Toltecs (master craftsmen) or to Teotihuacán (city of the gods) which is the site of the great Mexican pyramids; or even, eccentrically, whether he was Mediterranean or Irish or Chinese or, as some very respectable authorities have held, the apostle Thomas evangelising beyond the known world. The problem is nothing more than the hoary Bacon-Shakespeare controversy translated to Mexico. The question 'Who was Quetzalcoatl?' fades into the background as the myth speaks for itself.

To begin with there is the name, which has been analysed by Domingo Martínez Paredez. It is made up of *quetzal*, a rare bird with green feathers inhabiting the highlands of Chiapas and Guatemala, living in the tops of trees, seldom visible, and distinguished from other birds in having only

To hold the hearts of the sacrificed, *cuauhxicallis* or 'eagle vessels' were used, carved from stone and carefully decorated. The sides show eagle feathers, human hearts are represented on the rim, and signs signifying 'jewelled water' (blood) embody the idea of sacrifice. The glyph in the bottom represents the present universe. From Tenochtitlán, *c.* 1500 A.D.

The rain god Tlaloc scattering seeds. A prayer, or incantation, is indicated by the speech scroll issuing from his mouth. Mural painting from Teotihuacán, first to sixth centuries A.D.

Right: a pottery figure of Xipe Totec from one of the tombs at Monte Albán. He is shown here as the supreme penitent,his face scarred in a line from the eyebrows to the jaw and wearing a grimace of pain. Zapotec culture, eighth to eleventh centuries A.D.

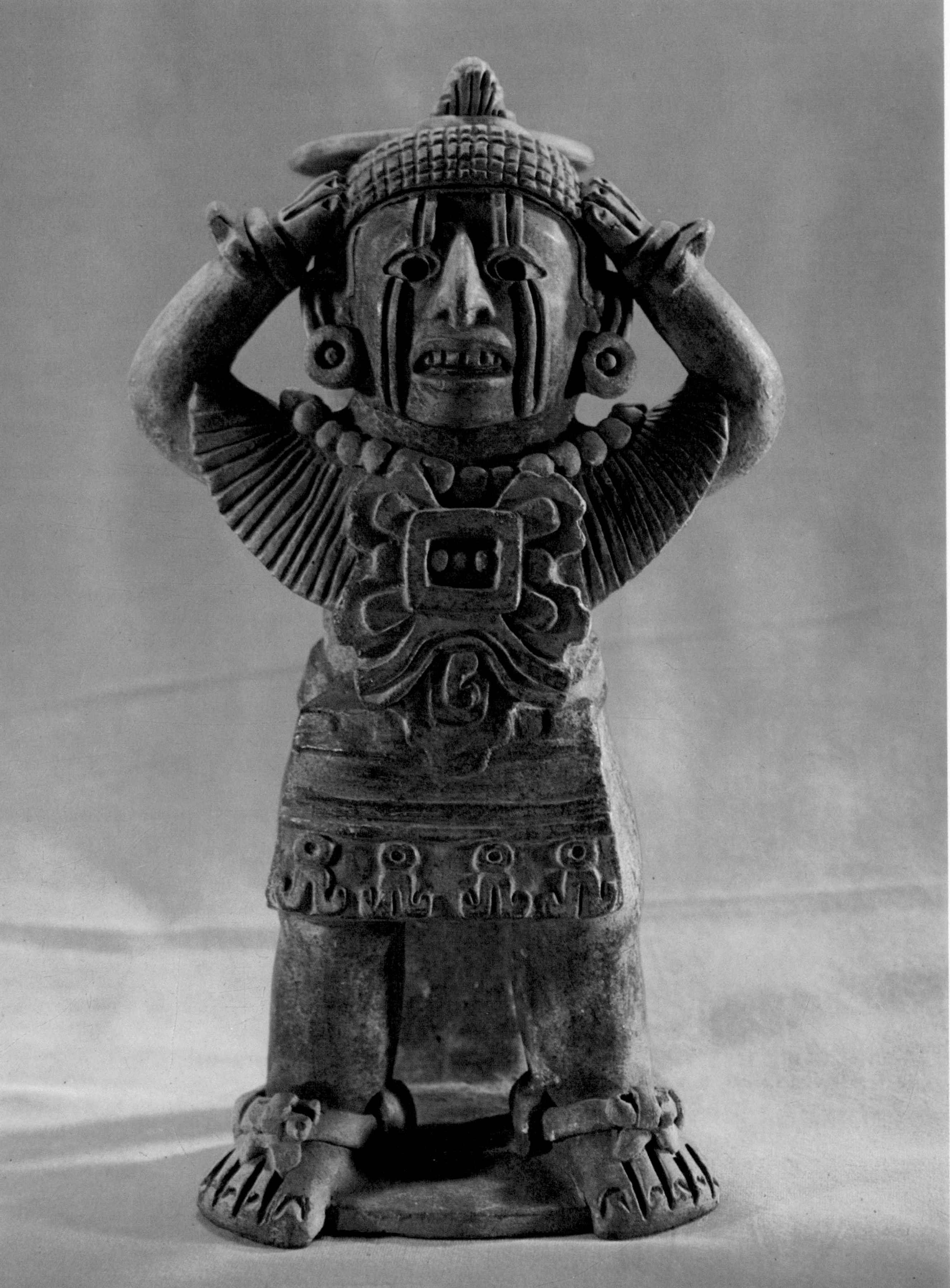

two front toes and almost no claws; and *coatl*, which is the Nahua word for snake but which is itself a combination of *co*, generic term for serpent or snake in the Maya language, and *atl*, the Nahua word for water.

From this derivation it is evident that the Mayas and the high-plateau Nahua-speaking peoples were in close contact by the time of the first Quetzalcoatl. The Mayas had their equivalent of Quetzalcoatl, who was Kukulcan but the curious thing is that the word Quetzalcoatl, the Nahua name for the god, includes the symbolism of the quetzal bird which belongs to the Maya lands and is not found on the high plateau. Both Mayas and Nahuas had erected a consistent, meaningful, and cosmically complete mythological figure who was at once water, earth (in the crawling snake), and bird. Quetzalcoatl was described as being the colour of jade or of some precious stone. He was the wind god, and also the god's messenger and road-sweeper. He discovered maize which allowed man – in the most mature sense of the word – to come into being. His heart was consumed by a bonfire which he himself built, whence it rose to become the planet Venus. His identification with the later Aztec sun god, Huitzilopochtli, gives him a claim to have passed beyond the planets into the solar world, source of life and light for our planet.

Below and right: Quetzalcoatl, lord of life and death, depicted in an elaborately carved 'apotheosis' statue of the Huastec culture, *c.* 1000 A.D.

Quetzalcoatl was thus a composite figure describing the many orders of matter in creation: a kind of ladder with man at the centre, but extending downward into animal, water, and mineral; and upward to the planets, the life-giving sun, and the god creators. This ladder is very similar to the orders of matter and life described by the modern palaeontologist Pierre Teilhard de Chardin. It is not unsimilar to the seven powers of nature in Hindu philosophy. And it can be likened to Pico della Mirandola's Renaissance description of man: 'the intermediary between creatures, familiar with the gods above as he is lord of the beings below'. Quetzalcoatl is an embodiment of Mahommed's affirmation that God created the angels (stars, planets) and set reason in them, and He created the beasts (serpent) and set lust in them, and He created the sons of Adam (man, eater of maize) and set in them both reason and lust to war with one another until reason (Quetzalcoatl as king) prevails.

Quetzalcoatl's very name, then, seems to be a symbol of man's condition and of his possibilities. The story of his discovery of maize fits this general hypothesis. Man was not created until the gods had first bestowed upon him that special human food, sought and found by Quetzalcoatl, who stole the tiny precious grain that could transform the life of humanity. In the shape of a black ant, he stole the grain from the red ants; and maize became the symbol of manhood in all its fullness. The maize god Cinteotl is but another aspect of Quetzalcoatl.

Evidently the story of the discovery of food fit for men is more than a mere agricultural description. It is another expression of the ancient Mexican aim: to create a deified heart, and a face that shall be a true expression of the inner life of man. The temple to Quetzalcoatl, as described by Sahagún, must in its beauty have expressed the myth's inner meaning. It had four rooms; one all of gold and facing toward the east; one of turquoise and emeralds opposite to this, facing westward; one of sea shells looking to the south; and one of silver for the north.

The walls of another of the plumed serpent's temples were lined throughout with quetzal feathers. In this the room facing eastward was of yellow feathers; the western room was blue; the southern, white; and the northern, red.

Quetzalcoatl's physical description is recorded in detail. He was tall, robust, broad of brow, with large eyes and a fair beard, though there is at least one description of him that makes him black-haired. He wore a conical ocelot-skin cap. His face was smeared with soot, and he wore a necklace of seashells and a quetzal bird on his back. His jacket was of cotton, and on his feet he wore anklets, rattles, and foam sandals.

From a hill in Tollan his voice could be heard for a distance of ten leagues. In his time maize grew so tall that every cob was as strong and firm as a human being. Pumpkins reached to a man's height and cotton grew in all colours.

In so far as he was man, he was of the breed of heroes from whom myths are created. In so far as he is symbol, he presides like the wind over all space. He is the soul taking wings to heaven, and he is matter descending to earth as the crawling snake; he is virtue rising, and he is the blind force pulling man down; he is waking and dream, angel and demon (but in his demoniac form, as we shall see later, he is Tezcatlipoca). He represents daylight and also, when he journeys to the underworld, night. He is love with its transmuting power, and carnal desire that wears chains.

Life carries with it the possibilities of eternity and the threat of death, the seed and the flower and the fruit. Quetzalcoatl is time itself, the serpent, yet paradoxically he exists beyond time. With his coming he brings to earth the possibility of a miracle. One South American statesman – now many years dead – told a journalist who was searching for the solution to his country's problems that Latin America would discover and fulfil her true destiny only when the plumed serpent learned to fly. To Latin Americans with perceptiveness to catch the subtlety of the symbol, Quetzalcoatl's message remains valid.

In the Vienna Codex (*Codex Vindobonensis*) we see a naked Quetzalcoatl raised to the high heavens and receiving gifts from the Dual Lord and Lady above all. He is given four temples one of which is that of the morning star, his symbol. One belongs to the moon and is round in plan like the observatory at Chichén Itzá. The third is for healing, Quetzalcoatl's priests being called healers or physicians. Lastly, there is the temple of the knot of Xipe, only open to those of Toltec descent.

Among the gifts are a seed; a shell and a wind mask for the god of air; a spear-thrower and an arrow to give him power; a jewel and a feather-fringed shirt of the kind worn by high priests; a black feather with a pair of eyes, and Quetzalcoatl's distinctive conical hat. To the left, behind his naked back, are the mountain of the sun and the double-peaked hill of sunset and evening star.

From this heavenly plane Quetzalcoatl drops to earth by a ladder knotted like a sacrificial lash. Two gods follow him to the earthly regions. In Quetzalcoatl's hand is a staff sprouting life, and he also carries the spear of the morning star.

Like King Arthur of England, he is half man, half legend. His most enthusiastic modern devotee and student, Laurette Séjourné, believes that as a man he lived perhaps about the time of Christ; but, as we have pointed out, if it was he who discovered that maize was a fitting food for man, he must have lived many centuries earlier.

The name Quetzalcoatl, plumed serpent or water-bird-serpent, has also a secondary meaning: precious twin. The god's mythical twin, a dog called Xolotl (mythologically Venus as the evening star), may have derived originally from a Chichimeca explorer and king of that name; but the twinship theme has probably meanings on another level connected with the double appearance of Venus in the morning and the evening sky, and with the double nature of most of the gods in the pantheon under the dual god-above-all.

There are two main versions of the Quetzalcoatl legend. The first tells how the god-man fell from grace and allowed himself to be coaxed into a drunken orgy, during which he had sexual intercourse with his sister. When he recovered he repented, built his own funeral pyre, and rose to heaven as the planet Venus. The second version, according to Bernardino de Sahagún, tells how the great king Quetzalcoatl was attacked by enemies and had to flee from his lands. There follows a struggle between Quetzalcoatl and his arch-enemy Tezcatlipoca, whom we shall discuss later. For all its symbolic interest, Sahagún's version of the legend is of minor importance compared to the better-known story of drunkenness and transformation which appears in the Legend of the Suns.

Quetzalcoatl was born of Coatlicue, one of the five moon-goddesses; or she may have been a single goddess represented as a five-fold symbol, or quincunx, signifying Earth with her four directions and her centre. In her – as later in a different sense in her offspring Quetzalcoatl – spirit and matter fused. But whereas the fusion in the case of Quetzalcoatl allowed matter to be redeemed in spirit, his mother's function was precisely the converse: to solidify spirit into the tangible planet on which we live. Coatlicue thus made life possible, but not without the help of certain mysterious magicians and of the Sun. Until the magicians guessed the mystery of her existence, she remained hidden in cloud, alone and sterile. But when the Sun appeared to take her for a bride, all the instinctive forces of life came into being in Quetzalcoatl. Thenceforth Earth is both mother and myth; fruit and energy; seed and flower; gentle breeze and wrecking hurricane; loving caress and rending claw; stone and water. In her, through her son, the transcendent became tangible and coarse materiality took wing. Moreover, by becoming her consort, the Sun acquired new and unforeseen strength. Together with Earth and with Quetzalcoatl (as represented by the planet Venus), the Sun formed part of a trinity in which a balance and a concord was achieved. Sun was the male force impregnating the female Earth, and out of them was born a son, merciful and loving.

The statue of Coatlicue

If this description seems too kindly to fit the awesome statue of Coatlicue in the Mexican Anthropological Museum, we must remember that the statue is describing a vast cosmic process. Whereas it looks cruel to human eyes, it is aloof from either cruelty or compassion because it is describing an objective fact: eat and be eaten, for all will return to the basic skull form in death. A modern Mexican art critic, Justino Fernández, has described how humanity – mankind – is symbolised in the goddess's skirt of entwined serpents which hang from two creative gods forming the belt. In the skulls with which Coatlicue is decked we see the rhythm of life merging into death. Behind hang thirteen leather thongs encrusted with snails, and these are the mythical heavens on which rests the shield of Huitzilopochtli, the Sun god.

In the statue Coatlicue is clad about the thorax in human skin, to remind us that she is connected with Xipe Totec, the flayed god, god of spring. Her necklace of hands and hearts is a symbol of the sacrifice needed to maintain the gods and uphold the cosmic order. Two aspects of Venus are shown in the hands in the form of serpent heads, one being Quetzalcoatl himself, and the other his twin Xolotl.

At the highest point of the statue we find Omeyocan, the place in which the divine god-above-all lives with his consort. This is represented by a bicephalic mass which takes the place of the head and in a sense represents the Moon. Justino Fernández ends his description of the goddess: 'The

Left: a view of Uxmal from the summit of the House of the Magician, looking down on the quadrangle of the 'Nunnery'.

Below: the statue of Coatlicue, over eight feet high, in the National Museum of Mexico. The mother of the gods, she is pictured here as the description of a cosmic process rather than as a female deity. The statue was discovered in Mexico City on the site of Tenochtitlán, the Aztec capital destroyed by the Spaniards.

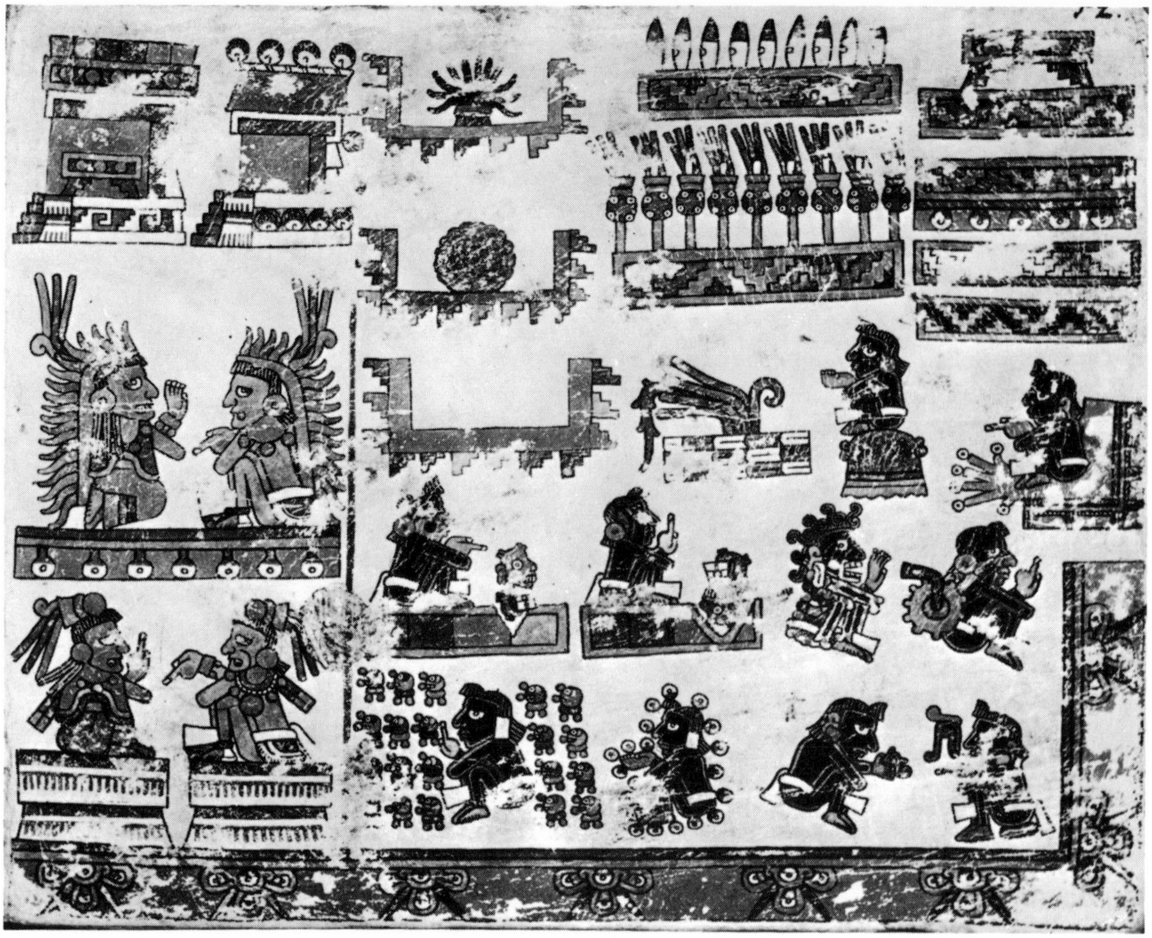

48

whole of her vibrates and lives, inside and out, the whole of her is life and is death; her meaning stretches in all possible directions... Coatlicue is the dynamic-cosmic force giving life and maintained by death in the struggle of opposites which is so necessary that its final and most radical meaning is war... Thus the dramatic beauty of Coatlicue has ultimately a warlike meaning, life and death; and that is why she is supreme, a tragic and a moving beauty.'

Tragic and warlike, one would add, only if she is looked upon with mortal eyes. On the cosmic level she is, like her statue image, a great pyramid or triangle representing stability and endurance.

Left: two leaves from the *Codex Vindobonensis*. In the upper one the Old Ones, male-female aspects of the god-above-all, can be seen on the left. They bestir themselves and are manifest. To them, in the lower picture, has come the naked Quetzalcoatl. He is given four temples and the insignia of his various attributes, and returns to earth by a knotted ladder accompanied by two gods. At the bottom of the lower picture he can be seen wearing his wind mask (as the god Ehecatl) and his distinctive conical hat. He carries a staff sprouting life and the spear of the morning star. British Museum.

Birth of the plumed serpent

Coatlicue, goddess of the serpent petticoat (as distinct from the goddess of the star petticoat, goddess-above-all), was both mother of the Sun and also the Sun's wife and sister. The suffix *cue* means petticoat and is a graphic word to describe a lady. One day Coatlicue and her four sisters, whose names are not recorded, were doing penance on a hill called Coatepec (Snake Hill – the name occurs as far south as Guatemala). Coatlicue, a virgin, gathered some white feathers and placed them in her bosom.

In another version the mother goddess swallows not a feather but an emerald – but the idea of something small and precious from which Quetzalcoatl arises remains. By this act his mother became pregnant and gave birth to Quetzalcoatl or Huitzilopochtli according to whether we are thinking in early Nahua or late Aztec terms.

In one dramatised version of the story, the goddess is called La, and she is alone, a widow, so she tells us, for her husband has died. As to her sons, they have gone away and live only in her memory, all four hundred of them. Then a feather announces itself, falling from the sky, lovely and soft and many-coloured. She places it in her bosom and begins to sweep the heavens so that her sons may come. All this appears to happen at twilight, a time when the Sun, her husband one supposes, has departed, but the stars, her sons, have not yet appeared. When night falls she lays aside her broom saying that it is useless to try to sweep night away. Sitting on the ground, she casts about for something to ponder, and remembers her feather. If she strokes it, she thinks to herself, perhaps the four hundred sons will come. But the feather is not there. It does not answer to her call. She begins to weep. Suddenly she becomes aware that she is pregnant and her face lights up with joy. She feels the baby quickening within her just as the four hundred had quickened before they were born.

In the next scene of the play the four hundred clamour to be told who has made their mother pregnant. Whoever he may be, they demand his death. The child, now sprung from the womb, declares himself to be Huitzilopochtli. As in the myth itself, he proceeds to kill the four hundred sons of Tezcatlipoca. The number four hundred, it is sometimes rendered as four thousand, need not be taken literally. It is used to signify the multitude of stars that are put out when the Sun enters the sky at dawn. On another level of meaning the number implies the diversity in the heavens that become unified by the birth of Quetzalcoatl-Huitzilopochtli.

In one version of the story the hero does not meet and vanquish the four hundred until he is nine years old. At that time the four hundred warriors who inhabited the Milky Way were filled with hatred against the boy's father – the Sun himself, though Quetzalcoatl is also the Sun. The anomaly fits the cosmic fact. Stars and Sun kill one another alternately as night follows day. So the four hundred killed the nine-year-old god's father and buried his body in sand. Quetzalcoatl was informed by

Below: a warrior, possibly a priest, decorated with plumes and flowers and with a characteristic Maya nose. The Mayas' ideal of physical beauty led them to flatten the head by tying boards to it in infancy. This head is from one of the tombs in the Temple of the Inscriptions at Palenque and may represent a priest of Kukulcan, the Quetzalcoatl of the Mayas. Seventh century A.D.

vultures of the murder; and with the help of a coyote, an eagle, a wolf, and an army of moles who bored a hole in the ground so that he could reach the skeleton, he recovered the bones.

Quetzalcoatl's temptation

As the boy grew up, evil magicians tried to tempt him to perform human sacrifices, but he would have none of this, being so filled with love toward all living things that he could not even be persuaded to kill a forest bear or to pick a flower. Then Tezcatlipoca, his chief enemy, showed Quetzalcoatl his image in a mirror. Quetzalcoatl was astonished to find his eyelids inflamed, his eyes sunken in their sockets, and his skin wrinkled. The face seemed not to be human at all, and Quetzalcoatl began to fear that if his subjects saw him thus they would destroy him. He went into retreat, thus conceding Tezcatlipoca the advantage.

Tezcatlipoca now decked his rival in finery so that he looked very splendid in a garment of quetzal feathers and a turquoise mask. With red dye he coloured Quetzalcoatl's lips, and with yellow dye he painted small squares on his forehead. A wig, and a beard of red and blue guacamaya feathers, completed the effect. When Quetzalcoatl looked into the mirror he saw so handsome a youth that he was persuaded to come out of his retreat.

The evil ones now tempted him with wine, but after a first refusal he dipped his little finger into the potion, and it tasted so good that he agreed to drink three times, then a fourth and a fifth. His servants followed suit, and soon they were all gloriously intoxicated. Growing ever merrier, Quetzalcoatl called for his sister, Quetzalpetlatl, and she too drank five times. The slippery path to carnal excess was begun; Quetzalcoatl and Quetzalpetlatl ceased to live ascetically and in cleanliness. They no longer pierced themselves with thorns, nor performed their daily rites at dawn.

But when the effects of the drunkenness had worn away, Quetzalcoatl repented and his heart was filled with sadness. He remembered his mother, the goddess of the serpent petticoat who ruled over the starry spheres, and it seemed to him that he was no longer truly her son. His servants grieved with him, until Quetzalcoatl ordered that he and his whole retinue should leave the city, and that a stone casket should be built in which he was to lie four days and nights in strict penance. This done, the pilgrims marched to the seashore; and there Quetzalcoatl dressed himself in his feathered robes and his turquoise mask. Building a funeral pyre he threw himself upon it and was consumed in flames. The ashes rose into the sky as a flock of birds, bearing his heart which was to become the planet Venus. It is said that when the morning star saw the birds fly aloft, it dipped down below the horizon to the region of the dead, and remained there for four days while Quetzalcoatl gathered arrows for his use in heaven. Eight days later he appeared again as the great star; and it is well known – says the myth – that since that time he has always been upon his throne.

The two Quetzalcoatls, mythical and historical, blend in a certain confusion. The myth of his virgin birth has several variants including one in which his mother swallows a sliver of jade. But all these events evidently happened both on the outer margins of history and somewhere in the high heavens. On the other hand at least one of the possible flesh-and-blood Quetzalcoatls was king of Tula, ruler over the Toltecs, and he lived during the tenth century of our era. But this was far too late for him to have discovered corn, and much later than early images of the god-man. Quetzalcoatl had by that time become a generic name for the priest-kings of

Tezcatlipoca, the god who brought about the temptation and fall of Quetzalcoatl. Aztec statue, thirteenth to fifteenth centuries A.D.

Mexico; and the name derives from the symbolism of the myth, not from any one of the historical figures, whether existing at the time of Christ, or earlier or later.

The symbolism of the god

One of the chief clues to the meaning of Quetzalcoatl is to be found in the story of the creation of the Fifth Sun, for the humble god with his crop of boils is none other than the plumed serpent in embryonic form. This can be seen from the images of the humble god that appear in the codices always with the insignia of Quetzalcoatl – the very insignia possessed by the king of Tula.

The Fifth Sun was the sun of movement. Quetzalcoatl presides, therefore, over the era of movement – that is, over a period in history when the elements became fused, when 'burning water' came to represent the living spirit of matter in constant activity. The perpetual and necessary round of movement in the heavens which creates our day and night is represented by the passage of Quetzalcoatl as an eagle across the sky, his sinking into the underworld as an ocelot and his emergence again at dawn. But here, as in every aspect of the myth, we must be careful not to take the phenomenal meaning as the only one. The passage from sky to underworld and back is still another representation of the dark-light, spirit-matter dualism that so preoccupied the ancient Mexicans.

We have already touched on the triple symbolism of bird-water-serpent; but this needs further analysis. As bird, Quetzalcoatl represents the heavens, or the heavenly characteristics of man. Besides being associated obviously with his own bird, the mysterious quetzal so difficult to capture, Quetzalcoatl is often portrayed together with a humming bird which represented to the Nahuas the human soul released from its bodily scaffolding, sparkling in the sky and lighting upon whatever flower will provide it with the honey that is its pleasure.

Birds, however, are only one aspect of the god, for at a certain stage of its development the human soul must have a scaffolding or armature, in other words matter, which is symbolised by the god's serpent scales. In this aspect, as Laurette Séjourné has pointed out in an illuminating study called *The Universe of Quetzalcoatl*, the connection with the deities of water and of femininity are constant. Thus Quetzalcoatl connects with the great earth monster whom we have seen as a symbol of time and who is represented hung with the skulls of physical death. But it would be quite misleading to take this symbolism as implying any negation of material creation, for matter is an essential phase in the cosmic cycle and cannot be escaped – nor, if it were possible, would escape be desirable. It is precisely the 'movement' of the Fifth Sun that gives matter life and form and the glowing, jewel-like beauty of the myth. There is no question of denying natural laws at a certain stage in the soul's pilgrimage and transformation. The plumed serpent must learn to fly. In other words, matter must transcend itself and be transmuted into pure spirit. But so equally must the quetzal bird descend into matter and join with the serpent to become part of the whole instinctive movement of organic life. In other words, spirit must enter matter to infuse it with life.

The most solid matter is the most unchanging, and yet it contains, even in its immutability, the glow and brilliance of life. Therefore it is represented in the Nahua myth by jade, beads of which were placed in the mouths of the dead. Jade represents on the one hand inert matter which has not yet been infused with spirit, and on the other the deified heart which passes beyond movement to perfect stillness and which it is

A clay vessel in the form of a man blowing a conch shell, from Colima in western Mexico. The conch shell was one of the insignia of Quetzalcoatl, symbolising both his aspect as the wind god and – in the spiral – the growth of natural things.

to be hoped has been created by man on his journey through this mortal life. A notable characteristic of the Nahua symbolism is that it gathers opposites into one whole and thus shows us simultaneously the apparently contradictory facets of a single truth. The contradictions exist only because of our limited minds. On another plane stillness and movement, matter and the most illuminated spirit, the physical and the holy, all meet. Between inert matter and pure life there stretches a chasm bridged by the whole vast range of creation. Moreover matter and life, though at opposite poles, can look outwardly very much alike. Jade represents both.

So it is too with the symbolism of the flower. At a superficial assessment it would seem that the blossoms adorning Quetzalcoatl's headdress are the converse of the stone and represent growth and life rather than death and inertia. But flowers in much Nahua poetry remind us also that all created life on earth must perish. Life is ephemeral, we are reminded, and not to be made immortal unless the deified heart, the jade in the mouth, is formed.

For the most part flowers appear to symbolise a fairly high but still intermediate state of the soul on its journey upward to full godhood. There are wall decorations showing the blood stream flowing within the body of the serpent; and in the blood are painted flowers, as if within the god-man's blood something had grown and flowered but had not yet at this stage become permanent, as in the jewel or precious stone.

It is odd that with their constant reference to 'flower and song' the ancient poets scarcely ever specified particular varieties of growing things, though there is occasional reference to 'the cocoa flower' or 'the flower that makes us drunk'. The frequent mention of scent, though again never specifically, suggests that this was an important attribute of the plant, and it seems that in our day there exists in certain parts a very detailed 'scent lore', for the Guatemalan novelist Miguel Angel Asturias, in his *Hombres de Maiz* describes a 'pharmacy for concealing scent'. According to him, Indian warriors or hunters smell of their *nagual* or protective animal. In order to put their enemies off the scent when they are being pursued, they anoint themselves with a special aromatic water or with some ointment or fruit juice that will disguise the natural body odour. The root of the violet is specifically mentioned in this connection, together with heliotrope water for concealing the smell of venison. Even more potent are said to be spikenard, jasmine (against snakes), wild lily, tobacco, fig, rosemary, and orange water.

An Aztec shield made of gold and feather-work, a fine example of a unique craft. The plumed coyote shows this creature's connection with the Quetzalcoatl legends telling how he helped the god recover the bones of his father from the underworld.

A central symbol in Quetzalcoatl's insignia is the conch shell, especially in its transverse section which in many stylised forms becomes the god's pectoral. As a transverse cut, it looks like half a star – half of the planet Venus to which Quetzalcoatl's heart was to rise. It can also look like the spiral so common in the growth of natural things, as d'Arcy Thompson showed us with abundant illustration in his *Growth and Form*. The conch holds sound and wind, and every child knows how, if put to the ear, it will reproduce the pulsations of surf beating on the shore. It is a fitting symbol for Quetzalcoatl in his role of wind god.

It is said that to ancient Mexicans the shell spiral represented birth; and Laurette Séjourné reminds us in this connection that Quetzalcoatl was the procreator of man, who endowed human kind with the special food, maize. What has not been pointed out is that the shell becomes a permanent record of the trace of its own growth. The chalky deposit of which it is made fixes the movement of growth's spiral so that we can see, in a single instant, the whole process from its tight, curled inception to its outermost whorl. It is thus a symbol of the permanence of time, of that space-time which is beyond either, which is eternal and unchanging, within and beyond the movement of organic life. In Nahua symbolism the shell represented the end of one era and the beginning of another, so that even permanence has its limitations. No time we can conceive of is absolutely unending, and all time is marked off by the passage of the great heavenly cycles. So the shell represents the relatively – not the absolutely – eternal. It is one completed cycle, visible and tangible.

The shell can also be the outer covering of hard matter within which the spirit is enclosed and from which, if it is to fulfill itself, it must at some stage emerge in splendour. The plumed serpent as man is he who seeks fulfillment whatever the cost may be. As Laurette Séjourné says: 'What makes Quetzalcoatl a king is his determination to alter the course of his existence, to initiate a journey to which he is forced only by inner necessity. He is the Sovereign because he obeys his own law instead of that of others; because he is the source and origin of *movement.*'

This is the central reason for Quetzalcoatl's existence as king and as god, and it puts him among the tiny band of the elect who, through all the ages have preferred freedom to bondage, immortality to imprisonment in passing time, lasting instead of transitory happiness.

Quetzalcoatl: Venus and Sun

Significantly, it is the lower half of the transverse cut of the conch shell that is represented in the pectoral of Quetzalcoatl. His connection with Venus is very specifically with the planet when it dips below the horizon into what the Nahuas regarded as the underworld, or outer darkness. Quetzalcoatl was not pure divinity, not Ometeotl, the one god-above-all, but rather a god in the making, who had to 'descend into hell' and there suffer transformation. As a boy he penetrated into the underworld in search of his father's bones, which were rediscovered and thus revived by the son's persistence and with the help of those very earthy and instinctive animals – the wolf (or coyote), the tiger (or ocelot), and the mole. The eagle helped too, an indication that Quetzalcoatl would rise again on wings to heaven.

Later, when Quetzalcoatl had committed the carnal act and then repented, he had to descend for eight days into the stone casket, the underworld, before he rose into the sky. We have here on the one hand a physical description of the passing of the planet Venus below the horizon and its reappearance; and on the other a symbolic representation of a stage in the soul's pilgrimage.

The disappearance of Venus in the blinding light of the sun's rays suggests that the planet is swallowed up in the sun, becomes the sun – just as Quetzalcoatl is both Venus and sun. We see this aspect of his symbolism especially in his Aztec successor, Huitzilopochtli, who is the sun god demanding to be nourished on human hearts. In reality the hearts that Quetzalcoatl required were divine creations after the pattern of his own, purged and deified through suffering. It has always been a necessary part of the task of every religious teacher to help his followers to the same degree of illumination that he has reached himself. Thus Quetzalcoatl had to construct a bridge by which his disciples might follow him into the promised land. His message would have been nothing if he had not been able to teach others the art of creating a deified heart.

The twinhood of Quetzalcoatl is a complex affair. As Venus, his twin is the dog Xolotl (the word means both twin and dog); as sun his twin is a tiger or ocelot. Nevertheless, the passage both of sun and planet through the underworld is usually represented by the ocelot and not the dog.

The eagle and the ocelot (tiger) carrying standards and crowned with flowers. The orders of Knights Tiger was originally a caste of initiates whose purpose was the attainment of spirituality. The Knights Eagle were their higher companions, warriors of the Sun. *Codex Borbonicus.*

The ocelot is the nobler animal and must be taken to represent a higher form. Quetzalcoatl as Venus in the underworld journey is less noble than when he represents the sun – or so one would think; and yet as Lord of Dawn (Venus) he is represented as the ocelot. Why? The ocelot howls at dawn to welcome the sun. Probably Xolotl represents the lowest bodily instincts, nonetheless necessary and nonetheless to be purified; whereas the ocelot represents certain higher instincts, or perhaps even the deepest feelings of man – feelings that cause so much trouble if they are not tamed and transformed. The ocelot, representing these higher feelings, must therefore pass through the underworld before being worthy of association with the redeemer, Quetzalcoatl.

The Mexican order corresponding to the Knights Templars of Europe was that of the Knights Tiger. It has often been mistaken for a warrior caste in an ordinary military sense. In fact it was a caste of initiates fighting for the attainment of spirituality. The special insignia of the knights was a thunderbolt, or flash of light illuminating man and his world; and their higher companions were the Knights Eagle, warriors of the Sun.

The Pochtecas

There was also a band of followers of Quetzalcoatl whose apparently humbler role was a decisive one in the society of ancient America. These were the *pochtecas*, or itinerant vendors who formed a guild or brotherhood with the material purpose of trade but with a central set of ethical principles that were more important to them than money-making. Wandering from their centre in Cholula near the Mexican capital, down into the Gulf lands and into Maya territory to the south, they were carriers of ideas as well as goods, and undoubtedly account for the enormously widespread cult of their god and protector. They seem to have been hard-headed business men who were yet never allowed to accumulate wealth, their main mission being to search for the 'Land of the Sun'. They were transmitters of ideas. Quetzalcoatl's kingdom was not of this world but it worked within it, and very efficiently.

One poem in a lesser *Chilam Balam* manuscript (for the *pochtecas* had wandered as far as the Maya lands) makes it clear that their function was not merely that of salesmen:

You are to wander,
entering and departing
from strange villages...
Perhaps you will achieve nothing anywhere.
It may be that your merchandise
and your items of trade
find no favour in any place...
Do not turn back, keep a firm step...
Something you will achieve;
Something the Lord of the Universe will assign to you...

The *pochtecas* were closely linked with guilds of craftsmen, and all the guilds together may have had some inner teaching and purpose similar to the masons and other guilds of mediaeval Europe. That the *pochtecas* were highly esteemed is evident from the following poem:

When the vendors reached
the coast...
the nobles who lived there presented them
with great round jade stones,
very green, the size of tomatoes;
also jade, the colour of quetzal,
emeralds like black water,
turquoise shields,
turtle shells,
guacamaya feathers
and others from a sea-black bird;
and red tiger skins.
When they returned to Mexico,
they presented to the king Ahuitzotl
everything they had brought.

. . . .

That is why king Ahuitzotl
held the vendors in great esteem
and made them equal to the knights of war.

Ahuitzotl was emperor of the Aztecs from 1486 to 1502. The *pochtecas* never made a show of their riches or power, but always behaved humbly. If they accumulated too much wealth, they organized religious banquets and quickly got rid of it. They were mysterious people in the ancient world, exercising their influence silently, behind the scenes, but acting as a thread binding the whole pattern of Nahua-Maya culture together and using coastal towns as centres from which to radiate their varied influences. Sahagún tells us that they had free entry into all manner of places, and that they were often afflicted by the intense coast heat and the lashing winds as they struggled to transverse mountain and canyon. He also describes their sacrifice of victims, but the esteem in which they were held makes us suspect that this was either a late aberration or an exaggeration of Sahagún's. Their god was Yiacatecuhtli, Lord of the Vanguard, or Nose and their own name means 'merchants who lead'.

Left: two Pochtecas, members of the guild of travelling merchants, from the *Codex Fejervary-Mayer*. They had a unique importance in the empire, being the only privileged class apart from the priests and the nobles. Their position might ultimately have led to the establishment of a true merchant middle class.

Left, below: Lord of the Vanguard, or Lord of the Nose, Yiacatecuhtli, from a pre-conquest manuscript. He was the particular god of the Pochtecas, the travelling merchants of ancient Mexico. As followers of Quetzalcoatl, they were carriers of ideas as well as goods, and helped to spread the cult of the plumed serpent over a widespread area. *Codex Fejervary-Mayer*.

The figure of Macuilxochitl, from a ceremonial vase. He was the god of games and feasting and an aspect of Xochipilli. Mixtec ceramic, from Miahuatlán in the state of Oaxaca.

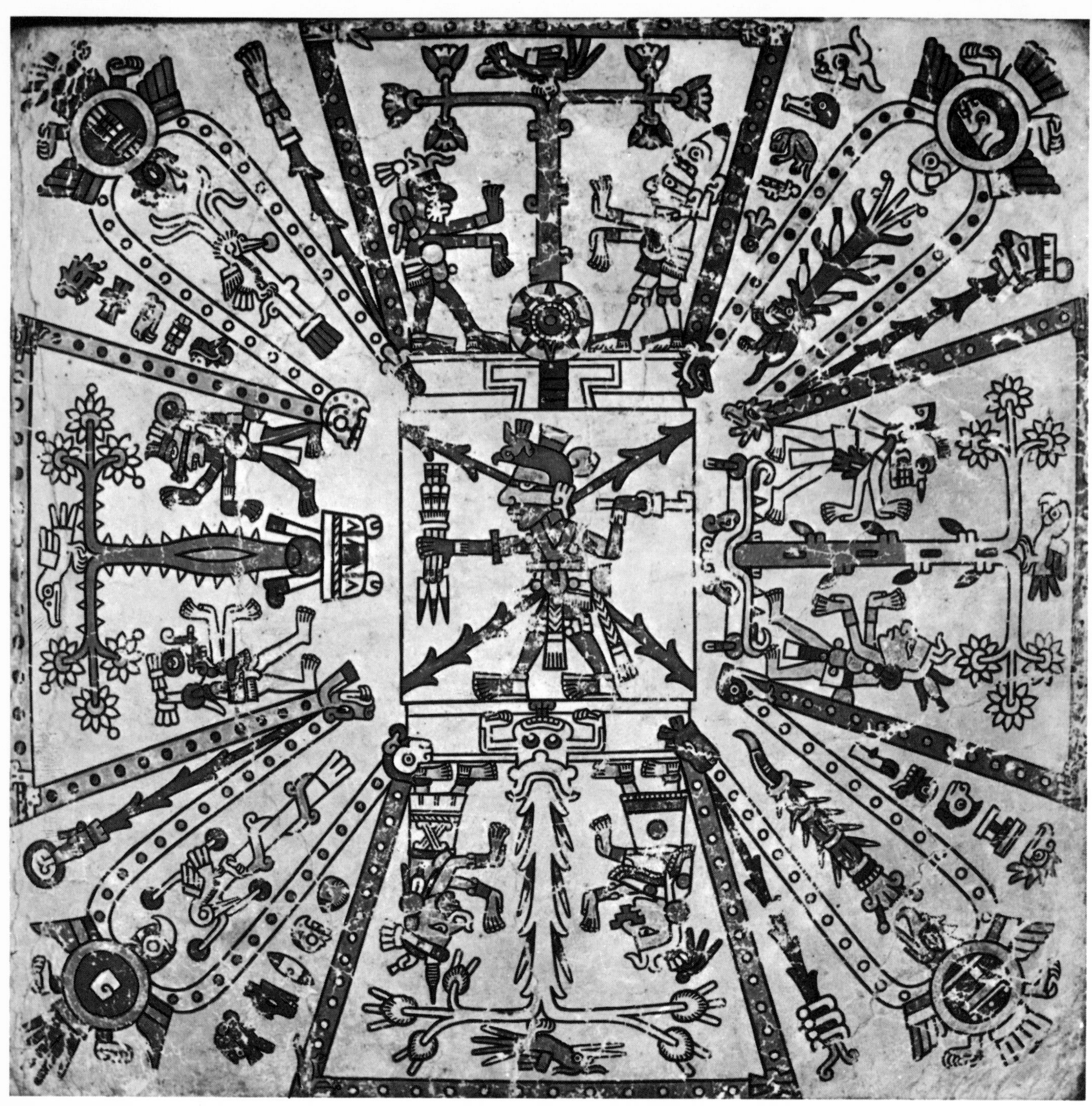

The five world regions. A leaf from the *Codex Fejervary-Mayer*. At the centre stands Tepeyollotl, the god who was Heart of the Mountain and one of the Lords of Night. The four cardinal points were associated with the four sons of the dual god-above-all; Quetzalcoatl, Xipe Totec, Camaxtli, Huitzilopochtli. They were also connected with the four Suns which preceded our own world and ended in destruction. The fifth and central region was that of the present world and represented instability – Tepeyollotl was also the god who caused earthquakes.

Four Aspects of Nature

At one time the Mexican gods who stood at the cardinal points of the compass were all Tezcatlipocas of various colours, though oddly the colours of the god do not seem to fit the normally accepted compass colours: white, north; red, east; yellow, south; and black, west.

Tezcatlipoca is black in his northern aspect, red in his eastern, blue in his southern, and white when he stands at the west. Later these four offspring of the one god-above-all and his consort became differentiated. The blue Tezcatlipoca of the south became Tlaloc, the god of rain. The red Tezcatlipoca belonging to the east, the point of sunrise, became Xipe Totec, the flayed god, or sometimes Tonatiuh the Sun itself. Quetzalcoatl was associated with the sunset, and Tezcatlipoca remained to rule the black land of the north. Alternatively Quetzalcoatl remained to conquer three Tezcatlipocas at the other points. Each god represents an aspect of nature. It seems that in the land of the four directions beneath the great heaven there were three basic principles of nature more or less in constant warfare, or at least in opposition and collision which had to be resolved by the coming of the great humaniser and restorer of harmony, Quetzalcoatl. We can think of all four gods as Tezcatlipoca in various stages of the god-man's pilgrimage, or as Quetzalcoatl at various degrees of redemption.

(In parenthesis one might note that the four Tezcatlipocas had their Maya parallel in four Bacabs, also belonging to the points of the compass; but the Nahuas appear to have taken this idea of a quadruple 'compass-god' – in certain aspects possibly representing something very like the mediaeval 'four humours' – to a much higher degree of development.)

The idea of the four Tezcatlipocas standing at the four corners of creation is graphically expressed on a page of the *Codex Fejervary-Mayer* which has been neatly interpreted by Cottie Burland who regards the god as 'continually hopping round the pole star', prowling about some desirable centre but never able to reach it. In the Codex painting the centre is represented by the god Tepeyollotl, the Heart of the Mountain, one of the Lords of Night who ruled over part of the Aztec calendar. Around this figure the four Tezcatlipocas revolve. Curiously, however, while east is placed at the top of the page, north is to the east's right and not to the left as we would normally expect. Burland suggests that this is intended to be a night-time vision so that we ought to look at it as if we were lying on our backs and gazing upward at the sky. In contrast, the time sequence that occurs at the points of the square in the picture proceeds in the direction of the sun's apparent movement across the sky, from east to west (taking east as established by the night positions).

The topmost of the cardinal points can be identified as east because of its temple, which tells us that this is the holy place of the rising Sun. A quetzal bird is perched on a flowering tree. This is the holy land whence Quetzalcoatl arose. Two gods face one another: the god of the sharp-cutting stone, Itzli, and the god of the rising Sun. Throughout the picture we shall find this same preoccupation with dual forces in opposition. Moving now to the right we find, at the north point of the compass, the land of souls. Here Cinteotl, the maize god, faces Mictlantecuhtli, Lord of the Dead. The tree is rigid, contains a yellow parrot, and is decorated with what Burland thinks are bloodstained stone knives. They might equally well be hearts. Either way, the dual death-life theme is emphasised: knives that look like hearts, or hearts that look like knives, the god of resurrection meeting the god of death.

At the foot of the picture, at the western point of the compass, Xochiquetzal, goddess of flowers, is paired with a goddess of drunkenness and witchcraft. Beauty is set in contrast with ugliness. The tree is long and spikey and the bird perched in it is the humming bird.

At the southern point, to the left of the picture, there is a split tree. South is sometimes regarded as a place of redemption, and the split may represent the crack through which man can escape. The bird is white, and the figures are Tlaloc the rain god and an unidentified god probably of the underworld. Rain, necessary to the growth of organic life, is paired with the underworld where nothing grows at all.

At the corners, around these four Tezcatlipoca positions, are grouped various calendar signs. The sign *Acatl* is carried by a quetzal bird feeding on a white plant where a bird carries a seed in his back. *Tecpatl* is carried by a red parrot, and a yellow vine winds about a blue shrub on which

A Huastec statue of the god of maize, Cinteotl. Eleventh to thirteenth centuries A.D.

sits a yellow bird. The sign *Calli* shows a falling eagle eating the fruit of the tuna cactus, symbol of sacrifice. *Tochtli* carries a parrot, and a maize plant is being gnawed by a mouse.

Whereas the interpretation of details must be speculative, there can be no doubt that the growing, dying, regenerative and destructive contrasts in organic life were strongly in the artist's mind. This picture thus leads us to consider another aspect of Quetzalcoatl-Tezcatlipoca, embodied in Xipe Totec, god of spring, who in his ceremonial representations used to wear a human skin. Just as the seed breaking its husk and the earth's crust to emerge as a tender shoot must inevitably go through a period of struggle and of overcoming (though neither need be interpreted anthropomorphically, so Xipe Totec, god of spring though he might be, did not escape sorrow and conflict. He was the god who suffered his skin to be flayed in order that the active, growing principle hidden within matter could be freed. He is that same pustule-ridden god who redeemed the Sun. In other words, he is Quetzalcoatl as the stricken, humble redeemer, suffering – as Sahagún tells us – a series of diseases including smallpox and an eye infection.

When Xipe is rid of his pock-marked skin he can be clad in gold, symbol of pure spirit or light. Having passed through the epoch of penitence, he becomes Quetzalcoatl in his redeemed form. According to Sahagún he was worshipped by the Zapotec Indians of Oaxaca and the Tehuantepec Isthmus where men jousted and played happily in front of his temple.

A clay figure of a priest of the Mayan rain god, Chac, wearing an elaborate headdress. From the island of Jaina, seventh century A.D.

The symbol of the growth of maize from the seed is one of the most important in ancient Mexican religion, as it was in the Greek mysteries. In the Maya *Popol Vuh* the creators are supposed to have needed maize for the making of man; and the grain was brought to them by four wild creatures: Yac, a forest cat; Utiu, a coyote; Quel, a parrot; and Hoh, a crow: 'And these four creatures brought the news of the yellow ears and the white... Thus they discovered food, and this it was that entered into the flesh of man created, of man made man. This was his blood, of this was man's blood made...'

Both Xipe and the corn god Cinteotl are important figures in the Nahua pantheon, and in the *Codex Fejervary-Mayer* there is a fourfold picture showing the varying fortunes of a maize plant and bearing a remarkable likeness to the Biblical parable of the sower. The pictures should be read from below upward, first the left-hand column and then the right. If studied in this order we see first a red maize plant burnt by the scorching sun. The soil is dry and the crop is being attacked by various birds including one with notes issuing from its beak. Underground an animal and a bird are burrowing, eating at the roots. This is the worst state of the sown seed, which dries and is attacked by enemies and has no resistance. The second picture shows the soil only half cultivated so that the maize plant produces only one ear. But even this gives reason to hope, and a jewelled god tends it. By the third picture we have entered the era of *ollin*, movement, the sign of the age of Quetzalcoatl as redeemer. However there is too much water, which prevents the maize from giving of its best. The rain goddess presides. In the fourth picture the soil is well tilled and the maize flourishes under the god Tlaloc who gives it just the right amount of water.

Tlaloc, god of rain, is the most benign of the four gods. In his purely agricultural aspect he is described by Sahagún as causing trees and plants to bud and flower and ripen. His face was painted with black, liquid rubber into which amaranth seeds were encrusted. His jacket was a net

Right: a vase bearing the image of the rain god Tlaloc. Toltec culture, from Tula. Below: an Aztec clay cup from Cholula, probably for the drinking of the intoxicating pulque.

symbolising clouds, and his crown was of heron feathers. He wore a green necklace and foam sandals, and carried rattles, to create thunder, and a braided red pendant. Stylised images of him show large circular eyes that give the appearance of goggles, so that he is sometimes known as the spectacled god. Under various names, Tlaloc appears throughout Mesoamerican mythology. To the Mayas he was Chac; to the Totonacs, Tajín; to the Mixtecs, Tzahui; and to the Zapotecs, Cocijo. Whereas the energy most essential to life is wind, or Quetzalcoatl, the next is water, or Tlaloc. Both are essential.

Tezcatlipoca, whose favourite disguise was that of a turkey, and one of whose feet, amputated by the great Earth Monster, had been replaced by a mirror, was Quetzalcoatl's greatest enemy but not entirely a personification of evil. If we think of Xipe as the necessary struggle and the suffering in nature, and of Tlaloc as the reviving rain, whether violent or gentle, then Tezcatlipoca becomes not the personification of evil but rather the whole capricious unpredictability of matter which is at one moment heavy and inert, at another light and dancing. His mirror-foot is shaped like a rabbit curled up in the womb, and the rabbit, 'which jumps in all directions', is symbolic of unpredictability. Some say that Tezcatlipoca dropped from heaven on a spider's web, so light must he have been. He was god of sin but also of feasting. He rewarded good men and brought diseases upon the evil. He was invisible and impalpable; born out of cloud but nevertheless bringing to mankind the gift of intelligence. He could at a glance pierce stones and trees and even the hearts of men, so that it was possible for him to read our innermost thoughts. It was said that he had only to think of something and he invented it forthwith. Seats were placed for him at the corners of all roads. Men, it was said, were mere actors on a stage whose plays were designed to entertain Tezcatlipoca. The sacrifice of the virgin youth to this god was the culmination of a year-round cycle of festivities intended to placate all the conflicting forces in nature; but it is clear from the symbolism of the breaking of the flutes as the youth ascends the temple steps that the ceremony is a dramatic enactment of some inner process that man must undergo, and not merely a superstitious eternal offering to gods who were feared.

The Maya god of sacrifice, shown on one of the great stelae at Copán in Honduras, *c.* seventh century A.D. His name remains undeciphered but he was probably the patron of the day Manik. His nearest equivalent among the Nahua gods was Xipe Totec.

Sahagún's story of the struggle between Quetzalcoatl and Tezcatlipoca shows the latter to be a wayward god possessing enormous if unbridled power and able to control much of the destiny of man and of organic life. He was finally conquered by Quetzalcoatl but only after exacting trials of strength, and because of the latter's greater purity and loftiness.

It is said that Tezcatlipoca, having descended from heaven on his rope of cobwebs, transformed himself into an ocelot while playing a game with Quetzalcoatl, then drove the latter from Tula and pursued him from city to city until finally they reached Cholula, which stands close to Puebla on the road from Mexico City and was one of the chief centres of the cult of Quetzalcoatl.

There came a time when Quetzalcoatl's people, the Toltecs, fell into slothful habits and became an easy prey to the machinations of demons sent to bring their downfall. The demons are evidently all Tezcatlipoca, whose first appearance was as a crooked old man with white hair. Thus disguised, Tezcatlipoca offered Quetzalcoatl intoxicating liquor which, he said, would ease the heart and banish thoughts of death. Quetzalcoatl, sensing that his mortal time was ending, asked where he should go. To Tollantlapallan, Tezcatlipoca told him, where an old man would be waiting for him and where Quetzalcoatl would become youthful again.

Quetzalcoatl accepted the drink, said to have been made of the maguey cactus which today still provides Mexicans with the distilled tequila and the fermented pulque.

Although Quetzalcoatl had allowed himself to be tempted with wine, the disguise did not really deceive him, and the demon had to resort to a more indirect trick. Quetzalcoatl possessed a daughter whom all men desired, but he would give her to no man. One day in the market place she saw a stranger selling green chilli and with his sexual organ erect and uncovered. Sick with desire, she returned to the palace and so pined away that her father ordered the chilli-vendor to be found. A town crier was sent out, to no avail, for the man had vanished. It was only when the search had been abandoned that the chilli-vendor reappeared of his own free will, just at the spot where he had first been seen. He was brought before Quetzalcoatl, questioned, reprimanded, and ordered to cover himself with a loincloth; he replied that in his homeland it was the custom to go about naked. Quetzalcoatl accused him of having caused his daughter's illness and demanded that she be healed, but he answered, 'I am not the only man who sells green chilli.'

Quetzalcoatl continued to importune him. At his command, his valets dressed the itinerant vendor's hair, bathed and anointed him, and gave him a loincloth. Thus suitably arrayed, he was taken to the maiden and lay with her. Later he was acknowledged as Quetzalcoatl's son-in-law, and this angered the Toltecs. Still sure that the man was an enemy even though he had allowed him to be taken into the family, Quetzalcoatl did not discourage the Toltecs from doing battle with the impostor. To Quetzalcoatl's delight the Toltecs at first seemed to be gaining the upper hand; but the army of Tezcatlipoca finally conquered. Quetzalcoatl admitted defeat and went out to meet his son-in-law, announcing that the virile young man had proved himself and was now definitely accepted into the family.

So powerful was this Tezcatlipoca that for long he seems to have dominated the Toltecs. For instance, he caused them all to sing. From dusk to midnight they went on singing, taking the cue from his own lips; and the music was so vibrant and intense that many fell into the caves and canyons and were turned to rock. Like the children lured by the Pied Piper of Hamelin, the Toltecs seemed to become hypnotised, and could not imagine how such disaster had befallen them. They seemed to be without resistance to the forces engulfing them.

Time and again they fell into this besotted state until they almost destroyed themselves. Tezcatlipoca now took the form of a warrior and called all that remained to assemble in Quetzalcoatl's field of flowers. Without question the Toltecs did as they were bidden, and Tezcatlipoca descended on them and began to massacre them. Many were slain, and many were trampled to death as they tried to flee.

Altering his disguise once more, Tezcatlipoca went into the market place and began entertaining the people by holding a dancing figure of the god Huitzilopochtli (or Quetzalcoatl) in the palm of his hand. Many Toltecs crowded forward to see the spectacle. But Tezcatlipoca cried out to them, 'What kind of sorcery is this? Is it not just a ruse to make men dance? You ought to stone us!' So the Toltecs stoned the marionette-worker until the body fell, apparently dead. It stank, and wherever the wind carried the stench the common people died. Not until many had perished from the fumes did Tezcatlipoca – who of course, in true mythical and fiendish fashion, went on living quite independently of the temporary form he had assumed – ordered the body to be thrown away.

Overleaf, left: head and shoulders of a hollow figure in painted clay of Xipe Totec, the flayed god. Totonac style, from the Veracruz region.
Right: Tlacolteutl, goddess of childbirth and the mother of Cinteotl and Xochiquetzal. This figure probably shows the birth of one of these. In another aspect she was the goddess of carnal sin – but as the 'Eater of Filth' she consumed the sins of mankind, receiving confession of their misdeeds. This was rewarded with total absolution but could only be made once in a lifetime. Aztec statuette with garnet inclusions.

A wooden mask covered with turquoise mosaic. The fangs suggest that it was a cult object associated with the Jaguar caste and probably used in religious rites. Very few exist; most were hidden from the Spaniards and the secret of their whereabouts subsequently lost. Mixtec, from Tilantongo, eighth to eleventh centuries A.D.

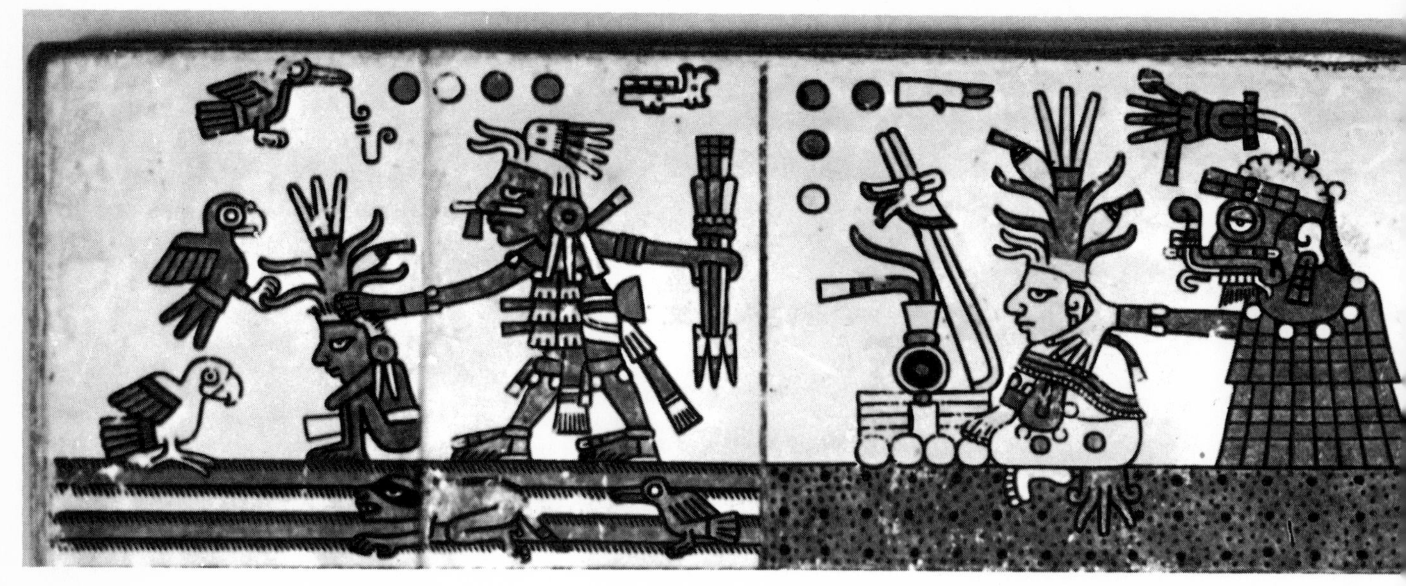

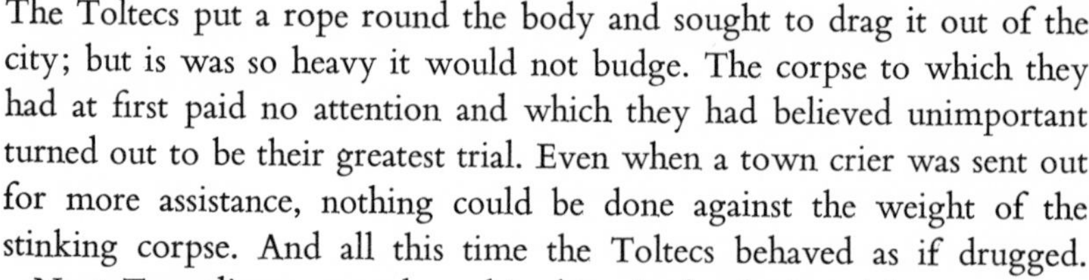

The Toltecs put a rope round the body and sought to drag it out of the city; but is was so heavy it would not budge. The corpse to which they had at first paid no attention and which they had believed unimportant turned out to be their greatest trial. Even when a town crier was sent out for more assistance, nothing could be done against the weight of the stinking corpse. And all this time the Toltecs behaved as if drugged.

Next Tezcatlipoca caused a white kite, its head pierced by an arrow, to fly to and fro as an evil omen over the heads of the Toltecs. He also caused a volcanic eruption. A mountain is said to have burned and stones to have rained down upon his enemies. Later still he became a little old woman selling paper flags among the crowds. Those who asked to buy one were sent immediately, at Tezcatlipoca's orders, to the sacrificial stone; they did not protest, nor could they help themselves for they were 'as if lost'.

Finally, after all the food had turned acrid and people were in danger of starving, an old woman came and began toasting delicious maize which sent out such a fragrant scent that crowds appeared from the most remote places to taste it. All the Toltecs left alive were now gathered in one place, so she – or rather he, for the old woman was Tezcatlipoca in disguise again, as we might have surmised – was able to go among them and slay them all.

The first trial endured by Quetzalcoatl is evidently a test of his power to overcome sensual pleasures, symbolized by wine. After that comes the temptation of sex, which is not suffered by Quetzalcoatl directly but by his daughter, and which finally puts all the Toltecs into a state of stupor. Then comes the desire for glory in battle, which Tezcatlipoca makes use of in order to lure the Toltecs to the 'field of flowers', a field of glory. After this comes an interesting trial, depending upon whether the Toltecs will be persuaded to mock even their own god Quetzalcoatl. They actually enjoy the degrading spectacle when he becomes Tezcatlipoca's plaything. It is only when Tezcatlipoca himself orders them to stone the marionette-worker that they do so, and then the result is disastrous, a stinking burden none can move. The besotted, drugged condition of Quetzalcoatl's followers goes from bad to worse, until they are unable to detect the evil quality in the fragrant maize brought them by an enemy. The very food given to them by their god Quetzalcoatl, as being fitting sustenance for man, becomes their downfall.

The growth of maize. Reading from right to left; the water goddess Chalchihuitlicue provides too much abundance, then the seed struggles with the harshness of a dry soil, manifest in the god Tepeyollotl who was Heart of the Mountain. Next the rain god Tlaloc brings the life-giving water in the right amount and, finally, the seed breaks through – Xipe Totec – and flourishes. *Codex Fejervary-Mayer.*

Bottom left: the rain god of the Zapotec culture was called Cocijo, represented here in a funerary urn from Monte Albán. Clay, ninth to fourteenth centuries A.D.

The departure

With his subjects all slain by the woman who brought them the fragrant maize, Quetzalcoatl decided finally to abandon Tula. He burned his houses of gold and coral and hid away all his treasures in the canyons and mountains, changing the cacao trees into dry mezquite fit for the desert, and sending the birds away. Taking the road, he and his remaining subjects set out for Anáhuac, the 'place at the centre, in the midst of the circle'. In other words, they now began their pilgrimage back to the source and inspiration of their being – the other holy place of the Toltecs, Tula, having become untenable.

They reached a spot where there was a stout, tall tree. Calling for his looking glass, Quetzalcoatl inspected his face and saw that he was now an old man, and he hurled stones at the tree, where they remained embedded in the trunk.

Flute players accompanied him as he proceeded forward. He rested on a stone and wept; hailstones rolled down his cheeks and gouged holes out of the stone, which also received the imprint of his hands and buttocks. Coming to a broad, long river, he laid stones to make a bridge, and after crossing over he came to a spot guarded by devils who sought to urge him back. But Quetzalcoatl said, 'I must go to Tlapallan, for I go to learn.'

'What wilt thou do?' the devils asked him, and he answered, 'I am called hence. The Sun calleth me.' They told him he would be allowed to go on condition that he left all his famous craftwork behind. They wrested from him all his skills; the casting of gold, the cutting of precious gems, wood carving, stone sculpture, the knowledge of the scribes and the art of feather work. At last in despair Quetzalcoatl cast his personal jewels into the water. Evidently in order to reach the place where he would 'learn' it was necessary for him to be deprived of this world's riches and of the crafts he had taught to his subjects. He must arrive poor. He encountered yet more devils, and when they accosted him replied that he was on his way to Tlapallan in order to learn. One devil tempted him with wine, but Quetzalcoatl refused until the devil insisted that nobody was allowed to proceed beyond that spot if he did not become drunk and stupefied. So Quetzalcoatl drank the wine, and fell asleep by the roadside, thundering as he snored.

Waking, he set off once again, and climbed the two snow volcanoes Popocatépetl and Ixtaccíhuatl, leading all the dwarfs and hunchbacks up

Xolotl, twin brother of Quetzalcoatl, represents the planet Venus as the evening star. This Aztec jadeite carving shows him as the death spirit on the obverse, while the reverse carries the sun, which dies at the rising of the evening star.

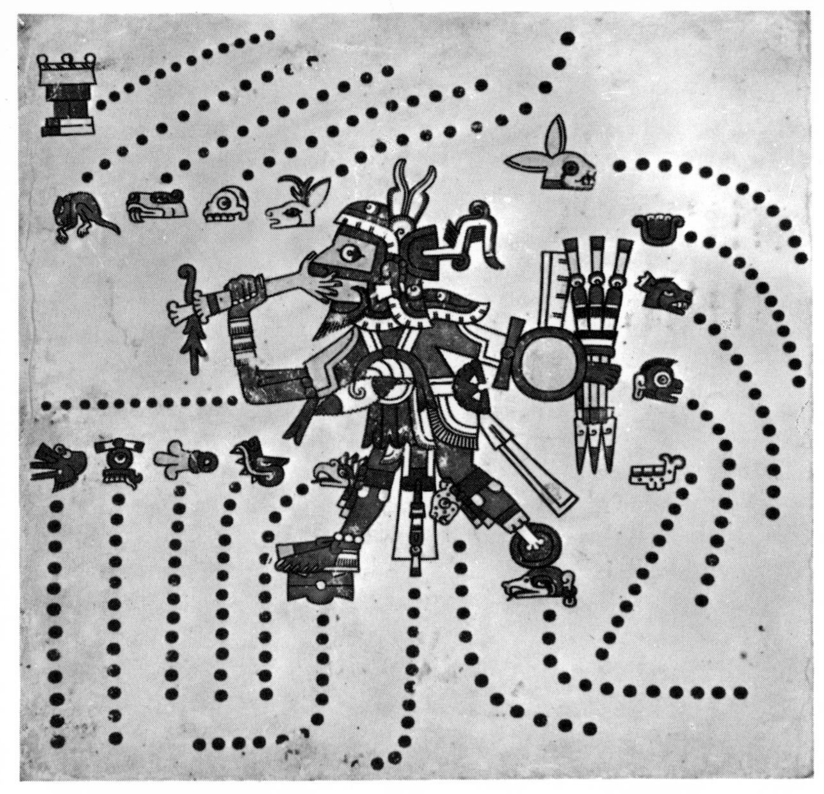

Tezcatlipoca eating flesh. The smoking mirror can be seen behind his ear in this leaf from the *Codex Fejervary-Mayer*.

the mountain until they died of cold. The dwarfs must have been a great loss to Quetzalcoatl, for in Mexican mythology they represent the tiny creatures of great power that we find in legends all over the world – the ants, the Tom Thumbs, the little fairies who do good deeds for people unseen. Veneration of dwarfs extended to Yucatán, where a small temple at Uxmal is known as The Dwarf's House. It is said that an old woman found an egg which she wrapped in cotton cloth and placed in a corner of her hut. One day the shell broke and a tiny mannikin crawled out. He went to court, and challenged the monarch to a trial of strength. The monarch asked him to lift a heavy stone, which he easily did. Vexed, the monarch then ordered him to build a palace taller than any in the city. Next morning there it was, for the mannikin turned out to be a sun dweller born of a cosmic egg.

No wonder then that on losing his dwarfs Quetzalcoatl wept and sang to himself as he gazed across at the third snow mountain – the one now called Orizaba but known in former days as Citlaltepetl. Elsewhere he planted maguey, and built a ball court with its stone ring, and shot at two silk-cotton trees and pierced them. He built a house in Mictlan, Land of the Dead. He proved his strength by pushing with his little finger a great rock that no other man had been able to budge from its place. And finally he set off on his raft of serpents to an unknown destination. The question has been asked, 'Why a raft of serpents?' Perhaps it was because he had conquered time and the lower ranges of the body.

Thus did the plumed serpent, Quetzalcoatl, triumph over the lord of the noumenal world Tezcatlipoca. Not without a struggle. Not without near defeat. But proving in the end the force of spirit over the illusory or only partially 'real' world of matter. Tezcatlipoca, sprightly, elusive, ever-changing, wore sandals of obsidian to show how firmly he was based on matter; whereas the wind-god and redeemer Quetzalcoatl had white sandals which – when interpreted together with the rest of his symbolism – may be taken to mean that wherever he trod he purified.

Characteristics of Tezcatlipoca

There was a statue of Tezcatlipoca said to have been of black stone like jet and to have been covered with gold and silver sequins. From the lower lip hung a glass bead in which was encased a green and blue feather which at first sight looked like a jewel. His hair was tied with a golden band, his headdress was of quail feathers, and he wore golden earplugs tinted with smoke to represent the prayers of the afflicted (whispered to him, presumably, in the intimacy of some Nahua confessional). From his neck hung a golden pectoral and he wore gold bracelets on his arms. An emerald marked his navel. In one hand he held a fly-whisk made of precious feathers, or else a spear; and in the other a shield and four arrows. In a disk burnished like a mirror he was able to see all that went on in the world. His stone was obsidian (*tezcat* means obsidian) used as late as the eighteenth century by Nahua-speaking Indians who regarded it as one member of a trinity together with the serpent and the dawning sun.

Sometimes he was represented seated in front of a red curtain on which were painted skulls and bones. He ruled over night and was in one aspect the Moon. The jaguar was his anvil, and he sometimes cried out like a bird of foreboding.

Tezcatlipoca presided over the school of plebeians, whereas Quetzalcoatl was patron of the academy of nobles where the army leaders, priests, and judges of the Aztec-Nahua establishment were trained. Tezcatlipoca is thus more immediately popular and human, less aloof than Quetzalcoatl. His smoking mirror, together with another opaque disk replacing the foot amputated by the earth monster, showed that he belonged to the world of noumena, the clouded world of half-perception and half-truth. In a sense he was a necromancer (and in that guise he tempted Quetzalcoatl), and he had some affinity with the Maya god Huracán whose very name suggests great energy unleashed and uncontrolled.

Tezcatlipoca sowed discord, but in a mischievous and not in a malevolent sense. He stimulated sexual activities but also received the confessions of lovers and others. He was lord over the material possessions of this world, and he could at will dispense or withhold them. He was a friend of the powerful, but also of slaves who were the humblest members of the community. Even more significant, those born under his sign were not ruled by fate but could be happy or accursed according to what they themselves were able to make of their inheritance.

It seems, therefore, that Tezcatlipoca, far from being a satanic figure, represented a kind of neutral energy. Like electricity it flowed freely and untrammeled, ready to be tapped and used, or wasted and left dangerously unharnessed, according to the individual whim, or the individual capacity, of each man who came under his power. The myth shows, like electricity, an interplay of positive and negative forces. Thus Quetzalcoatl was vanquished by Tezcatlipoca, and passed beneath the earth, and was again reborn; and in his rebirth he conquered his conqueror so that Tezcatlipoca's fate was finally to fall in a cascade of star-dust: the stars visible in the night sky. Although he was Lord of the Smoking Mirror, if the mirror were used as it ought to be it could reflect all the beauties of nature. In his breast there were two little doors meeting at the centre. A brave man might be able to open them and take hold of the heart within, in which case he was allowed to ask from Tezcatlipoca whatever ransom he chose; but any weakling who challenged Tezcatlipoca and failed to reach his heart would certainly die.

He is sometimes called the god of fire, although there was another god of fire in his own right – Xiuhtecuhtli also called Ixcozauhqui, of the yellow

face. Tezcatlipoca's paradoxical nature is never more clearly underlined than when we find him falling in love with Xochiquetzal, goddess of flowers and love, who lived on a mountain top surrounded by dwarfs, musicians, and dancing maidens, and who enticed all men by her charm. Tezcatlipoca snatched her from her true husband, Tlaloc. Tenderly Tezcatlipoca sang of her:

> She seems to me indeed a very goddess,
> she is so lovely and so gay.
> I must catch her, not tomorrow nor any time after
> but now in the very instant;
> I myself in person order and decree it shall be so.
> I, the warrior youth, shining like the sun
> and with the beauty of dawn.

Tezcatlipoca recognised that to achieve one's aim, to win the most precious thing in life, it is essential not to delay a single moment but to act forthwith. He also felt instinctively that beauty merits beauty, that he – so handsome as to be likened to the dawn – was destined for the flower goddess, lovely and gay.

Tezcatlipoca had thus a direct link with the merriest deities in the Nahua pantheon. Flower and song represented the words of the gods, manifest to mankind only through revelation. The deities of flower, dance, and games were precisely Xochiquetzal and her male twin Xochipilli. They were particularly closely associated with the later Aztec representation of Quetzalcoatl – Huitzilopochtli. At the feast of the flower gods, a bower of roses was built in Huitzilopochtli's temple. Here Xochiquetzal was

A ceremonial axehead – *hacha* – representing a warrior wearing an eagle headdress. The eagle represented the powers of light. From Itzapa, Guatemala, seventh to ninth centuries A.D.

Left: a gold pendant found in Tomb No. 7 at Monte Albán by Alfonso Caso. The disk represents the sun; above it are two ball players on either side of a serpent head. Below the disk is a moon glyph, followed by a representation of the Earth Monster which was seized by Tezcatlipoca and Quetzalcoatl. A fine example of Mixtec art, eighth to eleventh centuries A.D.

enthroned, and youths masquerading as birds and butterflies danced about her and climbed the artificial trees that had been erected for the occasion.

One version of the flower goddess story is that a flood destroyed all creatures except a god called Coxcox or alternatively Teocipactli and the goddess Xochiquetzal. The couple had many children, all of whom were born mute until a dove living in a high tree gave them each a voice and a different language.

Butterflies were particularly associated with Tezcatlipoca transmuted – in other words with Quetzalcoatl. In Teotihuacán, where a palace has been discovered evidently belonging to the priestly caste dedicated to Quetzalcoatl, there is a frieze showing the god's first entry into the world in the shape of a chrysalis, out of which he breaks painfully to emerge into the full light of perfection symbolised by the butterfly.

A Nahua triumvirate

On one side of his neutral but always ebullient nature, Tezcatlipoca links with song and flowers and butterflies; on the other with wickedness and sin. He is the direct opposite of Itzlacoliuhqui, the god of the curved obsidian knife (which also represents Tezcatlipoca himself so that Itzlacoliuhqui and Tezcatlipoca are sometimes taken to be one). Itzlacoliuhqui, god of ice and blindness and cold and obstinacy, represented matter in its most inert state, dead and immobile; and Tezcatlipoca that spark which gives uncontrolled, undisciplined vitality to stone and flower. Quetzalcoatl, making in this context a third in the triumvirate, is the saviour of a situation that, if left to itself, can lead to grave dangers, to chaos, and even to crime. He is the inspirer of values, of direction, and of discipline.

In the *Codex Cospiano*, Itzlacoliuhqui is seen making an offering to the powers of darkness, at the base of whose temple there is a human heart torn out. Inside it sits Tlacolotl, the great horned owl, omen of deepest evil. He represented to the Nahuas something far worse than the ordinary owl, who is merely the harbinger of death. Terrible as Tlacolotl is, however, the fumes that rise from him cannot obscure the sun which shines nevertheless. As Itzlacoliuhqui offers him a dark cloud of incense, blood flows from the god's self-mutilated ears. Like a fallen angel, this god had been cast down from heaven and blinded, so that on earth he was said to strike indiscriminately at his victims like the blind Greek fates. In the picture, his jaguar-skin mouth identifies him also with Tepeyollotl, Heart of the Mountain or of earthquakes; and by the same token he walks on lava rock. His evil appears to be that of material calamity, and not the more insidious evil of inner corruption, represented by certain female deities we shall refer to presently.

This god had his feminine counterpart, Itzpapalotl – the obsidian butterfly, the soul in the most permanent form, crystallised into rock. So the god of the sacrificial knife is also the soul god, for soul-making requires sacrifice of our lower natures. Perhaps because the soul is invisible, men cannot see Itzpapalotl entire, but only her jaguar claws. She seems to represent those delights that man, fallen from grace, has been deprived of; for there is a story that one day while picking roses in a garden she pricked her finger. Blood having once been caused to flow, she was obliged to deprive man of his happy pleasure-ground. But she may also be said to have fallen in another sense, for obsidian (the soul) was believed to have dropped from the stars. Obsidian is very important in ancient symbolism, and there is one story of the goddess of creation giving birth to an obsidian knife from which sprang sixteen hundred demi-gods who peopled the earth. Maize is often pictured in the form of an obsidian knife

Left: the Lord of the Region of Death portrayed on a remarkable piece of Mixtec gold work. This pectoral ornament shows Mictlantecuhtli with an elaborate headdress and there are two dates recorded on the breast pieces. He presided over the northern regions as well as over the hells below the earth. Eighth to eleventh centuries A.D.

The Plumed Serpent, god of learning, the planet Venus, great sky god – Quetzalcoatl was also the culture hero of the ancient Mexican peoples and a king of that name who ruled the Toltec people of Tula. He was also a great god of the Mayas. Aztec carving, thirteenth to fifteenth centuries A.D.

Xilonen, goddess of the young corn, and female counterpart of Cinteotl. Aztec carving.

and obsidian was often connected with lightning; it was the dark mirror of Tezcatlipoca, whereas Quetzalcoatl is rather connected with greenery and with jade.

In these three gods – Quetzalcoatl, Tezcatlipoca, and Itzlacoliuhqui-Itzpapalotl – we can see the different states of creation, always moving, always changing, always dying and being reborn. As the late Paul Westheim, a loving student of Mexican art, pointed out, life perishes but the energy of life is indestructible. The universe is composed of dynamic forces that are at once destructive and creative. The clash of such forces creates all cosmic events, and their interaction creates the world of nature. In this play of forces one against the other, all physical phenomena – not only man but even the stars in the sky – sooner or later die. But the vital energy (which we may surely equate with soul, obsidian) continues independently of space, time, and matter. It is the vital energy that is real: nothing else. Material things are mere appearance, simply one of the forms this energy can assume. Everything that exists is changing constantly; and change itself, life, is eternal.

According to Westheim, this idea of the constant clash of forces, of change on one level and constancy on another, is a fundamental concept of precolumbian thought. We find it expressed everywhere in the myths, particularly in the clashes between Quetzalcoatl and Tezcatlipoca. We find it also in the symbolism of eagle and tiger (ocelot) – the latter representing the powers of darkness and the underworld, the former of light. The knightly Orders of Eagles and Ocelots express the same inherent struggle in nature, and both are in a sense equally important. Light cannot exist without darkness, nor darkness without light. Man triumphs when he accepts and goes along with the contradictory forces in his nature, not when he tries to impose upon them some kind of artificial logic.

Yielding the forces of nature

The idea of yielding to the forces of nature is contained in the parallel roots of the words *atlatl* (arrow), and *atl* (water). Atlaua, an obscure god, is known as the 'master of waters', but he is also associated with arrows, and he sings: '...I leave my sandals behind. I leave my sandals and helmet... I cast off my arrows, even my reed arrows. I boast that they cannot break. Clad as a priest, I take the arrow in my hand. Even now I shall rise and come forth like the quetzal bird.

'Mighty is the god Atlaua. Truly I shall arise and come forth like the quetzal bird.'

Armed with arrows, by derivation soft as water and thus unbreakable, this god needs no helmet. Armed only with reed arrows he can emerge as the quetzal bird, the holy symbol of regeneration. Thus is duality eventually conquered.

We find duality again in the concept of the Moon god-goddess presiding over both the death and the regeneration of plant life on earth. Moon rules the drunken man asleep, and also his awakening; the human being hypnotised into a soporific state when he has no control over his actions, and at the same time the awakened 'man made man' who is lord over creation on earth. The Moon – Tecciztecatl, was observed by the Nahuas in all his contradictions. They saw how, when he first appeared he was 'like a bow, like a bent straw lip ornament, a very tiny one. He did not yet shine'. Slowly he grew larger until after fifteen days he was quite plump, and then he appeared in the Sun's place. When the night sky darkened he appeared 'like a large earthen skillet, very round and circular, seeming to be a bright, deep red. And after this, when he was already

The image of the plumed serpent, Toltec-Maya style. From the Temple of the Warriors at Chichén Itzá. The figure above is a standard-bearer.

some way on his travels, when he had risen, he became white'. It was said, 'Now he puts out moonbeams.' Then, so it was noticed, something that looked like a rabbit appeared on his face. If it was cloudless, not overcast, he shone like the Sun and it seemed to be day.

Then little by little he grew small again, becoming as he had first appeared, waning and vanishing. It was said, 'The Moon sleeps soundly now, falls into deep sleep. It is already near morning, near daybreak when he rises.' When he had vanished completely the Nahuas said, 'The Moon has died.'

There is a sequel to the story of the humble god Nanautzin who with the reluctant Tecciztecatl saved creation by burning himself up and thus allowing Sun and Moon to continue (Nanautzin as Sun and Tecciztecatl as Moon). The gods while playing with the two stars (at first they were both suns), struck Tecciztecatl's face with a rabbit, maiming and dimming him, so that thenceforth he was Moon.

It was necessary to bow before these cosmic facts, to yield to them, to go along with them. But it was not always easy, and at eclipses of either Sun or Moon there was profound fear and much weeping lest the powers of darkness should overcome the world. At an eclipse of the moon especially, it was thought that unborn children might be turned into mice. Women placed obsidian in their mouths so that their children would not be born deformed.

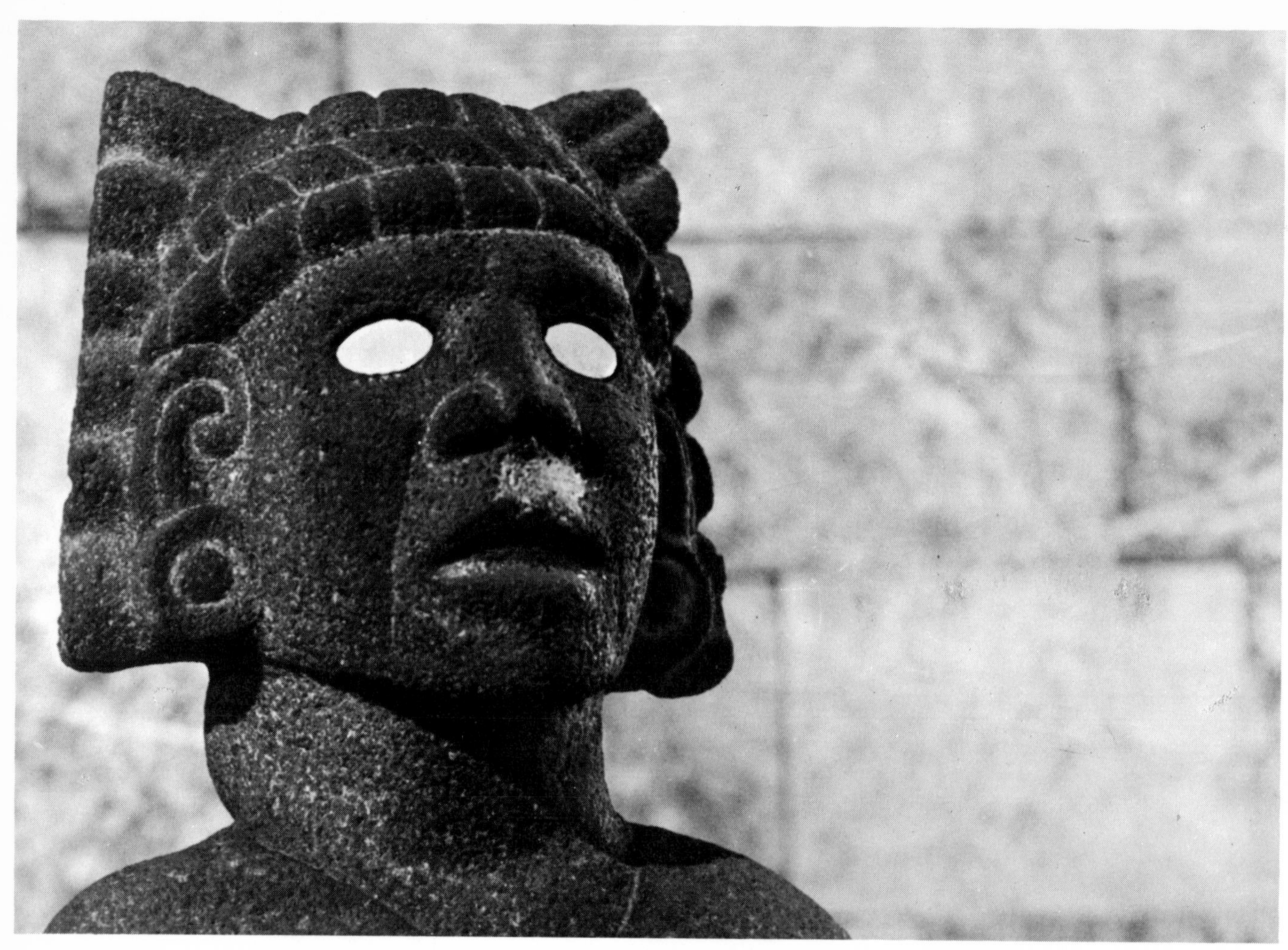

Tonantzin, the Aztec goddess of motherhood. There is a shrine to the Christian mother of god near Tenayuca on the very site where in ancient days the Mexicans worshipped this deity. Aztec basalt carving, with eyes of mother-of-pearl.

Some Female Deities

Strangely enough it was sometimes the female deities who personified cruel and evil forces, the darkest side of nature. The great mother goddess, it is true, was the patron of physicians, midwives, and owners of steam baths. From the liquid rubber on her lips and the circles of rubber on her cheeks we might think that she bore some relation to Tlaloc; but she was also decorated with flowers and a shell-covered petticoat, and she carried a broom, all of which suggests that she may have been a kind of female equivalent of Quetzalcoatl, wind-god and road-sweeper of the gods. There was another goddess more closely associated with Tlaloc – Chalchihuitlicue, goddess of the jade petticoat and elder sister of the rain gods. Her colouring – she was painted blue and yellow and wore a green stone necklace and turquoise earplugs, and a blue cap with a spray of quetzal feathers – gives her a watery shimmer. Her skirt and shift were painted like water, she was ornamented with waterlilies, and she carried clappers which were always a sign of the water deities.

Chicomecoatl, savage snake woman, in charge of man's nourishment, was also a benign goddess ornamented with water flowers and carrying a sun shield. She can be equated with Coatlicue herself, the great earth mother who engenders and nurtures all things. But there were other goddesses on a lower level who were more truly sinister. Chief of these was the terrible Ciuacoatl who, though she was dressed all in white and 'gave men the hoe and the tump line' (the means of labour), went weeping and wailing through the night, forecasting wars and misery. Her face was painted half red, half black, but her horrible appearance was somewhat alleviated by her feather headdress, her golden earplugs, and the turquoise weaving stick she carried. Was she a darker side of Quetzalcoatl, a savage instead of a redeeming serpent? And was perhaps Tlacolteutl, goddess of vice and eater of filth, a dreadful corollary to the impish Tezcatlipoca? Parallel to the four Tezcatlipocas there were four sisters, all of them aspects of Tlacolteutl: Tiacapan the eldest, Teicu, Tlaco, and Xocutzin the youngest. All these were but four faces of a witch who rode a broomstick in true European style only that she went naked except for a peaked hat. The four sisters hovered at the cross-roads of life, ready one supposes to lure the unwary away from their appointed destination. Turning fearfully from their evil influences, men used to go as penitents to Tezcatlipoca, and the priest would speak to the penitent saying: 'Thou hast come into the presence of the god, protector of all. Thou hast come to confess and to deliver thyself of thine evil and corruption. Thou hast come to unburden thyself of thy secrets. Be sure to commit no fault nor sin. Take off thy clothes; show thy nakedness to the god, the protector, our Lord Tezcatlipoca. Being a mortal, probably thou shalt not see the god; probably he will not speak to thee, a mortal. For he is invisible and impalpable. So thou comest to the god to uncover thy secrets and to explain thy way of life and thine actions... May our Lord, protector of all, take pity on thee, stretch forth his arms to thee, embrace thee, carry thee on his back. Be daring, be not timid nor shameful nor bashful.'

Then the penitent said: 'Our Lord, protector of all, who is aware of my evil smell and my vices, in thy presence I remove my clothing and lay bare my nakedness... Can these things be hid and made dark when they are reflected and clear in thy sight?'

Here is evidence that Tezcatlipoca, although the opponent of Quetzalcoatl who often frustrates the redeemer in his desire for the good and holy life, is in himself not evil. Among the goddesses there are truer personifications of evil, each the converse of some higher god, Quetzalcoatl or Tezcatlipoca, due warnings of what may happen when the free energies on the cosmic scene are deliberately distorted and become sin. From them there is no redemption unless the penitent is prepared to strip himself naked, to show himself as he is, without pretence and without concealment. Only then may he be saved. But the positive and negative poles of natural energy are not in themselves the cause of evil. They are simply opposed poles – 'burning water' and 'blossoming war'. By these two paradoxical concepts the Nahuas sought to express the war and conciliation inherent in all natural phenomena.

Tlacolteutl, like earth and fertility goddesses everywhere, has many of the aspects of a witch. In this leaf from the *Codex Fejervary-Mayer* she can be seen on a broomstick. The serpent was coloured red – the Aztec symbol of sex.

The goddess of flowers and love, Xochiquetzal was loved by Tezcatlipoca, who stole her from the rain god Tlaloc. She is seen uttering 'flowery words', characterised by the decorated speech scroll. *Codex Fejervary-Mayer.*

The dual god-above-all seen in the *Codex Zouche-Nuttall*. Though regarded as the bestower of all life the supreme god was too remote for ordinary man. The male-female deity can be seen on the left, seated by the waters – but it is to the rain god and his consort, seated on the right, that the four priests bring offerings.

Tloque Nahuaque

That is why the gods on the level of the four compass points, the gods belonging to the world of organic life, such as Quetzalcoatl and Tezcatlipoca, are in a sense more important in the Nahua pantheon than Ometeotl, sometimes called Tloque Nahuaque, the dual god-above-all. Even though he is called 'the god of the near and close', he remains to the ordinary man somewhat remote. He is 'invisible as night, impalpable as wind', and the ordinary man likes to see more clearly defined images of his god than the footprints and hands that appear in some Teotihuatecan frescoes. All the same, Tloque Nahuaque is the original bestower of all life, including his own. He is even said to have invented himself. He is the god who feeds us, and the serious seeker after truth must thus regard him as essentially accessible and merciful. The temple to him was all gold and precious feathers within, black and crusted with stars on the outside. His consort is the goddess of the starry petticoat, of all the heavens. There was never a statue of any kind made in his likeness. As Ometeotl, the supreme dual lord and lady, he is described as the Lord of the Ring, 'self-willing, self-enjoying':

Even as He wills, so shall He desire that it shall be.
In the centre of the palm of His hand He has placed us,

He is moving us according to His pleasure.
We are moving and turning like children's marbles, tossed without direction.
To him we are an object of diversion...

From one point of view, it seems a terrible thing for man to be no more than the plaything of the gods; from another, there could be no more kindly fate than to be a child's marble in the hands of the all-powerful.

There was a tendency to bring the great god-above-all down onto a level of visible creation; for example, he may sometimes be identified with the old god, the fire god, his consort becoming the earth or moon. The tribe of the Otomí Indians regarded the dual pair as the parents of five different nations, themselves among them. Even so, they give their great god, whom they call Otonteuctli a headdress representing an obsidian butterfly, symbol of the most complete permanence within the transitory.

In a lesser-known codex (the Huamantla) there is a drawing of Otonteuctli and Xochiquetzal, goddess of flowers but also of the obsidian butterfly, seated together inside a cave. At the top of the arched entrance there is a split or fault, and the inscription reads 'This is the cave from which we came forth'. The impression is of the male and female principles of permanence in transience – of noumena behind phenomena – enclosed in a curved space that looks like a skull. Out of the split at the top of the skull or cave these two energies, male and female, immortal and at the same time ephemeral in all their palpable manifestations, can come forth. In one hymn the god of fire says:

I tie a rope to the sacred tree.
I plait it with eight strands so that I –
a magician –
may descend to the magical house.
Intone your song in the Hall of Flames;
Intone your song in the Hall of Flames.
Why does the magician not come forth?
Why does he not appear?
May his vassals serve him in the Hall of Flames.
He comes, he comes, let his vassals serve him.

What is this eight-stranded rope by which the god of fire must descend in order to release the magician? It is impossible to answer this question dogmatically, but the whole impression is of a downward plunging of fire, or some primaeval energy, to release the magician, creator of all possibilities in the universe.

More usually, however, the great god-above-all is not concerned with energies and matter, being too distant, too rarified. In his purest form he is never depicted in images, and only his footprints and his hands are permitted to be drawn. It would seem to be impossible to describe his face. He is not to be looked at by human kind. He belongs to a different order, and it is to the gods on a lower level – especially to Quetzalcoatl – that man must turn if he would ask for mercy.

One extant hymn to Quetzalcoatl's successor Huitzilopochtli describes him as 'only a mortal', and in many respects he was. He is also said to be 'a magician, a terror, a disturber of life' – but this is more true of him in his aspect of Tezcatlipoca. His kindlier qualities are closer to those of Cinteotl, the corn god, with whom he is also identified, especially in a hymn that was sung only every eight years when there was a period of fasting on bread and water. Out of the fasting seems to have arisen joy and fertility and plentitude, for the hymn is one of the happiest:

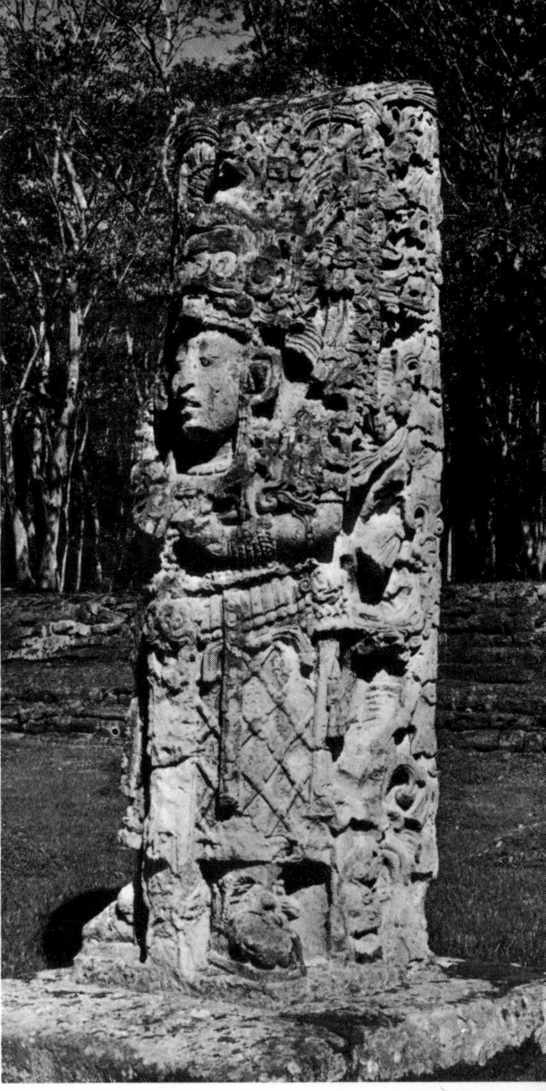

The Maya water goddess Ixchel, seen on a colossal stele from Copán, Honduras. She differs from her Nahua counterpart Chalchiuhuitlicue in being the consort of the chief god of the pantheon, and she is also the goddess of childbirth and weaving.

A game played by the Aztecs was *patolli*, not unlike our game of ludo. This leaf from the *Codex Magliabecchi* shows four players round a board. Macuilxochitl, god of games and feasting, presides.

My heart blossoms and propagates in the middle of the night...
I, Cinteotl, was born in Paradise. I come from the place of flowers.
I am the only flower, the new, the glorious one.
Cinteotl was born of water; as a mortal, as a young man, he was born from the sky-blue home of fish. A new, a glorious god.
He shone like the Sun. His mother lived in the house of dawn, many-coloured as the quetzal bird, a new and lovely flower.
On earth, even in the market place like any mortal, I – Quetzalcoatl – appeared, the great and the glorious.
Be ye happy under the flower-bush, many-coloured like the quetzal bird.
Listen to the quechol bird singing to the gods.
Listen to the quechol singing by the river.
Listen to its flute by the river in the house of reeds.
Would that my flowers might never die. Our flesh is as flowers; flowers in the flower land.
He plays ball, plays ball, the servant so marvellously skilled.
He plays ball, the servant highly prized. Mark him. Even he who rules over the nobles follows him to his home.
O youths, O youths! Follow the example of your forbears.
Emulate them in the ball court. Establish yourselves in their houses.
She goes to the market place. They carry Xochiquetzal to the market...
She astounds my heart. She astounds my heart.
She has not finished. The priest knows her. She is to be seen where the merchants sell ear-rings of jade.
In the place of wonders she is to be seen.
Sleep, sleep, sleep. I fold my hands in sleep. I – a woman – sleep.

Out of the jumble of names here – Cinteotl, Quetzalcoatl, Huitzilopochtli (to whom the hymn is said to be dedicated), Xochiquetzal – we may extract the basic message that Quetzalcoatl is the god of fertility and, on a deeper level, of regeneration; Xochiquetzal as well as Quetzalcoatl. This dual principle is born out of the basic element of water, a flower out of the happy land of flowers. It becomes incarnate in human form, and plays ball, the game that teaches mortals how to manipulate the predestined trend of events.

The sudden appearance of Xochiquetzal at the end of the hymn may appear arbitrary. The final stanzas sound like a separate song accidentally strung onto the earlier one; but it must have been part of the fasting ceremony, the final culmination announcing the birth of the goddess of flowers who then sleeps, returns to quiet, returns to her origins.

The sciences of astronomy and mathematics were developed to an extraordinary degree in Mexico, as the remarkable accuracy of their calendars demonstrate. This circular tower at Chichén Itzá is believed to have been part of a Maya observatory.

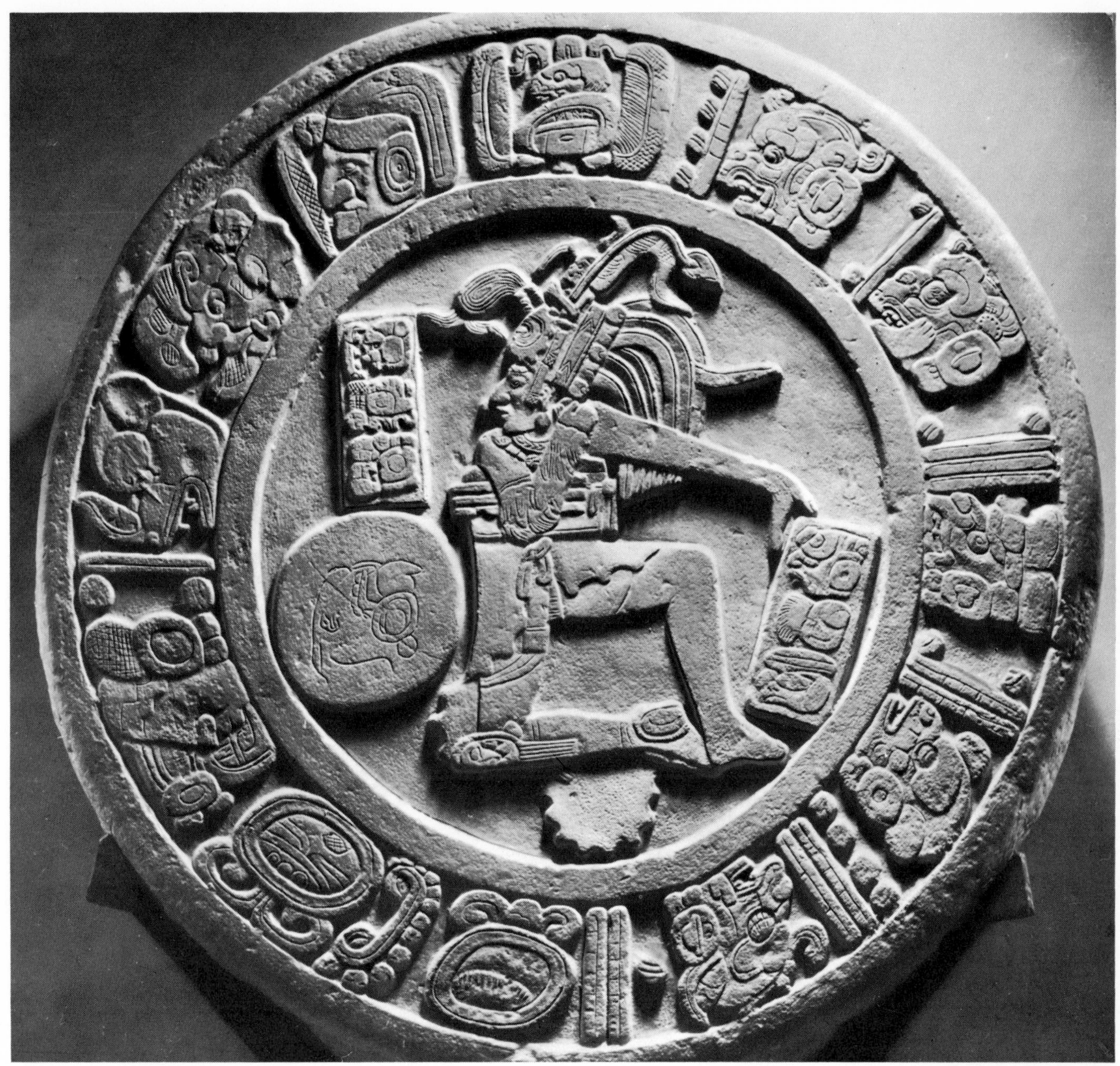

The Ball Game

In every part of old Mexico and Central America, wherever a temple stood, there existed a ball court. They have been found from Honduras to south-eastern Arizona. In the *Annals of Cuauhtitlán* it is said that Topiltzin, the incarnate King Quetzalcoatl, invented the game played in them, but its real age and origin are unknown.

The urge toward symbolic representation was so strongly developed in the Mexican people that every human act, even the games they played, reflected something deeper.

If the interpretation of the ball game as a symbolic working out of man's struggle to master fate seems arbitrary, we should remember the association of games with religious practice and not think of them as mere pastimes, though it is certain that they also provided pleasure. The exact symbolism of the ball game is unknown, but Cottie Burland has suggested that it represents the play of cosmic forces. Since the ball is

A carved stone medallion from Ratinlixul, Guatemala. The ball player is Maya and the glyphs surrounding him probably commemorate a festival. Pre-classic Maya, *c.* 750 A.D.

at the mercy of the players, who with elbows and buttocks (not with arms, hands, or feet) must try to send it through one of the stone hoops placed high on the court walls, it seems that there was a loophole for change in the cycle of heavenly movements. In one of the very few ancient poems that mentions the ball game, there is a suggestion of this free will within the predestined motion of the heavenly bodies. A sacred pheasant, representing the sun, hesitates at a crossroads wondering which road to take:

> Above the field of the ball game
> beautifully the peerless Pheasant sings:
> he is answering the Corn God.
> Now sing our friends,
> now sings the peerless Pheasant:
> at night the Corn God shone.
> 'Only he who wears bells on his ankles
> shall hear my song.
> Only she shall hear my song
> whose face is masked,
> the sign of the new year beginning.
> I give the law in Tlalocan
> I am the purveyor of riches.
> I am the purveyor in Tlalocan.
> I give the law.
> Oh, I have reached the point
> where the road divides:
> I am the Corn God!
> Where shall I go?
> Where continue my road...?'

The usual interpretation of the ball game is more sanguinary, and is based partly on frieze sculptures apparently showing the captain of the losing team beheaded, with blood spurting from seven vessels. The game, according to this view, was a physical battle. So too are football or tennis. But games have a symbolic origin, the pre-Hispanic ball-game no less than snakes and ladders, which had incidentally its ancient American counterpart in *patolli*, played on a crossshaped 'board' drawn out on the ground.

The symbolic nature of the game is evident in a story of how Quetzalcoatl played one day against Tlaloc the rain god and his children. Quetzalcoatl won, and Tlaloc offered him maize as his prize; but Quetzalcoatl would have nothing less than jade and fine feathers. Tlaloc gave him these, but warned him that jade could not compare in value with maize as food for man. Maize – organic and growing – was more appropriate a reward for victory than petrified jade.

Here a warning is needed. The symbolism of the ancient myths can never be regarded as rigid. Jade and precious stones seem sometimes to represent atrophy and loss of life, at others the fixing of spiritual qualities in the 'deified heart' so that it is no longer transient, like a flower or a butterfly, but endures like some precious or semi-precious stone. Nothing in the Quetzalcoatl symbolism is static. Everything is moving, everything is changeable, and in interpreting its many facets one has always to be watchful of the total context, remembering that the aim is the creation of man in the fullest sense of the word, 'man made man' as one poem has it: man with all his potential fulfilled.

Maya Parallels with the Nahua gods

Quetzalcoatl's religion extended into the Maya lands to the south and became confounded with that of the authors of the *Chilam Balam* and the *Popol Vuh*. But this was possible only because there was already a similarity in their thinking. The Maya god above all, sometimes known as Hunab-ku (the Great Hand, the God Behind the Gods, invisible and impalpable), is the exact parallel of Ometeotl (or Tloque Nahuaque). Quetzalcoatl was translated by the Mayas into Kukulcan, but was also identical with the earlier Itzamná, son of Hunab-ku. Itzamná introduced maize and cocoa into the human diet. He also saw the usefulness of rubber, invented writing, and generally established culture just as his Nahua counterpart had done further north.

The Bacabs, deities of the four compass points, who were placed there to give the world a firm support, seem to be the Maya equivalents of the four Tezcatlipocas, or Quetzalcoatl and three Tezcatlipocas. Each had personal names: Kan (yellow), Chac (red), Zac (white), and Ed (black). They had also the generic name Balam and were linked with the four winds.

Kinich Ahau is the fire bird, or Quetzalcoatl as sun god. Chac is the equivalent of Tlaloc, god of rain. Yum Kaax is the Maya corn god, and so on through the whole pantheon – which makes one suppose (though

A leaf from one of the rare Maya sacred books, *Codex Tro-Cortesianus*, showing the maize god, left, and the rain god Chac, right.

Left: a Mayan ball player, attired with elaborate yoke at his waist and wearing a headdress. He is probably performing a ritual in honour of the sun god before the game begins. The god of death can be seen in the lower right-hand corner. Monument III from the island of Cozumel, *c.* 1000 A.D.

Right: the Maya god of death, God 'A', seen holding a death's head in his hands. Painted pottery figure from Tikal, Guatemala.

A stone sculpture from Quiché, Guatemala, of the mask of Itzamná, the Maya god-above-all sometimes identified with Quetzalcoatl. He gave the Mayas cocoa and maize and invented writing.

the special protagonists of one or other religion will not have it so) that the Maya and the Nahua deities came originally from a single source possibly further back than either. Certainly there was no basic difference in the two systems of thought, both of which point to the need for refining man's emotions until they are capable of praising the creator – as in the Maya myth of creation – or of forming a deified heart as in the Nahua philosophical concept.

The name Mayapan, given to the Maya New Empire which endured from 987 to 1697 A.D., means 'the Standard of the Not Many', from Maya (not many) and pán (standard). It was sometimes called Ichpa, meaning 'within the enclosure', an exactly parallel idea to the Nahua description of Tloque Nahuaque as Lord of the Ring.

Like the Nahuas, the Mayas had an hierarchical caste system related to their gods. There were the ruling intellectual nobility on the one hand, and the priestly caste of the Sun on the other. Each of these hierarchies was in turn split into different grades according to their degree of advancement in religious and civic understanding. At the very top were the priests of Kukulcan (Quetzalcoatl). Immediately underneath these were the caste of nobles known as the *Halach uinic*, meaning 'true man', and the priestly caste *Ahuacan*, lord serpent. The 'true men' sat in judgment on those rising in the caste system in order to decide which among them should qualify to be *Almenhenob*, 'those who had fathers and mothers'. Evidently the parents referred to are the true men themselves, and in order to qualify as sons of these high men it was necessary to possess the key to a special language called *Zuyua* – the language of the Xiu people.

The Xiu were an important ruling Maya family centered in Uxmal and one member of it, Ah Kukum Xiu, helped Francisco Montejo the younger in his conquest of Yucatán. The language to which the Xiu gave their name may well have been much older and more venerable than the family itself.

The 'true men' who were the 'fathers and mothers' of lesser mortals, carried in their right hands a sceptre in the shape of a mannikin, one leg ending in a serpent which is the sceptre's handle. In the left hand they carried a shield of the sun god, seal and proof of their high status.

The *Almenhenob*, children of the 'true men' had their parallel in the priestly hierarchy: *Chilanes*, or diviners. The *Almenhenob* could be either hereditary or elected, but all the *Nacom* were elected for three years during which time they could have no relations with women, not even with their wives; they could not eat red meat, must not get drunk, and were not served by any woman. They lived in a place apart, with their own special cooking utensils. The *Nacom* were the lowest order of priesthood but on the lay side there was a caste called 'those at the head of the mat', *Ah holpopoh*, who stood in an intermediary position between the nobles and the common people. Their name suggests that they presided at ordinary gatherings consisting of the three lowest castes: the *tupiles* (town constables), the common people, and the slaves. All these lived outside the towns and villages, so that the distance of a man's house from the central plaza showed his position in the social-religious scale.

Somewhere at the level of Kukulcan were a host of other gods who are usually known to modern scholars only as a series of initials. God A is Hunhau or Ahpuch, the god of death who ruled over Mitnal, a name similar to the Nahua death country Mictlan. Hunhau is sometimes represented with a human body and the head of an owl, and present-day Indians of Mexico and Central America believe that when the owl screeches somebody will die.

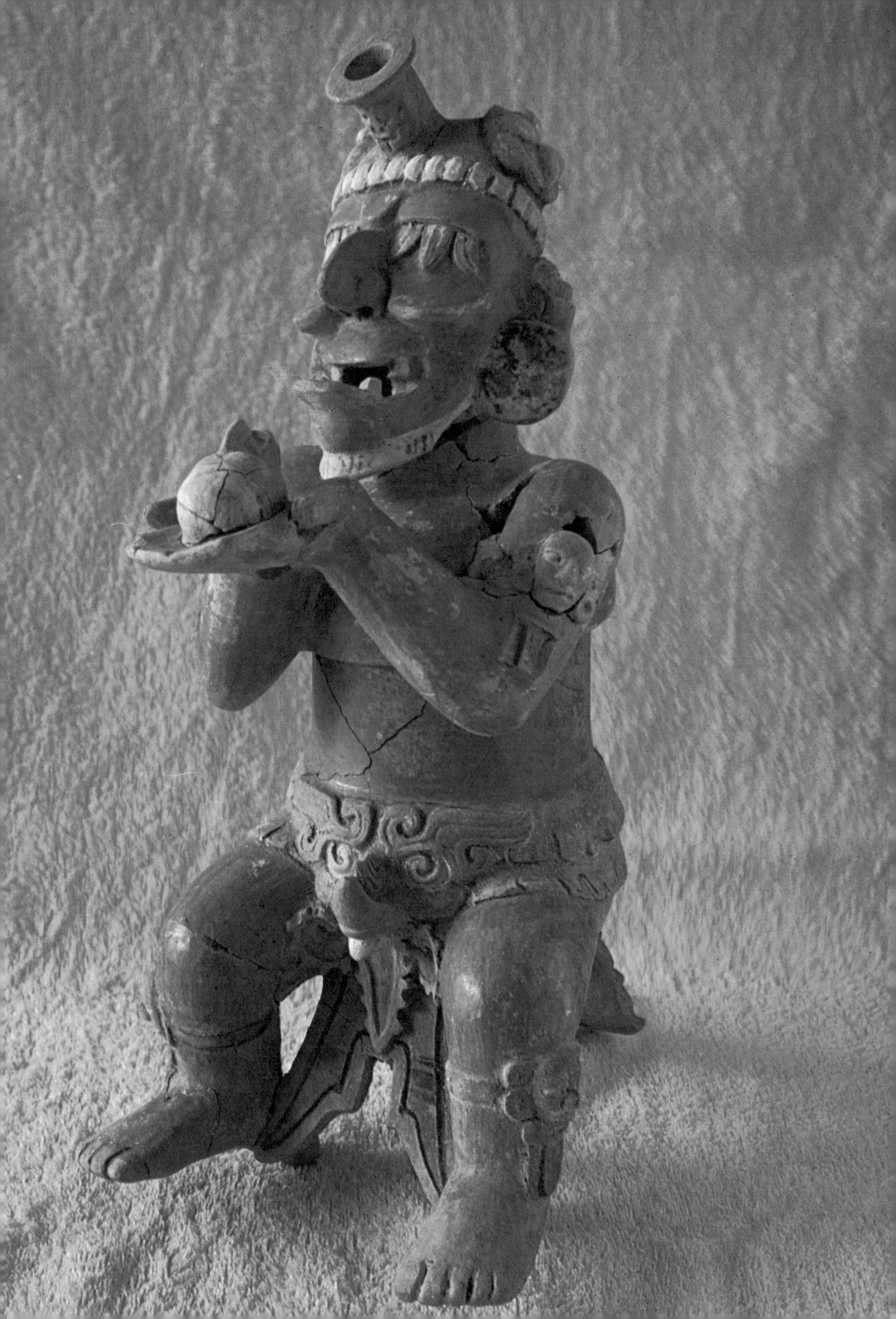

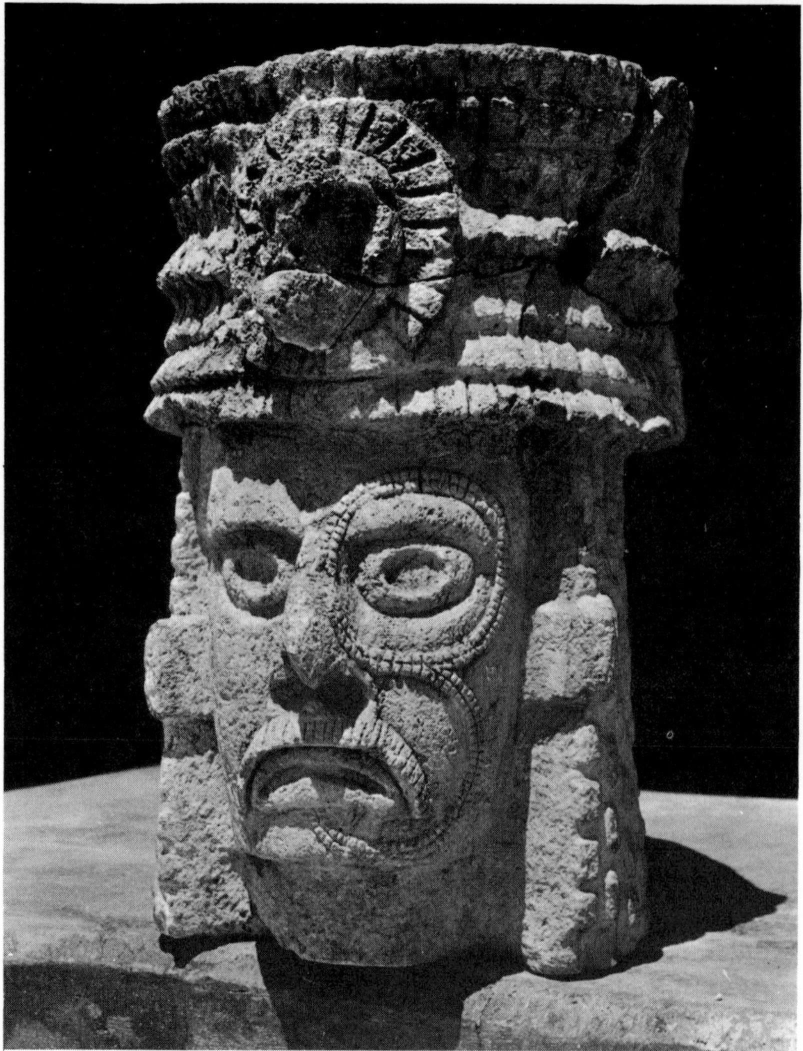

The Mayan god of sacrifice, God 'F'. He is also a warrior god, and his distinguishing mark is the line encircling the eye and extending down over his cheek. Temple carving from Kabah.

Below: a clay statuette from the Jalisco, Mexico. This ball player is simply attired but common to all is the heavy waistband. He carries the ball here, but during the game it was never touched by hand. The ball was made of rubber, and it was a description of the game by Oviedo in the sixteenth century that acquainted Europeans with this unique substance.

The Mayas were as preoccupied with death as the Nahuas, and both peoples believed that suicides went to paradise, not to hell. The Mayas thought they went to the goddess Ixtab, goddess of the noose or gallows. It is tempting to wonder whether originally the idea of suicide was related to the killing of a man's lower nature, whether it is an idea parallel to that of the hanged man of the Tarot pack. In this case the happy after-death fate of suicides would be explained.

Hunhau is usually associated with the dog, who is a symbol of death and the bearer of lightning. The Lacandón Indians, a few of whom still survive in the forests of Chiapas though the race is dying out, still place an image of a dog on their graves. Eduard Seler thought that the dog was buried with men because he had in life been their faithful companion, and that this practice gave rise to the animal's association with death. In the day names of the calendar the dog is the Maya *Oc*, the last day of the series, signifying the lowest point reached by the soul on his spiritual journey. If we take the pilgrimage as beginning with the first day of the Nahua series then *Itzcuintli*, the dog, falls on the same day. The Nahuas and the Mayas evidently had their equivalent of Cerberus.

God B is Kukulcan, the equivalent of Quetzalcoatl and the most important deity in the Maya pantheon. Some characteristics link him also with Tlaloc; and conversely there are other Maya gods that can be associated with Quetzalcoatl in certain particular aspects of his nature.

Kukulcan has a proboscis-like nose and serpent fangs at either side of

A fine stucco head from Tabasco. Remarkable for the European features, the nobility of the face and the unusual beard suggest that it may be a portrait of Kukulcan. Pre-classic Maya.

Below: an ancient Maya stone carving, sixth to ninth centuries, of the god of virility, a rare example of ithyphallic presentation. He was probably an early manifestation of Itzamná.

his mouth. His chief symbol is a torch, or fire; but he has also four others that seem to represent the four elements. They are the sprouting maize (earth), the fish (water), the lizard or salamandar (fire), and the vulture (air). In his heraldry there are four colours that also seem to represent the elements: yellow (air), red (fire), white (water), and black (earth). He sits at the centre of a cross-shaped tree, at the centre of the four compass points or of the quincunx. Sometimes he is earthy, planting maize, going on a journey with staff and bundle, and armed with axe and spear. At other times he is watery, being enthroned in clouds or riding in a canoe from which he goes fishing. He alternately devours or is devoured by a serpent. His day is *Ik*, the day of breath and of life, and he never on any account appears in conjunction with the frequent death symbols of Maya mythology. Like Quetzalcoatl he is essentially the god of resurrection and rebirth.

Little is known about god C except that his face is ornamented, that he hangs from the sky by a rope, and that his day is *Chuen*. This is the first created day of the Maya series, when the god-above-all brought forth divinity from himself and created heaven and earth. It is thought that this is a star god and one is inclined to think that he may be the planet Venus, in which case he would be another aspect of Kukulcan (Quetzalcoatl), though some have equated him with the Pole star. However, the more we study the Maya gods the more we find the kaleidoscopic central figure proliferating in a multitude of patterns, as if his full meaning were

Victorious Maya warriors – a detail from one of the mural paintings at Bonampak. The scene depicted is probably a successful raid on another tribe to obtain prisoners for sacrifice.
Right: a head carved in trachite from the stairway of Temple 26 at Copán, Honduras. It represents the young maize god Yum Caax and embodies all the Maya ideals of masculine beauty. Classic Maya style.

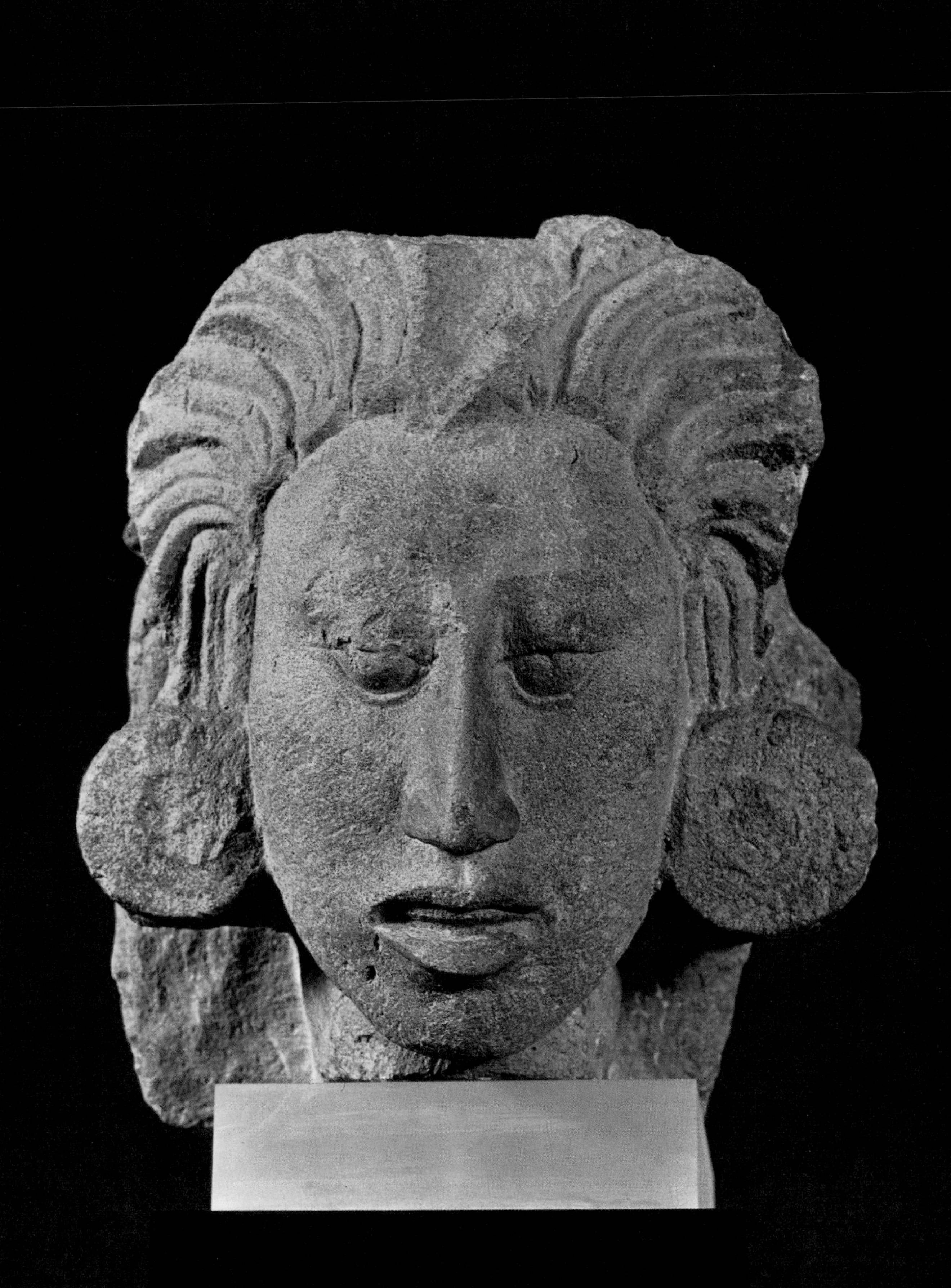

too vast for the human mind to grasp entire.

God D, for example, can also be equated with Kukulcan-Quetzalcoatl, though he is an old man with sunken cheeks and a mouth devoid of teeth except for one in the lower jaw. He is god of the Moon and of night, and his day is *Ahau* when bad men go to hell. Contradictorily however he never appears with death symbols. Sometimes he wears on his head a conch shell, symbol of birth and one of the distinctive signs for breath or life. Perhaps he represents the perpetual cycles of death and rebirth.

God E is *Ghanan* or Yum Caax, the maize god, god of the harvest fields, equivalent to the Nahua Cinteotl and thus also an aspect of Kukulcan-Quetzalcoatl. He is a handsome god with the long profile and elongated, flattened forehead cultivated by the Maya aristocracy and found in stone portraits from Palenque and in the paintings of Bonampak.

A carved lintel from Yaxchilán, *c.* 700 A.D. An offering, rather like the medicine bundles of North America, is being presented to a priest in elaborate robes and headdress, probably representing Kukulcan.

Skulls of Maya children were artificially flattened by tying boards to them when the bones were still soft. The resulting long oval shape is said to have represented an ear of maize. God E is associated with life, prosperity, and fruitfulness, never with death.

God F has a resemblance to Xipe, the flayed god. He is distinguished by vertical marks on his face. God G, who is Kukulcan in his aspect of sun god, is at times linked rather oddly with death. He has a snake-like tongue obtruding from his mouth.

God H, with a spot or snake scale on his forehead, seems to be Kukulcan-Quetzalcoatl in his serpent aspect. His day is *Chicchan*, associated with the serpent.

The deity lettered I is female, goddess of water, floods, and cloudbursts. She wears a knotted serpent on her head.

Although god K, with his elephant trunk, has been given a separate letter, he may be one more variant of god B, or Kukulcan. At any rate the two are closely related. God K may have been rather a god-man like Quetzalcoatl in human form. Some workers have identified him with Itzamná, a god who said of himself, 'I am the dew of heaven, I am the dew of the clouds.' He was also called Lakin Chan, serpent of the east, and was said to have been the creator of men and of all organic life and to have founded the Maya culture. He invented writing and books, had a knowledge of herbs and healing, and some say he was the son of Hunab-Ku, the invisible god above all.

God L is old and black with a sunken mouth. He is Ekchuah, god of travellers. God M is a black god with red lips, the lower one large, drooping, almost negroid. He appears to be Ek Ahau, or the black lord, and to have had some connection with war though he was also god of merchants like the Nahua god Yiacatecuhtli.

The headdress of god N bears the sign of the 360-day year, and he is evidently the deity who presides over the year's end. O is female with wrinkles round the eyes, and she is usually represented with a loom. Perhaps she is a goddess of fate. God P is known as the frog god, and he seems to be connected with the calendar, for his headdress, like that of god N, contains the sign for the 360-day year.

Besides these numbered gods there are several others, notably Zotz the bat god, patron of the Zotzil Indians who live today in Chiapas, and of some Guatemalan Indians. The Maya twenty-day period was called Zotz. In Copán there is a relief-carving of a struggle between him and Kukulcan, so that in some ways he seems to be parallel to Tezcatlipoca, opponent of Quetzalcoatl.

There were many Maya war gods, though some may have had a purely symbolic connection with war. Among them are Ahulane the archer, who is shown holding an arrow and whose shrine was on the island of Cozumel; Pakoc, the frightener, and Hex Chun Chan, the dangerous one, both of whom were gods of the usurping Itzá dynasty; Kac-u-Pacat, who carried a shield of fire; Ah Chuy Kak, the fire destroyer; Ah Cun Can, the serpent charmer; and Hun Pic Tok who held eight thousand spears.

Like the Nahuas, the Mayas had their god of intoxication. There was also a god of medicine, Cit Bolon Tum; a god of song, Xoc Bitum; and a god of poetry, Ab Kin Xoc or Ppiz Hiu Tec. The female deities were more benign than the Nahua ones, and included Ix Tub Tun, goddess of workers in jade and amethyst; Chebel Yax who invented woven colour designs; and Ix-huyne, the moon goddess.

The name Aztec means 'the heron people', and may have some bearing on the origins of the tribe which was somewhere to the north of the present boundaries of Mexico. But this stone carving suggests that the heron may have been a symbol in other parts of Mexico; it comes from the Veracruz region where these birds haunt the low-lying marshlands.

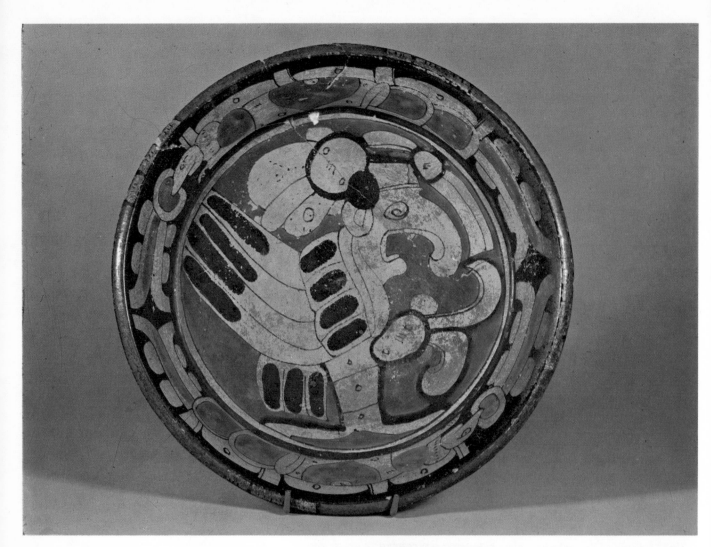

Above: the interior of a polychrome bowl with tripod legs. The bird shown here is Moan, the vulture who was the harbinger of death. Late classic Maya. Right: a Maya vase in the shape of a snail with a figure emerging. It probably represents the wind god, an aspect of Kukulcan in the Maya pantheon just as the Nahua wind god is an aspect of Quetzalcoatl. Far right: the Maya sun god wearing an elaborate headdress. This presentation of Kinich Ahau appears on a cylindrical carving from Palenque, *c.* 700 A.D.

A relief from Palenque. A triumphant lord, or king, is seated on the prostrate forms of the vanquished, while priests offer him a crown and a sceptre.

The Aztecs' Journey to Anáhuac

We have left until the end of the book the story of the Aztec migration to the land of Anáhuac because this half-history, half-legend fittingly sums up the all-pervading idea of a spiritual pilgrimage from darkness to light. Many historians have interpreted the legend of the arrival of the Aztec people on the high plateau as a simple narrative of events. But the tale is too poetic, and the events take place on too many different levels, for such a literal interpretation to have validity. Even the Aztecs, a barbarous people from the north who later took over the culture, the language, and the religion of the high plateau, had an understanding of the place of legend in history, and knew that myth and symbolism can and should be larger than life.

According to Francisco Xavier Clavijero, who was born near the beginning of the eighteenth century in Veracruz, the Aztecs came from somewhere far to the north of the Colorado river. Their migration southward was instigated by a bird who sang to them from a tree, calling *tihui* – which in the Aztec tongue means 'let us go'. Following upon the bird's instructions, the elders called Tecpaltzin, 'a distinguished man', who told them that they ought indeed to go looking for another homeland. About 1160 the Aztecs set out, and after crossing the Colorado river they made an image of their war god, or sun god, Huitzilopochtli, and placed this on a chair of rushes. Servants of the god, priests working in relays of four, carried this image at the head of the migrating caravan, which consisted of seven sub-tribes including the Mexicans. At one stage a test was made of their understanding. The tribes were presented with two bundles, in one of which was a jewel and in another only sticks. Those who chose the bundle with the sticks were the wisest, the moral being that utility is better than beauty. Or so Clavijero tells us; it is rather an odd thesis to be sustained by a people who wove so much myth about their daily lives. The moral may really go deeper.

Six of the travelling tribes went directly to the land of Anáhuac – the 'place within the ring'. The Mexicans, however, like Peer Gynt, seemed determined to go 'round and about'. After spending some years in Tollan they finally reached Zumpango in the Valley of Mexico in 1216. The ruler of this place, a man called Tochpanecatl, asked the Mexicans if they would provide a wife for his son, Ilhuicatl. A marriage was arranged and the royal house of Mexico was established.

Some of this, evidently, is history; but the story is interlocked with strands of pure mythology. The task of the pilgrims is to find a site where an eagle with a snake in its mouth will be sitting on a nopal cactus in the midst of a lake. This suggests a symbolism of time dominated by some higher force (the snake eaten by the eagle) at the centre of the universe.

Huitzilopochtli speaks to his subjects and tells them (in the transcription by Alfonso Caso, the Mexican anthropologist):

'Verily I shall lead you where you must go. I shall appear as a white eagle; and wherever you go, you shall go singing. You shall go only where you see me, and when you come to a place where it shall seem to me good that you stay, there I shall alight, and you shall see me there. Therefore in that place you shall build my temple, my house, my bed of grasses – where I have come to rest, poised and ready for flight. And in that place the people shall make their home and their dwelling. Your first task shall be to beautify the quality of the eagle, the quality of the tiger, the Holy War, the arrow and the shield. You shall eat what you have need of. You shall go in fear. As payment for your courage you shall conquer, you shall destroy all the villages and hamlets that are there already, wherever you see them...'

We note that the pilgrims of the sun god have a very specific and high task: '...to beautify the quality of the eagle, the quality of the tiger, the Holy War, the arrow and the shield'. It has been a gross misunderstanding to equate the 'holy' war with the later bloodthirsty ones by which the Aztecs held the surrounding tribes in subjection. The holy war was not this, but a psychological war waged within the consciences of specially chosen men capable of conquering their own lower natures.

The pilgrims, evidently chosen people in this spiritual sense, were rewarded by being shown a place of dazzling whiteness. They saw a white cypress tree from which issued a fountain, and all around were white willows, white reeds and bullrushes, white frogs, white fish, white watersnakes. This is certainly not a description of any geographical site on the high Mexican plateau, where rich greens and bright colours abound and white is notably absent.

When the priests and elders saw the place, they wept for joy and said: 'Now we have reached the promised land, now we have seen what

A detail of one of the colossal stone warriors at Tula, Hidalgo, Mexico.
The people of Guatemala believed that they came from 'the place of the sun', and the name Tula, which in various forms is given to a number of cities in Mesoamerica, had that meaning.

comfort and rest has been bestowed upon the Mexican people. Nothing more remains for us. O be comforted, sons and brothers, for we have now discovered and achieved what our God promised you, for He told us we should see wonders among the bullrushes and reed grasses of this place, and lo, these are they. But brothers, let us be silent and return to the place whence we came, and wait for our God's command, and He shall tell us what we have to do.'

Then Huitzilopochtli told them: 'O Mexicans, here must be your task and your office, here must you keep guard and wait, and the four quarters of the earth you must conquer, win, and subject to yourselves. Have command of body, breast, head, arms, and strength, for likewise it shall cost you sweat, work, and pure blood, if you are to reach and enjoy the fine emeralds, the stones of much value, the gold and silver, the fine

A wooden drum of the *teponaztli* type, much used in beating ceremonial rhythms. This one is Mixtec, with a year sign on the bottom right-hand corner. Tenth to fifteenth centuries A.D. British Museum.

feathers, the precious many-coloured feathers, the fine cocoa which has come from afar, the cotton of many colours, the many sweet-scented flowers, the different kinds of soft and delectable fruits, and many other things that give much pleasure and contentment.'

It may appear that we are back on an historical level, with the god offering a paradise of material prosperity. But we still cannot ignore the earlier symbolism, nor the fact that it is the god who is speaking. The eagle, representative of Hiutzilopochtli, is the sun. The nopal cactus with its red fruit is the human heart. The heart and the sun's light are at the centre of man, and from this inner sanctuary they hold Time, the serpent, in its rightful and lowly place. Self-subjection is the task. In ancient Mexican poetry, emeralds signify a fixing of beauty and purity in the human being, as when one poet sings:

Coral is my tongue
and emerald my beak:
I esteem myself highly, my fathers: I, Quetzalchictzin.
I open my wings
and weep before my fathers.
How shall we ever reach the heart of heaven.

It may be objected that the Aztecs arrived late on the scene, and that the symbolism of heart and precious jewel was created long before by the Nahua-speaking people they conquered. However, the narrative of the pilgrimage is retrospective, told by the Aztecs after they had already subdued the people of the high plateau and after they had borrowed a symbolism and a religion from the conquered people.

Thus the story of the pilgrimage has to be read on two levels, and on

one of these it is a beautiful example of Nahua practical mysticism – one more version of the recurring theme of death in the outer, phenomenal world and rebirth on another plane. The thread of the story of a real pilgrimage and war and conquest is often so closely interwoven with the thread of myth that it is difficult to disentangle them; but this does not mean that they are one and the same thing. Huitzilopochtli, who directed the expedition, was a god and was revered in ceremonies of communion in which images of his body were eaten. Amaranth was crushed into a powder, sifted of all chaff and foreign bodies, and made into a dough that was placed in earthen vessels until it was ready to be shaped into the god's image. The priest then pierced the heart of the image, and the body was broken up, to be eaten by the faithful who were known as 'keepers of the god'. Their task was onerous, for they

The great calendar stone of the Aztecs, thirteen feet in diameter, which was discovered in Mexico City on the site of Tenochtitlán. The outer border contains two serpents representing time, within which are the sun's rays. At the centre is the sign Four Motion – the present era, and preceding ages are indicated by the four arms, which also bear the 'motion' sign. The twenty day-names surround the central symbol. The stone was carved just after the year 1502.

The burial chamber in the Temple of the Inscriptions at Palenque, *c.* 700 A.D. The city was founded according to legend by Votan, who was probably a local Maya form of Quetzalcoatl. The carved stone, which depicts the young maize god Yum Caax, weighs more than five tons.

A polychrome vase, classic Maya style, showing the god 'N' seated in a conch shell. This was the Maya deity who ruled over the five unlucky inter-calendary days at the end of the year.

had to fast a whole year during which one of their number impersonated Huitzilopochtli and wore his garments. The climax of the feasting was a procession with dancing. One of the penitents marched ahead of the 'god', the others bringing up the rear with pine torches held aloft. In a place called The House of Mist the idol was set down on the floor and flutes were played while offerings of water and grasses were made to him. The image was then bathed, and this ceremony brought the year's penance to an end. From year to year the role of the performers rotated. The man who took the part of the god was called Paynal, he who hastens. He was dressed in a cape and head-ornament made of quetzal feathers. Bars and a star design were painted on his face, and he wore a turquoise nose-plug. On his breast was a shield set with turquoise mosaic, and a mirror.

It is true that in Christendom men have undertaken arduous pilgrimages and have waged wars in the name of their religion and their god, but the conquerors and military leaders have not been the god himself, as with the Mexicans in whose chronicles the worlds of god and man are inextricably interrelated.

The mingling of history and legend can be understood better if we remember a simple fact of human existence often forgotten in the modern, scientific world: that deep truth may exist unrelated to chronology and to material things. The story of the Aztec pilgrimage is history whose psychological and emotional overtones lend it another dimension.

A parallel Guatemalan pilgrimage

Another example of this two-level history common to most ancient peoples is to be found among the Guatemalan Indian tribes called the Cakchiquels of the Xahila family, who say they came 'from over the sea, from Tulan'. They may have come, geographically, from the Nahua lands to the north, where Tulan or Tula existed as an ancient capital. However, we need not take their specified place of origin as necessarily a physical one. The words Tula, Tollan, Tonalan, mean 'the place of the Sun'. The Cakchiquels, then, may have come either from the Nahua lands, or from over the sea to the east or west (sunrise or sunset), or from the metaphorical land of the Sun, of wisdom and knowledge. Their annals say: 'Four men came from Tulan. At the sunrise is one Tullan, and one is at Xibalbay (underworld), and one is at the sunset; and we came from the one at the sunset, and one is where God is.'

Although this suggests that they came physically from the west, they must in their own minds have had a connection with the man who came 'from where God is'; for the chronicle goes on to tell the old story of how the deities made various experiments to create a being who could honour and praise them. Finally he evolved the creature called man, ancestor of all people on earth including the Cakchiquels:

'And now the Obsidian Stone is created by the precious Xibalbay, the glorious Xibalbay, and man is made by the Maker, the Creator. The Obsidian Stone was his sustainer, when man was made in misery, when man was given shape. He was nurtured on wood, he was nurtured on leaves. He desired only the earth. He could not speak, he could not walk. He had no blood, he had no flesh.'

The obsidian stone seems here to represent the solid structure of material life upon which man is based. But man's nourishment was not yet satisfactory for he could not continue to live on wood and leaves. Once again, as in the story of Quetzalcoatl, a search had to be made for a more specifically human food.

A coyote was cleaning his maize field when a hawk called Tiuh Tiuh killed him. The hawk obtained the blood of a serpent and a tapir and kneaded the maize with these ingredients. This was how the flesh of man was formed. For the creation of man it was necessary to kill the lower animal, the coyote, and to incorporate into the maize the blood of the serpent, representing our instinctive nature perhaps, and the tapir.

After this food had been obtained, thirteen men and fourteen women were created and they multiplied. The obsidian stone was made to become 'the enclosure of Tulan' guarded by the Zotzils, the bat people who can see in the night. The human beings were separated into thirteen divisions of warriors and seven tribes. 'Sleep not, rest not, my daughters, my sons,' they were told, 'for to you, the seven rulers, I shall give power in equal shares.' And again, 'Great shall be your burden. Sleep not, rest not, be not cast down, my sons. You shall be rich. You shall be powerful. Let your round shields, your bows and your bucklers be your riches.'

However, a bird living in Tulan and called 'the guardian of the ravine' prophesied their extinction. An owl also declared himself an evil portent, but they refused to believe him. A parakeet foretold their death, but they answered, 'No, you are only the sign of spring.'

All the warriors of the seven tribes reached the sea but were unable to cross it. The two eldest sons called Gagavitz and Zactecauh fell asleep and were conquered. However, these two sons, the heroes of the migration, had in their possession a red staff which they had brought with them from Tulan. They drove it into the sea and caused sand and sea to separate so that a line of firm ground appeared above and below the waters, and they were able to pass across to the far shore.

As related in the annals, the subsequent adventures of the pilgrims seem to have been more or less historical until they met the 'spirit' or 'heart' of the forest, the fire spirit called Zakiqoxol, who was a robber and killer of men. The two warriors would have liked to do away with him, but they deferred to his supernatural quality and his title; instead of trying to destroy him they gave him clothing and a blood-red dagger and shoes. With these he descended into the forest:

'Then there was a disturbance among the trees, among the birds. One could hear the trees speak and the birds call. If we listened we could hear them say "What is this we hear? Who is this?" Therefore that place is called the Place of Restlessness.'

Zakiqoxol seems to be one more representation of the powerful instinctive energy deep in the forest of man's being, creating disquiet within him.

After this the brothers met a nobleman who told them, 'You have come to be the stone scaffolding and the prop of my house. I will give you lordship...' But later Zactecauh suffered an accident, leaving Gagavitz to continue alone. Like those of the Mexicans, the journeyings of this tribe seem to have had a round-and-about quality. For the second time they arrived at a particular mountain described, like the scenery met by the Aztecs, as white. It must have been volcanic, for it spewed fire througout an entire year. Only Gagavitz and a personage named Zakitzunun

Jadeite stilettos representing the head and beak of a humming bird. Acts of self mutilation were practised for many centuries by the peoples of ancient Mexico, blood probably being drawn from the tongue or the ears. The humming bird was associated with Huitzilopochtli in Aztec times. Olmec jadeite carvings.

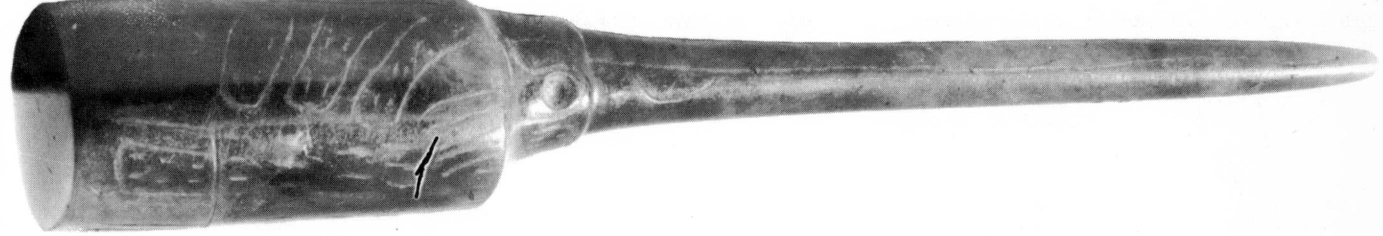

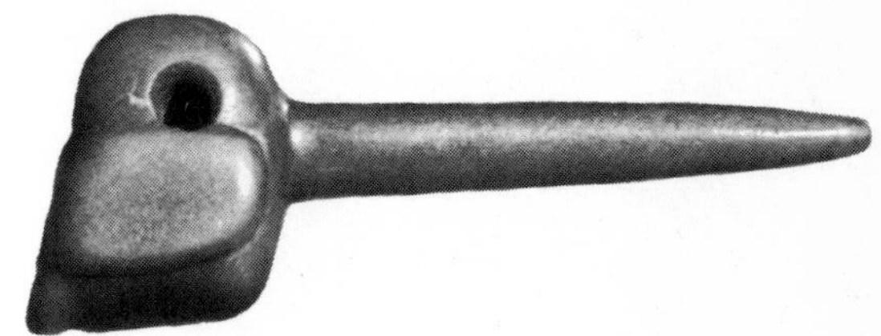

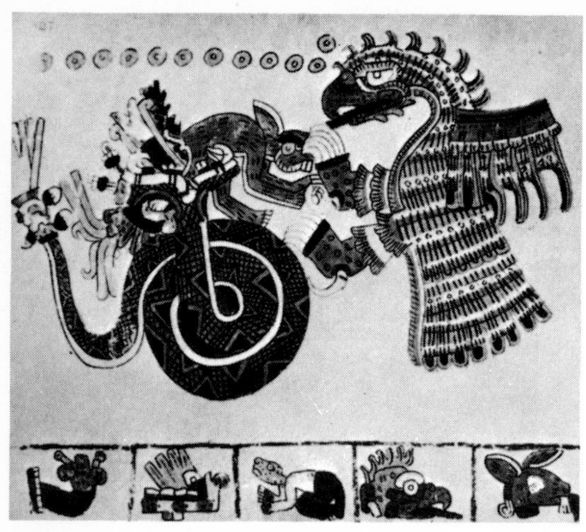

The eagle, the sun, draws life from the serpent, the earth. Life itself is represented by the rapid animated rabbit. The sun and war god of the Aztecs was Huitzilopochtli, and the Knights-Eagle were under his patronage. *Codex Vaticanus.*

dared go forward. All this has the quality of straight history, but suddenly we are back in the land of legend, with Gagavitz spending a lone vigil on the mountain. As the day faded, the courage of those waiting died in their hearts. Only a few sparks descended to where they were.

But suddenly their hero appeared from inside the mountain, so that all the warriors cried out, 'Truly his power, his knowledge, his glory and majesty are terrible. He died, yet he has returned.' So Gagavitz was acknowledged to have conquered the heart of the mountain, that mysterious creature who had descended into the forest with his red dagger and shoes: 'When the heart of the mountain is opened the fire separates from the stone...'

From this point on the chronicle is mainly historical, but the tradition of a holy origin in the place of the sun was not lost. Speaking of one of the tribe's rulers, the document says, 'Not only was he a king in majesty, but he impressed by his learning and the depth of his spirit, derived from Tullan.'

The origins were always in this centre, geographical or legendary, from whence all knowledge came, and the history derived from these origins was always more important to pre-Hispanic peoples than the simple statement of events.

The travels of Votan

The wanderings of Quetzalcoatl plainly come into the same category as these half-historical, half-mythical tales of journeys. There is one Maya tale about the travels of one, Votan, who seems to have been none other than Quetzalcoatl himself and who declared himself to be 'a serpent'. From some unknown origin he was ordered by the gods to go to America to found a culture. So he departed from his home, called Valum Chivim and unidentified, and by way of the 'dwelling of the thirteen snakes' he arrived at Valum Votan. From there he travelled up the Usumacinta river and founded Palenque. Afterwards he made several visits to his native home, on one of which he came upon a tower which was originally planned to reach the heavens but which was destroyed because of a 'confusion of tongues' among its architects. Votan was, however, allowed to use a subterranean passage in order to reach 'the rock of heaven'.

Detail from one of the frescoes at Bonampak. A priest is being arrayed as the plumed serpent, Kukulcan or Quetzalcoatl.

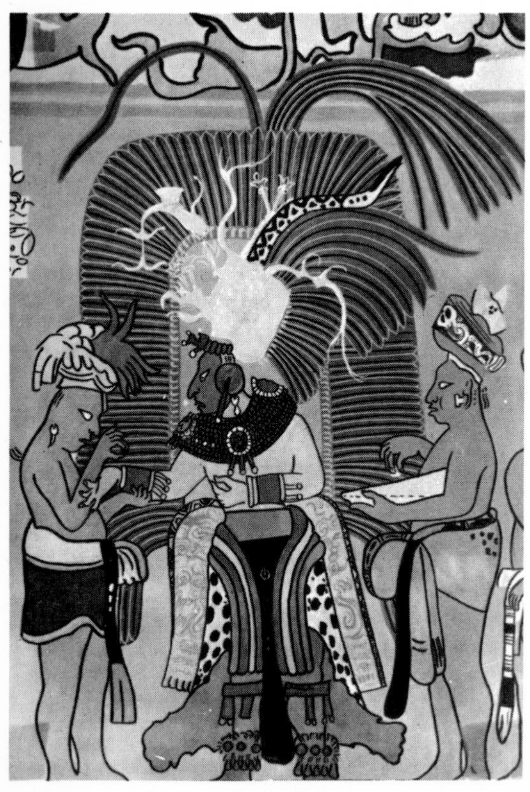

This Votan was supposed to be guardian of the hollow wooden instrument called *tepanaguaste* which is similar to the Mexican *teponaztli* drum. He was greatly venerated and was called by some 'the heart of the cities'. His consort was Ixchel, the rainbow, but she was sometimes known as Ix-kanleom, the spider's web catching the morning dew.

Votan's priests were of the caste of 'tigers' as Quetzalcoatl's were; and it is evident that he was a great enough leader to have extended his religious beliefs through a vast Maya-Nahua territory, so that they endured for many centuries, only gradually becoming distorted from their original redeeming message. It is a universal tragedy that we know so little of this great religious leader, Quetzalcoatl-Kukulcan-Votan: plumed serpent, quetzal bird, Venus and sun god, who sacrificed himself that true manhood might be created in the hemisphere of the west.

In spite of the great gulf that separates precolumbian thought from our own in many of its external aspects; in spite of distortions, irrelevancies, decadence and subsequent annihilation by European conquerors of a great part of it; the culture which this mysterious leader established shines down to our own day. Its message is still meaningful for those who will take the trouble to make their way, through the difficulties of outlandish names and rambling manuscripts, to the essence of the myth.

One of the elaborately carved lintels from Menché. The standing figure is probably a priest (the headdress suggests the plumed serpent – Kukulcan to the Mayas) and the kneeling one a penitent. The date of the inscription corresponds to 223 A.D. of our era.

South American Mythology

Harold Osborne

Introduction

A prehistoric stone statue from San Agustin, Colombia, in which the main figure is surmounted by a second head. Though the iconographical significance of these carvings is unknown, it may be that here the second head represents a controlling spirit or god. In style and expression these figures lie between the horrific and menacing supernaturalism of Mexico and the greater urbanity of Peru.

The peoples of South America

Speculation about the origin of human beings in the Western Hemisphere has been rife ever since the discovery of America. In an age when the Old Testament was accepted as inspired history the discovery of populations in the New World raised a theological rather than a scientific problem – or at any rate a scientific problem which had to be settled within an established theological framework. The naive speculations of the early Conquistadores were inevitably committed to the traditional Biblical world-picture and had to find a place for the native peoples of America within that picture. Thus within a few years of the Conquest the *Biblia Poliglota* (1569-73) recorded the view that the populations of the Americas were descended from Shem, son of Noah, after the Biblical deluge. An alternative view was that certain of the tribes of Israel, dispersed by the Assyrians, had found a refuge and a new home in the Western Hemisphere. Others derived the origin of the American peoples from the 'lost continents' of Mu in the Pacific or Atlantis in the Atlantic. While these wild and groping guesses are no more than a historical curiosity today, the attitude of mind which they represent is of interest to us since it was antipathetic to the serious preservation of native cosmological myths and local beliefs about origins. In so far as these were in conflict with Biblical 'truth', they were contemptuously rejected by the early chroniclers as pernicious follies and deceits of the devil. Thus a wealth of material which might have been of inestimable value to the modern student was irretrievably lost.

Only slightly later 'nativist' views were put forward which took the form of locating the Biblical Creation and the Garden of Eden in the New World. An early view of this type was propounded in the seventeenth century by a Spaniard, Antonio de León Pinelo, who settled in the Province of Charcas, now Bolivia, and in his book *El Paraíso en el Nuevo Mundo* asserted that the Earthly Paradise was situated and the Creation according to Genesis took place in the then little known province of Mojos in eastern Bolivia and that the rest of the world was populated from there. A similar view was put forward a century ago by the Bolivian scholar Emeterio Villamil de Rada, who in a book entitled *La Lengua de Adan* tried to prove on etymological grounds that Aymará was the original language of mankind and that from it all other tongues were derived. He thought that the human race had originated in Sorata, a canton at the foot of Mt Illampu in the eastern Cordillera of the Bolivian Andes.

The first scientific defence of the view that mankind originated in South America was argued by the Argentinian palaeontologist Florentine Ameghino in 1880, and various claims to have found palaeontological evidence of ancient man in South America – though without going so far as to assert that these were the original progenitors of all mankind – have persisted until recently. These claims have not stood up to criticism and it is now generally accepted to be pretty well beyond dispute that man first entered

The Altiplano, with its forsaken aspect of a landscape on some vaster and more ancient planet where life has long been obsolete. It is a harsh, inhuman land, inhabited now by a dour, unsmiling, toiling race; a high, bleak, barren, windswept tundra with the paradox of a tropical sun blazing through the frigid air. Yet the Altiplano was the home of the greatest civilisations and cultures which South America has known: the Tiahuanaco culture and later the Inca. It was the Collasuyu of the ancient Inca empire and the Collao of the Spaniards. It runs roughly north to south at an elevation of 12,000 to 13,000 feet above sea level from northern Peru to the southern tip of Bolivia, a distance of 520 miles, and averages eighty to a hundred miles across. There are no trees and except during the brief season of the rains there is no green.

America by migration across the Bering Strait during the last phases of the final glacial period, probably about 20,000 B.C. At that time the ice-cap held captive vast quantities of water with the result that the sea level was three hundred feet lower than at present. Thus the present Bering Strait was a broad isthmus forming a land bridge between Asia and North America.

The native peoples of America, who were of predominantly Mongoloid stock, immigrated from the region of Siberia and slowly spread from Alaska southwards, reaching Tierra del Fuego not later than about 5,000 B.C. They brought with them the elements of a Stone Age culture, which included the use of fire, techniques of cutting and grinding bones, flint chipping, the dressing of skins and perhaps various shamanistic religious observances and rituals such as birth, puberty and death rites. It is not possible to determine over what period the waves of immigration by way of the Bering Strait continued, but we can be confident that they did not go on after the melting of the last great ice-cap. They therefore ceased before agriculture was known anywhere in the world and the hunting and food-gathering stage of development lasted in America some 10,000 to 15,000 years – or in some regions which are unsuited to agriculture virtually until the present day.

Probably between 4,000 and 3,000 B.C., at a reasonable estimate, native American plants began to be domesticated in a few areas and the three prime American food products, maize, beans and squash, spread widely over South and North America in a large number of varieties adapted to local conditions. The pastoral stage, during which the llama, alpaca and cavey or guinea-pig were domesticated to man's use, is thought to have been roughly contemporary. Relics of a pre-ceramic culture from about 2,500 to 1,800 B.C. have been studied chiefly in Huaca Prieta at the mouth of the Chicama valley on the northern coast of Peru. Woven and decorated cotton textiles were found, gourds, mats and baskets of reeds and wide-meshed fish nets. Small carved figures of equal or greater antiquity have been found farther north. From archaeological evidence a general pattern of progress in civilisation and cultural techniques has been traced for the Central Andean region from about the middle of the second millennium B.C. and extending up to the conquest of the Inca empire by the Spanish in A.D. 1532. Elsewhere in South America the patterns were widely different and less clearly marked.

Pottery figure of a man carrying a foal. It is probably a llama, one of the few animals of the South American continent suitable for domestication. It originated in the Altiplano but its cultivation spread rapidly when its value as a draught animal was realised. The skin was only used after the creature died and its working life was rarely more than ten years duration. Chimu culture.

There has been considerable controversy between anthropologists who believe that South American culture was in the main indigenous and others who have claimed that its basic features were derived from outside the Western Hemisphere, being carried by trans-Pacific migrations from China, Indonesia or elsewhere in the Far East. A few traditions preserved by the early Spanish chroniclers have sometimes been thought to provide evidence of such contacts. For example, Sarmiento tells a curious story that in his expedition against the coast of Manta, the island of Puna and Tumbez, Topa Inca Yupanqui encountered merchants who had come over the western sea in boats and who told of two wealthy and populous islands, Ayachumbi and Ninachumbi, whence they came. After verifying their story by means of a magician, Topa Inca manned a large expedition of 20,000 men, sailed to the islands and returned with black people, much gold, a chair of brass, and the skin and jawbone of a horse. The horse's skin and jawbone were said to be still in the possession of the Inca noble who told Sarmiento the story. Such legends cannot be regarded as conclusive and together with legends of a race of white invaders and the giant invaders of Puerto Viejo might preserve memories of contacts with Northern or Central America. While today few anthropologists would deny completely the possibility of transoceanic contacts, the most authoritative opinion now is that any such cultural influences, particularly up to the Christian era, must have been at most casual and intermittent and can have

One of the large, flat, unshaped stone slabs carved with large human figures and heads in outline relief engraving, found at the Cerro Séchin, in the valley of the Casma. Although apparently contemporary with the Chavín culture, they follow a different tradition of stylisation. The figure in this representation holds before him a staff of office or a ceremonial axe and has certain affinities with the running figures in the frieze of the Gate of the Sun at Tiahuanaco.

The art of the Mochica potters found inspiration in every walk of life. This stirrup vessel, showing a twisted, scarred face is believed to represent a beggar.

Right: Common to all the great pre-columbian cultures was a genius for construction. This detail from the ruins of Machu Picchu shows the extraordinarily fine stonework found in the great Inca sites, where huge blocks were held together by the precision in fitting – no mortar was used.

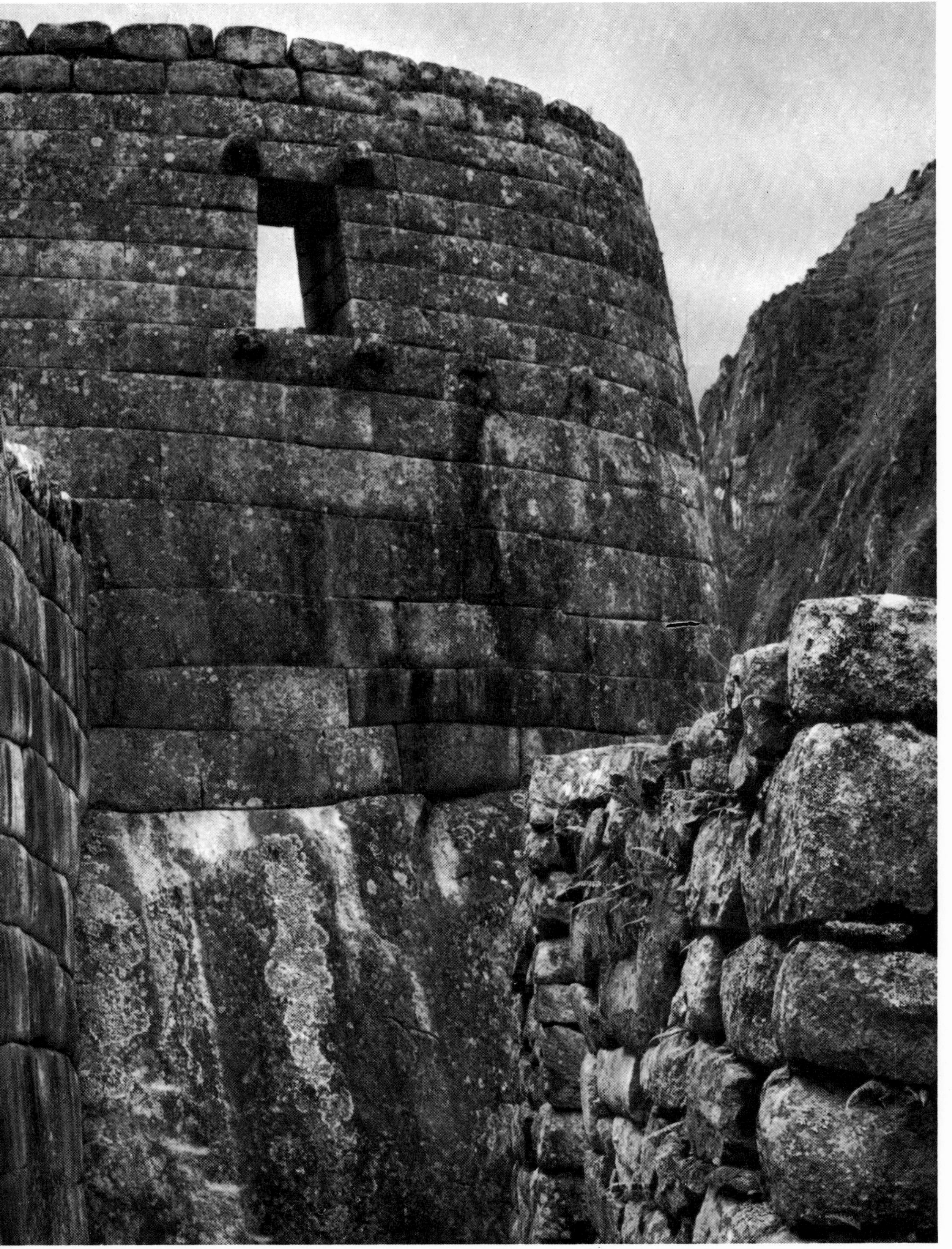

exerted no important impact on the total picture of South American culture. It therefore seems most likely that the mythology of the South American peoples developed from the beliefs of the original Stone Age immigrants and was elaborated without significant influences from outside the continent up to the time of the Conquest. From the time of the Conquest there was very rapid and extensive syncretism of native mythology with Christian doctrine and to a lesser extent with European folk stories and superstitions. This fact accounts for the great importance which today is attached to the rather scanty records of native myth and legend left by the early Spanish chroniclers. Before them nothing was recorded to indicate their religious beliefs or practices.

The picture presented by South American aboriginal culture as it was recorded at the time of the Conquest and as it has been studied since is so diversified that classification has proved very difficult. Extreme differences of geographical and climatic conditions – as for example between those of the pampas, the tropical rain-forests, the dry forested regions, the high valleys and plateaus of the Central Andes, and so on – were a major influence on most of the material aspects of the relevant cultures. But there is no simple co-ordination between these aspects and socio-political and religious patterns. No general pattern of culture development applicable to the subcontinent as a whole has been found and analogies drawn from temporal sequences based on Old World prehistory are suspect and dangerous when applied to the culture history of the New World. In these circumstances much of the work of modern anthropologists in South America has been restricted to detailed examinations of individual cultures or particular culture elements. Such a method of historical particularising tends to treat each culture or tribe as unique and to emphasise its peculiarities, while eschewing generalisations.

There have been some studies of the mythology of particular areas or tribes but no general study of mythology over the whole subcontinent has been attempted hitherto, and even the particular and limited studies form a very minor and unimportant part of anthropological investigation as a whole. It is the object of this book to present a sample of what is known about the mythological beliefs of the aboriginal peoples throughout South America. A complete survey would be both tedious to the general reader and impossible in the space, so no more than an illustration is attempted.

Three stone vessels in the form of alpacas. Like the llama this animal originated in the Altiplano, and was prized for the long abundant wool. Shearing took place two or three times a year. Inca period.

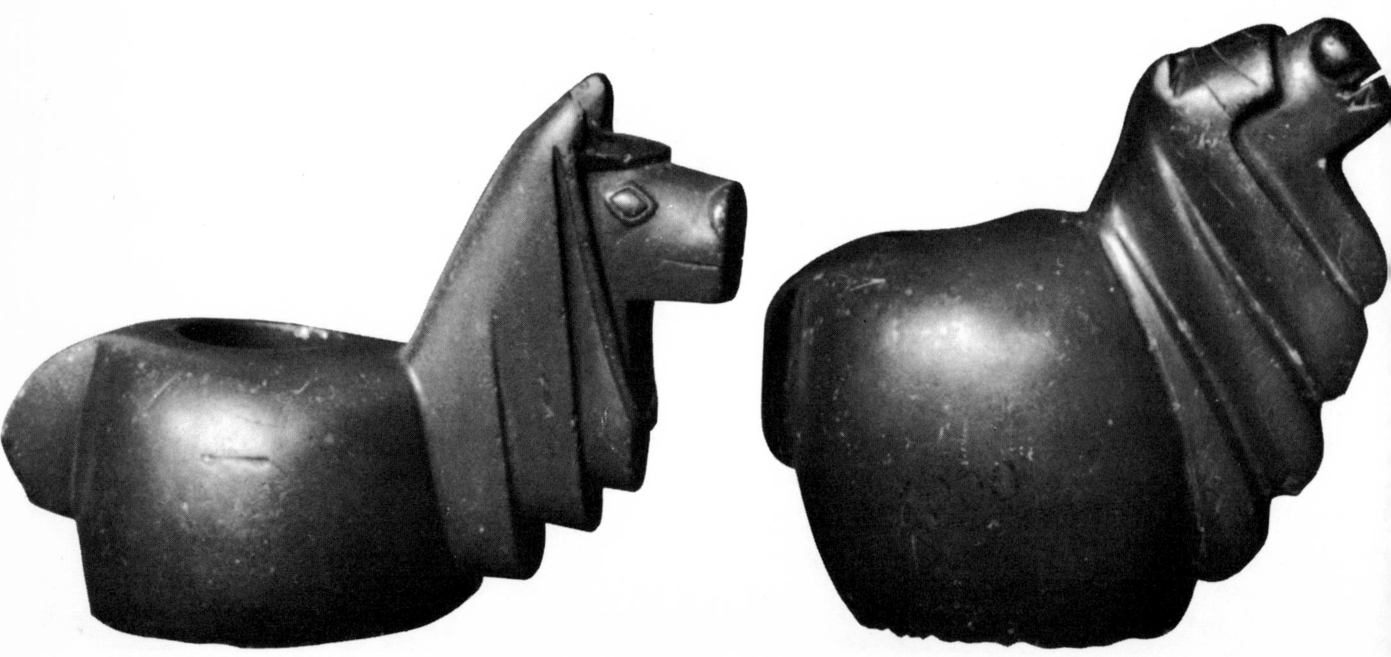

While certain striking parallels and similarities among the mythologies of distant and culturally diverse peoples will leap to the eye, wide generalisations must in the present stage of our knowledge be avoided.

Nevertheless in order to bring some order into what might otherwise appear a chaotic hotch-potch of haphazard and random variations it will be convenient to suggest some general cultural classification as a background to structures of mythological belief. For this purpose we will adapt the classification proposed by Julian H. Steward, editor of the Smithsonian *Handbook of South American Indians*. We shall omit the Circum-Caribbean peoples, who for our purposes are classed with the Central American areas, and we shall place the Southern Andean tribes in a separate category. This gives a fourfold classification into Marginal and Semi-Marginal tribes; Tropical Forest peoples; Southern Andean tribes; and Central Andean civilisations.

Marginal tribes

These occupied comparatively unproductive regions, which they exploited by simple technologies. Hunters and food-gatherers without developed agriculture, they were frequently nomadic or semi-nomadic and their social units were generally small and unstable, varying in size and permanency according to subsistence conditions but without uniform pattern. Their material culture remained rudimentary and they lacked the more advanced manufacturing processes found elsewhere in South America such as weaving, building and ceramic techniques, and the domestication of animals, except where – as in parts of the Chaco – certain of these were borrowed from more advanced peoples.

Their religious outlook had a broadly similar structure based on shamanism, though with innumerable local variations of particular features. Specific magical practices, witchcraft procedures, devices for controlling the spirit world and concepts of the supernatural varied from tribe to tribe. Crisis rites and magical practices played an important role but there was no organised priesthood or social cult. Although magico-religious rites were used in some areas to control sickness or the weather, in general these peoples were without group ceremonies and rituals. Among the Archipelagic tribes of the extreme south and those of Patagonia and the Pampas

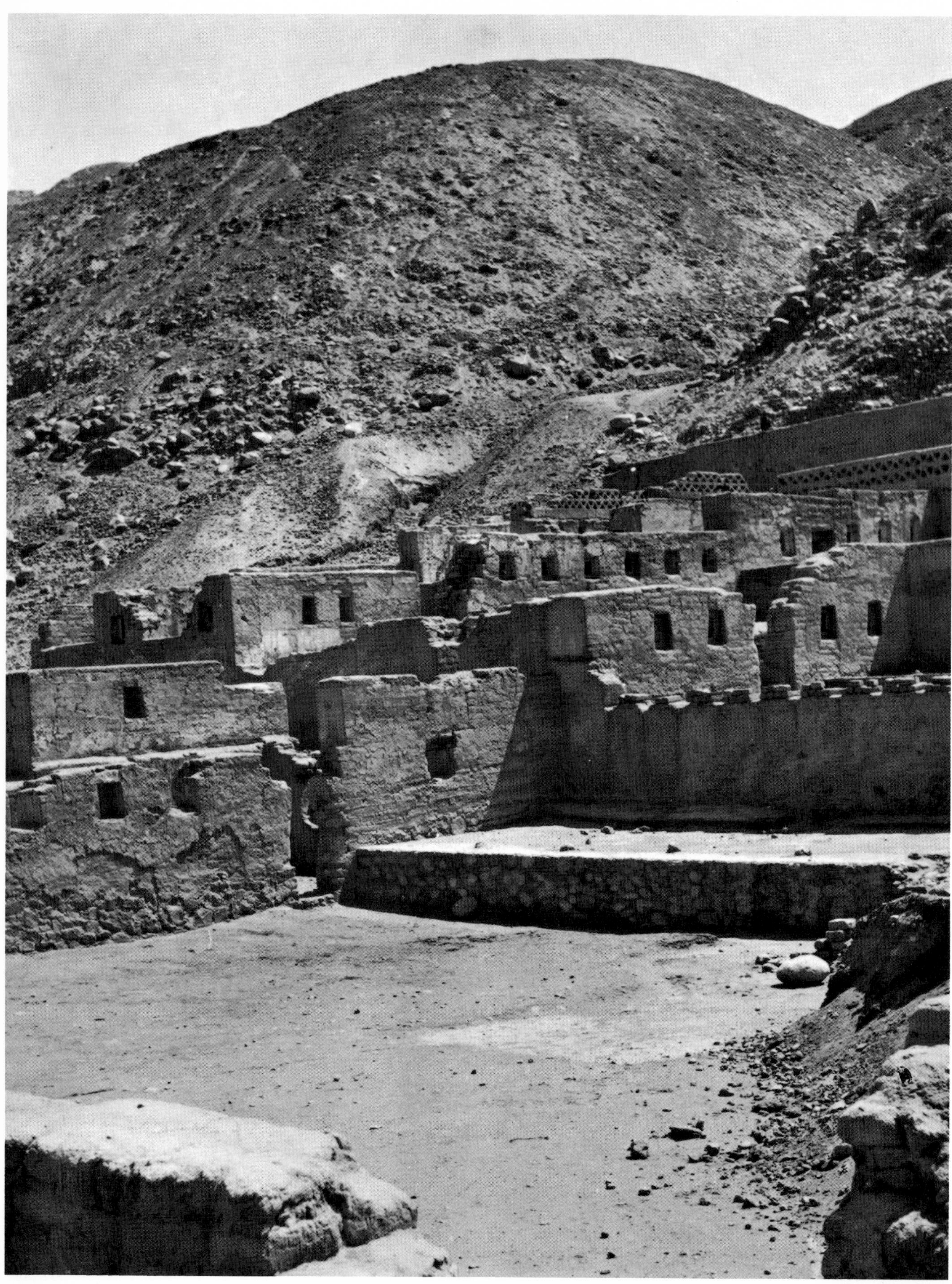

there is now believed to be clear evidence of an aboriginal belief in a Supreme God, although lesser spirits – particularly spirits of evil – played a more prominent role in practical everyday life and the Supreme Deity was not the object of an organised cult. Among the tribes of the upper Xingú, the Nambicuara of western Brazil bordering the Guaporé river and the northern Ge groups there was a belief in a creator-god, sometimes identified with the sun or moon, but whether this belief was aboriginal or derivative cannot be determined. The Bororo and certain tribes of eastern Bolivia attached great importance to the spirits of the dead, who were supposed to be invisibly present at mortuary ceremonies, and some believed that the spirit-helper of the shaman was the soul of a dead shaman.

We believe it to be probable, though it is certainly not provable, that the attitudes of belief towards the supernatural which prevailed among the Marginal peoples, and the rather elementary and unembroidered mythological structure which was generally associated with it, may have remained closest to that of the Stone Age immigrants who first populated the Americas and may have undergone least differentiation from the aboriginal structure of belief. If this is so, the pattern of myth and supernatural lore found among the Marginal tribes may be regarded as a primitive foundation upon which the more complicated mythological systems of other peoples were elaborated. Any such theory must be treated with the utmost caution since the basis of cultural classification is at best highly arbitrary, representing a compromise between socio-political features, levels of material culture and magico-religious elements, and also because the nature and extent of influences from one area to another in the matter of mythology and belief can only be conjectured.

Left: Tambo Colorado, on the desert plain of Peru. The building here was accomplished without the stone so readily available in the highlands but equal skill was shown in the use of adobe bricks. In the desert air the colours have lasted and much of the decoration can be seen in its original state. Inca culture.

Below: Camayura Indians of the Xingú River of Brazil. The tribes of the Amazon basin were well used to river travel and it is likely that there was some trading contact between them and the Andean civilisation. But the way of life of the river people would seem to have changed little over the centuries. The Camayura are a healthy and vigorous tribe of hunters, and are seen here preparing for a wrestling game which is their favourite sport.

Tropical forest peoples

These comprise in the main the tribes who inhabited the tropical rain-forests of Guiana, the Amazon basin, the Paraná delta and the area watered by the Paraguay. They developed advanced techniques of agriculture by the slash-and-burn method, which necessitated periodical movement within an area. They had more advanced exploitation devices than the Marginal tribes and utilised the rivers for transport in dug-out canoes. They cultivated tropical root crops and built frame houses with thatch. Though they lacked wool, metal and stone and were without domesticated animals, they had developed techniques of loom weaving, basketry, bark cloth and ceramics. Their social units were larger and more stable, often including large and semi-permanent villages, but they lacked political federations and empires.

The structure of religious belief remained in general similar to that of the Marginal peoples, being centred on the shaman who, with an invisible supernatural helper, controlled magical practices, cured the sick, performed functions of prognostication and divination and in general safeguarded tribal tradition, particularly in regard to the relations of the living with the world of the supernatural. Crisis rituals were important for defining social status, differentiating the functions of the sexes, and so on. There were no temples or idols and few of the Tropical Forest tribes had tribal gods or public religious ceremonies. The principal deities and celestial beings were mythological personages rather than objects of cult. The main mythological

A party of Indians on a fishing trip in the small canoes used for local travel. The great rivers served the Indians of the tropical rain-forest and the Amazon basin as highways; travel by canoe was highly developed.

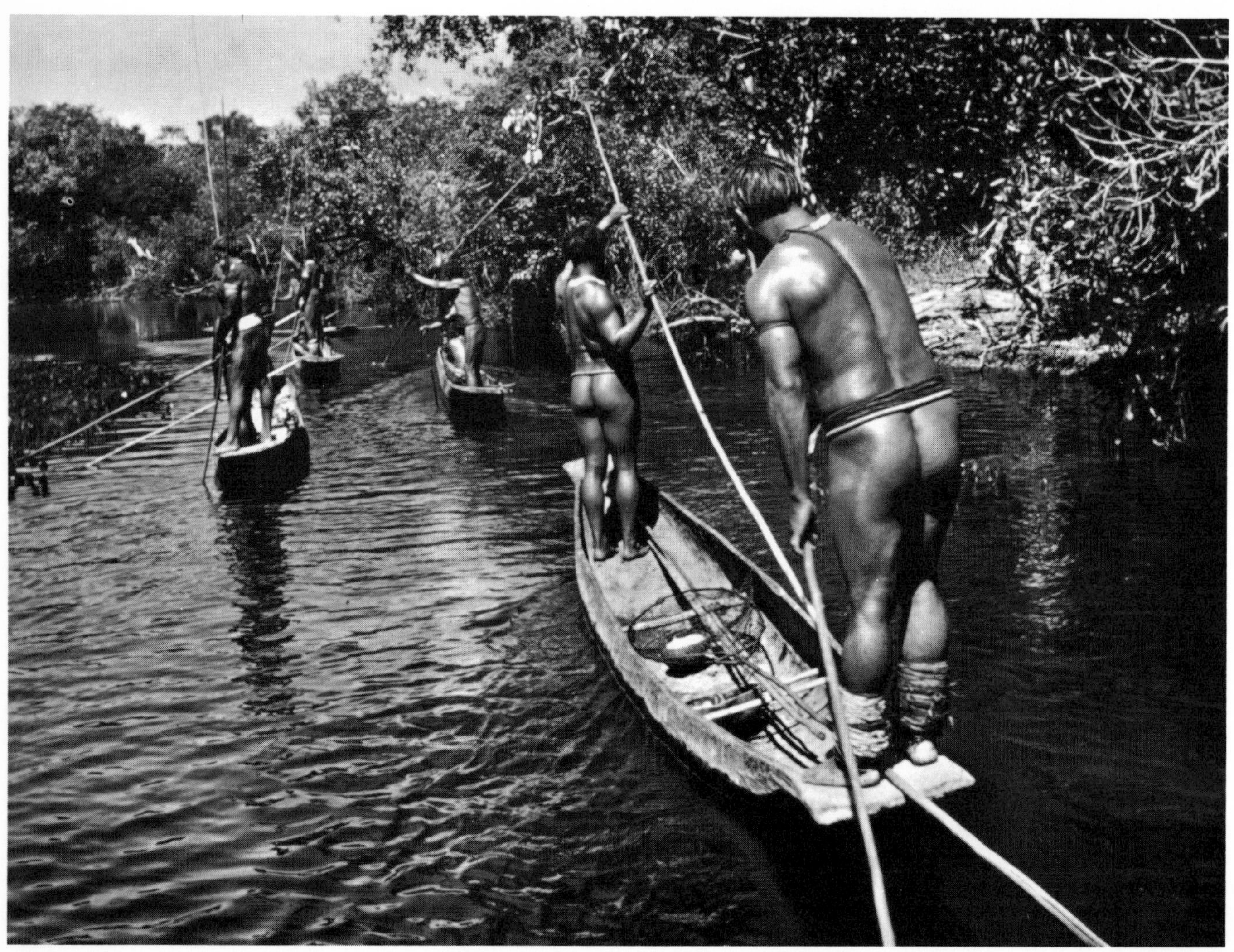

beings were personifications of the sun, the moon, the stars, thunder or rain, and some anthropologists believe these to have been the prototypes of the tribal deities of the Andean peoples. Belief in a multitude of nature spirits was general, though spirits of mountains, streams, rocks, springs and place spirits in general seem to have been less important than they were among the more settled peoples of the Andes. Belief in a supernatural jaguar spirit or were-jaguar was widespread in some areas, surviving until very recent times in parts of eastern Bolivia, and may have been the source of a jaguar cult in the Central Andes.

Southern Andean tribes

These comprise chiefly the peoples of the Atacama desert, the Diaguita of northern Argentina and of the states of Atacama and Coquimbo in Chile, and the Araucanians of central Chile. In socio-political structure and perhaps in popular religious belief their culture had affinities with the peoples of the Tropical Forest. But in material aspects it was closer to that of the Central Andes. They shared with the Central Andes techniques of metallurgy, building in stone, breeding of llamas, and wore Andean types of clothing. Their agricultural techniques were also Andean, based on the cultivation of the potato and of cereals such as maize and quinoa. During the expansion of the Inca empire, and perhaps even before, strong cultural influences spread directly from the Central Andes to northern Argentina and Chile. Over large parts of the Chaco direct influences from the Central Andes overlapped with those from the Tropical Forest peoples of Brazil.

There is little evidence of organised priesthood or temple religion among the Southern Andean peoples apart from agricultural ceremonies. The Diaguita conducted agricultural ceremonies and the Atacameño had fertility rites for their fields. The Araucanians had a public ceremony conducted by priests who said prayers and offered animal sacrifices to a Supreme Being and creator-god for good crops and the health of the people. These public ceremonials may well have grown up under influences from the Central Andes and we know little in detail about them. The religion of the Araucanians in particular seems to have been dominated by belief in witchcraft, magic and by the propitiation of ill-disposed supernatural beings. Shamans were important and the Araucanian shaman was a transvestite. Shamans used divination, cured disease and brought rain. Diseases were thought to be caused by the intrusion of some foreign object, possession by an evil spirit, by magic or ill-wishing, or by the loss of a man's soul. The shaman obtained his powers in the supernatural realm, among them magical and curative powers, from association with a dead shamanistic helper and also from the Supreme Being, to whom he offered prayers.

A man of the Suya tribe from the Xingú river. He wears a large lip disk as well as the ubiquitous ear-plugs.

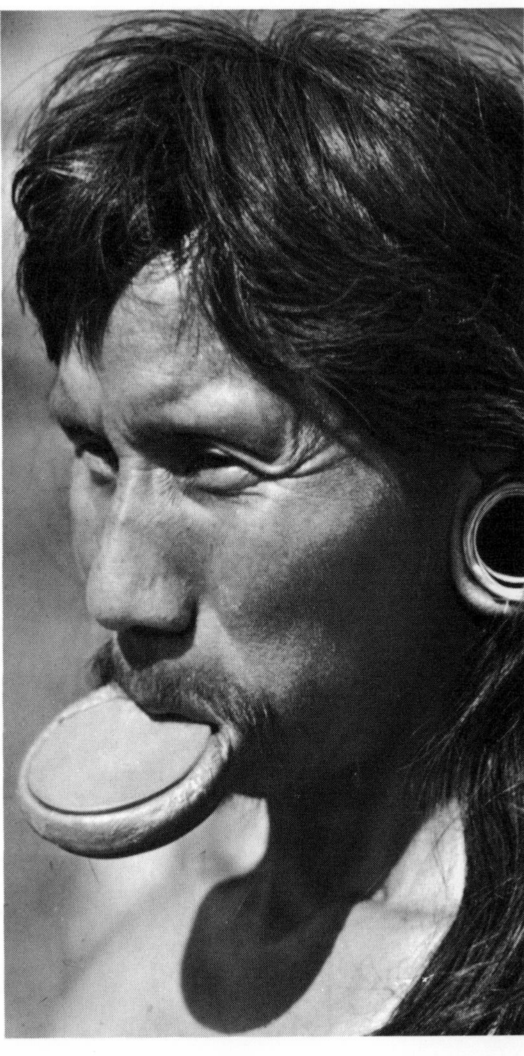

Central Andean civilisations

The most advanced civilisation of the subcontinent of South America was developed in the Central Andean region, roughly coextensive with the territories of the modern Bolivia and Peru. It was centred in the coastal valleys of Peru, the high valleys which seam the western slopes of the Cordillera and the rather bleak and arid plateau which is now known as the Altiplano. It was a civilisation based on agriculture: semi-tropical fruits and root crops in the hot coastal valleys, maize and other cereals in the highland valleys, and potatoes and quinoa on the high plateau. The llama, the alpaca, the guinea-pig and the duck were domesticated; other animals were preserved and hunted. Specialised agricultural techniques were developed, including large-scale irrigation systems and terracing, and agricultural surpluses were produced which supported the densest aggregation of population found anywhere in the Americas and allowed for large non-productive

Right: A mask of beaten gold from one of the Nazca graves. The shape of this funerary offering suggests devotion to the cult of the sun, but neither the remarkably beautiful Nazca ceramics nor the accomplished use of weaving techniques offers a positive answer. Knowledge of this culture only dates from 1901, when it was discovered by Max Uhle.

Below: Chanchan, capital of the Chimu kingdom, the ruins of which lie to the north of the Moche river, not far from the modern town of Trujillo. The name Chimu is given to the most splendid of the coastal kingdoms of Peru preceding the rise to power of the highland Inca. At the time of its greatest expansion, from about A.D. 1000 to 1400, Chimu was the dominant power over a strip of land stretching 600 miles along the coast, from the river Chicama to the Patavilca valley and reaching inland 30 to 100 miles, to include, among others, the highland valleys of Recuay and Huaras. The kernel of the Chimu kingdom was the extensive and fertile valley of the Chicama. The imposing ruins of the walled capital, Chanchan, cover an area of some eight square miles. There are relics of innumerable canals and aqueducts leading to city squares in which once were large gardens and green parks, as well as extensive harbour installations, now well above the tide mark.

classes of nobility, priesthood and warriors. Mechanical processes of production in the crafts were brought to a level which has been surpassed nowhere in the world before the age of machine manufacture and the aesthetic quality of the work was such that surviving examples have a place of honour in museums and collections throughout the world today. Agricultural and manufacturing processes developed in the Central Andes spread southwards into northern Argentina, the fringe of the Chaco and northern Chile; to the north they permeated into Central America and Mexico; and from the Caribbean they were carried down the Atlantic coast and up the great rivers to leave their mark here and there among the tribes of the Tropical Forest area. It is not unreasonable to suppose that elements of myth and legend were disseminated along with the spread of trade and manufacturing processes.

Although the mountainous nature of the terrain made for scattered population centres, this was the only part of South America which developed a civilisation on a genuinely urban pattern. Society was organised on a stratified basis with kings, nobility, priesthood and classes based on occupation. Unlike the rest of South America, unification over large areas was effected by military conquest resulting in permanent domination and empire. The basis of social organisation was the land-owning village community, the *ayllu*, a settlement cemented on grounds of kinship. In the earlier stages of development there were important centres of religious pilgrimage and cultural dissemination at Chavín de Huantar in northern Peru, at Tiahuanaco on the borders of Lake Titicaca in northern Bolivia and at Pachacamac near Lima. During the so-called 'Urbanist' period, from about A.D. 1000, important urban centres were built. The powerful coastal kingdom of Chimu had its capital at Chanchan, near the present city of Trujillo, and the still impressive ruins cover an area of eight square miles. Cuzco, the highland capital of the Inca empire, based on military conquest, extended a unitary social organisation and administration from northern Ecuador to the river Maule in Chile.

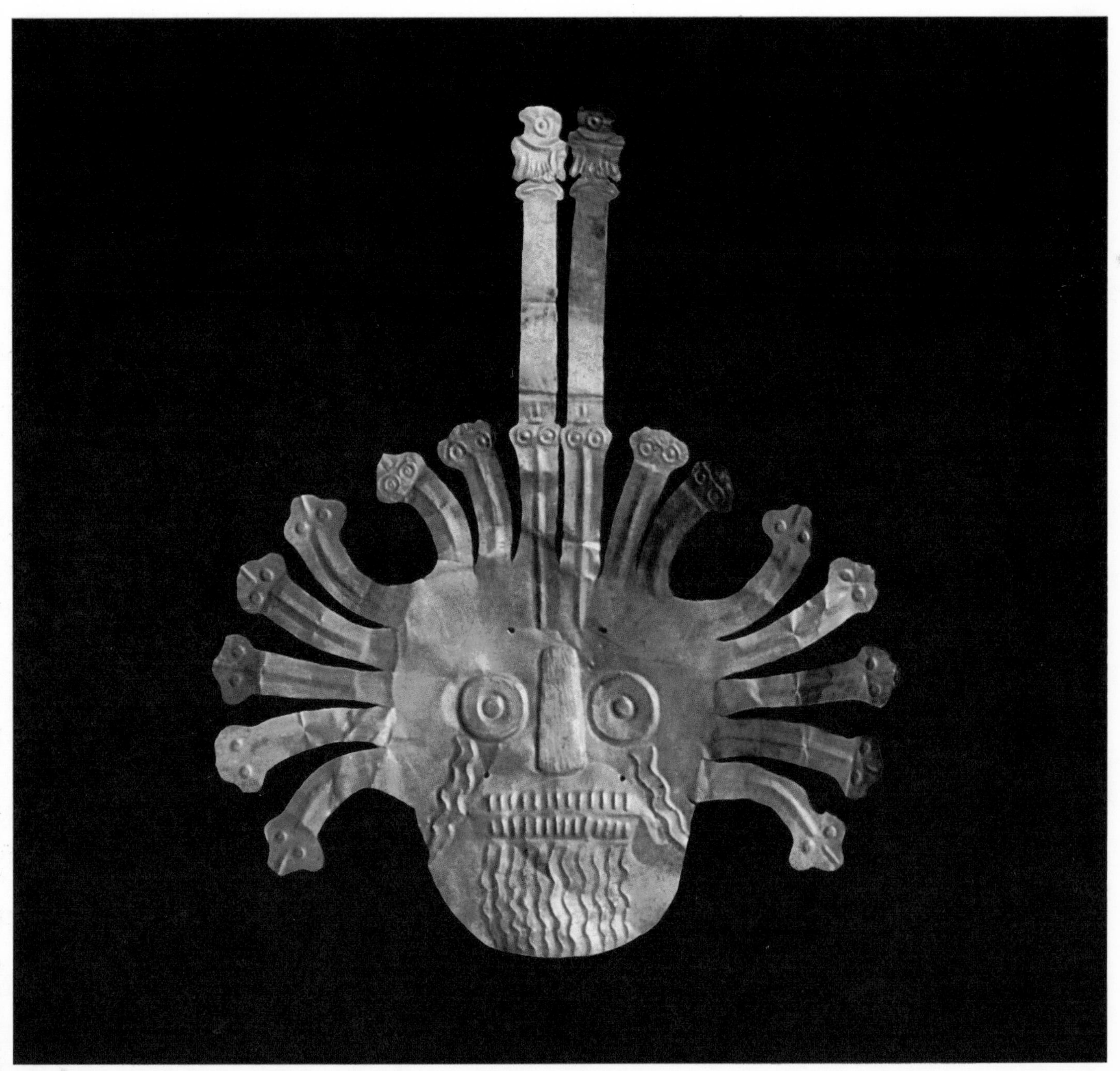

There are several good and easily accessible accounts of the Central Andean civilisations of South America. We shall restrict ourselves here to giving some details of the structure of religious belief and ceremonial which have most relevance to mythology. But readers of popular and unscientific literature about pre-columbian South America should exercise the utmost caution in view of the extreme hazards which beset historical reconstructions based on archaeological material alone without written records – and the art of writing was nowhere practised in South America. How closely population movements or social developments can be correlated with changes in artistic styles or manipulative techniques is a matter of speculation where exact verification is virtually impossible.

In the field of mythology and religious belief the difficulties are still more serious. Without outside clues in the form of written records or comparisons with closely related cultures where the significance is known, it is not possible to determine the nature of religious belief from surviving cult objects or to derive the content of myths from pictorial representations. All attempts to do so must remain purely subjective and unverifiable. Indeed it is never possible in these circumstances to be certain that an artistic representation or motif has in fact a religious significance, or to be certain that the subject of a pictorial scene has any relation whatever to myth or legend.

The dangers of basing mythological reconstructions on archaeological evidence may be illustrated by the following difficulties. They are illustrations only of a very general problem. Students of archaeology tend to take it as more or less certain that the Chavín culture was predominantly religious in character and that the cult of a feline deity, perhaps also a condor-deity and a snake-deity, spread widely over the coastal area of Peru. Yet the surviving records from the early years of the Conquest, sparse as they are, afford little or no support for such cults. The records do suggest the worship of a supreme creator-deity who may have been named Con or Viracocha, but the archaeological material provides no evidence which could with reasonable probability be ascribed to this cult. The very elaborate burial customs – almost all our archaeological material has been recovered from burials – might well lead one to suppose that there must have been a fairly well developed mythology of the after-life. Yet the records which survive are extremely meagre on this matter. The sculptures at Tiahuanaco and the highly formalised relief carvings and artistic motifs have led archaeologists to suppose a well organised religious control for this culture, which spread – perhaps by conquest – to the coastal areas of Peru from the Bolivian highlands.

However, though the Spanish chroniclers who visited the area in the

Below: Relief from the Chanchan ruins, perhaps depicting a man performing a ritual ceremony. In the absence of contemporary records it has proved impossible to derive from these reliefs any specific facts of mythological or religious beliefs among the Chimu.

Below right: Relief from Chanchan: one of many giving evidence of an intense and alert preoccupation with the limited fauna – feline, snake fox, falcon, condor, guinea-pig, badger and marine animals. The method of stylisation and the expressive impact made by the conventionalised patterns seem to indicate a religious as well as an aesthetic interest.

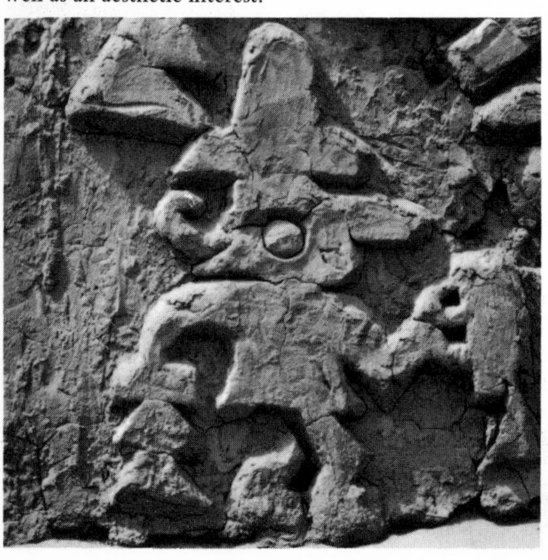

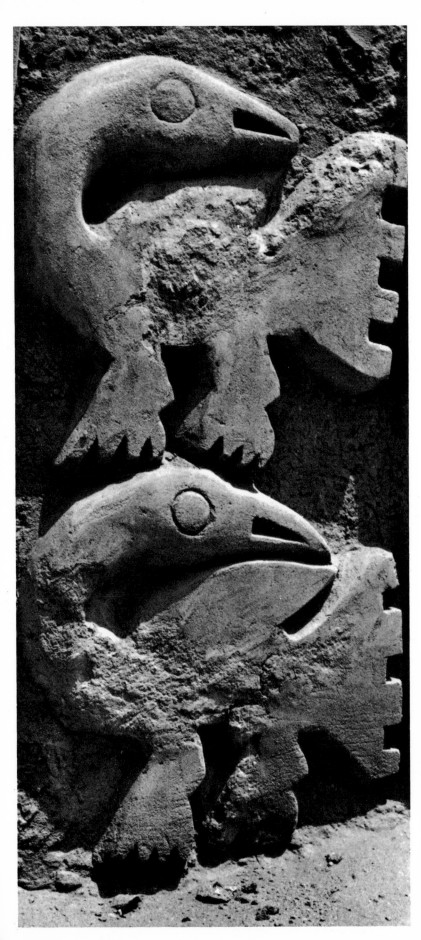

Left: Detail of the central wall decoration from one of the two Chanchan palaces, showing a stylised bird pattern. According to Hermann Leicht, the historian of the Chimu civilisation, the walls of the palace courtyards 'were covered with fine white plaster painted with vivid scenes such as one can still admire today on much of the pottery. Other walls were covered with geometrical arabesques, chequered and rhomboid patterns as well as complicated patterns in severely hieratic style, reminiscent not only of Tiahunaco but . . . of the burial city of the Zapotec kings'.

Below: Relief from Chanchan; an example of the patterns which approach the complicated symbolism which, from the Chavín times to the Nazca, features in the design of sculptured figures and of painted pottery.

Right: Polychrome pottery jar from Pachacamac, showing Tiahuanaco influence. The neck is in the form of a stylised human head with headdress and the body is decorated with conventionalised symbols of animal forms. Pachacamac, on a hill near present-day Lima, was the site of a famous temple and cult centre of the god Viracocha. The enormous value of the offerings deposited there by worshippers in pre-Inca and Inca times excited the greed of the Spanish invaders.

A clay figure from one of the tombs in the Cauca River valley of Columbia. The shield suggests a warrior and the slit eyes are like those of the Quimbaya gold figures; but nothing is known of the people who built the tombs, and made figures like these, about the sixth century A.D.

early years after the Conquest gathered some elements of indigenous Aymará mythology from the local inhabitants, they gleaned nothing which could throw light on the religious or mythological significance of Tiahuanaco. It is not until Inca times that we can get a more detailed picture based on written memories of cult and myths. It is for this reason that the study of South American mythology, if it aspires to be more than a subjective fancy picture, must depend almost entirely on written records (or on the field researches of ethnologists in more modern times), even though these are very scanty for some of the most interesting areas and times.

In the religion of the highland farmers, the village communities or *ayllus*, animistic beliefs, sorcerers and medicine-men were most prominent. Crisis events in the life of the individual were treated as family affairs rather than as matters of public ritual. The major communal religious ceremonies and rituals were connected with the agricultural cycle and many of these have persisted in a reduced form until the present. They were systematised and elaborated by the Inca and we have fairly detailed accounts by Cristóbal de Molina, Felipe Guamán Poma de Ayala and others of the early chroniclers. Popular religion was dominated by the conception of the *huaca*, which meant basically anything at all which was supposed to be holy or fraught with spiritual force, or the dwelling place of a spirit. *Huacas* varied enormously from household fetishes, charms, any strange or unusual objects, to temples and symbols of the gods, things to do with the cult of the dead, and objects important in tribal tradition such as the shrine of Ayar Ucho

at Huanacauri and the stone relic of Ayar Auca which became the field-guardian of Cuzco and the stones from the battlefield where the Inca defeated the Chanca, which in Inca legend were supposed to have been turned into men to aid the forces of Cusi Inca Yupanqui.

Huacas of locality were particularly important in the highland religion. They might be mountains, springs, trees, caves or any other natural feature. A particular class were the cairns of stones, called *apachitas*, which even today are built up by travellers at dangerous spots or at the highest point of a road. The preservation of the bodies of ancestors or founders of the clan, dried and half-mummified by the cold air of the highland plateau, was a general feature. In the four years from 1615 to 1619, according to a letter from Francisco de Borja to the King of Spain, the Spaniards took from the Indians of Peru 1,365 such 'mummies of ancestors'. The bodies of the dead Inca were preserved and became the objects of a cult. Even today the word *huaca* is in general popular use for anything connected with an ancient burial, as for example the textiles and ceramics which find their way into museums and private collections.

During a period lasting roughly from 850 to 400 B.C. the art products of the coastal and highland valleys of Peru were dominated by a style and motifs which spread from the temple site of Chavín de Huantar in northern Peru and this has led to the supposition that the cultural advances which took place in these centuries were associated with a religious movement superimposed on the amorphous local cults. It is thought that Chavín was a centre of pilgrimage and that associated with it was the worship of tribal deities, with some form of organised priesthood and temple cult, in the shape of a feline (jaguar) deity, a condor, a snake and possibly certain fish deities. The evidence is entirely archaeological and nothing in detail is known about the nature of the beliefs associated with the cult or the mythological background.

Our ignorance of the nature of the highland religion which centred on

A grave discovered in the sand near the mouth of the River Loa in northern Chile. The practice of interment in deep sandy graves was common to all the peoples of the coast, among the unknown race represented here no less than the sophisticated cultures to the north. The body was put into a coarse cloth with simple belongings, the whole being wrapped before burial in the skin of a sea-lion.

Tiahuanaco is almost as great. Even the dates are uncertain. Some authorities place the Tiahuanaco period from about 300 B.C. to about A.D. 500, others from about A.D. 400 to about A.D. 1000. The little we know about the highland Aymará mythology does not bear an obvious or close relation to the Tiahuanaco religion as manifested in archaeological remains.

We know more about the Inca religion. It was a hierarchical theocratic state religion based on the principle of divine kingship. The Sun was the tribal god of the Inca aristocracy and the Inca monarchs were personifications, representatives, or 'sons' of the sun-god. The religion also recognised a creator-god Viracocha, a moon-god, gods of stars and weather – in particular the god of thunder – and a host of minor gods and spirits. In relation to conquered peoples the Inca adopted the system of syncretism and absorption, bringing their local deities and cults within the organised state religion, so that it becomes almost impossible to disentangle genuine Inca features from syncretistic elements. Even the basic Inca mythology and cult seem to have been largely borrowed or linked with the highland sun-worship (possibly part of the Tiahuanaco religion) which centred upon Lake Titicaca. The Inca state religion was highly organised, with temple worship, a priestly class, elaborate rituals to cover almost every aspect of life, a class of Sacred Virgins of the Sun, rites of confession, penitence, excommunication, and so on. It did not suppress the more primitive *huaca* religion, and did not make much inroad on the widely spread beliefs in sorcery and magic, but was a superimposed national cult and ritual fostering the divine majesty of the Inca monarchs and their empire.

Sources for mythology

Among the Inca there was a special class of wise men, *amautas*, whose duty it was to compose and perpetuate from generation to generation the traditions of the people, history and legend combined. A similar practice existed among the Aymará tribes of the Bolivian Altiplano and almost certainly some such practice existed among the coastal peoples, although details of it are more sparse. The Spanish chronicler Cieza de León, writing some fifteen years after the Conquest, gives the following account of it among the Inca.

'I understood, when I was in Cuzco, that it was the custom among the king Incas, that the king, as soon as he died, should be mourned with much lamentation, and that great sacrifices should be offered up in accordance with their religion. When these ceremonies were over, the oldest people of the country discussed the life and acts of the recently deceased king, considering whether he had done good for the country and what battles he had gained over the country's enemies. Having settled these questions, and others which we do not entirely understand, they decided whether the deceased king had been so fortunate as to merit praise and fame, and to deserve that his memory should be for ever preserved. They then called for the great *quiposcamayos*, who preserve the records and understand how to give an account of the events that occur in the kingdom. Next they communicated with those who were most expert and who were selected for their skill in rhetoric and the use of words. These knew how to narrate the events in regular order, like ballad singers and romance writers. These compose the songs, so that they shall be heard by all at marriage ceremonies and other festivities. Thus they were instructed what to say concerning the deceased lord, and, if they treated of wars, they sang in proper order of the many battles he had fought in different parts of the empire. And for other events there were songs and romances to celebrate them on suitable occasions, so that the people might be animated by the recital of what had passed in other times. These Indians who by order of the kings had learnt the romances were honoured and favoured and great

'Tupa Inca speaks with all the *huacas*'. *Huaca* was the name given to anything believed to be imbued with spiritual force, or the dwelling place of a spirit. They could be simple household charms, or temples, or rocks and other natural features such as caves and springs. In this drawing from Guamán Poma de Ayala the Inca enters into communication with the spirits in order to learn the past and the future.

care was taken to teach their sons and other men in their provinces who were most able and intelligent. By this plan from the mouths of one generation the succeeding one was taught, and they can relate what took place five hundred years ago as if only ten years had passed.'

Tribal history, legend and the background of mythology were preserved by word of mouth, and among the more organised peoples special classes of professional historians and reciters were fostered. As the Inca extended their conquests their ubiquitous passion for organisation did not neglect the structuring of history and legend. In some cases they combined and syncretised, adopting myth and legend of subject peoples as their own; in other cases they suppressed. They exercised a deliberate and systematic policy of distorting recorded history by obliterating the achievements of their predecessors in the advancement of civilisation, truncating the remembered traditions and representing themselves – or their legendary tribal ancestors – as the original bearers and inventors of culture to peoples living at a pre-agricultural stage of hunting and food-gathering, without manufacturing crafts or social organisation. From the official Inca corpus of legend the contributions of the coastal peoples – the Chavín culture and the great coastal kingdoms which followed it – and of the southern

Left: A beautiful Inca *keru*, or painted and lacquered wooden beaker, with a small bird figure and human figures in attitudes of amazement with birds perched on their heads. It seems to represent some scene of magic or cult of the *huaca* of the birds.

Centre: Indians of the western part of the empire, according to Guamán Poma de Ayala, had their own idols and *huacas* whom they honoured as well as those of the official Inca religion. They sacrificed gold and silver, coca, the fruit of the molle tree, flamingo feathers, twelve-year-old children, and black llama kids. Here, they bring offerings to the *huaca* Cocopona.

Below: A mace head with four blades and eight spikes made of diorite, from the Chavín culture which flourished on the north coast of Peru c. 850–500 B.C. Later weapons were more sophisticated but the club persisted, hand-to-hand fighting playing a large part in the warfare of peoples who lacked both projectiles and mobility.

highland peoples, the megalithic builders of Tiahuanaco, have disappeared.

We depend for our knowledge of myth and legend, even in this systematically distorted form, entirely on the records of the chroniclers who wrote during the early decades after the Conquest. In general they lacked the objective and scientific interest which we have today, and even the sort of impartial curiosity which is nowadays taken for granted was rare among them. Some were genuinely eager to find out what the Indians themselves believed about their origins and took the trouble to question Indian authorities and record what they said. In some cases their motive was to justify the destructive Spanish occupation by showing that the Inca themselves had held their domination by conquest and not by right. Others had a less partial interest. But all were hampered by a rigid belief in the literal truth

A nut-shaped vessel of the Nazca culture, which flourished in the fertile valleys some fifty miles inland of the south coast of Peru. The shape may have been for decorative purpose only but it was possibly used for storing oil.

of Biblical records and a horror of anything which conflicted with Christian dogma. As we have said, owing to this reason a great deal of mythological and legendary material which we should have valued today was contemptuously passed by in silence as trivial or immoral. Again and again our sources stop short just at the point where we should have found the continuation of most interest. The following passage from Sarmiento is typical of the attitude with which they approached their sources of information.

'As the devil, who is always striving to injure the human race, found these unfortunates to be easy of belief and timid in obedience, he introduced many illusions, lies and frauds, giving them to understand that he had created them from the first and afterwards, owing to their sins and evil deeds, he had destroyed them with a flood, again creating them and giving them food and the way to preserve it. By chance, they formerly had some notice, passed down to them from mouth to mouth, which has reached them from their ancestors, respecting the truth of what had happened in former times. Mixing this with the stories told them by the devil, and with other things which they changed, invented or added, which may happen in all nations, they made up a pleasing salad, and in some things worthy of the attention of the curious who are accustomed to consider and discuss human ideas. One thing must be noted among many others. It is that the stories which are here treated as fables, which they are, are held by the natives to be as true as we hold the articles of our faith, and as such they affirm and confirm them with unanimity and swear by them.'

The few Indian or half-Indian chroniclers wrote under a strong impulse to assert their Christian orthodoxy and were inclined to emphasise aspects of native mythology which seemed to parallel Christian doctrine. For instance Juan de Santa Cruz Pachacuti-yamqui Salcamayhua prefaces his *Account of the Antiquities of Peru* with the statement: 'When the first Apostolic Priests entered this most noble province of Ttahuantin-suyu [the Inca Empire] inspired by the holy zeal of gaining a soul for God our Lord, like good fishers with their loving words, preaching and catechising on the mystery of our holy Catholic Faith, then my ancestors, after having been well instructed, were baptised. They renounced the Devil and all his followers and his false promises, and all his rites. Thus they became Christians, adopted sons of Jesus Christ our Lord, and enemies of all the ancient customs and idolatries. As such they persecuted the wizards, destroyed and pulled down all the *huacas* and idols, denounced idolaters,

Above: 'The Great Sorcerer'. With some confusion of symbolism – the book was compiled after the conquest – the Inca master sorcerer is shown ceremonially burning a very Christian-looking devil. The Inca symbols of the Sun, Moon, and Morning Star look on approvingly. Illustration by Guamán Poma de Ayala.

Below: The ruins of Sacsahuamán, the fortress of the Inca capital of Cuzco. The walls stretched for over a third of a mile and the terrace walls reach a height of over sixty feet. The buildings for the populace and the towers for defence were on the highest terrace, and also water reservoirs. Most of this part of the fortress was plundered for building stone by the Spaniards.

and punished those who were their own servants and vassals throughout all that province. Therefore our Lord God preserved these my ancestors and to their grandchildren and descendants, male and female, He has given His holy benediction. Finally I am, through the mercy of his divine majesty, and by his divine grace, a believer in this holy Catholic faith, as I ought to believe...'

The manuscript of the *Nueva corónica y buen gobierno* by Don Felipe Guamán Poma de Ayala was discovered in the Royal Library, Copenhagen, in 1908. A facsimile edition was published by the Institute of Ethnology, Paris, in 1936 and a new edition was issued by the Tihuanacu Institute, La Paz, in 1944. The manuscript consists of 1,179 pages and is illustrated by full-page pen and ink drawings which provide our best visual evidence of Peruvian life and manners during the time of the Inca and the early years of the Conquest. This is the only illustrated Peruvian codex that is known. It was probably written in 1613. The author was an Indian who claimed descent on his mother's side from the Inca monarchy and through his father from an ancient line of monarchs who ruled in the northern parts of Peru before the domination of the Inca. Guamán (falcon) and Poma (lion) may both be royal titles. Rather more than a quarter of the manuscript deals with conditions in Peru before the Conquest and the work as a whole was intended as a bitter denunciation of the cruelty and oppression of the Spanish rule. The text is confused and illiterate, but is best on matters of religion and daily life. The drawings, however, which often reveal real talent, are of unique importance for the vivid impressions they give of Indian customs and belief.

With the exception of the mestizo Garcilaso Inca de la Vega, who wrote many years later in Spain, these native chroniclers were not men of high education, and were poorly versed in the language. Moreover, as is usual wherever tradition depends on oral memory and is not yet fixed by written records, the mythopoeic faculty was still active and there is no doubt that from the very early years of the Conquest the local mythology and legends were conflated with and coloured by the Christian teachings of the missionaries. This is particularly noticeable with the Thunupa legends which were gathered somewhat later by Spanish missionaries who had settled on the Altiplano.

Outside the Central Andean region our early knowledge depends in the main on the records made by the Jesuits who extended their missions over the tribes of the upper Amazon, eastern Bolivia, the province of Chiquitos, the Chaco, Paraguay and the Pampas, and who were particularly successful with the Guarani Indians of the middle and upper Paraguay and Uruguay rivers. Their descriptions of the cultures of the Indians whom they converted are invaluable and are often scientific and objective in character. Some useful information about mythological beliefs is embedded in these descriptions, but here too it is often difficult to determine the extent to which the original material has been conflated with the new Christian teaching. The desire of the Indian to please causes him to adapt his account to his hearer.

Myth, legend and folklore

The anthropologist Bronislaw Malinowski once said: 'Myth is the constant by-product of a living faith in need of miracles, of sociological status which demands precedent, of moral rule which demands sanction.' Myths are often more or less closely linked with religious beliefs and cults, social customs including crisis and other rites, and magical and medicinal lore. In addition to genuine myth South American cultures contained a great wealth of folk story, including animal stories of all kinds, and an abundance of legendary material, much of which embodies confused traditions of tribal

Left: Detail of a finely painted Inca wooden *keru* depicting a scene from a ceremonial procession. Inca painted and lacquered wooden beakers, known as *kerus*, are usually dated shortly after the Spanish Conquest of America. They often represented ceremonial or ritual scenes in vivid colours and with lively figuration.

Below: A pottery vessel of the Inca period showing a labourer going forth to the fields. All cultivation was done with hand tools and the plough was unknown.

movements or the emergence and decline of cultures and technologies. It is not possible to make any precise line of demarcation between folk story, legend and myth, and indeed a great deal of the material which has survived combines features of each. In the following survey no attempt has been made to cover South American folk story, legend or religious belief as such; but myth elements have not been excluded simply in the interests of academic preciseness because they incorporate features which belong more properly to legend or story. For example, the myths of Inca origins, which rank among the most interesting of the Central Andean material, have the appearance of incorporating a considerable body of legend artificially conflated with both earlier legendary and genuine mythological cycles.

Nowhere in South American cultures do we find an elaborate polytheistic mythology associated with a divine pantheon such as the Olympic deities of the Greeks and the animal-shaped gods of Egypt. The innumerable ghostly and supernatural powers by which men's lives were swayed belonged in the realm of popular or organised occultism and were not so highly personalised as to attract genuine mythological cycles. On the other hand cultural and causal myth was more fully developed, and cycles on the borderland between myth and legend were cherished and preserved through the generations. Mythological pictures about the after-life are not well developed among the advanced civilisations and among the more primitive cultures are little elaborated beyond the bounds of folk story. Perhaps the most ubiquitous features in South American myth are the stories of a deluge and variant accounts of the origins of advanced agricultural and social culture with or without a divine culture hero. It is, however, difficult to determine how far such generalisations belong to the original character of the mythological material and how far they are accounted for by the conditions of preservation.

For the sake of convenience South American myth may be classified into the following categories.

The origin of the world. Myths of the origins of the universe are not well developed. Apart from infrequent stories of fabulous mythological animals, the origin of the sun and constellations is usually attributed to a creator-god and often connected with a deluge.

The deluge. Myths of a deluge are very widespread both among the highland peoples and the tribes of the tropical lowlands. The deluge is commonly connected with the creation and with an epiphany of the creator-god. It is often associated with the creation of mankind or of the present races of man. It is sometimes regarded as a divine punishment wiping out existing mankind in preparation for the emergence of a new race.

The creation of man. The origin of human beings as they are now is commonly attributed to the act of a creator-god and often connected with the deluge. Some mythological cycles feature a primitive age of darkness before the existence of the sun, when human beings lived in a state of anarchy without the techniques of civilised life. Sometimes myths in this category appear to embody a confused racial memory of a hunting and food-gathering stage. It is not uncommon for them to be associated with a tradition of the destruction of the primitive food-gathering race by a creator-god and the creation of new races, usually following a deluge. In the mythology both of the highland peoples and of the tropical forest tribes the creation of the present human race is very frequently connected with natural features, such as mountains, rivers and caverns or even trees and rocks, in a way which appears to indicate a close relation with the animistic religion of *huacas*, or the worship of natural features, which preceded the more organised cults of national divinities but persisted with them.

The culture hero. Myths of a culture hero who brought the arts of civilisation to the present races of mankind are often connected, as in the official Inca myth, with the legendary ancestor of a tribe. Sometimes the culture

Right: A Mochica clay vessel from a grave site near the north coast, decorated in terracotta and yellow paint. The praying figure is probably a priest, and the mask suggests a feline cult; but in spite of the wealth of artistic objects which have survived from this brilliant culture nothing is certain about its religious practices.

Below: An Inca record-keeper using his *quipu*, a string from which hung down variously coloured cords. By means of knots tied at different intervals in the various cords and by different methods of twisting and differences in the size and kind of knot, the Inca and other South American peoples used the *quipu* as a mnemonic device. It could be used not only for statistical, calendrical and other records, but also as a reminder of verses memorised to perpetuate the record of history and events. Thus, though writing was unknown to the peoples of South America before the conquest, among the more stable cultures of the Central Andes legends, traditions and mythology were preserved over many generations. Illustration by Guamán Poma de Ayala.

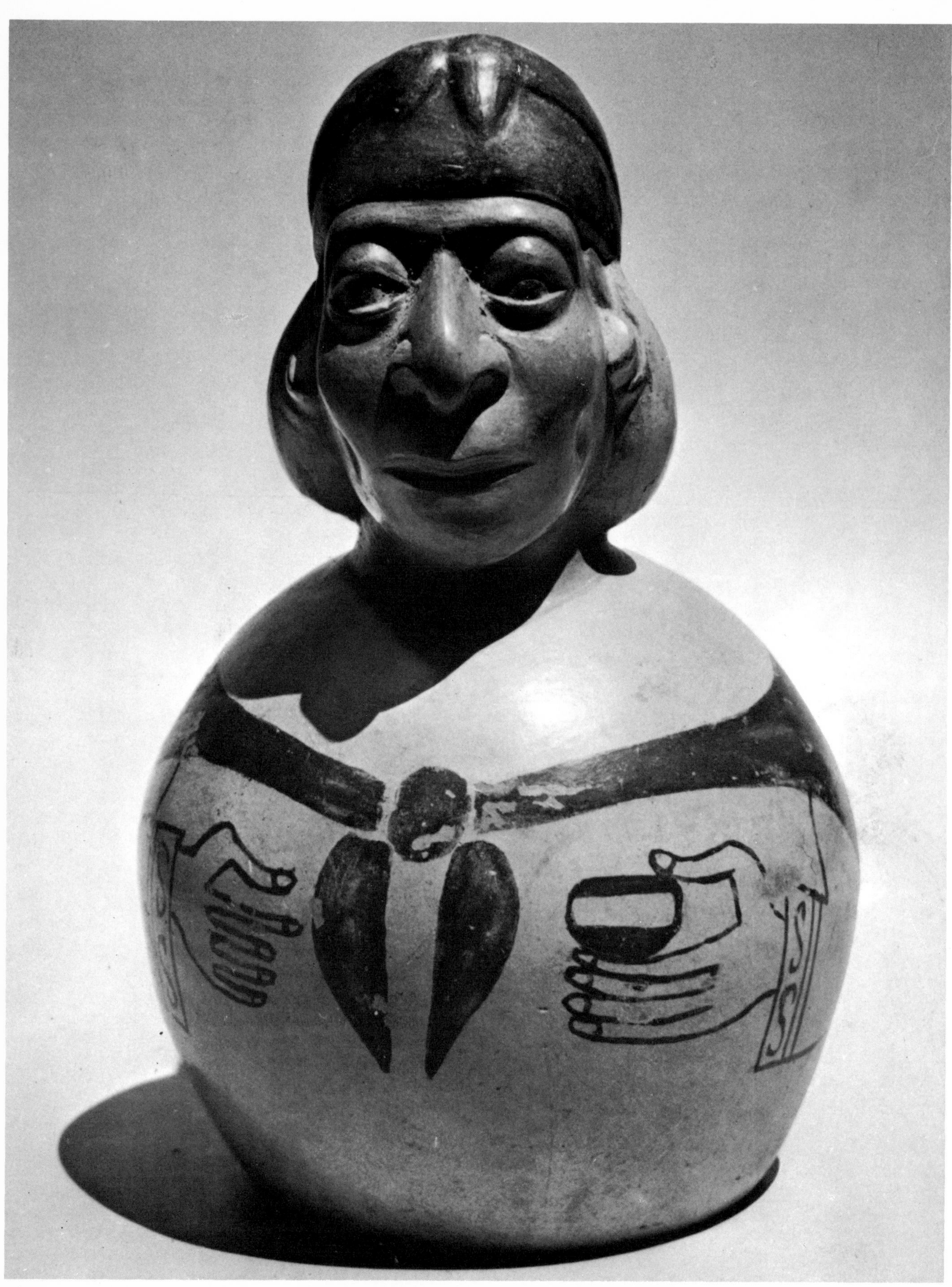

hero is identified with the creator-god. The creator was also called Pachayachachic, meaning Teacher of the World, in Peru. More often he is represented as the semi-divine son of the creator or as a human being with miraculous powers. His appearance generally follows the deluge and the creation of the present races.

Aetiological myths. Myths purporting to explain the origin of tribes, dynasties, religious or magical rituals, animals, unusual natural features, social institutions and the like are to be found throughout the continent. Indeed all myths of the foregoing categories tend to take on an aetiological character.

In addition there is a great wealth of folklore, including stories which conform to the world-wide type of animal story illustrating the typical characteristics of various species of animal life, and there is an abundance of legendary material, much of which incorporates confused traditions of the movements of tribes or the emergence and decline of cultures. It is not possible to make any precise line of division between folk story, legend and myth. As will be apparent, the myths themselves do not fall clearly into one or the other of the above categories but almost always combine features from several. In quoting the myths, therefore, as reported by the ancient chroniclers or the ethnologists it is not possible to arrange them in the categories as defined. The great majority of reports will be seen to bring together elements from several categories and this is undoubtedly the way in which the mythology has survived in native tradition.

Left: A highland Indian depicted on a glazed vase of the Mochica culture which flourished on the north coast of Peru, A.D. 400–1000. The Quechua Indian of today (below), here seen playing a *quena* flute, is distinctly of the same race. The Quechuas are the same people who, under the lead of the Incas, achieved greatness with the empire which the Conquistadores plundered in the sixteenth century.

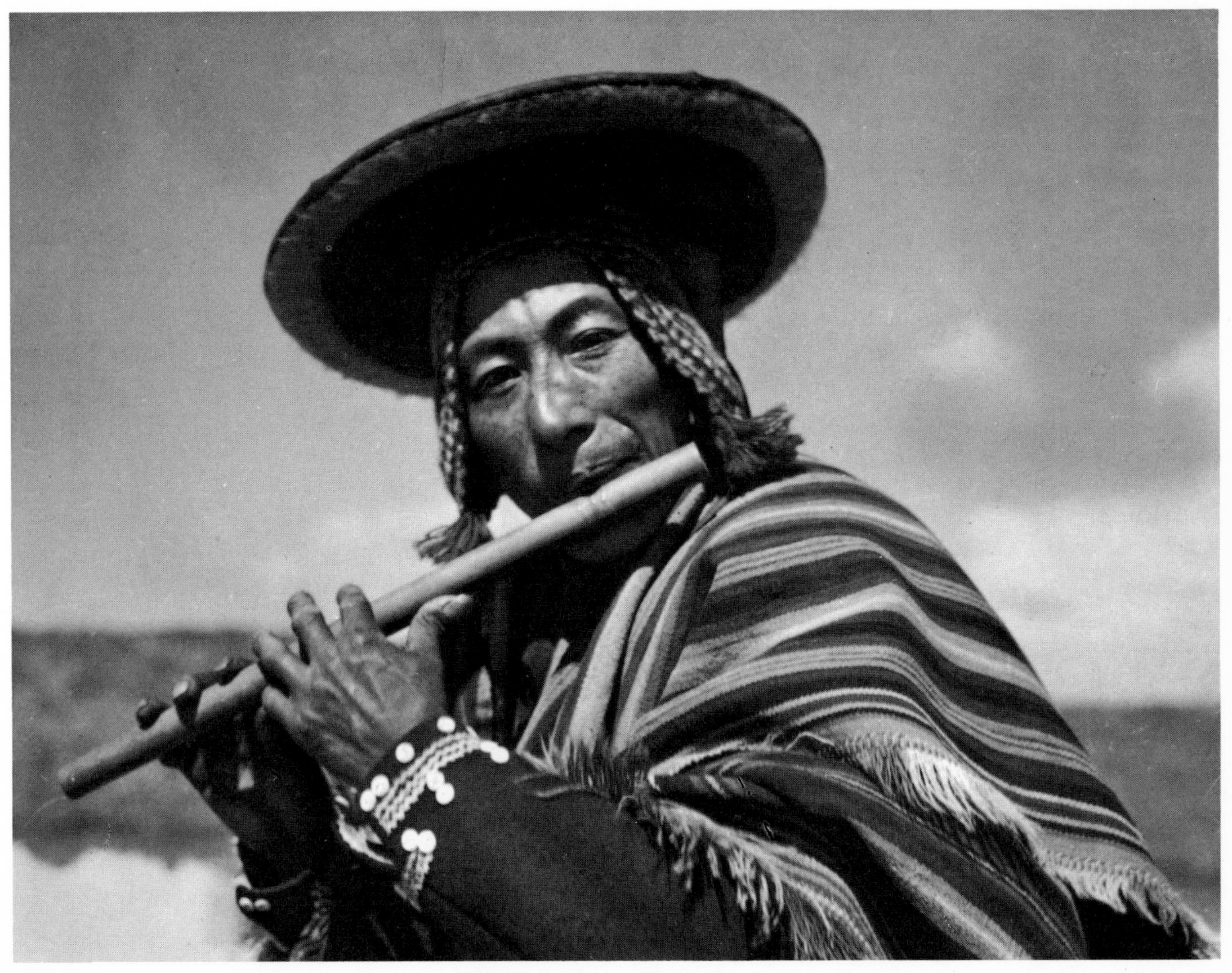

The Divine Origin of the Inca

We begin with the myths of Inca origins both because these have been recorded most frequently and in some cases most carefully by the early chroniclers, and also because when mythological material of greater antiquity survives it has often come down to us conflated with Inca legend. Indeed the official Inca accounts of their legendary origins may fairly be surmised to have taken their shape largely by the appropriation of folk stories which long antedated the rise of their dynasty.

There are three main legends of Inca origins. They all contain a large admixture of mythical elements and all establish a claim for a special relationship of the Inca nobility to the sun-deity. The Inca monarchs expanded and stabilised their empire with an organising genius and technological brilliance not inferior to the Romans'. The social system which they imposed was based on the hierarchical principle of divine kingship, and the prestige of their authority went hand in hand with the cult of the Sun which they propagated. At the pinnacle of the hierarchy were the Inca rulers, who were themselves worshipped as children of the sun. The mythical origins of the dynasty confirmed and supported this cult. It will be seen that many of the details of the stories incidentally provided a rationale for Inca institutions and rituals, e.g. the marriage of the reigning monarch to a sister, the cult of Huanacauri.

The first version tells of a cliff with three small cave mouths, or a building with three exits, about twenty miles from the present city of Cuzco. It was called Paccari-tambo (Inn of Origin) or Tambotocco (Place of the Hole). In prehistoric times four brothers and four sisters, who were to be the founders of the Inca dynasty, emerged from the middle orifice. Their names and numbers are differently given – according to some versions the ancestors of other, non-royal Inca clans emerged from the other two orifices. These brothers and sisters differed in costume and appearance from the local population and were able to gain a moral ascendancy over them. They proceeded slowly in the general direction of Cuzco, looking for good land on which to settle. One of the brothers, Ayar Cachi, incurred the resentment of the others by his feats of strength and his boastfulness. In particular he climbed to the top of a mountain, Huanacauri, and hurling stones from his sling at the neighbouring hills, he opened up ravines where none had been before. The brothers therefore induced him to return to the cave to fetch objects which they had left behind and walled him up inside it. The other brothers went on and made a temporary settlement at Tambu Quiru. Here they were visited miraculously by the spirit of Ayar Cachi, who after exhorting them to proceed with the foundation of Cuzco turned himself to stone on the hill Huanacauri and became the object of a later Inca cult. According to another version it was the brother Ayar Uchu who, after instructing Manco Capac in the maturity ritual for Inca youths, turned to stone on Huanacauri. Manco Capac (or Ayar Manco) went on with the sisters until they eventually reached the site of Cuzco. Here they found the terrain suitable to their needs and, after driving off

Left: The Inca royal arms, according to Guamán Poma de Ayala. In the first drawing can be seen, top left, *Inti* the Sun and *raymi* the festival of the Sun celebrated in Cuzco in June. Top right: Coya was the wife and sister of the reigning Inca, whose children inherited the throne. The name also described the sacred virgins, wives of the Sun. Here the moon is pictured as the divine sister-wife of the Sun, and Queen of Heaven. Bottom left: the morning star. The word *uillca* is a term of divine honour. These symbols indicate that the Inca claims the divine Sun as his father, the Moon as his mother and the Morning Star as his brother. Bottom right: this shows Tambotocco, Paccari-tambo and the 'idol' Huanacauri – which figure in the legendary origin of the Inca dynasty. The second drawing shows, top left, the bird whose feathers are like bright flowers. Top right: the *chunta*, or hard chonta tree, and at its foot an *otoronco*. Bottom left: the pouch for coca. Bottom right: two amaru snakes with the royal *borla* (tassel) in their mouths.

Below: Machu Picchu, the Lost City of the Inca, which was rediscovered by Hiram Bingham in 1912. It lies at the end of the gorge of the Urubamba river, on the edge of the tropical rain-forest. Behind it towers the peak of Huayna Picchu, flanked by precipices which rise 2,500 feet from the rapids. There are more than a hundred stairways in the ruins, the most imposing being that which leads from the central Plaza to the top of the hill on the left, on which still stands the *Inti-huatana* or 'hitching post of the Sun'. The illustration shows stepped terraces leading up to the platform.

the Indian tribe which was settled there, they founded their city. Manco Capac with his wife and sister Mama Ocllo were the first rulers.

The idea of human ancestors emerging from rocks and caves is common among the peoples of South America. The story of brothers – often involved in fratricidal strife – as cultural heroes or founders of the tribe is also very widely disseminated and is met far beyond the Central Andean area. The Inca may have taken over and adapted the story from local folklore or they may have furbished up a legend which had been perpetuated from more ancient times in their tribe.

In a second version the sun-god, seeing men living in a state of primitive barbarity, felt pity for them and sent to earth on an island in Lake Titicaca his two children Manco Capac and Mama Ocllo, brother and sister, to instruct them in the arts of civilised life. These two journeyed northwards over the Altiplano carrying with them a long golden rod, and were to settle when they came to a place where the rod could be buried entirely in the soil. (In a region where for the most part the earth is thin, stony and unprolific the test for deep and penetrable soil makes sense.) When they reached the valley of Cuzco (a highland valley some 11,000 ft above sea level) they first stopped at Huanacauri. Proceeding further, they came to the site of Cuzco, where the rod sank into the ground. Here they founded the city as the seat of their empire, won over the native peoples by teaching them the arts of civilisation, and instituted the religion of the sun.

This version of Inca origins bears a close affinity with a common form of creation myth. Creation – or at any rate the origin of civilisation – seems to have been linked with the story of a flood. Before the flood men lived in a state of primitive barbarity. After the world had been destroyed by the flood the creator brought into being a new race of men and sent down to earth a culture hero to teach them the arts of civilisation. In the Inca version the sun god takes the place of (or is closely linked with) the creator, and the founders of the Inca race are depicted as culture heroes, assuming the characteristics of divine agents who elsewhere bear other names such as Viracocha or Thunupa or Pachacamac. The Inca myth is obviously conflated most nearly with the creation story in the southern Altiplano and ties up the origin of the Inca with the sacred Lake Titicaca in whose basin stood Tiahuanaco, the capital of an earlier religious culture.

One effect of this version was to suppress the memory of the important pre-Inca culture and to represent the Inca as universal benefactors who brought civilisation and culture to the whole of mankind.

According to a third version, Inca divine kingship originated in an astute deception practised by an early Inca king, who dressed himself in a shining cloak of gold or beads and, parading before his ignorant subjects, so impressed them with his majesty in the glittering rays of the sun that they were prepared to worship him as the offspring and representative of the sun-god. Some chroniclers, for example Ramos Gavilan in his *Historia del célebre Santuario de Nuestra Señora de Copacabana*, published in Lima in 1621, and Martín de Morúa in this century, tell this story of the first Inca king, Manco Capac. Others tell it of Sinchi Roca, who is the second monarch in the usual version, and assign the credit for the trick to his mother. She spread the word that the Sun was about to send a ruler and then produced the boy Sinchi Roca from the mouth of a cave, dressed in resplendent garments. The gullible people thereupon accepted him as a heaven-sent ruler and he thus became the first Inca monarch. Montesinos, whose version we quote, assigned the story of the four brothers to the dynasty of the Piruas, which according to him preceded the Inca by many centuries, and used the 'Shining Mantle' myth to account for the origin of the Inca dynasty with Sinchi Roca. Although the historical interpretations given by Montesinos have not so far been taken seriously, there is no reason to doubt that he has preserved genuine legendary material.

The Inca capital and sacred city of Cuzco, the heart of the Inca empire and of the religion of the Sun with which the Inca monarchy was identified, was constructed of fine megalithic architecture. Two styles were used: in one the stone blocks were rectangularly shaped and in the other style they were polygonal. In both styles the huge stones were fitted together with such accuracy that it is said a knife-blade cannot be thrust between them. The impressive Inca building can still be seen in Cuzco streets, where it often serves as the foundation for later Spanish Colonial building.

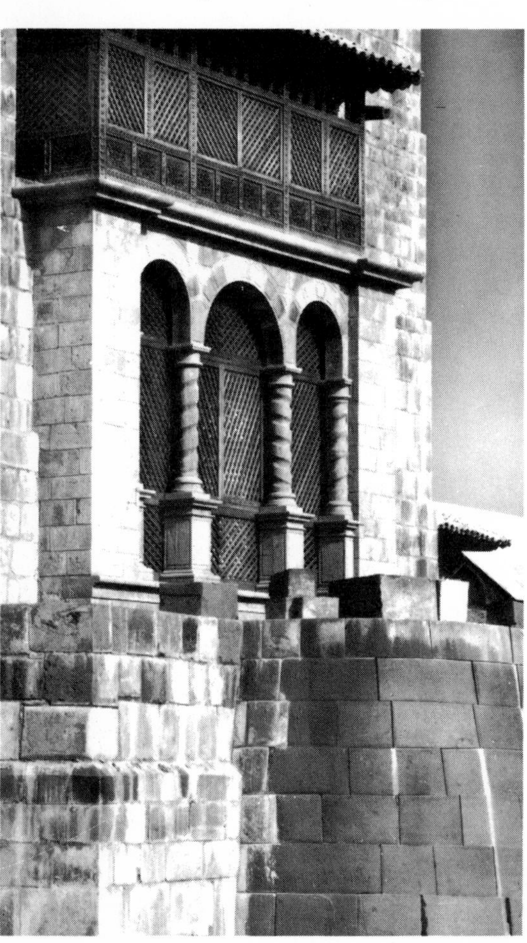

The Inn of Origin

'I have already stated more than once how as an exercise to escape from the vices caused by idleness I took the trouble to describe all that I obtained touching the Incas and their system and good order of government. As I have no other account nor writing beyond what they gave me, if another should undertake to write more certainly than I have on this subject, he may well do so. At the same time I have not spared pains to make what I write clear; and to ensure greater accuracy I went to Cuzco when the Captain Juan de Saavedra was Corregidor. [i.e. A.D. 1550] Here he arranged that Cayu Tupac should meet me, who is one of the surviving descendants of Huayna Capac. For Sairi Tupac, son of Manco Inca, has retired to Viticos, where his father took refuge after his great war with the Spaniards at Cuzco. I also met others of the Orejones, who are those that are held to be most noble among themselves. [Orejones (large-ears) was the Spanish term for the Inca nobility on account of their custom of enlarging the ear-lobes, in which they wore golden plaques.] With the best interpreters that could be found I asked these Lords Incas of what race they were and of what nation. It would seem that the former Incas, to magnify their origin with great deeds, exaggerated the story they had received in their songs. It is this.

'When all the races who lived in these regions were in a state of disorder, slaughtering each other and sunk in vice, there appeared three men and three women in a place not far from the city of Cuzco which is called Paccari-tambo. And according to the interpretation Paccari-tambo is as much as to say the House of Origin. The men who came forth from there were, as they relate, the one Ayar Ucho and the other Ayar Cachi Asauca and the other, they say, was named Ayar Manco. Of the women one had

The enormous row of faced stones set up on one of the highest platforms at Ollantaytambo. They are upwards of ten foot high and must have had a ceremonial significance, though this has been lost.

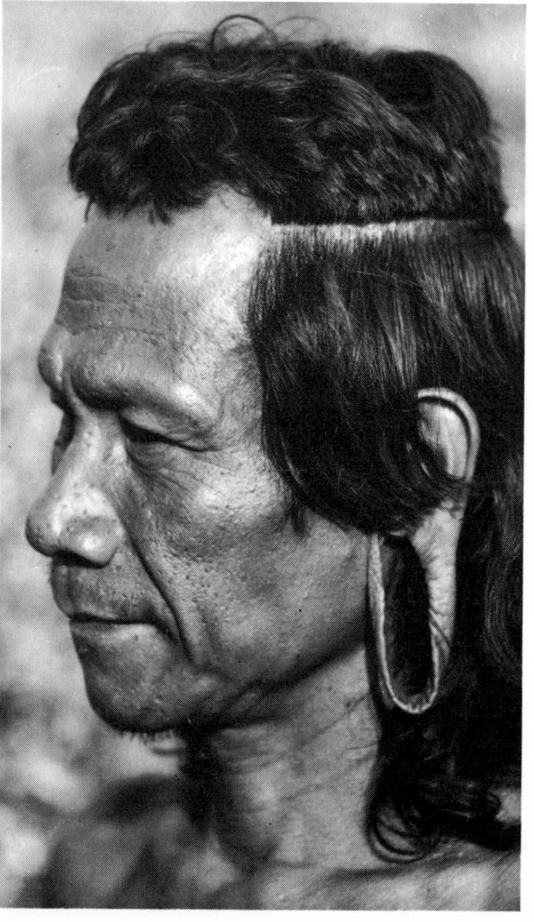

the name of Mama Huaco, the other Mama Coya, the other Mama Rahua.

'Some Indians give these names after another fashion and in greater number but I have put them down from the informations of the Orejones, who know better than any one else. They say that these people came forth dressed in long mantles and some vestments like a shirt without collar or sleeves, made of very fine wool with patterns of different kinds, which they called *tapacu* and in our language the meaning is "vestures of kings". And each of these lords held in the hand a sling of gold with a stone in it. The women came out dressed very richly like the men and they had much gold. Going forward with this, they further say that they obtained great store of gold and that one of the brothers named Ayar Ucho spoke to his brethren that they should make a beginning of the great things that they had to do; for their presumption was such that they thought they were to make themselves sole lords of the land. They were determined to make in that place a new settlement, to which they gave the name of Paccaritambo, and this was soon done, for they had the help of the inhabitants of the surrounding country. As time went on they put great quantities of pure gold and jewels with other precious things into that place, of which the fame goes that Hernando Pizarro and Don Diego de Almagro the younger obtained a large share.

'Returning to the history, they say that one of the three named Ayar Cachi was so valiant and had such great power that with stones hurled from his sling he split the hills and threw them up to the clouds. When the other brothers saw this they were sorry, thinking that it was an affront to them who could not do such things and they were enraged by reason of their envy. Then they asked him sweetly and with gentle words, though full of deceit, to return and enter the mouth of a cave where they had their treasure, to bring out a certain vase of gold which they had forgotten, and to pray to their father the Sun that he would prosper their efforts so that they might be lords of that land. Ayar Cachi, believing that there was no deceit in what his brothers said, joyfully sent to do what they required of him; but he had scarcely got into the cave when the other two so filled up the mouth with stones that it could not be seen. This done, they relate that for a certainty the earth trembled in such a manner that many hills fell into the valleys.

'Thus far the Orejones relate the story of the origin of the Incas because they wished it to be understood that as their deeds were so marvellous they must have been children of the Sun. Afterwards, when the Indians exalted them with grand titles, they were called *Ancha hatun apu intipchuri*, which means "O very great Lord, child of the Sun". That which for my part I hold to be the truth in this matter is that as Zapana rose up in Hatuncollao and other valiant captains did the same thing in other parts, these Incas must have been some three valiant and powerful brothers with grand thoughts who were natives of some place in those regions or who had come from some other part of the mountains of the Andes; and that they, finding the opportunity, conquered and acquired the lordship which they possessed. Even without this supposition it might be that what they tell of Ayar Cachi and the others was the work of magicians, who did what is told of them through the Devil. In fine, we cannot get from the story any other solution than this.'

This is significant of the mentality of the Spanish chroniclers on whom we rely for recording South American mythology. They accepted the active intervention of the devil in human affairs and did not doubt the reality of magic.

'As soon as Ayar Cachi was secured in the cave, the other two brothers with some people who had joined them agreed to form another settlement, to which they gave the name of Tambo Quiru, which is as much as to say "Teeth of a residence or of a palace", and it may be supposed that these settlements were not large nor more than sufficient for a small force. They remained at this place for some days, being now sorry at having made away with their brother Ayar Cachi, who was also called Huanacauri.

'Proceeding with the narrative that I took down in Cuzco, the Orejones say that after the two Incas had settled in Tambo Quiru, careless now about seeing Ayar Cachi again, they beheld him coming in the air with great wings of coloured feathers and they, by reason of the great fear that this visit caused them, wanted to flee away; but he quickly removed their terror by saying to them: "Do not fear, neither be afflicted; for I only come that the empire of the Incas may begin to be known. Wherefore leave this settlement that you have made and advance further down until you see a valley, and there found Cuzco, which will be of great note. For here are only hamlets of little importance; but that will be a great city, where the sumptuous temple must be built that will be so honoured and frequented and where the Sun will be so worshipped. I shall always have to pray to God for you and to intercede that you may soon become great Lords. I shall remain in the form and fashion that you will see on a hill not distant from here and will be for you and your descendants a place of sanctity and worship, and its name shall be Huanacauri. And in return for the good things which you will have received from me I pray that you will always adore me as god and set up altars in that place at which to offer sacrifices. If you do this, you shall receive help from me in war; and as a sign that from henceforward you are to be esteemed, honoured and feared your ears shall be bored in the manner that you now behold in mine." And when he had so spoken they say that he appeared with ear ornaments of gold set round as with a gem.'

We see here the genesis of an aetiological myth explaining the origin of the Inca ceremony at the *huaca* of Huanacauri and of the custom of enlarging the ear-lobes.

Above left: 'In Cuzco', a drawing by Guamán Poma de Ayala which shows the Inca and his queen ceremoniously acknowledging the origins of their race and of the royal house at Paccari-Tambo (Inn of Origin) or Tambotocco (Place of the Hole) as it was variously called.

Below left: A Karaja Indian of Brazil. The enlarged earlobes usually hold large flat ornaments. The Inca nobility of times past also wore them, fashioned of gold and precious stones, and this led to their being dubbed *orejones* (long ears) by the Spaniards.

Below: A pair of ear ornaments from the Mochica culture. The mosaic design is contained in gold. A liking for large ear ornaments seems to be a feature of the South American Indian character. They are represented in all the pre-columbian cultures, and are much worn by the primitive tribes of today.

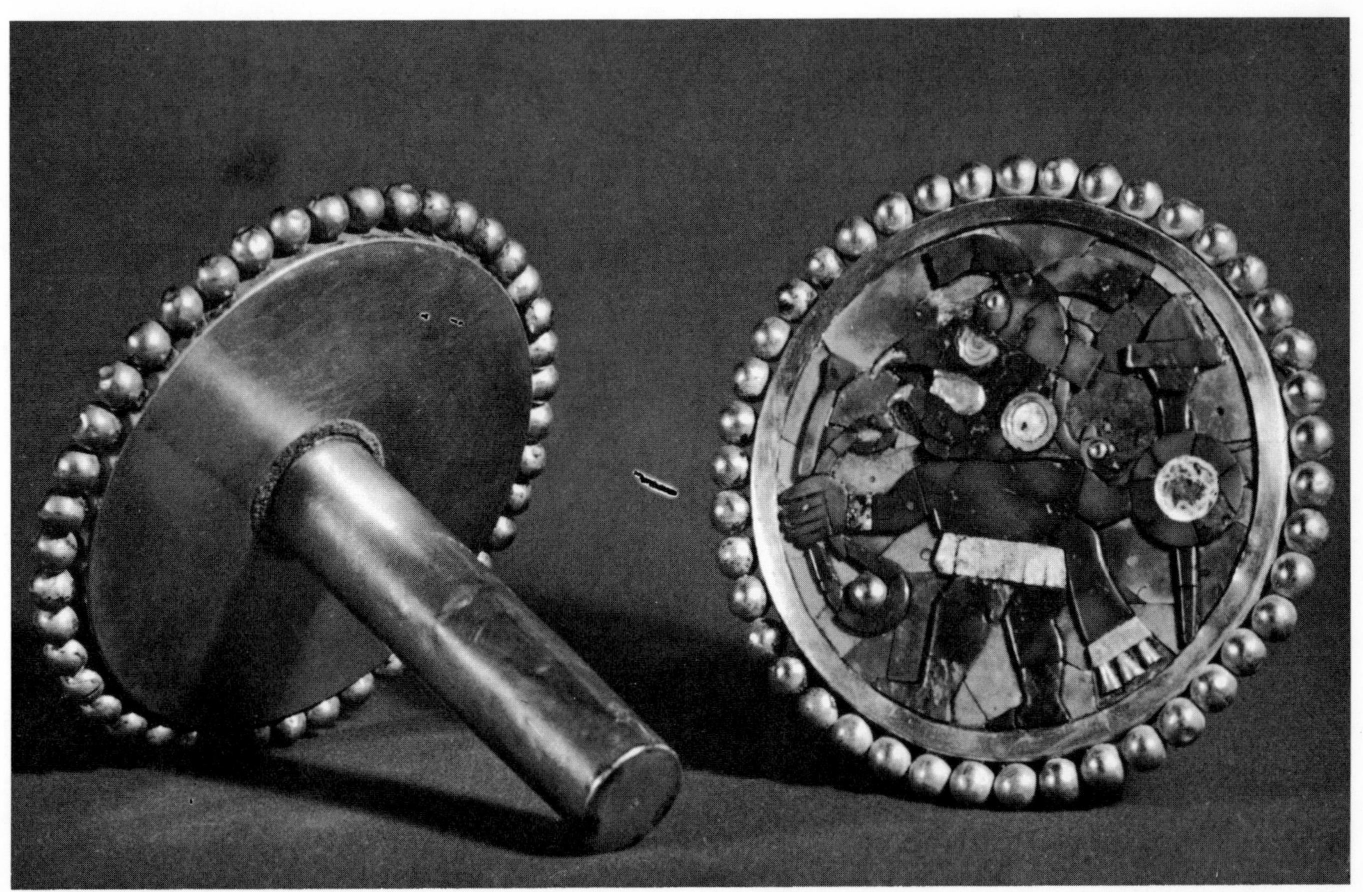

Right: The *Intihuatana* at Machu Picchu. These curiously cut stones of enormous size have been found set up on the summit of several Inca fortresses. They appear to be connected with calendrical calculations and so perhaps indirectly to have had significance in the cult of the sun-god. The *Intihuatana* may have been what the chronicler Montesinos referred to when he said of the Inca Capac Raymi Amauta that he 'called a great assembly of his wise men and astrologers and, with the king himself (who was deeply learned), they all studied the solstices with care. There was a sort of shadow-clock by which they knew which days were long and which were short, and when the sun went to and returned from the tropics.' Owing to the importance of the *Intihuatana* in Inca religion, the Spanish conquerors used to break off the stone wherever they found one. But Machu Picchu was never discovered by the Spanish and the *Intihuatana* is intact.

Below: Ollantaytambo, an Inca pueblo and fortress in the Urubamba valley guarding the approaches to Machu Picchu. This is one of the most impressive examples of Inca building, a magnificent structure of stone terracing.

'The brothers, astonished at what they saw, were as men struck dumb and without speech. When their perturbation had ceased they replied that they were content to do as he commanded and presently they went in haste to the hill called the Hill of Huanacauri, which from that time forward was accounted sacred. In the highest part of it they again saw Ayar Cachi, who without doubt must have been some devil if there is any truth in what they relate; and, God permitting, he made them understand his desire that they should worship and sacrifice unto him under these false appearances. They say that he again spoke to them, telling them to assume the fringe or crown of empire, [known as the *llautu*] such of them as were to be sovereign lords, and how they should order the arming of youths to make them knights and nobles. The brothers answered that they would comply with all his commands as they had already promised, and in sign of obedience with hands joined and heads bowed down they made the *mocha* or reverence that he might the better understand them. The Orejones further say that the practice of assuming the fringe and of arming the knights began here, so I put it in this place that there may be no necessity for repeating it further on...

'Returning to those who were on the hill of Huanacauri, after Ayar Cachi had spoken of the order that was to be taken for the arming of knights the Indians relate that, turning to his brother Ayar Manco, he told him to go on with the two women to the valley he had pointed out and to found there the city of Cuzco without forgetting to come and perform sacrifices in that place as he had commanded. And as soon as he had done speaking both he and the other brother were turned into two figures of stone in the shape of men. This was seen by Ayar Manco, who taking the women with him went to the place where now stands Cuzco and founded a city, naming himself from that time forward Manco Capac, which means the rich King and Lord.

'When Manco Capac had seen what had happened to his brothers and had come to the valley where now is the city of Cuzco, the Orejones say that he raised his eyes to heaven and with great humility besought the Sun that he would favour and aid him in forming the new settlement. Then turning his eyes towards the hill of Huanacauri he addressed the same petition to his brother, whom he now held and reverenced as a god. Next he watched the flight of birds, the signs in the stars, and other omens, which filled him with confidence so that he felt certain that the new settlement would flourish and that he would be its founder and the father of all the Incas who would reign there. In the name of Ticci Viracocha and of the Sun and of the other gods he laid the foundation of the new city. The original and beginning of it was a small stone house with a roof of straw that Manco Capac and his women built, to which they gave the name of Curicancha, meaning the place of gold. This is the place where afterwards stood that celebrated and most rich temple of the Sun, and now a monastery of the monks of the order of St Domingo. It is held for certain that at the time when Manco Capac built this house there were Indians in large numbers in the district; but as he did them no harm and did not in any way molest them, they did not object to his remaining in their land but rather rejoiced at this coming. So Manco Capac built the said house and it was devoted to the worship of his gods and he became a great man and one who represented high authority.

'One of his wives was barren and never had children. By the other he had three sons and one daughter. The eldest was named Sinchi Roca Inca and the daughter Ocllo. The names of the others are not recorded nor is more said than that the eldest was married to his sister and that he taught them how to make themselves beloved by the people and not hated, with other important matters.' Pedro de Cieza de León: *Crónica del Perú*, Part II, Chs. 6-8.

The Children of the Sun

Garcilaso Inca de la Vega, the author of the following account, claims to have been taught the official Inca legends as a boy by his uncles, who belonged to the Inca aristocracy.

'Know then, cousin, that in centuries past all this part of the earth consisted of great mountains and brushwood and the people in those times lived like wild animals without religion or polity, without houses or cities. They did not sow or cultivate the earth or clothe their bodies, for they did not know how to work cotton or wool for garments. They lived in twos and threes as they chanced to come together in caves and hollows and crevices of the rocks. Like beasts they ate wild plants and roots, the fruits which were produced by the bushes without cultivation, and human flesh. They covered their bodies with leaves and bark and skins of animals; others went naked. In a word they lived like wild animals and like the brutes they even had their women in common...

'Our Father the Sun, seeing men as I have described them, was moved to pity and sent from the sky to earth one of his sons and daughters to instruct them in the knowledge of Our Father the Sun, that they might adore him and have him as their God, and to give them laws and prescriptions whereby they might live as men in reason and comity, that they might dwell in houses and cities, learn how to till the earth, cultivate and harvest food-plants, domesticate animals and enjoy the fruits of the earth like rational beings and no longer like animals. With this injunction and mandate Our Father the Sun sent down his two children to Lake Titicaca, which is eighty leagues from Cuzco, and told them to pass where they would and wherever they stayed to eat or to sleep they should sink in the soil a rod of gold which he gave them. This rod, half a yard long and two fingers thick, was to serve as a sign, for where it sank in the earth with a

The shores of Lake Titicaca, at 12,500 feet above sea level the highest navigable lake in the world, stretching between Peru and Bolivia. The lake is 138 miles long and 70 miles across at its widest, and its waters, of exceptional diaphaneity, reflect the intense blue of the sky with extraordinary depth and purity. Its serene beauty in the midst of the parched dreariness of the Altiplano has won it an almost mystical significance in the eyes of the Indians, and a mass of myth and legend centres on it. In the foreground of the picture is the curious rock structure popularly known as the *Horca de los Inca*, the 'Inca Gallows'.

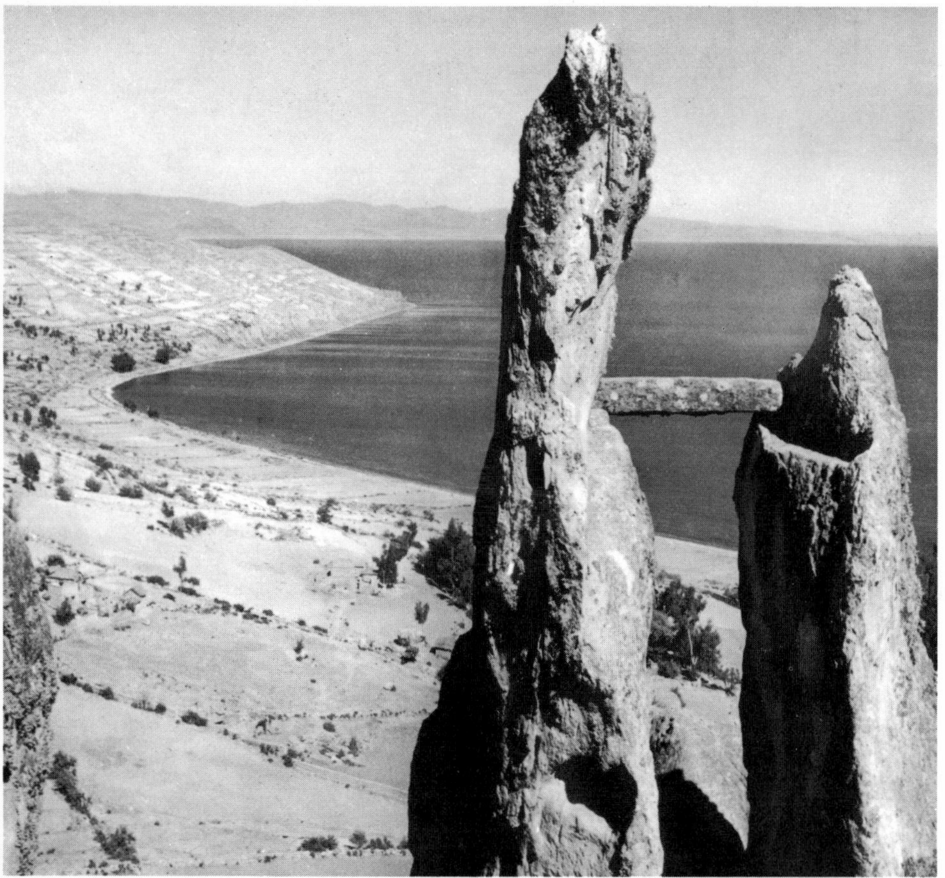

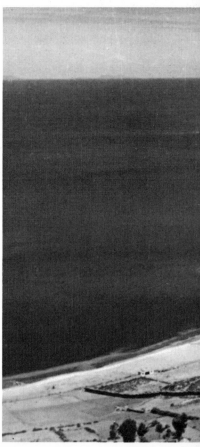

single blow there they were to stop and found the sacred city of the Sun. He concluded his instructions as follows:

' "When you have reduced these peoples to our service, you shall maintain them in reason and justice with devotion, clemency and tenderness, playing in all things the part of a loving father to his beloved children, modelling yourselves on me. For I look to the well-being of the whole world, since I give men my light by which they see and warm themselves when they are cold and make their pastures and fields to grow, their trees to bear and their flocks to multiply. I bring rain and fair weather in their season and each day I traverse the whole surface of the earth in order that I may see the needs of the world to succour and provide for them as the supporter and protector of men. It is my will that you my children follow this my example, sent to the earth solely to teach and aid these men who live like beasts. And to that end I name and establish you lords and kings of all races whom you thus benefit with your instructions and good government."

'Having thus declared his will, Our Father the Sun took leave of his children. They set out from Titicaca and journeyed to the north and throughout the whole journey wherever they stopped they tried to sink the rod of gold. But nowhere would it bury itself in the soil. So they came to a small roadside inn seven or eight leagues south of Cuzco, which today goes by the name Paccari-tambo or Inn of the Dawn. The Inca gave it that name because he left this inn at dawn, and the villagers today are very proud of the name. From there he and his wife, our Queen, came to the valley of Cuzco, which at this time was wild and unpopulated highland.

'The first stop they made in this valley was on the height called Huanacauri, south of the city. There the bar of gold sank entirely into the earth at a single blow and was not seen again. Thereupon our Inca said to his sister and wife:

View over Lake Titicaca from the modern hamlet of Copacabana, one of the most popular centres of pilgrimage in South America. Today the Indians come to worship before the Virgin of Copacabana, whose image is, according to tradition, the work of an Indian craftsman. But the lake has older religious associations. In the most ancient mythology of the Collao, the lake was the birthplace of the Sun, and from it the creator-god brought forth the races of men in the days of primeval darkness. Later Titicaca was associated with the origin of the legendary founders of the Inca dynasty, and Copacabana became one of the centres of Inca religion. And to this day there is a tenacious belief that in order to avoid the rapacity of the Spanish Conquistadores the Inca threw into the lake fabulous stores of gold from the temple on the Island of the Sun and from the palace of the Nustas (Virgins of the Sun) on the island of Coati.

Right: Reed boats on Lake Titicaca. These boats have been used for lake transport by the Indians of the highlands from time immemorial. Constructed from bundles of the totora reeds which grow beside the lake, they are often fitted with masts to carry a sail. The reeds were also used for making hawsers, bridges and so forth.

Below: Hammered gold plaque from the Mochica culture. While Mochica pottery was naturalistic, the drawing and design followed the formalistic and symbolic tradition initiated by the Chavín culture. This design appears to represent two ritualistic figures with bird or animal masks, surmounted by animal headdresses, and carrying a dance staff topped by a human head whose square features are reminiscent of the carved stone head of Chavín. The figure on the right has a girdle terminating in a snake's head.

' "It is in this valley that Our Father the Sun commanded us to make our abode in accordance with his will. Therefore, Queen and sister, it behoves each of us to go his way and draw the people to him in order to instruct them and care for them as Our Father the Sun enjoined." From the height of Huanacauri went forth our first monarchs, each in his own way, to gather together the peoples. And for this reason, since it was from there they sallied abroad to care for the well-being of mankind, we have erected there, as is common knowledge, a temple to the Sun in memory and honour of his beneficence to the world of men. The prince went towards the north and the princess to the south. To all the men and women they came upon in those barren regions they told how their Father the Sun had sent them from the sky to be lords and benefactors to the inhabitants of that land, removing them from the life of brutes which they had led and teaching them to live like men in towns and villages, eating the victuals of men. In this fashion our Kings spoke to the first savages they found in the mountain plateaus, and the latter, seeing these two persons clothed and adorned with the ornaments which Our Father the Sun had bestowed upon them, with their ears pierced and the lobes drawn low as is the fashion with us their descendants, and seeing that in their words and demeanour they showed themselves to be children of the Sun, marvelling at what they saw and won over by the promises made to them, they believed them in all things, according them reverence and worship as children of the Sun and obedience as Kings. Thus the word passed from one to another until large multitudes assembled ready to follow where our Kings might lead.

'Seeing the large numbers who flocked to their banner, our chiefs ordered some to gather food of the fields lest hunger should disperse them again and instructed others to make cottages and houses according to the model they supplied. In this fashion began to be built our imperial city, divided into two halves which they called Hanan Cuzco (which means upper Cuzco) and Hurin Cuzco (which is lower Cuzco)...

'Meanwhile, as the city grew up, our Inca taught the male Indians the duties pertaining to the male, how to break and cultivate the soil, to sow the crops and grain and vegetables which he showed them were good for food. For this he taught them how to make ploughs and other necessary tools, instructed them in the manner of digging irrigation channels from the streams which water this valley of Cuzco, and even taught them to make the type of footgear we wear. The Queen on her part instructed the females in womanly offices, sewing and weaving cotton and wool, making garments for themselves and for their husbands and children. In a word there is nothing belonging to civilised life which our first chiefs omitted to teach their vassals, the Inca making himself instructor of the men and the Queen Coya instructress of the women...

'How many years ago the Sun Our Father sent these his first children I cannot tell you exactly. It was so long ago that it was not possible to retain the memory: we believe it was more than four hundred years. Our Inca was called Manco Capac and our Mama Coya was called Ocllo Huaco. As I have told you, they were brother and sister, children of the Sun and the Moon, our ancestors.' Garcilaso Inca de la Vega: *Comentarios Reales de los Incas.* Book I, Ch. 15.

The Shining Mantle

'Because of its distance in time the beginning of the Inca cannot be surely known except that they would tell in fable that from a cave or window in a certain building near Cuzco which they call Tambotocco or Paccari-tambo there came forth eight Inca brethren (others say only six, but the more general and plausible view is eight). The four males were thus called: the eldest Huana Cauri, the second Cusco Huanca, the third Manco Capac and the fourth Topa Ayar Cachi. The sisters were thus called: the eldest Topa Huaco, the second Mama Coya, the third Cori Ocllo, the fourth Ipa Huaco. These eight came forth to adventure together in search of lands which they could populate and before arriving at Cuzco they stopped at a place called Apitay, which some call Huana Cauri. The third sister, Cori Ocllo, being considered the most intelligent by the rest, went ahead in search of territory suitable for their purpose. And coming to the hutments of this city of Cuzco, which at that time was occupied by low and poor tribes of Indians called Lares, Poques and Huallas, before she arrived there she came upon a Poque Indian and slew him with a weapon called *macana*. She then cut him open and took out the lungs and blew them up and with these all bloody in her mouth she entered the town. Terrified at the sight, thinking that she fed on human flesh, the Indians abandoned their houses and fled. Judging the place to be good for settlement and that the natives were tame, she returned to where she had left her brethren and brought them there, except the eldest brother who wished to remain in Apitay, where he died. And they named the hill Huanacauri in his memory. The others occupied Cuzco without resistance and named the second brother, Cusco Huanca, chief of the city, for which reason the settlement was called Cuzco, being named before that Acamama. He died in Coricancha and was succeeded by the third brother, called the great Manco Capac.

'This valiant Inca Manco Capac held sway over all that city of Cuzco, although he conquered no new territories. Yet some tell of these ancient Indians that there came from the great Lake Titicaca, which is in the prov-

A brightly decorated poncho from the region of Lake Titicaca. Inca period.

ince of Collao, to the said cave of Paccari-tambo certain brothers and sisters, called Cusco Huanca and Huana Cauri, noble and valiant persons and very warlike, who had their ears pierced and pieces of gold in the holes. The great Manco Capac was one of them and they say that he had beaten out two thin plaques of silver, placing one on his chest and the other on his back, and on his head he wore the diadem which they call *canipo*. He sent a certain Indian to the city with the message that he was the son of the Sun and he went to the top of a high peak where he showed himself walking to and fro with the silver plaques gleaming and flashing in the sun. When they saw this the Indians accepted him for the son of the Sun and a divine being and gave him much riches and all that he wished for. Thus he became rich and powerful and sallied forth to conquer peoples in the neighbourhood of that city... Afterwards they say this great Manco Capac was changed into a stone which they greatly venerate.' Fray Martín de Morúa: *Historia del origen y genealogía real de los reyes Incas del Perú*. Chs. 2 and 3.

Alternative accounts

The following stories of Inca origins were recorded by Garcilaso. They appear to reveal conflation of Inca legend with other local mythologies, or the adaptation of local mythologies by the Incas for purposes of their own glorification. It was the general practice of the Incas to reinforce their military dominance of a subject people by using religion and legend to justify their pre-eminence. Few dared, therefore, to question the right of the Incas to rule over them.

'Another fable about the origin of the Incas is told by the common people who live in the district south of Cuzco, called Collasuyu, and to the west in the district called Cuntisuyu. They say that after the flood –

Stone lintel found at Chavín de Huántar carved with a crude and semi-naturalistic representation of a feline figure – the puma, jaguar or mountain cat which is the most frequent motif in Chavín art and which archaeologists regard as evidence of a feline cult, though snakes, condors and other animals are also used in designs. The feline's broad flat nose, staring eyes, claw feet and square mouth of grinning teeth with overlapping fangs are all typical of what was later stylised into a convention which was taken up by the Paracas and Nazca and perpetuated into and through Inca times.

and about this they can tell no more than that it took place and don't know whether it was the general flood of the time of Noah or some other local flood (and for this reason we shall omit what they tell about it and about other similar things which seem from the way they tell them more like dreams or disordered fables than historical events) – they say, then, that after the waters abated there appeared a man in Tiahuanacu, which lies to the south of Cuzco, and that his might was so great he divided the world into four parts and gave them to four men whom he called kings. The first of these was called Manco Capac, the second Colla, the third Tocay and the fourth Pinahua. They say he gave the northern region to Manco Capac, the southern to Colla (from whose name that great province was afterwards named Collao), to the third, named Tocay, he gave the east and to the fourth, Pinahua, he gave the west. He ordered each of them to go into his district and to conquer and govern the people he found there. And they don't bother to say whether these Indians had been drowned in the flood or had been resuscitated in order to be conquered and instructed – most accounts of those ancient times are similarly vague. It is said that from this partitioning of the world arose the later division which the Incas made of their empire, called Tahuantinsuyu. They say that Manco Capac went forth to the north and came to the valley of Cuzco and founded that city and reduced and indoctrinated the surrounding peoples. After this beginning they give practically the same account of Manco Capac as we have given above...

'Still another account of the origin of the Inca is current among the Indians who dwell to the east and the north of Cuzco. They say that at the beginning of the world four men and four women, brothers and sisters, came forth from windows in some crags near the city in a place called Paccari-tambo. There were three openings and they came through the middle one, which is called the "royal window". Because of this fable they lined that window with large plaques of gold and precious stones. The side windows were edged with gold but not with jewels. They called the first brother Manco Capac and his wife Mama Ocllo. They say that he founded the city and called it Cuzco, which in the common language of the natives means "navel", that he subdued the surrounding tribes and taught them the arts of civilisation and that all the Inca are descended from him. The second brother is called Ayar Cachi, the third Ayar Ucho and the fourth Ayar Sauca. The word 'Ayar' has no meaning in the general language of Peru [i.e. Quechua]; in the esoteric language of the Inca it must have had a meaning. The other words belong to the general language. *Cachi* means salt; *ucho* is the seasoning they use in their food, what the Spanish called *pimiento*; *sauca* means joy, happiness or gladness. When the Indians are pressed to say why they made those three brothers and sisters their first monarchs they talk nonsense and finding no better solution allegorise the fable, saying that by salt they mean the instruction which the Inca gave them in the natural life, by *pimiento* they understand the taste they acquired for it and by joy they symbolise the happiness and contentment in which they lived thereafter.' *Comentarios Reales de los Incas*. Book I, Ch. 18.

The island of Titicaca

This account by Garcilaso illustrates how the Inca incorporated elements of Tiahuanaco myth in their own legends.

'Among other famous temples to the Sun which existed in Peru and which in the richness of the ornament of gold and silver could rival the temple of Cuzco, there was one in the island called Titicaca. It is in the lake of the same name rather more than two crossbow shots distant from the mainland, and five to six thousand paces in circumference. It is in

Left: Detail from Paracas Necropolis woven textile. The very complicated feline and snake motif seems to indicate a developed and mature iconographical tradition, and thus a long established cult with associated mythology and beliefs. Unfortunately neither oral nor written records throw light on the mythological background of this early culture.

Stone head found at Chavín de Huántar. It is over life-size, about two feet high. The broad nose and prominent nostrils, the square mouth and the large, eccentric eyes are all typical of this culture, as is the strange curvilinear decoration of the eyebrows, hair and cheeks. Although plainly symbolic, Chavín art is never anecdotal or pictorial and for this reason it tells nothing about mythological beliefs or religious ritual.

this island that the Inca say the Sun set down his two children, male and female, when he sent them to earth to instruct in the arts of civilised life the barbarous peoples who up to then inhabited that land. With this fable they join another from centuries earlier. They say that after the flood the rays of the sun appeared in that island and that great lake before they were seen in any other part... Seeing that the Indians believed this ancient fable and regarded the island and the lake as a sacred place, the first Inca, Manco Capac, in his natural ingenuity and sagacity took advantage of it and composed the second fable, saying that he and his wife were children of the Sun and that their father had set them down in that island so that they could go out from there all over the earth teaching the people, as has already been recorded. The Inca *amautas* – who were the philosophers and wise men of that kingdom – reduced the first fable to the second, treating it as a prophecy or prognostication. They said that the fact that the Sun cast his first rays on that island to illuminate the world had been a sign and promise that there he would send down his first two children to teach and enlighten those peoples, freeing them from the bestialities in which they lived – as in fact the Inca monarchs did. With these and other similar inventions the Inca caused the Indians to believe that they were the children of the Sun and they confirmed the belief with the many benefits they conferred.

'Because of these two fables the Inca and all the people of their empire held that island for a holy place and so they ordered a splendidly rich temple to be built there and dedicated to the Sun. It was all lined with plaques of gold and all the provinces subject to the Inca offered there every year much gold and silver and precious stones in thanksgiving to the Sun for the two benefices which he had vouchsafed in that place. That temple had the same service as the temple at Cuzco. So much gold and silver from the offerings was heaped up on the island, in addition to what was fashioned for the temple service, that what the Indians say about it causes more astonishment than belief. Father Blas Valera, speaking of the wealth of that temple and the great surplus which was heaped up outside it, says that the transplanted Indians (called *mitmac*) living at Copacabana assured him that the surplus of silver and gold was such that another complete temple could have been made from it without the use of any other material. And they say that when the Indians learned of the entry of the Spaniards and that they came seizing any wealth they found, they threw it all into that great lake...

'The Inca Kings did much to raise the prestige of this island apart from the temple with its rich adorment, since – as they claimed – it was the first soil that their forbears had trod when they came down from heaven. They smoothed its whole surface as far as possible, removing rocks and boulders; they constructed terraces which they clothed with rich and fertile soil brought from afar so as to raise maize, since all that region on account of the cold is unable to support it. On these terraces they sowed it along with other grain and with constant attention raised a few paltry ears, which were dedicated to the King as a sacred thing, and he bestowed them on the temple of the Sun. Some was given to the Sacred Virgins of the Sun and sent to all the convents in turn so that all could enjoy the grain brought down from the heavens. The grain was sown in the gardens of the temples and the convents of the Chosen Virgins throughout the provinces and the grain which grew from it was shared among all the people of the province. They used to put a few grains in the granaries of the Sun and in those of the King and in the public depositories so that as a holy thing it might protect, increase and keep free from rot the grain stored for public consumption. And any Indian who could obtain one grain of that maize for his allotments believed that he would not be short of bread his whole life through – so superstitious were they in anything touching their Inca.'
Comentarios Reales de los Incas. Book III, Ch. 25.

Left: Roughly carved, primitive figure of a man from Chavín. The straight flat nose later became conventional. Although this highly individual art style is conventionalised and sophisticated, the effect is massive and strong – often expressive and urgent.

The most common form of Mochica ceramic was the 'stirrup' vase, in which a semicircular handle rises from the body of the vase and is surrounded by a single spout; they are first found in the Chavín horizon. Early Mochica stirrup vase in the form of a feline, perhaps a puma. The flat nose, prominent eyes and overlapping fangs are treated more naturalistically than in the Chavín style. The significance of the 'benedictory' gesture of the hands can only be conjectured, but the expression of the figure may well be benevolent rather than horrific. It may represent a priest or celebrant wearing a feline mask.

Carved stone figure from Chavín de Huántar. The broad flat nose and enlarged eyes have some resemblance to the early sculptured figures found at Tiahuanaco, although the face lacks the high cheek bones of the Tiahuanaco figures. The engraved decoration is less stylised than most of the Chavín carving which has come down to us.

What the Indians report of their beginnings

'It is no matter of any great importance to know what the Indians themselves report of their beginning, being more like unto dreams than to true histories. They make great mention of a deluge which happened in their country ... The Indians say that all men were drowned in this deluge, and they report that out of the great Lake Titicaca came one Viracocha, who stayed in Tiahuanaco, where at this day there is to be seen the ruins of ancient and very strange buildings, and from thence came to Cuzco, and so began mankind to multiply. They show in the same lake a small island, where they feign that the sun hid himself and so was preserved; and for this reason they make great sacrifices unto him in that place, both of sheep [i.e. llamas] and men.

'Others report that six, or I know not what number of men, came out of a certain cave by a window, by whom men first began to multiply; and for this reason they call them Paccari-tambo. And therefore they are of opinion that the Tambos are the most ancient race of men. They say also that Manco Capac, whom they acknowledge for the founder and chief of their Incas, was issued of that race and that from him sprang two families or lineages, the one of Hanan Cuzco and the other of Urin Cuzco. They say moreover that when the King Incas attempted war and conquered sundry provinces they gave a colour and made a pretext of their enterprise, saying that all the world ought to acknowledge them for that all the world was renewed by their race and country; and also that the true religion had been revealed to them from heaven. But what availeth it to speak more, seeing that all is full of lies and vanity, far from reason?'
Father José de Acosta: *The Natural and Moral History of the Indies.* Book I, Ch. 25 English translation by Edward Grimston, 1604.

The origin of nations and cults

'And as to the origin of their idolatries it is thus that these peoples had no usage of writing but in a house of the Sun called Poquen Cancha, which is hard by Cuzco, they possessed paintings done on boards of the life of each one of the Incas and the lands he had conquered and also their origin. And among these paintings the following fable was also depicted.

'In the life of Manco Capac, who was the first Inca and from whom they began to boast themselves children of the Sun and from whom they derived their idolatrous worship of the Sun, they had an ample account of the deluge. They say that in it perished all races of men and created things insomuch that the waters rose above the highest mountain peaks in the world. So it was that no living thing remained except one man and one woman. And what time the waters subsided the wind cast them up at Tiahuanaco, which will be more than seventy leagues from Cuzco, a little more or less. The creator of all things commanded them there to remain as *mitmacs* [colonists; persons transplanted and settled elsewhere than in the place of their birth.] And there in Tiahuanaco the Creator began to make the peoples and tribes who are in the land, fashioning of clay one of each nation and painting the garments which each was to wear and keep to. Those that were to go with long hair he painted with long hair and those that were to wear it short with short. This done, he gave to each nation the language it was to speak and the songs they were to sing and the seeds and foodstuffs they were to grow.

'When he had finished painting and creating the said nations and lumps of clay he gave being and soul to each one as well the men as the women and commanded each nation to sink below the earth. Thence each nation passed underground and came up in the places to which he assigned them.

Above: The Indians of the Collao sacrifice a black llama and coca to the spirit of Villcanota. This drawing by Guamán Poma de Ayala reflects what he knew of the religious practices of the region in Inca times. The true Tiahuanaco period pre-dates this however, and was probably suppressed by the Incas.

Below: A Chimu figurine in gold, possibly a votive offering. The headdress suggests a priest, who carries a maize plant and a spade. Maize was the staff of life of the high civilisations of Peru.

Thus they say that some came out of caves, others from hills, others out of fountains, others from lakes, others from tree boles and other rubbish of this kind. They say that because they issued forth from these places and began to multiply, and had the beginning of their lineage from them, they made *huacas* and places of worship of them in memory of the beginning of their lineage which proceeded out from them. Thus every nation of people uses the dress with which they clothe their *huaca*. And they say that the first to be born from that place returned there and was turned into stones, or others into falcons and condors and other animals and birds. Thus the *huacas* they use and worship are of different form.

'There are other peoples who say that when the deluge was ended mankind was destroyed by the waters except those – and they were very few – who had been able to escape on hills or in caves or trees and that from them they began to multiply. And in memory of those first progenitors who had escaped in these places they made idols of stone and to each *huaca* they gave the name of him from whom they claimed their race was

Double spouted vase in black Chimu ware. The upper half of the body is decorated with conventionalised animal and human figures analogous in style and iconography to the relief decorations on the walls of Chanchan. On the bridge is the head of a deity or crowned king with prostrate worshipping figures.

descended. ,Thus they worshipped and made sacrifice of such articles as each tribe used. Yet there were some tribes who retained a tradition even before they were subjected by the Inca of a Creator of all things, and although they made sacrifices to him it was not in such quantity or with such reverence as they sacrificed to their *huacas*.

'But to return to our myth. They say that the Creator was in Tiahuanaco and that was his principal abode. Hence there are there superb edifices deserving of wonder in which are painted many dresses of those Indians and many stone figures of men and women whom he turned into stone for not obeying his commands. They say that over all was the darkness of night and there he created the Sun and the Moon and stars and that he commanded the Sun, the Moon and the stars to go to the island of Titicaca which is near by and from there to ascend to the sky.

'And at the moment when the Sun was about to ascend in the form of a man all shining and resplendent, he called to the Incas and to Manco Capac and said: "Thou and thy descendants are to be lords and subdue

Mochica stirrup vase with a human-headed crab on a platform. The face shows great character despite the bulging eyes and prominent jaguar fangs. It wears a high headdress and snake or feline ear pendants. Some historians presume that this represents a 'crab-deity' but we have no evidence for deity or ritual apart from the representations.

A ceremonial knife, fashioned in gold and originally inlaid with turquoise, from the Lambayeque Valley where a seaborne hero called Naymlap is said to have founded a kingdom in the twelfth century. It was once believed that the figure portrayed was of Naymlap himself but this is now regarded as unlikely since this decorative theme also appears in the art of the other coastal cultures.

many nations. Regard me as thy father and yourselves as my children and reverence me as thy father." Having said these words he gave to Manco Capac as his insignia and arms the *suntur paucar* and the *champi* [royal Inca headdress and mace] and the other insignia which they used in the manner of a sceptre. At that point he commanded the Sun, the Moon and the stars to ascend to the sky and take their proper places there; and they did so. And at the same moment Manco Capac and his brothers and sisters, at the command of the Creator, sank beneath the earth and came out at the cave of Paccari-tambo, which they regard as their place of origin, although it is said that other races also came out of the said cave at the point where the Sun rose on the first day after the Creator had divided night from day. From this they obtained the name children of the Sun and worshipped and reverenced the Sun as their father.

'The Indians also have another myth in which they say that the Creator had two sons, one of whom they called Imaymana Viracocha and the other Tocapo Viracocha. When the Creator had fashioned the peoples and nations, giving to each their appropriate appearance and language, and had sent the Sun, Moon and stars to their places in the sky from Tiahuanaco, as has been said, the Creator, whom the Indians in their own language call Pachayachachic [Teacher of the World] or Ticci Viracocha, which means the Unknowable God, went along the highland road and visited the tribes to see how they had begun to multiply and to fulfil the commandments he had given them. Finding that some tribes had rebelled against his commands, he changed a large part of them into stones in the shape of men and women with the same costume that they had worn.

'The changing into stone occurred at the following places: in Tiahuanaco, in Pucara and Jauja, where they say he turned the *huaca* called Huarivilca into stone, and in Pachacamac, in Cajamarca and other regions. Indeed today there are huge figures of stone in these places, some of them almost the size of giants, which must have been fashioned by human hands in times of great antiquity and as the memory failed and in the absence of writing they invented this legend saying that the people were turned into stones by command of the Creator on account of disobeying his commands.

'They also say that at Pucara, which is forty leagues from Cuzco on the Collao road, fire came down from heaven and burnt a great part of them while those who tried to escape were turned into stone. The Creator, who they say was the father of Imaymana Viracocha and Tocapo Viracocha, commanded Imaymana Viracocha, the elder of his two sons, in whose power all things are placed, to set out from that place and traverse all the world by the road of the mountains and forested valleys. As he went he was to give names to all the trees large and small, to the flowers and fruit they were to bear, and to indicate to the people which were edible and which not and which had medicinal properties. He also gave names to the herbs and flowers, and the time when they were to produce flowers and fruits and taught people which could cure and which would kill. His other son named Tocapo Viracocha, which in their language means "the Maker", he ordered to go by the road of the plains, visiting the peoples and giving names to the rivers and trees and instructing them as to the fruits and flowers. And thus they went to the lowest parts of this land until they came to the sea, where they ascended into the sky after having finished making all that there is in the land.

'In the same myth they also say that at Tiahuanaco, where he created the tribes of men, he created all the different kinds of birds, male and female of each, giving them the songs which each kind was to sing. Those that were to inhabit the forests he sent to the forests and those which were to inhabit the highlands to the highlands, each to the region proper to its kind. He also created all the different species of animals, male and female of each, and all the snakes and creeping things there are in the land and commanded each to its proper habitat. And he taught the people the names and properties of the birds and snakes and other reptiles.

'These Indians also believed that neither the Creator nor his sons were born of woman and that they were unchanging and eternal. The various tribes of this country have many other nonsensical beliefs and fables about their origin insomuch that if we were to record them all, it would be very prolix and there would be no end to it. I will merely mention a few to illustrate the folly and blindness in which they lived.' Cristóbal de Molina of Cuzco: *The Fables and Rites of the Yncas.*

A stirrup vase from the middle period of the Mochica culture, apparently expressing in a different vein the symbols which recur again and again and which suggest a priest and a feline cult. It is quite possible that the creatures painted on the ascending spiral are decoration merely; but these together with the elaborately dressed figure at the top suggest something more.

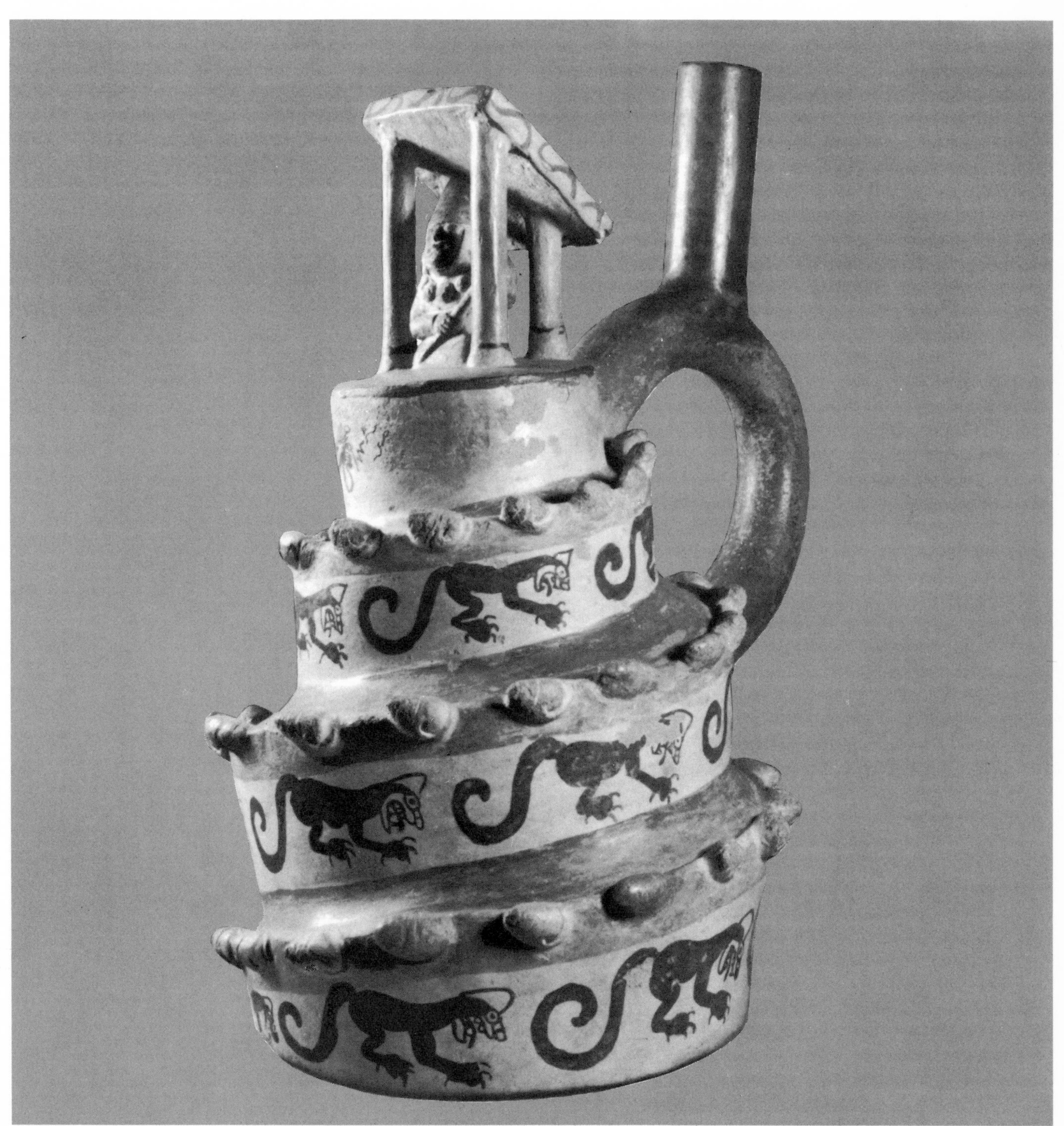

Mythology of the Collao

Tiahuanaco

The village of Tiahuanaco, now a few miles from the shores of Lake Titicaca on the Bolivian Altipiano, or Collao, is the site of some of the most astonishing and enigmatic megalithic remains of South America. They were the centre of an important highland civilisation and religion, thought to have been later than the coastal culture of Chavín but earlier than the flourishing coastal kingdom of Chimu which preceded the Inca. The culture and the art styles of Tiahuanaco spread, perhaps by conquest, to the coastal regions of Peru and may have swamped the early coastal cultures of Mochica and Nazca. The collapse of Tiahuanaco was followed by a period of political anarchy and regional warring groups on the Altiplano until the area was conquered and unified by the Inca monarchs. The cause of the collapse is obscure. Almost everything to do with the Tiahuanaco civilisation has been a matter of conflicting theories among modern archaeologists and nothing can be regarded as certain.

By the time the first Spaniards visited the Bolivian Altiplano all detailed memory of the Tiahuanaco culture had passed from men's minds. The absence of recorded traditions is not due to incuriosity on the part of Spanish chroniclers, as it was in the case of the coastal kingdom of Chimu and Pachacamac near Lima. For the Spaniards were impressed by what they saw at Tiahuanaco – the most sensational archaeological remains of the continent – and at other localities in the neighbourhood of Lake Titicaca.

It is one of the mysteries of South American mythology and legend that, although they questioned the local Indians closely, no traditions from the period of Tiahuanaco ascendancy were available to them. The local Indians – who according to Cieza de León and other chroniclers were by no means unintelligent – themselves regarded the unfinished ruins as a thing miraculous and foreign to them. They knew with complete assurance that they dated from a time far more ancient than the Inca monarchy. But they did not know what people had been responsible for them – except only that it was not their own ancestors. They possessed a cycle of cosmological myth incorporating stories of a deluge, creation and a divine culture hero. They also retained legends of their past history which embodied memories of a hunting and food-gathering stage before the introduction of agriculture and handicrafts. But they had no traditions from the Tiahuanaco culture.

The evidence of archaeology points certainly to the existence of a highly centralised social organisation, whether religious or political, which must have preceded the Inca regime and must have lasted many centuries on the Bolivian Altiplano with its centres at Tiahuanaco and other sites in the vicinity of Lake Titicaca. This must be assumed in order to account for the high level of megalithic technology, the stone carvings, the elaborately developed iconography, the exquisite handicrafts and the perfection

Left: A figure of a water-carrier in gold from the Inca period.

The rim of a shallow plate of the Mochica culture from Chimbote. Soldiers are seen tormenting their prisoners, who are forced to run naked with halters round their necks, their noses mutilated. The desert location is plainly indicated, and the formalised design gives the whole the look of some sadistic rite.

of a distinctive artistic style which spread from the highlands over much of the coastal area of Peru. The oblivion in which this great civilisation was submerged is the more astonishing in a people generally notable for the length and retentiveness of their racial memories.

Two theories have been advanced to account for the loss of this tradition. One supposes that the people who built up the Tiahuanaco civilisation were overthrown by warlike immigrants, who wiped them out and liquidated their culture and traditions. The other theory suggests that, in accordance with the policy of moving populations, when the Inca sovereigns conquered the Collao, they transplanted the local peoples and settled on the Altiplano other races who had no traditions about the Tiahuanaco past. Both these theories are necessarily speculative.

Three facts tell slightly in favour of the former. First, the building at Tiahuanaco was left unfinished and seems to have stopped abruptly. There are still partly worked stones at the site and one may still see roughly fashioned stones of great size left lying at the quarries from which they came. The second is the legend that during a time of disturbance and anarchy (apparently between the fall of Tiahuanaco and the dominance of the Inca), two chieftains, Cari and Zapana, rose up and made war on each other; and that as a result of this the then Inca king was able to obtain easy control. This story would seem to indicate the existence of some

Monolithic gateway at Tiahuanaco, known locally as the Gateway of the Sun. The elaborately carved frieze with large central figure and rows of subsidiary figures in highly conventionalised relief is typical of the Tiahuanacan art style and iconography. The megalithic ruins and the surviving statuary are the most imposing archaeological remains of South America. With the expansion of the highland power, whether by conquest or by trade, the style and iconographic motifs spread northwards into Peru and influenced much of the coastal area, where it is known as 'coastal Tiahuanaco'.

historical memories from before the Inca conquest, though without any traditions from the time of Tiahuanaco greatness. The third fact, for what it is worth, is a curious legend of an early race of 'white and bearded' people in the region of Titicaca, who were entirely destroyed as a result of a war with a later arriving people and disappeared without leaving any trace of their existence. The recurrent story of a 'white and bearded' race (the peoples of South America are of various shades of bronze and lacking in facial hair) is no doubt best regarded as an indication that the mythopoeic fancy was still active at the time of the Spanish Conquest; existing legends of an earlier race who were conquered and liquidated in the distant past by the present inhabitants might well have been conflated (so far as the appearance is concerned) with stories which were circulated of the new and terrifying white arrivals.

The accounts of the Spanish chroniclers

'Although the temple of Tiahuanaco was a universal shrine and *huaca*, ... the Indians esteemed it chiefly on account of its size and antiquity, for indeed the buildings are the most magnificent and spectacular of any in this kingdom ... The ruins are about two hundred paces to the south of the village. Its name before it came under the sway of the Incas was

Below left: Detail of the Gateway of the Sun, showing the central figure and the subordinate running figures, all carrying sceptres or staffs of office, topped by what are perhaps formalised condor heads. The meaning of the figures and the symbols has been lost, for the memory of the Tiahuanacan people and their empire was systematically overlaid with the official Inca legend and the remains were already a matter of mystery and astonishment to the local Indians when the site was first visited by Spanish Conquistadores. We know, at least, that the site was connected with the origin myths of the highland Indians; and the powerful central figure may represent their supreme creator-deity before the Inca cult of the Sun was introduced to the Callao.

Below: Seated figure from Pokótia at the foot of the mountain ridge of Quimzachata south of Tiahuanaco. It is now in the open-air Tiahuanaco museum of La Paz. It belongs to the earlier of the two periods of sculpture found at Tiahuanaco, which produced impressive over life-size heads and kneeling figures. The faces are not Aymara in type, but memory of the people who made them is lost. Spanish chroniclers say the native populace connected them with local creation mythology, with belief in an earlier race of giants and a race of men turned into stone by the creator.

Paypicala, a word from the Aymará which is the language of the natives of that district and which means "the stone in the middle". For the Indians of the Collao believe that that village was at the middle of the world and that from it set forth the men who were to repopulate the world after the deluge. It got the name Tiahuanaco for the following reason. The locals say that, when an Inca king happened to be there, there arrived from Cuzco a runner; and when the Inca learned the extraordinary speed with which he had run the distance he said to him: "Tiay huanacu", which in the Inca tongue means: "Sit down and rest, guanaco". [A guanaco is an animal of the alpaca family.] He called him this because the guanaco is the speediest animal of the country, and this sentence became the name of the village ...

'I find two things worthy of especial note in connection with these edifices: the first is the astonishing size of the stones and the whole work and the second their great antiquity ... The principal cause for the great veneration in which the Indians hold this shrine must have been its great antiquity. The natives have considered it sacred from time immemorial before they were conquered by the kings of Cuzco, as also did those kings after they became lords of this province. The latter made Pumapuncu a famous temple, ennobling it and enriching it, increasing its adornment and the number of priests and sacrifices. And near to it they built the Royal Palaces in which they say Manco Capac was born, the son of Huayna Capac, and their ruins can be seen today. It was a very large edifice with many rooms and compartments.

'The rumour that great abundance of riches was buried in these buildings has induced some Spaniards to excavate them in search of it and they have found at various times many pieces of gold and silver, though not as much as was thought to be there. And in truth this greed to possess the treasures which common belief supposes to be hidden there has been a chief cause for the destruction and spoiling of this structure. They have also despoiled it in order to make use of the stones. For the church of Tiahuanaco was built from them and the inhabitants of the town of Chuquiago [La Paz] carried off many to build their houses, and even the Indians in the village of Tiahuanaco make their tombs from beautiful stone tiles which they obtain from the ruins ...

'I cannot pass over in silence a very remarkable thing which happened in these buildings. It was as follows. The first encomendero [Spanish overseer] of the village of Tiahuanaco was an inhabitant of Chuquiago called Captain Juan de Vargas [an uncle of the chronicler Garcilaso]. Having been sent to Spain during the civil wars here and being very upset at the Court because his private affairs were not going ahead with as good dispatch as he would have wished, an unknown man came up to him one day in the patio of the Palace and asked him why he was sad, since he was Lord of the richest town in the world, namely Tiahuanaco. He then gave him a map of these buildings which indicated the position of the riches he said were there. When the Captain returned from Spain after concluding his business he had excavations made according to the indications given him by that man or demon in human shape (as he was thought to have been) and his discoveries there seemed to show that the map was entirely accurate. At first he took out many large jars full of finely woven cloth (cumbí), jars and pitchers of silver and a quantity of chaquira [finely wrought beads of gold] and vermilion. He unearthed a human skeleton of gigantic size and, continuing with his discoveries in great contentment, one day he found a large human head of gold whose features were very like those of the stone statues at Tiahuanaco. Greedy to obtain still more wealth, he could not contain his pleasure. But it lasted but a little, for the following night death cut short his career although he had ailed nothing when he went to bed. This eventually caused much alarm and abated the greed of those who would have continued the excavations in search of the treasure which was thought to be buried in those edifices.' Padre Bernabé Cobo: *Historia del Nuevo Mundo.*

'It is my belief that these ruins are the most ancient of all Peru and the general opinion is that some of these edifices were made a long time before the reign of the Inca. Indeed I have heard it stated by the Indians that the Inca constructed the great buildings of Cuzco on the model of the wall which can be seen here. More, they say that the first Incas were in two minds whether to make the seat of their empire at Tiahuanaco ... I asked the natives in the presence of Juan Vargas (who has the *encomienda* over them) whether these edifices were built in the time of the Inca and they laughed at the question, affirming that they were made long before the Inca reign but they could not say who had made them, only that they had heard from their forbears that everything to be seen there appeared suddenly in the course of a single night. From this, and from the fact that they also say bearded men had been seen in the island of Titicaca and that similar people had made the edifice at Vinaque, I would say that perhaps it may have been that before the Inca rule a civilised and intelligent people may have immigrated to this region, though where they came from is not known, but being few, and the native population so numerous, they may have been wiped out in the wars. Pedro de Cieza de León: *Crónica del Perú,* Part I, Ch. 105.

'The largest river near the town of Guamanga [now Ayacucho] is called Vinaque, near which are some large and very old buildings and to judge by the ruinous state they are now in they must have endured from great antiquity. When the Indians of the district are asked who made that ancient monument they reply that they were made by other peoples, bearded and white like ourselves, who came to that region and settled there many ages before the reign of the Incas. These and some other ancient buildings in this area seem to me to be of a different style of architecture from the buildings which were put up by order of the Inca; for these are square while the Inca buildings are long and narrow. There is also a rumour that an inscription was found on a tile from these buildings. I neither affirm this nor do I abandon my belief that in the distant past there immigrated into this region a people with sufficient intelligence and judgement to have made these things and others which are no longer to be seen.' Cieza de León. Part I, Ch. 87.

Origin myths of the Collao

'Many of these Indians [i.e. of the Collao] tell that they have heard from their ancestors that in times past there was a great deluge ... and give it to be understood that their ancestors are of great antiquity, and they relate so many stories and fables about their origin that I shan't stop to write them down. For some say that their ancestors came forth from a fountain, some from a rock, some from a lake, so that it is impossible to get anything else from them about their origins. But they all agree that their forbears lived in a state of anarchy before the Inca held sway over them. Their stongholds were high in the mountains and from there they made war and their manners were corrupt. Later they learned from the Incas everything that their other subjects were taught and they began to build their villages in the same manner as now ...

'Before the Incas reigned over them many of these Indians of the Collao say that there were two great lords in their province, one called Zapana and the other Cari, and that these conquered many *pucaras,* which are their fortresses. And one of them entered the larger of the two islands

Left: Monolithic figure now set up on the Kalasasaya, or Temple of the Sun, at Tiahuanaco. It is known locally as El Fraile, 'the Friar'. Posnansky nevertheless believed that it represented a female figure, perhaps dedicated to lacustrine worship since the decorations engraved upon it appear to be connected with the fauna of the lake. The waist band, for example, is carved with stylised crustaceans which may be the *hyalela* found in Lake Titicaca. The right hand holds a sceptre and the left carries an object which may be a ceremonial *keru.* Carved from a single block of red sandstone, the statue is over six feet high.

'Devil' mask worn by a participant in a Corpus Christi procession; it incorporates the jaguar fangs which were a feature of Peruvian iconography from the earliest Chavín times and is surmounted by a headdress embroidered with a Sun symbol. In the processions for such Christian festivals the traditional costumes and masks are often worn by those following the Cross and other Christian symbols. Among the highland Indians of the Altiplano the ancient religions, superstitions and ritual customs persist in synthesis with the Catholic Christianity brought by the Spaniards.

in Lake Titicaca and found there a race of white people with beards and fought with them until he had killed them all. And after that they say there were heavy battles against the Canas and Canchas. And after they had done notable exploits these two lords who had arisen in the Collao turned their arms against each other. They sought the support of the Inca Viracocha, who then reigned at Cuzco, and he made an alliance with Cari at Chucuito and displayed such adroitness that he made himself master over many peoples of the Collao without fighting ...

'These natives of the Collao say the same as all the highland peoples that the Creator of all things is called Ticci Viracocha and they know that his principal abode is in heaven. But deceived by the Devil, they adored various other gods, as all the heathen did. They have a kind of romances or songs by means of which the memory of events is preserved and they do not forget it in spite of the lack of writing. And among the natives of this Collao are men of good understanding who show their intelligence when they are questioned. They keep count of time and know something of the movements both of the sun and the moon ...' Cieza de León. Part I, Ch. 100.

Right: Large Nazca jar with what may be a demon face and arm gripping a severed head. The vase is surrounded with modelled heads in three different colours. Whether this has a religious and mythological significance in connection with a sacrificial cult or whether it has rather a military significance can only be conjectured.

'I often asked the natives of these regions what they knew about their condition before they were subjected by the Inca. They say that men lived in those times in a state of disorder, many went naked like savages; they had no houses or other dwellings than caves (many of which can be seen high in the mountains) and from these they went forth to gather whatever they could find to eat in the countryside. Some made fortresses, called *pucara*, in the highlands and they sallied forth from these to fight one another. Many were killed and they carried off the spoils and women of the conquered. They were in a state of anarchy without political cohesion and had no overlords but only petty chiefs who led them in battle. Their clothing was primitive, but they say that the headbands or *llautu* by which one tribe is nowadays distinguished from another were used even then.

'When they were living in this state there rose up in the province of the Collao a powerful chief named Zapana, who brought many people

Two of the high masonry towers, *chullpas*, thought to be burial towers whcih are found in Bolivia and around Lake Titicaca. They date from the period, about A.D. 1000 and after, when the power of Tiahuanaco had been broken but the Inca ascendancy not yet established. The admirable masonry and structure suggest that, while the strength of the state had gone, the skill of the Tiahuanaco artisans had certainly survived.

under his command. One other thing they say, but whether it is true or not only the Almighty God knows who understands all things; as for me, my only authority is the testimony of the Indians. They assert with assurance that after this great captain arose in Hatun Colla there appeared in the district of the Canas, which is between the Canchas and Collao, near the village of Chugara, women who were as valiant as men. These women took up arms and made themselves masters of the district, where they lived without husbands almost as it is told of the Amazons. After some years these people clashed with Zapana, who had made himself lord of Hatun Colla, and built walled fortresses, which still exist, to defend themselves against him. But after they had done all they could they were defeated and killed and their name died out ...

'They also relate that long ago in the island of Titicaca there were people with beards like ourselves. And coming from the valley of Coquimbo, their captain, who was called Cari, came to the place where Chucuito now stands, and after making a new settlement there crossed over to the island ...

'Before the Incas ruled or had even been heard of in these kingdoms these Indians relate a thing more noteworthy than anything else that they say. They assert that they were a long time without seeing the sun and, suffering much hardship from this, they offered prayers and vows to those whom they held for gods, beseeching of them the light they lacked. At this the sun very brilliant rose from the island of Titicaca in the great lake of the Collao, and all were rejoiced. After this had happened they say that there suddenly appeared, coming from the south, a white man of large stature and authoritative demeanour. This man had such great power that he changed the hills into valleys and from the valleys made great hills, causing streams to flow from the living stone. When they saw his power they called him Maker of all things created and Prince of all things, Father of the sun. For he did other still more wonderful things, giving being to men and animals; in a word by his hand very great benefits accrued to them. This is the story that the Indians themselves told me and they heard it from their fathers who in their turn had it from the old songs which were handed down from very ancient times.

'They say that this man travelled along the highland route to the north, working marvels as he went and that they never saw him again. They say that in many places he gave men instructions how they should live, speaking to them with great love and kindness and admonishing them to be good and to do no damage or injury one to another, but to love one another and show charity to all. In most places they name him Ticci Viracocha, but in the province of Collao he is called Tuapaca [Thunupa] or in some parts of it Arunaua. In many places they built temples to him and in them they set up statues in his likeness and offered sacrifices before them. The huge statues in the village of Tiahuanaco are held to be from those times. Although they relate what I have recorded about Ticci Viracocha based on the tradition of past time, they can say no more about him nor whether he ever returned to any part of that kingdom.

'They relate further that after much time had passed they saw another man like in appearance to the first but they do not mention his name. They have it from their forbears that wherever he passed he healed all that were sick and restored sight to the blind by words alone. Thus he was beloved by all. So, working great miracles by his words, he came to the district of the Canas and there, near a village called Cacha ... the people rose up against him and threatened to stone him. They saw him sink to his knees and raise his hands to heaven as if beseeching aid in the peril which beset him. The Indians declare that thereupon they saw fire in the sky which seemed all around them. Full of fear, they approached him whom they had intended to kill and besought him to forgive them; for

Right: Square-cut head, almost four feet high, belonging to the later period of Tiahuanaco sculptures, in which highly stylised gigantic figures were often covered with symbolic relief carving or engraved decoration. This head is now in the open-air museum of La Paz.

Pottery beaker from Tiahuanaco. The relief design of a conventionalised human figure seems to belong in style to a somewhat earlier period than the classical style illustrated by the iconography of the Gate of the Sun. It is not known whether the figure represents a deity or a priest-king.

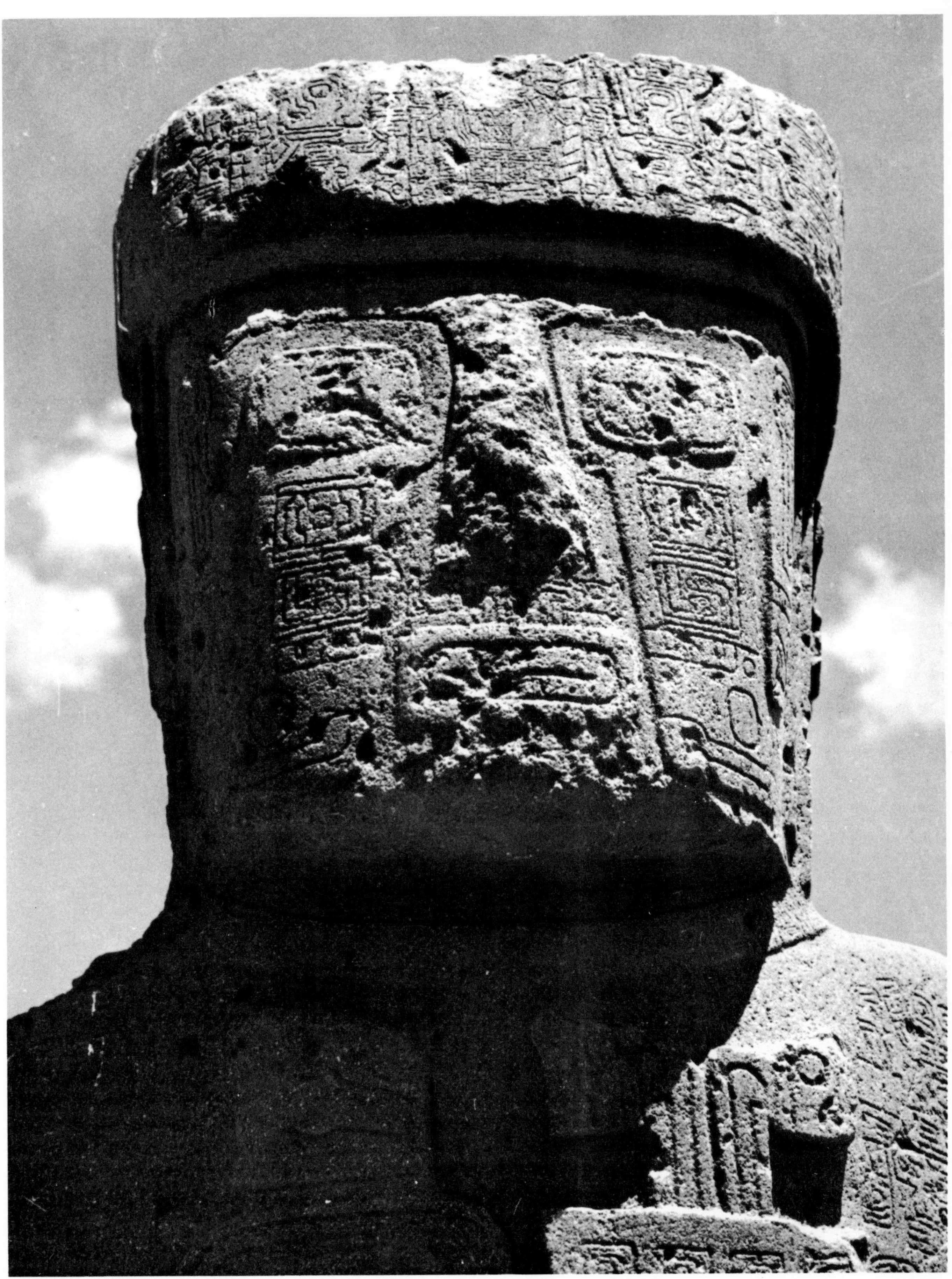

they regarded this as a punishment for their sin in seeking to stone a stranger. Presently they saw that the fire was extinguished at his command, though the stones were consumed by fire in such wise that large blocks could be lifted by hand as if they were cork. They narrate further that, leaving the place where this occurred, he came to the coast and there, holding his mantle, he went forth amidst the waves of the sea and was seen no more. And as he went they gave him the name Viracocha, which means "foam of the sea".' Cieza de León. Part II, Chs. 4 and 5.

Creation myths of the Collao

'They say that in ancient times the land of Peru was dark and there was no light nor day in it. In those times there dwelt there a certain people who owed allegiance to an overlord whose name they no longer remember. And they say that in those times when all was night in the land there came forth from a lake in the district called Collasuyu, a Lord named Con Ticci Viracocha bringing with him a certain number of people, though they don't remember how many. And after emerging from the lake he went to a place nearby, where is now the village they call Tiahuanaco in the Collao. And while he was there with his followers they say that he suddenly made the sun and the day and commanded the sun to follow the course which it does follow. Then he made the stars and the moon. They say that this Con Ticci Viracocha had emerged on an earlier occasion and that on this first appearance he made the heaven and the earth and left everything dark. It was then that he created this race of men who lived during the times of darkness. And this race did something which angered Viracocha, so he came forth the second time as has been said and turned that race and their overlord to stone as a punishment for the anger they had caused him.

'So, as has been said, when he emerged he made the sun and day and moon and stars. This done, he made at Tiahuanaco stone models or patterns of the peoples he was afterwards to produce, and he did it in the following way. He made from stone a certain number of people and a lord who governed them and many women who were pregnant and others who had young children in cradles after their custom. When this was done he set the stone figures apart and made another province there in Tiahuanaco also of stone in the same manner. When this was done he commanded all the people with him to journey forth, keeping only two with him, and these he commanded to look at the stone figures he had made and the names he had given them, saying to them: "These are called so and so and will issue forth from such and such a fountain in such and such a province and shall increase and populate it; these others shall issue from such and such a cave and shall be named such and such and shall populate such and such a region. As I have them here painted and fashioned of stone, so shall they issue from fountains, rivers, caves and rocks in the provinces that I have indicated to you. And all you my people shall go in that direction (indicating the direction of sunrise), dividing them up and indicating the title which each is to bear."

'Thus those viracochas went off to the various districts which Viracocha had indicated to them and as soon as each arrived in his district he called those stone figures which Viracocha had commanded in Tiahuanaco were to issue forth in that district, each viracocha taking up his position close by the site where he had been told they were to come forth. When this was done, the Viracocha at Tiahuanaco spoke in a loud voice: "So and so, come forth and people this land which is deserted, for thus has commanded Con Ticci Viracocha who made the world." Thereupon these peoples came forth from the places and regions which the Viracocha had instructed. Thus they went on calling forth the races of men from

Right: Early Nazca vase shaped in the form of a human figure with a foxskin headdress and stylised snake decorations. The figure wears what appears to be a necklace of silver plaques. Although we can only conjecture, it seems likely that these accoutrements indicate a ceremonial or ritualistic function in connection with local cult.

Polished clay stirrup jar. The scene depicted is open to numerous interpretations but the most likely one is religious ritual. The priest(?) is grasped by a man or worshipper wearing a mask on his head. The beast represented is like no known animal of the Pacific coast; the central crest suggests that it was purely imaginary.

caves, rivers and fountains and the high sierras and peopling the earth towards the east.

'And when Con Ticci Viracocha had accomplished this, then he sent forth the two who had remained behind with him in Tiahuanaco, to call forth the races of men in the same manner aforesaid. One he sent through the province of Cuntisuyu, that is to the left if one stands in Tiahuanaco with one's back to the sunrise, to bring forth the Indians native to the province of Cuntisuyu in the manner as aforesaid. The other he sent through the province of Antisuyu, which is on the right hand if one stands with the back to the sunrise.

'When he had despatched those two they say that he himself left towards Cuzco, which lies between those provinces, travelling by the royal road over the sierra in the direction of Cajamarca. As he went he called forth the races of men in the manner you have heard. When he came to the district called Cacha, the district of the Canas, eighteen leagues from the city of Cuzco, and when he called forth these Canas they came forth armed; and when they saw Viracocha, not knowing him, they rushed upon him weapons in hand, intending to kill him. Understanding their purpose, when he saw them coming thus upon him he suddenly made fire fall from heaven, burning a mountain peak in the direction where the Indians were. The Indians saw the fire, and were terrified of being burned, so they cast their weapons on the ground and fled straight towards Viracocha. When they reached him they all cast themselves on the ground. And when he saw them so, he took a staff in his hand, went to where the fire was and gave it two or three blows, whereupon it died out.

'Afterwards he told the Canas that he was their creator and they made a sumptuous *huaca* (that is, an idol or place of worship) in the place where it happened, and they and their descendants offered much gold and silver to the *huaca*. And in memory of this Viracocha and what happened they set up in the *huaca* a huge sculpted stone figure on a large stone base about five yards long by one yard wide. I myself have seen the burnt mountain and the stones from it and the burn extends for more than a quarter of a league. And when I saw this marvel I called together the chief and most ancient Indians of the village of Cacha and asked them about it; they told me what I have recounted. The *huaca* of this Viracocha is a stone's throw to the right of the burn on a level patch the other side of a stream which runs between it and the burn. Many persons have crossed the stream and have seen the *huaca* and the stone.

'I asked them what their tradition had to tell about the appearance of the Viracocha when he was seen by the first men of their race and they told me he was a man of tall stature clothed in a white robe which came down to his feet and which he wore belted at the waist. He had short hair and a tonsure like a priest. He went unshod and carried in his hands a thing which, in the light of what they know today, they liken to the breviaries which priests carry. And I asked them what was the name of the person in whose honour that stone was set up and they told me it was Con Ticci Viracocha Pachayachachic, which means in their language "God, Creator of the World".

'To return to our story. They say that after this miracle in the district of Cacha he went on his way, intent on his work, until he came to a place which is now called the Tambo of Urcos, six leagues from Cuzco, and there he climbed a high mountain peak and sat down on the top of it. From there he commanded to be produced and to come forth from that height the Indians who today live in that region. And in that place, because Viracocha sat down there, they have made a very rich and sumptuous *huaca*. They have made there a throne of fine gold and the statue which they have set up in honour of Viracocha – also of fine gold – sits on the throne.

An unusually large vessel (twenty inches high and ten in diameter) in painted terracotta of the Mochica culture. These figures, with the huge ear plugs and a mace in the right hand, are commonly called 'warriors' but they may equally represent noblemen or chieftains.

'From there Viracocha pursued his way, calling forth the races of men, until he came to Cuzco. There he made a Lord, to whom he gave the name Alcaviza, and he also named the site Cuzco. After leaving injunctions how after his departure the Orejones should be produced, he passed on further to continue his work. When he came to the district of Puerto Viejo he was joined by his followers whom he had sent on before as has been said, and when they had joined him he put to sea in their company and they say that he and his people went by water as easily as they had traversed the land. There are many other things I could have written about this Viracocha according as they were told me by the Indians, but to avoid prolixity and great idolatry and bestiality I have omitted them ...' Juan de Betanzos: *Suma y Narración de los Incas.*

'I declare that from childhood I have heard ancient traditions and histories and fables and barbarities of heathen times and they are as follows according to the unvarying testimony of the natives about past events.

Cast copper plaque representing in highly stylised form a human figure between two felines. Above are two conventionalised figures which may represent a fox or ant-eater motif. Aguada culture of the north-west Argentine, A.D. 700–1000.

'In the age of *Purunpacha* [the savage world] all the tribes of the *Tahuantinsuyu* [the four parts of the Inca empire, i.e. the inhabited world] came from beyond Potosí in four or five armies prepared for war. As they advanced they settled in the various districts. This period was called *Ccallacpacha* or *Tutayacpacha* [the beginning of the world; or the age of darkness]. Since each band chose a place where to make its home they called this *Purunpacharacyaptin* [multitudes before the age of savagery]. This age lasted a vast number of years. As the people poured into the country there was a shortage of land and wars and quarrels became frequent. Then they began to make fortresses and there were daily clashes and the people knew no peace. Then it was that in the middle of the night they heard the *Hapi-ñuñus* [demons: lit. seizers of women's bosoms] making off with mournful cries and saying: "We are defeated! We are defeated! Ah that we should lose our subjects!" We are to understand by this that the demons had been conquered by Jesus Christ upon Calvary. For they say that in ancient times, in the age of savagery, the *Hapi-ñuñus* walked to and fro in visible form over all the land so that it was not safe to go abroad at night, for they carried off men, women and children like the enemies of the human race that they are.

'Some while after the devils called *Hapi-ñuñus Achacallas* had been driven from the land, there arrived in these territories of the *Tahuantinsuyu* a bearded man of medium height and long hair dressed in a rather long cloak. They say he was past his prime, with grey hair, and lean. He walked with a staff and addressed the natives with love, calling them his sons and daughters. As he traversed all the land he worked miracles. He healed the sick by his touch. He spoke every tongue even better than the natives. They called him *Thunupa* or *Tarapaca* ... *Viracocharapacha yachipachan* or *Pachaccan* [chief steward]. This means servant, and *Vicchaycamayoc*, which means preacher. He preached to the people but they took little notice, for they held him in low account. He was called *Thunupa Viracocha nipachan*, but surely he was the glorious apostle St Thomas.

'They say that this man came to a village called Apo-tampu [this is *Paccari-tambo*], very weary, and they were celebrating a marriage feast there. The chief listened to his teaching in a friendly spirit but the people were unwilling to listen. The traveller became a guest of the chief Apo-tampu, to whom he gave a branch from his staff, and under the influence of the chief the people heard him willingly ...

'This good man Thunupa visited all the districts of the Collasuyu, preaching always to the people, until one day he came to the town of Yamquisupa. There he was treated with contempt and driven out. He often slept in the open without any covering but his cloak and a book. He cursed that town and it was submerged in the water. The place is now called *Yamquisupaloiga*. It is now a lake and the Indians knew that it had once been a village. On a high hill called *Cacha-pucara* [the fortress of Cacha, a town in the valley of Vilcamayo] there was an idol shaped like a woman and Thunupa disliked it bitterly, set fire to it and destroyed it with the hill on which it stood. The signs of this awful miracle are said to be visible today.

'Another time he began to preach with loving words in a town where they were celebrating a wedding, and they would not listen to him. Therefore he cursed them and turned them into stones, which are still to be seen. The same thing occurred at Pucara and other places. They say further that when in his wandering Thunupa came to the mountains of Caravaya he set up a large cross and carried it on his back to the mountain of Carapucu, where he preached in a loud voice and wept. The daughter of the chief had water sprinkled on her head, which was misunderstood by the Indians. So Thunupa was put in prison and his head was shorn, near the great lake of Carapucu. The name Carapucu is derived from the *pucupucu*,

Left: Woven textile from Chancay in the central coastal region of Peru. The pattern is formed from stylised feline (puma ?) and bird motifs, with possibly also deer. The traditional pattern has here a purely decorative function and is treated light-heartedly and even humorously. The religious and ritualistic impact made by the feline motif in earlier Chavín and Paracas art is no longer present.

An example of the pottery work found in the desolate Paracas peninsula, where nothing exists today but red sand. But buried under this lay the remains of a people unknown to history, undiscovered until 1925, who produced remarkable textiles and the mask shown here. The decoration is resin paint and was applied after firing. First century B.C.

a bird which sings at dawn. When Thunupa was in prison they say that at daybreak a beautiful youth came to him and said: "Fear not, for I come to you from the mistress, who watches over you and who is about to go to the place of rest." So saying he touched with his fingers the bonds which bound Thunupa hand and foot. There were many guards, for Thunupa had been condemned to a cruel death, but at five in the morning he entered the lake with the youth, his mantle bearing him up on the waters in place of a boat.

'When he reached the town of Carapucu the leaders were annoyed that their idol had been cast down and destroyed. They say that the idol flew like the wind to a deserted place which was never visited. There the idol or *huaca* was mourning and lamenting with lowered head and was so found by an Indian, and his story made the chiefs excited at the arrival of Thunupa, who had been put in prison. They say that after he had been freed from these savage men Thunupa remained for a long time on a rock called Titicaca and then went by Tiquina to Chacamarca, where he came to a town called Tiahuanaco. The people of that town were singing and dancing when he came and were unwilling to listen to his preaching. Then in anger he denounced them in their own language and when he left the people were turned to stone, as they can be seen to this day. This is told by the ancient Incas.' Juan de Santa Cruz Pachacuti-Yamqui Salcamayhua: *An Account of the Antiquities of Peru.*

Cosmological myths

The cosmological stories recorded from the Collao have much in common with those from other parts of the Central Andes but with some characteristic features of their own. In many cases they have come to us conflated with legends of Inca origins and it seems that the Inca took over these legends among others to explain and justify the supremacy they arrogated to themselves. The basic form of the myth ran somewhat as follows.

In the most ancient times the earth was covered in darkness and there was no sun. For some crime unstated the people who lived in those times were destroyed by the creator. Or they were destroyed in a deluge. After the deluge the creator (or his divine embodiment) appeared in human form from Lake Titicaca. He then created the sun and moon and stars. After that he renewed the human population of the earth. He first fashioned in stone prototypes of the different races, paying great attention to details of costume and deportment.

In the Central Andean highlands the natives of each district, sometimes even each village, are distinguished by small differences of costume, chiefly headdress and hair-styles. This custom persists to some extent even today. To many, a state of affairs in which a person's place of origin is not apparent from his costume is synonymous with anarchy. The origin of the practice is sometimes attributed to the Inca. However, many myths describing human origins and dating from pre-Inca times, as this one, lay great emphasis upon it.

Tribes of living people corresponding to these prototypes were then brought forth by the creator from rocks and rivers, caves, trees and fountains through the length and breadth of the highlands. To these he gave names and instructions in civilised life. In some versions he acts alone and in others in conjunction with subordinate divine beings who put his instructions into effect. The method of creation depicted in this and similar myths points pretty clearly to a race memory of a period of religious animism, a stage when people ascribed spiritual powers to natural features to which they attributed their origin as a group and to which they were specially attached in a symbolic way. The *huaca* in this most primitive sense was some natural feature or object to which the group gave partic-

A rock engraving from the Atacama Desert showing a vicuña hunt. The wool of this small cousin of the llama is so fine that in Inca times its use was restricted to the nobility, when the animals were released after being shorn. But llamas, alpacas and vicuñas were commonly hunted in primitive times.

ular reverence and which they connected both with the origin of the group and its continued safekeeping.

Achachilas

Among the Aymara who still inhabit the Bolivian highlands, natural objects of reverence are called *Achachilas*. Chief among them are the great mountain peaks of the Cordillera; Illimani, Illampu, Huaynu Potosí, and the rest. The Aymara Indians still perform acts of worship to them, claim them as tribal ancestors and tell traditional fables about them. People have often seen Indians, travelling by lorry from Lake Titicaca to La Paz, remove their woollen caps and take up the attitude of prayer when they came within sight of the Cordillera. Pilgrims to the shrine of the Virgin at Copacabana on the Lake still make a weekly ascent of the hill Calvario, led by the *yatiri* doctor-diviners, and from the top, along with Christian ceremonies, pay tribute to the mountain peaks which are imposingly visible from there.

The story is currently told that Illimani, the mountain which looks down on La Paz, was the favourite of Viracocha and roused therefore the envy of the neighbouring peak which was taller and larger. This peak, Mururata, grumbled to Viracocha, who in anger broke off its top with his sling so that it is now truncated, and the upper part sailed through the air to form the present Sajama. Both the Omasuyus and the Pacajes claim Illimani as their ancestor.

When two peaks stand facing each other Indian myth often represents them as male and female, as with the two mountains Sicasica and Churu-

Illimani, one of the majestic peaks of the Cordillera Real which are worshipped as *Achachilas*, objects of reverence in Aymara mythology and religion. Illimani, which overlooks La Paz, is regarded as the tutelary spirit of the city and is said to be the favourite of Viracocha.

quilla, *Achachilas* for the Sucre region. The natives of this region believe that the spirit of the former shows itself from time to time, and particularly at night, in the form of a young and beautiful female, who smiles seductively at those who come upon her but who cannot be approached. Indians who are found dead in these mountains are believed to have been punished for not showing due reverence towards this mountain spirit. The mountains San Juan de Parichata and Tata-Turqui outside Potosí are also worshipped as *Achachilas*, male and female, of the region. As an instance of the continuation of the native mythopoeic fancy during colonial times, the following story about Parichata may be told. It is given by M. Rigoberto Paredes in his *Mitos, Supersticiones y Supervivencias populares de Bolivia.*

Formerly the Spaniards worked silver mines on Parichata and treated the Indian labourers so harshly that in despair they appealed to the mountain. The mountain took pity on them and resolved to help them. One night an Indian muleteer was mounting the path up the mountain when he heard the clatter of carrier animals. An Indian met him and told him to go back under pain of death as the road ahead was blocked. This he did. But later he returned to the place and hiding beside the path, he saw go by an enormous troop of mules laden with silver ore. One of the beasts collapsed under its load. The muleteer went to its aid and found it had broken a bone of its shin. He therefore unloaded the silver and, taking care to mark the spot, returned to his lodging. Next day he returned but both the silver and the mule had disappeared. In the place where the mule had been lying was a beetle moving painfully with a broken leg. The spirit of the mountain had transformed all the beetles of the region into mules to cart away all the silver ore in the mountain. From that night the veins of silver in Parichata dried up and the Indians were no longer worked to death mining it for the Spaniards. The silver was removed to Tata-Turqui, where it was mined until recently, but the abuse of the Indians ceased.

Some tribes still trace their first beginnings from lakes. Thus the Quillacas say they are descendants of Lake Poopo, sacred to the moon. The despised Urus, whose language is not Aymara, are said to have been born

Left: Detail of woven textile from Paracas Necropolis in the southern coastal zone of Peru, about 400–100 B.C. It appears to represent three demon figures half humorously conceived. The long trailers descending from the headdresses terminate in conventional snake heads. The figures carry what may be a ceremonial axe or knife in one hand and a bent staff, whose significance is lost, in the other.

Neither the provenance nor the interpretation of this curious terracotta is known. It appears to represent a boat; not the usual balsa boat made from the totora rush, but a boat of skins. In it are laid out figures of the dead. It may indicate a myth comparable to Egyptian and Greek myths in which the dead were taken by boat to the other world – but in the absence of confirmatory evidence the symbolism must remain obscure.

from the slime of Lake Titicaca when it was first heated by the sun. Yet another tradition holds that the Urus were originally transplanted from the Pacific coast as slaves and settled near Titicaca by a highland chieftain called Tacuilla.

Thunupa

The mythological cycle of the Collao also contains stories of a culture hero, the bringer of civilisation and an advanced social code. He is variously named Thunupa, Tonapa and Taapac. Although a fair amount is told about him, it is excessively difficult to disentangle for several reasons. First, many of his activites are elsewhere attributed to the creator-god Viracocha and no clear distinction of function is made between them. Second, the official Inca syncretistic mythology arrogated to the founders of the Inca dynasty the attributes of a culture hero and sought to heighten the prestige of the dynasty by connecting its origin with Titicaca and the Collao. Thus the Thunupa myth was conflated with the myth of Inca origins. Thirdly, much of our information about the myth comes from the researches of the Augustinian Fathers (themselves by no means lacking in credulity), and in particular Antonio de la Calancha's *Crónica moralizada del orden de San Agustín en el Perú*, which was published in 1638.

Indian legend was still plastic and creative during the Colonial period and there is no doubt that many of the attributes ascribed to Thunupa in the stories preserved by Calancha were assimilated to the stories told by the Fathers to the Indians about the Apostles. Even Salcamayhua and Guamán Poma de Ayala were Christian converts. The former identifies Thunupa with St Thomas and the latter with St Bartholomew. So the *persona* of Thunupa acquires a twofold character in the stories. On the one hand he is the acme of loving kindness and invites martyrdom. On the other hand when he is angered or rejected he punishes the guilty ones by turning them to stone or drowning them in a flood. The myth runs as follows.

The monument known as the Huaca del Sol (Temple of the Sun), outside the modern town of Trujillo, the largest and most impressive of the enormous ceremonial structures in the form of platforms surmounted by terraced pyramids built of adobe bricks by the Moche people. The base platform measures 750 feet by 450 feet and is 60 feet high. It rises up in five terraces and is surmounted by a stepped pyramidal structure 340 feet square and 75 feet high. It has been estimated to contain 130 million adobe bricks. The Mochica culture of the northern coast of Peru was roughly contemporary with Paracas and Nazca in the southern coastal area, about 300 B.C. to A.D. 500. It was preceded by the Gallinazo and, after a period of Tiahuanaco influence, was succeeded by Chimu. It was centred in the same area as the Chimu empire, the valleys of Chicama, Moche, Viru and Santa.

Thunupa appeared on the Altiplano in ancient times, coming from the north with five disciples. He was a man of august presence, blue-eyed, bearded, without headgear and wearing a *cusma*, a jerkin or sleeveless shirt reaching to the knees. He was sober, puritanical and preached against drunkenness, polygamy and war. He first came carrying a large wooden cross on his back to Carapucu, the capital of the famous chief Makuri, and reproved the latter for his warlike deeds and his cruelty. Makuri took no account of him, but the priests and soothsayers set up an opposition to him. Thunupa then went to Sicasica, where his preaching annoyed the people and they set fire to the house where he was sleeping. Escaping from the fire, Thunupa returned to Carapucu. But during his absence one of his disciples had fallen in love with and converted the daughter of Makuri, and on his return Thunupa had her baptised. Angered at this, Makuri martyred the disciples and left Thunupa for dead. Calancha then takes up the story:

'They put his blessed body in a boat of totora rush and set it adrift on Lake Titicaca. [Totora is a strong rush which grows on the shores of Lake Titicaca. The Indians fashion it into bundles from which they still make their boats.] There the gentle waters served him for oars and the soft winds for pilot, and he sailed away with such speed that those who had tried so cruelly to kill him were left behind in terror and astonishment. For this lake has no current... The boat came to the shore at Cochamarca, where today is the river Desaguadero. Indian tradition asserts that the boat struck the land with such force it created the river Desaguadero, which before then did not exist. And on the water so released the holy body was carried many leagues away to the sea coast at Arica.'

There was also a tradition that his enemies tried to destroy Thunupa's cross, both by fire and by hewing it to pieces, but were unable to do so. They tried to get rid of it in the Lake but it would not sink. They then buried it in the ground and it was unearthed and discovered to the Augustine Fathers in 1569, as related by Ramos Gavilán in *Historia del célebre y milagroso Santuario de la insigne imagen de Nuestra Señora de Copacabana*, published in 1621.

In his *Account of the Antiquities of Peru* Salcamayhua tells of a visit by the Inca monarch Capac Yupanqui to the highlands around Titicaca.

'It is said that the Inca sent men to search for the place called Titicaca, where the great Thunupa had arrived, and that they brought water thence to pour over the infant Inca Roca while they celebrated the praises of Thunupa. [This is the only account I have found pointing to a cult of Thunupa.] In the spring on the top of the rocks the water was in a basin called *ccapacchama quispisutuc una* [rich joy of crystal drops of water]. Future Incas caused this water to be brought in a bowl called *curi-ccacca* (rock of gold) and placed in the middle of the square of Cuzco called Huacay-pata, where they did honour to the water which had been touched by Thunupa.

'In those days the *curacas* [village headmen] of Asillu and Hucuru told the Inca how in ancient times a poor thin old man with a beard and long hair had come to them in a long tunic and that he was a wise counsellor in matters of state and that his name was Thunupa Vihinquira. They said that he had banished all the idols and *Hapi-ñuñu* demons to the snowy mountains. All the *curacas* and chroniclers also said that this Thunupa had banished all the idols and *huacas* to the mountains of Asancata, Quiyancatay, Sallcatay and Apitosiray. When all the *curacas* of the Tahuantinsuyu were assembled in the Huacay-pata, each in his place, those of the Huancas said that this Thunupa Varivillca had also been in their land and that he had made a house to live in and had banished all the *huacas* and *Hapi-ñuñus* in the provinces of Hatun Sausa to the snowy mountains in Pariacaca and Vallollo. Before their banishment these idols

Detail of a wooden totem-like pile showing a feline motif. Pachacamac.

had done much harm to the people, forcing the *curacas* to make human sacrifices to them.

'The Inca ordered that the house of Thunupa should be preserved. It was at the foot of a small hill near the river as you enter Jauja from the Cuzco road, and before coming to it there are two stones where Thunupa had turned a female *huaca* into stone for having fornicated with a man of the Huancas.'

Ekkekko

Ekkekko was a domestic god of good luck and prosperity among the highland Indians. He was represented by small figures of a pot-bellied man radiating happiness and goodwill, usually loaded with all manner of objects of domestic use. Going back before the Conquest, the cult of the Ekkekko has always been connected with things in miniature. Small images of the Ekkekko had a place of honour in every Indian house during the colonial period and are still popular today. In his *Vocabulario de la Lengua Aymará* Ludovico Bertonio connects him with Thunupa, and says that the Indians tell innumerable stories about good fortune caused by the Ekkekko. Tiny figures of the god are still widely worn as amulets and charms.

The cult of the Ekkekko is especially connected with annual fairs in La Paz, Cochabamba, and Oruro, called Alacitas. At these fairs all things are sold in miniature and are much sought after by the natives and cholos. An Indian or chola woman, for example, will buy a miniature pottery house at the Alacitas in order to make certain that she will obtain a husband and a house of her own. The word 'alacita' is said to be derived from an Aymará cry *alacita*, meaning 'Buy me!' and the La Paz festival of Alacitas is said to derive from a fair instituted by Sebastian de Segurola in 1781 to celebrate the relief of the city from siege by Tupac Catari during the insurrection of Tupac Amaru.

Apart from innumerable miraculous good luck stories, there seems to be no myth associated with Ekkekko himself.

Fine Chimu black ceramic vase shaped as a human head with geometrical decoration. There is a distinct bulge in the right cheek caused by a quid (*jacchu*) formed of coca leaves, which is usually masticated in conjunction with a paste of quinoa stalks, which heightens the effect. Though Garcilaso says that in Inca times the use of coca was restricted to the nobility and to certain *curacas* (village headmen), it was certainly used widely before the Inca, as this head testifies, and equally widely since the conquest.

Coca

The coca plant has been cultivated from time immemorial in the semi-tropical valleys of the Andean Cordilleras. The dried leaves of the coca are masticated by the Indians and produce a state of euphoria which, they believe, enables them to sustain hunger, cold and fatigue. Coca leaves have been found in early coastal burials. During Inca times it was known as the 'divine plant' and it is said that its use was reserved for the Inca aristocracy. But the habit of chewing coca was so general and so ingrained among the native population even in the first decades of the Conquest that attempts to eradicate it were ineffective and to this day its cultivation is a major part of agricultural industry in Bolivia. (For a fuller account, see the author's *Indians of the Andes*, pp. 237-51.)

Cieza de León wrote about it as follows. 'In Peru, in all its extent, it was the custom, and is, to carry this coca in the mouth and from morning until they retire to sleep they carry it without emptying it from their mouths. And when I enquired of certain Indians why they keep their mouths ever filled with that herb (the which they eat not neither do they more than carry it between their teeth), they say that they have little sense of hunger and feel great vigour and strength. For my part I believe that it must have some effect, though rather indeed it seems a vicious custom and the sort to be expected of a people such as these Indians are. In the Andes from Huamanga to the town of Plata this coca is cultivated and it grows on small bushes which they tend much and cherish that they shall produce the leaf they call coca; and they dry it in the sun and then pack it in certain long and narrow bales, each one a little over one arroba [about 25 lbs] ... There are some in Spain now rich with the profits they have made from this coca, buying it up and selling it to the markets of the Indians.'

Coca is the object of semi-religious awe and reverence among the Indians. The leaves were used by the wise men or *amautas* for divination and were burnt as a sacred fumigant before religious ceremonies and to purify suspected places from evil spirits or the spirits of diseases. They were offered in ritual sacrifices to the gods, to propitiate the earth goddess Pachamama, and to ward off ill luck. A tincture of coca is thought to have been one of the ingredients in the process of mummification practised by the Inca and still imperfectly understood. Plasters of coca leaves were applied, then as now, to wounds and contusions, and infusions of coca were given, as they are today, as a remedy for stomach and intestinal afflictions.

Among the modern Indians coca has lost nothing of its former medical and magical importance. It is still used by the diviner (*yatiri*) to foretell the future and by the magician (*pako*) and the doctor (*kollasiri*) to diagnose the cause of disease. Coca is still offered to Pachamama to ensure her favour for the crops and to bring good luck when a new house is built. Coca leaves are offered to the dead and to all the supernatural powers. A simple offering consists of six perfect leaves placed green side up one above the other (*aita*). A more elaborate offering consists of 144 *aita* in twelve rows of twelve. The most perfect offering of all is to burn a block of llama fat with coca at midnight inside a ring of dried llama dung and to throw the ashes into a stream. Today as heretofore coca is no less an essential part of the ritual life of the Indian than it is a daily necessity and indulgence.

There are two myths told of the origin of coca. One, referred to by the Peruvianist Julio Tello, comes from a report of the Viceroy Toledo (1568-72). 'About its origin they all say they know nothing except six who say that among the natives there was a legend that before the coca tree was as it is now there was a beautiful woman and because she lived a loose life they slew her and cut her in two. From her body grew the bush which they call Mama-coca and from that time they began to eat it. They carried it in a small bag and it was forbidden to open the bag and eat it until after they had had relations with a woman in memory of that woman. For this reason they call it coca.'

Another legend says that Indians of the Altiplano found their way over the crest of the mountains and settled in the high valleys, called Yungas, of the eastern clopes of the Cordillera. In order to clear land for cultivation, they set fire to the teeming forest and undergrowth. The smoke from the fires rose and polluted the peaks of Illimani and Illampu, the ice-mansions of Khuno, the god of snow and storm. Angered at this, Khuno sent down torrential rain and hail on the Yungas, which destroyed the houses and farms, opened up ravines and caused swift rivers and streams which swept everything away. They also destroyed the mountain roads and cut off the Indians from the highlands. Coming out from the caves in which they had taken refuge, the Indians found nothing but desolation around them until, weak with hunger and despair, they at last came upon an unknown shrub with leaves of a brilliant green. Gathering the leaves of this plant, they put them in their mouths to stay their hunger and immediately were invaded by a sense of supreme wellbeing. They no longer felt the hunger, the weariness or the cold. Refreshed with new energy, they were able to return to Tiahuanaco, where they revealed the secret of this wonderful new plant to the elders (*auquis*) and wise men (*amautas*); and thus the knowledge of coca spread throughout the sierra. (José Agustin Morales, *El Oro Verde de los Yungas*, 1938, and M. Rigoberto Paredes, *Mitos, Supersticiones y Supervivencias populares de Bolivia*, 1963.)

Mochica stirrup vase with skull head wearing the usual 'snood' headdress tied beneath the chin. Painted on the body are a coca pouch like the *shuspa* in which the modern Indian carries his daily coca ration, and hands holding a chilli pepper, or *aci*. The custom of representing a death's head, often in conjunction with living figures, has persisted to the present day, though its significance is no longer understood.

Myths and Legends of the Coast

The invasion of giants

'As there exist rumours of giants in Peru, who landed at the point of Santa Helena, near Puerto Viejo, I will report what I have myself been told without paying attention to the stories current among the vulgar, who always exaggerate what happened. The natives recount the following tradition, which they heard from their fathers and the latter from ancient tradition.

'There arrived by sea in balsa boats made of rushes [totora, see p. 87], but as large as ships, men so enormous that from the knee downwards they were the size of an ordinary man of good stature. Their limbs were in proportion to the size of their bodies and it was a monstrous thing to see their huge heads and the hair which came down to their shoulders. Their eyes were as large as saucers. They say they had no beards. Some were dressed in the skins of animals, others had no other costume than nature gave them. They brought no women with them. When they landed they made some sort of settlement at this point and the sites of their houses are still pointed out. As they found no water, they bored some extremely deep wells in the rock – a work truly worthy of remembrance, since only men of their outstanding strength could have done it. For they dug these wells in the living rock until they found water and then lined them from bottom to top with masonry such as would resist the wear and tear of time for many centuries. In these wells there is excellent and wholesome water, so cool that it is always a delight to drink.

'But these giants ate so much that they soon exhausted the resources of the district – since one of them devoured more meat than fifty of the natives. As they could not find enough to satisfy them, they slaughtered large quantities of fish in the sea with their nets and other gear. They were hated by the natives because they killed their women in associating with them, and the men also for other causes. They leagued together to resist this new race of giants who had come to occupy their lands, but were not strong enough to engage them. So many years passed and the giants were still in the land.

'Since they lacked women and the natives would have nothing to do with them because of their size, they practised sodomy with each other openly and without shame or fear of God ... The natives assert that God visited on them a punishment befitting the enormity of their crime. When they were all together and indulging in their homosexual practices fearful and terrifying fire came down from the sky with a huge noise and from the midst came forth a shining angel, a sharp and glittering sword in his hand. With a single blow he slew them all and the fire consumed them, so that there remained only a few bones and skulls which God permitted to stay unconsumed by the fire as a memory of this punishment.

'This they say about the giants. The which we believe is true, for in this part there have been found and are still found enormous bones, and

Left: A tintinabulum fashioned out of copper and surmounted by the head of possibly a chief or priest. North coast of Peru.

Bale of coca in an Altiplano street market. The habit of masticating coca is almost universal among the highland Indians, for its euphoric effect does something to alleviate the harsh conditions in which they live their lives. Even during the most rigorous periods of Spanish oppression it was impossible to deny this indulgence to the mining and agricultural labourers.

I have heard tell of Spaniards who have seen a piece of a tooth which complete would have weighed half a butcher's pound.' Pedro de Cieza de León: *Crónica del Perú*. Part I, Ch. 52.

Myths of Huarochiri

Huarochiri or Warachiri is a highland district on the western side of the coastal Cordillera of Peru, east of Lima, and their own legends, as reported, indicate that the Indians migrated there in distant times from the coastal valleys. An unfinished manuscript written in Quechua in 1608 was left by Francisco de Avila, priest of San Damian, the principal parish of the district of Huarochiri. It is described by him as '*A Narrative of the Errors, False Gods, and other Superstitions and Diabolical Rites in which the Indians of the Provinces of Huarochiri, Mama and Chaclla lived in ancient times, and in which they even now live, to the great perdition of their souls*'. The fragment is a somewhat confused account of the myths and legends which survived among these people at the beginning of the seventeenth century, and was obtained by Father Avila 'from trustworthy

Detail of the bridge of a double-spouted Chimu vase. On either side of the crowned head are frog and monkey figures. There is no portraiture in the Chimu period, and animals and birds are sometimes so formalised as to be difficult to identify. Technical skill has outlasted the spontaneity of the earlier craftsmanship. Particularly characteristic of the Chimu is a beautifully modelled black ware richly various in design and subject.

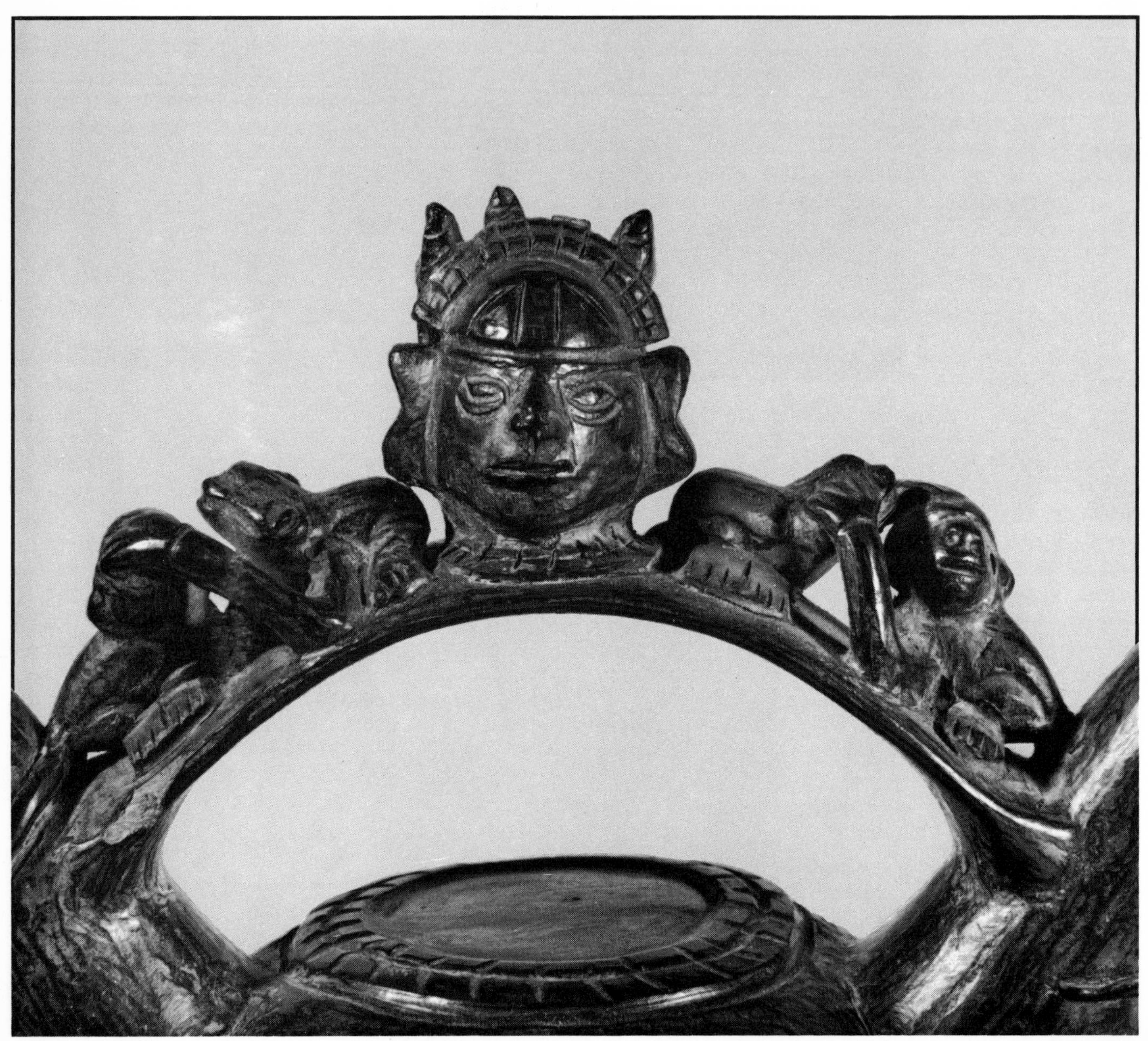

persons who, with special diligence, ascertained the whole truth'. The manuscript was first published in the English translation by Clements R. Markham issued by the Hakluyt Society in 1873. The manuscript begins as follows in Markham's translation.

'It is a most ancient tradition that, before any other event of which there is any memory, there were certain *huacas* or idols, which, together with others of which I shall treat, must be supposed to have walked in the form of men. These *huacas* were called *Yananamca Intanamca*; and in a certain encounter they had with another *huaca* called Huallallo Caruincho, they were conquered and destroyed by the said Huallallo, who remained as Lord and God of the land. He ordered that no woman should bring forth more than two children, of which one was to be sacrificed for him to eat, and the other – whichever of the two the parents chose – might be brought up. It was also a tradition that in those days all who died were brought to life again on the fifth day and that what was sown in that land also sprouted, grew, and ripened on the fifth day; and that all these three provinces were then a very hot country, which the Indians call *Yunca* or *Ande*; and they say that these crops were made visible in

The peoples of South America, like those of every land and culture, used the forms of the creatures most familiar to them for their decorative art. This shell pendant is Chimu, from the north coastal plains of Peru. The inlay, showing two birds eating a fish, is turquoise.

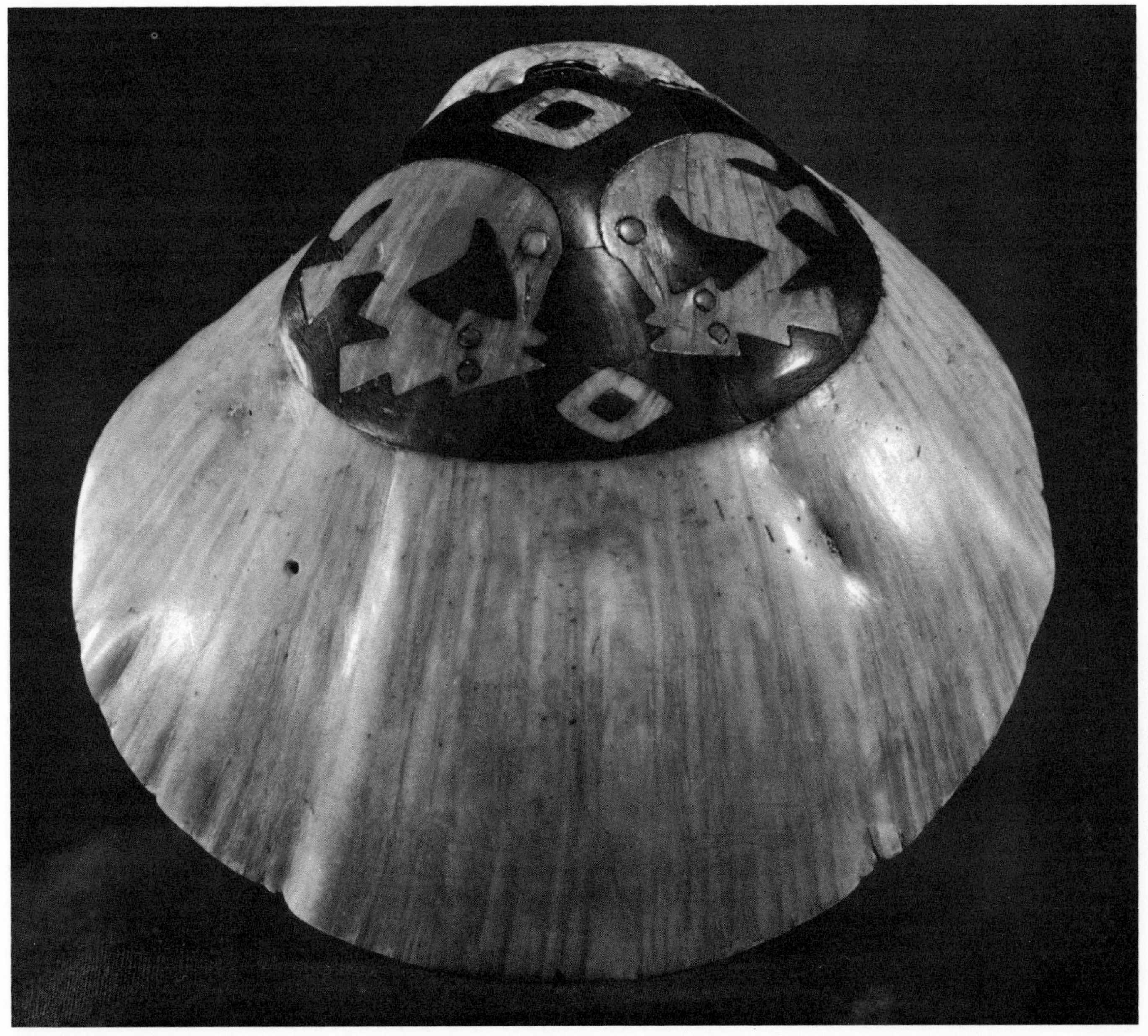

the deserts and uninhabited places, such as that of Pariacaca and others; and that in these Andes there was a great variety of most beautiful and brilliant birds, such as macaws, parrots and others. All this, with the people who then inhabited the land (and who, according to their account, led very evil lives), and the said idol, came to be driven away to other Andes by the idol Pariacaca, of whom I shall speak presently and of the battle he had with this Huallallo Caruincho.'

Yunca – or as it is nowadays spelled 'Yungas' – are the wet and fertile valleys of the coastal region or the eastern slopes of the Cordillera. Avila rightly discredits the legend that the harsh highlands had formerly been tropical and fertile. He does not see the implication of the tradition he reports, namely that the Indians of Huarochiri had in ancient times lived on the coast and had been driven back by invaders into the highlands.

The time of primitive darkness

'A long time ago the sun disappeared and the world was dark for a space of five days. The stones knocked one against another. The mortars, which they called *mutca*, and the pestles, called *marop*, rose against their masters,

who were also attacked by their sheep [llamas], both those fastened in the houses and those in the fields [i.e. wild auchenids, vicuña].'

Avila takes this to be an account of an eclipse. It may well have been, however, a myth of a time of primeval darkness analogous to the stories of the darkness before the deluge in Collao mythology.

The deluge

'An Indian tethering his llama where there was good pasture noticed that it displayed signs of grief, refusing to eat and crying *yu' yu'*. The llama told him it was sad because in five days the sea would cover the whole earth, destroying everything in it. [This prognostication of the deluge by a llama is paralleled in the account reported by Morúa.] Under the guidance of the llama the Indian went to the top of a high mountain called Villcacoto, taking food for five days. There he found so many animals and birds assembled that there was barely room for them all. The sea began to rise, the waters filled the valleys and covered all the hills except Villcacoto. They were so crowded that the fox's tail dipped into the water, which is the reason why the tips of foxes' tails are black. After five days the waters abated and from this sole survivor are descended all the people now in the world.'

Stories of Pariacaca

'At the time of the primitive anarchy called *Purunpacha* which followed the deluge, when there was no centralised authority but each group chose the strongest man as their leader, five large eggs appeared on a mountain called Condorcoto. In one of these was the god Pariacaca.'

Huathiacuri

'Huathiacuri was a poor Indian dressed in rags. He was the son of Pariacaca and learnt many arts from his father. In the area there was a rich and powerful Indian, who made himself out to be very wise and to be

Left: Rock engraving of a double llama, with the two heads facing in opposite directions. The masked head above may be intended to represent a Supreme Deity or a god of agriculture and cattle. Atacama desert.

Quechuas pouring *chicha*, an intoxicating drink made from maize and widely drunk throughout South America, both in times past and today. The 'heaven' believed in by some Indians is a realm where the dead souls are forever plied with *chicha* but do not become drunk.

the creator-god. His house was roofed with yellow and red birds' feathers and he had a great number of coloured llamas so that it was unnecessary to dye the wool they produced. This rich man fell ill with a foul disease. As Huathiacuri was travelling towards the sea he overheard a conversation between two foxes and learned the cause of the great man's illness: his wife had committed adultery and two serpents were hovering over his house eating his life away, while a two-headed toad was hiding under the grinding stone. Huathiacuri caused the wife to confess, the monsters were destroyed, Tamtanamka recovered and Huathiacuri married the daughter.'

Right: Pottery stirrup vase formed in the shape of a seated man, an example of the very fine portrait sculpture characteristic of the Mochica culture. The large ear plaques and the expression of arrogant dignity seem to indicate that this was a personage of importance. From the right wrist is slung what may be a pouch for carrying coca leaves. From the northern coastal area of Moche, most probably early centuries of the Christian era.

Mochica stirrup vase with painted decoration of stylised snails. The treatment is both observant and humorous. The Mochica culture is notable for a surprisingly varied naturalistic pottery, which gives us a better and more intimate picture of the people and their day-to-day life than of almost any other prehistoric culture.

Pariacaca and Huallallo Caruincho

'From the five eggs on Mt Condorcoto came forth five falcons, who turned into men. They were Pariacaca and his brothers. They went about doing many marvellous things. Among others, Pariacaca raised a storm and flood which destroyed Tamtanamka and his family.

'Pariacaca decided to try his strength against the rival god Huallallo Caruincho, and went in search of him. Pariacaca's strength lay in wind and rain and flood, Caruincho's in fire. Passing through a village called Huagaihusa in the guise of a poor man, he was not well received except by one young woman who brought him *chicha* to drink. He therefore destroyed the place by rain and flood, having first warned the woman and her family so that they escaped the disaster. He defeated Huallallo Caruincho and caused him to flee towards the Amazonian forest.

'But Caruincho only pretended to enter the forest. He turned himself into a bird and hid on a cliff of Mt Tacilluka. This time the five sons of Pariacaca swept the mountain with a storm and thunderbolts and Caruincho had to flee again, but he left behind an enormous serpent with two heads. This was changed to stone by Pariacaca. Closely pursued, Caruincho this time took refuge in the jungle. The sons of Pariacaca returned to Mt Llamallaku, where they called together all the peoples and established the cult of Pariacaca. Long afterwards when the Inca came to power they took over this cult and fostered it.'

The loves of Coniraya and Cavillaca

'There was a very ancient *huaca* called Coniraya, but whether his worship preceded or was more recent than that of Pariacaca is not known. He was worshipped under the name of Viracocha up to the time of the Spaniards.

'Coniraya Virachocha came to earth as a poor man dressed in rags and was held in contempt by all. He was the creator of all things and he was responsible for the system of agricultural terracing and irrigation. Coniraya fell in love with a beautiful goddess Cavillaca, who lived as a virgin. One day Cavillaca was sitting under a *lucma* tree and Coniraya turned himself into a beautiful bird and made some of his sperm into the likeness of a *lucma* fruit, which was eaten by Cavillaca. Of this she became pregnant while still a virgin. When the child was a year old she called an assembly of the principal *huacas* of the land to find who was its father. They all turned up in their best clothes, but none admitted the paternity of the child. She therefore let the child free, declaring that the man to whom it would crawl was the father. The child crawled to Coniraya, who sat in rags in the lowest seat. [This myth, the identification by an infant of its divine father, is found in the Chaco and among some tribes of the tropical forest.] Shamed and angered at having been made pregnant by so poor a creature, Cavillaca fled with the child to the sea coast at Pachacamac and, there entering the sea, both she and the child became rocks.

'She was followed by Coniraya, who enquired for news of her flight from the various animals he met on his way. He met a condor, who told

A stone sculpture from Manabi on the coast of Ecuador. The seat borne on a crouching beast is nearer to Mesoamerican art rather than to Andean, but some authorities maintain that there is a connection between the culture of the Manabí area c. A.D. 1000, and the later Chimu culture of the north coast of Peru.

him she was near and he would soon catch up with her. He therefore blessed the condor and gave it power to fly over mountains and ravines, to build its nest where it would not be disturbed, and to eat all things dead or neglected by their owners, and he gave it immunity. Then he met a fox, who told him that the goddess was far off and he would pursue her in vain. So he cursed the fox and caused it to emit a bad smell and be persecuted and disliked by all men. [According to Rigoberto Paredes the fox is still an animal of ill omen among the Indians of the Altiplano.] Next the lion told him that if he made haste he would soon overtake Cavillaca. So he blessed the lion saying: "You shall be respected and feared by all and I assign to you the office of punisher and executioner of evil doers. You may eat the llamas of sinners, and after your death you shall still be honoured; for when they kill you and take your skin they shall do so without cutting off the head, which they shall preserve with the teeth, and eyes shall be put in the sockets so as to appear to be still alive. Your feet shall remain hanging from the skin with the tail, and above all those who kill you shall wear your head over their own and your skin shall cover them. This shall they do at their principal festivals so that you shall receive honour from them. I further decree that he who would adorn himself with your skin must kill a llama on the occasion and then dance and sing with you on his back." [This is one of the very few passages bearing on the place of the feline in coastal ritual. There is a comparison with customs reported from Mojos and Chiquitos in the eastern lowlands of Bolivia.] He then met a falcon, who was also blessed. Lastly, parrots gave him bad news, and they were cursed, given loud voices which would put them in danger when feeding and were made hateful to all people.

'When he came to the coast Coniraya found that Cavillaca and her son were turned into stone. He met the two daughters of Pachacamac, who were guarded by a snake. Their mother, Urpi-huachac, was away visiting Cavillaca. Coniraya had intercourse with the elder daughter and wished to do the same with the other, but she turned into a pigeon and flew away. At that time there were no fishes in the sea but Urpi-huachac kept a few in a pond. Angry at her absence, Coniraya emptied them into the sea and from them all the fish in the sea have been born.'

Coniraya and Huayna Capac

'Coniraya went to Cuzco and took Huayna Capac [an Inca monarch] to Lake Titicaca. There he persuaded the king to send a commission to the lowlands of the west. The commission consisted of descendants of the condor, the falcon and the swallow. After five days one of the descendants of the swallow reached his journey's end. There he was given a coffer with instructions that it was to be opened only by the Inca in person. On the outskirts of Cuzco he could contain his curiosity no longer. On taking off the lid he was greatly surprised to see inside a radiantly beautiful woman with hair like gold and dressed as a queen. The vision lasted only an instant before it disappeared. When he reached Titicaca the Inca spared his life because he was descended from the swallow and sent him back to the lowlands. This time he brought the coffer intact into the hands of the Inca, but before the latter could open it Coniraya said to him: "Inca, we must both leave this world. I go to this other world and you shall go to another in the company of my sister. We shall not see each other again." When the coffer was opened an immediate splendour covered the world. The Inca determined not to return to Cuzco. "Here I will stay with my princess," he said, and sent back one of his relations to Cuzco in his place with the command: "Go thou to Cuzco and say that you are Huayna Capac." In that moment the Inca disappeared with his spouse, as did Coniraya.' Father Francisco de Avila: '*A Narrative of the Errors, False*

A male figure from Manabí on the coast of Ecuador, from the Manteño culture of the tenth century A.D. Ithyphallic representation is frequent in the smaller art forms of the pre-columbian cultures.

Right: The characteristic naturalism of Mochica ceramics is shown in this figure of a warrior of A.D. 1–900. Warriors appear to have enjoyed an eminent place in Mochica society.

A Mochica stirrup vessel in the shape of a man with two parrots perched on his head. Among the coastal myths there is a story of two brothers who escaped to a high mountain peak where they were sustained by two birds, parrots or macaws, who showed their true faces – of beautiful women – when they believed themselves unobserved. The younger brother captured the smaller bird, and the people of the province of Canaribamba, near Quito, are their descendants.

Gods, and other Superstitions and Diabolical Rites in which the Indians of the Provinces of Huarochiri, Mama and Chaclla lived in ancient times, and in which they even now live, to the great perdition of their souls'.

Deluge myths of the Coast

'In the province of Quito there is a district called Cañaribamba and the Indians are called Cañaris from the name of the country. These Indians say that at the time of the deluge two brothers escaped on a very high mountain peak there called Huacayñan. According to the fable, as the waters rose the mountain kept increasing in height so that the water could not reach them. When the deluge was over, since the foodstuffs which they had gathered there were finished, they sallied forth over the mountains and valleys seeking food and they built a tiny hut in which they lived,

supporting themselves on roots and herbs and suffering much from hunger and fatigue.

'One day, when they had been out to search for food, they returned to their hut and found there a meal prepared to eat and *chicha* to drink [a fermented drink brewed from maize, which is still the 'beer' of the country]. They did not know where it came from or who had prepared it and brought it there. This happened for about ten days, at the end of which they discussed together how to find out who was their benefactor in such great necessity. So the elder of the two remained hidden in the hut and saw two birds arrive of the kind called *aguaque* or *torito*, or in our tongue macaws. They came dressed like Cañaris, with long hair fastened in front as they now wear it. When they came to the hut the Indian in hiding saw the larger of the two take off her *lliclla* (which is the cloak the Indians wear) and begin to cook the food they had brought. When he saw they were beautiful and that they had the faces of women he came out of his hiding place and threw himself upon them. But when they saw the Indian they flew away in anger without leaving anything to eat that day. When the younger brother returned from the country, where he had been looking for food, and found nothing ready and prepared as on previous days he asked his brother the reason and the latter told him what had happened. So the younger brother determined to remain in hiding to see whether the birds returned.

'After three days the macaws returned and began to cook. When he saw that the time was ripe, after they had finished preparing the meal, he leapt to the door and closed it, shutting them inside the hut. The birds became very angry and while he grasped the smaller one the larger flew

A stealite cup of the Cupisnique (coastal Chavín) culture. It bears a carving of two were-jaguars each holding a snake-like body which loops across the base of the vessel.

Right: *Quipu* from Peru, showing the different types of knots. Like most pre-literate peoples, the Indians had excellent powers of memory, which they cultivated systematically and professionally. Their knowledge of past history and legend was embodied in epic poems and genealogical traditions, which were composed, memorised and handed down by experts, called *quiposcamayos*, who used *quipus* as mnemonic devices. *Quipus* were not a real substitute for writing, for they could not be 'read' by others. They were solely an aid to the trained memory of the men who made them, not an independent recording device. When under the Spanish dominion the expertise lapsed and the techniques were no longer passed from father to son, the lore embodied in the *quipas* was lost beyond recovery.

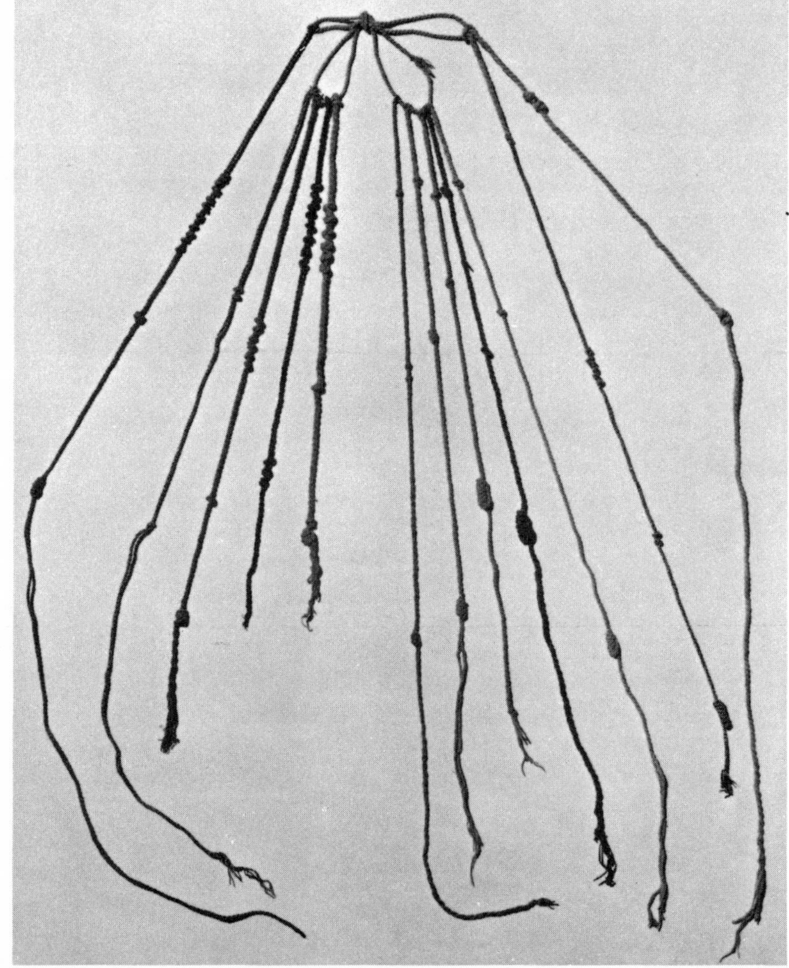

away. And they say that he had carnal relations with this smaller one and in due course begot by it six sons and daughters. They lived together for a long time on that mountain, supporting themselves on grain which they sowed, the seeds being brought by the macaw. They say that from these six sons and daughters born of the macaw, all the Cañaris are descended, and therefore they regard that mountain as a *huaca* and pay much veneration to the macaw, whose feathers they value highly for their festivals.

'In the country of Ancasmarca, which is five leagues from Cuzco in the province of Antisuyu, they have the following myth.

'A month before the coming of the deluge their sheep [i.e. llamas: there were no sheep before the Conquest] appeared very sad. They ate nothing during the day and all night long they gazed at the stars, until at last the shepherd in charge of them asked them what they were looking at. They replied that they were looking at the conjunction of the stars, which portended that the world was to be destroyed by water. When he heard this the shepherd consulted with his six sons and daughters and agreed with them that they should assemble all the food and livestock they could and go to the top of a high mountain called Ancasmarca. They say that as the waters kept on rising and covering the earth, the mountain kept getting higher, so that they never covered it. Afterwards, when the floods receded, the mountain also grew lower. And from those six children of the shepherd who escaped, the province of Cuyos was peopled again.

'These and similar follies they used to tell and still tell. To avoid prolixity I omit them. Besides the chief cause of this, which was their ignorance of God and their abandonment to idolatry and vices, it was also due to the

Mochica stirrup vase in the form of a seated figure with the head or mask of a falcon and playing a skin drum. This *may* represent an incident in ceremonial ritual. But despite the lively realism for which the Mochica ceramics are prized in all museums and private collections, it is not possible to obtain from them exact knowledge of beliefs and ritual.

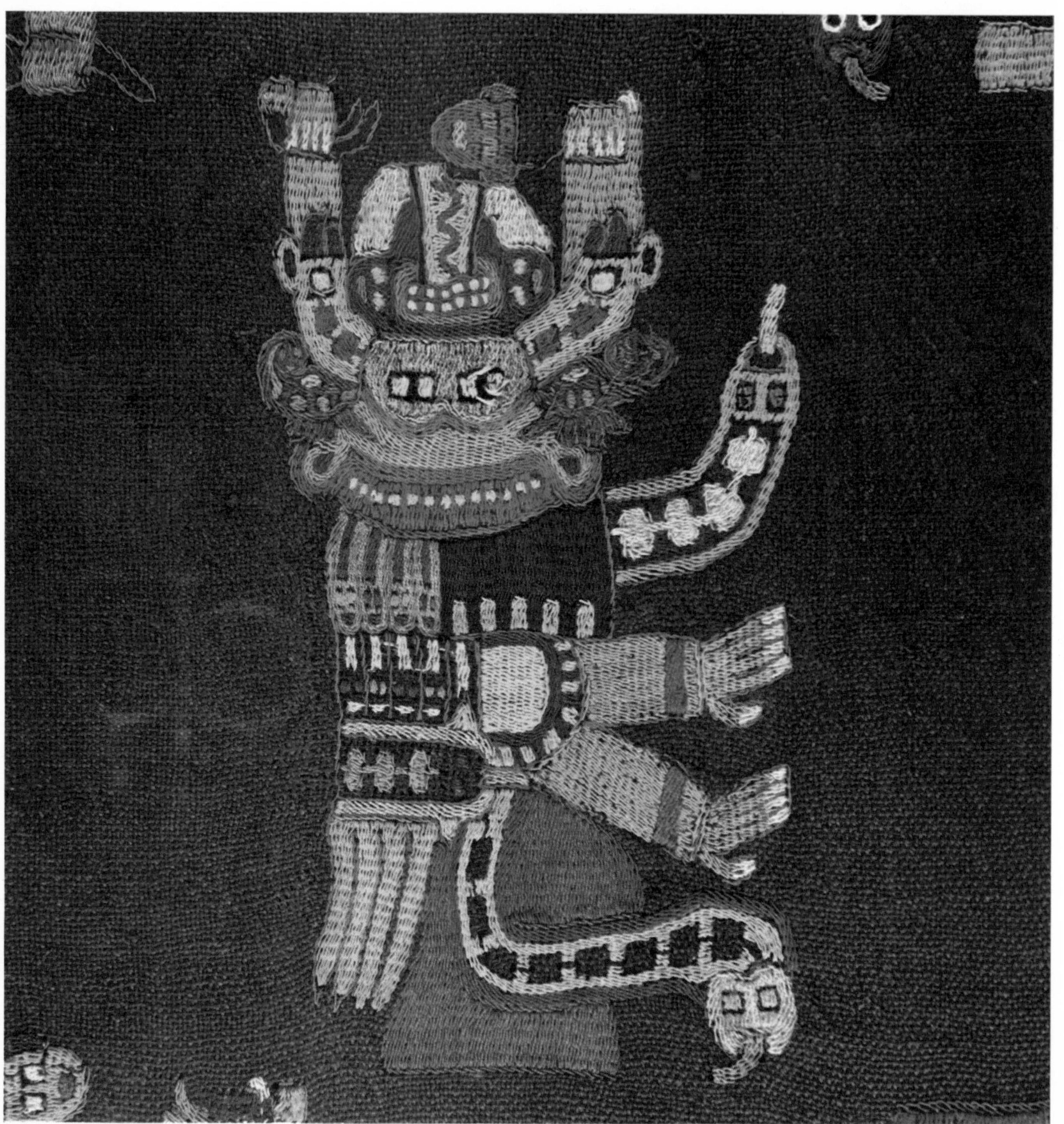

fact that they had no writing. If they had known how to read and write they would not have been addicted to such blind and stupid nonsense and fables. Nevertheless they made use of a very cunning method of counting by means of strands of wool with two knots and different coloured wool in the knots. By means of these *quipus*, as they call them, they understand so much that they can give an account of everything that has happened in this land for more than five hundred years. They had Indians who were trained and expert in the *quipus* and these handed down knowledge of the past from generation to generation, soaking it into the memory of those who were apprenticed to the task so that very little indeed was forgotten [see Introduction, p. 31]. In these *quipus*, which are rather like the strings used instead of rosary beads by old women in Spain, except that the *quipus* had small strands hanging from them, they kept so accurate a record of years and months that no mistake found its way into them. But the system was less well organised before the Inca Yupanqui who first extended the Inca sway beyond the Cuzco region.' Cristóbal de Molina of Cuzco: '*The Fables and Rites of the Yncas*'.

Left: Detail from Paracas woven textile, about 400 B.C. to A.D. 200. The colours in these very fine textiles recovered from burials have been preserved by the near-desert conditions in which they have lain. The iconography cannot be interpreted with assurance. This seems to be an example of the 'killer-whale' motif, which some scholars associate with the cult of a trophy-head deity.

A dog of the pointed-nosed, long muzzled type familiar to us from the art of pre-columbian South America. Both a household pet and a scavenger, the dog appears in numerous creation myths and was often offered as a sacrifice.

A creation myth from the Coast

'They say that at the beginning of the world there came from the north a man called Con, who was without bones. [Probably a supreme deity of pre-Inca mythology who was incorporated into the Inca pantheon.] He was quick and agile and journeyed far. He eased his path by lowering the mountains and raising the valleys simply by the power of his will and word, as became the child of the Sun, which he declared himself to be. He filled the land with men and women whom he created, and gave them much fruit and bread and the other necessities of life. Nevertheless, because some of them caused him annoyance, he turned the good land he had given them into dry and barren deserts, like those that are by the coast, and caused the rain to cease so that from that time it has not rained in those parts. He left them only the rivers in his clemency that they might support themselves by irrigation and toil.

'There next came Pachacamac (which means Creator), also son of the Sun and Moon, and he drove out Con and changed his men into monkeys, after which he created anew the men and women who exist today and furnished them with all things they have. In gratitude for such benefits, they made him their god and used to worship him at Pachacamac [the site, near the modern city of Lima, of one of the most renowned of pre-Inca temples and a centre of pilgrimage in pre-Inca times], until such time as the Christians came and cast him out of there, whereat they were much astonished. The temple of Pachacamac near Lima was most celebrated in those lands and was much frequented for worship and for its oracles, for the devil would appear and used to converse with the priests who lived there. The Spanish who went there with Hernando Pizarro after the capture of Atabaliba [Spanicised form of Atahuallpa, the last of the Inca monarchs] robbed it of all its gold and silver and then brought to an end the visions and oracles with the coming of the cross, a thing which caused the Indians horror and alarm.

'They say too that it rained so long a time that all the lowlands were submerged and all men were drowned except those who took refuge in caves high in the mountains whose narrow entries they blocked so that the water could not get in. Inside they stored many provisions and animals. When they no longer heard the rain they sent out two dogs, and as they came back clean but wet they knew that the waters had not subsided. They then sent out more dogs, and when these came back covered with dried mud they knew that the flood had ended and came forth to people the earth. Their greatest trouble and nuisance was caused by the many great snakes which had been bred by the wetness and slime of the deluge, but at length they killed them and were able to live in safety.

'They also believe in the end of the world. But they think it will be preceded by a great drought and that the Sun and Moon, which they worship, will be lost. And for that reason they howl and weep when there is an eclipse, especially an eclipse of the sun, thinking they are about to lose it and that this will be the end of themselves and the world.' Francisco López de Gomara: *Historia General de las Indias*, Ch. 122.

Pachacamac

The god Pachacamac was worshipped at a temple built on a small hill in a fertile coastal valley of the same name south of the present site of Lima. The cult was earlier than the Inca religion of the Sun in the coastal valleys of Peru and had great prestige, rivalling that of Tiahuanaco. A powerful priesthood was attached to the temple and the ritual included sacrifices and an oracle. Pachacamac was worshipped only at this one temple (according to Garcilaso) and it was a centre of pilgrimage from many parts

Left: One of the statues standing before the small rectangular temples built of roughly hewn stone slabs in the highland district of Huila, around San Agustin. Apart from these figures, Colombia has rather little of interest in the way of prehistoric architecture or stone sculpture. However, the rude but powerfully expressive vigour of these statues has made an enormous impact on modern observers. Often carved in the round, they are squat and powerful, square cut and formidable. They have round, staring and deep-set eyes, broad strong noses with wide nostrils and prominent feline fangs. They wear a loin cloth or a girdle and usually carry a mace or other object.

A family of Indians worshipping Pachacamac. The cult of this creator god pre-dated the Inca supremacy, but was incorporated by them in their cult of the sun. The temple of Pachacamac was in a valley south of the present city of Lima, and was a centre of pilgrimage. Devotion to this god persisted and he was later identified by the Indians with the Christian god. Drawing by Guamán Poma de Ayala.

of the country. Pilgrims brought gifts to the god and it was held to be an honour to be buried in the vicinity of the temple. A very large number of burials has been recovered by archaeologists in the present century. When the Inca kings extended their empire over the coastal regions of Peru they maintained the temple of Pachacamac, joining his cult with their own worship of the Sun. The temple was sacked by Pizarro.

Pachacamac seems to have had the functions elsewhere ascribed to Con and Viracocha of creator, preserver and culture hero. According to Cieza de León the name comes from *camac*, 'creator' and *pacha*, 'the world'. Garcilaso disagrees with this and asserts that *camac* means 'animator'. He says: 'If I were asked today what is the name of God in your language, I would reply "Pachacamac", for in the general language of Peru there is no other word which so well expresses the concept of God.' After the Christianisation of the region, memories of the prestige of Pachacamac survived and he was sometimes identified by the Indians with the new God of the Christians.

No more than tantalising hints of the Pachacamac mythological cycle have survived. Cieza de León gives the following account.

'Four leagues from the City of the Kings [Lima], travelling down the coast, is the valley of Pachacamac, which is very famous among these Indians. This valley is fruitful and pleasant and in it there was one of the grandest temples that is to be seen in this part of the world. They say that although the Incas built many other temples besides that of Cuzco and embellished them with great riches, none equalled that of Pachacamac. It was built on a small artificial hill made of adobes and soil. The temple had many doors and both they and the walls were painted with figures of fierce animals. Inside, where they placed the idol, were the priests, who pretended to much sanctity. When they performed the sacrifices before the multitude of people they went with their faces towards the doors and their backs to the idol, with eyes cast down and filled with great awe and trembling ... They say that they sacrificed many animals and some human beings before the statue of this demon, and that in their most solemn rituals it gave oracular replies which were accepted as truth. The priests were held in great reverence and the chiefs and caciques obeyed them in many things.

'The report goes that near the temple there used to be many rooms built for the pilgrims and that only the chiefs and pilgrims bringing gifts were considered worthy to be buried in the temple vicinity. At the annual festivals a great concourse of people assembled and amused themselves to the sound of music.

'It was the custom of the Inca to build temples to the Sun in all the territories they conquered. But when they came to Pachacamac, seeing the majesty and antiquity of this temple and the respect and devotion it aroused in all the neighbourhood, they thought it would be very difficult to abolish it and therefore agreed to its continuance on condition that a temple to the Sun was set aside on the loftiest part ... When the governor Don Francisco Pizarro (God permitting it) seized Atahuallpa in the province of Cajamarca, hearing wonderful reports of this temple and the quantity of riches that were there, he sent his brother Captain Hernando Pizarro with a force of Spaniards to seek it out and seize the gold that was there. And although Hernando made all diligence, it is common talk among the Indians that the chiefs and priests of the temple had already taken off more than four hundred loads of gold before he arrived. This has not reappeared and the Indians alive today don't know where it is ... From the time that Hernando Pizarro and the other Christians entered this temple the devil has had little power and the idols that were there have been destroyed. The buildings, including the temple to the Sun, have fallen into ruins and few people now remain in the district.'

Left: Wooden face with inset shell eyes, painted with red pigments and originally surmounted by human hair. Despite the crude carving these faces make a powerful impact even today. They may have been used with mummy bundles, or dressed as votive or tomb offerings. Inca period.

A bound mummy discovered in a burial tower in the region of Lake Titicaca.

Marginal, Forest and Southern Andean Peoples

Right: A gold pectoral of the Chibcha culture showing a figure wearing a fan-shaped headdress.

Mochica stirrup vase with relief modelling representing what may be either a warrior slaying an opponent or a scene of ritualistic sacrifice. The standing figure has a tail or pendant terminating in a snake's head and the face with prominent fangs may indicate a jaguar mask. On the other hand the 'defeated' figure also carries what seems to be an axe and this would indicate a scene of combat.

The Chibcha

The Chibcha territory lay in the upper valleys of the rivers Suárez and Chicamocha in what is now Colombia and consisted of three states, the southernmost of which was ruled by the Zipa; to the north was a state ruled by the Zaque, and the smaller realm of the Iraca lay beyond this. The Chibcha had a socio-political organisation more advanced than anything in South America other than the Inca empire and possibly the earlier coastal kingdoms of Peru. But their religion and mythology appear to have been little systematised and were far less adequately reported than those of the Inca.

The creation

In the beginning the world was in darkness and the light was shut up within a being called Chiminigagua, who was the creator of all things that are. The beginning of creation was the shining forth of the light he held inside him. He first created large black birds, which flew over the mountain peaks breathing forth light. Chiminigagua played an unimportant part in the cult and this, according to Pedro Simón in *Noticias historiales de las conquistas de tierra*, was explained by them as being because the Sun (Zuhé) and the Moon (Chía) were more beautiful and therefore more deserving of worship.

The origin of mankind is connected with the goddess Bachúe ('she of the large breasts') or Fura-chogue ('the beneficent female'). Shortly after the origin of light and the creation of the world there emerged from a mountain lake the goddess Bachúe with a three-year-old child. She went with him to the nearby village of Iguaque, north-east of Tunja, the capital of Zaque, and there she brought up the child. Years later when he came to maturity she married him and bore him four to six children at each birth. These and their offspring populated the land. After many generations Bachúe and her husband decided to leave the village. They retired to the mountains and, after exhorting the people to live together in peace and instructing them in the arts of civilisation and social organisation, re-entered the sacred lake as snakes. Bachúe was worshipped as a protector of agriculture and images of her and her child-husband were the objects of a cult.

A variant myth of the origin of mankind states that the first men were the cacique of Iraca and his nephew the cacique of Ramiquiri who lived when the world was still dark before the creation of light. Bored by the lack of other human beings in the world, they made small statues of yellow clay, which became men, and they cut figures from the stalks of *keck*, which became women. And from these descended the Chibcha peoples. As the world was still dark Ramiquiri, on the orders of Iraca, went up into the sky and turned himself into the Sun. Then Iraca followed him into the sky and became the Moon.

Right: A large grave-stone from the highlands of Colombia. The semi-circular headdress and accompanying necklace are familiar features of the art of the region, and suggest that statues like this were placed on the graves of chieftains or kings. The slit eyes are a feature which look back to primitive times; the headdress, on the other hand, is also found in the gold work of Lambayeque, and another theory postulates a lunar cult in the region.

A Chibcha *tunjo* c. A.D. 1400. These figures were cast from gold and are believed to have represented deceased Chibcha rulers. The Chibcha culture was probably the last in Colombia before the arrival of the Spaniards, when these figures were still being made.

Bochica

Bochica was recognised as the chief of the gods. Though invisible, he was worshipped under the image of the Sun, Zuhé or Xué ('Lord'). In addition, he was sometimes identified with the culture hero Nemterequeteba or Chimizapagua.

Chibchacum or Chicchechum, patron deity of the labourers and merchants, grew angry against the people of the Bogotá plateau and sent a deluge which flooded the land. In their distress they appealed to Bochica, who showed himself in the rainbow near the town of Soacha and sent the sun to dry the waters. With his staff he struck the rocks and opened a deep chasm through which the flood-waters receded. The great waterfall Tequendama was formed at this time and is a memorial of the event. Chibchacum went underground and since that time he has supported the world on his shoulders; before that the world had been supported on strong pillars in Lake Guayacán. When Chibchacum gets tired and changes his burden from one shoulder to the other he is often careless and that is the cause of earthquakes.

The culture hero

Nemterequeteba (sometimes identified with Bochica or the Sun) was a culture hero who came to the country of the Chibcha from the plains of Venezuela to the east. He came twenty ages of seventy years each before the Spanish Conquest. One tradition claims that he entered in the Iraca region, another that he came to the Bacatá region at Pasca in the south. He traversed the Zipa country and then by Muequetá to Cota, where he lived in a cave and had to be protected by a parapet from the large crowds who flocked to hear his preaching. From there he went north to Guane, south through Tunja and east to Gameza and Sugamixi, where he organised a cult, appointed a high priest and then disappeared from view. He was represented as an old man with long hair and a beard down to his girdle. He taught chastity, sobriety, good social order and the arts of spinning, weaving and painting textiles.

Nemterequeteba was also called Sugumonxe or Sugunsúa (the person who disappears) and Chimizapagua (the messenger of Chiminigagua), though records indicate some doubt whether these were two culture heroes or one.

Huitaca

Huitaca was the goddess of indulgence, drunkenness and licence. In myth she was described as a beautiful woman who came after Nemterequeteba and whose teachings were the opposite of his. She was sometimes represented as the wife of Bochica, sometimes as the Moon (Chía), wife of the Sun. Some versions of her myth tell how she was converted by Bochica (or by Chiminigagua or by Nemterequeteba) either into an owl or into the Moon).

The after-life

The Chibcha believed that the soul leaves the body at death and travels to the kingdom of the dead at the centre of the earth through gorges of yellow and black soil. As in some other mythologies, the souls have to first cross a wide river to reach the underworld – in this case they ford the river in boats made from spiders' webs. In the other world each district has its own place and every person upon entering the world of the dead finds a site ready for him to cultivate.

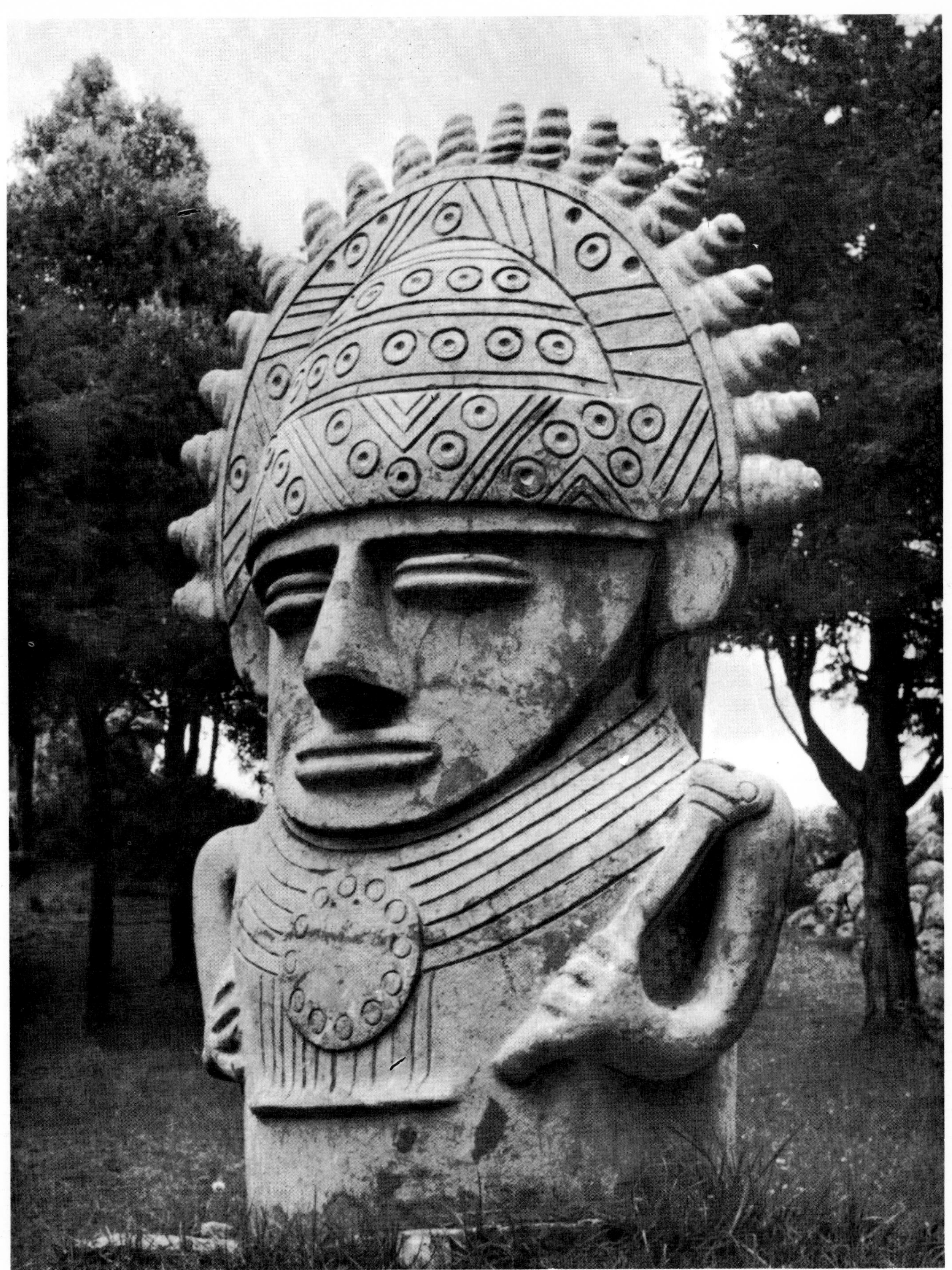

Divine kingship

The Chibcha tradition also contained a number of myths which, like the myths of Inca origins, supported the institution of divine kingship and connected the dynasties with the gods. The following are examples.

When Nemterequeteba (or Bochica) came to Sugamixi, Nompanem was Iraca. He received Bochica with honour and Bochica dictated the laws, founded the ritual, taught a way of life and introduced the industrial arts. He was succeeded by Firavitoba, husband of his sister. In his time reigned the High Priest Idacanzas, who originated the priestly dynasty.

Hunsahua was the most powerful chief of Tunja, uniting it with Ramiquiri and founding the dynasty of the Zaque. He fell in love with his own sister. The mother refused to countenance the match and therefore the two fled to Chipatae and lived as husband and wife. They returned to the maternal home and the mother in indignation attacked her daughter with the stick used for stirring *chicha*. The girl avoided the blow. The measure of *chicha* was upset and formed a lake north of the city of Tunja. The two lovers then left for the south, where at Susa their child was born. The child was turned to stone. The parents in despair wandered south-

wards until they came to the waterfall Tequendama on the frontier. Here they determined to settle, but were themselves turned to stone in the middle of the river.

Lake Guatavita was the site of a famous temple. It was said that the deity who inhabited the lake used from time to time to come to the surface in the form of a serpent to receive the offerings brought to the shrine. A certain chief of Guatavita discovered his favourite wife was unfaithful. He had her lover impaled and caused her to eat his private parts. He had songs sung publicly about the matter in order to shame her. Overcome by shame, she threw herself with her infant daughter into the lake. The chief, who was still fond of her, ordered the principal magician to bring mother and daughter back from the lake. The chief magician made a ritual sacrifice, threw heated stones into the lake and dived in after them. He then returned and told the cacique that he had found his wife and the child alive at the bottom of the lake living in an enchanted palace and tending the dragon. He was sent back again to bring them up and returned with the little girl, dead and blind. The dragon had eaten out her eyes. The supposed custom of throwing the lavish offerings of gold into the lake led in time to its identification with the El Dorado of legend.

Characteristically stylised mask in red ceramic from the Chibcha Indians of Guatavita in Colombia. The general shape has affinities with a common Mexican and Central American style. But the rectilinear type of pattern and the stylisation is typical of the regions north of Peru.

The Araucanians

The Araucanians of Chile are renowned for having put up the most obstinate resistance first to Inca and later to Spanish domination. Their folklore and legend were influenced both by Inca (perhaps also by pre-Inca) tradition and by Christian teaching. It is virtually impossible to determine what part of the reported mythology belongs to the original strata of belief. *Mitos y Supersticiones*, by Julio Vicuña Cifuentes, a collection gathered from oral tradition, consists almost entirely of folk stories centred for the most part on magic and superstition.

The Araucanians believed in a Supreme Being called Guinechén ('master of men') or Guinemapun ('master of the land'), who controlled the forces of nature and gave life to men and animals. There was also a cult of Pillan, to whom were attributed natural catastrophes such as storms, floods, volcanic eruptions, and perhaps epidemics and the care of crops. The forces of evil, impersonal and personal, under the name Guecufü, were the subject of elaborate deterrent magical practices.

Myth of the deluge

Many centuries ago there was a deluge. The people took refuge from the rising waters on a high peak called Tenten, the animals assembled on another peak, Caicai. The flood was caused by the evil power Guecufü. But in order to frustrate him, the higher the waters rose the higher Guinechén raised the mountains. Those who survived the flood were the ancestors of the Araucanians. According to another version the flood was caused by strife between two serpents, Tenten and Caicai, and the higher Caicai raised the waters, the higher Tenten raised the mountains thus saving the people and animals from drowning. The human beings who had taken refuge on one of the two mountains were then transformed into animals, fishes, birds, and so forth.

Mochica stirrup vase representing a human figure playing a drum. The mutilated nostrils and lips and the cuts on either side of the mouth would seem to indicate some ceremonial punishment, perhaps of a captured enemy.

Araucanian folklore

The following stories are typical of surviving folklore.

The Manta or Huecú is a cuttlefish that lives in deep lakes, cries and causes the water to boil. It has the appearance of the spread out hide of an ox (or of a goat). The edges are covered with innumerable eyes and it has four enormous eyes in the part which corresponds to the head. When any person or animal enters the water it rises to the surface, drags them down and devours them. If it has intercourse with animals, their offspring are monsters. Sometimes it suns itself on the banks; it is dangerous because it will drag a person back into the water with it. In order to kill it you must throw it branches of a bush called in Chile *quisco*, which is covered with spines.

There is also a cuttlefish called Trelque-huecuve, whose tentacles end in hooves. It will seize and squeeze to death anything which comes within its reach.

The Huallepén or Guallipén is an amphibious animal about thirty inches high, with the head of a calf and the body of a sheep. It is fierce and strong. It covers both sheep and cows, taking them by surprise, and begets on them offspring of the same type as the mother; but the feet and sometimes the muzzle are deformed. If a pregnant woman sees a Huallepén or hears it bellowing, or dreams of one on three successive nights, her child will be deformed. The same happens if she sees an animal begotten by a Huallepén. According to another version the Huallepén is the offspring of a sheep and a bull with twisted hooves. It is very ugly and is an animal of ill omen.

The peoples of the far south

The habitat of the Yahgan is the mountainous archipelago of Tierra del Fuego, which is the most southerly tip of the Andean mountain chains. They are people of whom Charles Darwin stated that they were lacking any religious concept. Later investigation has shown that they believe in a Supreme Being Watauineiwa ('the Most Ancient One'), called also 'The Powerful, The Most High', and commonly prayed to under the title 'My Father'. He is a benevolent god, who has no body but lives above the heavens. He is not conceived as a creator, but as the giver and sustainer of life. He is the protector of the social and moral code. In rites of mourning complaints are addressed to Watauineiwa for having allowed the person to die. The Alacaluf believe that the Supreme Being Xolas puts the soul into each new-born baby and that on a man's death his soul is reabsorbed by Xolas. The Yahgan believe that on death the spirits of the dead (*koshpik*) fly away to the east. Watauineiwa features importantly in initiation ceremonies but is not the centre of a cycle of myth.

The cosmological mythology includes a deluge and a culture hero. The origin of civilisation is explained by the myth of two brothers, Yoalox, and their sister. The elder brother was stupid and the younger brother, the culture hero, was clever. This myth functions importantly during the initiation ceremony, called *ciexaus*.

The Yahgan have no cult of ancestors but a certain fear of the dead, and their *kina* rite has analogies with ghost rituals of other tribes such as the Alacaluf. Women are excluded from the *kina* rituals and an elaborate myth is told in explanation of this practice, envisaging an earlier time when the women were the masters and in order to maintain their supremacy wore spirit masks which hoodwinked the men. The myth tells how the deception was discovered and all the women killed except one young child. In the ceremonies the men wear elaborate spirit masks and threaten the women with penalties if they are not submissive.

The Ona, who inhabit Tierra del Fuego, believe in a Supreme Being Temaukel, who is without body, wife or children, who has always existed and sustains the universe and the socio-moral code. He lives above the stars, is invisible, benevolent and the recipient of individual prayers in time of trouble. Souls (*kaspi*) go to the place of Temaukel after death.

The first man, Kenos, was the agent of Temaukel in bringing civilisation and culture to mankind. The myth also tells of the early ancestors of the Ona, who turned into rivers, mountains and lakes; of a hunter-hero Kwanyip who overcame the spirit of evil, Chenuke, and who waged perpetual war against a giant black and invisible cannibal who ranged the hills. The Ona initiations rite *kloketen*, like the Yahgan *kina*, exclusively for men, was associated with a myth featuring the conquest of superiority by the men after a period when women were dominant. The myth is in the form of a victory of the sun over the moon.

No mythology is recorded of the Chono and Alacaluf of southern Chile and information from the Tehuelcho and Puelcho tribes of the Patagonian pampas is very sparse. Among the Puelcho the Sun and Moon were brothers. The Sun, the elder of the two, was the intelligent one and beneficent to man. They believed in a Supreme Being, whose name has been very variously reported, and in a supreme spirit of evil sometimes called Ellal. Their mythology is said to have included a story of a flood, after which the world was populated by men issuing from mountain caves. The Tehuelcho had a Supreme Being, sometimes reported by the name Guayavacuni, and a good spirit, who may or may not have been identified with him and who created the tribes of men at a hill called God's Hill and dispersed them from there. Alternatively Heller, son of the Sun, is reported as creator of men and bringer of civilisation.

Mochica whistling jar of red ceramic representing a house or shelter within which are a man and suckling mother. Birds are perched on the corners of the roof, and the roof tiles are decorated with relief modelling.

The Tupari

In 1948 a young Swiss ethnologist, Franz Caspar, visited the Tupari Indians, a primitive Stone Age people living up the Rio Branco in the Mato Grosso region of Brazil, and remained with them for four months as a guest-member of the tribe. The author, who had known him in La Paz, happened to be in Guayaramerín on the Rio Mamoré when he came out, and travelled with him overland to Cachuela Esperanza. In his book *Tupari* Caspar has given a brief account of what he learnt, despite severe linguistic difficulties which attended the exchange of ideas on other than practical matters, about their beliefs concerning the spirits of heaven and the origins of man and concerning the souls of the dead.

The spirits of heaven

Once upon a time no men were yet on earth and no *kiad-pod* in heaven. There was only a big block of rock, beautiful and smooth and shining. Now this block of stone was a woman. One day it split and brought forth a man amid streams of blood. This was Valedjád. And again the rock split and brought forth a second man. His name was Vab. Both were magicians. But they had no wives, so they made themselves stone axes and cut down two trees. They then killed an agouti, took out its front teeth and from them each carved himself a woman.

Thus too did the other primitive magicians arise – the *vamoa-pod*, some from water and others from the earth.

Valedjád was a wicked magician. He very often grew angry and whenever he did it rained. So he flooded the whole land and many *vamoa-pod* perished. The survivors racked their brains to think how they could rid themselves of Valedjád. One of the primitive magicians, Arkoanyó, hid in a tree and poured liquid beeswax on Valedjád as he went past. This sealed up his eyes, nostrils and fingers so that he could do no more mischief. And then they wanted to remove him far, far away. Many birds tried to pick him up and carry him off. But they were all too small. At last they found a large bird which was strong enough. He seized Valedjád and flew with him far away to the north. There he put him down and there to this day Valedjád lives in a stone hut. And when he becomes angry we have rain here.

Another evil magician was called Aunyain-á. He had great tusks like a boar and used to eat the children of his neighbours. These neighbours at last decided to escape from this monster and leave the earth. One day Aunyain-à went into the forest to shoot a mutum fowl and while he was away they climbed up a creeper which hung from the sky down to the earth. At that time the sky was not as far up as it is today, but hung down quite near the earth.

When Aunyain-á came back from the hunt he could no longer find his neighbours. He asked a parrot where they had gone. The parrot sent him to the river, but Aunyain-á found no traces in the sand. Then the parrot laughed him to scorn and said that all his neighbours had climbed up into the sky. Aunyain-á grew furious and tried to shoot the parrot, but he did not hit him.

Then Aunyain-á seized the creeper in order to overtake the fugitives. But the parrot quickly flew up high and began to gnaw through the creeper. Aunyain-á plunged down to the ground and lay there shattered. From his arms and legs there grew caymans and iguanas and from his fingers and toes little lizards of many kinds. The vultures ate the rest of him. Since that time the primitive magicians live up in heaven. A few of them still live on the earth but very far away from here.

Many of the *kiad-pod* look like men but they have their peculiarities.

Right: Terracotta figurine with incised decoration and high conical headdress, from the Paracas peninsula. The statue gives some idea of the racial types who inhabited the southern and central coast of Peru about 500 B.C. At that time the Paracas people were making some of the finest pottery and textiles ever produced in South America.

A street in Cuzco surviving from Inca times. The remarkable use of cut stone blocks is plainly seen and, on the lintel, two serpents. According to Guamán Poma de Ayala the people of this period believed that snakes (and foxes) had the power to absorb evil, drawing it away from man. The snakes seen here were probably a device to protect the family who lived there.

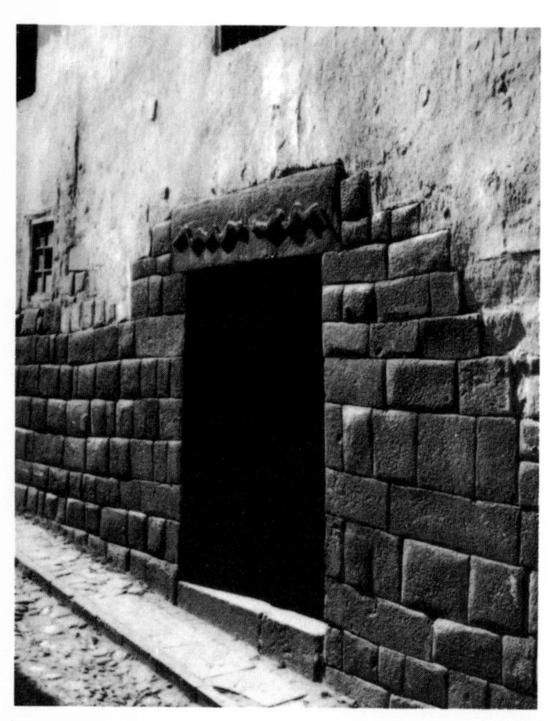

One talks through his nose, another has a twisted mouth and a third, Vamoá-togá-togá, has a navel a span long. And none of them has any hair on the back of his head.

But there were some primitive magicians in this heaven who had animal form. There was a sapajou monkey, a black monkey, a howler monkey and many others. They too were proper magicians, said the Indians.

'They can't talk and sing like men. And when here in the *maloca* [village] the magicians sniff tobacco and *aimpeh*, then the powder also goes up into the noses of those monkeys in heaven: they sneeze and come down from heaven to take part in Vaitó's magic ceremonies.

'Ordinary people cannot see these dwellers in heaven. Only our magicians have dealings with them during the raising of spirits. Then the *kiad-pod* come into the *maloca* and the souls of our magicians go to heaven and wander through the most distant places of the world. There they receive from the spirits mysterious yellow grains, the *pagab*. With the *pagab* the magicians bewitch and kill their enemies.'

The origins of man

About their own origins the Tupari said:

'Long ago there were on earth no Tupari or other men. Our ancestors lived under the ground where the sun never shines. They suffered great hunger, for they had nothing to eat but wretched palm fruits. One night they discovered a hole in the earth and climbed out. This was not far from the tent of the two primeval magicians Aroteh and Tovapod. There they found peanuts and maize. They ate some and next morning they vanished again into the hole between the stones from which they had emerged. This they did night after night. Aroteh and Tovapod believed that it was the agoutis which were stealing their crops, but one morning they saw the tracks of men and found the holes through which they used to creep out. With a long pole they dug about in the hole and prised out the stones. Then men began to stream out in great hordes until the primeval magicians closed up the hole again.

But the men were ugly to look upon. They had long canine teeth like those of wild boars and between their fingers and toes the flesh was webbed like a duck's. Aroteh and Tovapod snapped off their tusks and shaped their hands and feet. Since then men have no longer had long tusks or webs but beautiful teeth and fingers and toes.

Many men remained in the earth. They are called *kinno* and still live there. One day, when all the people of the earth have died, the *kinno* will come out of the ground and live here.

But the men whom Aroteh had let out of the earth did not all find room in the same place. We Tupari remained here, the others wandered far away in all directions. They are our neighbours: the Arikapú, Yabutí, Makuráp, Aruá, and all the other tribes.

The souls of the dead

When a Tupari dies, then the pupils of his eyes leave him and change into a *pabid*. The *pabid* does not walk the earth like living men but his path to the realm of the dead leads over the backs of two great crocodiles and two giant snakes, a male and a female. Ordinary folk cannot see these crocodiles; only the magicians see them in their dreams. Often the snakes rear up towards the sky and when it rains they become visible to everybody; that is the rainbow. The *pabid*, then, strides over the backs of the snakes and the crocodiles to the village of the dead. He also passes two huge jaguars who frighten him with their roars, but who cannot do anything to him. At last the dead man reaches his new home, which lies on the big river Mani-mani. But he sees nothing of all this, for his eyes are still closed. He is received by two fat worms, a male and a female. They bore a hole in his belly and eat all his intestines. Then they crawl out again.

Now comes Patobkia, the head magician and chief of the *maloca* of the dead. He sprinkles stinging pepper juice into the newcomer's eyes and now for the first time the *pabid* sees where he has come to. In astonishment he looks about him and sees nothing but strangers. They all have hollow bellies because the worms have eaten their bowels and their teeth are nothing but short stumps. Sadly he asks Patobkia: 'Where am I and who are all these people?' 'These are your parents! These are your brothers and sisters!' laughs Patobkia scornfully. But this is a cruel lie. The *pabid* sees neither parents nor brothers and sisters but only strange beings, staring dully at him. 'Then I really have died and gone to the *pabid*,' says the dead man. And with horror he notices that he too has only short stumps left for teeth and no bowels. Then Patobkia hands him a bowl of *chicha*. The new *pabid* drinks it and Patobkia leads him further into the village of the dead. There an old couple of giant primeval magicians await the newcomer. If he is a man he must in full view of everyone copulate with the ancient giantess Vaugh'eh, but if the *pabid* is a woman she must give herself to old Mpokálero ... Later the *pabid* no longer have intercourse in the usual human manner but the men breathe on a bundle of leaves and throw it at the backs of the women and in this way they become pregnant and bear children.

The *pabid* live in large, round huts; they have no hammocks but sleep standing up in the huts. They lean against the supporting posts and cover their eyes with their arms. They clear no woods and plant no fields. Patobkia does all this with a magic gesture of his hand and with his magic breath.

The *chicha* which the *pabid* women brew from peanuts does not ferment, so the dead men cannot get drunk. However, they frequently sing and dance in their full array of feathers, and the Tupari's magicians hear their songs when they visit the *pabids*' village in their dreams. If ever a *pabid*

Right: Man of the Waura tribe preparing special feathers, which he keeps in a rolled fibre mat. These peoples attached much importance to the various spirits of good and evil, and each tribe or group evolved magical practices to try to control them.

Suyá Indians with bundles of timbó which have been crushed and will be used to poison a nearby lake. Later the Indians will return to collect the dead fish floating on the surface.

falls ill he eats papaws. The *pabid's* papaws are much bigger and sweeter than those of the living and make sick men well and old men young again.

In addition to the *pabid* the Tupari believe that the dead have a second ghostly existence in the region of the body. Caspar reports as follows:

'When someone dies and the pupils of his eyes go off to the *pabid*, then we bury him in the hut or where we have burnt down an old hut. Immediately the heart begins to grow in the dead man's body and after a few days it is as big as the head of a child. Inside the heart springs up a little man who grows bigger and bigger and bursts open the heart, just as a bird breaks its shell. This is the *ki-apoga-pod*. But he cannot crawl out of the ground and weeps with hunger and thirst. The relatives of the dead man therefore go hunting. When they come back they hold three sessions of snuff-taking with the magicians. The chief magician draws the *ki-apoga-pod* from the ground, cleans him and shapes his face and limbs, for when he comes out of the ground he is still unformed clay. Then the magician gives him something to eat and drink and lets him loose in the air. Up there the *ki-apoga-pod* live.

'But if the dead man was a magician, then his *apoga-pod* does not float away to those distant places but stays in the *maloca*. There the souls of the dead magicians eat our food and drink our *chicha*. Down from the dome of the hut they cast a spell on us at night and produce our dreams. The souls of the dead wives of the magicians also hover up there.'

A typical mummy bundle from Peru, elaborately tied up with fibre rope. Bodies for burial – the so-called 'mummies' – were carefully wrapped in many layers of cloth with sand between, and the whole was roped into a 'bundle'. Inside it were often placed mortuary gifts of pottery, fine robes, utensils, costume jewellery, toys, and so forth. The bundles have been found buried in extensive cemeteries, preserved by the hot dry atmosphere of the coastal desert.

The Chaco tribes

The Chaco, said to be derived from a Quechua word meaning 'hunting ground', is a name loosely applied to the large plain which extends from the edge of the Mato Grosso region to the Argentine pampas. The greater part of the territory is now divided between Bolivia and Paraguay. The early mythology of the Chaco tribes is very unevenly reported. Such records as there are point in the direction of a lively, not to say exuberant, fancy but have the appearance rather of a colourful and diversified folklore than any systematised mythology.

The reports of missionaries from the seventeenth century give no clear evidence of belief in a Supreme Being, although the Chamacoco had a supreme goddess who was the Mother of all spirits (*guara*), controlled the sun and saw that men had water. The Mocobi had a benevolent spirit Cotaá, invisible in the sky, who made the earth, maintained the sun, moon and stars in their courses and made the earth fruitful. It is, in such cases, particularly difficult to determine how far such attributes reflect missionary teaching or to what extent they belonged to indigenous belief.

The sun, moon and certain constellations were often personified and made the subjects of folk tales. The Pleiades were called 'Grandfather', their annual disappearance being attributed to illness and their reappearance hailed with rejoicing. In some myths of the Pilaga the rainbow was thought to kidnap children and kill people by its tongue. Among most tribes of the Chaco the sun was female and the moon male. The typical story of two brothers, one clever and successful the other stupid and blundering, the sort of story which is found throughout South America, was among the Chamacoco and Mataco told of the Sun and Moon. The Sun was the successful brother and the Moon was his unsuccessful twin. Many stories were told illustrating these qualities.

The thunderbolt – or the lightning – was a hairy old woman who fell to the earth during a storm and could only return to the sky in the smoke of a fire. The rain was produced by a red ant-eater, or by a female spirit called Kasogonaga hanging in the sky, or by thunderbirds from a celestial jar. Eclipses were thought by some to be caused by an attack of the celestial jaguar on the Sun or Moon. The Lule thought that a large bird was hiding the heavenly body with its wings. The Lule attributed all illnesses to a mountain grub of imaginary form called Ayacua, armed with bow and stone-tipped arrows. According to the folklore of several tribes there was once an enormous tree connecting earth with the sky and men used to climb the tree in order to reach the celestial hunting-grounds. The tree was burnt by a vengeful woman, and the men who were caught in the sky were changed into stars.

Creation

Creation stories were no less various and unorganised. The Lengua attributed the creation of the world to a gigantic beetle, which also created the spirits and produced the first man and woman (originally stuck together) from particles of soil he threw away. The Mbaya told that men were hatched from eggs laid by a large bird on the top of a mountain; or they came from a large cave in the north; or they first lived underground and were released by a dog. The Chamacoco said that men lived underground and reached the surface by a rope made from the fibre of a plant named caraguata. The first to come were very tiny. There was little food on the earth to support them, so when a few had come to the surface a dog gnawed through the cord. Later the Chamacoco and other peoples climbed to the sky by an enormous tree trunk and they all fell to earth again. That is why the Chamacoco are now so few. Alternatively the Chamacoco were at first shut up inside a quebracho tree so huge that they could play ball in it. A man came and split the trunk and let them out. According to the Matado and Toba, women came down from the sky by a rope in order to steal the food of the men, who were at that time animals. The rope was cut by a bird and the women had to remain. The Tereno tradition is that two supernatural brothers were hunting birds and came to a deep crevasse; from this hole the Tereno came, shivering with cold and blinded by the sun.

The destruction of the world and culture heroes

There are myths of a deluge, caused by a menstruating girl; a destruction of the world by cold; a destruction by fire caused by the fall of the sun. There are numerous folk tales of the origin of fire. It was the property of the thunderbirds, and men learnt its uses when they tasted snails which had been roasted by the birds. The Chamacoco attributed it to a culture hero Carancho, who had received it from the owl.

The culture hero Carancho, sometimes identified with the hawk, features in the folk myth of several tribes. He is clever and benevolent. In

The lives and beliefs of the Indians of the Mato Grosso are heavily influenced by the ever-present moisture of the tropical rain-forest. The scene shown here is typical of the region, where both the need for food and methods of communication have been satisfied by the Indians' adaptation to an exacting environment.

many stories he is accompanied by the stupid or mischievous fox in adventures analogous to the 'two brothers' stories which are a common theme of South American folklore. Other culture heroes were Peritalnik, Asin (a bald, large-bellied warrior who produced food from under his robe), the aquatic bird Nedamik. The figure of the 'trickster' is a common feature; he is a vainglorious, boastful and malicious individual, but easily tricked in his turn. A little man called Kosodot taught men to hunt, his wife Kopilitara for her part taught women the art of pottery, and weaving was learned from the Spider.

Mythical trees

It is a matter for no surprise that peoples whose ecology was closely linked with the semi-tropical forest had many folk legends of trees, in addition to the mythical trees which connected the earth with the sky. The following are examples.

There is a rare fern or lliana called Yobec Mapic which is burned and the ashes used as salt. It is told that the god Cotaá created a miraculous tree which would yield food and drink to the hungry people. The mischievous spirit Neepec tipped over it a pitcher filled with tears and spoiled the taste. When the god Cotaá returned and saw what was done, he turned the damage into good and explained that the salty taste might serve for seasoning meat dishes.

There is a large and beautiful tree called Timbo whose crest is like a huge umbrella. Its wood is used for canoes and pirogues. Its fruit is a black berry shaped like an ear, and for this reason the tree is called 'black ear'. The Guaraní say that in the past a famous chief Saguaa had a daughter Tacuareé of whom he was very fond. Tacuareé fell in love with a distant chief of another tribe and left her father to travel through the forest to join her lover. Saguaa set out to follow her and constantly put his ear to the ground in the attempt to hear her steps across the forest. At last, unable to travel any farther, he collapsed in exhaustion and lay with his ear still glued to the ground. The ear put down roots and from them grew the Timbo tree.

The Matacos have a different version. They tell that when the first strangers invaded the territories of the Chaco the daughter of a chieftain, the most beautiful woman in the land, put herself at the head of the repelling forces. Her father remained at home and, overcome by anxiety, constantly put his ear to the ground listening for the sounds of the returning force. But it never did return and the chief at last died with his ear still to the ground. Thence grew the Timbo tree.

The Chane have a story which seems to carry echoes of the Tree of Life theme which was common in the Guianas. In former times there was a huge yuachan tree in which swam fish, which the men of old times used to shoot. They were not allowed to kill the larger ones but the Trickster, true to character, disregarded this prohibition and shot a large dorado. This caused the earth to be flooded. But the Trickster fortunatly put an end to the flood by opening up with his spear a passage through which the waters were able to flow into the sea.

The foregoing are samples of material which has been reported in some abundance, together with animal stories and some legends of tribal chieftains. Most of the material is on the borders between folk story and myth. The coexistence of various alternative stories on the same theme has led to the supposition that much of the folklore of the Chaco tribes was imported from other cultural centres – particularly the Aymará and Quechua. This would also account in part for its variety and its fragmentary and unsystematised state.

Right: Man of the Karaja tribe wearing a special feather headdress used during a boy's initiation. Crisis rituals played an important part in both personal and social life among the Marginal and Tropical Forest peoples.

Engraving of a puma from the Atacama desert. Behind it is what may be a demon figure or the figure of a magician, carved on a stone of what is believed to be a cult site of great antiquity.

Some Riddles of South American Myth

Right: Gold plaque from the north coast of Peru, Chimu or Lambayeque; 'Urbanist' period, eleventh to twelfth centuries. It may represent the sun with rays spreading outward from the head. In accordance with convention, the rays terminate in a snake's head surmounted by a human head with conical headdress.

A specimen of cotton embroidery from the Paracas peninsula. Discovered by J. C. Tello in 1925, the Paracas graves have yielded a wealth of beautiful textiles which have strong suggestions of deities and spirits. But without definite knowledge nothing can be stated, and further doubt on the idea is cast by the skill of the Paracas weavers in repeating as a formal design the most complicated figures.

Jaguar cults

Archaeological evidence tells overwhelmingly in support of a widespread religion based on a feline deity – probably a jaguar or mountain cat – from the Cultist period (*c.* 850 B.C.) onwards. The feline motif dominated in the Chavín culture and is common on early Paracas textiles. Wendell C. Bennett and Junius Bird in their *Andean Culture History* call the feline design the 'primary symbol of the [Chavín] religion'; and in the later, Experimental Period (*c.* 400 B.C.) through to the Mastercraftsman Period (*c.* A.D. 0-900) – in the Nazca and Mochica styles for example – they say that 'the feline is the most universal religious figure represented'. J. Alden Mason in his *Ancient Civilisations of Peru* states that in the Cultist period: 'A religious cult in which a feline deity, puma or jaguar, played the most prominent role was the common element, for otherwise the small villages had no political bond and the local cultural variations from valley to valley were considerable'. G.H.S. Bushnell commits himself to the statement that the frequency of feline features in the carvings 'makes it virtually certain that the jaguar was a very powerful god, perhaps the most powerful of all'. Such is the voice of archaeology. And some of the representations of the jaguar motif make so strong an impact even now that it is difficult not to suppose that they had a profound religious significance. Yet in the absence of written records the supposition of an organised religion featuring a jaguar-god must remain speculative.

Some writers have derived the name 'Titicaca' from the Aymará *titi*, a general term for a feline. But this etymology is hardly more convincing than the derivation, given for example by Garcilaso, from the Quechua word *titi*, which means 'lead'. In the early and classical periods of Tiahuanaco art the head of the puma (South American lion) was a frequent motif. There have been found at Tiahuanaco zoomorphic stone figures, called locally *Chacha-puma* or Lion-man, representing a man with a feline head, often with an expression of exaggerated ferocity. These are usually about three feet high and sometimes carry a cudgel in the right hand and a human head in the left. Examples of these figures may be seen in the Tiahuanaco Museum at La Paz.

Garcilaso says that the Indians of the Bolivian Altiplano worshipped the tiger and the lion among many other animals during the stage of naturalistic animism, and that if they met one of these animals (or a bear) they would offer no resistance but fall down before it. Cieza de León and Bernal Diez de Casillo mention sacrifical worship of the tiger after the fall of the Inca, the former as far north as Quito. Polo de Ondegardo speaks of forest Indians who worshipped a star called Chuquichinchay, which he says 'is a tiger in whose charge are the tigers, bears and lions'. José de Arriaga states that the Devil appeared to the native sorcerers in the form of a lion or tiger. Guamán Poma de Ayala asserts that in very early times

the Yarohuillka had a complete hierarchy based on the puma, and Juan de Betanzos mentions a city which was called 'Body of the Lion' and its inhabitants the members. In his *Descripción biográfica, histórica y estadística de Bolivia* Alcides d'Orbigny described survivals of a tiger cult as late as 1815. To this day in the traditional dances performed at Carnival throughout the Altiplano the tiger mask is prominent.

In eastern Bolivia, where the jaguar is indigenous, men still go out to kill the jaguar single-handed and armed only with a wooden spear in order to win the status of warriors. The archaeologist Leo Pucher reported a belief that such men are believed to have the power to turn themselves into tigers at night. The Chiriguani still believe in a fabulous green tiger Yaguarogui, which causes eclipses of the sun and moon by attempting to eat them, as reported by Dorotéo Giannecchini in *Diccionario Chiriguano-Español*. A ceramic representation of what was believed to be the Yaguarogui was found by Julio Tello at Chavín. The common practice of howling and

Left: An Indian of the Amazon basin, fully painted. This young man of the Waura tribe is wearing painted hair, feather ear-tassels, and a necklace of jaguar claws. Belief in jaguar spirits – or were-jaguars – was once widely held among the more primitive tribes, and may have been the source of a jaguar cult in the Central Andes.

Hammered sheet gold ornaments in the shape of humming-birds from the Paracas burial site. Precious metals, as well as the remarkable ceramics and textiles, were buried with the deceased.

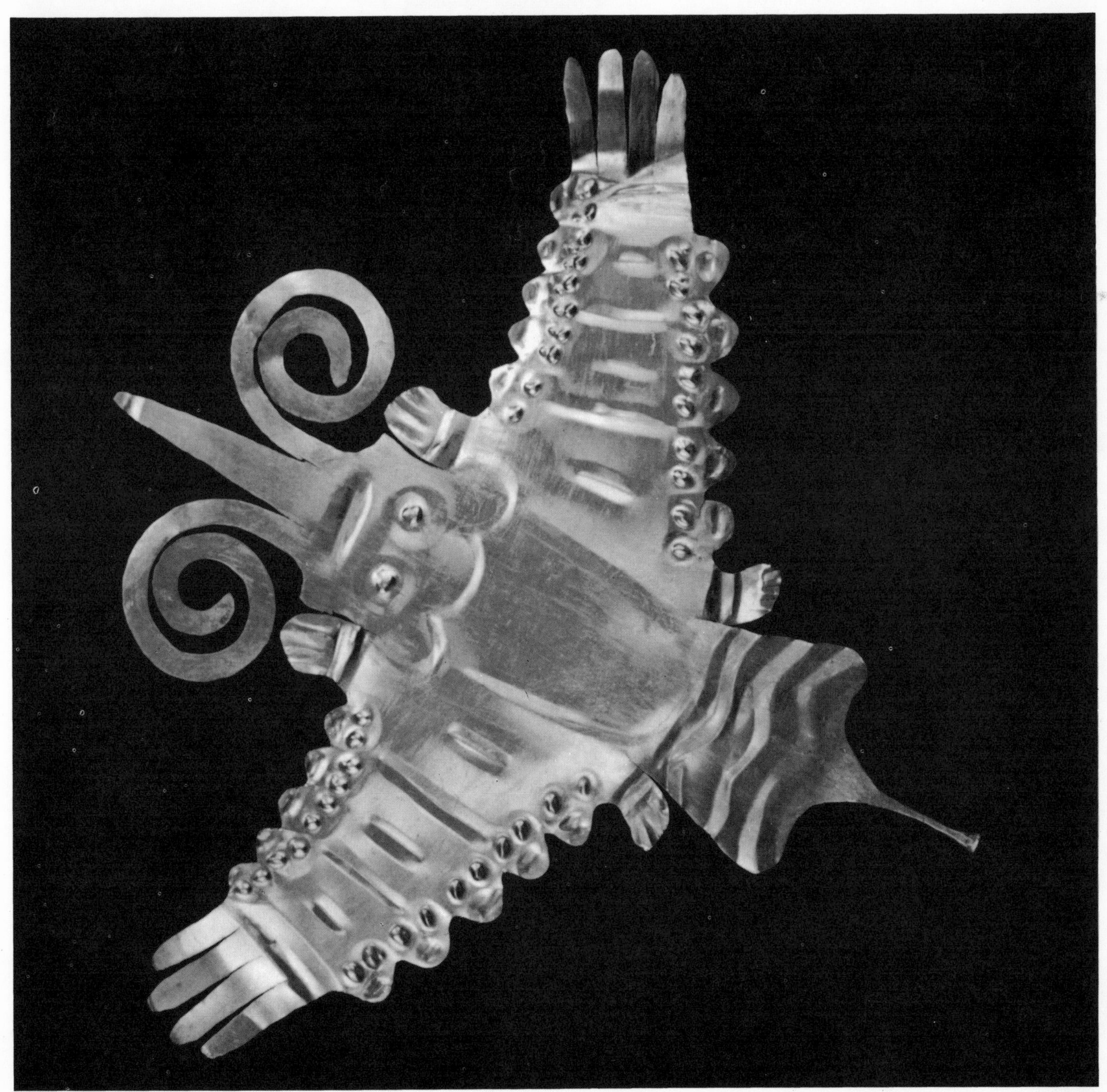

shouting during an eclipse is sometimes explained as an attempt to scare off the jaguar which is eating the sun.

Among the Mojo and some other peoples of the eastern lowlands of Bolivia the jaguar was regarded with superstitious awe and was the object of a cult. Persons who had been wounded by a jaguar and had escaped with their lives constituted a special class of magicians or shamans called *camacoy*. They warned the people when a jaguar was about to prey on the community and were thought to have supernatural contact with the jaguar spirits. Sometimes they were believed to be able to turn themselves into jaguars. The belongings of persons killed by a jaguar were sacred to the jaguar cult. A hunter who had killed a jaguar acquired great prestige. The secret name of the jaguar was revealed to him by the shamans and was adopted by him as his own. The claws and skull were kept as trophies in the communal drinking hall. But no developed jaguar mythology is recorded from these peoples.

There is no lack of evidence of a superstitious worship of the feline along with the worship of many other animals and natural objects. But there is lacking a tradition of an organised religion of the jaguar or of a feline god such as the archaeologists suppose, and no myth of the jaguar bulks at all important in the recorded mythology. While the mythological records are distressingly fragmentary, such as they are they do not offer support to the interpretations of archaeology which suggest a religious culture based on the worship of a feline deity.

Mythology and cult of the dead

Few peoples anywhere in the world have given evidence of so universal a care for the dead as the tribes of the Central Andean region. Methods of burial varied widely from one place to another. In the highlands the bodies of the dead were dried in the cold air and kept in the houses or put away in caves; the Inca had an elaborate ceremonial of burial and the mummified bodies of the kings were preserved each in its own shrine and brought forth from time to time in ceremonial procession. By far the greatest part of the art objects and handicrafts which now fill public museums and private collections throughout the world were recovered from the cemeteries of the sandy coastal valleys.

While it is thought to have existed from very early times, the cult of the dead became more elaborate and more highly organised as civilisation progressed. By analogy with what we know about similar practices elsewhere, it is generally presumed that this complex ceremonial care for the dead points towards a well-developed belief in an afterlife. For example, J. Alden Mason says of the Salinar, a people of the Chicama valley in northern Peru from the transition period between the Cultist and Experimental: 'The better care of the dead indicates a belief in the afterlife, and probably early phases of the cult of ancestor worship which later became of maximum cultural importance. The bodies were interred wrapped in or covered with textiles, and provided with pottery vessels and gourds containing food and drink. They wore their ornaments and a piece of beaten gold was often put in the mouth. Dogs were sometimes placed at the feet, together with pieces of chalk, quartz and other stones, generally of a white colour. Red powder (cinnabar?) was found in most graves. The body was almost always laid at full length, on the right side, in elliptical graves covered with great stone slabs'.'

An elaborate mortuary ritual indicating care for the dead and attention to the needs of the departed in the future life implies a developed mythology of the afterlife. Yet in the recorded mythology the life after death plays so insignificant a part that one can but wonder whether the Indians

Right: In the highlands of the Antisuyu'. The Indians of the eastern part of the empire, the high valleys of the eastern slopes of the Andes, worship at their sacred places. They sacrifice to the tiger, to whom they burn the fat of snakes, coca, maize, and the feathers of birds. Guamán Poma says that these forest Indians worship the tiger and the snakes not because they are *huaca* but in fear because they are fierce animals which eat men and they hope that by worship they can placate them. Illustration by Guamán Poma de Ayala.

Below right: A mummy mask from the Mochica culture, c. A.D. 500. The face is made of beaten copper and the eyes of shell.

Pottery jar from the great adobe frontier fortress of Paramonga on the river Paravilca at the southern extremity of the Chimu kingdom. The fortress may have been built as a defence against the growing power of the highland Inca. The neck of the jar is in the form of a human head naturalistically treated. On the body is relief decoration representing the crowned figure of a priest-king, or possibly a deity, dancing with two felines.

withheld from the Spanish this most cherished sector of their beliefs, or whether the Spanish chroniclers were uninterested in eliciting and recording beliefs which differed from the orthodox Christian picture of the afterlife. What has survived on this matter is summed up in the following passage from Cieza de León.

'I have frequently mentioned in this history that in the greater part of this kingdom of Peru it is a custom much practised and cherished by the Indians to bury with the bodies of the dead all their most prized possessions and some of the most beautiful of their women and those most beloved by them... From the lofty and magnificent tombs they have made, adorned with tiles and vaulted roofs, from the fact that they place with the dead all their goods and their women and servants, an ample store of provisions and numerous jars of *chicha* (that is the wine they use), and also their weapons and personal adornments, one can gather that they had understanding of the immortality of the soul and knew that there was more to a man than the mortal body.

'Deceived by the Devil, they accomplished his commands, for he gave them to understand (as they themselves say) that after death they would return to life in another place which he had made ready for them; and there they would eat and drink at their pleasure as they had done before they died. And in order that they might believe what he told them was true and not a lie and deceit, from time to time, when the will of God is served by giving him the power and allowing it, he would take the form of one of the chiefs who was dead and, showing himself in the chief's true shape and

figure with the appearance he bore during life, ornaments, decorations and all, he gave them to believe that this chief lived on in another world, happy and at peace, just as they saw him. Because of these sayings and illusions of the Devil these blind Indians, taking those false appearances for reality, give more attention to beautifying their tombs and sepulchres than to anything else. When one of the chiefs dies they bury with him his treasure, his women and youths and other persons whom he held in close friendship while alive. Thus from what I have related it was the general opinion of these Indians of the valleys and even those of the highlands of Peru that the spirits of the dead do not die but live on for ever and that they would all come together again in the other world, and there they believed they would live at ease, eating and drinking, which is their chief delight.'
Pedro de Cieza de León; *Crónica del Perú*, Part I, Ch. 62.

The Amazons

The tenacious myth of the Amazon women originated with the historic voyage of Francisco Orellana up the 'river of the Amazons' in 1540, though rumours going back much earlier predisposed the Spanish Conquistadores to the belief. When he returned to Europe Christopher Columbus himself claimed to have discovered an island of the Antilles which in the words of Bartolomé de Las Casas, 'was inhabited solely by women, who are visited by the men at a certain time of the year; and if they bear a female child they keep it with them, if a male they send it away to the island of the men'. He believed that he had come across the source of the classical Greek myth of the Amazons. Before Orellana set out and during the early stages of his voyage he came across constant stories from the Indians of tribes whose women were trained to battle. Gaspar de Carbajal, who wrote a Diary of the voyage, reports an encounter they had with Indians on St John the Baptist's day, 1542.

'Here were seen Indian women with bows and arrows who fought as vigorously, or more so, than the men and goaded on the men to fight. They acted as leaders, took the foremost place in the battle, struck those who wished to flee and encouraged the others to do battle. What is certain is that these women, who fought like Amazons, are the source of the stories widely disseminated among the Indians of a warlike race of women who have their kingdom somewhere in this district without commerce with men... They are tall and well built, go naked in war... but in peace they wear very comely mantles of thin cotton cloth.'

The myth had no firmer basis than the practice of certain tribes of the Amazon basin whose women took part in battle. Stories of these current among the Indians of Peru reached the Spaniards, who misunderstood their informants and too readily associated the rumours with the Greek myth. Carbajal himself says: 'We obtained many intimations about these women during all the voyage and even before we left the domains of Gonzalo Pizarro the existence of a kingdom of women was regarded as certain. But we improperly called them "Amazons" among ourselves.' In Chapter 86 of his *Historia General de las Indias* Gomara says:

'Among the nonsense he spoke he [Orellana] affirmed that there are Amazons on this river, with whom he and his comrades fought. That some of the women there carry arms and fight is a small matter, for this they are accustomed to do in many parts of the Indies. But I don't believe that any woman cuts or burns off her right breast in order to be able to draw the bow, for they can do this quite well without. Nor do they kill or deport their male children or live without husbands. Others besides Orellana have bruited such stories of Amazons since the discovery of the Indies but no such has been seen or ever will be seen along this river. But it is these reports which cause many to speak of it as the "river of the Amazons".'

Left: Suyá hunter and fisherman from the Xingú river, adorned with a flower headdress to celebrate good fishing. The Indians of the tropical rain-forest and the Amazonian area had a culture of their own well adapted to the conditions of their environment. It was thus different in most important essentials from that of the Central Andes.

One of the remarkably explicit Mochica vessels of painted pottery. Cats of different kinds appear frequently in Mochia art, and the protesting creature so firmly held in this illustration, possibly a sacrifice, would seem to lend strength to the theory of a feline cult.

El Dorado

Right: Figure which may have been used with a mummy bundle, or as a temple or tomb offering. The wooden head and body, thirty-two inches high, was made by the Huacho Indians in the fourteenth century A.D. The cap and headdress are of llama wool, the shawl of cotton and the hair is made from plant fibre.

Below: a gold plaque from Ecuador decorated with four feline figures.

It was in the early stages of the conquest of the New World that Spanish explorers first heard from native tribes on the fringes of Central America whispered stories of a mysterious people in the south whose cities were paved and palaced in solid gold and of a kingdom ruled over by a mighty priest-king, called El Dorado – the Gilded Man – because his body was covered in powdered gold. There is no reasonable doubt that these stories were garbled and misunderstood accounts of the Inca, the fame of whose empire, percolating along the trade routes, had reverberated far beyond the ordered civilisation they had built up and was current among the more primitive peoples of the fringe in exaggerated rumours of marvel and wonder. It was these stories which lured the Conquistadores to push south

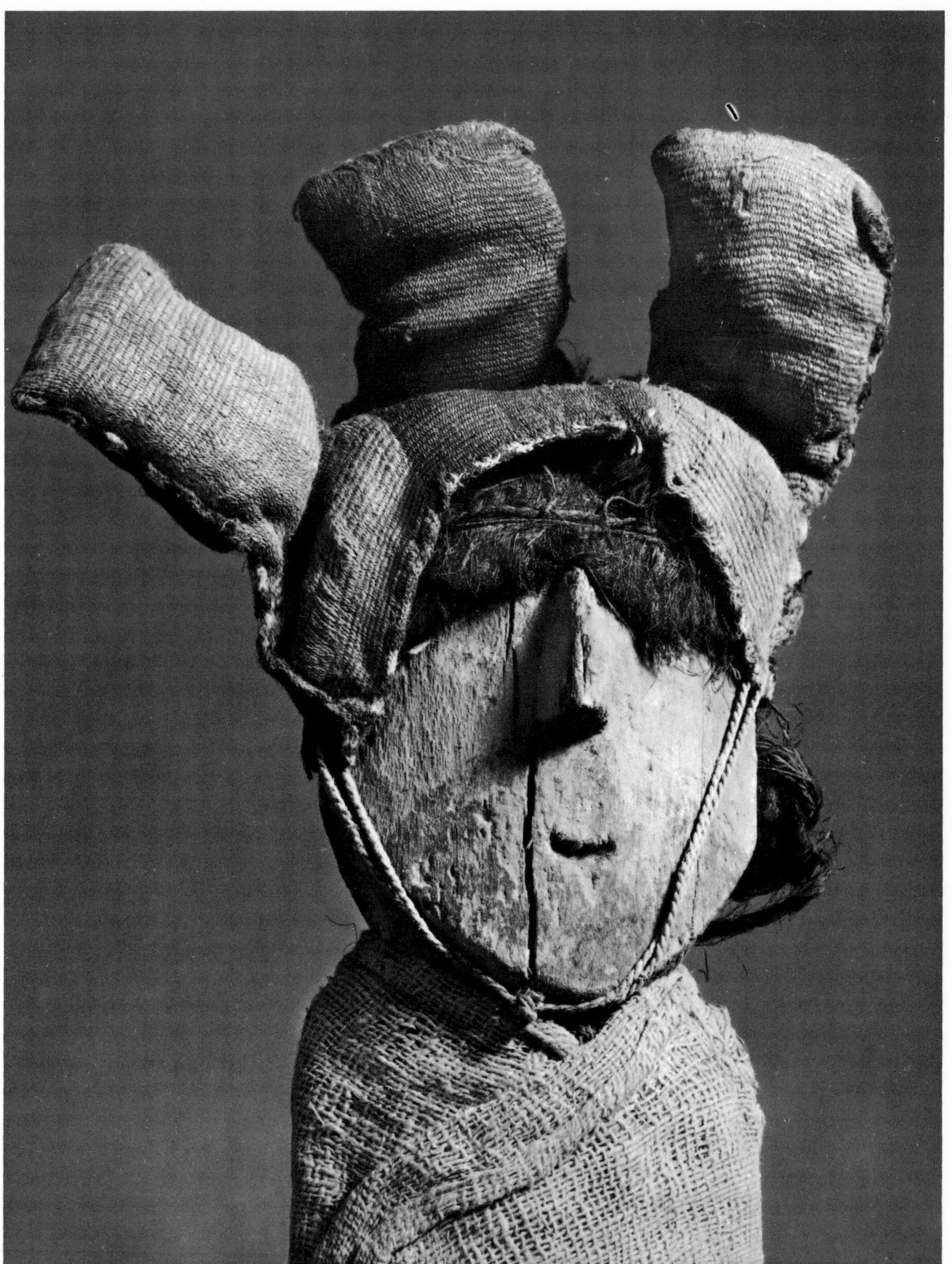

from Panama. Then having set themselves in the seat of the Inca and seized the Inca gold, they had achieved the goal they sought. But they did not recognise it for the goal and, with the reality already in their grasp, they still sought the illusion. For the legend of El Dorado persisted – and has persisted to this day – luring countless intrepid romantics to their death in the pathless jungles and fevered swamps of the Amazon valley, searching for the rumoured land of gold.

One of the most persistent rumours was centred about the mysterious Lake Guatavita, high in the mountains behind Santa Fé de Bogotá, into whose waters pieces of gold were cast as offerings to the god. From Gonzalo Ximenes de Quesada, who sought to recover the secret in 1569, roasting the local Chibcha chieftain over a slow fire, to the British company which in 1913 sank £15,000 in a vain attempt to drain the lake, Guatavita has proved a will-o'-the-wisp to many sanguine hopes. There is a long list of those who perished in the forests beyond, seeking the country where the legendary gold of Guatavita had its origin.

No less tempting proved the fabulous country of Manoa or Omoa, located in the unexplored hinterland of the river Orinoco near the mythical Lake Parima, which was marked in maps of South America on the borders of Venezuela and Guiana until its existence was disproved by von Humboldt. Among the most famous expeditions in search of the El Dorado of the Omaguas, as it was called, was that of Diego de Ortaz in 1537. One of his men, a certain Juan Martínez, who became separated from his companions, reappeared many years later from the jungle, exhausted and emaciated, and swore on his deathbed that he had been entertained by El Dorado himself. In 1541-5 the expedition of Philip von Hutten followed the trail of the old German knight Georg von Speier into the country beyond

Above right: A tiny but finely wrought gold figure of a man wearing a visored helmet and a semicircular headdress. It was possibly worn as a decoration (it is scarcely two and a half inches high), probably by a chieftain or a warrior. Tairona culture of the north-east coast of Colombia.

Below right: A Quimbaya gold figure from Colombia, possibly an amulet. Little is known of this culture beyond its existence between the Cauca and Magdalena rivers at the time the Spaniards arrived in the New World. Gold work in this style has been discovered as far north as Panama.

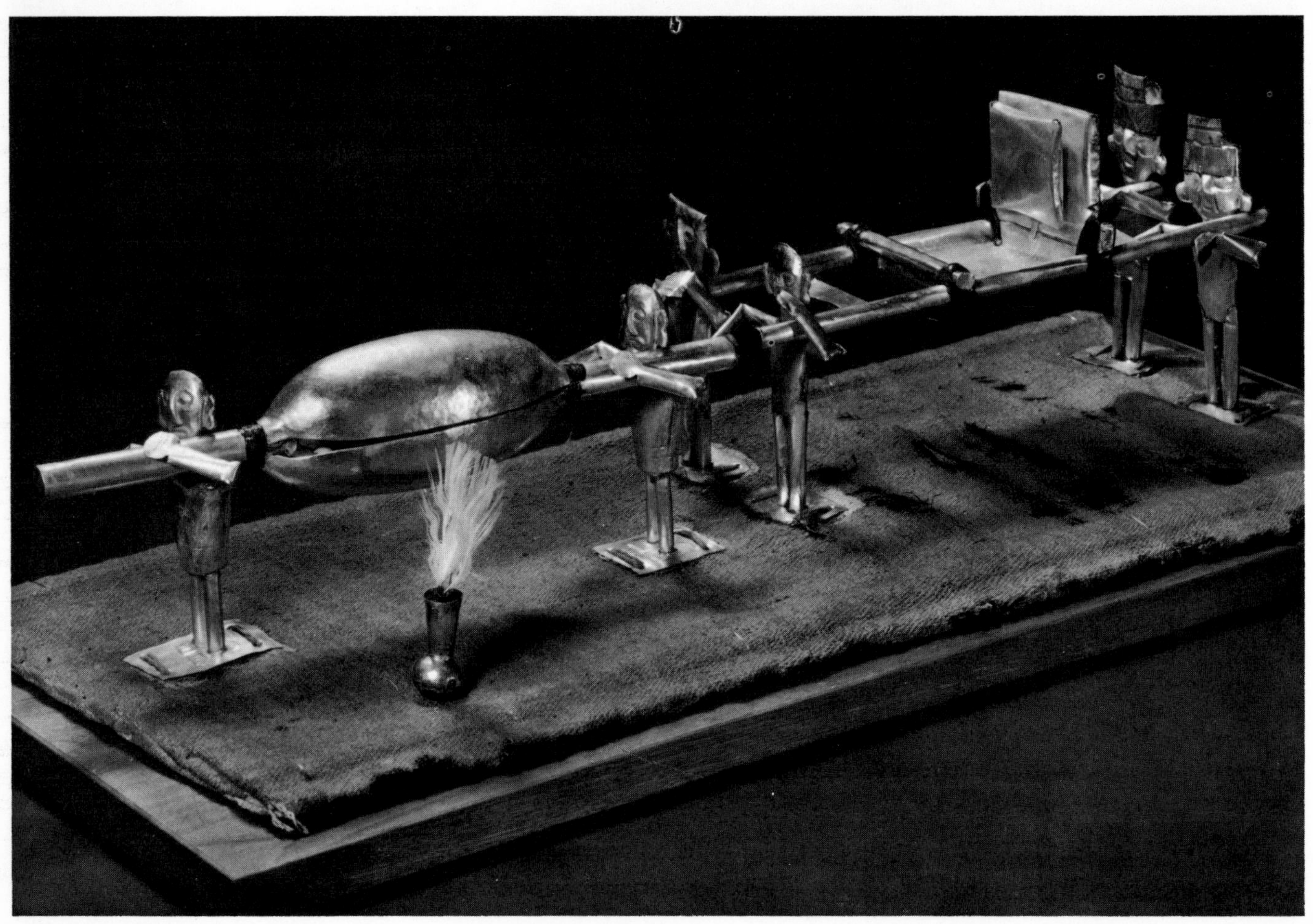

A procession of small figures in silver found in a grave of the Inca period in the Chicama valley in Peru. It is believed to represent a funeral procession: the container preceding the litter (which probably carried the body) would have held the material belongings which were also interred.

the Putumayo, a river later to become infamous as the scene of the worst atrocities of the rubber boom. In 1595 Sir Walter Raleigh declared his faith in the legend of Omoa and hoped to renew the search.

All the expeditions into the Amazonian basin – and they were many – came upon rumours of El Dorado among the native tribes, rumours which directed them always a little further on. What they did not realise was that these rumours were tribal lore handed down from generation to generation which had their origin in the fame of the great empire of the Inca at Cuzco – whence many of the expeditions of discovery had come. Though they did not know it, they were being directed back to the point of their departure.

The myth was also current among the Guaraní Indians of the Rio de la Plata basin. At the end of the fifteenth century bands of Guaraní raided across the Chaco and brought back silver and gold looted from the peaceful tribes within the Inca empire. From this arose the rumour of a 'people of metal' far in the north, the Sierra de Plata. The myth of Paititi, the land of gold, ruled over by El Gran Moxo (the Musu of Quechua legend) became indigenous in Paraguay. It was supposed to be situated in a magic lake Cuni-Cuni at the sources of the river Paraguay and guarded by the jaguar-lizard, Teyú-Yaguá. When Sebastian Cabot landed at Pernambuco in 1526 he heard these rumours from companions of an earlier adventurer Alejo García, stories of Indians who lived east of the Cordillera of Charcas and who 'wore silver crowns on their heads and gold plates hanging from their necks and ears and attached round their belts'. Convinced that this was El Dorado, Cabot sailed the Paraná and then the river Paraguay to its junction with the Pilcomayo.

Although his expedition was a failure, reports of the Quechua Indians of the Inca empire who traded gold and silver with the Guaraní continued to incite the covetousness of the Spaniards. In 1536 the Adelantado Pedro de Mendoza sent Juan de Ayloas with an expedition up the Paraguay and across the Chaco in search of the Caracaras (i.e. Quechuas of the Charcas). In 1553 Nuñez Cabeza de Vaca sent a certain Hernando de Ribera up the Paraguay and in the marshes of Xaragues at the entrance to Chiquitos the latter came across Inca trade goods and brought back the usual stories of a great and powerful people to the north-west, a land of gold and unlimited wealth, a country of Amazons, a race of white Indians and the land of El Dorado. Curiously enough Spanish already established on the Altiplano got rumours of these stories and in turn believed that El Dorado lay to their east in the lowlands of Mojos. Expeditions from Sucre into Mojos were led by Lorenzo de Figueroa in 1580 and by Gonzalo de Solis de Holguín in 1617 and 1624.

The Chilean folklorist Julio Vicuña Cifuentes reports a legend of a magical city of gold, another version of the El Dorado myth, which he declares to be widespread in Chile. In the south of Chile on the borders of a mountain lake whose whereabouts no one knows there exists a magic city whose streets and palaces are of solid gold. The inhabitants are ideally happy, do not have to work to support themselves and live for ever. The city is invisible. Travellers who come upon it forget all about it after they leave and cannot remember the way back to it. Its church has a great bell so large that if it were to be rung it would be heard the whole world over. There is there an inexhaustible tobacco plantation. The people never travel from it. This golden city will become visible only at the end of the world. It is commonly known as the City of Caesars.

The name derives from Francisco César who, sponsored by Cabot, led an expedition of fourteen men to discover the land of gold in the interior. It is supposed that the Chilean myth combines memories of the fame of the Incas with features from the mythical abode of the dead and with memories of the expedition of César.

Further reading List

North American Indian Mythology

Carpenter, E. *Eskimo*. Oxford Univ. Press & Toronto Univ. Press, 1959.

Catlin, George. *Letters and Notes on the Manners, Customs, and Condition of the North American Indian*. 2 Vols. Published by the author, London, 1842.
Illustrations to the Letters and Notes on the Manners, Customs, and Condition of the North American Indian. 2 Vols. Chatto & Windus, London, 1876.
Life amongst the Indians. Gall & Inglis, London and Edinburgh, 1874.

Clark, E. E. *Indian Legends of the Pacific North-west*. Cambridge Univ. Press, 1958.

Coccola, R. de. *Ayorama*. Oxford Univ. Press & Toronto Univ. Press, 1955.

Collier, John. *The Indians of the Americas*. W. W. Norton & Co., New York, 1947.

Grinnell, George Bird. *The Cheyenne Indians, their History and Ways of Life*. 2 Vols. Cooper Square Pubs. Inc., New York, 1962.

Judson, K. B. *Myths and Legends of Alaska*. Chicago Univ. Press, 1911.

La Farge, Oliver. *A Pictorial History of the American Indians*. Spring Books, London, 1962.

Macmillan, C. *Glooskap's Country*. Oxford Univ. Press., 1956.

Martin, Paul Sydney. *Indians before Columbus*. Chicago Univ. Press, 1947.

Palmer, Wm. Rees. *Why the North Star stands still*. Baily Bros & Swinfen, London, 1957.

Simmons, Leo W. Editor of *Sun Chief: The Autobiography of a Hopi Indian*. Yale Univ. Press, 1942.

Spence, Lewis. *Myths and Legends of the North-American Indians*. Harrap, London, 1914.

John A. MacCulloch and Louis H. Gray. *North American Mythology* in *The Mythology of all Races*. 13 Vols. Cooper Square Pubs. Inc., New York, 1922.

Special studies on the subject of the North American Indian are published by: The American Museum of Natural History, New York. The Chicago Natural History Museum. The Los Angeles County Museum. The Museum of Navajo Ceremonial Art, Santa Fe, The National Museum of Canada, Ottawa. The Smithsonian Institution, Bureau of American Ethnology, Washington.

Mexican and Central American Mythology

Asturias, Miguel Angel. *Hombres de Maiz*. Losada, Buenos Aires, 1957.

Burland, Cottie A. *Art and Life in Ancient Mexico*. Bruno Cassirer Ltd., Oxford, 1947.
The Gods of Mexico. Eyre & Spottiswoode, London, 1967.
Magic Books of Mexico. Penguin Books, Harmondsworth, 1953.

Bushnell, G. H. S. *Ancient Arts of the Americas*. Thames & Hudson, London, 1965.

Caso, Alfonso. *The Aztecs, People of the Sun*. Oklahoma Univ. Press, 1958.

Castellanos, Rosario. *The Nine Guardians*. Faber & Faber, London, 1959.

Coe, Michael D. *Mexico*. Thames & Hudson, London, 1962.
The Maya. Thames & Hudson, London, 1966.

Collis, Maurice. *Cortes and Montezuma*. Faber & Faber, London, 1954.

Diaz, Bernal. *The Conquest of New Spain* trans. by J. M. Cohen. Penguin Classics, Harmondsworth, 1963.

Goetz, D. and Morley, S. G. *Popol Vuh* trans. from the Spanish of Adrian Recinos. William Hodge, London, 1951.

Grimal, P. *Larousse World Mythology*. Paul Hamlyn Ltd., London, 1965.

Hagen, Victor W. von. *The Ancient Sun Kingdoms*. Thames & Hudson, London, 1962.

Lothrop, S. K., Foshag, W. F., and Mahler, Joy. *Pre-Columbian Art*. Phaidon Press, London, 1958.

MacCulloch, John A. and Gray, Louis H. *The Mythology of all Races*. 13 Vols. Cooper Square Pubs. Inc., New York, 1922.

Morley, S. G. *The Ancient Maya*. Oxford Univ. Press, 1946.

Nicholson, Irene. *Firefly in the Night*. Faber & Faber, London, 1959.
The X in Mexico. Faber & Faber, London, 1965.

Parkes, H. Bamford. *The History of Mexico*. Eyre & Spottiswoode, London, 1962.

Peterson, Frederick. *Ancient Mexico*. Allen & Unwin, London, 1959.

Séjourné, Laurette. *Burning Water*. Thames & Hudson, London, 1957.
El Universo de Quetzalcoatl. Fondo de Cultura Económica, Mexico, 1962. (*The Universe of Quetzalcoatl*.)

Soustelle, Jacques. *Daily Life of the Aztecs* trans. by Patrick O'Brian. Weidenfeld & Nicolson, London, 1961.

Thompson, J. E. *The Rise and Fall of Maya Civilisation*. Oklahoma Univ. Press, 1956.

Vaillant, G. C. *The Aztecs of Mexico*. Penguin Boks, Harmondsworth, 1952.

Wuthenau, A. von. *Pre-columbian Terracottas*. Methuen & Co. Ltd., London, 1970.

South American Mythology

Avila, Father Francisco de. *A Narrative of the Errors, False Gods, and other Superstitions and Diabolical Rites in which the Indians of Huarochiri lived in Ancient Times.* Translated and edited by Clements R. Markham in 'Rites and Laws of the Yncas'. Hakluyt Society, London, 1873.

Baudin, Louis. *A Socialist Empire: The Incas of Peru.* Princeton, New Jersey, 1961.

Baumann, Hans. *Gold and Gods of Peru.* Oxford University Press, London, 1963.

Bellamy, H. S. and Allen, Peter. *The Calendar of Tiahuanaco.* Faber & Faber, London, 1956.

Bushnell, G. H. S. *The Ancient People of the Andes.* Penguin Books, Harmondsworth, 1949.
The Arts of the Ancient Americas. Thames and Hudson, London, 1965.
Peru. Thames and Hudson, London, 1956.

Cieza de León, Pedro de. *The Travels of Pedro de Cieza de León, Contained in the First Part of his Chronicle of Peru, AD 1532–1550.* Hakluyt Society. No. 33. London, 1864

Cieza de León, Pedro de. *The Second Part of the Chronicle of Peru.* Hakluyt Society, No. 68. London, 1883.

Flornoy, Bertrand. *Inca Adventure.* Allen and Unwin, London, 1956.
The World of the Inca. Vanguard Press, New York. 1957.

Guppy, Nicholas. *Wai-Wai: Through the Forests North of the Amazon.* Dutton, Inc. New York, 1958

Hagen, Victor W. von. *The Ancient Sun Kingdoms.* Thames and Hudson, London, 1962.
The Desert Kingdoms of Peru. Weidenfeld and Nicolson, London, 1965.

Kirkpatrick, A. *The Spanish Conquistadores.* A. and C. Black, London, 1946.

Leicht, Hermann. *Pre-Inca Art and Culture.* MacGibbon and Kee, London, 1960.

MacCullouch, John A. and Gray, Louis H. *The Mythology of all Races.* 13 Vols Cooper Square Pubs. Inc, New York, 1922.

Mason, John Alden. *The Ancient Civilisations of Peru.* Penguin Books, Harmondsworth, 1957.

Molina (of Cuzco), Cristóbal de. *The Fables and Rites of the Yncas* translated and edited by Clements R. Markham in 'Rites and Laws of the Yncas'. p.1–64. Hakluyt Society, London, 1873.

Owens, R. J. *Peru.* Oxford University Press, London, 1963.

Prescott, William Hickling. *History of the Conquest of Peru.* Everyman Library, London, 1963.

Salas, Mariano Picon. *A Cultural History of South America.* University of California Press, Los Angeles, 1965.

Steward, Julian H. (editor). *Handbook of South American Indians.* Smithsonian Institution, Bureau of American Ethnology. Bulletin 143, vols. 2, 5, and 6. Washington, 1946–50.

Steward, Julian H. and Faron, Louis C. *Native Peoples of South America.* McGraw-Hill, New York, 1959.

Tschiffely, A. S. *Coricancha.* Hodder and Stoughton, London, 1949.

Acknowledgments

For permission to quote an extract from *The Nine Guardians* by Rosario Castellanos (translated from the Spanish by Irene Nicholson), the Nahua poems on pp. 203, 242–3, 246 and 260 from *Firefly in the Night* by Irene Nicholson, and the latter's translations of passages from *Coatlicue, estética del arte indígena antiguo* by Justino Fernandez (Centro de Estudios Filosóficos, Mexico, 1954) and *El Pueblo del Sol* by Alfonso Caso (Fondo de Cultura Económica, Mexico) on pp. 213 and 259, the publishers gratefully acknowledge Messrs Faber & Faber Ltd.

The Publishers also acknowledge the following sources for permission to reproduce the illustrations indicated.

Colour plates

Philip C. Gifford, American Museum of Nat. Hist.: 99 top right. Ferdinand Anton: 360. Andy Bernhaut: 103. British Museum: 164. Chicago Museum of Nat. Hist.: 52. Dumbarton Oaks, Robert Woods Bliss Collection: 229, 253. Arpad Elfer: front cover left, 309. Giraudon: 183. Hamlyn Group Library: front cover bottom, frontis, 25, 57, 76, 98, 99 left, centre right, bottom right, 121, 128, 129 bottom, 357. Heye Foundation, Museum of the American Indian: 56, 60, 73, 80, 124, 125. Michael Holford – Hamlyn Group Library: 285, 288, 292, 312, 316, 329, 333, 340, 353, 364. Fondo Editorial de la Plástica Mexicana: 205. Irmgard Groth Kimball 187, 208, 209, 225, 228, 256 top. Eugen Kusch: 249. Musée de l'Homme: 281, front cover right. Museum of Navajo Ceremonial Art: 107. Peabody Museum, Harvard University: 252. Paul Popper: 176, 212. Constantino Reyes-Valerio: 157, 161, 236, 256 bottom, 257. Harald Schultz: 377, 381, 384, 388. Smithsonian Inst., Bureau of American Eth.: 129 top. J. C. Spahni: 305, back cover. Henri Stierlin: 153, 179. University Museum, Philadelphia: 32, 33, 36. Western Ways & Features, Camera Press: 84, 106, 132. Württemburgisches Landesmuseum, Stuttgart: 232.

Black and white

Pierre Allard – Les Films du Château: 383. Paul Almasy: 369. Roy Atkisson-Rex Features: 22. American Museum of Natural History: 155, 181 top, 221, 301, 358 right, 362, 391, 392. Mike Andrews: 276, 280, 304. Ferdinand Anton: 295, 332. Art Institute of Chicago: 334, 354, 387 bottom. Ashmolean Museum: 110 bottom. M. & E. Baumann: 347. Biblioteca Apostolica Vaticana: 173. Bodleian Library: Oxford: 195. British Museum: 9, 28 top, 43 bottom, 55 bottom, 113, 150, 169, 196 bottom, 242, 244 top, 264 top, 265. The Brooklyn Museum: 46 bottom, 126, 127 right, 210, 211. Camera Press: 108, 116, 277, 302 bottom, 327, 376, 379. Canning House Library: 324. Cincinnati Art Museum: 11, 112 top. City of Liverpool Museums: 197, 220, 222, 230-31, 233, 241. Cleveland Museum of Art: 190, 393 bottom. Deutsche Fotothek, Dresden: 131, 323. M. Desjardins-Réalités: 269. Dumbarton Oaks, Roberts Woods Bliss Collection: 140 bottom, 145, 162 bottom, 177, 180, 227, 262 bottom, 263, 289 right, 308, 337, 349, 358 left, 385, 393 top. Faber & Faber, Ltd.: 136-7. Fondo Editorial de la Plástica Mexicana: 158 bottom, 171, 186, 192, 193, 199, 200, 218. Giraudon: 142, 149, 159 top, 176, 203 top, 216, 223, 250 bottom, 251 bottom, 321. Glasgow Art Gallery: 15 top, 90. Raúl Flores Guerrero: 238. Hamlyn Group Library: 14, 19, 21 top, 26, 28 bottom, 30, 35, 38, 42, 46 top, 61, 65, 69, 72, 101, 110 top, 112 bottom, 114, 115, 119 bottom, 143, 144, 152, 175-6, 182, 196 top, 214, 244 top, 260, 284, 303. Stephen Harrison: 271. Johannes Hartmann: 268. Michael Holford: – Hamlyn Group Library: 287, 288, 289 left, 291 top, 294, 298, 302 top, 315, 317 top, 318, 319, 330, 341, 344, 345, 352, 359, 363, 366, 372, 373, 386, 387 top. Kansas State Historical Society: 12 top. Irmgard Groth Kimball: 141, 146 top, 155 top, 156, 158 top, 159 bottom, 163, 172, 184, 185, 188, 191, 194, 198, 202, 206, 224, 226, 228, 243, 244 bottom, 254. Eugen Kusch: 151 bottom, 181 bottom, 235, 237, 245, 247, 259, 274-5, 283, 290, 300, 311, 313, 314, 325 right, 343, 356. Larousse: 77, 119 top, 160, 219. L.E.A., H. Armstrong Roberts: 48, 100. Linden-Museum, Stuttgart: 78. Robt. H. Lowïe Museum of Anthropology, University of California: 34-5. Mansell Collection: 64, 66.

Marburg, Bildarchiv: 44, 50 top, 91, 104 left. Musée de l'Homme: 74, 75, 293, 310, 342, 346, 365, 367, 370–71, 378, 390. Museo Nacional de Antropología y Arquelogía, Lima: 382. Museo de Antropologia de la Universidad Veracruzana, Jalapa: 154 bottom, 170. Museum of the American Indian, Heye Foundation: 8–9, 10, 17 top, 18, 24, 29, 49, 51, 58 top, 85, 105, 109 top, 114 top, 127 top, 136, 166, 248. Museum of Navajo Ceremonial Art: 96 right, Museum of Primitive Art, N.Y.: 71, 122. Museum für Völkerkunde, Berlin: 246. Museum für Völkerkunde, Munich: 50 bottom. Museum für Völkerkunde, Vienna: 207. National Museum, Copenhagen: 58 bottom, 59, 133. National Museum of Canada: 34 bottom, 37, 40–41, 55 top, 70. National Museum of Anthropology, Mexico City: 261. N.Y. State Museum: 64. Irene Nicholson: 140 top, 189. Ohio Development Board: 109 bottom. Harold Osborne: 297, 351. Peabody Museum, Harvard University: 12 bottom. Philadelphia Museum, Arensburg Collection: 217. Philbrook Art Centre, Tulsa: 135. Paul Popper: 250 top, 306–7, 326. Public Archives of Canada: 62, 63 top. Radio Times Hulton Picture Library: 31. Ivor Rees Photo: 306, 339. Constantino Reyes-Valerio: 146 bottom, 151 top, 201, 213, 215m 251 top, 264 bottom. Rietbergsmuseum, Zurich: 361. Rijksmuseum voor Volkenkunde, Leiden: 53, 93, 150. Rochester Museum of Arts and Sciences, N.Y.: 63. Roger-Viollet: 138. Royal Albert Memorial Museum, Exeter: 88. Runcie Graphs: 291 bottom. M. Serrailler: 299. Harald Schultz: 278, 279. Smithsonian Inst., Bureau of American Eth.: 15 bottom, 23, 39, 67, 68, 79, 83, 117, 118. J. C. Spahni: 270, 272 bottom, 282, 283 right, 286, 296, 317 bottom, 322, 328, 338, 349, 380, 389. Kurt Stavenhagen: 255. Walter Steinkopf: 320, 328. Henri Stierlin: 139, 147, 148, 162 top, 165, 167, 168, 230 bottom, 234, 239, 240, 258, 262 top. Taylor Museum, Colorado Springs: 27, 43 top, 87, 89, 94, 95, 100, 104 right, 123. University Museum of Arch. and Eth., Cambridge: 335, 355. Mireille Vautier: 325 left, 331. Hirst von Irmer: 272 right. Z.F.A.: 92, 96 left, 97.

Index